Essential Public Affairs for Journalists

READ ALL ABOUT IT!

Available to buy direct from **www.oup.com**, or your local bookshop

Essential Public Affairs for Journalists

FIFTH EDITION

James Morrison

OXFORD
UNIVERSITY PRESS

OXFORD
UNIVERSITY PRESS

Great Clarendon Street, Oxford OX2 6DP,
United Kingdom

Oxford University Press is a department of the University of Oxford.
It furthers the University's objective of excellence in research, scholarship,
and education by publishing worldwide. Oxford is a registered trade mark of
Oxford University Press in the UK and in certain other countries

© James Morrison and the NCTJ 2017

The moral rights of the author have been asserted

Second edition 2011
Third edition 2013
Fourth edition 2015

Impression: 1

All rights reserved. No part of this publication may be reproduced, stored in a retrieval system, or transmitted, in any form or by any means, without the prior permission in writing of Oxford University Press, or as expressly permitted by law, by licence or under terms agreed with the appropriate reprographics rights organization. Enquiries concerning reproduction outside the scope of the above should be sent to the Rights Department, Oxford University Press, at the address above

You must not circulate this work in any other form
and you must impose this same condition on any acquirer.

Public sector information reproduced under Open Government Licence v3.0
(http://www.nationalarchives.gov.uk/doc/open-government-licence/open-government-licence.htm)

Published in the United States of America by Oxford University Press
198 Madison Avenue, New York, NY 10016, United States of America

British Library Cataloguing in Publication Data
Data available

Library of Congress Control Number: 2017932659

ISBN 978–0–19–878551–4

Printed in Great Britain by
Bell & Bain Ltd., Glasgow

Links to third party websites are provided by Oxford in good faith and
for information only. Oxford disclaims any responsibility for the materials
contained in any third party website referenced in this work.

For my beloved Annalise, Scarlet, Rosella, and Ivor Munro

New to this edition

- Detailed analysis of the result of the 'Brexit' referendum and its most likely outcomes for the UK, the devolved nations, and their future relationships with the rest of the world.
- Major updates on the legislative and political changes flowing from the 2015 general election; the 2016 local and devolved assembly polls; and the post-referendum change of government.
- New-look, fully revised chapters on the NHS, political parties, and the European Union and other international institutions.
- Revised key points sections, topical feature ideas, and lists of current issues at the end of each chapter.

Preface: it never rains but it pours

Seasoned readers of these short 'welcome letters' to successive editions of *Essential Public Affairs for Journalists* will be familiar with the author's habit of bemoaning the relentless flux and change in British politics—and the headaches involved in keeping a textbook on this subject as up to date as possible. But if the last edition presented its challenges—the Scottish referendum helpfully took place several weeks after the official copy deadline, while the book appeared in shops barely a month before the 2015 general election—these were as nothing to the gargantuan task of compiling its fifth incarnation.

At risk of labouring the sympathy act, even before the earthquake of 'Brexit' (the referendum's date, if not outcome, could at least be planned for), the long list of beckoning chapter rewrites included three (to record the demise of the Coalition and the return to single-party government 'business as usual'); five (to reflect the *breakdown* of 'business as usual' in the party-political make-up of Westminster, with the decimation of the Liberal Democrats and the Scottish National Party insurgency); and six (to introduce the latest twists in NHS reform—notably the devolution of health to combined authorities and increasing moves towards integrating health and social care). And that is to say nothing of this edition's 'big', pre-planned change: the decision to entirely remove the chapter dedicated to international relations beyond the bounds of the EU, in order to align the textbook even more closely to the National Council for the Training of Journalists (NCTJ) programme of study.

Before turning to 'Brexit' (the subject can only be avoided for so long!), it is probably worth signposting some of the other changes in a little more detail. Chapter 5, in particular, has undergone a very substantial rewrite, with the result that it has been necessary to sacrifice large chunks of more 'distant' historical background in the service of a more nuanced and representative (and much less two-/three-party centred) overview of the increasingly diverse political landscape at Westminster, Holyrood, Cardiff—and, of course, European level. Elsewhere, sections in almost all chapters that touch on the increasingly marked differences in public administration (and policy) between England and the devolved nations have been substantially revised and amplified. And this is to say nothing of the need to chronicle the recent (at time of writing, ongoing) turmoil inside the Labour Party: now the biggest political party anywhere in Europe (perhaps even the world), yet also among the most volatile, fractious, and ill-disciplined. Throughout the book loom a number of ghosts of the recent political past: that of George Osborne, so unceremoniously ejected from Theresa May's embryonic administration, in the abundant references to combined authorities, the new generation of metropolitan mayors, and the 'Osborne Doctrine' that might offer the UK one potential route through the labyrinthine post-Brexit negotiations to come; and, of course, David Cameron, who, having scraped the Tories their first Commons majority for twenty-three years, fell limply on his sword scarcely a year later, after his political judgment failed him with a referendum gamble that so spectacularly backfired.

Naturally, Brexit's outcome was only ever going to necessitate an extensive re-framing of the European Union chapter (now re-cast, in any case, as a look at all the major international institutions of which Britain is a member) and, for this reason, that particular rewrite was left until last. But, if rewriting a chapter dedicated to the EU was challenging enough, it was nothing to the task of adjusting many of those that had already been drafted to reflect the ripple effects flowing from the UK's historic decision—from the rapid change of government personnel to the much more prolonged period of mutiny and fratricide that then engulfed Labour.

This, then, is the most heavily revised edition yet of *EPAFJ*—and one which, for all the additional material it necessarily contains, has somehow come in around 10,000 words shorter than its predecessor. Not yet quite the 'pocket guide' some might hope for, perhaps, but (one hopes) as succinct as it is possible to be while trying to cover so much (ever-shifting) ground.

Praise for *Essential Public Affairs for Journalists*

An essential guide for everybody in our trade. Finding your way around public bodies and laws is to discover how much of Britain works. And his time in journalism has taught James Morrison what journalists need to know: where and how to find stories.

Kevin Maguire, Associate Editor, *The Daily Mirror*

A work of extraordinary range and ambition that brilliantly succeeds in laying bare the workings of our nation. Above all else this is a readable, useable book; the information is accessible and the analysis is snappy and fair-minded.

Justin Webb, Presenter, The Today Programme, BBC Radio 4

If this compendious volume had been at my elbow, explaining how all the bits join together as I started out in journalism, many things would have been easier to understand and write about.

Michael White, Assistant Editor and former Political Editor, *The Guardian*

Journalists need to know what they need to know. Government, at every level, and public bodies are where they will find the stories that really affect their readers, listeners, and the viewers. This is a practical guide to help cut through the bureaucracy, jargon, smokescreens, and secrecy.

Bob Satchwell, Executive Director, Society of Editors

Acknowledgements

I would like to thank my colleagues on the NCTJ's public affairs board. Thanks, too, are due to the various other lecturers and journalists who reviewed the chapters as I wrote them, for their invariably salient advice. Special mention must go to Ron Fenney and to David Kett (the nearest that Britain has, surely, to a public affairs guru) for the huge amount of legwork that they both did before me to make sense of the tangle of legislation and 'officialese' that bedevils local and central government today. I would also like to thank the Department for Communities and Local Government (DCLG), the National Archive, and the Economic and Social Research Council (ESRC) for their prompt responses to requests for data, and their willingness for us to reproduce tables and charts (which we have credited where this is the case). Finally, thanks to the various other government departments, executive agencies, and quangos that have helped with enquiries in one way or other both in relation to this and the previous editions: HM Treasury; the Department for Work and Pensions (DWP); the Foreign and Commonwealth Office (FCO) Europe Delivery Group; the School Improvement Division of the Department for Education (DfE); the Care Quality Commission (CQC); the Department of Health (DoH); the United Nations Department of Public Information (UNSPI); the Directorate General for Budget of the European Commission (DG Budget); and the Institute for Fiscal Studies (IFS).

Finally, I'd like to thank the 'class of 95' on my first paper, the *North Devon Journal*—James Cornish, Mark Devane, Tahira Yaqoob, Kent Upshon, Matt Radley, and Rob Baker—for keeping my spirits up.

Grateful acknowledgement is made to all the authors and publishers of copyright material which appears in this book, and in particular to the following for permission to reprint material from the sources indicated:

This book contains public sector information licensed under the Open Government Licence v3.0., on which, see http://www.nationalarchives.gov.uk/doc/open-government-licence/open-government-licence.htm. Crown Copyright material is reproduced with the permission of the Controller, HMSO (under the terms of the Click Use licence).

The Birmingham Mail (www.birminghammail.co.uk): extract from Anuji Varma, 'Bed blocking crisis as number of patients 'trapped' at hospitals doubles in year' (February 2016) at http://www.birminghammail.co.uk/news/midlands-news/bed-blocking-crisis-number-patients-10876109

Grant Thornton UK LLP: extract from 'The Annual Audit Letter for Worcestershire County Council' (October 2015) at http://www.psaa.co.uk/wp-content/uploads/AAL/2015/Worcestershire%20County%20Council.pdf

The Guardian (www.guardian.com): extract from Katie Allen, 'Nearly one in six workers in England and Wales in insecure work' (June 2016) at https://www.theguardian.com/money/2016/jun/13/england-wales-zero-hours-contracts-citizens-advice-insecure-work

The Institute for Fiscal Studies (IFS): extract from 'Central Cuts, Local Decision Making: Changes in Local Government Spending and Revenues in England, 2009–10 to 2014–15' (March 2015) at https://www.ifs.org.uk/uploads/publications/bns/BN166.pdf

The Torquay Herald Express (www.torquayheraldexpress.co.uk): extract from Tina Crowson, ''Slash and burn' claims over Paignton Hospital closure rejected' (April 2016) at http://www.torquayheraldexpress.co.uk/slash-burn-claims-paignton-hospital-closure/story-29111882-detail/story.html

Wirral Metropolitan Borough Council: extract from 'Savings proposal for consultation—libraries re-provision' (2016)

Every effort has been made to trace and contact copyright holders prior to going to press, but this has not been possible in every case. If notified, the publisher will undertake to rectify any errors or omissions at the earliest opportunity.

Brief contents

Detailed contents

Guide to the book's features

Each chapter in *Essential Public Affairs for Journalists* contains a selection of features to help you to navigate your way through the book and to direct you to sources of further information.

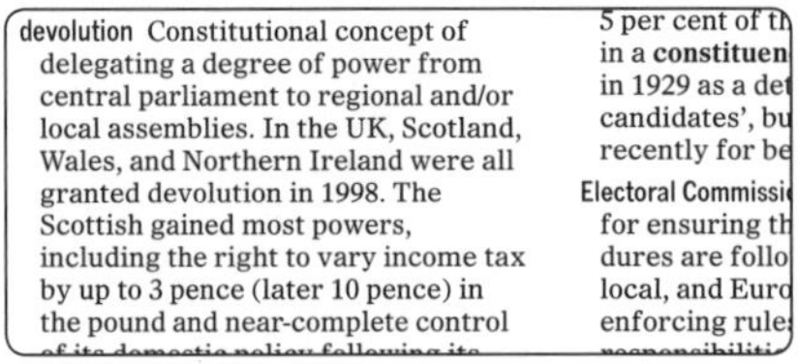

devolution Constitutional concept of delegating a degree of power from central parliament to regional and/or local assemblies. In the UK, Scotland, Wales, and Northern Ireland were all granted devolution in 1998. The Scottish gained most powers, including the right to vary income tax by up to 3 pence (later 10 pence) in the pound and near-complete control

Glossary terms

Key terms are emboldened in the text and are defined in a glossary at the end of the book.

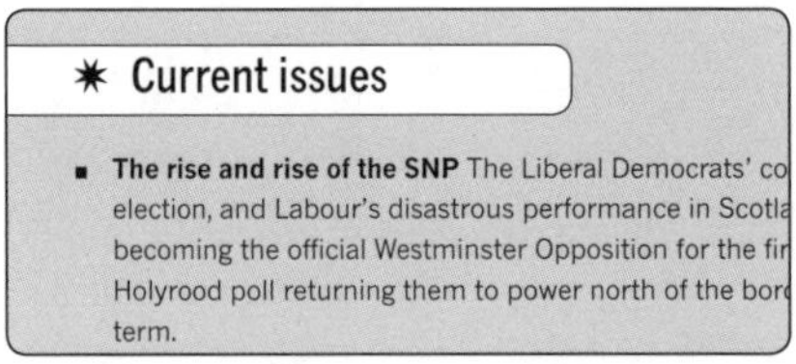

Current issues
The rise and rise of the SNP

Current issues

Current issues highlight contemporary topics that are particularly relevant to journalists and provide a starting point for further exploration.

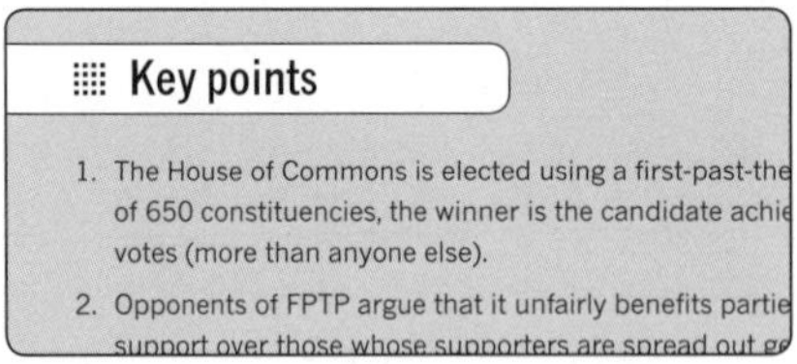

Key points

A bulleted list outlining core facts and figures most vital to success in the Essential Public Affairs exam is supplied at the end of each chapter.

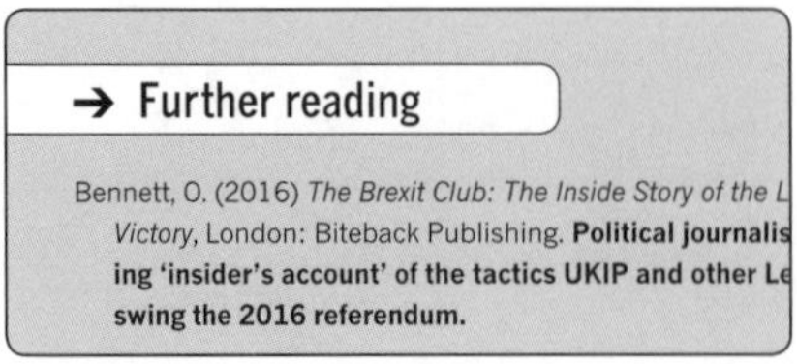

Further reading

Take your learning further by using the reading lists at the end of each chapter to find more detailed information on a specific topic.

Topical feature ideas

Topical feature ideas at the end of chapters suggest possible sources for a story on each subject.

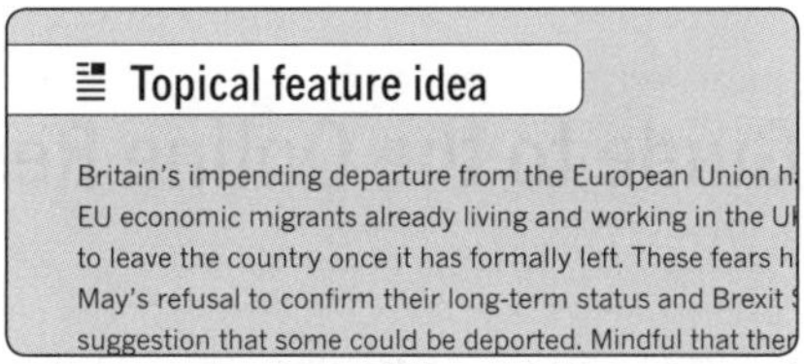
Topical feature idea

Britain's impending departure from the European Union h
EU economic migrants already living and working in the U
to leave the country once it has formally left. These fears h
May's refusal to confirm their long-term status and Brexit
suggestion that some could be deported. Mindful that the

In the margin, you will also find a number of icons with the following meanings:

This icon indicates discussion of an issue concerned with **devolution** in the United Kingdom. It allows you to see at a glance where devolved subjects are explored.

This icon occurs where there is discussion of public affairs **reporting in practice**.

The **Online Resource Centre** icon appears to remind you when additional or updated material can be found on the book's accompanying website: www.oxfordtextbooks.co.uk/orc/morrison5e/

Guide to the Online Resource Centre

Essential Public Affairs for Journalists is accompanied by an Online Resource Centre that features a range of helpful additional materials to augment the printed text. These resources are available free of charge and can be found online at:

www.oxfordtextbooks.co.uk/orc/morrison5e/

News feeds

Links to real articles from various news sites are provided via RSS.

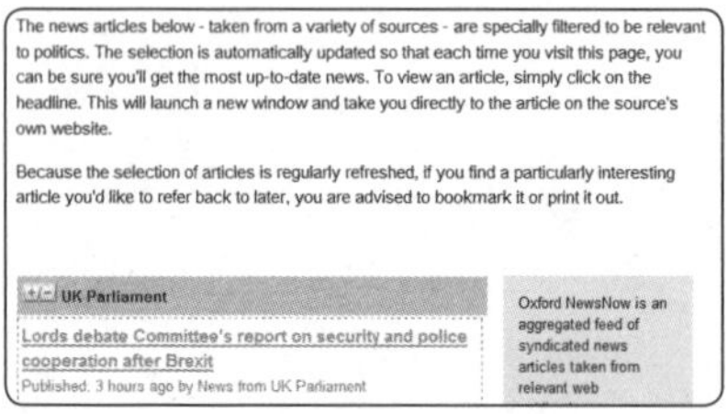

Additional and updated tables

Tables with information that changes regularly can be found in an updated form online, alongside additional tables that do not appear in the book.

Chapter 7: The Treasury, industry, and the utilities

Types of direct taxation in the UK - and how they work

Tax	How administered	Rates (2014–15)	Notes
Income	Paid by working people through either Pay As You Earn (PAYE) contributions deducted from their gross salaries by their employers, or as retrospective payments to HM Revenue and Customs (HMRC) by self-employed	Personal allowance—£10,000 Basic rate—20% (20p in £) on earnings up to £41,865 Higher rate—40% (40p in £) on earnings above £41,866 Additional rate—45% (45p in £) for those earning £150,000 or more	As of the 2015-16 tax year (6 April-5 April), the income tax 'personal allowance' (the amount a person can earn before paying tax) is due to increase to £10,600. The higher rate of tax for 2015-16 was raised to £42,385 in the 2014 autumn statement. The Chancellor cut the additional rate of income tax from 50% to 45% in 2013.

Topical feature ideas

Further topical feature ideas are provided to help you to consider where to find a story or to prepare for the NCTJ portfolio assessment.

Morrison: Essential Public Affairs for Journalists 5e

Topical feature ideas

A report by the Independent Commission for Aid Impact (Icai) has found that money invested by the UK government overseas is funding corruption. Icai, the independent body responsible for scrutinising the UK aid budget, ruled that while DfID had recognised and wished to tackle corruption, it had not "developed an approach equal to the challenge, nor has it focussed its efforts sufficiently on the poor," before adding: "While some programmes show limited achievements, there is little evidence of impact on corruption levels or in meeting the particular needs of the poor."

DfID's budget for international aid was ring-fenced and protected from the budget cuts faced by other government departments, however, critics argue that some countries that the UK has traditionally given aid to, such as India, should lose their funding because of financial

Web links

Useful websites relating to the topics in each chapter are listed to allow you to find further information.

Morrison: Essential Public Affairs for Journalists 5e

Web links

www.bis.gov.uk/
Website of the Department for Business, Innovation and Skills (BIS), outlining its key policy areas and the roles of individual ministers.

http://www.fca.org.uk/
Official website of the Financial Conduct Authority, outlining its role and responsibilities, and the procedure by which complaints should be addressed to it. The FCA took over responsibilities from the now-defunct Office of Fair Trading in April 2014.

https://www.adviceguide.org.uk/
Website of Citizens Advice, a charity which provides a consumer advice service. The charity

Introduction

Confessions of a local council reporter

I'll always remember the name Mervyn Lane. From the moment I arrived as a naive raw recruit on the *North Devon Journal* in Barnstaple—bristling with high ideas, most of them hugely unrealistic and some more than a little 'conspiracy theorist'—Mervyn and I were destined to clash. I'd been taken on as a junior reporter without a car (or, for that matter, a driving licence) and was hired only on condition I passed my test within six months of starting. Logically enough, I was immediately posted to Bideford—the area's 'second town', some ten miles west of the paper's Barnstaple headquarters—but still expected to soldier into head office each day, and to cover a sprawling patch of rustic terrain into the bargain.

To top it all, I was required to generate a district edition single-handedly each week, filling three pages of news and finding at least one front-page lead without fail. Bideford being Bideford, there were few obvious sources of scoops: the edgiest events tended to be an annual Easter fair, known dubiously (but all too descriptively) as 'Cow Pat Fun Day', and the occasional drugs raid on a pint-sized sink estate at East-the-Water, the town's ungrammatically named answer to Moss Side.

Unsurprisingly, it wasn't long before I was turning to the local authority for inspiration (or, more accurately, out of desperation). Little did I know how fruitful this would be. Those wintry evenings spent pinching myself awake through meetings of Torridge District Council's planning committee invariably threw up a last-minute gem that, with a bit of creative editing (and barring news of an international sheep-rustling scam), would generate enough ire to merit a splash.

From the humdrum ('Supermarket Threat to Town Centre') to the absurd ('Ships in Our Back Garden'), Torridge seldom failed to deliver the goods. Inevitably, it was only a matter of time before I crossed swords with the venerable Mr Lane—at that time leader of the district council's ruling Liberal Democrat group, chairman of its powerful policy and resources committee, and both a Bideford town councillor and Devon county councillor to boot.

The first of our many run-ins was sparked by a front-page story I wrote about a decision to award free parking permits to all Torridge councillors and ninety-two senior officers (dubbed 'essential users' by the council) for use in council car parks in central Bideford whenever they were on local authority business. As controversies go, this may sound small beer—there was nothing illegal or improper about the policy—but, boy, did it upset the locals. To understand the scale of the furore among residents and businesses, a little context is needed. Parking and the wider subject of transport were perhaps the most toxic issues facing Bidefordians. For various reasons, driving was pretty much the only way most people had of gaining access to the town for shopping or tourism, thanks to a train line that was (literally) a museum piece (take a bow Dr Beeching) and an antediluvian bus service. The notoriously perilous North Devon Link Road and a winding, hazardous 'coastal route' were all that connected it to civilization (or Barnstaple, at any rate)—providing lifelines for those living in outlying villages. Yet, in central Bideford—in the words of one councillor, 'a medieval town with a twentieth-century traffic problem'—any street wide enough to admit vehicles seemed to have been daubed with double yellow lines, putting the limited parking spaces available at a premium. Hence the incendiary reaction.

My parking story was one of many to irritate Mr Lane during my eighteen-month tenure as Bideford district reporter. But he wasn't the only local dignitary to be the focus of embarrassing headlines on the *Journal* during this time . . .

Let's not forget George Moss, the Bideford mayor who arrived in full regalia to turn on the town's Christmas lights one November only to find that a timer switch had done so automatically several hours earlier—the moment dusk had descended. He didn't fare any better a year later, when the precautions that council engineers took to avoid a similar fiasco proved so watertight that the lights couldn't be switched on at all.

Of course, council stories don't need to emanate from committee meetings—or, for that matter, councillors. Take the example of Les Garland, a community activist from Northam—a strip of suburban housing, pockmarked with scrappy golf courses, which runs along the Torridge Estuary to the east of Bideford. Armed with little more than a tape measure, he led a one-man campaign to rid the whole of Devon of the peril of 'hazardously placed' A-boards. (To the uninitiated, A-boards are the signs one finds outside newsagents bearing misspelt headlines from papers such as the *Journal*.)

Insisting that they posed a hazard to pedestrians, by blocking pavements and tripping people up, Les set about scouring the small print of Devon County Council's highways regulations—not to mention various Acts of Parliament—in search of a clause that would back his assertion that they contravened health and safety legislation. I clearly remember a conversation with an apoplectic county councillor, who stormed into the *Journal's* Bideford office to inform me that the county could be faced with rewriting its entire highways policy, at a cost of tens of thousands of pounds, if Les were to force the issue.

Perhaps inevitably, Les had the last laugh. When I last visited North Devon, in 2003, I picked up a copy of that hallowed Bideford edition of the *Journal*. Turning to the district pages, I was greeted by a familiar visage, grinning at me over a caption about a good citizenship award he'd received for serving the local community. As I wandered down Bideford high street later that day, I couldn't help noticing that several shops still had A-boards placed perilously distant from their doorways—but the memory of Les's beaming face reminded me that, in one way or another, his dogged devotion to civic duty had paid off.

My purpose in highlighting these anecdotal examples is to illustrate a simple point: that knowledge of public affairs (and, for the rookie journalist, local government especially) *matters*. Whether it be protests by angry parents over changes to school catchment areas, demands from worried residents for 'speed bumps' to prevent accidents on dangerous roads, or controversies about New Age traveller camps, waste disposal sites, or parasitical out-of-town superstores, local newspapers are chock-full of council-related stories on a daily and weekly basis. And to identify, research, and write up these stories in a way that is comprehensible and meaningful to their readers, journalists first need to grasp the basics of how government works and the parameters within which it operates.

This book aims to make that process easier.

1

The British constitution and monarchy

1.1 What is a 'constitution'?

For any state to achieve a sense of order and identity, it requires its subjects to recognize a shared set of values. Such values tend to be instilled by fundamental laws and principles, and upheld by parliaments, courts, and other institutions established to maintain and reinforce them.

This notion of shared membership, of collective rights and responsibilities—as common to commercial companies and supranational organizations such as the European Union (EU) as states or governments—is known as a 'constitution'.

Constitutions come in various guises. They can be formal or informal, long or short, absolute or merely advisory. Most significant, though, is the difference between the two broad types: *written* and *unwritten*. For any set of ideas related to one's citizenship of a state to be sustained, a form of written record must exist. Yet there is an important distinction between constitutions regarded as 'written' and those that are not. All constitutions worth the name comprise elements written in a *literal* sense—for example, laws recorded in documentary form. But this does not make them 'written constitutions' per se. Written constitutions are *codified* frameworks: single manuscripts summarizing the rights, values, and responsibilities attached to 'membership' of a state.

For historical reasons, some states have adopted written constitutions while others have eschewed them. Generally, written constitutions emerge in countries that undergo sudden transformations in their entire systems of government following political upheavals such as wars or revolutions. This was certainly the case for two nations with which the term is perhaps most closely associated—France and the United States—both of which adopted codified constitutions following popular uprisings against oppressive elites (the French royal family and the British government respectively).

1.1.1 Origins and sources of the British constitution

Britain—more formally, the 'United Kingdom of Great Britain and Northern Ireland'—is a different case entirely. The story of its constitutional evolution is of the gradual unification of disparate kingdoms under one national sovereign (monarch), followed by a long struggle for supremacy between monarchy and Christian Church and, ultimately, Crown and Parliament. More recently, the union of Britain's four component nations—England, Scotland, Wales, and Northern Ireland—narrowly avoided dissolution, after Scottish residents voted to reject independence in September 2014. Questions remain, though, about the long-term durability of the union.

As these various power struggles have played out through time, Britain has repeatedly come close to adopting a formal statement of principles specifying its citizenry's rights and responsibilities. In defiance of campaigns by pressure groups ranging from the Chartists of 1848 to the coalition of liberal thinkers who revived their name 140 years later with Charter 88, officially Britain's constitution remains unwritten.

As such, the British constitution has clear advantages: it is *flexible* enough to be amended or supplemented by Parliament, without any of the tortuous procedures required whenever the slightest break with tradition is sought in the United States, France, or Ireland. The narrowness of Scotland's 'No' vote means this flexibility is certain to come into play with the impending transfer of significant additional legislative powers from Westminster, as detailed later in this chapter. Conversely, unwritten constitutions have the disadvantage of provoking as much wrangling among lawyers, politicians, and historians as they ever circumvent, by leaving layers of ambiguity around sometimes crucial issues relating to their subjects' liberties and entitlements. Former Prime Minister Gordon Brown's controversial decision to sign the European Union's 2007 Lisbon Treaty—seen by some as a 'European constitution' in all but name—demonstrates how easily Britain can adopt significant changes to its constitutional fabric without any of the debate rendered necessary by the rigid frameworks that apply in other countries. Meanwhile, the perceived assault on individuals' civil liberties represented by the rash of anti-terror legislation following the attacks on the Twin Towers on 11 September 2001 were viewed by some human rights campaigners as examples of the dangers of failing to enshrine core principles in a solid constitutional statement.

So what are the primary sources of Britain's constitution? Its main components fall into the following five categories:

- *statute*—individual laws or 'Acts of Parliament';
- *common law*—sometimes known as 'judge-made' or 'case' law, or 'precedent';
- *conventions*—customs, traditions, and long-standing practices;

- *treatises*—historical works of legal and/or constitutional authority; and
- *treaties*—EU and other international agreements.

1.1.1.1 Statute

Magna Carta (the Great Charter), signed by King John in 1215, is often cited as the foundation-stone of Britain's constitution, because it invokes the principle of **rule of law**. This embodied the inalienable right of any citizen accused of a crime to a free and fair trial before his peers and, crucially, enshrined the principle that no one—even a reigning sovereign—was 'above the law'.

Perhaps more significant even than Magna Carta was the 1689 Bill of Rights, which ended a turbulent forty-year period stemming from the execution of King Charles I in 1649, and the eleven-year interregnum that followed under Puritan 'Lord Protector' Oliver Cromwell. Although titular head of the Church of England, Charles was seen by many as too sympathetic to Roman Catholicism, having married the Catholic Princess Henrietta Maria of France. There was also deep unease about his invocation of the loose medieval principle of the 'Divine Right of Kings'—a notion that the sovereign's authority was incontestable because it derived from his or her relationship to God. In the event, the Parliamentarians vanquished Charles's Royalist supporters in the ensuing English Civil War (1642–51), ending centuries of rule under this premise.

The Bill of Rights itself arose out of the alliance between the Protestant-dominated Parliament and William of Orange, the Dutch king. This led to the deposition of Charles's younger son, James II, during the 'Glorious Revolution' of 1688. Having worked in an uneasy stalemate with James's elder brother, Charles II, following his return from exile after Cromwell's death in 1660, Parliament used the ascension of his uncompromising sibling (a devout Catholic) as a pretext for cementing its constitutional supremacy.

To this end, it effectively mounted a coup—replacing James with his Protestant daughter, Mary. In exchange for Parliament's loyalty, they permitted the passage of the Bill, which formalized for the first time the transfer of constitutional supremacy from Crown to elected Parliament. Its central tenet ratified the principle that future sovereigns could rule only *through* Parliament—rather than by telling it what to do, as before. Monarchs would have to seek formal consent from members of Parliament (MPs) before passing legislation (Acts), declaring war, or invoking other sovereign powers that they had traditionally wielded. The Bill ended centuries of 'royal sovereignty' and ushered in the concept of **parliamentary sovereignty**, which still prevails.

This core constitutional principle symbolizes the oft-cited flexibility of an unwritten constitution. The term 'sovereignty'—or **political sovereignty**—refers to the notion of an individual or institution exercising supreme control over a geographical realm or people. Parliamentary sovereignty flows from this: as well as asserting the authority of the *institution* of Parliament over

British subjects, it confers on *individual* parliaments—the bodies of MPs elected at given general elections—authority to make their own laws and repeal any of those passed by previous parliaments. To this extent, it prevents any one parliament being bound by the actions of a predecessor.

Many constitutional experts argue that this idea is incompatible with a conventional written constitution, because if we had such a document, one parliament could theoretically use its sovereignty to repeal the Act that introduced it. Advocates of a codified document dismiss this argument, contending that many countries with written constitutions manage to maintain them alongside their own versions of parliamentary sovereignty without encountering such conflicts. One way of embedding a written constitution into a state's political fabric is to compose a web of interlocking legislation, rather than simply passing individual Acts—making it harder to repeal. Another might be to set up an independent superior court to adjudicate in constitutional disputes. Britain's Supreme Court (see 2.3.3) could conceivably fulfil this role.

In addition to formalizing parliamentary sovereignty, the Bill of Rights granted several privileges to all 'Englishmen'—with the exception (in certain cases) of Roman Catholics. Its main tenets are listed in table 1A, to be found on the **Online Resource Centre** that accompanies this book.

The Bill also specified conditions governing the future succession of the monarchy (see 1.2), and established a further constitutional principle that today remains fundamental to the workings of Parliament. Often incorrectly described as a 'convention' (rather than a product of statute, which it is), this is **parliamentary privilege**. In brief, parliamentary privilege enables any MP sitting in the House of Commons or peer in the House of Lords to make accusations about individuals or companies in open debate in the chambers without fear of prosecution for defamation.

Recent years have seen several high-profile examples of parliamentary privilege being used by members to 'name and shame' private individuals in ways that would be considered defamatory (and invite legal action) if repeated outside Parliament. In 2001, for example, Peter Robinson, then deputy leader of the Democratic Unionist Party (DUP), used it to 'out' Brian Keenan and Brian Gillen as members of the Provisional Irish Republican Army (IRA) ruling Army Council.

A flipside of the legal protection afforded by parliamentary privilege is the fact that certain words and phrases are construed as unacceptable 'unparliamentary language' if directed at fellow members in either chamber. Most notorious is the word 'liar', which is held to conflict constitutionally with the privilege members otherwise enjoy to speak their minds. In November 1993, the then DUP leader, Reverend Ian Paisley, was famously suspended from the Commons for five days for accusing Prime Minister John Major of lying after it emerged that, despite previously insisting that the idea of negotiating with Northern Irish 'terrorists' would 'turn his stomach', he had held secret talks for more than a year with Sinn Féin, the main republican party.

The present Commons Speaker, John Bercow, has frequently berated MPs for hurling insults: in April 2016, he ordered veteran Labour backbencher Dennis Skinner out of the chamber for refusing to withdraw an insult branding David Cameron 'dodgy Dave' during a statement in which the then prime minister set out his financial affairs to dispel allegations of tax avoidance by his family made in a leak of 11.5 million documents from a Panama-based law firm, Mossack Fonseca (see also 7.1.1).

Just as parliamentary privilege protects MPs and peers from being sued for defamatory statements made in Parliament, it also safeguards the media from action arising out of repeating those claims: contemporaneous reports of what is said in either chamber, as well as parliamentary committee rooms, are covered by *qualified privilege*. By way of further complicating explanations of this privilege, however, according to a literal interpretation of the Bill of Rights it also protects the press from proceedings arising from 'a report alleging wrongdoing in Parliament by an MP'. This legal argument enabled *The Guardian* to defend a libel action brought in 1996 by former Conservative minister Neil Hamilton over its allegations two years earlier that he had accepted cash from Harrods owner Mohamed Al Fayed for asking parliamentary questions designed to advance the latter's business interests. As a sitting MP, Mr Hamilton had to obtain formal permission to sue the newspaper—which he did (ultimately unsuccessfully) through a new clause inserted into the 1996 Defamation Act (section 13), enabling him to waive his right to parliamentary privilege by taking action as a private citizen.

Parliamentary privilege can also operate in ways that are more obscure. In November 2008, a row erupted when it emerged that the then Opposition immigration spokesman Damian Green had been arrested over allegations that he unlawfully solicited leaks about government policy from a Home Office civil servant. Both Opposition and government MPs united in criticizing the police action, which many saw as an abuse of the long-established constitutional right of members to conduct free and open conversations with officials in the Palace of Westminster—and a throwback to Charles I's challenge to parliamentary freedoms in the seventeenth century. Members on all sides turned their fire on the then Commons Speaker, Michael Martin, who, as its overall custodian, was accused of allowing officers to search Mr Green's office—potentially jeopardizing the confidentiality of sensitive information relating to his constituents.

Perhaps the most contentious attempt to use parliamentary privilege as a legal protection, however, was the interpretation cited by Labour MPs Elliot Morley, Jim Devine, and David Chaytor, and Tory peer Lord Hanningfield after being charged with false accounting over their Commons expenses claims. They invoked Article 9 of the 1689 Bill of Rights to argue that, because any alleged wrongdoing had been committed by them while performing official duties, it was for Parliament alone to try and (if necessary) punish them. In the event, the courts dismissed their argument and all four were convicted (see 2.2.6).

Of Britain's other key constitutional statutes, the most historically significant are the 1701 Act of Settlement and 1706–7 Acts of Union. The former built on the newly introduced rules relating to monarchical succession in the Bill of Rights by setting out the conditions for future sovereigns, as outlined in table 1B to be found on the **Online Resource Centre**. Its principal condition—that Roman Catholic heirs or those who married Catholics should be barred from inheriting the Crown—remained in place for 324 years, until the Succession to the Crown Act 2013 (see 1.2.5).

The Acts of Union, meanwhile, were twin laws passed first in England, then Scotland, in 1706 and 1707 respectively, which formalized the overarching Treaty of Union: the agreement unifying the countries as one United Kingdom under a single sovereign and Parliament. Key Acts absorbed into UK law more recently include those listed in Table 1.1.

The Human Rights Act (HRA) 1998—justifies some discussion here, given the growing contention by many lawyers, human rights campaigners, and constitutional experts that it conflicts with Britain's constitution as it previously stood. For this and other reasons, the Conservatives entered both the 2010 and 2015 elections with a manifesto commitment to replace it with a new Bill of Rights tailored specifically to UK citizens. Their plans to repeal the HRA were repeatedly frustrated during the five years from 2010 in which they shared power with the Liberal Democrats (committed supporters of the Act). But to this day, tensions continue with the European Court of Human Rights (ECtHR)—the principal court of the Council of Europe, the body that established the European Convention on Human Rights (ECHR—see 9.8.3). The Court has repeatedly demanded that Parliament abandon its long-standing opposition to allowing convicted prisoners the vote (see 4.1.1). Spurred on by the narrow parliamentary majority they achieved five years on, in their May 2016 Queen's Speech the Conservatives revived their previous pledge to abandon the existing HRA, by announcing a formal consultation on a proposal to replace it with a new Bill of Rights and Responsibilities. The

Table 1.1 Key statutes absorbed into the UK constitution in the twentieth century

Statute	Effect
Race Relations Acts 1965, 1968, and 1976	Outlawed racial discrimination
Government of Scotland and Government of Wales Acts 1998	Paved the way for national referendums to establish devolved power in Scotland and Wales
Human Rights Act (HRA) 1998	Incorporated into British law the European Convention on the Protection of Human Rights and Fundamental Freedoms (the European Convention on Human Rights, or ECHR), signed by the Council of Europe in 1950
House of Lords Act 1999	Removed all but ninety-two hereditary peers then remaining and created 'transitional' Lords to remain until decisive reform agreed by both Houses (see 2.3.2)

addition of the latter term symbolically rebalanced the emphasis in the current Act away from freedoms individuals can expect their UK citizenship to bring them towards the duties and behaviours expected *of* them. Within 24 hours of the announcement, an Amnesty International petition calling on ministers to keep the HRA had already topped 110,000 signatures—10,000 more than is needed to trigger a potential debate in Parliament (see 2.2.1).

Although it received royal assent in November 1998, the HRA only came into force in October 2000. Among its stipulations was that every future Bill put before Parliament must now include a preface confirming that the relevant secretary of state is happy that it conforms with the Convention. The individual rights safeguarded by the Convention—which include a 'right to liberty and security of person' (Article 5) and 'freedom of expression' (Article 10)—are as outlined in table 1C, to be found on the **Online Resource Centre**.

In addition, the UK has accepted the First and Sixth (now Thirteenth) Protocols to the ECHR, of which there are fourteen altogether. The First Protocol includes additional rights for property (Article 1), education (Article 2), and free and fair elections (Article 3). The Thirteenth Protocol formally abolishes the death penalty.

Although the HRA has theoretically strengthened the ability of ordinary people to challenge the actions of governments, public bodies, and private companies in British and EU courts, there are limits to its pre-eminence, as test cases have demonstrated. By general consensus, the principle of parliamentary privilege remains unaffected by the Act. In addition, British judges—although required to take account of ECtHR judgments when making rulings in UK courts—may not simply override extant parliamentary legislation that appears to contravene the Convention.

Further, the following formal qualifications exist in relation to the Act's enforcement:

- claims must be brought against offending states or public bodies 'within one year of the action about which the complaint is being made';
- some rights can theoretically be breached if not 'in accordance with the laws of the country' that is a signatory; and
- breaches are tolerated 'in the interests of national security, public safety, or the country's economic well-being; for the prevention of crime and disorder, the protection of health or morals, or to protect the freedom and rights of others'.

In Britain, the HRA has arguably been breached repeatedly. The Anti-terrorism, Crime, and Security Act 2001 allowed the detention and deportation without trial of people suspected of terrorist links, and the then Prime Minister Tony Blair repeatedly threatened to amend the Act to prevent judges blocking further crackdowns—particularly on the activities of extremist Islamic preachers, following the 2005 London bombings.

In Scotland, the Act came into force in 1998—two years before England. By November 1999, the High Court had already declared unlawful the appointment of 129 temporary sheriffs (judges in the Scottish criminal courts) because they had been hired by the Lord Advocate, at that point still a member of the Scottish Executive—a clear conflict with one of the constitution's fundamental guiding principles, the separation of powers.

Besides the showpiece constitutional Acts listed in Table 1.1, several others have contained key clauses with serious implications for the workings of the British constitution. Among these are the myriad Parliament Acts passed before the Second World War (see 2.3.1). Perhaps the single most significant constitutional reform introduced by any of these was the stipulation, in the Parliament Act 1911, that general elections must be held *a maximum of five years after the previous Parliament was convened* (in other words, a little over five years after the previous polling day). Until then, parliaments could theoretically last up to seven years, under the terms of the Septennial Act 1715. It would be another century, however, before 'fixed-term parliaments' were introduced by the 2010–15 Liberal Democrat-Conservative Coalition (see 4.1.1).

1.1.1.2 Common law

For several centuries before the emergence of parliamentary democracy many English laws were decided, on a case-by-case basis, by judges. When this system began emerging in the eleventh and twelfth centuries, judicial decisions were often taken ad hoc and locally, leading to wide disparities between one area and another—both in terms of what was (and was not) perceived a criminal offence and the range and severity of punishments applied when laws were broken.

In 1166, the first Plantagenet king, Henry II, began institutionalizing a unified national framework of common law derived from 'case law' or 'precedent'—in essence, what he regarded as the more reasoned judgments made in individual local hearings over previous decades. This new framework—which came to apply throughout England and Wales—elevated some local laws to national status, eliminated arbitrary or eccentric rulings, and established a great enduring constitutional right of citizens charged with criminal offences: a jury system, enshrining defendants' entitlement to be tried by 'twelve good men and true' from among their fellow citizens. To ensure that these practices were implemented consistently nationwide, Henry appointed judges at his own central court and sent them around the country to adjudicate on local disputes.

Many statutes that were passed—and constitutional conventions that evolved—subsequently were rooted in common law. Even now, common law is still sometimes 'created', when judges have to make rulings based on interpretations of ambiguously worded Acts or conflicts between domestic and international laws. Such 'test cases' are, in their way, common law hearings.

1.1.1.3 Conventions

Another feature of Britain's unwritten constitution is its incorporation of all manner of idiosyncratic, quaint, and occasionally absurd traditions and customs. These well-worn practices have become accepted as part of the constitutional framework through little more than endless repetition.

Many key conventions operating in Parliament and government today are discussed in detail elsewhere in this book. These include the doctrines of collective responsibility and individual ministerial responsibility (see 3.2.2) and the tradition that sovereigns accept Parliament's will by rubber-stamping legislation with the royal assent (see 2.5). More amusing conventions include the fact that the Lords Speaker sits on a woolsack and wears a wig. The annual State Opening of Parliament by the monarch is heralded by a procession led by a ceremonial officer known as 'The Gentleman Usher of the Black Rod'. It is the task of Black Rod—as he is commonly known—to lead MPs ('strangers') from Commons to Lords to hear the Queen's Speech. On arriving at the Commons to summon MPs, he has the door slammed in his face and is forced to gain entry by rapping on it three times with (what else?) a black rod. This ritual derives from a famous confrontation between Parliament and the sovereign in 1642, when King Charles I tried to arrest five MPs in what the Commons saw as a breach of parliamentary privilege. Within Parliament today, a form of light 'class warfare' between the chambers remains: MPs refer to the Lords only as 'another place'.

1.1.1.4 Treatises (works of legal authority)

Just as judges often have to disentangle contradictory elements of Britain's unwritten constitution when ruling on cases, so too are constitutional historians, philosophers, and political scientists forever debating it.

Of the myriad books and theses written about the UK constitution down the centuries, a handful have become so revered that they now qualify as constitutional documents in their own right. Some are considered so indispensable that they are effectively used as 'handbooks' by everyone from the Speaker of the House of Commons to High Court barristers and judges. Many of today's new laws and court judgments are framed in reference to the wisdom imparted in such tomes, the most celebrated of which are listed in table 1D to be found on the **Online Resource Centre**.

1.1.1.5 Treaties

Britain has signed many international treaties in recent decades, only a handful of which are 'constitutional', in that they are legally binding. Most—like the 1945 Charter of the United Nations and the North Atlantic Treaty, which established the North Atlantic Treaty Organization (NATO) in 1949 (see 9.8.2)—are little more than membership agreements and, as such, could theoretically be 'opted out of'.

However, some—like the ECHR—have effectively been incorporated into Britain's constitution and would require legislation to remove the obligations that they impose on it. There has also been considerable debate about the growing powers of the EU (see Chapter 9), which Britain joined (amid some controversy) in 1973, when it was still known as the 'European Economic Community' (EEC). Recent treaties—notably the 2007 Lisbon Treaty—have solidified the relationship between member states and the EU's governing institutions, leading 'Eurosceptics' to claim that Britain has signed up to an 'EU constitution' by the back door and is now part of a 'European super-state' governed from Brussels, rather than an independent sovereign nation.

1.1.2 The separation of powers in the UK

Perhaps the most fundamental guiding principle underlying the British constitution is the **separation of powers**. Based on the theories of French political thinker Baron de Montesquieu (1689–1755), the *Trias Politica* is a notional model that splits the state into three branches:

- the 'executive' (the government);
- the 'legislature' (Parliament); and
- the 'judiciary' (the courts).

The idea is that, to avoid arbitrary or dictatorial government, a constitutional framework is needed that does not confer too much power in too few hands. In theory, if the executive is wholly 'separated' from the legislature, and in turn the judiciary, each acts as a 'check and balance' on the other.

Montesquieu purportedly formulated his theory based on the workings of the UK system, although Britain's democracy arguably adheres less strictly to this model than many established since. In practice, numerous overlaps have emerged over time between the roles, powers, and even memberships of key institutions charged with preserving the separation of powers. These include that:

- constitutionally, the reigning monarch (as 'head of state') is titular head of all three branches of the constitution;
- for centuries, until the post was reformed in 2007, the Lord Chancellor was a member of all three institutions, as Speaker of the Lords (legislature), 'manager' of the legal profession (judiciary), and a Cabinet minister (executive);
- most ministers, including the prime minister, are members of both government (executive) and Parliament (legislature); and
- before the independent Supreme Court was established in October 2009, the Law Lords collectively constituted Britain's highest court of appeal (judiciary), as well as being voting peers (legislature).

Such constitutional overlaps are not confined to Britain. Many other parliamentary democracies—particularly those of Commonwealth countries that directly mimic the UK's—display a similar fusion of powers, rather than the 'separation' to which they aspire. Constitutional historians increasingly distinguish between jurisdictions that practise 'presidential government' and those characterized by 'parliamentary government'. In the former (including the United States, France, South Africa, and Australia), separation is felt to be both more practised and practicable than in countries like Britain, where the most senior politician (prime minister) is today drawn from the ranks of ordinary MPs and represents a constituency in the same way as his or her peers.

In Britain, executive decisions are taken primarily by prime ministers and ministers, before being presented for approval to Parliament (where they also tend to be present, as voting MPs and peers). In the United States and other states, in contrast, the most senior elected politician is the president—who, in the absence of a monarch, is also head of state. Crucially, unlike in Britain and other parliamentary states, presidents are usually elected on different timetables from those of their national parliaments. Separation of powers in the United States is more pronounced than in Britain because Congress (the Senate and House of Representatives—the US equivalent of Parliament) is largely elected on a different date, in a different manner, from the president. More crucially, the president (unlike the British prime minister) is not a member of either House; so while he or she may present policies to Congress for approval, he or she does not lead or participate in ensuing parliamentary debates in the way that prime ministers do in the Commons.

Another feature of the separation of powers enjoyed by presidential states is the fact that, historically, they tend to develop more genuinely independent judicial systems than prime ministerial ones. The United States has long had a Supreme Court that is entirely separate from the political process. Notwithstanding controversies over the president's ability to nominate judges to replace those who retire (President Bush was castigated in 2005 for choosing a former adviser, who later withdrew her candidacy), this system is felt to be more appropriate than one in which judges straddle the divide between legislature and judiciary by serving in both a legal and law-making capacity. To this end, Jack Straw, as inaugural Secretary of State for Justice (and de facto Lord Chancellor), removed the Law Lords from Parliament in 2009, to sit in the then new Supreme Court.

1.2 The monarchy

Britain's reigning sovereign is head of a 'constitutional' monarchy. This means that while he or she remains head of state, with the notional prerogative to govern and take major constitutional decisions, in practice he or she does not.

Unlike in presidential countries, Britain's head of state is a figurehead with little real power; instead, day-to-day decisions regarding domestic and foreign policy are left to Her Majesty's government (see Chapter 3).

Authority invested in successive prime ministers to appoint their ministers, devise and draft legislation, and decide whether to take Britain to war is derived from another key constitutional principle: the **royal prerogative**. This is the body of customary privileges and powers historically acquired by reigning monarchs (predominantly in the Middle Ages). Today, most 'prerogative powers' derived from this principle are exercised not by the Crown itself, but by Parliament.

1.2.1 The origins of the modern British monarchy

Queen Elizabeth II reputedly traces her ancestral line directly to King Egbert—the ruler who united England under one throne in AD 829. However, she is also descended from several powerful families with roots outside the UK.

Despite the relative security of the institution of the British monarchy today, the 'English Revolution' marked a break with the past that would change its role forever. Beforehand, the prevailing rationale for the primacy of the sovereign derived from the 'Divine Right of Kings'. By propagating the idea that they should not be answerable to 'man-made' institutions, European medieval monarchs sought to reign with minimal interference—their authority matched (and occasionally challenged) only by the Church. Parliaments were generally regarded as little more than tools enabling kings and queens to raise taxes, pass edicts, and declare wars with impunity.

In England, all this changed after Charles I's execution. While his eldest son, Charles II, ultimately succeeded him following the eleven-year interregnum, the concept that any monarch had a God-given right to rule unchallenged had by then been decisively quashed. Through a succession of landmark constitutional statutes—principally the Bill of Rights and Act of Settlement—a newly liberated Parliament stamped its authority on the state and (in all but name) the monarch.

1.2.2 The role of the monarchy today

In *The English Constitution*, Bagehot (1826–77) memorably summed up the constitutional role of the sovereign as embodying 'the right to be consulted, the right to encourage, the right to warn'. Today, the powers and purposes of the monarch fall into two broad categories: *actual* and *notional*.

1.2.2.1 Actual prerogative powers: those exercised by the monarch

Despite huge upheavals in recent centuries, the sovereign still holds the following constitutional positions:

- head of state;
- head of the executive, legislature, and judiciary;

- commander-in-chief of the Armed Forces;
- supreme governor of the established Church of England;
- head of the Commonwealth (and head of state of fifteen of its fifty-three members); and
- the authority from which the Royal Mint derives its licence to coin and print money in the monarch's image.

So much for the official titles, though: what do monarchs actually *do*? More specifically, which prerogative powers do they still personally exercise in an age when governments take most key political decisions for them?

The core roles and duties of the monarch—many largely ceremonial—include:

- reading Her Majesty's Most Gracious Speech or 'Gracious Address'—known as the **Queen's Speech**—at the annual State Opening of Parliament (historically in October or November, but generally now held in May or June) or after a general election;
- overseeing the Church of England and formally approving senior appointments;
- 'creating' peers and conferring knighthoods and honours;
- meeting the prime minister weekly (usually on Tuesdays) to discuss Cabinet business and to offer advice on affairs of state;
- entertaining visiting heads of state at Buckingham Palace;
- touring other nations on official state visits as Britain's premier overseas ambassador;
- chairing meetings of the Privy Council (a body of advisers made up of members of current and previous Cabinets, plus other distinguished individuals, which issues Royal Charters and Orders in Council—see 2.4.2); and
- attending 'Trooping the Colour' (the monarch's annual birthday parade, led by regiments of HM Armed Forces).

Although this list of 'powers' may appear feeble in the scheme of things, anecdotal evidence suggests the present monarch has discharged her duties rigorously. In her first audience with the then newly elected Labour Prime Minister Harold Wilson in 1964, she famously wrong-footed him by expressing interest in proposals for a 'new town' near Bletchley—something about which he knew nothing, having not yet read his Cabinet papers. In his 1976 resignation speech, Wilson joked about the episode, advising his successors to 'do their homework' before meeting the Queen.

As well as retaining some prerogative powers, the sovereign has traditionally been called on to fulfil a unifying role as a national figurehead at times of crisis. The late HM Queen Elizabeth the Queen Mother toured bomb sites in

London's East End to provide comfort to dispossessed families during the Blitz, while the Queen's annual televised Christmas Day address is designed as much to 'sum up' the past year and look to that ahead on the whole nation's behalf as to update her subjects on her own regal affairs. Such is the onus placed on the sovereign to 'speak for Britain' at times of tragedy or disaster that the Queen's initial silence following the death of Diana, Princess of Wales, and her lover, Dodi Fayed, in a Paris car crash in 1997 became a cause célèbre among her critics—allegedly prompting newly elected premier Mr Blair to appeal to her to issue a tribute.

In terms of public profile, the reigning monarch must retain the appearance of political neutrality at all times—in particular, standing 'above' *party* politics. However, concerns have been raised that her heir, the Prince of Wales, has repeatedly expressed his personal political views to government ministers. In 2015, a number of letters were published showing how the Prince had lobbied various government ministers for changes in government policy (see 19.1.1.1), while in May 2014 he sparked a diplomatic row with Russia after reportedly comparing the country's president, Vladimir Putin, to Adolf Hitler in a private discussion (leaked to the media) with a woman who fled the Nazis.

Although she has generally been careful to avoid such scrapes, the Queen herself was embroiled in controversy after delivering the June 2014 Queen's Speech. Labour formally complained to the head of the Civil Service that the speech contained Conservative Party slogans, including the phrase 'long-term plan' repeatedly used by ministers to promote their economic strategy. This echoed a similar complaint by Mr Cameron about Gordon Brown's final Queen's Speech, in 2009, which he had dismissed as a 'Labour press release on Palace parchment'.

1.2.2.2 Notional prerogative powers: those delegated to government

Most sovereign powers are exercised 'on the advice of ministers', meaning that it is they—and the prime minister mostly—who actually take decisions. In practice, then, the monarch offers 'advice' to prime ministers, rather than the other way round, and premiers discharge the following functions:

- dissolving and summoning Parliament—calling elections and forming new parliaments after elections;
- giving royal assent (the final 'rubberstamp' of approval) to Bills passed by Parliament;
- appointing ministers and other senior public officials, including judges, diplomats, governors, military officers, police chief constables, and Church of England bishops and archbishops;
- devising the legislative agenda for each parliamentary session (year of Parliament) and *writing* the Queen's Speech, which outlines that agenda and is read out by the sovereign at the State Opening of Parliament;

- declaring war and peace;
- proroguing Parliament—that is, suspending its activities over holiday periods, such as the summer recess, and annual Christmas and Easter breaks; and
- drawing up lists of nominations—in consultation with Opposition party leaders—for peerages, knighthoods, and other honours to be confirmed by the sovereign in the New Year Honours List and Queen's Birthday Honours List.

In addition, the monarch occasionally issues 'royal pardons'—formally known as 'royal prerogatives of mercy'—to convicted criminals. This tends to happen either when convicts are pardoned in light of new evidence or (rarer still) when their actions are deemed to merit their early release from jail. Unlike all other sovereign powers exercised by the government on the monarch's behalf, pardons are issued on the advice not of the prime minister but the Justice Secretary (in England and Wales), Scottish First Minister (Scotland), or Northern Ireland Secretary (Northern Ireland). In 2006, a blanket royal pardon was posthumously given to families of all British soldiers executed for cowardice during the First World War.

1.2.3 How the monarchy is funded

For forty years before the 2012–13 tax year, the income of the reigning monarch and his or her immediate family—the 'Royal Household'—derived from the following:

- the Civil List;
- grants-in-aid;
- the Privy Purse; and
- personal income.

However, the Sovereign Grant Act 2011 introduced a rationalized funding regime, which has seen the first two sources of sovereign income (both funded by taxpayers) supplanted by a single annual payment: the **sovereign grant**.

1.2.3.1 From old to new: finances in transition

Often invoked by those who favour abolishing the monarchy as shorthand for the Royal Family as a whole, the Civil List originated in the Bill of Rights. With William and Mary's accession, Parliament voted to pay the Royal Household £600,000 to aid it in 'civil government'. The List in its more recent form was established in 1760, during George III's reign. In return for the king surrendering to Parliament his 'hereditary revenues'—income generated by the Crown Lands (estates owned previously by the monarch)—MPs agreed a fixed annual income for the Royal Household. In practice, this exchange has reaped huge dividends for Parliament: in 2015–16, the income generated for the Treasury by the Crown Lands (as administered by the Crown Estate Commissioners) hit a record £304.1 million, compared to the £42.8m paid to the monarch in sovereign grant.

In 2001, the List itself was fixed at £7.9 million a year for the Queen until at least 2011, with her husband, the Duke of Edinburgh (Prince Philip), receiving a separate £359,000 annuity. In a deal struck with then Chancellor Mr Brown, the Queen agreed to finance increases in her outgoings from a 'reserve fund' worth up to £30 million, accumulated over the previous decade. In return, her and Prince Philip's 'fixed' incomes would rise by 7.5 per cent a year to keep abreast of inflation (which, was 3 per cent in 2001). As a result, by the end of 2009–10, the List had swelled to £14.2 million. Like many households, though, the royals emerged from the recession less solvent than beforehand: Buckingham Palace's 2009–10 accounts revealed that the Queen had supplemented the official Civil List pot by a record £6.5 million during that year, reducing her reserve fund to £15.2 million. Even before replacing the old funding system with the sovereign grant, the then Chancellor George Osborne made the Royal Family's taxpayer-funded income subject to the same scrutiny as government departments, amending the Civil List Audit Act 1816 to hand auditing powers to the National Audit Office and the influential Public Accounts Committee of MPs. And in his subsequent Comprehensive Spending Review (CSR) (see 7.1.2), he revealed that the Queen had agreed to a two-year freeze in her grant funding, in 2011–12 and 2012–13, necessitating a 14 per cent reduction in the Royal Household's spending.

In the years immediately prior to its abolition, the List funded the following expenses:

- salaries of the retinue of 645 servants, butlers, and other Royal Household employees (70 per cent); and
- costs of royal garden parties (attended by 48,000 people each year) and hospitality during state visits (30 per cent).

In addition, several parliamentary allowances were issued annually to individual Royal Family members, including the Duke of York (Prince Andrew) and the Princess Royal (Princess Anne), under the Civil List Acts. These generally amounted to £2.5 million extra, although from April 1993 the Queen refunded £1.5 million to Parliament in practice, using her personal pot of money, the Privy Purse (see 1.2.3.2). The remaining £1 million was retained as income for the Duke of Edinburgh and, until her death in 2002, the Queen Mother. All other senior royals performing official duties received annuities from the Privy Purse rather than the Civil List.

Perhaps surprisingly, one of the few key Royal Household members who did not benefit from these annuities was Prince Charles: as Duke of Cornwall, he earns substantial income from his sprawling 130,000-acre Duchy of Cornwall estate. Originally bestowed on the Black Prince in 1337, the Duchy extends over twenty-three counties. According to the Prince of Wales and Duchess of Cornwall's Annual Review 2016 (available online at www.princeofwales.gov.uk), in 2015–16 it generated income of £20.5 million (including departmental subsidies and the portion of the sovereign grant spent on the couple's main residence, St James's Palace). This was a year-on-year rise of 3 per cent.

While the Civil List covered the Royal Household's day-to-day living costs, the other customary pot of taxpayers' money, grants-in-aid, maintained the 'occupied royal palaces'—those, including Buckingham Palace, Kensington Palace, and Windsor Castle, in which Royal Family members still lived—and its personal transport, primarily the Royal Air Force (RAF) aircraft of the No. 32 (The Royal) Squadron, the Royal Train, and numerous chartered and scheduled flights used by senior royals for official visits. These were awarded by the Department of Culture, Media, and Sport (DCMS) and the Department for Transport (DfT) respectively.

In recent years, disclosures of the Royal Family's travel expenditure in the preceding twelve months has attracted heavy media attention, though its 2015–16 accounts, published in July 2016, showed it had dropped by £1m since the previous year, to around £4m. Its most notorious globetrotter has generally been the Duke of York, Prince Andrew—nicknamed 'Airmiles Andy'—and, true to form, he racked up some impressive expenses in 2015–16, including a trip on behalf of his mother to celebrate the fiftieth anniversary of Singapore's independence, costing £20,238.

The remaining grants-in-aid budget, as was (typically one tenth of the total), was spent on royal 'communications': letters, telephone bills, and other correspondences (including party invitations).

For its first five years, the sovereign grant was set at 15 per cent of the net revenue generated each year by the Crown Estates: a settlement which, left unchecked, would result in a 6.5 per cent 'pay rise' for the Queen in 2017–18, to £45.6m. The more generous nature of the grant, compared to the combined value of the old Civil List payments and grants-in-aid, was designed to enable the Queen to finance future repairs to her palaces without the need for further public subsidy. An early example of this was the £4.5 million renovation of the Kensington Palace apartment used by the Duke and Duchess of Cambridge revealed in her 2013–14 accounts. The parliamentary annuities that the Queen used to receive for family members have also now ceased. If there is money left from the sovereign grant in a given year, this is paid into a reserve fund overseen by the Royal Trustees (up to a maximum value of half of the grant awarded). Conversely, if the Queen requires more money one year, she can dip into this fund to meet any unforeseen expenditure. At the time of writing, the Royal Household was awaiting the outcome of the first five-year review of the grant, and with a new Chancellor of the Exchequer, Philip Hammond, in charge of the purse strings.

1.2.3.2 The Privy Purse

Dating back to 1399, the Privy Purse derives from income generated by the Duchy of Lancaster—a huge expanse of land covering 19,268 acres and the sole surviving Crown estate still 'owned' by the monarch. It is kept under lock and key by her personal accountant, and administered by the Chancellor of the Duchy of Lancaster—usually a senior Cabinet minister—and the Keeper of the Privy Purse (currently Sir Alan Reid). The most recent Duchy of Lancaster accounts show that, in 2015–16, the Privy Purse's net income was £17.8m—up 7.7 per cent on the previous year—while the estate's value rose to £495m (£472m in 2014–15).

1.2.3.3 Personal income

Senior Royal Family members, despite deriving significant income from the state, are free to generate earnings—provided they pay income tax on these. Personal incomes earned by individual members include the military salaries drawn at various times by Prince Charles, his brothers Princes Andrew and Edward, and both the Duke of Cambridge and Prince Harry. Other examples include income earned by the Duchy of Cornwall from rent and sales of its produce.

More sporadic sources of income might include everything from share dividends to windfalls from betting on the races (the Queen Mother famously liked a flutter).

1.2.4 Taxation and the monarchy

Like everyone else, the Queen has always paid indirect taxes—value added tax (VAT) and other tariffs levied on consumer goods and services. She also voluntarily pays Council Tax. It was not until 1993, however, that she agreed to pay income tax—prompted by a public backlash over the revelation that much of the £60 million cost of repairing Windsor Castle after a devastating 1992 fire was funded by taxpayers, despite the fact they already heavily subsidized her household.

The monarch and certain immediate family members do, though, enjoy substantial tax breaks not granted to her subjects. While the Privy Purse pays tax and the Queen's personal estate incurs inheritance tax, the sovereign grant is untaxed, as is any property transfer 'from sovereign to sovereign'. Hardly surprising, perhaps, that when, in November 2016, it emerged that Buckingham Palace required repairs totalling £369m, an online petition was launched urging the Royal Household to foot the bill itself, and some senior Labour figures, including Shadow Chancellor John McDonnell and Shadow Business Secretary Clive Lewis, added their voices to the calls.

1.2.5 The succession

As in other European nation states, the monarchy has, for centuries, passed from father to son in Britain, through a process known as 'eldest male primogeniture'.

When a male line (going through the eldest son) is exhausted, the crown passes to the eldest male sibling of its originator, and only after his male line ends will it ever reach a woman. Under this system, Prince Charles would have inherited the throne from his mother and, after his death, it would have passed to his eldest son, William, and then to *his* son, George. The only way it would ever have reached William's daughter, Charlotte, was after passing through any other son he later had and *his* line. It would finally have passed to William's younger brother, Harry, only after going through each of the former's offspring.

This was the route the Crown *would* have taken after the death of Queen Elizabeth based on the original eldest male principle. However, in a radical constitutional departure, the Coalition dispensed with centuries of tradition by passing the Succession to the Crown Act 2013, which will end eldest male primogeniture with effect from the succession of Prince William. Had Princess Charlotte been the Duke and Duchess of Cambridge's eldest child, she would automatically have succeeded to the throne following William's death, rather than losing out to any younger brother. In a further significant change, the Bill of Rights, Act of Settlement, and Royal Marriages Act 1772 were all amended at the same time to allow future sovereigns to marry Roman Catholics without forfeiting their titles. The legal obligation of every descendant of George II to seek the monarch's permission before getting married has also been limited to the six family members closest to the Crown.

1.2.6 Monarchy versus presidency: which way forward?

Although Britain has had a monarchy for some 1,500 years, today it is one of the few 'developed' nations to retain one—let alone boast an extended Royal Family, funded largely by taxpayers. Recent years have witnessed growing calls for it to be replaced by an elected head of state. These have been fuelled by a succession of controversies surrounding the Royal Household, in particular that relating to Prince Charles's divorce from Diana, Princess of Wales, and revelations about his long-standing relationship with Camilla Parker-Bowles (now his second wife and Duchess of Cornwall). Further succour was given to those arguing for Britain's hereditary figurehead to be replaced by an elected one by the Australian electorate's narrow decision to retain the Queen as Australia's head of state in November 1999.

The argument for an elected head of state is self-explanatory: in a modern democracy (so the republican case goes), it is surely only right that the state's ultimate ambassador—the individual who publicly represents its interests on the global stage—should seek a 'mandate' from his or her subjects. But what are the arguments for retaining a monarch? Opinions differ among constitutional historians about the institution's merits, but an oft-cited argument favouring the hereditary principle is that it produces heads of state capable of maintaining an objective, independent-minded *distance* from the day-to-day workings of the political process—rather than being hidebound by the narrow, short-term thinking that constrains politicians reliant on the votes of a fickle electorate. In addition, the presence of Queen Elizabeth II through sixty years of changing governments and shifting political priorities has provided, some argue, a degree of continuity absent from presidential states.

1.3 Devolution: from union to government in the nations

Most of this chapter has focused on outlining the process by which the modern British state came into being, and the rules, customs, and laws that have evolved to determine the balance of powers between Parliament, monarchy, and citizens.

The UK is a 'representative democracy'—a state that exercises its power through democratically elected representatives (MPs in the House of Commons). There are two main types of democracy: *federal* and *unitary*. In federal democracies, countries are divided into separate political units, each with considerable autonomy over its own affairs. The United States is one such democracy: major foreign and domestic policy decisions are taken by the national government (president and Congress), but many day-to-day matters are decided on a state-by-state basis. The most oft-cited example of **federalism** in action relates to the way in which different states punish felons convicted of serious crimes such as murder and rape: while fourteen US states favour custodial sentences, the remaining thirty-six still practise capital punishment.

Britain, by contrast, has long been a unitary democracy. Since the passage of the 1706–7 Acts of Union, most power has resided with its central government and Parliament. But while its constitutional story since the late medieval period has mostly been one of the gradual unification and consolidation at the centre, in recent decades this has been compromised by gradual decentralization, with power shifting incrementally closer to the people from whom it derives. This trend is in the process of being consolidated following Scotland's 2014 independence referendum, with further devolution north of the border and the introduction of a new upper tier of local government in metropolitan areas, in the form of combined authorities with sweeping powers which, in some cases, will include local management of the National Health Service (NHS) and even the ability to levy their own taxes (see 2.9.1.2).

The story of the emergence of local government—elected councils, funded by local taxpayers, which run local services—is told in Chapter 10. But, at a higher level than the strictly 'local', there now exists in Scotland, Wales, and Northern Ireland self-governing institutions to which significant powers have been devolved by Westminster. This statutory transfer of power from central government to the separate nations that make up the UK alongside England is known as **devolution**.

Before proceeding further, it is important to make the distinction between devolution and **independence**. Although the parties most enthusiastically embracing devolution in Scotland, Wales, and Northern Ireland tend to be 'nationalist' ones—that is, those that would ultimately like to break away from Britain to become independent states—devolved power does not amount to independence. Neither does it inevitably follow that, having gained devolution, a country will one day become independent. Indeed, a principal argument used by Labour to justify devolution was that, in granting it, the party was safeguarding the union, by permitting a limited degree of autonomy that would answer many frustrations with over-centralized power voiced by otherwise loyal British subjects in those countries. Conversely, advocates of independence have argued that, in the long term, it makes little sense for national assemblies in Scotland or Wales, which take most of their own day-to-day decisions, to remain Westminster's vassals, making fuller self-government of one kind or another a logical next step. To this end, barely an hour after the Scottish referendum result was announced, Mr Cameron confirmed plans to set Britain on a more federal course, as part of a 'devolution revolution'—with Scotland rapidly gaining significant additional devolved powers, as outlined below, and Wales, Northern Ireland, and England also earning greater autonomy over their own distinctive internal affairs (see 1.3.6).

1.3.1 The unification of Great Britain

Like much of Britain's constitutional heritage, the concept of devolution originated in the Middle Ages, when Wales and Scotland first began demanding the right to govern themselves independently of the English sovereign. Of the two countries Wales has the longest formal association with England. The main stages in its moves towards incorporation into the UK are outlined in table 1E to be found on the **Online Resource Centre**.

Scotland's progress towards integration in the UK was more complex—in part because it had never been formally absorbed into the Roman Empire. It took centuries of conflict during the medieval period for it to succumb finally to the authority of the English Crown. A timeline showing this is outlined in table 1F to be found on the **Online Resource Centre**.

Northern Ireland's incorporation was still more problematic, encompassing as it did its split from Southern Ireland (Eire). The early stages of the process are outlined in table 1G to be found on the **Online Resource Centre**.

1.3.2 The path to Scottish devolution

Of the three UK countries besides England, Scotland has the most extensive powers, following enabling legislation passed to formalize devolution in 1998 and the extension of its powers after the 2014 referendum. In part, this reflects the fact that, for complex historical reasons, the country has long had certain devolved functions—notably a distinct legal system. More significantly, however, it came about in response to growing calls north of the border, after eighteen years of Conservative rule at Westminster, for greater autonomy from a national Parliament that seemed increasingly remote (both politically and geographically) from Scottish interests.

The path to Scottish devolution began in the 1960s, when the then Labour government established a Royal Commission to examine the arguments for some form of 'home rule'. The sequence of events leading to devolution—and later agreement to extend the scope of the Scottish Parliament's devolved powers—is outlined in Table 1.2.

Unlike Wales and Northern Ireland, where devolved powers have been limited, the Scottish Parliament has considerable authority, with only foreign affairs, defence, social security, and overall tax policy initially outside its

Table 1.2 Timeline for the introduction of devolution in Scotland

Date	Event
1973	Royal Commission on Constitution recommends devolution to Edward Heath's Conservatives
1978	Re-elected Labour government passes Scotland Act, allowing referendum on Scottish self-government: 40% of Scottish electorate must vote for devolution for it to be granted
March 1979	Devolution put on hold because, although 52% of those who voted supported it, this was equivalent to only 32% of total electorate
July 1997	Newly re-elected Labour government publishes Scotland's Parliament White Paper advocating devolution
11 September 1997	New referendum attracts 60% turnout, with 74% of voters backing devolution and 64% voting 'Yes' to second question, backing Scottish Parliament's having tax-varying powers
1998	Government of Scotland Act passed, conferring devolution
12 May 1999	Queen opens new Scottish Parliament after its remit confirmed by consultative steering group
7 September 2004	Grand opening of £420 million purpose-built Scottish Parliament at Holyrood, by foot of Edinburgh's Royal Mile
18 September 2014	Scottish electorate votes in referendum to remain in UK and Alex Salmond resigns as First Minister and leader of the Scottish National Party (SNP)
27 November 2014	Publication of the report of the Smith Commission, recommending further devolution for Scotland
23 March 2016	Passage of the Scotland Act, conferring new powers recommended by Smith Commission—including control of key areas of social security, the ability to set income tax rates, and control over areas including rail franchising and other areas

remit. But most of these restrictions are in the process of being lifted, following passage of the Scotland Act 2016. This devolves to Holyrood half of the VAT receipts raised in Scotland; authority to set income tax rates on non-savings and non-dividend income; control over many aspects of welfare policy and administration; and a raft of other powers relating to everything from the awarding of rail franchises to road speed limits and onshore oil and gas extraction.

Since its inception, the Scottish Parliament's powers have included determining its own education, health, environment, and transport policy, and being able to 'vary'—raise or lower—income tax by up to 3 pence in the pound (the so-called 'Tartan Tax' option). The Scotland Act 2012 conferred more extensive tax-varying powers (up to 10 pence in the pound) but, despite calls from Scottish Labour, the Lib Dems, and the Green Party to raise the basic and higher rates of income tax, the ruling SNP has shied away from introducing a distinctive 'Scottish rate'—suggesting that wealthy people would find ways of avoiding paying it, thereby reducing the government's overall 'tax take' (intriguingly, an argument the Conservatives had used to justify lowering the UK-wide top rate from 50 to 45 pence in the pound). It remains to be seen whether extended fiscal powers devolved over landfill tax in 2015, and income tax and air passenger duty in 2016, will lead to wider variations emerging between Scotland and elsewhere, but the first signs of Holyrood preparing to flex its muscles came when MSPs voted in November 2016 to approve raising bills for households in the top four Council Tax bands from April 2017 (see 11.2.4.1).

1.3.3 The lingering question over Scottish independence

Although Parliament's approval is technically required for independence to be granted, demands for a breakaway Scottish government became a clamour when Alex Salmond, the then dynamic leader of the SNP, was elected First Minister in May 2007—eradicating Labour's majority share of the vote in Scotland for the first time in fifty years. The clamour grew even more acute when, four years on, his party achieved an outright majority.

Mr Salmond's repeated pledges to hold a referendum were addressed in part by a draft Bill published in February 2010, outlining proposals for two separate ballots of Scottish voters. The first would have asked if they supported the Scottish Parliament being granted more devolved autonomy, with two alternative models proposed: one—dubbed 'devolution max', or 'devo max'—involving the handover of all remaining Westminster powers to Holyrood (apart from defence policy, foreign affairs, and financial regulation); the other envisaging a more limited extension of devolution, along the lines of changes suggested in June 2009 in a report published by Sir Kenneth Calman. This included a proposal that 10 pence should be top-sliced from the basic and higher rates of income tax in Scotland, with the Scottish Parliament left to decide whether to make up the shortfall by levying its own top-up tax. Mr Salmond also proposed to ask voters, in a second ballot, if they wanted Holyrood’s powers extended to full-blooded independence. But, even under these plans, the Queen would have remained Scotland’s head of state and the country would have sought to stay in the European Union (although the European Commission later made clear that it could not do so without formally ‘reapplying’ as an independent state).

Mr Salmond renewed his calls for independence in January 2012 when, challenged by Mr Cameron to ‘put up or shut up’, he published a Consultation Paper setting out a detailed timetable and the desired wording of his referendum ‘question’. Stating that he intended to hold the crucial vote in autumn 2014, he revived the notion of putting more than one scenario to the Scottish people, including a ‘devo max’ option. The main item on the ballot paper, however, would be an ‘in or out’ question, worded as follows:

‘Do you agree that Scotland should be an independent country?’

Buoyed by opinion polls suggesting that seven out of ten Scots wanted to preserve the union, Mr Cameron argued that the referendum should concern itself solely with gauging support for full-blown independence. After intense negotiations, Mr Salmond finally agreed a deal in October 2012 to put a single ‘yes or no’ question to the Scottish people. His preferred wording was also amended, after the **Electoral Commission**—the body responsible for ensuring that elections and referendums are conducted fairly—argued that it could be seen as a ‘leading’ question. The final wording was as follows:

‘Should Scotland be an independent country?’

In return for dropping his demand for a second question on ‘devo max’, Mr Salmond secured the Coalition’s promise that the vote’s outcome would be binding, under an obscure constitutional instrument known as ‘Section 30’. In the event, the Scots voted by a margin of 44.7 to 55.3 per cent against independence on 18 September 2014, and Mr Salmond resigned hours later—paving the way for his deputy, Nicola Sturgeon, to succeed him as SNP leader and First Minister.

Though the referendum was ultimately lost by the ‘Yes’ camp, by the time of the vote it had long been clear that, whatever its outcome, the referendum would have major ramifications for the future of Britain’s system of government—not least because opinion polls had shown the gap between the two sides tightening by the day. Moreover, unlike in any previous election, 16- and 17-year-olds were allowed to take part, making it difficult to portray a close result, let alone a win for the ‘Yes’ campaign, as anything less than a clear (and legitimate) expression of dissatisfaction at the status quo.

Since the referendum, the drumroll for independence has continued to build, with an emboldened SNP skilfully keeping alive the prospect of a ‘second referendum’ at some point in the near future. Several recent political events have conspired to make this more likely, most notably the near-wipeout Labour suffered in Scotland—one of its traditional 'heartlands'—in the 2015 general election, when it lost forty seats to the SNP (and retained only one). Its rout was widely put down to its decision to share platforms, and mount a joint 'Better Together' campaign, with the Tories and other pro-union parties in the run-up to the 2014 referendum, rather than make its own case for retaining a powerful, more fully devolved, Scotland in the UK—an ironic charge, in some respects, given the widespread praise heaped on former prime minister (and Scottish MP) Mr Brown for a series of late interventions that were judged to have swung the vote for the 'No' camp. Nonetheless, the nationalist case remained a potent one at time of writing, in light of two further developments. These were the further collapse of Labour support in Scotland in the May 2016 Holyrood elections, which saw the party slip into third place (see 4.5.1) for the first time in nearly a century—ceding the status of 'official opposition' in the Scottish Parliament to the Tories—and the European Union referendum a month later, which saw the SNP cast as one of the most vociferous advocates of continued EU membership (see 9.7.4). In the eyes of SNP supporters, each of these electoral advances only furthered its ultimate cause—both by *reflecting* a continued appetite for independence in Scotland and, in strengthening the party's power base, *legitimating* its demands and keeping them on the Westminster agenda. This appetite intensified after the Scottish electorate voted by 68 to 32 per cent to remain in the European Union in the June 2016 'Brexit' referendum—defying the slender UK-wide majority in favour of leaving (see Chapter 9). With Britain entering previously uncharted constitutional waters, Ms Sturgeon signalled her intention to open negotiations with the EU over the possibility of Scotland's being allowed to stay a member, even if the UK as a whole continued on its path to withdrawal. Tenuous though this option may sound, it is not entirely without precedent: back in 1985, it effectively happened in reverse, when Greenland left the then European Economic Community (EEC), but Denmark (the state of which it is part) remained. During her first meeting with new prime minister Theresa May, barely three weeks after the vote, Ms Sturgeon warned that, if the British government instigated the formal process of withdrawing from the EU before Scotland had had a chance to secure its continued membership, she was prepared to demand a second referendum on Scottish independence as early as the following year 2017.

1.3.4 The path to Welsh devolution

Welsh devolution was introduced as outlined in Table 1.3.

1.3.5 The rocky road to Northern Irish devolution

As a result of the fallout from 'The Troubles', the devolution process in Northern Ireland has been more drawn out, with various parties unable to agree

Table 1.3 Timeline for the introduction of devolution in Wales

Date	Event
July 1997	White Paper entitled A Voice for Wales outlines proposals for Welsh devolution
18 September 1997	Referendum attracts low turnout of around 50%, but 50.3% approve devolution
1998	Government of Wales Act passed to lay out framework
1999	National Assembly for Wales (Transfer of Functions) Order introduced, providing a legal and constitutional framework
6 May 1999	First election for National Assembly for Wales
12 May 1999	National Assembly for Wales meets for first time
1 March 2006	Queen officially opens new, purpose-built £67million Welsh Assembly building in Cardiff
November 2012 and March 2014	Publication—in two parts—of the report of the Commission on Devolution in Wales (the Silk Commission), recommending devolved tax powers, including ability to vary income tax, and devolution of policing, regulatory transport policy and youth justice
March 2014	Wales Act passes into law most of main recommendations of Silk Commission

a workable framework for devolved rule until a landmark 'power-sharing' agreement was finally signed in 2007. With the ruling DUP accepting the IRA had decommissioned its weapons, the Northern Ireland Assembly was restored at this point—cementing a unique governmental arrangement in which all elected parties have seats at the top table, regardless of who 'wins' an election, in an enforced truce designed to reconcile once implacably opposed sectarian interests.

The saga that led to the granting of meaningful devolution to Northern Ireland lasted decades, so it would be impractical to list every twist and turn here, but the most significant events are outlined in Table 1.4.

Ironically, the *level* of power devolved to the province has, so far, been much more limited than that of Scotland or Wales. As in Wales, before it gained greater autonomy over health and education policy, Northern Ireland has largely been restricted to:

- determining budgetary priorities in education, health, etc.;
- funding, directing, and appointing managers of its NHS bodies;

- administering any EU structural funds; and
- determining the content of its version of the National Curriculum in schools.

However, in a highly symbolic development, April 2010 saw the devolution of policing and justice powers. Defying trenchant opposition from the Ulster

Table 1.4 Timeline for the introduction of devolution in Northern Ireland

Date	Event
1968	Dawn of 'The Troubles'—paramilitary struggle between Protestants and Catholics
1972	Most notorious explosion of violence in Troubles history—'Bloody Sunday'—occurs in Derry/Londonderry, culminating at Catholic ghetto the Bogside
1972	Northern Ireland constitution, prime minister, and Parliament suspended for year owing to escalating violence
November 1985	Anglo-Irish Agreement ('Hillsborough Agreement') signed by Britain and Ireland, recognizing that constitutional change can occur only with agreement of population through referendum
December 1993	UK Prime Minister John Major and Irish Taoiseach Albert Reynolds issue Joint Declaration from 10 Downing Street ('The Downing Street Declaration'), stipulating that future participation in discussions about government of Northern Ireland should be restricted to parties committed to 'exclusively peaceful means'
August 1994	IRA announces 'complete cessation of military operations'; Combined Loyalist Military Command confirms own ceasefire
February 1995	British and Irish governments launch proposals for new democratic institutions
February 1996	Docklands bomb ends IRA ceasefire
June 1996	Former US Senator George Mitchell convenes Northern Ireland Forum, outlining six 'Mitchell Principles' for peace process; Sinn Féin excluded until IRA formally readopts ceasefire; two further IRA blasts follow, in Manchester and County Antrim
July 1997	Sinn Féin president Gerry Adams and vice-president Martin McGuinness elected Westminster MPs, and IRA resumes its ceasefire; International Commission on Decommissioning set up under Canadian General John de Chastelain to oversee process
September 1997	Sinn Féin signs up to Mitchell Principles and multiparty talks start at Stormont; after switching to Lancaster House, London, deadline of 9 April 1998 set for agreement
10 April 1998	'Good Friday Agreement' (Belfast Agreement) enables dual referendums on devolution in Northern and Southern Ireland; constitutionally, way is paved by Northern Ireland (Elections) Act 1998 and nineteenth Amendment to Irish Constitution (renouncing Eire's claim on the north)
22 May 1998	Referendum of all Ireland produces 94% backing for devolution in Eire and 71% 'Yes' vote in Northern Ireland
25 June 1998	First elections for Northern Ireland Assembly
1 July 1998	New Assembly meets for first time, with Lord Alderdice as Presiding Officer and David Trimble, Ulster Unionist Party leader, First Minister Designate; at least three nationalists and three designated unionists to be included in government under devolution deal known as 'd'Hondt procedure' (after Belgian Victor d'Hondt); each party allocated seats on 'largest average' basis relating to number of votes it receives
15 August 1998	Twenty-nine people die in Omagh bomb planted by 'Real IRA' splinter group

Table 1.4 *(continued)*

Date	Event
1 December 1999	Direct rule of Northern Ireland from Westminster ends with Queen's signing of Northern Ireland Act 1998
2 December 1999	Anglo-Irish Agreement replaced by British-Irish Agreement, formally creating North–South Ministerial Council and British–Irish Ministerial Council envisaged in Good Friday Agreement; on same day, Irish Parliament replaces Arts 2 and 3 of Irish Constitution—formally abandoning Eire's historic claim to Northern Ireland
11 February 2000	Assembly suspended owing to disagreement about pace of weapons decommissioning; prolonged period of intermittent direct rule resumes
March 2007	After third set of elections in Northern Ireland and power-sharing talks, agreement finally struck to restore devolution
April 2007	Loyalist Volunteer Force follows IRA's declaration of 'final cessation of hostilities' in August 2005 by announcing its end
May 2007	Power-sharing resumes in Assembly

Unionists, the ruling DUP–Sinn Féin coalition won sufficient cross-community approval to drive the process to its next, decisive stage: the appointment of a Justice Minister.

A month later, another watershed was reached, with the long-awaited publication of the final report of an official inquiry set up by Mr Blair into 'Bloody Sunday'—after twelve years of hearings, costing £200 million. The 5,000-page report concluded that when, on 30 January 1972, British paratroopers fired on a civil rights march in Londonderry, killing thirteen civilians, none of the dead had been armed, the paras had shot first and without warning, and some had lied about their actions.

1.3.6 The West Lothian or English Question—and the revival of English devolution

The growing assertiveness of devolved assemblies has raised significant constitutional issues for the UK as a whole. None is more explosive than the 'West Lothian Question': the argument that it is unfair for MPs representing Scottish (or, indeed, Welsh and Northern Irish) constituencies to be able to vote on matters that affect only England, while English members have no say over issues particular to devolved nations. Although devolution was only introduced in 1998, this quandary was first raised in the Commons by Labour backbencher Tam Dalyell in the 1970s. It was dubbed the 'West Lothian Question' by then Tory MP Enoch Powell after the name of Dalyell's constituency.

Under devolution, Westminster governments have bolstered shaky Commons majorities in votes on controversial legislation with the help of Scottish, Welsh, and/or Northern Irish MPs—including, at times, those who did not support the same policies being applied in their own countries (see 6.2).

Today, debate over the West Lothian Question rages louder than ever, reignited by the Scottish referendum. Within an hour of the result, Mr Cameron pledged to give the 'question' of 'English votes for English laws' a 'decisive answer'. To this end, he set up a new commission, led by Lord Smith of Kelvin, to draft further Scottish devolution plans, with then Leader of the House of Commons, William Hague, chairing a cabinet committee devoted to ironing out the practicalities of giving English MPs exclusive jurisdiction over English-only matters. Despite both inquiries swiftly reporting in favour of an 'English votes' plan, it was not until the Conservatives were re-elected in 2015, as a single-party government, that they were taken forward. In October 2015 in defiance of claims by SNP Members that they would be reduced to 'second-class status' in the House—the Commons voted by 312 to 270 to introduce a modified legislative process for Bills (or parts of Bills) certified by the Speaker as applying only to England or England and Wales. Under the new arrangements—introduced by amending the standing orders governing parliamentary procedures—Bills that do not concern Scotland, or Scotland and Northern Ireland, are now considered at committee stage only by English MPs or 'grand committees' comprising MPs from the relevant nations. A fuller explanation of this new system is outlined in Chapter 2.

Despite the strong arguments of principle in favour of this latest stage in Britain's democratic evolution, it is not just the SNP that has taken issue with it. Although it fared very poorly in Scotland in the 2015 general election, Labour has traditionally relied for Commons majorities on the forty-plus MPs it customarily musters there, so any further extension of 'English votes for English laws' would raise the prospect of future Labour governments failing to pass radical domestic legislation in England. To do so, the party would also need to win a majority of English MPs—a feat several Labour governments (notably Wilson's 1964 and 1974 administrations) failed to manage. Fears about such an eventuality were heightened in November 2014, when the Smith Commission recommended that Scotland be given full control of its own income tax and VAT rates—and allowed to keep all the money it raised to spend as it chose. Such enhanced devolution might notionally lead to Scottish MPs being barred from voting on the overall UK Budget—increasing the likelihood that a minority Labour government (or one with a small majority) might struggle to fund its policies.

Leaving aside the wider issue of England's 'national' autonomy (see 'The West Lothian or English Question—and the revival of English devolution' on page 33), the introduction of devolution in Scotland, Wales, and Northern Ireland has led to periodic demands for major English *regions* outside London to be given similar legislative powers. Tentative moves towards embryonic English regional devolution actually emerged under the Tories, when Mr Major set up regional offices manned by civil servants seconded from the main Whitehall departments. When Labour returned to power in 1997, steps were taken to introduce elected English regional authorities, but the first region to hold a referendum on the proposals, the North East, decisively rejected them—kicking regional devolution into touch for years. However, on the back of the recent 'England-only' changes to the parliamentary legislative process, a far wider extension of the devolution principle is now under way in metropolitan areas through the aegis of new 'super-councils' called combined authorities. This has effectively reintroduced the idea of a form of regional government—and with levels of autonomy more commensurate with federalism than mere devolution. A fuller explanation of combined authorities, and the two Acts of Parliament that paved the way for them, follows in Chapter 10.

Topical feature idea

With Scotland gaining enhanced devolved powers, and Greater Manchester becoming the first English region to take on significant new powers—including control of its own £6bn NHS budget—there is a growing appetite for comparable devolved powers among political leaders of a group of 'core cities'—Birmingham, Bristol, Cardiff, Glasgow, Leeds, Liverpool, Manchester, Newcastle, Nottingham and Sheffield—as well as some unitary and county councils. What do people living in your area think about the prospect of regional, or more local, devolution?

✷ Current issues

- **English devolution** To address the 'West Lothian Question' and the associated issue of 'English votes for English laws', the Conservatives have begun the process of introducing full-blooded devolution south of the border, with the Greater Manchester Combined Authority taking on a slew of Greater London Authority-style powers, as well as control of its own NHS budget. Other major northern cities are in talks with the Treasury to take on similar powers as part of Chancellor George Osborne's drive to foster a 'northern powerhouse' to rebalance Britain's economy away from London.
- **A new Bill of Rights?** Following their May 2015 election victory, the Conservatives revived plans to replace the Human Rights Act with a new Bill of Rights and Responsibilities. An in-depth review designed to pave the way for this was announced in the 2016 Queen's Speech.
- **The prospect of another Scottish independence referendum** The triumph of the SNP in Scotland at the 2015 general election, and its re-election at Holyrood, have emboldened its leader, Nicola Sturgeon, and led to calls from some quarters for a

second independence vote—especially in the event of Britain (but not Scotland) voting to leave the European Union in the 2016 EU referendum.

Key points

1. Britain has a flexible, 'unwritten' constitution that derives from a number of sources—principally statute, common law, works of legal authority, and convention.
2. The British constitution is underpinned by two key principles: the *rule of law* stipulates no individual is 'above the law', while the *separation of powers* ensures that executive/government, legislature/Parliament, and judiciary/courts act as 'checks and balances' on each other. Members of Parliament are part of the legislature and their role includes approving or rejecting legislation.
3. Britain has a constitutional monarchy. The reigning sovereign is head of state, commander-in-chief of the Armed Forces, and supreme-governor of the Church of England, but most of his or her prerogative powers are exercised in practice by the government and prime minister.
4. The monarchy today has two principal sources of funding: the *sovereign grant*, an annual payment to the Queen and the Duke of Edinburgh; and the *Privy Purse*, a personal income derived from the income of the Duchy of Lancaster estate.
5. Scotland, Wales, and Northern Ireland have been granted differing levels of devolution: the ability to govern their own affairs in relation to a wide range of policy areas, such as health and education. Scotland also has growing power over its income tax rates.

→ Further reading

Bogdanor, V. (2009) *The New British Constitution*, Oxford: Hart Publishing. **Insightful critique of New Labour's constitutional reform and how it fits into Britain's established constitutional framework.**

Jowell, J., Oliver, D., and Ocinneide, C. (2015) *The Changing Constitution*, 8th edn, Oxford: Oxford University Press. **Revised eighth edition of essay collection focusing on recent developments in the British constitution, incorporating evaluation of the Coalition's reform programme.**

Leyland, P. (2016) *Constitution of the United Kingdom: A Contextual Analysis*, 3rd edn, Oxford: Hart Publishing. **Fully updated third edition of acclaimed analysis of the historical and cultural context of the British constitution, taking account of developments since the 2010 election.**

Loughlin, M. (2013) *The British Constitution: A Very Short Introduction*, Oxford: Oxford University Press. **Concise, punchy, and up-to-the-minute introduction to all aspects of the UK's evolving constitution.**

Olechnowicz, A. (2007) *The Monarchy and the British Nation, 1780 to the Present*, Cambridge: Cambridge University Press. **Informative cultural history of Britain's relationship with its monarchy down the ages.**

Turpin, C. and Tomkins, A. (2011) *British Government and the Constitution: Text and Materials*, 7th edn, Cambridge: Cambridge University Press. **Fully updated guide to the impact of the UK constitution on day-to-day government, replete with extracts from case law and parliamentary documents.**

Online Resource Centre

www.oxfordtextbooks.co.uk/orc/Morrison5e/

Visit the Online Resource Centre that accompanies this book for web links and regular updates.

2

Parliamentary democracy in the UK

2.1 The origins of the British Parliament

As explained in Chapter 1, the reins of power in Britain no longer lie with the sovereign, but with the Houses of Parliament and, specifically, **members of Parliament (MPs)** elected to its primary legislative chamber: the House of Commons.

But what are the origins of today's 'bicameral legislature'—a Parliament comprising twin chambers, each with its own distinct constitutional role? What role does it play in developing and passing legislation and how does it hold ministers accountable for their use of prerogative powers vested in them by the Crown? And how is the authority of Parliament being affected by the onward march of devolution in Britain's nations and regions?

The UK Parliament, famously dubbed the 'mother of parliaments' by nineteenth-century social reformer John Bright, is rooted in successive institutions that emerged in the medieval period—initially to bolster, but ultimately to counteract, the power of monarchy. The most significant of these originated in Norman times, an era of root-and-branch constitutional upheaval that saw the publication, in 1086, of the Domesday Book—England's first great population census. To provide mechanisms through which the sovereign could tax and rule his subjects, a succession of bodies was established. These included the *Magnum Concilium* and *Curia Regis*—early forerunners of Parliament—and the **Privy Council**, a conclave of the sovereign's personal confidantes, at which meetings they continue to officiate to this day. For more detailed explanations of the roles of these bodies, see table 2A to be found on the **Online Resource Centre**.

The role of Parliament has since been greatly, if incrementally, enhanced—and it long ago took precedence over the sovereign in the day-to-day exercise of constitutional power. By the fourteenth century, monarchs were already being forced to recognize that the earls and barons on whom they relied to maintain their authority had a right to be consulted on major affairs of state. It was during this century that kings reluctantly came to accept the need to gain consent from their landed supporters to levy taxes and, in ensuing decades, a newly assertive Parliament of 'Commoners' secured an active role in converting royal petitions (Bills) into statutes (Acts).

Then, in the seventeenth century, came the English Civil War and with it the sequence of decisive constitutional changes outlined in Chapter 1. It would be another 200 years or more, though, before ordinary citizens began to be granted a true stake in parliamentary democracy: a vote.

2.1.1 Parliament today

The above developments are discussed in Chapter 4, which explores the British electoral system. It is this chapter's task to examine two key aspects of Britain's parliamentary democracy: the nature and composition of the various institutions of Parliament; and the roles, duties, and responsibilities that its members discharge on the country's behalf.

2.1.2 Hansard

The workings of the Houses of Parliament—the House of Commons and the House of Lords—are a source of day-to-day news stories and, as such, are routinely covered by gallery reporters for the Press Association and national newspapers, whose job involves sitting through often lengthy debates to tease out newsworthy quotes and angles. A huge aid to the work of today's round-the-clock newsrooms, though, is the way in which the official record of parliamentary business—**Hansard**—has adapted to the demands of the 24-hour news cycle through its near-contemporaneous publication on the Parliament website, at **www.publications.parliament.uk/pa/cm/cmhansrd.htm**.

First published by Parliament itself in 1909, Hansard's origins actually date back to 1771, when a printer named Miller was hauled before the Lord Mayor of London for producing illicit reports of parliamentary debates. The first detailed parliamentary reports appeared in pamphleteer William Cobbett's *Political Register* in 1803, courtesy of one Thomas Curson 'TC' Hansard—the printer from whom the 'official' record derives. But how thorough a record of parliamentary business does today's Hansard offer us? Excepting the words of serving prime ministers, it is not quite verbatim—'repetitions, redundancies, and obvious errors' are omitted—yet it remains the nearest we have to a definitive account of Parliament's business. A more critical overview of individual voting records of MPs and peers—a boon for journalists researching stories or background features on particular political issues or MPs—can be found at the crowd-sourced site **www.theyworkforyou.com**.

2.2 The House of Commons

The linchpin of modern constitutional government in Britain is the 'lower house', or House of Commons. It currently comprises 650 MPs, each representing a **constituency** or 'seat' (electoral district) averaging 70,000 inhabitants. This number is due to be cut to 600 before the 2020 general election, following the latest in a series of periodic reviews of constituency boundaries by Britain's four national Boundary Commissions (see 4.4)—a complex exercise that is meant to update the sizes and shapes of individual seats to make them more 'equal' in terms of the number of voters they cover. In practice, wide disparities are likely to continue to exist between a handful of relatively underpopulated seats, such as the Scottish islands, and those in densely occupied urban areas, but the stated aim of the review is to ensure that no future constituency represents more than 78,507 voters or fewer than 71,031.

Unlike many other parliaments, Commons Members sit along two sets of opposing benches, presided over by a chairperson, the **Speaker**. To the right of the Speaker's chair are the government benches, while on the left are those occupied by 'Her Majesty's Loyal Opposition' (the Opposition)—generally the second biggest party after a general election. All MPs not allied to the governing party (or parties) sit along this side.

The Commons' adversarial layout mirrors the 'two-party politics' that (barring occasional interludes) has characterized Britain's parliamentary scene for centuries. Since the later medieval period, debate has been divided broadly along conservative versus radical/reformist lines with, at various times, Royalists ranged against Parliamentarians, landowning Whigs battling an upwardly mobile, entrepreneurial breed of Tories during the Industrial Revolution, and, latterly, Liberal, then Labour, MPs championing the rights of the 'common man' against the forces of a more establishment 'big C' Conservatism.

In modern times, two-party politics has generally prevailed, largely due to the inequities of the electoral system. As we will see in Chapter 4 (4.2.1), the 'first past the post' (FPTP) voting process sees only candidates who win a *relative majority* of votes cast in their constituencies—that is, more than any of their rivals—elected to the Commons; all votes cast for anyone else being effectively 'wasted'. As a result, the electoral process favours parties that can muster sufficient concentrations of support in enough constituencies to form a government—so discriminating against minority interests and independent candidates.

While Commons debates are chaired by the Speaker, its business timetable is set by a Cabinet minister: the **Leader of the House**. The typical Commons year is outlined in Table 2.1, while its usual weekly sittings are set out in Table 2.2.

Table 2.1 Annual House of Commons timetable

Date	Event
May (one week over spring bank holiday)	Whit recess
May/June	State Opening of Parliament and Queen's Speech
July–September (two months)	Summer recess
September/October (three weeks)	Party conference season
October/November	Prorogation
December–January (for four weeks)	Christmas recess
February (one week)	Half-term recess
March/April (two weeks)	Easter recess

Table 2.2 Weekly House of Commons timetable

Day	Time of sitting
Monday	2.30–10.30 p.m.
Tuesday	2.30–10.30 p.m.
Wednesday	11.30 a.m.–7.30 p.m.
Thursday	10.30 a.m.–6.30 p.m.
Friday (thirteen days a year for private members' business, including private members' Bills)	9.30 a.m.–3.00 p.m.

2.2.1 The role of a member of Parliament (MP) in relation to constituents

As of 1 April 2016, ordinary MPs each receive salaries of £74,962—a rise of 1.3 per cent on the previous July, when members were awarded a corrective 10 per cent rise by the Independent Parliamentary Standards Authority (IPSA) to make up for the preceding five-year period of capped pay introduced by the Coalition in a show of solidarity with public-sector workers whose wages had been frozen as part of the government's austerity drive (see 7.1.2).

At any time, the serving government numbers between eighty and 100-odd MPs. All other members—save Opposition 'shadow ministers'—are known as 'backbench MPs' or **backbenchers**. Once elected, it is the duty of every MP—whether backbencher or frontbencher—to represent the concerns and interests of *all* his or her constituents, regardless of individual voters' political affiliations. Following the parliamentary expenses scandal (see 2.2.6), the Coalition introduced a Bill giving constituents the power to 'recall' MPs found guilty of 'serious wrongdoing' between elections—potentially forcing them to defend their seats in by-elections (see 4.5). Though criticized by many (including the then Tory MP Zac Goldsmith) for including only watered-down versions of the original proposals, the resulting Recall of MPs Act 2015 applies to members who are either sentenced to prison terms or suspended from the Commons for twenty-one or more sitting days. Under such circumstances, the Speaker (see 2.6) gives notice to a petitions officer to inform electors in the MP's constituency that a petition is being published recalling him or her for a by-election. If, after eight weeks, 10 per cent or more of eligible voters in the constituency have signed, a by-election is called.

So what duties are MPs *meant* to perform? Members' constituency responsibilities include:

- holding weekly 'surgeries' for constituents;
- writing to departmental ministers to try to resolve grievances voiced by constituents;
- asking written or oral questions in the Commons at Question Time—both 'Prime Minister's Questions' on a Wednesday and other regular slots, during which senior ministers answer for their departments;
- canvassing support among fellow MPs for early day motions (EDMs)—formal parliamentary records expressing strong views on issues dear to them;
- requesting leave from the Speaker for adjournment debates, urgent debates, or debates on e-petitions;
- introducing private members' Bills (PMBs)—primary legislation that, if passed, would change the law of the land (see 2.4.1.2); and
- coordinating e-petitions on behalf of constituents and/or the wider public interest.

The main forms of debate that may be tabled or promoted by backbenchers are explained in Table 2.3, but certain of their roles justify more detailed explanation.

2.2.1.1 Surgeries

Also known as 'clinics', these weekly drop-ins may be attended by constituents wishing to voice concerns. They are normally held on Thursdays or Fridays (when little parliamentary business is timetabled), or Saturdays in the case of MPs whose constituencies are distant from London. Although many MPs hold surgeries in their constituency offices, they frequently take place in more informal surroundings, such as church halls, libraries, community centres, and even pubs.

Given that surgeries provide forums for constituents to air grievances and to come into direct contact with representatives who might at other times seem somewhat 'distant' has occasionally led to their customary civility breaking down, to be replaced by a tenser, more confrontational, atmosphere. Most dramatically, Labour MP Jo Cox was stabbed and shot dead outside a constituency

Table 2.3 Types of Commons debate that may be tabled or promoted by backbenchers

Name	How it works	Example
Early day motion (EDM)	'Paper' record of strong view expressed by number of MPs. Rarely results in actual 'motion' (vote) or wins sufficient signatures to warrant full debate (for which at least half of sitting MPs must support motion), but, as part of official Commons record, has official status greater than minor procedures. Often gives journalists stories—and can, over time, influence government. Most importantly, enables backbenchers to highlight issues of personal concern, gauging colleagues' support for more definite attempts to initiate change through PMBs (see 2.4.1.2)	Most significant EDM of recent times was tabled by then Opposition leader Margaret Thatcher in 1979, censuring Jim Callaghan's ailing Labour government. Callaghan's administration had been unstable since the collapse of the 'Lib–Lab Pact' negotiated with David Steel's Liberal Party the previous August, and Mrs Thatcher's motion precipitated a 'vote of no confidence' that brought it down. What followed for Labour, on 4 May 1979, was election loss to Tories. Other EDMs have included an influential motion signed by 412 of 646 MPs, days after the 2005 election, calling for a Climate Change Bill, which followed in 2006. Only three other EDMs had ever received more than 400 signatures.
Adjournment debate	Half-hour debate on motion that 'this House do now adjourn', held either in Commons or neighbouring Westminster Hall at end of day's business. Presents opportunity for a backbencher to raise issue of concern to his/her constituents—and to 'summon' a minister to respond. As with EDMs, adjournment debates rarely result in votes, other than when debate raises a nationally significant issue over which strong disagreement exists.	Conservative Prime Minister Neville Chamberlain, signatory to the Munich Agreement with Nazi Germany, was brought down by a motion flowing from adjournment debate: while the government won the vote—effectively a motion of confidence in his leadership following Hitler's breach of agreement by invading Poland—he resigned, and was replaced by Winston Churchill.

(continued)

Table 2.3 (*continued*)

Name	How it works	Example
Urgent debate	A backbencher may apply to the Speaker for urgent debate 'on a specific and important matter that should have urgent consideration' under Standing Order No. 24. In practice, far more MPs apply than are granted debates and the Speaker allows only one or two per session. If granted, debate takes place within twenty-four hours.	Recent urgent debates have included one called by David Cameron in August 2013 to determine whether Britain should back military action against the government of Syria, amid claims that it had used chemical weapons on its civilians.
e-petition debate	The Coalition introduced e-petitions to boost public engagement with Parliament. Anyone can start e-petitions by setting them up online at http://epetitions.direct.gov.uk. If it receives 100,000 or more signatories, e-petition is referred to the Backbench Business Committee for consideration for full Commons debate on one of thirty-five days each session. Campaigning backbenchers increasingly help to coordinate e-petitions to win parliamentary time for debates on pet issues.	Several parliamentary debates have been prompted by e-petitions, with grass-roots campaign groups such as 38 Degrees and Avaaz leading calls for MPs to debate issues ranging from the 'Robin Hood Tax' on big banks to electoral reform. Labour used justification of an e-petition attracting 170,000 backers for an urgent debate on the Coalition's NHS reforms to table a last-minute attempt to halt them in March 2012—weeks after ministers blocked an e-petition debate on this issue, arguing that it had already been debated in Commons. Backers of an e-petition demanding reinstatement of the death penalty (coordinated by political blogger Guido Fawkes via his order-order.com website) failed to secure debate after attracting j ust 26,000 signatories.

surgery in her West Yorkshire seat on 16 June 2016 by an armed constituent subsequently charged with her murder (see 4.5).

2.2.1.2 Question Time

An opportunity to quiz senior departmental ministers directly about their policy decisions and the day-to-day workings of their ministries, **Question Time** is held for at least one hour a day whenever the Commons sits. On Mondays and Tuesdays, it takes place between 2.30 p.m. and 3.30 p.m.; on Wednesdays, from 11.30 a.m. to 12 p.m.; on Thursdays, from 10.30 a.m. to 12.30 p.m. (the two-hour slot on this day is intended to make up for the fact Parliament rarely sits on Fridays).

Each department takes turns to answer questions from the Commons floor on a fortnightly rota. In addition to these *departmental* question times, the prime minister answers questions on Wednesday lunchtimes, from 12 noon to 12.30 p.m. Between its introduction in 1961 and Mr Blair's election in 1997, 'Prime Minister's Questions' (PMQs) occupied a twice-weekly 15-minute slot: on Tuesdays and Thursdays, between 3.00 p.m. and 3.15 p.m. Mr Blair's decision to combine the two into a single session was widely criticized as a high-handed presidential-style gesture calculated to limit opportunities for Parliament (and his own party) to scrutinize him publicly. Nonetheless, the bumper Wednesday PMQs slot—which, since 1989, has been televised live on BBC2—remains a knockabout media highlight of the weekly Commons timetable.

Questions posed at departmental question times tend to be for verbal ('oral') responses. They are answered by ministers according to a rota called the 'Order of Oral Questions'. Prime Minister's Questions, in contrast, take one of two forms: oral or written (officially 'questions for a written answer').

Posed, as they are, in front of television cameras, oral questions attract most media attention—often more for their 'Punch and Judy' nature than substance. Because PMQs can be very oversubscribed, MPs keen to ask questions are advised to give the Speaker three days' advance notice of their intentions to ensure that their names appear sufficiently early on the order paper for them to be called in the allotted time. Giving such notice does *not* mean that MPs must specify the *exact wording* of their questions in advance; merely that they let it be known that they wish to ask them.

PMQs follow curious conventions. The opening question tends to be one asking the prime minister about his/her other engagements for the rest of the day. This is immediately tailed by the 'real' question the MP who began with the procedural one wants to ask. Should the PM refer, later in the session, to 'the reply I gave some moments ago', he or she is alluding to the fact that the next MP to pose a question has also used the formality of asking about his or her engagements as a device to get onto the order paper.

While the prime minister may have prior notice of the subjects to which questions relate, he or she rarely knows exactly how they will be phrased—which can occasionally lead him or her to falter or stumble, even in these heavily choreographed political times. That said, PMQs is often criticized by serious-minded observers for being superficial and insincere, and playing to the cameras. And it is not only the prime minister and his or her would-be Opposition replacement who are accused of this: the most derided questions are often those asked by jobbing backbenchers using the session as an opportunity either to curry favour with their constituents by focusing on local issues, or to massage ministers' egos in the hope of gaining promotion.

In general, MPs genuinely seeking to hold ministers to account for their actions and influence decision-making on their constituents' behalf will pose *written questions* (which, as well as being 'put on paper' themselves, are intended for written answers). This enables them to be forensic—seeking more detailed replies than are delivered during the theatrical point-scoring exercise that PMQs often resembles. Although ministers invariably put a positive gloss on their policies—and the luxury of being able to map out a considered written answer gives them ample scope to do so—they are under a constitutional obligation to reply to these questions thoroughly and accurately. From a journalistic viewpoint, while snappy oral 'sound-bites' may generate easy headlines, stories that emerge from skilfully worded written questions can be more newsworthy in the long run.

An alternative is to table 'urgent questions'. These are on issues that have suddenly come to light and do not require MPs to give the usual three days' notice. In recent times, this device has increasingly been used by shadow ministers, as well as backbenchers, to hold ministers to account: since entering Opposition in 2010, Labour has tabled numerous urgent questions, grilling first the Coalition then the Conservative government on everything from its controversial welfare reforms to its attempted imposition of a new junior doctors' contract in April 2016 (see 6.3.3).

None of this is to downplay the importance of straightforward oral questions—PMQs in particular. As a weekly barometer of the political weather, there is nothing to rival it. While ordinary backbenchers may ask just one question, the Leader of the Opposition is allowed to pose six supplementaries and that of the second largest opposing party (presently the SNP) two. Between May 2010 and 2015, Mr Clegg, then head of the third biggest party, the Liberal Democrats, forfeited his right to ask questions for the duration of the Coalition—and, as deputy prime minister, stood in at the despatch box when Mr Cameron was abroad.

PMQs have long generated lively exchanges between serving prime ministers and the pretenders who would dethrone them—and are said to make or break party leaders. Despite a shaky start, Mr Blair became an adept Question Time operator in his decade in power. Nonetheless, on stepping down in summer 2007, he confessed he had always privately dreaded the weekly ordeal. More recently, the style of PMQs changed somewhat, at least for a time, with the election of

Mr Corbyn as Labour leader. The old-school backbencher initially eschewed the theatrical approach of his predecessors, and for the first few months even went so far as crowd-sourcing questions from his supporters, rather than using the weekly session to hurl the usual sound bites at Mr Cameron.

2.2.2 The role of an MP in relation to Parliament and party

Constitutionally, an MP's primary duty of care lies with his or her constituents. In addition, MPs have a responsibility to Parliament, and the British people generally, to participate in debate and scrutinize the workings of the executive (government and Cabinet). A chief way in which they discharge this responsibility is through the committee system—a key 'check and balance' built into the workings of the legislature to ensure government transparency and accountability.

In practice, however, the nature of Britain's party system means that these constitutional responsibilities can conflict with the pressure MPs encounter to support and defend their parties' policy positions. This instilled 'party loyalty'—increasingly enforced by a strict whip system—is known as 'toeing the party line'. The archaic expression refers to the clearly delineated lines drawn along the length of the Commons in front of each set of benches, behind which members are required to stand while debating. It relates to the principle that opposing MPs should be made to stand sufficiently far apart to ensure that if they were to draw swords in the heat of debate, they could hold their arms fully outstretched without their weapons clashing.

2.2.3 Parliamentary scrutiny and the committee system

Most backbenchers—and peers, who have an equivalent system in the Lords—are members of at least one committee. Each comprises a minimum of eleven members, one of whom is elected to chair. The proportion of committees chaired by MPs or peers drawn from one party or other has customarily reflected the distribution of Commons seats. Between May 1997 and May 2010, therefore, Labour had proportionately more chairpersons than all other parties put together, reflecting its majority, while the same is currently true of the Tories.

Although committees have become more 'fluid' in the forms that they have taken recently—a Committee against Anti-Semitism was formed in 2005—they can generally be divided into three types:

- select committees;
- general committees (including public and private Bill committees, and grand committees); and
- joint committees.

2.2.3.1 Select committees

The most frequently publicized type, **select committees** scrutinize the workings of individual government departments and Parliament itself, and as such are permanent (at least until the department to which they relate is renamed or disbanded). At time of writing, there were forty-seven select committees, covering a mix of departmental matters, interdepartmental policy issues, and internal parliamentary and wider constitutional matters. This latter category includes the Backbench Business Committee, which decides how the (limited) time allotted to backbenchers is divided up, Departmental committees include the Education Committee—which scrutinizes the Department for Education (DfE)—and the Culture, Media, and Sport Select Committee. There is also a Commons Liaison Committee, comprising the chairpersons of all other select committees, to which prime ministers submit themselves for questioning on government policy twice a year.

Select committees have powers to summon MPs, senior civil servants, and other public officials as witnesses, and publish reports on their findings, which are printed, delivered to the Commons, and placed on the Parliament website. Dissembling though their responses might be, governments have only sixty days to reply formally to committees' recommendations. One of the most explosive hearings of recent times occurred on 15 July 2003, when the late weapons inspector David Kelly was grilled by the Foreign Affairs Select Committee amid the controversy over a dossier compiled by the Blair government to justify its case for war against Saddam Hussein's Iraq. Members subjected Dr Kelly to intensive questioning about whether he was the source of a report by BBC defence correspondent Andrew Gilligan for Radio 4's *Today* programme. This programme claimed that senior intelligence sources were concerned that ministers had 'sexed up' the dossier by exaggerating the likelihood that Saddam's forces could unleash weapons of mass destruction (WMDs) within forty-five minutes of being ordered to do so. Dr Kelly was found dead in a wood near his Gloucestershire home two days later.

Because they are permanent, the composition of select committees has been contentious, in light of their customary inbuilt bias towards governing parties. During the Thatcher and early Blair years, Parliament was often criticized for failing to hold ministers adequately to account, and committees in particular often seemed neutered—not least because premiers had a habit of using their party whips to parachute favoured placemen and women into chairperson roles. It was against this backdrop (and the general loss of public trust in MPs sparked by the expenses controversy) that the Commons Parliamentary Reform Select Committee recommended in 2010 that all future chairpersons should be formally elected by fellow MPs. The Coalition implemented this recommendation, introducing elections by alternative vote (AV—see 4.6) for most chairs and extending the scope of elections further, to cover all members of such committees. Henceforth, committee seats allotted to each party proportionally would be filled by MPs elected by their fellow party members.

2.2.3.2 General (including public and private Bill) committees

The other most influential type of committee is the **general committee**—an overarching category embracing public Bill committees, private Bill committees, and grand committees. Most numerous are the first of these (previously known as 'standing committees'). The role of **public Bill committees** is to scrutinize, comment on, amend, and/or refer back to the Commons for further consideration Bills in the process of becoming Acts. Unlike the standing committees of old, they have enhanced powers, including the ability to summon expert witnesses and officials from outside Parliament to give evidence.

Because the work of public and **private Bill committees** can take weeks or months, governments sometimes try to bypass them by rushing through legislation they deem urgent. If agreed by the Speaker, in such cases the Commons itself takes on the role of such a committee, as a 'Committee of the Whole House'—an approach that the Lords uses more routinely for its own committee stages. This crucial stage in the passage of a Bill is explored in more detail in section 2.5.

Most **grand committees** are concerned with debating the impact of legislation on specific geographical nations and regions. There are, for example, grand committees for the East Midlands and Scotland. Grand committees also exist for delegated legislation, European documents, and the House of Lords—which uses them for committee stages not taken on the floor of the House.

2.2.3.3 Joint committees

So-called because they are composed of both MPs and peers, joint committees include the Joint Committee on House of Lords Reform, formed in 2002 to consider a range of alternative options for the composition of the 'Upper House' in the wake of the as-yet-incomplete Lords reforms (see 2.3). Since 1894, there has been a joint committee devoted to assisting the swift passage of laws designed to rationalize the number of Acts on the statute book (the record of all parliamentary legislation in place at any one time). These 'consolidation Bills', normally introduced in the Lords rather than the Commons, seek to combine disparate Acts on the same subjects into single statutes.

2.2.4 Into the twenty-first century: juggling parliamentary and constituency work

A significant development approved in October 2011 was the use of Twitter in the Commons. After the House Procedure Committee recommended that portable electronic devices be permitted in the main chamber, MPs voted 206 to 63 against a motion to block the use of social media—defying warnings by opponents, including the then Lib Dem Deputy Leader Simon Hughes, that this could lead to tweeting members appearing 'disconnected' from debates.

In theory, using Twitter (and SMS text messaging and email) could prove revolutionary, enabling MPs to juggle parliamentary duties with answering constituents' queries and receiving feedback. In practice, questions remain about whether most members are up to such multitasking. Even as the Commons voted in favour of tweeting (provided it was done silently), the *Huffington Post* ran a news feature revealing that MPs who tweeted most frequently and/or had the greatest number of followers tended to be those with the poorest parliamentary attendance. Meanwhile, in July 2012, members of the Commons Treasury Committee were widely criticized in the media for tweeting while they were supposed to be concentrating on questioning former Barclays chief executive Bob Diamond over the Libor-rigging scandal (see 7.3.4.1).

2.2.5 Party loyalty and the whip system

As noted earlier, British MPs tend to be affiliated to political parties. Notable exceptions have included Martin Bell, the one-time BBC foreign correspondent who overturned disgraced former Tory minister Neil Hamilton's huge majority in Tatton in 1997, standing as an independent candidate on an 'anti-sleaze' ticket. But, mostly, the nature of Britain's electoral system tends to guarantee candidates backed by major party machines the best chances of election. The 2010 election saw Caroline Lucas elected as Britain's first Green Party MP in Brighton Pavilion (she was re-elected in 2015), while in March 2012 former Labour backbencher George Galloway trounced his old party in a dramatic by-election win for Respect in Bradford West (though Labour regained the seat five years later). Moreover, following the defection to UKIP of Tory MPs Douglas Carswell and Mark Reckless, and their successful defence of their seats in later by-elections, a new 'minority' force entered the Commons just months before the 2015 election.

Party membership is a double-edged sword. Being selected as a candidate for a major party grants an individual access to a huge support network, including significant financial backing in election campaigns. By contrast, Independents must largely fund themselves. But being a partisan MP also comes at a price. Parties in Britain have traditionally been 'broad churches' representing people united by common ideals but holding a variety of shades of opinion on specific issues. In recent times, however, party leaders have been criticized for stifling dissent in their ranks by using the whip system to force their MPs to back the party line when voting.

There are three broad definitions of the term **whip**:

- whips;
- party whip; and
- three-line whips.

Whips are individuals (MPs or peers) charged with 'whipping into line' backbenchers when a debate or vote that the leadership regards as important is pending. It is the job of whips, led by a chief whip, to persuade MPs whose views are known to differ from those of their leadership to attend debates and vote with their party at the appropriate time.

Whips have frequently been accused of cajoling or bullying MPs into doing their leaders' bidding. When John Major was struggling to pass the Maastricht Treaty into British law in May 1992, following a backbench rebellion by Eurosceptic Tories (see 9.5), ailing loyalists—including one who had just had brain surgery—were taxied to the Commons to act as 'lobby fodder' for the government. The media dubbed this the 'stretcher vote'. Under New Labour, whips would notoriously bombard MPs with pager alerts urging them to turn up and vote along party lines, and to stay 'on message' when speaking publicly.

Mr Blair's prolonged honeymoon with his backbenchers after his 1997 election victory ended abruptly in his second term, when he faced a succession of knife-edge votes on controversial reforms, despite retaining a large Commons majority. Mr Cameron faced similar problems on squeezing back into power in May 2015 with a wafer-thin majority: threatened rebellions by relatively small numbers of MPs against the proposed tax credit and disability benefit cuts were enough to deter his government from pursuing these policies, in the face of opposition benches united against them (see 8.5).

In addition to being fixers, the whips also play a more constructive role. Crucially, they act as unofficial personnel officers for the party leadership—talent-spotting potential future ministers and frontbench spokespeople, and providing important lines of communication between leader and party.

The term 'party whip' effectively refers to an MP or peer's 'membership' of his or her parliamentary party. Like any such affiliation, this can be withdrawn if he or she breaks the 'rules' attached to membership. Mr Major temporarily withdrew the whip from the twenty-two 'Maastricht rebels'—including future party leader Iain Duncan Smith—as a punishment for their disloyalty. More recently, several Labour backbenchers convicted for bogus allowance claims in the fallout from the 2009 expenses scandal lost it permanently, while in 2012 another Labour backbencher, Eric Joyce, was expelled from the party after assaulting four fellow MPs in the Commons Strangers' Bar—an incident leading to his subsequent conviction. In May 2016, meanwhile, Bradford West MP Nadine Shah was temporarily suspended from the Labour Party for allegedly posting 'anti-Semitic' tweets prior to her election in 2015.

Votes judged to be of the highest importance are highlighted—and underlined three times—in a weekly circular sent to MPs and peers, *The Whip*. These votes are known as 'three-line whips', and attendance and voting along party lines is regarded by party leaders as mandatory. There are two lower levels of voting:

- 'one-line whips' (or 'free votes') tend to be called on 'matters of conscience'—non-party political issues, such as fox hunting or euthanasia; and
- 'two-line whips', under which MPs are told that they 'must attend' unless they have made legitimate arrangements to be absent under the *pairing* system.

Pairing is a traditional parliamentary convention allowing one MP sitting on one side of the House to miss a vote on which he or she would have voted one way if an MP with opposing views on the opposite side of the chamber also misses the vote—each missing vote 'cancelling the other out'. Although regarded as acceptable, leaders would obviously prefer all of their MPs to attend and vote with their party, regardless of whether members on the other side are absent, to increase the leader's chances of winning votes. In turn, certain 'tribal' MPs—notably the late Labour firebrand, Tony Benn—have historically refused on principle to participate in pairing.

For a number of years, Labour called a halt to pairing—in retaliation for a 1996 incident in which, while Mr Major's government was in power, three Conservative MPs cheated by each pairing up with Members from both major Opposition parties (thereby cancelling out six, rather than three, votes). Despite reviving the convention more recently, the party remains guarded about using it. In December 2010, Mr Miliband sparked a row with the Coalition by refusing to pair one of his own MPs with the then Environment Secretary Chris Huhne to let him miss a crucial vote on the proposed tripling of undergraduate tuition fees while he attended a United Nations climate change summit.

Three-line whips have long been used as the ultimate call to arms (and disciplinary device) by party leaders—so much so that the term has passed into popular vernacular to denote engagements at which attendance is compulsory. But, as with collective responsibility (see 3.2.2.1), the Coalition compromised established practice in areas of principled disagreement between the parties, in the interests of preserving the overall alliance. For example, the official 'Coalition agreement' included provision for a three-line whip to force through the Referendum Bill, which paved the way for the 2011 public vote on electoral reform—although Tories went on to (successfully) campaign *against* changing the voting system in the run-up to the referendum.

2.2.6 MPs, conflicts of interest, abuses of privilege—and how to avoid them

Recent years have seen MPs accused of compromising their responsibilities to their constituents and Parliament by affiliating themselves to 'outside interests' other than those to which they have democratic obligations. To promote greater openness about such interests—and avoid charges of corruption or deceit about their motives—since 1974 they have been expected to declare any gifts or income received over and above their parliamentary salaries on a register of members' interests, today called the **register of members' financial interests**.

The idea that MPs might have financial or non-pecuniary interests in organizations other than the Commons is hardly new. Eighteenth- and nineteenth-century MPs were often industrialists, agriculturalists, and/or landlords first and foremost, and elected representatives second—their decision to stand in the first place motivated as much by ego and self-promotion as any concern to improve the welfare of their fellow man. Conversely, when the Labour Party was formed, one of its aims was to get working-class candidates elected to the Commons, to counter the long-standing dominance of the middle and upper classes. To enable people from poorer backgrounds to fight elections, the trade union movement (one of several bodies that united to form the party) offered to 'sponsor' them—a traditional source of funding that continued for more than a century, but recently switched from MPs themselves to their constituencies. Even Mr Blair—one of his party's most determined 'modernizers'—was sponsored by the (now defunct) Transport and General Workers' Union (TGWU, later T&G) for much of his time as an MP, while the constituencies of around 100 current Labour MPs receive funding from its successor, Unite.

While Labour has long been accused of being in the unions' pockets, similar charges have been levelled at the Conservatives in relation to big business. Jonathan Aitken, Minister for Defence Procurement in Mr Major's government, notoriously signed a 'gagging order' during the 'Iraqi Supergun' affair, preventing it being disclosed that a British arms company of which he was a non-executive director, The British Manufacture and Research Company (BMARC), had sold weapons to Saddam's regime. Another major lobbying saga under Mr Major erupted over 'cash for questions': in October 1994, Trade Minister Neil Hamilton and a colleague, Tim Smith, were accused in *The Guardian* of receiving money in brown paper envelopes from Harrods owner Mohamed Al Fayed in exchange for asking parliamentary questions on his behalf—a clear breach of Commons rules. Both had to resign, and although Hamilton was granted immunity from parliamentary privilege to sue the paper and Al Fayed, he was unsuccessful.

Following the Hamilton debacle and a series of personal scandals involving other ministers, Mr Major established a new Committee on Standards in Public Life under distinguished judge Lord Nolan. After six months' deliberation, the Nolan Committee published seven 'principles' MPs (and peers) should be expected to adhere to, as outlined in table 2B to be found on the **Online Resource Centre**.

But if 'cash for questions' marked a low point for Mr Major, its fallout was nothing compared to that from the MPs' expenses scandal that erupted under

Gordon Brown. What began as a trickle of minor revelations about the questionable claims of a handful of MPs—exposed by requests under the Freedom of Information Act 2000 (FoI) from journalists Ben Leapman, Jon Ungoed-Thomas, and Heather Brooke—soon became a flood, with the release of unexpurgated details of the accounts of hundreds of MPs in a flurry of front-page scoops by *The Daily Telegraph*.

An early casualty of the furore was Conservative backbencher Derek Conway, who had the whip withdrawn by Mr Cameron after it emerged that he had used his parliamentary allowance to pay his sons tens of thousands of pounds for purportedly working as his 'researchers'. The scandal centred less on their being employed by their father—it soon emerged that such nepotism was commonplace at Westminster—than on whether they actually carried out the duties, of which no records were kept. The three main parties swiftly ordered their MPs to declare any relatives whom they were employing, the nature of their engagement, and details of their remuneration.

It transpired that many MPs—including then Speaker Michael Martin—were claiming up to £22,000 a year to help with mortgage repayments on second homes in their constituencies, despite the fact that some had long since repaid the loans. Scenting blood, the media was soon chasing every shred of information about the obscure rules governing MPs' expenses. An early twist in the saga came when it emerged that MPs claiming £250 or less on expenses were not even required to submit receipts to the authority then in charge, the Operations Directorate of the House of Commons Department of Resources ('Fees Office' for short). Although Mr Brown immediately slashed the minimum receipted claim to £25, this change came into effect only in June 2009—by which time the saga had moved on with the disclosure of a so-called 'John Lewis list' of perks for which MPs were eligible in relation to second homes: MPs could claim (at taxpayers' expense) for furnishing the properties, including around £10,000 for a new kitchen, £300 for air-conditioning units, and £750 apiece for television sets.

Two months later, the High Court ruled that a request for full disclosure of MPs' expenses, made some two years earlier under FoI, should be granted. Under intense media pressure, the custodian of this information, Mr Martin, reluctantly agreed to publish a receipt-by-receipt breakdown—in so doing, revealing that Mr Brown had claimed £4,471 to modernize his kitchen in 2005, with Mr Blair reimbursed £10,600 for one at his former constituency home in Sedgefield. Only weeks after these disclosures, husband-and-wife Tory MPs Nicholas and Ann Winterton were found guilty by Parliamentary Commissioner John Lyon of breaching rules introduced two years earlier to stop MPs reclaiming rent on properties owned by family members. Having paid off the mortgage on their £700,000 London flat in the early 1990s, the couple had placed it in a family trust to avoid inheritance tax. But since 2002 they had occupied it again as tenants, paying the trust £21,600 a year out of a Commons entitlement known as the 'additional costs allowance' (ACA)—a subsidy of up to £24,000 a year to help MPs who needed second homes because of the distance between their constituencies and Parliament. It soon emerged that 'abuse' of the ACA by MPs was widespread—with many Members deliberately 'flipping' the houses and flats they designated as second homes to claim help with the cost of furnishing/refurbishing more than one residence. Among the serving and shadow ministers exposed for misusing the ACA were then Communities Secretary Hazel Blears, Transport Secretary Geoff Hoon, and future Tory minister Michael Gove. Some Members had even added value to properties at taxpayers' expense before selling them—avoiding capital gains tax (see 7.1.1) by designating them 'first' homes.

And 'home-flipping' turned out to be only part of the picture. Under intense pressure from its critics, the government finally relented and ordered full details of all MPs' expense receipts going back to April 2004 to be published on 1 July that year, but two months before its (heavily redacted) disclosure was published, *The Telegraph* unleashed the first of numerous sensational instalments revealing the extent of abuse of the allowance system—after obtaining a leaked disc containing data on all 646 serving MPs from former SAS officer John Wick. For weeks, the news was dominated by unravelling details of the sometimes lavish, more often trivial, and occasionally downright bizarre expenses claimed by MPs and peers. Among the most outlandish were the purchase of a £1,645 'duck island' by Conservative MP Peter Viggers, the £2,115 reimbursement to ex-minister Douglas Hogg for the cost of cleaning his moat, and a rejected claim made by then Home Secretary Jacqui Smith (apparently unwittingly) for a £67 Virgin Media bill that included two pornographic pay-per-view films ordered by her husband. She eventually resigned (officially for family reasons) ahead of the 2009 European elections, but after losing her seat in the 2010 Westminster poll conceded that one of her reasons for quitting had been her elevation to the status of expenses 'poster girl'.

In the end, Mr Brown's response to the scandal was threefold:

- commissioning Sir Christopher Kelly, chairman of the Committee on Standards in Public Life, to examine the existing expenses regime and to recommend reform;
- establishing an Independent Parliamentary Commission for Standards (IPSA) to assume responsibility for policing the expenses system from the existing in-house Commons authorities, the Members Estimate Committee and Fees Office; and
- ensuring that questionable second-home expenses claimed since 2004 were repaid by MPs in full, by authorizing retired permanent secretary Sir Thomas Legg to conduct a backdated audit—invoicing anyone whom he judged to be in breach of existing rules.

Sir Christopher Kelly's report, published in October 2009, led to the following key reforms:

- replacement of the ACA with an allowance of up to £1,450 per month for renting (not buying) a second home, with effect from the 2010 election;
- a crackdown on MPs employing family members, with each member now only allowed to hire up to one relative;
- an end to generous 'resettlement grants' to which retiring MPs had been entitled, which had been worth up to a year's salary (around £65,000) depending on their age and length of service—the first £30,000 being tax-free, with only those unseated at an election entitled to help, up to a maximum of six months' pay; and
- the transfer of responsibility for determining MPs' expenses, salaries and pensions, as of 2010, to the new **Independent Parliamentary Commissioner for Standards (IPSA)**.

Not all MPs 'outed' for excessive or inappropriate claims took their punishments meekly. When, in February 2010, Sir Thomas Legg issued individual letters demanding repayment from 390 MPs (who had collectively 'over-claimed' £1.3 million), some said that they did not have enough money available, while others criticized the 'injustice' of applying a new set of rules to claims made in good faith under old ones. By the time his final report was published—exposing a 'culture of deference' at the Fees Office—seventy MPs had lodged appeals against his demands (at least nine winning them). In the end, the most substantial repayments that Sir Thomas requested included £42,458 from then Communities Minister Barbara Follett and £24,878 from future minister Liam Fox.

More unedifying still was the prosecution for false accounting of five Labour MPs—former Fisheries Minister Elliot Morley, David Chaytor, Jim Devine, Eric Illsley, and Margaret Moran—and Conservative peers Lord Hanningfield and Lord Taylor. All but one of these parliamentarians were subsequently convicted (Ms Moran was judged unfit to stand trial owing to depression)—but not before Messrs Morley, Chaytor, and Devine had tried to invoke the constitutional protection of parliamentary privilege (see 1.1.1.1), arguing that allowing a law court to try them would breach the principle of the separation of powers between judiciary and legislature.

Their efforts to avoid a high-profile trial were short-lived, however: in June 2010, Mr Justice Saunders ruled that there was no 'logical, practical, or moral justification' for their immunity. Devolved chambers are not immune to similar scandals: although members concerned were ultimately vindicated, a probe was launched into expenses claims by Northern Irish Members of the Legislative Assembly (MLAs) in 2014, following revelations in two BBC *Spotlight* films.

2.2.7 The Parliamentary Commissioner for Standards

To reinforce his determination to stamp out the perceived culture of 'sleaze' among certain party members, Mr Major had a formal code of conduct for MPs drawn up and appointed Sir Gordon Downey as first **Parliamentary Commissioner for Standards** in 1995. The Commissioner's job is to oversee the register of interests, summoning and holding to account any member who may have breached the code. The current Commissioner is Kathryn Hudson, who assumed the role on 1 January 2013. To ensure that the Commissioner is correctly discharging his or her duties, a further layer of oversight exists, in the guise of the Committee on Standards and Privileges. Not to be confused with the Committee on Standards in Public Life, this is composed of sitting MPs and has the same membership as the House of Commons Commission (see 2.6). A separate Lords Commissioner for Standards (currently Paul Kernaghan) oversees probity in the Upper House. Among his recent investigations was a probe into the accommodation expenses of Conservative co-chairman Baroness Warsi, after she referred herself to him in June 2012 amid allegations that she had claimed her allowance while staying with a friend, rent-free, in 2008. She was subsequently cleared of expenses irregularities, but found to have breached the Lords' code of conduct for failing to register properly a property with it.

2.3 The House of Lords

Before describing the means by which Parliament passes legislation, it is necessary to look at the nature and composition of the 'second chamber', or **House of Lords**. Since the passage of the House of Lords Act 1999, which Labour introduced to start the process of reforming or replacing this institution, it has been in a state of prolonged limbo—and currently remains a 'transitional House', despite successive attempts to revive the reform agenda (see 2.3.1).

2.3.1 What is the point of the Lords?

Even among parliamentarians who dispute the Lords' current make-up there is widespread support for the principle that the main law-making chamber in a bicameral legislature should be held accountable by a second. The ongoing arguments over whether the Lords should be reformed or abolished are less about any real desire to scrap the Upper House altogether than a growing recognition that, in a modern democracy, a second chamber composed primarily of political appointees and members by birthright is an anachronism.

As long ago as the early twentieth century, the Lords had begun to seem outmoded to many. But it was Herbert Asquith's Chancellor, David Lloyd George, who brought the case for reform to a head when his 1909 'People's Budget', which sought to raise taxes to fund social reform, was rejected by the disproportionately Conservative Lords. Following his 1910 election victory, Asquith sought to prevent the Lords ever again vetoing primary legislation (Bills) outright and, backed by a threat from George V to force through reform by creating sufficient Liberal peers to overcome its inbuilt Tory majority, succeeded in passing the Parliament Act 1911. This replaced the Lords' power of veto with a right merely to *delay* Bills—and for a maximum of two calendar years (or three parliamentary sessions). Subsequently, the Lords voluntarily ceded further powers in recognition of the unequivocal mandate for change following Labour's landslide 1945 election victory. In a constitutional tweak that became known as the 'Salisbury convention', or 'Salisbury doctrine', the then Tory leader in the Lords, Viscount Cranborne (later Lord Salisbury), agreed that the Upper House should not oppose the second or third readings of legislation promised in a governing party's election manifesto.

The Lords' delaying period was further truncated by the Parliament Act 1949 to two sessions over thirteen months—though, intriguingly, it has up to now retained the right to veto some secondary legislation. This little-known constitutional quirk came to light for the first time in some years when, in October 2015, peers decisively rejected then Chancellor George Osborne's attempt to cut working-age tax credits using a statutory instrument (see 8.5). Any attempt to veto *primary* Bills, however, today sees governments threaten to 'invoke' the 'Parliament Act'. The Lords' repeated attempts to thwart Labour's hunting ban during Mr Blair's second term were defeated in this way.

Since 1949, little decisive action to further reform the Lords was taken until the House of Lords Act 1999, which banned all but a handful of hereditary peers from continuing to sit in the House. Its long-term aim was to replace the hereditary principle with some form of membership entitlement based on individuals' contribution to society through public service or other major achievements.

The Lords' composition prior to 1999 was as follows:

1 **Lords Spiritual**—twenty-six peers, comprising:
   (a) the Archbishops of Canterbury and York;
   (b) the Bishops of London, Durham, and Winchester; and
   (c) the twenty-one next most senior Church of England diocesan bishops.
2 Lords Temporal—1,263 peers, comprising:
   (a) all 759 *hereditary peers* of England, Scotland, Great Britain, and the UK (not including Northern Ireland);

(b) the *Lords of Appeal in Ordinary (the Law Lords)*—twenty-seven peers 'created' by successive governments under the Appellate Jurisdiction Act 1876 to help the Lords to fulfil its role as the UK's final court of appeal; and

(c) 477 others with **life peerages** created in **honours lists** under the terms of the Life Peerages Act 1958.

Hereditary peers have been permitted to disclaim their peerages so that they may stand as MPs since Tony Benn persuaded Harold Macmillan's Conservative government to change the law through the Peerage Act 1963, after inheriting the title Viscount Stansgate from his father while sitting in the Commons. Following his lead, Tory MP Quintin Hogg (later Lord Hailsham) disclaimed his family seat to fight a by-election—ironically, in his father's old constituency of St Marylebone. But, most peculiarly, in 1963 Lord Home performed a double-flip by giving up an inherited title that had earlier forced him to resign a Commons seat to return to the Lower House as prime minister. His action—prompted by his election to replace Macmillan as Conservative leader—had the unique consequence of creating a two-week interval between his 'resignation' as a peer and re-election as an MP during which time Britain's prime minister was a member of neither the Commons nor the Lords.

2.3.2 The House of Lords Act 1999

The 1999 Act contained five key clauses designed to pave the way for an—at least partially—elected second chamber. After a series of run-ins between Mr Blair, his own backbenchers, the Tories, and the Lords itself, however, it was decided to move towards reform gradually by setting up a 'transitional' chamber that would initially merely remove the automatic membership rights of all but ninety-two hereditary peers. In the meantime, the question of what the final composition of a new Upper House should be was handed to a Royal Commission headed by former Tory minister Lord Wakeham.

Of the ninety-two hereditary peers permitted to remain in the House during the transition period, ninety were elected—but by their fellow peers, not the public. The aim was to retain individuals with a history of making valuable contributions to debates, rather than the many who seldom attended proceedings. Since 2002, whenever elected—or 'excepted'—hereditary peers have died, their places have been taken not by their heirs, but other hereditaries drawn from the pool of those initially debarred from the Lords in 1999. By-elections, conducted using the alternative vote (AV) system (see 4.5), must be held within three months of the peers' deaths. The only peers eligible to vote at such times are other serving hereditary members drawn from the same party grouping—or, in the case of cross-bench peers, fellow cross benchers. At the time of writing, the most recent 'new arrival' was the Lib Dem peer

Lord Thurso, who was elected to replace Lord Avebury following the latter's death in February 2016.

As well as the ninety lords with **excepted hereditary peerages**, however, a further two hereditary peers have remained *ex officio* members since 1999, based on their ceremonial significance to the chamber. These are the Earl Marshal, the Duke of Norfolk, and Lord Great Chamberlain, the Marquess of Cholmondeley. In addition, ten new life peerages were controversially created when the Act was passed to enable several hereditary peers *not* elected to remain. These included former Tory Leader of the House Lord Cranborne, ex-Foreign Secretary Lord Carrington, and the Earl of Longford. The process by which the transitional House was set up was brokered as a compromise amendment to the Bill by Lord Weatherill, a former Commons Speaker.

After the internal election following passage of the 'Weatherill Amendment', the composition of the Lords was as follows:

- 26 Lords Spiritual; and
- 598 Lords Temporal, comprising 27 Law Lords, two non-elected hereditary peers, 90 elected hereditary peers, and 477 life peers.

Since then, life peers have continued being appointed at a prodigious rate and the balance of power between parties has fluctuated, with Labour finally reaching the symbolic tipping point at which it had as many peers as the Tories and Lib Dems put together in 2009—twelve years after regaining power. Shortly after entering coalition in 2010, Messrs Cameron and Clegg unveiled plans to create up to 172 new party-affiliated peers between them to ensure the uninterrupted passage of their Bills through the Lords—a move condemned by Labour MP Chris Bryant, a former Deputy Leader of the Commons, as 'the single largest simultaneous act of political patronage probably since Charles II came to the throne in 1660'. As of August 2016, the Tories boasted 247 peers to Labour's 211, with the Lib Dems retaining 109—a disproportionate representation which has proved a source of controversy, in light of the party's near wipeout in the 2015 general election.

In practice, although the Lords' political composition tends broadly to mirror that of the Commons, members drawn from the governing party (or parties) often behave more independent-mindedly than their ministerial 'masters' would like. The Coalition weathered several embarrassing defeats at peers' hands over its controversial Health and Social Care and Welfare Reform Bills—some spearheaded by prominent Tories and Lib Dems. Following months of horse-trading with rebel Lib Dem peers led by veteran former minister Baroness Williams, the then Health Secretary Andrew Lansley finally dragged his Bill onto the statute book in 2012, but only after several attempts by those still wary of the legislation to frustrate it with eleventh-hour amendments (see 6.2.1). Rebellions in the Tories' own ranks, meanwhile, helped block aspects of the Coalition's Welfare Reform Bill and repeatedly threw back to the Commons attempts by the Conservative-only government to cut first tax credits for working households, then Employment and Support Allowance (ESA) payments for the sick and disabled. The Welfare Reform Bill only reached the statute book with the help of an obscure procedural rule designed to limit 'parliamentary ping-pong' between Commons and Lords. 'Financial privilege' rules allow governments to overturn amendments tabled in the Lords to public Bills that are intended to 'make significant changes to public expenditure' and/or 'affect national or local taxation or National Insurance [NI]' (see 8.1). Given that the Bill introduced the biggest shake-up of the welfare state since its inception—and related directly to NI-funded benefits—it was judged to have met this test.

Lords with no declared party affiliation are known as **cross benchers**. Appropriately, they sit on benches ranged in short rows across the width of the House, with the government benches to their left and the Opposition to their right. Although independent of party ties, cross benchers often flex their political muscles. During the choppy passage of the NHS reforms, persistent opposition to the Bill came from then cross bencher Lord Owen, ex-leader of the Social Democratic Party (SDP), which was set up by a splinter group that abandoned the Labour Party over its leftward drift in 1981. So opposed was he to the Coalition's NHS policies that, following Mr Miliband's reform of Labour's links with the unions (see 5.2), he publicly announced his renewed support for the party—informing the convener of the cross benchers that he would henceforth sit as an 'Independent Social Democrat'.

2.3.3 From Wakeham to the waste-bin? The future of Lords reform

What, then, are the prospects for democratizing the second chamber? Lord Wakeham's 2000 report, *A House for the Future*, made several recommendations, subsequently crystallized in a 2001 House of Lords White Paper. This advocated a neutered version of his proposals, including the removal of all remaining hereditary peers, the retention of existing life peers 'transitionally', and the eventual capping of Lords membership at about 600. The one concrete development that happened almost immediately was the establishment of an independent **House of Lords Appointments Commission** to ensure that while transitional arrangements remained, life peerages would be awarded principally on merit, rather than by political patronage. The Commission's main role was to vet individuals nominated by party leaders for any sign of rewards for favours—a power that it memorably used to block three of Mr Blair's nominees in 2005 (see 5.12). But it is also allowed to propose its own peers, focusing on non-partisan individuals with 'a record of significant achievement' in their 'chosen way of life'. To date, fifty-five 'people's peers' have been appointed, ranging from Baroness Howe of Idlicote (wife of former Tory minister

Geoffrey, now Lord, Howe) to the late disability rights activist Baroness Chapman.

During his third term, Mr Blair edged away from advocating a partially elected chamber toward a fully appointed one—in defiance of an all-party motion in March 1999 demanding that it be entirely elected. Although he cited well-rehearsed Conservative arguments—including the potential challenge an elected Lords might pose to Commons supremacy—the Conservatives branded his alternative an attempt to shore up his power base by appointing 'Tony's Cronies'. Unhappy memories were evoked of the 'Lavender List', a notorious string of honours for trusted allies that another Labour premier, Harold Wilson, had patronized on his retirement in 1976. This blatant display of nepotism would be echoed in 2016, when the resignation honours list of a Tory PM, Mr Cameron, rewarded an extended 'chumocracy', including his former Chancellor, Mr Osborne, who became a Companion of Honour; ex-Downing Street Director of Communications Craig Oliver, who was knighted; and his wife Samantha's stylist, Isabel Spearman, who was made an OBE.

The 'settled' view of MPs now appears to favour a largely or wholly elected second chamber, but the most recent attempt to introduce such reforms, by Mr Clegg, was formally abandoned by him in August 2012, after Mr Cameron told him that, despite previously pledging his personal support, he could not secure sufficient support from his MPs to take it forward. The Bill's fate was ultimately sealed by an unholy alliance of Conservatives and what Mr Clegg branded an 'opportunistic' Labour Party, intent on exploiting the situation to promote cracks in the then Coalition. Labour's leadership had indicated support for the legislation in principle (although it had argued for a national referendum first), but before voting 'yes' to the second reading it forced ministers into dropping a proposed 'programme motion' to limit scrutiny at that stage to ten days—a vote the government would have lost. In a final twist, though, Mr Clegg exacted his revenge on the Tories—by instructing his fellow Lib Dems to oppose Conservative proposals for changes to Commons constituency boundaries, a move which had the effect of kicking this plan into the long grass until after the 2015 election (see 4.2.1).

Determined campaigners continue to insist that the cause of Lords reform is still not lost—with former Liberal leader Lord Steel steering his long-cherished House of Lords (Amendment) Bill through the Lords in March 2012. This private member's Bill (see 2.4.1.2) proposed new rules removing the patronage of party leaders in creating future life peers, in favour of purely merit-based decisions by a statutory appointments commission; removing any members sentenced to more than a year in prison for serious crimes; and scrapping future by-elections to replace deceased hereditary peers (a move that would have gradually 'abolished' hereditary members as the ninety remaining incumbents died). In reality, until such ideas are picked up and pushed through the Commons by a willing government, it is unlikely to be implemented.

At time of writing, the prospect of further Lords reform was once again fading, after Theresa May's government abandoned plans introduced by her predecessor to stop peers blocking statutory instruments following their successful rebellion against proposed cuts to working-age tax credits in October 2015 (see 8.5). This plan had been roundly condemned by the Lords' Constitution Committee, which dismissed ministers' claims that a single policy defeat could be described as a 'constitutional crisis'—arguing instead that the questions raised by the row were more about the fundamental right of the Legislature to hold the Executive to account than the issue of unelected peers defying the will of elected MPs. A report by the Delegated Powers and Regulatory Reform Committee had been even more scathing—condemning what it saw as the growing trend for governments to publish 'skeleton bills' consisting of little more than 'delegations of powers' that, once passed by Parliament, allowed ministers to fill in the details with little or no parliamentary scrutiny, using executive edicts reminiscent of 'Henry VIII'. It, too, reduced the dispute, ultimately, to a constitutional question over the balance of power between Legislature and Executive (see 1.1.2).

The one significant reform since 1999 to have affected the Lords was the creation in the Constitutional Reform Act 2005 of a US-style Supreme Court—formally known as the **Supreme Court of the United Kingdom**. To reinforce the principle of separation of powers, then Lord Chancellor Mr Straw divested the Lords of its judicial function, transferred its status as Britain's highest court of justice to the Supreme Court, and installed twelve of the then twenty-seven Law Lords as inaugural Justices of the Supreme Court. The Court began work on 1 October 2009. For the duration of their service as Justices, its members are not permitted to sit in the Lords, although they are entitled to return to the chamber on retirement. Future appointees will not, though, be given seats in the Lords. Although the new Supreme Court is the ultimate bastion of English, Northern Irish, and Scottish law, and has taken over adjudicating devolutionary matters from the Judicial Committee of the Privy Council, Scotland retains its own criminal supreme court: the High Court of Justiciary.

2.4 Types of legislation

As Britain's legislature, the primary purpose of Parliament is to legislate. So how does it do this?

British legislation is divided into two broad types: primary and secondary. **Primary legislation** is the umbrella term for all Bills that pass through Parliament and (when successful) receive royal assent, becoming Acts. It is also known as 'enabling legislation', in that Acts must be passed to 'enable' governments/Parliament to issue the various rules, regulations, and instructions needed to implement changes in law on the ground.

2.4.1 Primary legislation

The four main categories of primary Bill are:

- public Bills;
- private Bills;
- hybrid Bills; and
- private members' Bills.

2.4.1.1 Public, private, and hybrid Bills

Public, private, and hybrid Bills all have one thing in common: they are initiated by the government. This, though, is where the similarities end. Whereas **public Bills** change 'the law of the land', **private Bills** affect only specific individuals or organizations—for example, companies or local authorities. Whichever category they fall into, these government Bills have traditionally been preceded by at least two draft versions—a Green Paper and a White Paper (see 2.5).

Briefly, the majority of new laws that gain media attention are public Bills. The earlier mentioned Welfare Reform and Health and Social Care Bills were both public Bills affecting the entire population of Britain. Private Bills, in contrast, are usually introduced at the request of specific individuals or bodies, either to exempt them from a law otherwise affecting the whole country or to grant them other discrete privileges. **Highways England** (formerly the Highways Agency)—the government-owned company responsible for building and maintaining major trunk roads, 'A' roads, and motorways (see 18.1.2)—has often been granted private Bills enabling it to extend, or introduce, roads in new areas. Hybrid Bills are a mix of the other two. Like public Bills, they affect the whole population, but resemble private Bills in that they impinge on some people more than others. Examples of hybrid Bills include the ones enabling work to begin on the successive stages of London's Crossrail project, which affects some residents of the country (those living along the link) more than others.

2.4.1.2 Private Members' Bills (PMBs)

Private members' Bills (PMBs) warrant a separate category because, unlike all other types of legislation, they are introduced not by governments but by backbenchers. PMBs may be introduced in one of the three ways listed in Table 2.4.

The primary purpose of **Ten-minute rule** Bills is to enable MPs to raise issues that they consider important—rather than get their measures onto the statute book. In practice, MPs usually struggle to persuade their parties, let alone governments, to allocate sufficient parliamentary time to take their Bills further.

Table 2.4 Three ways of introducing private members' Bills (PMBs)

Method	Procedure
PMB Fridays	Early in each parliamentary session, MPs enter 'ballots' for the chance to introduce their own Bills on one of thirteen 'PMB Fridays'. On these days, PMBs take precedence over other business. The first twenty names drawn in ballot may introduce their Bills. Six or seven at top of list likely to be discussed in detail in Commons.
The Ten-minute rule	Members may instead use 'Ten-minute rule' (officially, Standing Order No. 23), on most Tuesdays and Wednesdays at start of public business. Introducer makes ten-minute speech outlining proposals, provided they have ten other members' support. An opponent may make ten-minute speech in reply.
Presentation Bills	Members may introduce 'presentation Bill' (under Standing Order No. 57). This draws limited attention to an issue because—unlike other two methods—it does not allow MP to outline Bill's details in Commons.

To qualify to introduce a Ten-minute rule Bill, an MP must be 'the first member through the door' to the Public Bill Office on the Tuesday or Wednesday fifteen working days before the date on which they wish to present it. Their Bill must have a proposer and seconder, and the written backing of ten colleagues.

Many significant issues have been raised through PMBs. In 1997, after initial indications that he would receive government time, Labour backbencher Michael Foster introduced a PMB proposing a ban on hunting with dogs (a measure in his party's manifesto). This Bill was eventually passed into law as part of the government's official programme in Mr Blair's second term. The most celebrated PMB success story, though, was former Liberal leader Mr Steel's Abortion Bill 1967, which legalized terminations of unwanted pregnancies for the first time in Britain—albeit only up to twenty-four weeks after conception. Touching on an issue of huge public concern, it was allotted ample time for full debate and scrutiny by Harold Wilson's socially liberalizing Labour government, and duly passed.

2.4.2 Secondary legislation

It has increasingly been the convention for primary legislation to cover only the fundamental *principles* underpinning a change in the law. In contrast, **secondary legislation**—or delegated/subordinate legislation—refers to powers 'flowing from' Acts themselves, and rules, regulations, and guidelines drawn up to implement them. For primary legislation to be implemented, ministers need authority to introduce the measures it contains on the ground. This authority is exercised through 'delegated' legislative powers, the main types of which are listed in Table 2.5.

Table 2.5 Main types of secondary legislation

Name	Definition	Example
Statutory instrument	Rules, regulations, and guidelines issued by ministers to flesh out and implement new Acts. Although no further Act is required to implement measures, they still require Parliament's agreement. 'Parent' Act usually specifies whether affirmative or negative agreement required (former means the statutory instrument will not come into play unless Parliament formally approves resolution; latter that it will automatically do so if, after forty days, no motion passed objecting to it).	Complex instructions issued by Department for Culture, Media, and Sport (DCMS) to give local authorities and police responsibility for issuing liquor and public entertainment licences under Licensing Act 2003 (which took so long to come into force that '24-hour drinking' was introduced in pubs only in November 2005—two years after royal assent).
By-law	Localized laws passed on approval of relevant minister, according to scope enshrined in existing Act.	City-centre street-drinking bans introduced by councils in problem areas.
Order in Council	Submitted by ministers for sovereign's approval in Privy Council. Draft normally agreed by Parliament before being submitted by ministers.	Used to introduce much delegated anti-terror legislation relating to Northern Ireland in 1960s and 1970s.

2.5 The passage of a Bill

Before it is formally introduced in Parliament, prospective government legislation is customarily 'opinion-tested' in two early forms: a **Green Paper** and at least one **White Paper**. The former is a sketchy consultation document outlining the *broad spirit* of a proposed Bill. It is open to significant redefinition depending on the response it elicits from the public and other interested parties. The latter is a more crystallized outline of a proposed law—again issued for consultation purposes—that normally prefigures a Bill to be introduced in the next session.

Bills can be introduced in either the Commons or Lords, although they are normally instigated in the former. The passage of Bills affecting the whole of Britain is outlined in Table 2.6 but, since October 2015, new Bills concerning only England, or England and Wales, have been subject to a modified process which excludes Scottish and Northern Irish MPs from having a say at crucial stages (see 1.3.6). This 'English votes' process is described in Table 2.7.

2.5.1 Speeding up the legislative process

The legislative process can be very involved, and no parties are immune to the temptation to delay Bills to which they object. Traditionally, MPs conspired to do so by making excessively long speeches to frustrate governments' attempts

Table 2.6 The passage of a UK-wide Bill

Stage	Process
First reading	Reading of new Bill's full title in Commons.
Second reading	General principles of Bill read out, debated, and voted on for first time. This normally happens in 'an afternoon' between 4 p.m. and 10 p.m. Second reading can run over several days if Bill has major implications.
Committee stage	Public or private Bill committee consider main clauses of Bill in detail. Sometimes this stage occurs in Commons, sitting as Committee of Whole House (normally when treaty being ratified or Bill needs passing urgently). This happens automatically following annual Budget Speech, when main Finance Act provisions are fast-tracked.
Report stage	Committee's recommendations referred to Commons in written report and further amendments can follow before Bill proceeds to third reading, often involving late sittings.
Third reading	Bill reviewed and debated in final intended form. All opportunities for Commons to amend have now passed (although the Lords still can).
Bill now referred to Lords (or 'another place'), through which it follows similar sequence to Commons, but with committee stage usually taken on floor of House.	
House of Lords report to Commons	Amendments made by Lords must be agreed by Commons before it proceeds to statute book. Should there be significant differences of opinion between Houses, a joint committee is set up to resolve them. Under successive Parliament Acts, Lords cannot delay money Bills and can delay others only by thirteen months.
Royal assent	Final approval, turning Bill into Act, notionally still given by monarch, but last time this formally happened was in 1854. It is conferred in Norman French, La Reine le Veult, and has not been refused since 1707, when Queen Anne declined it for a Bill to settle militia in Scotland. Sentence preceding every Act reads: 'Be it enacted by the Queen's Most Excellent Majesty, by and with the advice and consent of the Lords Spiritual and Temporal, and Commons, in this Parliament assembled, and by authority of the same, as follows . . .'

to get through the various stages of a Bill's passage. Such 'filibustering' was at times used to delay new laws indefinitely—or even kill them off entirely. If a Bill is obstructed for long enough that the government championing it is voted out of office, this might well spell its end, because the Opposition waiting to take over will be unlikely to resurrect it. Similarly, 'wrecking amendments'

Table 2.7 The passage of an 'English-only' or English and Welsh Bill

Stage	Process
First reading	Reading of new Bill's full title in Commons.
Certification of Bill	Speaker will certify if Bill should be subject to new process as only applying to England or England and Wales.
Second reading	General principles of Bill read out, debated, and voted on.
Committee stage	England-only Bills considered by committees made up only of MPs representing English constituencies, with political make-up determined by spread of seats between parties in England. Bills applying to England and Wales only considered by committee comprising MPs from all nations as normal.
Report stage	Committee's recommendations referred to Commons in written report.
Consent motion	Any Bill affecting only England or England and Wales now considered by legislative **grand committee** comprising only English/English and Welsh MPs. This may veto any clauses affecting only these nations—potentially scrapping entire Bill.
Reconsideration stage	Bill passes back to whole House, like second report stage. Other MPs—including those from Scotland—could reinstate vetoed clauses at this stage.
Second legislative grand committee	English/English and Welsh MPs asked to consider any changes introduced by whole House. If they disagree with these, disputed parts of Bill fail.
Third reading	Bill reviewed and debated in final intended form. All opportunities for Commons to amend it have passed.
House of Lords	Same process followed as with other Bills.
Royal Assent	Bill becomes law.

have often been made by the Lords towards the end of parliaments in efforts to 'time out' Bills, in the hope that incoming governments will abandon them. Traditionally, Bills that fail to reach royal assent before the end of a parliamentary session have had to start the whole legislative process again the following year. However, since October 2004, it has been possible for the Commons to pass 'carry-over motions', allowing Bills that would otherwise have timed out in one session to continue their passage from the same stage in the succeeding one.

The term 'filibustering' was first coined in reference to pro-independence Irish MPs in the nineteenth century, who, in an effort to force the Westminster government to hand over 'home rule' for Ireland, would deliberately hold up Bills on other issues. Today, this and other forms of time-wasting, repetition, and drawn-out debate can be countered in various ways outlined in table 2C to be found on the **Online Resource Centre**.

2.6 The role of the Commons Speaker

The most important officer of the Commons, the Speaker, chairs its business. He or she presides over votes and debates, intervenes to restore 'order' when members become rowdy, and chooses which member should be next to speak when confronted by MPs waving their order papers to 'catch the Speaker's eye'. The Speaker is always drawn from the ranks of MPs, but, on taking office, discards his or her previous party allegiance for the duration of his or her tenure. Conventionally, this non-partisanship will continue if he or she is subsequently appointed to the Lords, with most ennobled ex-Speakers going on to serve as cross benchers. The only exceptional circumstance in which a Speaker becomes directly involved in a vote is in the unlikely event of a Commons vote resulting in a tie. On such an occasion, 'Speaker Denison's rule'—an obscure convention named after a nineteenth-century Speaker—stipulates that the incumbent use his or her casting vote to call for further debate or to uphold the status quo (for instance, voting against a motion of no confidence—see 3.1.3.4).

Today's Speakers are primarily responsible for:

- controlling debates, including deciding when those on specific subjects should end in a vote, and suspending or adjourning sittings that become unruly (for example, in May 2004 debate was suspended when activists from Fathers4Justice, a pressure group campaigning for equal access rights to children for separated fathers, threw a missile containing purple powder from the guests' gallery at Mr Blair);
- ordering MPs who break Commons rules to leave the chamber (for example, Mr Galloway was barred from the Commons for eighteen days in July 2007 for failing to declare his links to the United Nations' 'Oil for Food' programme—a charitable appeal allegedly part-funded by a supporter involved in the sale of oil under Saddam Hussein);
- certifying some Bills as 'money Bills' to give them swift approval;
- signing warrants to send members to jail for contempt of the House;
- chairing the House of Commons Commission—a body that administers the procedures of the Commons; and
- chairing the Speaker's Committee on the Electoral Commission, which recommends appointments to the Commission's board (see 5.11)
- certifying some Bills as applying to England or England and Wales only.

Traditionally, the Speaker (the first of whom, Peter de Montfort, was appointed Parlour of the Commons in 1258) is chosen by an election of MPs called by the 'Father of the House'—the backbench MP with the longest unbroken membership of the Commons. For nearly forty years it has also been customary for the two main political parties to alternate in providing Speakers, but when the post became vacant in October 2000 after Betty (now Baroness) Boothroyd's retirement, backbenchers grew so annoyed by the government's insistence that this tradition be upheld that they defied it by voting in another Labour MP, Mr Martin, instead of Mr Blair's preferred candidate, former Tory minister Sir George Young.

In the event, Mr Martin's tenure was most notable for the ignominy of his premature departure. A series of errors of judgment began in November 2008, with his mishandling of the Damian Green affair (see 1.1.1.1). More damaging still were revelations that he had claimed £20,000 of taxpayers' money to pay City law firm Carter Ruck to defend him against negative press stories, and subsequent disclosures that his wife had been reimbursed by taxpayers for £4,000 in taxi fares incurred on shopping trips to buy food and refreshment for receptions, and that refurbishments to the couple's official residence, the Speaker's House, had cost £1.7 million. The final straw, though, was Mr Martin's faltering response to the wave of revelations about MPs' expenses claims (see 2.2.6). After appearing to do too little too late—by proposing only a prolonged sequence of meetings between party leaders and other internal Commons bodies to decide how best to reform the system, rather than any larger-scale changes—on 12 May 2009, following a decisive no-confidence vote, Mr Martin became the first Speaker to be forced out of office since Sir John Trevor in 1695.

With Mr Martin's successor, the Commons reverted to its customary pendulum swing from Labour to Conservatives: in a hotly contested election that marked a break from the 'coronations' of past Speakers, John Bercow beat several hopefuls, including fellow Tories Ann Widdecombe and Sir George Young, and former Labour Foreign Secretary Margaret Beckett. He was reconfirmed in office in 2010, and again re-elected unopposed in 2015—defying an unsuccessful attempt by outgoing Leader of the Commons William Hague to pass a motion requiring him to win a secret ballot to stay on after that May's election in the dying days of the previous parliament.

Although the Speaker officially presides over the Commons, recent events have acted as a timely reminder of the presence of a more shadowy figure, whose constitutional role is also to oversee debate in the chamber—on behalf of a very particular vested interest. The 'City Remembrancer'—who has a chair reserved for him or her behind the Speaker's 'throne'—occupies an obscure office of state dating back to 1571. His or her task is to act as a channel of information between, on the one hand, the City of London Corporation and its chief dignitary, the Lord Mayor of London (see 10.5), and, on the other, Parliament and sovereign. Critics view this arcane post as a sinister manifestation of the grip that Britain's financial sector has long exercised over the seat of British democracy—a concern sharpened in the wake of the 2007–8 banking collapse (see 7.3.4) and, in February 2012, the eviction by Corporation authorities of a camp set up by supporters of anti-capitalist protest movement Occupy from the area surrounding St Paul's Cathedral.

2.7 The changing role of the Lord Chancellor

Officially the 'Lord High Chancellor of Great Britain', this ancient post—dating back at least to the 1066 Norman Conquest—has lately undergone significant changes. The Lord Chancellor is the second most senior 'Great Officer of State'—the highest ranking being the Lord High Steward (a post generally kept vacant, except during coronations). As explained in Chapter 1 (1.1.2), the post was for centuries a bastion of all three branches of Britain's constitution, being head of the judiciary, Speaker of the Lords (legislature), and, as Cabinet minister responsible for the erstwhile 'Lord Chancellor's Department', a member of the executive.

Even today, the Lord Chancellor still retains many ancient ceremonial roles. As 'Custodian of The Great Seal of the Realm', or 'The Great Seal of the United Kingdom', he or she can authorize the reigning sovereign's documents (most notably the royal assent) on his or her behalf—saving the monarch from having to sign each one personally. The Lord Chancellor also remains a minister.

Since 2003, however, postholders have ceased to retain quite the authority enjoyed by their predecessors (to the annoyance of the Lords, which sought initially to prevent Mr Blair denuding these powers). In a notoriously botched Cabinet reshuffle, Mr Blair replaced outgoing Lord Chancellor Derry Irvine with Lord Falconer of Thoroton. In doing so, he sought to rename the post 'Secretary of State for Constitutional Affairs'—effectively *abolishing* a constitutional role that had existed since the Middle Ages.

Mr Blair was forced to step back from scrapping the post outright, and although he did abolish the Lord Chancellor's Department, Lord Falconer retained the dual titles of Constitutional Affairs Secretary and Lord Chancellor throughout his four years in office. Further changes, however, occurred after the 2005 election, when the Constitutional Affairs Act 2005 handed responsibility for running the judiciary to the Lord Chief Justice and created a new post of **Lord Speaker**—elected by his or her fellow peers using the AV (see 4.6)—to assume the Lord Chancellor's role as chair of the Lords. The present Lord Speaker is former Conservative Cabinet Minister Lord Fowler.

During Mr Brown's first reshuffle, the Department for Constitutional Affairs was renamed the Ministry of Justice (MoJ). More significantly, Lord Falconer's successor, Mr Straw, became the first Lord Chancellor since the sixteenth century to not be a lord at all, but an MP. This 'new tradition' has continued with first Mr Clarke, then Chris Grayling, and now Liz Truss serving as successive Tory Lord Chancellors and Secretaries of State for Justice.

2.8 The Opposition

The party with the most Commons seats besides the governing one forms the Opposition. In recognition of its official status, the Leader of the Opposition, Opposition Chief Whip, and Opposition Deputy Chief Whip each receive allowances on top of their normal parliamentary ones to aid with their responsibilities.

The Opposition is expected to:

- hold the government to account by appointing a 'Shadow Cabinet' covering the main departmental briefs;
- contribute to the legislative process by proposing amendments; and
- set out its policies as an alternative government using designated 'Opposition Days', on which it, not the government, dictates Commons business. (In each session, there are twenty Opposition Days: seventeen customarily go to the largest Opposition party and three to the second largest.)

To help Oppositions carry out their duties they receive a taxpayer-funded allowance known as 'short money', which since 1975 has been allocated to each Opposition party with at least one MP on a proportional basis. Its value has traditionally been linked to annual changes in the retail price index (RPI) measure of inflation (see 7.1.4.1). However, in his November 2015 Comprehensive Spending Review, Mr Osborne announced plans to cut the fund by 19 per cent and freeze it for the rest of the Parliament (see 7.1.1). Amid howls of protest from Labour and the SNP, a deal was struck in March 2016 to instead link it to the customarily lower measure of inflation, the consumer prices index (CPI) (see 7.1.4.1), which translated into a more modest year-on-year real-terms cut of 5 per cent.

2.9 Devolution in practice—parliaments in the provinces

The first chapter laid out Britain's overall constitutional framework, while introducing devolution and how it applies in the UK's constituent countries outside England. This section explains how devolution works in practice through the aegis of new chambers created to implement it.

2.9.1 The Scottish Parliament

Comprising 129 **members of the Scottish Parliament (MSPs)**, the **Scottish Parliament** is a 'unicameral' legislature—meaning that it has only one House.

During the initial transition stage flowing from its establishment in 1998, some inaugural MSPs were permitted to hold 'dual mandates'—that is, to remain MPs as well. This swiftly changed, however, when they assumed their place as MSPs full time and by-elections were held to find replacements for their previous Commons constituencies. Similar arrangements currently exist in the Northern Ireland Assembly, following restoration of devolved government in that province, although they were due to end with the 2015 Assembly elections.

MSPs are elected using the additional member system (AMS) form of proportional representation (see 4.5), with seventy-three voted in via the UK's traditional FPTP system and the remaining fifty-six from a regional list designed to more fairly allocate seats to each party nationally. Each elector has two votes: one for his or her constituency; the other for a political party, the names of which appear on the list.

Members originally met in a temporary chamber at Edinburgh's Church of Scotland Assembly Hall on The Mound. This was belatedly replaced by a purpose-built Parliament in Holyrood, in 2004. One MSP is elected 'Presiding Officer' (equivalent to the Commons Speaker), supported by two deputies. Parliament is elected for fixed terms lasting four years from its election date, with each year constituting a parliamentary session, which is further split into 'sitting days' and 'recess periods'. On sitting days, Parliament tries to finish its business at 5.30 p.m., except on Fridays, which tend to end at 12.30 p.m.

Members can raise issues by:

- asking oral questions during parliamentary sittings;
- submitting written questions; and
- giving notice of, or moving, a motion.

2.9.1.1 Scottish parliamentary committees

Unlike at Westminster, much of the Scottish Parliament's work is performed by its eighteen committees: a system intended to make it easier for individual members to hold ministers to account. Committees comprise between five and fifteen MSPs, and are chaired by 'conveners'. Meetings take place in public and can be held anywhere in Scotland. This is meant to provide more direct access to the democratic process for ordinary people. One committee member is appointed as 'reporter' and MSPs may participate in meetings of committees of which they are not members (although they cannot vote).

Committees are charged with examining:

- policy, administration, and financial arrangements of the Scottish Government or Scottish Executive (see 3.4.1);
- proposed legislation in the Scottish and Westminster Parliaments; and
- the application of EU and international laws or conventions in Scotland.

2.9.1.2 The role and responsibilities of the Scottish Parliament

Until 2015, the Scottish Parliament was responsible only for domestic issues specifically relevant to Scotland, but not Britain as a whole. Roles retained by the Commons included:

- foreign and defence policy;
- most economic policy;
- social security; and
- medical ethics.

In the run-up to the narrow 'No' vote in the 2014 independence referendum, however, the main Westminster parties—alarmed at the prospect of defeat—promised a series of major concessions to Scotland, akin to a twenty-first-century version of 'home rule' (see 1.3.2). In reality, since the passage of the Scotland Act 2012—which formally renamed the Scottish Executive the 'Scottish Government', at the request of the ruling SNP—a series of incremental changes have edged Scotland towards a 'devo max-style' settlement. Moreover, in the aftermath of the close-run independence vote, its autonomy is slowly being extended further. The main enhancements of the Scottish Parliament's powers introduced by the 2012 Act included:

- authority to introduce a new 'Scottish rate' of income tax up to 10 pence in the pound above or below that applying to the rest of the UK from April 2016;
- full control (from April 2015) over levels of landfill tax and stamp duty;
- power to introduce new taxes, subject to the agreement of the UK government;
- control over policy relating to drink-driving limits, misuse of drugs, national road speed limits, and administration of Scottish parliamentary elections.

Even more significant devolution was conferred by the Scotland Act 2016—which Mr Cameron heralded as the birth of a new 'powerhouse parliament'. The main provisions of this Act were:

- unrestricted ability to set income tax levels—except those applying to savings and dividends;
- control over other taxes previously set by Parliament, notably air passenger duty;
- powers to vary UK social security policy—by, for example, topping up Jobseeker's Allowance (JSA), launching its own employment schemes, and creating new benefits (see also 8.8);

- the right to receive half the value-added tax (VAT) receipts (see 7.1.1) generated in Scotland;
- ability to amend aspects of the Scotland Act 1998 relating to the operation of the Scottish Parliament, including its electoral system (subject to a two-thirds majority at Holyrood).

Following prolonged wrangling between Scottish and UK governments, at time of writing Scotland also appeared to have been guaranteed indefinite continuation of the population-based 'Barnett Formula' (see 7.3.2), under which annual public spending per head north of the border tends to be higher than in England or Wales (though not Northern Ireland). This was despite recent protestations by its architect, the late Lord Barnett, that it should be scrapped in the interests of fairness.

2.9.1.3 The Scottish legislative process

The four main types of Bill that can be introduced into the Scottish Parliament are:

- *executive*—introduced by a minister;
- *committee*—introduced by the convener (chair) of a committee;
- *member's*—introduced by individual MSPs, like private members' Bills at Westminster, with the support of eleven fellow members; and
- *private*—introduced by private individuals or promoters.

When introduced in the Scottish Parliament, Bills must be accompanied by the documents listed in table 2D to be found on the **Online Resource Centre**. To become law, they must pass through the four stages outlined in Table 2.8, in a streamlined version of the Westminster process.

Table 2.8 Passage of a Bill through the Scottish Parliament

Stage	Process
Stage one	Examination of Bill's general principles, normally handled by specialist lead committee.
Stage two	Line-by-line examination of Bill and amendments, either by lead committee, another committee, or whole Parliament.
Stage three	Final consideration by full Parliament; amendments debated and Parliament decides whether to pass Bill; more than quarter of all MSPs must vote either way for it to pass.
Final stage	Parliament decides whether to approve Bill when referred back to full House; then automatically submitted for royal assent by Presiding Officer (there is no Lords stage).

2.9.2 The National Assembly for Wales

The Cardiff-based **National Assembly for Wales**—or Senedd—has sixty members. Forty of these represent constituencies, with the remaining twenty split equally over five larger regions. As in Scotland and Northern Ireland, these **Assembly members (AMs)** are no longer permitted to sit simultaneously as MPs. Like MSPs and MLAs, since 2011 AMs have been elected for five-year terms, rather than at four-year intervals as previously—to avoid any future prospect of devolved assembly elections clashing with UK-wide contests.

As in Scotland, each Welsh elector has two votes: one for a constituency member and the other for one from the relevant regional list. The Secretary of State for Wales retains a degree of responsibility for the province and, unlike in Scotland, the Assembly has, to date, only been able to vary income tax according to a 'lock-step' process, under which a change to one band must be applied to all others. The Secretary of State for Wales is charged with ensuring that devolution works effectively, by chairing a joint ministerial committee between Westminster and Cardiff.

The Assembly's responsibilities originally covered only the following:

- determining budgetary priorities;
- funding, directing, and appointing managers of NHS bodies in Wales;
- administering EU structural funds aimed at Wales; and
- determining the content of the National Curriculum in Wales.

Although its autonomy compares unfavourably to that of the Scottish Parliament, the Assembly gained notable new legislative powers through the Government of Wales Act 2006 and Wales Act 2014 respectively. The former introduced the 'Measure of the National Assembly for Wales' (known as the 'Assembly Measure')—a power allowing the Welsh Assembly Government to enact statutory instruments in relation to twenty 'fields' and 'matters' over which it has devolved authority. Assembly Measures can be proposed by any AM (including backbenchers) and must be scrutinized by committees, debated in plenary session, and approved in votes before adoption. Importantly, the 2006 Act also broadened the Assembly's powers to cover a wider range of areas (devolution of which had to be approved through a form of Order in Council known as a 'Legislative Competence Order'/LCO):

- agriculture, fisheries, forestry, and rural development;
- ancient monuments and historic buildings;
- culture;
- economic development;
- education and training;
- environment;

- fire and rescue services and promotion of fire safety;
- food;
- health and health services;
- highways and transport;
- housing;
- local government;
- public administration;
- social welfare;
- sport and recreation;
- tourism;
- town and country planning;
- water and flood defence;
- Welsh language; and
- the Assembly itself.

The Wales Act 2014 built significantly on the 2006 changes, following a 2011 referendum which saw Welsh electors vote 63.5 to 36.5 per cent to grant the Assembly powers to pass its own laws—or 'Acts of the Assembly'—on all twenty 'subject areas' over which it already had jurisdiction. The 2014 Act gave the Assembly control over stamp duty, business rates, and landfill tax—including the power to replace any or all of them with taxes specific to Wales—and permitted it to introduce a 'Welsh rate' of income tax, subject to a referendum. However, in November 2015 Mr Osborne removed the requirement for it to seek public approval for income tax changes and a year later newly installed Welsh Secretary Alun Cairns finalized a deal allowing Cardiff-based ministers to raise or lower rates within each band by up to 10 per cent from April 2019.

2.9.2.1 The Welsh legislative process

The law-making process in Wales in many ways resembles Scotland's. It too is overseen by a presiding officer and his or her deputy, elected by other AMs. Again, executive functions are wielded by a First Minister at the head of a devolved government. This was initially called the Welsh Executive, but is now referred to as the **Welsh Assembly Government**.

The Assembly meets in public plenary session in Cardiff Bay, and business is directed by the presiding officer through a business secretary and business committee. Each session allows at least fifteen minutes for oral questions of the First Minister and, every four weeks, similar sessions for each departmental minister. In addition, any AM can propose a motion once a week, before the conclusion of plenary business, and there are two forms of committee to consider matters in plenary session: 'subject committees' and 'regional committees' covering specific areas of the country.

Today's Acts are passed by the Assembly in a four-stage process almost identical to that used in Scotland. In addition, some subordinate legislation (statutory instruments) introduced by ministers must now be formally approved by AMs in plenary session—a process known as the 'affirmative procedure'. Alternatively, it can be challenged by a 'negative procedure' in the Assembly, if an AM tables a successful 'motion to annul' before a specified deadline upheld by a vote in the chamber.

2.9.3 The Northern Ireland Assembly

Devolved government in Stormont only finally came about in 2007, with the signing of a landmark power-sharing agreement between the two biggest parties—the late Ian Paisley's Democratic Unionist Party (DUP) and Gerry Adams's Sinn Féin—following fresh elections. The following year, Dr Paisley (a stalwart of Northern Irish politics for more than four decades) retired as First Minister and DUP leader, to be replaced by MP Peter Robinson. He subsequently lost his Westminster seat, but continued as First Minister until handing over to Arlene Foster in November 2015. She was reinstated after the May 2016 election, with Sinn Féin's Martin McGuinness continuing as Deputy First Minister-until his sudden resignation, in January 2017, over a botched green energy policy. His dramatic move was set to spark a fresh poll, as under the province's unique constitutional arrangements its ruling coalition collapses automatically if either a First Minister or his or her deputy quit.

2.9.3.1 Areas of responsibility retained over Northern Ireland by Westminster

The Secretary of State for Northern Ireland remains responsible for international relations, defence, and taxation.

Several Whitehall agencies remain responsible for overseeing specific areas, including the Northern Ireland Prison Service, Compensation Agency, and Forensic Agency of Northern Ireland. Policing and justice powers were devolved in April 2010 (see 1.3.5). The Northern Ireland Prison Service is overseen by a recently reconstituted Northern Ireland Policing Board, with members drawn from all of the main political parties.

2.9.3.2 The legislative process in Northern Ireland

The Northern Ireland Assembly is home to 108 elected representatives, known as **members of the Legislative Assembly (MLAs)**. The nature and titles of its senior politicians and officers, and the nature of its legislative process, are virtually identical to those in Wales.

Topical feature idea

Since 2010, ordinary citizens—and local MPs representing them—have been able to engage in a more 'direct' form of democracy than was previously possible, by launching e-petitions. Anyone who mobilizes at least 100,000 signatories to back an online petition supporting their cause can press the Commons Backbench Business Committee to timetable a full debate on that issue in the chamber. The advent of online activist movements such as Avaaz and 38 Degrees has made it easier for individuals and small community groups to mobilize support for e-petitions. But, in practice, petitions are usually 'presented' to the committee by backbench MPs representing particular constituencies or with personal interests in a campaign. Have there been any successful e-petitions mounted in your area? Are any current or pending? Why not set up your own e-petition as an experiment to see how much support can be rallied for a campaign on a local issue?

Current issues

- **English votes for English laws** Parliament recently began using a new, more drawn-out, process for legislation only aimed at England—or England and Wales—which gives English (or English and Welsh) MPs a final say over whether it should pass into law, and in what form. The aim is to act as a counterweight to increased devolution in Scotland and Wales.
- **The return of backbench rebellions** With the Conservatives now governing alone, but with a majority of just twelve seats and the thorny task of extricating Britain from the European Union, ministers have dropped a number of radical proposals from the party's 2015 manifesto, because of the risk of defeat by their own backbenchers. U-turns have included the abandonment of further cuts to working tax credits and disability benefits.
- **New tax powers for Wales** Having already gained incremental increases in its autonomy, with the introduction of first 'Assembly Measures' then 'Acts', the Welsh Assembly has now been granted authority to set its own income tax rate without first seeking public approval. As of May 2016, Assembly terms have also been extended from four to five years.

Key points

1. Britain's Parliament is a 'bicameral' legislature, comprising a primary legislative chamber, the House of Commons, and a secondary chamber tasked with revising legislation (the House of Lords). Scotland has a devolved Scottish Parliament, and Wales and Northern Ireland their own assemblies.

2. There are 650 MPs, each representing geographical areas known as 'constituencies', on average covering 65,000 people. Scotland has 129 MSPs; Wales, 60 AMs; Northern Ireland, 108 MLAs. The number of MPs will be cut to 600 by 2020.
3. The principal duty of an MP is to represent the interests of his or her constituents, by tabling questions in Parliament, lobbying ministers, and holding weekly constituency surgeries. Members are also expected to vote with their parties in Parliament and to sit on committees tasked with holding government to account.
4. The House of Lords currently comprises a mix of ninety-two hereditary peers (ninety elected by other peers), an ever-growing number of life peers appointed on merit, and twenty-six 'Lords Spiritual' (the most senior Church of England bishops).
5. Bills in Parliament go through a series of key stages, starting with the first and second readings, followed by a committee and report stage, a third reading, and consideration by the Lords. They become Acts of Parliament only after receiving royal assent. Each devolved assembly follows a similar sequence, but without the Lords stage.

→ Further reading

Jones, B. (2010) *Dictionary of British Politics*, 2nd edn, Manchester: Manchester University Press. **Thorough, accessible A–Z of terms and recent developments in British politics.**

Jones, B. and Norton, P. (2013) *Politics UK*, 8th edn, London: Longman. **Full-colour edition of established core text giving comprehensive overview of structure and workings of British political system up to 2005.**

Norton, P. (2013) *Parliament in British Politics*, 2nd edn, Basingstoke: Palgrave Macmillan. **Thoughtful evaluation of changing significance of British Parliament in light of recent constitutional developments, such as devolution and partial reform of the Lords.**

Rogers, R. and Walters, R. (2015) *How Parliament Works*, 7th edn, London: Longman. **Seventh edition of indispensable layman's guide to often complex, sometimes archaic, workings of British Parliament.**

Online Resource Centre

www.oxfordtextbooks.co.uk/orc/Morrison5e/

Visit the Online Resource Centre that accompanies this book for web links and regular updates.

3

Prime minister, Cabinet, and government

This chapter focuses on the make-up and workings of the executive branch of the UK constitution—the government—and particularly the role of the inner circle of ministers known as the **Cabinet**, and its titular head, the prime minister.

3.1 The origins of the role of prime minister

The role of **prime minister (PM)** emerged surprisingly recently, and owes its origins to historical accident. When German-born George I succeeded to the British throne in 1714, he could speak little English. Traditionally, the Cabinet had always been chaired by the monarch, but with the newly crowned king unable to speak the language of UK government a practical need arose for a senior minister to perform this duty in his place. Thus was born the post that became that of de facto head of government in Britain—or 'prime' minister. After some debate, the honour of assuming this role was handed to Sir Robert Walpole, then 'First Lord of the Treasury' (in effect, the Lord High Treasurer or official head of HM Treasury—the department responsible for raising taxes to finance government policy). His previous duties were generally assumed from this date by the Lord High Commissioners of the Treasury.

Despite assuming the day-to-day role of prime minister, however, Walpole retained his official Cabinet title, as did his successors for nearly a century. In fact, although the term 'prime minister' was used informally within government from 1714 onwards and started appearing on government documents in the 1860s, under Benjamin Disraeli, it was coined publicly only during the term of Liberal premier Sir Henry Campbell-Bannerman (1905–8).

Given the disproportionate power wielded by the PM, since the position arose it has been constitutionally contentious. Before its introduction, all ministers were regarded as equals, with shared responsibility for governing. The emergence of a Cabinet chairperson from within its own ranks made an immediate mockery of this idea, by implicitly elevating him or her to a level *more equal* than others. This somewhat contradictory position spawned the use of the Latin phrase *primus inter pares* ('first among equals') to describe the status of the premier. Prime ministers are 'equal' to their Cabinet colleagues—and all members of the House of Commons—in that, as elected members of Parliament (MPs), they must be voted in to represent constituencies and can be removed by local people if they become unpopular. In contrast, he or she is 'first among' those notional 'equals' by dint not of being both a senior government minister and the chair and convener of Cabinet meetings.

Monarchs have seldom even attended Cabinet meetings since the premier took on the chairman role. However, in December 2012, the Queen was invited to sit in on Cabinet for the first time since the reign of Queen Victoria, as a one-off gesture to mark her Diamond Jubilee.

3.1.1 The role of prime minister today

Today, there are many established conventions surrounding the office of prime minister, almost all introduced since Walpole's day. The PM tends to be leader of the party that wins the most seats in the Commons at a general election. To this extent, although British voters theoretically turn out to elect their local MPs on polling day (and, indirectly, contribute to the election of a national government), the implications of one party beating another in the contest are inherently 'presidential': in other words, everyone knows that if X party gets in, Y leader will become PM (a consequence that, intriguingly, is not nearly so certain in elections for the devolved assemblies—see 3.4.2). Historically, premiers have always hailed from one of the two biggest parliamentary parties at any given time. In the twentieth century, five PMs were Labour and twelve Conservatives, with both parties vying to establish themselves as the 'natural party of government'.

Although many prerogative powers exercised on the sovereign's behalf are discharged collectively by Cabinet (at least notionally), the PM is customarily the only minister ever granted private audiences with the monarch. Incoming premiers first meet the Queen when they visit her at Buckingham Palace to be offered the post formally after their election. This behind-the-scenes ritual is known as the 'kissing of the hands'. The PM's official London residence is at 10 Downing Street and he or she also has a sprawling country estate at Chequers in the Chilterns. Like many conventions, such rules are there to be bent when circumstances dictate: when Mr Blair came to power, he swapped domestic quarters with his Chancellor, Gordon Brown, whose official residence was

Number 11, where there is more living space. At the time, Mr Blair had a growing family, while Mr Brown was living alone.

By far the most important convention relating to the PM, however, is the fact that whoever holds the office has the authority to exercise, on the sovereign's behalf, most powers entrusted to him or her by royal prerogative. The principal **prerogative powers** discharged by the premier are to:

- appoint fellow ministers;
- chair weekly Cabinet meetings;
- appoint members of Cabinet committees;
- keep the sovereign informed of government business on a weekly basis;
- declare war;
- recommend passage of government Bills to royal assent;
- recommend **dissolution** of Parliament for general elections;
- recommend **prorogation** of Parliament for summer recess and other holidays;
- draw up his or her party's manifesto at elections and write the Queen's Speech—the annual announcement of proposed government legislation;
- recommend for sovereign's approval appointees to senior clergy positions, including the Church of England bishops and deans;
- recommend the appointment of senior judges;
- recommend appointees for senior positions in public corporations, including the British Broadcasting Corporation (BBC);
- recommend prospective recipients of honours and peerages in the Queen's Birthday Honours List and New Year Honours List; and
- answer for his or her government's actions at Prime Minister's Questions (PMQs).

The PM is also Minister for the Civil Service. The 'department' that he or she oversees in this capacity is the Cabinet Office (effectively the 'Ministry for the Civil Service') and, until recently, his or her **permanent secretary** (the most senior civil servant) was the Cabinet Secretary. On the retirement of the then incumbent Sir Gus O'Donnell, in 2011, his previous role was split three ways: with a new Cabinet Secretary, permanent secretary to the Cabinet Office, and formal Head of the Home Civil Service replacing him. But a further, more radical, reform was to come—and one emblematic of the Conservatives' wider agenda to shake up the policymaking process and inject a spirit of entrepreneurship into Whitehall. Alongside his dramatic July 2014 Cabinet reshuffle, then prime minister David Cameron introduced a new chief executive role at the top of the Civil Service, the first holder of which is John Mazoni, a former president and CEO of Canadian oil and gas company Talisman Inc. Manzoni, who is also permanent secretary to the Cabinet Office, is tasked specifically with promoting the 'digital transformation' of public services and ensuring British taxpayers get the best possible value for money from government commercial decisions and contracts with suppliers—in the spirit of the tight controls on public finances introduced by then Chancellor George Osborne (see Chapter 7). He reports directly to Cabinet Secretary Sir Jeremy Heywood, who has in turn resumed the secondary role of heading up the service traditionally held by his predecessors until the retiring Sir Bob Kerslake had been handed that role, as a part-time position, in 2011.

3.1.2 Towards 'elective dictatorship': are prime ministers now too presidential?

Britain's premier may not be its head of state, but to many observers he or she often appears so. No monarch has had the temerity to challenge the passage of a government Bill since Queen Anne more than 300 years ago. And the notion that sovereigns would defy the electorate's will to block appointments of PMs whose policies they opposed is the stuff of establishment conspiracy theories.

Perhaps unsurprisingly, power has been known to go to some PMs' heads. As long ago as 1976, Quintin Hogg—who, as Lord Hailsham, twice served as Conservative Lord Chancellor—used his Richard Dimbleby Lecture to criticize the 'elective dictatorship' of British governments. His argument was that successive PMs had accrued substantial additional power beyond that vested in them constitutionally and were increasingly using their parliamentary colleagues to steamroller policies through Parliament. Moreover, he argued those same policies were often decided upon behind closed doors—long before being debated in Parliament. At best, this backstage policymaking would take place around the Cabinet table, among premiers and their ministerial colleagues; at worst, it might be dreamed up informally between the PM and an inner circle of trusted confidantes, not all necessarily ministers. This mode of governing is often referred to as 'prime ministerial government'—or 'sofa government'—as opposed to the more collegiate traditional 'Cabinet government'.

Indeed, it was often said that 1960s and 1970s governments were prone to striking deals in 'smoke-filled rooms', with business leaders, trade union bosses, and other interest groups having a direct and unofficial input into policymaking.

But these tactics—increasingly common to all governing parties—are far from the only examples of perceived presidential behaviour by modern PMs. Occasional slips of the tongue by pressurized premiers have spoken volumes about their apparent sense of superiority. In 1989, Margaret Thatcher notoriously greeted news of her son Mark's fatherhood with the royal 'we', telling the waiting media: 'We are a grandmother.'

So much for the sound bites, though: in what ways do PMs *act* high-handedly? Examples of such presidential actions can broadly be grouped under four headings:

- bypassing or downgrading the Cabinet's role in devising policy;
- announcing policies to the media before informing Parliament or Cabinet;
- ignoring popular opinion and protest; and
- grandstanding on the international stage.

3.1.2.1 Bypassing or downgrading the Cabinet's role in devising policy

Prime ministers chair meetings of Cabinet. It is here that policies are traditionally thrashed out, before being announced to the press and public. In recent decades, however, there has been a tendency for premiers to downgrade the Cabinet's role in policymaking—or even bypass it entirely, instead seeking advice from select coteries of trusted friends known as 'kitchen Cabinets'.

'Kitchen Cabinets' have taken various forms, often closely reflecting the particular personalities of individual PMs. An early manifestation of a kitchen Cabinet was Conservative PM Ted Heath's Central Policy Review Staff (CPRS), a group of advisers within the Cabinet Office (see 3.2.4) entrusted with streamlining the formulation of government policy across departments. The formation of the CPRS had been recommended by the Fulton Committee, established by Mr Wilson in 1966 to review the workings of the Civil Service. The Committee had also suggested a separate 'policy unit' be formed to coordinate long-term planning in each ministry and, to this end, when Wilson returned to power in 1974 he formed the Downing Street Policy Unit (effectively a more formal kitchen Cabinet), chaired by journalist, academic and staunch Labour ally Sir Bernard Donoughue.

Indeed, Mr Wilson had a reputation for valuing the views of personal friends over those of Cabinet colleagues. His private secretary, Marcia Williams, was seen to exert an at times powerful influence on his managerial decisions. This fashion for consulting close allies—elected or otherwise—before presenting ideas to Cabinet (let alone Parliament) was also favoured by Mrs Thatcher, whose closest aides included her press secretary, Sir Bernard Ingham, and private secretary, former businessman Charles Powell—intriguingly, the brother of Mr Blair's loyal Downing Street chief of staff, Jonathan Powell.

More recently, kitchen Cabinets have become increasingly associated with the machinations of 'special advisers', in particular the **spin doctors** whom ministers employ to put a positive gloss on government policy. This development will be discussed more fully later, but it is worth considering here in relation to one particular casualty of the 'sofa government' favoured by Mr Blair: Cabinet decision-making. As with his weekly meetings with the Queen, when the Iraq War was in full swing, Mr Blair downgraded formal Cabinet meetings to such an extent that deliberations that traditionally took several hours were often reduced to thirty minutes or less. In addition, he left many detailed policy debates, customarily held in full Cabinet, to Cabinet committees—appointing his most loyal colleagues to chair these hearings to reduce the likelihood of his own ideas being disputed. It was for this and other 'undemocratic' tendencies that former Cabinet minister Clare Short later publicly dubbed Mr Blair a 'control freak'. Mr Cameron initially largely abandoned 'sofa government', but some senior Tories, such as Michael Gove, were periodically accused during the Coalition years of letting senior advisers brief against their Liberal Democrat colleagues. In March 2014, the then Education Secretary's outspoken former adviser, Dominic Cummings, became embroiled in a full-blown public row with then Lib Dem deputy prime minister Nick Clegg over what he dismissed as the latter's 'chaotic' and uncosted plan to introduce free school meals for infant school pupils from that September.

Mrs Thatcher and Mr Blair were also repeatedly accused of downgrading Parliament's role in the legislative process. By using the party whip system to coerce MPs and peers to back the party line, Mr Blair was frequently accused of abusing his large Commons majority to 'steamroller' through policies unpopular with the public (and his own backbenchers). Examples include various anti-terror measures introduced following the attacks on the Twin Towers in New York and the 7 July 2005 bombings in London—many rushed through in a matter of days, with committee stages taking place on the Commons floor (see 2.2.3.2). In October 2011, Mr Cameron used a three-line whip to stifle a backbench revolt by Conservative MPs demanding a referendum on Britain's European Union (EU) membership. Despite this, the resulting rebellion remained the single biggest over Europe since the Second World War, with eighty-one backbenchers defying the party whip to support it. Nine months later, ninety-one Tory MPs broke ranks to vote down Lib Dem proposals for Lords reform (see 2.3.3), while almost exactly a year after the 2011 EU rebellion by his backbenchers Mr Cameron suffered a Commons defeat over his proposal to argue for a freeze, rather than real-terms cut, in the Union's budget. The legacy of these first-term conflicts with the right of his party went on to shape some of the most eye-opening pledges in the Tories' 2015 election manifesto—notably Mr Cameron's ultimately fateful promises to withdraw the UK from the European Convention on Human Rights and hold an 'in-out' EU referendum (see Chapter 9).

3.1.2.2 Announcing policies to media before Parliament or Cabinet

Briefing the media (or sympathetic sections of it) on policy proposals before formally announcing them to Parliament and public has become a much criticized trend under recent administrations. In some instances under Mr Blair, ministers close to the PM spoon-fed policy details to favoured journalists before even the Cabinet (let alone the Commons) had deliberated them.

Arrangements for the briefings invariably involved spin doctors and/or special advisers—principally Mr Blair's official spokesman and long-time director of communications, Alastair Campbell, and/or Mr Powell.

The most widely used forms of 'off-the-record' briefings are explained in table 3A to be found on the **Online Resource Centre**.

An infamous example of serious policy proposals being released to the press prior to full Cabinet discussion occurred in 2002, when then Health Secretary and close Blair ally Alan Milburn gave *The Times* a detailed explanation of his 'Ten-Year Plan for the National Health Service'. Mr Cameron's government was repeatedly accused of similar leaks: Mr Osborne's 2012 'omnishambles Budget' was as notorious for the fact that little of substance was left for the Chancellor to announce in his statement as the perceived political folly of measures it introduced (see 7.2.2).

3.1.2.3 Ignoring popular opinion or protest

During his first term, Mr Blair frequently consulted opinion pollsters and focus groups before taking radical policy decisions. His critics (many within his own party) argued that this was, at best, a waste of the mandate he had achieved by winning such a large majority in the 1997 election and, at worst, a betrayal of Labour's manifesto pledges.

In his second term, Mr Blair developed a tendency to do precisely the opposite—becoming increasingly bold in his political judgments. The most notorious example of this was his pursuit of the case for war with Iraq, citing supposed evidence that Saddam Hussein was stockpiling weapons of mass destruction (WMDs). Defying huge opposition in the country—articulated by the biggest peacetime demonstration in Britain's history, when some 500,000 protestors converged on Trafalgar Square just days before the war—he persuaded a reluctant Commons to vote for invasion.

Mr Blair's appetite for defying public opposition echoed Mrs Thatcher's. The policy that most clearly demonstrated her stubbornness in the teeth of huge public opposition would ultimately—like the Iraq War for Mr Blair—hasten her downfall. Introducing the deeply unpopular Community Charge (see 11.2.4) to replace the age-old rates system provoked some of the largest-scale protests in British history. Mrs Thatcher remained resolute, however, and only when John Major succeeded her the following year was the tax abandoned.

3.1.2.4 Grandstanding on the international stage

As Britain's de facto head of state, the PM has the biggest global profile of any UK politician. Nonetheless, some premiers take to the role of international statesperson more than others. Of twentieth-century PMs, Winston Churchill was widely regarded as the greatest statesman, principally because of the leadership he gave to Europe during the Second World War.

Recent examples of 'presidential-style' grandstanding at a global level have included Mrs Thatcher's decisive handling of the Falklands War and high-profile White House 'love-ins' with US President Ronald Reagan. Her implacable opposition to communism and her determined negotiation of various British opt-outs from EU legislation also helped to maintain her high international profile. Mr Blair, meanwhile, waged four wars during his decade in Downing Street—pursuing a proactive defence policy known as 'liberal interventionism'. During his first term, he helped to launch two military campaigns: the North Atlantic Treaty Organization (NATO) intervention over alleged 'ethnic cleansing' of Albanians by Slobodan Milošović's Serbian forces in Kosovo, and a decisive move to halt civil war in the former British colony of Sierra Leone. In his second, he became forever wedded in the public eye to George Bush's US administration by pledging to 'stand shoulder to shoulder' with him following the 11 September terrorist attacks, and actively supporting the invasions of Afghanistan and Iraq.

Earlier, Mr Blair had stamped his international profile with 'missions' to tackle poverty in Africa, to forge peace in Northern Ireland, and to promote a decisive 'two-state solution' to the long-running stand-off between Israel and Palestine in the Middle East. In many ways, Mr Cameron continued this interventionist 'tradition'—drawing international praise for his Commons statement following publication of the long-awaited 'Bloody Sunday' report; making repeated high-profile visits to China and India to promote British business interests; and playing a leading role in pushing for military action against Muammar Gaddafi in Libya, and first Bashar Al-Assad then the so-called 'Islamic State' in Syria.

3.1.3 Holding the prime minister to account

Given the degree of power accrued by PMs, what mechanisms exist to hold them to account? As we know, monarchs have long since lost their inclination (if not constitutional 'right') to challenge premiers. Notwithstanding Queen Elizabeth II's predilection for wrong-footing Wilson and her reputedly frosty relationship with Mrs Thatcher, there has been little recent evidence for reigning monarchs displaying appetites for confrontation. Nonetheless, there remain significant ways in which the actions of PMs can be influenced, if not directly controlled. These can be divided into four areas:

- public;
- press;
- Parliament; and
- party.

3.1.3.1 Public

The primary means of holding premiers accountable returns to that first principle: that they are ultimately MPs like any other and must stand for re-election in their constituencies on polling day. Their parties are similarly dependent on mandates for their Commons majorities: if enough of their MPs lose their seats, other parties will supplant them in government.

Mr Major's resounding defeat in 1997 by Mr Blair's rebranded 'New' Labour was the clearest example in recent times of an ailing administration being unceremoniously ejected by a determined electorate. Not only did the Tories suffer a landslide defeat, but many senior MPs—including future political pundit Michael Portillo—lost their seats. Although Mr Major escaped this ignominy, it has been known for PMs in some countries to lose their own constituencies, not just their parliamentary majorities. For example, Northern Ireland First Minister Peter Robinson lost his parliamentary seat in the 2010 UK election (see 2.9.3).

Prime ministers are also accountable in other ways. It has long been the practice for local authority, European, and by-elections to be treated as anti-government 'protest votes'—giving PM's a 'bloody nose'. Other voters prefer to withhold their support from governing parties that they might still back at general elections by abstaining altogether. There was significant anecdotal evidence that protest votes rose under New Labour, especially among traditional party voters disillusioned by the Iraq invasion. The combined effect of protest votes and abstentions, on one side, and renewed determination to harness support, on the other, can lead to situations like that witnessed in the 2007 and 2008 local elections, both of which were 'won' by the then resurgent Conservatives.

Other forms of public pressure that can be heaped on PMs include demonstrations (such as the Stop the War Coalition marches over Iraq or the more recent student protests over the tripling of undergraduate tuition fees in England); industrial action by public sector employees; and rejections of key policies in national **referendums**. Although British governments have historically put few individual questions to the public vote—preferring to invoke the constitutional principle of parliamentary sovereignty, which leaves decisions to Parliament between elections—there have so far been three referendums under the post-2010 Conservative-led governments, focusing on electoral reform (2011), Scottish independence (2014), and Britain's EU membership (2016).

3.1.3.2 **Press**

If there is one thing guaranteed to send a PM scurrying in pursuit of populist policy ideas to regain public support, it is a run of negative tabloid headlines.

In recent years, the national press—particularly the biggest-selling daily papers, *The Sun* and *Daily Mail*—has arguably wielded disproportionate influence on successive governments' actions. Mrs Thatcher's hat-trick of election victories was attributed, in part, to the support of 'white van' or 'Essex' man—terms denoting a new breed of aspirational working-class voter weary of the class warfare espoused by old-school Labour politicians, and attracted by the entrepreneurial doctrines of share and home ownership she ushered in.

Although formerly a red-blooded Labour paper (the *Daily Herald*), under Rupert Murdoch *The Sun* came to epitomize this new spirit of aspiration, while the *Mail's* high moral tone appealed to more 'traditional' Conservatives.

Throughout the 1980s, *The Sun*, under bullish editor Kelvin Mackenzie, remained a staunch advocate of Thatcherism, using many memorable front-page headlines to bolster support for her resolutely patriotic brand of politics. His most controversial splashes included its celebration of the sinking of the Argentine warship *General Belgrano* with the headline 'Gotcha!', and one aggressively urging voters to support Mr Major rather than Labour leader Neil Kinnock on the morning of the 1992 election. After years of supporting the Conservatives, though, Britain's biggest-selling paper switched horses in the run-up to the 1997 election, backing Mr Blair (before eventually returning to the Tories on the morning after Mr Brown's speech to the 2009 Labour Party Conference).

Although this was strenuously denied by both Mr Blair and Mr Brown, the liberalization of UK media ownership laws enabling Mr Murdoch to buy a stake in ITV was rumoured to have come as a result of his behind-the-scenes lobbying. Mr Cameron also faced serious questions over his perceived closeness to the Murdoch empire following his decision, while in Opposition, to hire former *News of the World* editor Andy Coulson as his personal spokesman shortly after the latter's 2007 resignation over a (then incipient) scandal about the practice of reporters at the Sunday paper 'hacking' into their contacts' mobile phone messages. Although Mr Coulson quit his Downing Street post in February 2011 (amid growing allegations about his collusion in a cover-up at his old paper), the uncomfortably close relations between the Murdoch press and Mr Cameron's Tories was laid bare in detail during a series of hearings at the public inquiry convened in 2011 by Lord Justice Leveson to examine the culture and practices of the British media following further phone-hacking revelations. Among the nuggets to emerge were anecdotes about Mr Cameron's cosy chat with then News International chairman James Murdoch in a Mayfair club, during which he learned that the paper's sister title, *The Sun*, was reverting to supporting the Tories.

More controversial still were questions that emerged about the extent of the Coalition's unofficial endorsement of News Corporation's attempt to purchase the 61 per cent of shares that it did not yet own in UK-based satellite television broadcaster BSkyB. In his evidence to the inquiry, Murdoch junior disclosed a slew of email exchanges between Adam Smith (a special adviser to then Culture Secretary Jeremy Hunt) and News Corp lobbyist Frederic Michel, which appeared to reflect the minister's implied support for the bid. At a later hearing, Mr Smith revealed a memo sent to Mr Cameron by Mr Hunt, in which he apparently urged the PM to back the takeover. The note was sent on 19 November 2010—a month before Mr Cameron appointed Mr Hunt to succeed Lib Dem Business Secretary Vince Cable in determining the outcome of the BSkyB bid, following the latter's indiscreet confession to undercover reporters from *The Daily Telegraph* that he had 'declared war' on Rupert Murdoch.

Set alongside Mr Murdoch's recollection of chatting to Mr Cameron about the takeover plans over Christmas dinner at Mrs Brooks's Cotswolds home and the regular text messages she received from the PM, an impression emerged of unprecedented levels of intimacy between Britain's most powerful media company and the holder of its highest political office.

While it has long been commonplace for newspapers to take partisan stands, in Britain broadcasters are bound by a strict code of impartiality upheld by the Office of Communications, whose remit was extended to cover the BBC in May 2016 following publication of a ministerial review of the corporation's governance (Ofcom—see 7.5.1.1).

3.1.3.3 **Parliament**

Prime ministers are held to account by Parliament in various ways, the most demonstrable being Prime Minister's Questions (PMQs)—the Wednesday lunchtime session in which the PM is quizzed about his or her actions (see 2.2.1.2).

Most MPs also sit on committees. On select committees, they examine the workings of individual government departments—and, indirectly, the Cabinet. General committees, meanwhile, scrutinize prospective legislation, the bulk of which will have originated in the in-trays of the PM and his or her most senior ministerial colleagues. Prime ministers also now subject themselves to twice-yearly scrutiny by the Commons Liaison Committee.

In addition, MPs can use a variety of other parliamentary procedures outlined in the last chapter to influence or criticize PMs. But perhaps the single most powerful way in which MPs—and, to a lesser extent, peers—conspire to embarrass serving PMs is by voting down their policies in Parliament. Because most governments have working Commons majorities enabling them to marshal sufficient support from loyalists, historically government legislation is rarely defeated. Occasionally, however, PMs have found themselves so out of step with their parliamentary parties that (whatever their nominal majorities) they have struggled to get their proposals passed.

3.1.3.4 **Party**

When Parliament conspires to censure PMs, derail their legislative programmes, or otherwise undermine their authority, it usually succeeds only with the complicity of government backbenchers so dismayed at their leader's direction that they are prepared to vote against it en masse. During Mr Blair's second and third terms and the early phase of Jeremy Corbyn's leadership of Labour in Opposition, rebellions within the governing parties became so frequent at times that government backbenchers were often described as the 'unofficial Opposition'—particularly when the *real* ones were still under stuttering leaderships that often stood accused of missing open goals.

Among the most serious rebellions are those that threaten to overrule the Budget (see 7.2), the means by which governments finance their policies—an eventuality narrowly avoided by two recent Chancellors, Alistair Darling and Mr Osborne, over, respectively, the scrapping of the 10 pence starting rate of income tax in 2008 and the latter's (ultimately abandoned) 2016 plans to further cut disability benefits (see 8.5). Similarly perilous are rebellions that threaten to vote down part, or all, of the Queen's Speech. Mr Cameron narrowly averted this in May 2016, by agreeing to back an amendment supported by Labour, the SNP, and twenty-five Eurosceptic MPs from his own party expressing 'regret' that that year's speech—delivered barely twenty-four hours earlier—had failed to include a Bill exempting the NHS from the proposed Transatlantic Trade and Investment Partnership (TTIP), a sweeping free trade deal between the European Union and United States of America that critics warned could see swathes of the NHS privatized and/or made subject to the full force of commercial competition. Had the government lost a vote on this issue, it would have suffered the first defeat on a King's or Queen's Speech since 1924. Most ominous of all, though, is the prospect of a 'motion of no confidence' (also known as 'vote of no confidence', or 'censure motion'). This is when a device such as an early day motion (EDM) is put before the Commons—customarily by the Leader of the Opposition—inviting MPs to pass a motion (vote) expressing loss of 'confidence' in the PM. If he or she loses, this normally means that even his or her own MPs have withdrawn their support and an election must be called. The election that brought an end to Callaghan's Labour government in May 1979 was ultimately precipitated by a confidence vote tabled by Opposition leader Mrs Thatcher. Because Callaghan had been leading a minority government following the collapse of a fragile deal with the Liberal Party (the 'Lib–Lab Pact'), he was increasingly reliant on support from the Ulster Unionists and Scottish Nationalists. When his government refused to implement a proposed Scotland Act to introduce devolution (a referendum had backed it, but on only a relatively low turnout—see 1.3.2), the nationalists tabled a confidence motion, which Mrs Thatcher swiftly emulated.

Prime ministers in desperate straits have even been known to call their own confidence votes to instil discipline in their party ranks and force through unpopular legislation. In 1993, Mr Major tabled a 'back me or sack me' motion to force the hand of the 'Maastricht rebels' (see 9.5). In the event, he won—not least because most rebels represented marginal seats and could easily have lost them in the event of an election at that time.

Traditionally, confidence motions require only *simple majorities* of MPs' votes—50 per cent of those cast, plus one—to bring down a government. So it was with alarm that some constitutional experts and politicians initially greeted the Coalition's proposals in May 2010 to introduce not only five-year fixed-term parliaments (see 4.1.1), but also a new rule preventing elections being called mid-term unless 55 per cent of MPs voted in favour of dissolution. Critics argued that the proposed '55 per cent rule' could be used to insure Mr Cameron against the possibility of his coalition partners pulling the plug on it prematurely (between them, the Lib Dems, Labour, and all minority parties would have mustered only 53 per cent of Commons votes if the former had switched loyalties). They also complained that it would render the confidence procedure redundant: although a government could theoretically still be defeated by such a vote, the backing of a further 5 per cent of MPs would be needed to force an election, potentially leaving a 'defeated' administration limping on like a 'zombie'. But in the Coalition's defence, then Leader of the House Sir George Young argued that its opponents were missing the point: rather than enabling PMs to prolong their tenures against Parliament's wishes, the new rule would instead liberate the Commons by equipping it with a mechanism to demand dissolution without the formality of a confidence vote. Nevertheless, when Mr Clegg confirmed the final proposals in a Commons statement two months later, he announced that the 55 per cent rule was being dropped and elections would instead continue to be triggered by a no confidence vote alone. He did, though, introduce an important new lifeline for struggling minority governments—granting them a two-week breathing space after losing confidence votes to try to form alternative administrations and stay in power. At the same time, the Commons would still have the ability to prompt dissolution by a straight vote, although only if two-thirds of MPs (as opposed to the mooted 55 per cent) were to approve it. This provision, subsequently enshrined in the Fixed Term Parliament Act 2011, echoed one previously adopted by the Scottish Parliament.

There are, of course, various other ways in which governing parties can hold their leaders to account—and even depose them. Once a week when Labour is in government, and less regularly when in Opposition, leaders subject themselves to a lengthy meeting of the **Parliamentary Labour Party (PLP)**—a body representing all Labour MPs. Although Mr Blair was given a famously easy ride for his first few years in power, after the Iraq debacle PLP meetings became increasingly strained, while Mr Corbyn has endured frequent heckling and hostile questioning from high-profile backbench critics such as John Mann and Jess Phillips.

If anything, Conservatives have an even more ferocious means of grilling (and removing) their leaders. The **1922 Committee** is a body made up of all Tory MPs. Actually formed in 1923 (its name refers to the 1922 election), this has an eighteen-strong executive committee charged with overseeing the election of new leaders, which at times has replaced existing ones. As the 'voice' of Tory MPs, the 1922 Committee is seen to represent the collective 'mood' of the parliamentary party. If it passes a vote of no confidence, it is normally only a matter of time before the leader jumps (if he or she is not pushed first). Though it is examined in more detail in Chapter 5, the 1922 Committee is relevant here in relation to its role in unseating one particular premier: Mrs Thatcher. Her downfall was effectively instigated by her former Cabinet colleague, Michael Heseltine, who challenged her for the party leadership in November 1990. Although she won the first round of voting, she did so by too small a margin to seal the contest. To do so she had to secure an *absolute majority* (more than half) of all Tory MPs and achieve 15 per cent more votes than her nearest rival—a target she narrowly missed. Despite initially announcing her intention to continue into a second round, in the interim Mrs Thatcher was visited by a deputation of backbenchers who persuaded her that she had lost her MPs' backing. After taking counsel from fellow ministers, she withdrew her candidacy—paving the way for Mr Major's election.

3.2 Cabinet versus government: what's the difference?

Despite clear moves towards more presidential—or 'prime ministerial'—forms of government, the role of Cabinet remains of paramount importance in the exercise of elected power in Britain. So what exactly *is* the 'Cabinet', and how does it differ from and relate to the 'government'?

The simple answer is that the former is a 'subset' of the latter: while governments comprise *all* ministers appointed by the PM, Cabinets comprise only the most senior. Governments and Cabinets have varied wildly in size from one administration to another, with some favouring a more compact, rationalized approach and others one that is more all-embracing.

As explained in Chapter 2, governments can number anything between 80 and 100-plus ministers. In October 2011, the Coalition was criticized by the Commons Public Administration Committee for hitting record highs—with 119 ministers and 46 ministerial aides on the government's payroll. Historically, the average Cabinet size has been twenty. Yet, for much of the Second World War, Winston Churchill ran a Cabinet numbering sixty-eight ministers, while in 1922 Andrew Bonar Law formed a peacetime Cabinet of only sixteen. In contrast, Labour PMs have tended to appoint larger Cabinets—as a bulwark, in part, against what the party long saw as the intransigence of senior civil servants against implementing radical reform. Mr Brown appointed an enlarged 'hybrid' first Cabinet, effectively numbering twenty-nine—before expanding it still further, to thirty-four (including 'occasional' members such as the then Olympics Minister Tessa Jowell). Its numbers were boosted, in part, by his decision to create a new Department of Energy and Climate Change (DECC), and reinstate two distinct offices for Defence and Scotland, following criticisms from military chiefs and the devolved Scottish Government respectively of his earlier decision to combine the two under one minister. Under the Tories, the tally remains well over thirty—including eight ministers who, though not full members, were entitled to attend its meetings.

Cabinet ministers have, until recently, always been either MPs or peers. Although some critics and constitutional historians regard the idea of peers being entrusted with ministerial briefs as contentious, there have been many high-profile examples of such appointments, including Lord Young (Trade and Industry Secretary under Mrs Thatcher) and Lord Adonis (first Education Minister, then Transport Secretary, in Blair and Brown's administrations). Until the defeat of Lord Salisbury in the 1902 election, moreover, it was not uncommon for even prime ministers to sit in the Upper House. Though this would be unthinkable today, peers continue to be appointed to other Cabinet roles.

A more controversial recent trend, however, has been for PMs to appoint individuals who are neither MPs nor peers to senior positions. Mr Brown took his discretion to choose ministers from outside the Commons to a new level on entering office, by declaring his intention to form a 'government of all the talents'. This assertion (an extension of the 'big tent' politics for which Mr Blair was often criticized by Labour traditionalists) saw several individuals from outside his party appointed to senior advisory posts. Baron Jones of Birmingham, former director-general of the Confederation of British Industry (CBI), was appointed a minister at the then Department of Business, Enterprise, and Regulatory Reform (BERR)—despite openly refusing to join the Labour Party. Mr Brown also dispensed with another tradition: for the first time since 1963, Cabinet meetings switched from Thursdays to Tuesdays.

Most Cabinet ministers have the title **secretary of state**, rather than **minister of state**, denoting their seniority. This normally means that they head up a major spending department, such as health, and have several junior ministers beneath them. The choice of ministerial posts included in the Cabinet can vary greatly, depending on political priorities of the day. Until Mr Blair's 1997 victory, overseas aid/development was treated as a relatively minor ministerial area and was the responsibility of a lower-ranking Foreign Office minister. When Labour was re-elected, the post's incumbent was promoted to 'International Development Secretary', with his or her own dedicated ministry.

In addition to obvious senior departmental posts, the Cabinet traditionally contains one or two honorary ones awarded to loyal lieutenants of the prime minister whom he or she wants to keep close at hand, but for more general duties than overseeing specific portfolios. One such post is that of 'Chancellor of the Duchy of Lancaster'—a sinecure deriving from an office once involved in the daily management of the sovereign's one significant surviving estate following the handover of the Crown Lands to the state (see 1.2.3.2). Another such post is that of 'Minister without Portfolio'—an office briefly assumed after the 1997 election by Mr Blair's close ally Peter Mandelson (who made two subsequent returns to Cabinet). In forming his 2010 coalition, meanwhile, Mr Cameron dispensed with convention by appointing Lib Dem leader Mr Clegg deputy prime minister without allocating him a departmental brief. As of August 2016, fifteen months after the 2015 general election, the make-up of the Conservative-only Cabinet was as listed in Table 3.1.

So much for the Cabinet: what of the government as a whole? Its size can also vary, but in modern times it is customary for it to number up to 100 ministers. The most junior ministerial post is that of **parliamentary under-secretary**, ranking beneath both ministers and secretaries of state. Also included are government whips and any MP appointed a **parliamentary private secretary (PPS).** These are junior posts ascribed to ambitious MPs who aspire to ministerial office. They serve as points of contact or liaison in Parliament (or, as some would have it, 'spies') for serving ministers and are informally connected to their departments. The PM tends to have two.

3.2.1 Ministerial salaries

In recognition of their responsibilities, ministers who are MPs receive substantially higher salaries than backbenchers. Precise levels of ministerial salaries can vary widely, depending on their seniority and the complexity of their jobs. During his first week in power in May 2010, Mr Cameron cut Cabinet ministers' salaries by 5 per cent in absolute terms and froze them at those levels for the rest of the parliament—consolidating earlier moves by Mr Brown to curb his own and colleagues' pay in a show of solidarity with people whose incomes had suffered as a result of the 2008 financial crisis and ensuing recession (see 7.3.4). In so doing, Mr Cameron brought his own political earnings down to £142,500, those of Cabinet ministers to £134,565, and pay for ministers of state outside Cabinet from £100,568 under Labour to £98,740. As of the start of the 2016–17 financial year, Cabinet ministers were paid £135,527—£60,565 more than an ordinary MP—with Mr Cameron's successor as prime minister, Theresa May, earning £143,462 a year.

Although peers are unpaid, those occupying government positions do receive parliamentary remuneration. Cabinet ministers drawn from the Lords receive more than £100,000, while those at lower ranks in the government get around £80,000. Until 2007, the highest-paid minister of all was not the PM, but the Lord Chancellor (then still a peer), who earned £232,900. Substantial salaries are also paid to senior Opposition frontbenchers, although at a lower level than those of their government counterparts. The leader of the Opposition currently earns around £125,000 a year—though this was cut from over £130,000 at the request of Mr Corbyn's predecessor, Ed Miliband.

Table 3.1 The composition of the UK Cabinet (August 2016)

Title	Name
Prime Minister/First Lord of the Treasury/Minister for the Civil Service	Theresa May
First Secretary of State and Chancellor of the Exchequer	Phillip Hammond
Secretary of State for Foreign and Commonwealth Affairs (Foreign Secretary)	Boris Johnson
Secretary of State for Exiting the European Union	David Davis
Secretary of State for International Trade	Liam Fox
Secretary of State for Justice/Lord Chancellor	Liz Truss
Secretary of State for the Home Department (Home Secretary)	Amber Rudd
Secretary of State for Defence	Michael Fallon
Secretary of State for Health	Jeremy Hunt
Secretary of State for Business, Energy, and Industrial Strategy	Greg Clark
Secretary of State for the Environment, Food, and Rural Affairs	Andrea Leadsom
Secretary of State for International Development	Priti Patel
Secretary of State for Work and Pensions	Damian Green
Secretary of State for Transport	Chris Grayling
Secretary of State for Communities and Local Government	Sajid Javid
Secretary of State for Education	Justine Greening
Secretary of State for Northern Ireland	James Brokenshire
Secretary of State for Wales	Alun Cairns
Secretary of State for Scotland	David Mundell
Conservative Party chairman and Chancellor of the Duchy of Lancaster	Patrick McLoughlin
Secretary of State for Culture, Media, and Sport	Karen Bradley
Leader of the House of Lords	Baroness Evans
Chief Secretary to the Treasury	Greg Hands
Leader of the House of Commons	David Lidington
Chief Secretary to the Treasury	David Gauke
Parliamentary Secretary to the Treasury (Chief Whip)	Gavin Williamson
Attorney General	Jeremy Wright
Minister for the Cabinet Office	Ben Gummer

NOTE: A regularly updated version of this table can be found on the **Online Resource Centre**

3.2.2 Collective responsibility, ministerial responsibility, and the ministerial code

The actions of ministers, especially those in Cabinet, are governed by two constitutional conventions—collective responsibility and individual ministerial responsibility—and an increasingly strict statutory 'rule book', the Ministerial Code.

3.2.2.1 Collective responsibility

Cabinet ministers are expected to endorse publicly the actions of governments of which they are members, even if they privately disagree with them. This **collective responsibility** doctrine rests on the assumption that individual ministers broadly support the policy programme adopted by their government, but may occasionally disagree with specific proposals. It has therefore long been the custom for ministers to bite their tongues. On many notable occasions, however, individuals have found themselves increasingly out of step with the views of Cabinet colleagues and have ultimately resigned—freeing themselves to speak out.

In 1986, then Defence Secretary Mr. Heseltine theatrically quit Mrs Thatcher's Cabinet in full view of waiting television cameras over the proposed merger of Westland, Britain's last surviving helicopter manufacturer, with US company Sikorsky. In 2003, the late Robin Cook, then Leader of the House, resigned from government in protest at the invasion of Iraq. He was followed, months later, by International Development Secretary Clare Short, who blamed the country's chaotic reconstruction following Saddam's defeat for her decision. More recently, Tory Work and Pensions Secretary Iain Duncan Smith quit the Cabinet within days of Mr Osborne's widely criticized spring 2016 Budget, officially in protest at the Chancellor's 'indefensible' decision to proceed with £4.4 billion cuts to disability benefits by 2020 while simultaneously raising the threshold at which middle-income and higher earners began paying the 40p rate of income tax (see 7.1.1). The fact that Mr Duncan Smith was one of the most vociferous opponents of Britain's continued membership of the EU, however, led many observers to speculate that his resignation may have been motivated as much by a desire to free himself up to campaign more fiercely in the then live 'Brexit' campaign (see 9.7) as any sudden crisis of conscience after six years of leading the charge on welfare cuts.

In fact, for only the second time in living memory, the constraints imposed by collective responsibility had been formally waived for the duration of the referendum campaign, to allow Cabinet colleagues who held strong Eurosceptic views to argue against the government's official position without fear of reprisals. The last time this had happened was when, in 1975, Mr Wilson had adopted the same tactic to placate a similarly divided *Labour* Cabinet during his own campaign to persuade voters to support Britain's accession five years earlier to the then European Community.

In the early days of the 2010–15 Coalition, Messrs Cameron and Clegg came close to mimicking Mr Wilson's tactic in relation to several policies over which their parties were in clear disagreement. To win the latter's support, the

Conservatives agreed to let Lib Dem frontbenchers 'continue to make the case for' alternative policies in areas such as the proposed renewal of Britain's Trident nuclear programme, while Tory ministers were allowed to campaign against the introduction of the alternative vote (AV—see 4.6) prior to the May 2011 referendum on electoral reform. But while the Coalition agreement allowed for limited open Cabinet 'dissent' in specified areas, Lib Dem MPs (both front and back bench) were generally bound by an undertaking not to vote *against* policy proposals, but only to abstain.

3.2.2.2 Individual ministerial responsibility

The other major convention relating to ministers' work is that of **individual ministerial responsibility**. This is the doctrine that, should a serious error or scandal occur 'on the watch' of a departmental minister, he or she must do the honourable thing and resign.

Recent history has, however, been littered with examples of significant departmental errors for which ministers have been reluctant to take the blame. The fiasco over Britain's sudden withdrawal from the European exchange rate mechanism (ERM) in 1992 would, on many other occasions, have seen the immediate departure of the Chancellor of the Exchequer—the minister in charge of the economy. In fact, then Chancellor Norman Lamont stayed on for several months before belatedly being sacked by Mr Major. Culture Secretary Mr Hunt doggedly defied calls for his scalp following the Leveson Inquiry's revelations about email exchanges between his special adviser and a senior News Corp lobbyist focusing on the company's bid to take over BSkyB—an example of ministerial responsibility that some critics, including outspoken Culture, Media, and Sport Select Committee member Tom Watson, argued was also in breach of the Ministerial Code (see 3.2.3).

Those who have 'fallen on their swords' recently include Liam Fox, who was forced to resign as Defence Secretary in October 2011 following revelations that he had allowed his former best man, Adam Werritty, to accompany him on official overseas visits and attend sensitive meetings that might have aided the latter's business interests. Mr Werritty, a freelance corporate lobbyist who had not received Ministry of Defence security clearance, exacerbated the situation by handing out business cards falsely claiming to be Dr Fox's adviser. In practice, ministers are often sacked before they have a chance to quit. The premier's ability to remove colleagues unceremoniously dates back to a convention initiated by William Pitt the Younger in the early nineteenth century and perfected by a later Tory premier, Harold Macmillan, when, on Friday 13 July 1962—the notorious 'Night of the Long Knives'—he gave seven ministers their marching orders. Sackings almost always precipitate 'Cabinet reshuffles', during which other ministers are moved from one job to another to fill gaps created by their colleagues' removal.

3.2.3 The Ministerial Code

The most recent redraft of the **Ministerial Code** was agreed by the then newly formed Coalition government in May 2010. Its opening line sets the tone of the document, stating:

> 'Ministers of the Crown are expected to behave in a way that upholds the highest standards of propriety.'

The implication is clear: while Lord Nolan's *Seven Principles of Public Life* (see table 2B on the **Online Resource Centre**) are intended to encourage responsible behaviour by parliamentarians, the bar is raised higher for members of Her Majesty's government. To this end, the Code lays out the following ten additional principles governing ministerial conduct:

(a) The principle of collective responsibility, except when explicitly set aside, applies to all ministers.

(b) Ministers have a duty to Parliament to account, and be held to account, for policies, decisions, and actions of their departments and agencies.

(c) Ministers must give accurate and truthful information to Parliament, correcting inadvertent errors at the earliest opportunity. Those who knowingly mislead Parliament should offer their resignations.

(d) Ministers should be as open as possible with Parliament and public, refusing to provide information only when disclosure would not be in the public interest, which should be decided in accordance with relevant statutes and the Freedom of Information Act 2000.

(e) Ministers should require civil servants who give evidence before parliamentary committees on their behalf and under their direction to be as helpful as possible in providing accurate, truthful, and full information in accordance with the duties and responsibilities of civil servants as set out in the Civil Service Code.

(f) Ministers must ensure no conflict arises, or appears to arise, between their public duties and private interests.

(g) Ministers should not accept any gift or hospitality which might, or might reasonably appear to, compromise their judgment or place them under an improper obligation.

(h) Ministers in the Commons must keep separate their roles as minister and constituency member.

(i) Ministers must not use government resources for party political purposes.

(j) Ministers must uphold the political impartiality of the civil service and not ask civil servants to act in any way which would conflict with the Civil Service Code as set out in the Constitutional Reform and Governance Act 2010.

The Code stipulates that it is the PM's personal responsibility to refer alleged breaches to an independent adviser on ministerial interests (at time of writing, Sir Alex Allan), which Mr Cameron did in June 2012 in relation to the expenses claims of then Conservative Party co-chairman Baroness Warsi (see 2.2.7). It also describes at length the array of duties that accompany ministerial office—ranging from the obligation to chair departmental board meetings to responsibility for the conduct of appointees, including special advisers. It was in relation to this latter point that Mr Hunt faced calls for his resignation over the Murdoch emails affair. Even more important, perhaps, than their responsibility for their staff's conduct is ministers' obligation to ensure that no conflicts of interest arise—or 'could reasonably be perceived to arise'—between their ministerial positions and private interests, 'financial or otherwise'. To this end, a formal list of ministers' interests is now published online, and regularly updated, as an additional level of transparency beyond the register of members' financial interests to which all MPs are subject. Among the interests declared by Mr Cameron on the list as of December 2015 were his vice-presidency of the National Society for Epilepsy, elected membership of the Council of the Scout Association, and patronage of Witney United Football Club, based in his Oxfordshire constituency. In his last year in Downing Street, Mr Cameron also declared relevant roles held by his wife, Samantha—principally her £100,000-a-year part-time post as creative consultant of upmarket Bond Street stationers Smythson.

3.2.4 The Cabinet Office and Cabinet committees

The Cabinet Office is effectively the 'Civil Service of the Cabinet'—the administrative staff and machinery that organizes its meetings and business on a day-to-day basis. It comprises a Cabinet Secretariat, responsible for recording Cabinet minutes, and the Office of Public Service, which oversees overall government business. It is headed by the Cabinet Secretary.

In turn, the Secretariat is made up of six separate departmental secretariats, covering:

- Economic and Domestic Affairs;
- Defence and Overseas Affairs;
- Europe;
- the Constitution;
- Central administration; and
- Intelligence Support.

In addition, **Cabinet committees** are increasingly formed to deal with the finer points of policymaking. They tend to be chaired by ministers whose personal views are close to those of the PM. Under the Coalition, many of the nine full cabinet committees and their sixteen subcommittees were chaired by a so-called 'quartet' of senior ministers: Messrs Cameron, Clegg, Osborne, and Danny Alexander, the Lib Dem then Chief Secretary to the Treasury. There are several types of Cabinet committee, as outlined in table 3B to be found on the **Online Resource Centre**.

3.3 The Civil Service

If ministers are the government's 'architects'—brainstorming and formulating policies in Cabinet—civil servants are its construction workers, responsible for putting together the building blocks that transform their ideas into reality. The 'Civil Service' is the collective term for the administrative structure that carries out the work of government departments and the numerous agencies that implement policy.

Dating back to the secretariats that first emerged, piecemeal, in the eighteenth century, the Civil Service has become the one constant of UK government. The fact that government continues uninterrupted even after governing parties change at elections (and while the country is without MPs—though not ministers—during election campaigns) is a tribute to the continuity guaranteed by the professionals responsible for 'keeping things running'. This continuity role has rarely been more starkly apparent than during the five days between the May 2010 election and the formation of the Coalition, when caretaker PM Mr Brown agreed to give both other main parties access to then Cabinet Secretary Sir Gus O'Donnell and other high-level mandarins as they drafted their prospective deal. He also revealed the existence of a working document that he had asked Sir Gus to produce in the run-up to the election clarifying the constitutional position of sitting premiers in a hung Parliament.

The foundations of today's Civil Service were laid in the Northcote–Trevelyan Report 1854, which stipulated that:

- all appointments should be made on merit; and
- there should be fair and open competition for advertised posts.

Efforts were quickly made to establish a professional structure for the Civil Service and successive governments have made this progressively more rigorous. Senior civil servants—or 'mandarins'—are recruited by independent Civil Service Commissioners through the Civil Service Board. Some recruits rise to senior ranks swiftly, via the Fast Stream development programme.

Altogether, Her Majesty's Civil Service comprises around 500,000 officials working across anything up to sixty departments and 100 associated bodies—primarily executive agencies (see 3.3.2)—based principally at Whitehall and Millbank, a stone's throw from Parliament. Each department is headed by a permanent secretary. As with lower-ranking civil servants, they are employed because of their expertise in the particular areas overseen by their departments. Not to be confused with secretaries of state, they often have long records of departmental service, given that they are permanent Crown employees and will remain in post irrespective of changes of government. Although they come into close daily contact with ministers and often advise them on policy, as paid officials, permanent secretaries are expected to be politically neutral.

3.3.1 Political neutrality in practice

Although the 'political neutrality' doctrine is sacrosanct in the Civil Service, controversies have sometimes arisen over civil servants who have acted in politically motivated ways. The machinations of Sir Humphrey Appleby—the odious permanent secretary for the Ministry for Administrative Affairs in the classic 1980s BBC1 sitcoms *Yes, Minister* and *Yes, Prime Minister*—were inspired by real-life Whitehall shenanigans. More radical governments, from Clement Attlee's Labour to the Coalition, have also characterized civil servants as 'small-c' conservative. But perhaps the most significant Civil Service scandal of modern times occurred in 1985, when Clive Ponting, a civil servant in the Ministry of Defence, was tried under the Official Secrets Act 1911 for passing classified details to an unauthorized person about the sinking during the Falklands War of the Argentine ship the *General Belgrano*—allegedly while it was both retreating and outside the 'exclusion zone' declared by the British government around the islands. Although Ponting was acquitted of breaching section 2 of the Act, the case prompted the then Cabinet Secretary Sir Robin Butler to issue a 'Note'—as an addendum to the Civil Service code of conduct—emphasizing that policy decisions were the responsibility of ministers, and civil servants had a 'duty' to carry out their decisions, while respecting the confidence of their ministerial dealings.

Following the Ponting affair and a series of smaller-scale 'leaks' by other 'whistle-blowers', new stipulations were drawn up to clarify the *levels* of political neutrality expected of civil servants on different rungs of the professional ladder. While those of all ranks were expected to remain politically impartial in the workplace, it was decided that the extent to which they had to be entirely neutral *outside* it would depend on their seniority (see table 3C on the **Online Resource Centre**). In addition to the expectation of political neutrality, the most senior civil servants—notably permanent secretaries—and all those involved in dealing with the press or giving ministers policy advice are also politically restricted—that is, barred from participating in any direct political activity outside their day jobs, unless they first resign. This extends from election canvassing and leafleting, to standing as candidates in any election themselves, be they local, national, or European.

Despite these safeguards, apparently politically motivated policy leaks have continued. The Home Office was embroiled in controversy after a series of leaks to then Opposition MP Damian Green led to the police searching his office (see 1.1.1.1) in November 2008, and months later a disc containing details of MPs' expenses claims was leaked to *The Daily Telegraph* (see 2.2.6).

In running their departments on a day-to-day basis, civil servants are expected to abide by the 'three Es': 'economy, efficiency, and effectiveness'. This maxim has been underlined by two key milestones: the Efficiency Strategy published in 1979 by Sir Derek (now Lord) Rayner; and the 1982 Financial Management Initiative, which sought to provide departmental managers with 'a clear view' of the responsibilities of their individual ministries.

3.3.2 Executive agencies

The work of the Civil Service is so all-consuming that governments have often tried to rationalize departments, breaking them down into smaller, more manageable units. These units—effectively *subsets* of their parent departments—focus exclusively on *delivering*, rather than *formulating*, policy. Today most are known as 'executive agencies'.

Initially established in 1988 by Mrs Thatcher—who sought to abandon what she saw as an over-centralized, monolithic structure—these smaller-scale, breakaway bodies were designed to resemble commercial companies rather than traditional organs of government. As such, they were each given chief executives, who presided over boards of directors—a radical departure from the bureaucratic way in which the Civil Service had previously been run. Unlike commercial companies, agencies had no shareholders (and therefore no profit motive) and were staffed by civil servants seconded from their parent departments. But as time went on, their managers were increasingly drafted in from industry, rather than graduating from the Service itself (the theory being that importing talent from the private sector would increase efficiency). This approach would ultimately have a sweeping impact across the public sector that continues to be felt today, with everything from local NHS trusts to further education colleges adopting a 'chief executive and board' model.

Initially, there were only a handful of executive agencies, the first of which, the Vehicle Inspectorate—Driver and Vehicle Standards Agency (DVSA)—was established in August 1988. Their number mushroomed under Labour, which ended up with 130 in total—more than ninety reporting to government departments at Whitehall, with the remainder answering to the three devolved administrations in Scotland, Wales, and Northern Ireland. While some smaller spending departments have only one or two agencies beneath them, larger ones such as the Home Office and Department for Work and Pensions (DWP) allocate much of their day-to-day work to agencies. The single biggest agency, in terms of staffing and budget, is Jobcentre Plus (see 8.3.1), which employs 100,000 people and spends £4 billion a year of taxpayers' money. With thirty-six agencies, the Ministry of Defence (MoD) has the most.

One criticism of executive agencies is that they are used by ministers to absolve themselves from individual ministerial responsibility. By devolving power to 'breakaway' sections of their departments, they might disclaim personal liability for their mistakes. This arguably happened in November 2007 when then Chancellor Alistair Darling refused to accept culpability for the loss of two unencrypted computer discs containing the names, addresses, birthdates, National Insurance (NI) numbers, and bank details of 25 million families by HM Revenue and Customs (HMRC), an executive agency of HM Treasury (see 8.4).

3.3.3 Quangos

Long before executive agencies existed, there were already a large number of taxpayer-funded organizations carrying out work delegated by government departments. But, historically, these non-departmental public bodies (NDPBs) tended to be staffed not by seconded departmental civil servants, but their own employees, which they recruited as discrete entities, notionally independent of government. Over time, an umbrella term has evolved for these bodies: 'quasi-autonomous non-governmental organizations', or **quangos**.

Quangos are often confused with executive agencies and it is easy to see why. Like agencies, they have their own management boards—although these are headed by honorary chairpersons, rather than salaried chief executives. They also control significant, largely taxpayer-funded, budgets. But this is where the similarities end. As the term implies, quangos are 'semi-independent' of government and, for that reason, are tasked with overseeing areas of practical policy at an arm's length from ministers. They also have the freedom to be more outspoken than agencies: Culture Secretaries have often had to weather the barbs of chairpersons of Arts Council England (ACE), for instance, over cuts to regional theatres and museums.

Perhaps unsurprisingly, quangos are frequently condemned by the media for lacking accountability. Whereas agencies are at least answerable to ministers who can be ejected at elections, quangos have always been more autonomous. Yet, like agencies, they receive most of their funding from taxpayers—through the aegis of related departments.

Lack of accountability is one criticism levelled at quangos; another is nepotism. How can we be certain that board members appointed by ministers will be genuinely chosen on merit? The long-since disbanded BBC Board of Governors—charged with holding the Corporation to account for its public service broadcasting responsibilities—was a quango in all but name, and the board of Ofcom, the regulator which will soon replace the BBC Trust in overseeing the BBC alongside all other UK broadcasters, is also ultimately appointed by ministers in the Department for Culture, Media and Sport.

Sustained criticism of the 'quangocracy' has led to several recent moves to address the nepotism question. In 2000, the government introduced an Appointments Commission to propose chairpersons and non-executive directors (NEDs) of NHS bodies (see Chapter 6). It also has powers to vet appointees to other local, regional, and national quangos. These appointments are themselves regulated by an Office of the Commissioner for Public Appointments (OCPA).

In July 1996, a democratic audit identified 6,224 executive and advisory quangos, run by 66,000–73,500 people and responsible for spending £60.4 billion. On entering power, Mr Blair vowed to scrap 'unaccountable quangos' and Mr Brown spoke of a 'bonfire of the quangos'. But in August 2007 Cabinet Office figures revealed that quangos had spent £167.5 billion the previous year. The Coalition revived the 'bonfire' concept, with former Cabinet Office Minister Francis Maude promising to cull 192 and merge 118 in October 2010. While few can have lamented the passing of obscure bodies such as the Zoos Forum or the Government Hospitality Advisory Committee on the Purchase of Wines, there was widespread criticism of the decision to scrap the UK Film Council, which had co-funded numerous globally successful British-made movies, including that year's big Oscar winner, *The King's Speech*, while the government's pledge to replace the Audit Commission—the national quango responsible for auditing council accounts—with a patchwork of private contractors was seen by some as an example of free market ideology trumping transparency (see 13.2.2.1) In practice, the Coalition acted much like previous governments: liberally chopping quangos in some areas, while introducing new ones elsewhere. According to a widely reported exchange between Mr Cameron and Mr Miliband during PMQs on 29 June 2011, the Coalition's health reforms had seen the number of NHS quangos alone more than triple.

3.3.4 Taskforces and tsars

A new form of non-elected body created by Mr Blair's government was the 'taskforce': an ad hoc and/or temporary form of quango set up to tackle a particular topical policy issue. By 2000, the number of taskforces had already multiplied to forty-four. Taskforces tended to be headed by senior public figures dubbed 'tsars' (effectively, hired trouble-shooters). Examples included the Rough Sleepers' Unit, led by 'Homelessness Tsar' Louise Casey, which set out to tackle street homelessness, and a short-lived drugs taskforce run by 'Drugs Tsar' Keith Hellawell. Although the term 'taskforce' is seldom heard today, the Coalition continued the trend for 'tsars', allowing the term to be used to denote advisory roles given to former Labour MPs Alan Milburn and Lord Hutton (as 'Social Mobility Tsar' and 'Pensions Tsar', respectively), current Labour MP Frank Field ('Poverty Tsar'), and Will Hutton, ex-editor of *The Observer* ('Fair Pay Tsar').

3.3.5 Think tanks, the private sector, and the future of public policymaking

Even policymaking—long the preserve of Whitehall mandarins and their underlings—is now on the verge of being outsourced to the private sector. In May 2012, then new Cabinet Secretary Sir Jeremy Heywood floated the 'perfectly legitimate' idea of contracting private companies to devise future ministerial initiatives. In so doing, he appeared to be advocating a move that, critics argued, could open up the highly sensitive area of policy formulation to commercial conflicts of interest, dilute the institutional memory of the Civil Service itself, and relegate knowledgeable and experienced officials to the status of mere administrators. Within weeks, Mr Maude had published even more radical proposals, including allowing ministers to appoint future permanent secretaries, rather than relying on the Civil Service's own promotional structure—an idea that revived concerns about the 'politicization' of policy delivery.

3.3.6 Spin doctors and special advisers

Under the Ministerial Code, each Cabinet minister may employ up to two special advisers—or 'SPADs'—while other government ministers permitted to attend Cabinet meetings may appoint one. The total number of special advisers, in particular spin doctors, multiplied under Mr Blair, whose government consistently employed up to seventy-four at the highest level. At its peak, the advisers' salary bill topped £3.6 million, but their number has since declined.

Unlike civil servants, special advisers are normally *party*, rather than government, appointees. This was the case with most Downing Street big-hitters of the Blair years, including Mr Campbell and Mr Powell. Sometimes, however, the edges are more blurred: Sir Bernard Ingham began as a civil servant, before switching to the Conservatives' payroll under Mrs Thatcher. When a party is in opposition, it pays for its advisers, but once in government, they (like civil servants) are usually paid from public funds.

Under Mr Blair, some special advisers became bywords for cold-hearted calculation. Jo Moore, an adviser at the Department of Transport, Local Government, and the Regions (DTLR), resigned in February 2002 following a series of controversies about her management style, and in particular the publication of an explosive email she sent on 11 September the previous year—the date of the terrorist attacks on the Twin Towers—describing it as a 'very good day' to 'bury' bad news.

Mr Blair's reliance on advice from spin doctors and party appointees over senior civil servants frequently saw him accused of 'politicizing' the Civil Service. One of his first actions was to pass an executive order allowing senior advisers like Mr Campbell and Mr Powell to issue orders to civil servants. Mr Brown revoked this, symbolically, within hours of replacing him at Number 10, but cynics dismissed even this gesture as spin, in light of recent statistics indicating that the number of government special advisers, spin doctors, and press/marketing staff continued to climb during his tenure. A Whitehall audit found that sixty-eight additional advisers were employed by ministers during 2007 and all were still in post six months after Mr Brown took office. The overall number of press office staff (many civil servants, but nonetheless employed to put a positive gloss on government policy) had risen to 3,250. Between 1997 and 2007, Labour increased the annual cost of 'government PR' (public relations) to £338 million—with a £15 million rise in 2007 alone.

In July 2001, the Labour government finally published a Code of Conduct for Special Advisers. It defined them as 'temporary civil servants', who did not necessarily have to be appointed 'on merit', but were nonetheless expected to comply with the Civil Service Code and avoid using 'official resources', such as stationery, for party-political purposes. If they wished to campaign on behalf of their ministers during the lead-up to an election, they must first resign from their posts in recognition of their political affiliation. Mr Campbell did this in 2005.

3.3.7 The Parliamentary Ombudsman

Despite its title, the **Parliamentary Commissioner for Administration** (part of a wider regulatory body known as the **Parliamentary and Health Service Ombudsman**) investigates public complaints not about Parliament itself, but about government departments and other public bodies, including quangos. The basis of an individual's complaint must be that he or she has suffered an injustice owing to maladministration arising from delay, faulty procedures, errors, unfairness, and/or bias. Complaints against judges, police officers, and councils are investigated by separate bodies.

The Ombudsman is sometimes derided as 'a watchdog without teeth', because even though it can recommend that departments or bodies should 'remedy' mistakes, its maladministration rulings cannot be *enforced*.

As a result of devolution, there are now separate ombudsmen for Scotland, Wales, and Northern Ireland.

3.4 Devolved government—executive decision-making in the regions

Chapter 1 and 2 laid out, first, the manner in which devolution unfolded in Britain and the forms of government subsequently settled on in each of the three countries outside England. There follows a brief overview of the manner in which government is constituted in those countries.

3.4.1 The Scottish Government

Just as the legislative process prevailing in Scotland is distinct from those in Wales and Northern Ireland, so too is its executive framework. Scotland now boasts its own **Scottish Government**, headed by a First Minister (the country's prime minister in all but name). More fully formed than its cousins in Cardiff and Stormont, the Scottish Government has its own Cabinet, which meets on Tuesday mornings at Bute House in Edinburgh's Charlotte Square (the First Minister's official residence). The administration itself is based at St Andrew's House, with its own secretariat, and has two subcommittees: a Cabinet subcommittee on legislation, and an emergency room Cabinet subcommittee. Scotland's government was Labour-run for the first two terms of devolved rule, but since 2007 the SNP have been dominant—largely as a minority government, but from 2011–16 with a majority.

3.4.2 The Welsh Assembly Government

Like its Scottish equivalent, the Welsh Assembly was formally known as an 'executive', rather than 'government'. It too is led by a First Minister (currently Labour leader Carwyn Jones). After the 2007 Welsh Assembly election, Labour entered a coalition with the Welsh nationalist party, Plaid Cymru, under the banner 'One Wales', but since May 2011, when it scored its biggest victory since devolution began, it has governed alone. Despite Labour's continuing dominance in the Senedd, the Welsh constitution was briefly thrown into crisis days after the 2016 assembly election, when Mr Jones's anticipated 'automatic' re-election by fellow AMs as First Minister was temporarily blocked by the surprise decision of Tory and UKIP members to back Plaid Cymru's nomination of its leader, Leanne Wood—a self-declared 'socialist'—to take his place. This had the effect of forcing a tie between Jones and Wood, at twenty-nine votes apiece, in an election that should have been a formality. As Labour was by far the biggest party—with twenty-nine AMs to Plaid Cymru's twelve—it was only a matter of time before the deadlock ended. This happened the following week, when Plaid Cymru agreed to give tacit support to the formation of a minority Labour government, in return for some policy concessions, on education, health, and other areas. However, the fleeting limbo exposed a loophole in the post-devolution constitutional settlements not only for Wales but Scotland and Northern Ireland as well. Unlike in the UK Parliament, leaders of the biggest parties in the devolved nations must be formally elected as First Ministers before assuming (or resuming) office on the formation of new parliaments—raising the prospect of challenges when election results have been tight.

3.4.3 The Northern Ireland Executive

The 'power-sharing executive' in Northern Ireland, also lead by a First Minister, has been a coalition since its inception and began functioning properly only following the conclusion of a substantive peace agreement in spring 2007. Since May 2011, it has remained a coalition run by the two biggest parties: the Democratic Unionist Party (DUP) and Sinn Féin.

Topical feature idea

You work on a local evening newspaper in a metropolitan area in the north of England. The local combined authority has announced that it is in advanced talks with the Treasury about taking over control of almost all public services in the area, including the NHS, in exchange for introducing a new kind of leadership structure, topped by an elected mayor. Your editor wants you to write a background feature explaining how this new regional government approach relates to the wider picture of devolution outside England. Who would you contact and how would you approach writing this piece to keep its emphasis as relevant as possible to your readers?

Current issues

- **The return of single-party government at Westminster** After the exceptional five-year period of Lib Dem–Tory coalition, the Conservatives defied opinion-pollsters to secure a small overall majority of twelve in the May 2015 general election. With this, British parliamentary politics returned to its familiar rhythm and conventions, with a single-party government but the Lib Dems supplanted as second Opposition party by the Scottish Nationalists.
- **Compromise government in the devolved nations** The May 2016 devolved assembly elections saw Labour deprived (by a single AM) of its majority in Wales and the SNP suffered a similar fate in Scotland—where it nonetheless won, knocking its old rival, Labour, into third place behind the Tories, for the first time in a century. Compromise government also continues in Northern Ireland, where the DUP and Sinn Féin are once more in coalition.

- **The future of collective responsibility** Following five years in which ministers from the two Coalition parties—the Conservatives and Lib Dems—were routinely permitted to express differences of opinion on certain issues, collective responsibility has continued to be undermined under the Tory-only government, with high-profile resignations over issues of asserted principle, such as former Work and Pensions Secretary Iain Duncan Smith's, and a prolonged 'relaxation' of the principle to allow ministers on opposing sides of the 'Brexit' debate to campaign against each other.

Key points

1. Most prerogative powers are exercised on the sovereign's behalf by the government, in particular the prime minister (First Lord of the Treasury).
2. The government is the collective name for the ministers of the Crown who oversee departments of state. The most senior ministers, chaired by the prime minister, sit in Cabinet.
3. Government ministers must abide by two key constitutional principles: collective responsibility and individual ministerial responsibility. The first is the convention that all ministers should publicly support government policy, whatever their private misgivings. The second requires them to resign for major mistakes made by their ministries.
4. Civil servants are the paid officials employed to implement government policy and to administer departments on a day-to-day basis. They are expected to be politically neutral.
5. The most senior departmental ministers are known as secretaries of state. Top departmental civil servants are permanent secretaries. They are politically restricted—that is, barred from political campaigning or standing in elections.

→ Further reading

Bower, T. (2016) *Broken Vows: Tony Blair—The Tragedy of Power*, London: Faber & Faber. **Unvarnished character study of Labour's longest-serving prime minister by investigative journalist Bower, with a particular focus on political manoeuvring in the run-up to the Iraq War.**

Budge, I., Crewe, I., McKay, D., and Newton, K. (2007) *The New British Politics*, 4th edn, London: Longman. **Fourth edition of acclaimed critical introduction to British politics at the dawn of the twenty-first century, updated to cover Brown's administration.**

Burnham, J. and Pyper, R. (2008) *Britain's Modernised Civil Service*, Basingstoke: Palgrave Macmillan. **Thorough examination of recent Civil Service developments, incorporating analysis of the impact of changes introduced by the Thatcher, Major, Blair, and Brown governments.**

Crossman, R. (1979) *The Crossman Diaries: Selections from the Diaries of a Cabinet Minister, 1964–1970*, London: Book Club Associates. **Widely regarded as among the most incisive and revealing political diaries written by a British minister, these highlights are edited by one of Britain's foremost contemporary political biographers.**

Mullin, C. (2010) *View from the Foothills*, London: Profile Books. **Witty, warts-and-all account of the follies and foibles of the Blair government by a former junior minister. Best read as a counterpoint or companion piece to the more positive spin in Campbell's diaries.**

Online Resource Centre

www.oxfordtextbooks.co.uk/orc/Morrison5e/

Visit the Online Resource Centre that accompanies this book for web links and regular updates.

4

Britain's electoral systems

The legitimacy of the UK's Parliament and three devolved assemblies—and the executives drawn from them—today derives from more than mere historical precedent. It stems from the principle of liberal democracy and democratic elections that is the bedrock of modern UK government.

4.1 The origins of the British franchise

British social reformers were demanding the vote for centuries before it was granted. For John Lilburne's Levellers, who propelled Oliver Cromwell to power, the English Civil War was about far more than a tussle for constitutional supremacy between Parliament and Crown: parliamentary sovereignty meant nothing if it was not exercised by ordinary people. For this to happen, he argued, all 'free-born Englishmen' must be given a direct say in how Parliament was run, through the vote.

Lilburne's arguments would echo down the centuries before being slowly answered—through the writings of Thomas Paine, the marches of the nineteenth-century Chartists, the speeches of the Labour Party's firebrand first member of Parliament (MP), James Keir Hardie, and ultimately the campaigns of the suffragettes. But it would be another century before every adult (regardless of class or gender) was granted a say in the running of Britain's affairs. The slow extension of voting rights is charted in table 4A on the **Online Resource Centre.**

While the primary significance of these Acts was to extend voting entitlements to more people, the most radical went further. The 'Great' Reform Act 1832 owes its place in history less to a wholesale extension of the franchise than to its abolition of 'rotten boroughs'—by that point a shameful hangover from medieval times. The term 'rotten borough' was coined for areas in which constituency boundaries ought to have been altered to reflect dwindling population numbers, but had not—with the result that, in some areas, the number of voters was so minimal that candidates could bribe the whole electorate to vote for them. In 1831, the year before the Act was passed, the constituency of Old Sarum in Wiltshire had just three houses and eleven registered voters. Gatton, in Surrey, had twenty-three houses, but only seven voters. As a result, rotten boroughs became a byword for corruption, with some constituencies effectively being bought and sold, and others passed from father to son like inheritances. Rotten boroughs were memorably satirized in the BBC1 sitcom *Blackadder the Third*, in which a dog won the fictitious seat of 'Dunny-on-the-Wold'.

Another significant reform was the abolition of 'plural voting'. This was the tradition allowing individuals who owned properties in two or more areas—or those attending university in one area when their family home was elsewhere—to have a multiple say in an election's outcome, by voting in each constituency. This practice (not to be confused with that, still common today, allowing individuals in these positions to choose in which constituency they would like to vote) was ended by the Representation of the People Act 1948.

4.1.1 The British franchise today: who can vote?

Elections to the House of Commons are called **general elections**. Historically, voting used to occur over several days—raising the prospect that a bandwagon effect might occur, whereby political parties and their supporters might be able to persuade more people to back them on the basis that others had already done so. Since 1918, though, polling day has traditionally been held on a Thursday—the day of the week said to be least at risk of 'influence' by alcohol (Friday customarily being pay day) on the one hand and Sunday sermonizing by (Liberal-supporting) Free Church ministers on the other. For a century, between 1911 and 2011, elections also took place anything up to five years to the day after the previous Parliament was assembled following a poll—allowing prime ministers to 'quit while they were ahead' in the polls, by going to the country at times of their choosing, rather than on set dates. In earlier times, parliaments had lasted for up to seven years. However, variable terms came to an end with passage of the Fixed-term Parliaments Act 2011, which introduced new, immovable, five-year terms, commencing from the then next election, which took place on Thursday 7 May 2015. Despite the fact that fixed terms were introduced some six years ago, and an election has already been held under the new 'rules', political reporters still seem to be struggling to get their heads around the 2011 Act's implications. In the immediate aftermath of David Cameron's resignation following the June 2016 'Brexit' referendum (see 9.7), newspapers, broadcast news programmes, and social media were abuzz with speculation that his as yet unnamed successor would call a 'snap election' to secure a personal mandate and exploit divisions in the Labour Party over Jeremy Corbyn's lacklustre campaign for the 'Remain' side. In truth, no such snap election would have been possible—unless the very Labour backbenchers who claimed to be terrified about their party being annihilated at the polls were willing to join forces with the Tories to secure the two-thirds Commons majority needed to dissolve Parliament (see 3.1.3.4).

As the name implies, at general elections all sitting MPs formally resign to contest their seats. This means that elections are held simultaneously in every constituency and a new Parliament is normally summoned by the sovereign as soon as all votes are counted and seats allocated. The distribution of seats after the 2015 election is outlined in table 4B on the **Online Resource Centre**.

In defiance of almost all opinion polls, which had consistently placed Labour and Conservatives neck and neck, the 2015 result gave the Tories a narrow working majority of sixteen—thanks, in part, to the customary refusal of Sinn Féin MPs to take up their seats by swearing allegiance to the Crown. The decisive result spelt the end of Mr Cameron's five-year Coalition with the Liberal Democrats, whose number was brutally slashed from fifty-seven to a rump of just eight.

Whereas in local and European elections the franchise has gradually been extended to include UK-resident European Union (EU) citizens, voting is more restricted in general elections. Currently, it is open to British, Irish, and Commonwealth citizens normally resident in the UK, subject to their:

- names being on the electoral register for constituencies in which they live; and
- being over the age of eighteen on election day (although they may enter their names on the electoral register from age seventeen).

Despite these broad qualification criteria, the following individuals are barred from voting:

- peers entitled to sit in the Lords;
- foreign nationals (including citizens of other EU states);
- patients detained under mental health legislation for crimes;
- people detained in prison (other than those awaiting trial); and
- people convicted during the preceding five years of 'corrupt' or 'illegal election practices'.

General election voting rules also have the following quirks:

- Members of the Armed Forces and Crown servants of British embassies, the Diplomatic Service, and the British Council employed overseas (and their partners and family members) may vote in constituencies 'where they would normally live'.
- UK citizens living abroad ('ex-pats') for fewer than fifteen years can make annual declarations allowing them to vote in constituencies 'where they were living before they went abroad'. They can vote by proxy—appointing

friends or relatives to vote on their behalf. At time of writing, Theresa May's government had recently confirmed plans to remove the 'fifteen-year rule', allowing all British citizens living overseas to continue voting in parliamentary elections for the rest of their lives, potentially doing so online. A 'Votes for Life Bill' to make this change was due to be published later in the parliament.

- Holidaymakers are allowed 'absent votes' under the Representation of the People Act 1985—provided electoral registration officers are satisfied they cannot vote in person.
- Although there is nothing stopping monarchs and their heirs from voting, they have generally refrained from doing so, because this would be seen as unconstitutional.

Registers of electors are compiled by local electoral registration officers and filling them in is compulsory—although, unlike in countries such as Australia, voting is *not*.

The Representation of the People Act 2000 changed the way registration took place, to introduce rolling registration in addition to an annual canvass. But more recently, in the dying months of the Coalition an individual registration system was introduced, first in England and Wales, then in Scotland—modelled on a practice that had been in place in Northern Ireland since 2002. Since June and September 2014 respectively, every adult has had to proactively register him or herself by providing proof of identity (for example date of birth and/or National Insurance number) to his or her local electoral registration officer. This individual system—ostensibly designed to combat electoral fraud—replaces the long tradition of one person in each household taking responsibility for registering all eligible voters. But critics argue that the reform has skewed registration towards more proactive voters, many of them better-off middle-aged and older people (on balance, more likely to support the Conservatives) and away from transient ones, like students, and poorer people with patchier voting records—in other words, those more likely to back Labour or other parties. It was only in July 2015 that the simmering row over the transition to the new system erupted in earnest, though, when ministers announced they were bringing forward the deadline by which individuals had to register themselves by twelve months, to December that year. This was despite a warning from the voting regulator, the Electoral Commission (see 4.4.1), that up to 1.9 million people risked losing their votes as a result. The official reason for fast tracking individual registration was to enable Britain's four national boundary commissions to speed up the process of redrawing Commons constituencies to equalize them in size and cut MP numbers (see 2.2 and 4.4). To more cynical Labour observers, this rationale was proof positive of the Conservatives' real motives for introducing the new system in the first place: to gerrymander the electoral map in favour of their party by, first, reducing the number of left-leaning voters on the roll and then using the misleadingly small numbers recorded in certain (disproportionately 'Labour') areas as a basis on which to define where one constituency's boundary should begin and another's end. The first major hiccup in the individual registration system arose on the eve of the deadline for registering to vote in the June 2016 European Union referendum. With an estimated 7 million eligible voters yet to register, the website set up to handle online registration went down—forcing ministers to introduce emergency legislation to extend the deadline by a further forty-eight hours.

In terms of the rules about who can and cannot vote, Tony Blair's government was the last to significantly liberalize pre-existing disqualifications, while remaining strict about others. Many people detained in hospitals under mental health legislation used to be barred from voting, on the grounds that they were not of 'sound mind'. This is no longer the case, unless they are convicted criminals. Homeless people were also enfranchised formally for the first time under the 2000 Act, and may now vote subject to a 'declaration of local connection'. Following repeated appeals by convicted prisoners against their prohibition from voting under the European Convention on Human Rights, Coalition ministers were ordered to address this issue by letting at least some of them vote, but at time of writing this matter was still the subject of a prolonged game of 'ping-pong' between a reluctant UK Parliament and both the European Union and European Court of Human Rights.

Although its stance was more liberal than those of previous governments in some respects, Labour tightened up certain qualifications. The Representation of the People Act 1989 made it easier for ex-pats to vote in general elections—allowing them to do so up to twenty years after emigrating. After the 2001 election, Labour reduced this entitlement period to fifteen years.

4.2 General elections and candidacy: who can stand?

Any citizen of Britain, the Irish Republic, or a Commonwealth country resident in Britain and over eighteen on the day he or she is nominated may stand for election—provided he or she is not disqualified on account of being:

- a peer retained in the House of Lords;
- an undischarged bankrupt subject to a bankruptcy restriction order under the Enterprise Act 2002 in England and Wales (because he or she has acted dishonestly or in another 'blameworthy' way), adjudged bankrupt in Northern Ireland, or someone whose estate has been sequestered in Scotland;

- a mental patient detained for crimes;
- someone sentenced to or currently serving more than one year's imprisonment;
- someone found personally guilty of *corrupt* election practices during the preceding ten years (if in the same constituency) or the last five years (if a different one);
- someone found personally guilty of *illegal* election practices in the last seven years (if in his or her constituency) or five years (elsewhere); or
- a holder of the offices listed in the House of Commons Disqualification Act 1975—that is:
  - a **politically restricted post** in the Civil Service (see 3.3.1);
  - a member of the regular Armed Forces or Ulster Defence Regiment;
  - a serving police officer;
  - a holder of judicial office; or
  - a member of a specified commission—for example the Equality and Human Rights Commission (EHRC) or the Independent Police Complaints Commission (IPCC).

Some disqualifications are more liberal than others. While convicted prisoners have long been denied the vote in general elections, they may stand as candidates—provided they are serving twelve months or less. This 'loophole' was once even bigger: Provisional Irish Republican Army (IRA) member Bobby Sands was imprisoned for fourteen years for possessing firearms in 1977, yet managed to get himself elected as MP for Fermanagh and South Tyrone in April 1981, after standing on a so-called 'Anti-H Block/Armagh Political Prisoner' ticket. He was on hunger strike at the time, however, and died several weeks later. After his death, Margaret Thatcher's government hastily passed the Representation of the People Act 1981, which introduced the current 'maximum twelve-month sentence' qualification for serving prisoners with parliamentary ambitions.

4.2.1 How the Commons electoral system works

The system used to elect MPs is colloquially known as 'first past the post' (FPTP)—or, more technically, *plurality voting*. In each constituency, the candidate receiving most votes—a relative majority—is elected. Similarly, the political party gaining the most Commons seats once all constituency votes are counted nationally normally forms the government. Historically, one party has tended to win an *overall majority* nationally—more seats than all other parties and independent MPs put together (or a majority 'over all'). More rarely, one party emerges with only a handful more seats than its nearest rival—and can form only a *minority* administration (as Labour did temporarily in February 1974) or a coalition with another party/parties. This result is known as a **hung Parliament**.

Britain's most recent hung Parliament followed the 2010 election, when the Conservatives secured 307 Commons seats, Labour 258, and the Lib Dems 57. With Lib Dem leader Nick Clegg holding the balance of power—despite a disappointing election-night result, which saw his party make a net loss of five seats—he was invited into swift negotiations with Mr Cameron. After five days of furtive deal-making (which, at one point, saw Mr Clegg holding parallel talks with Labour), the Lib Dems agreed to join a Conservative-led government—marking the start of the UK's first formal coalition since the Second World War.

The British electoral system has long been controversial, because of the frequent imbalance between shares of the vote cast for particular parties and the numbers of seats into which these translate. Because only first-placed candidates in each constituency are elected, all other votes cast (often tens of thousands) are 'wasted'. For many years, it has been only the Conservatives and Labour who have stood realistic chances of forming governments alone, because in order to win sufficient seats parties have to rely on *concentrations* of support. Traditional heartlands—for the Tories, the south-east; for Labour, the north—have tended to swing the pendulum between them.

General elections have also produced governments with majorities vastly disproportionate to their voting shares. The 2005 poll saw Labour win well over half the available seats, despite gaining only 35 per cent of the vote (equivalent to just over one-fifth of registered voters, given the low turnout). The then inbuilt Labour bias under FPTP was underlined further in 2010, when the Tories won 36 per cent of the votes, compared to Labour's 29 per cent and the Lib Dems' 23 per cent, but were nineteen seats short of a majority. Detailed analysis of the 2005 results had found that the average Labour MP needed only 26,858 votes to be re-elected at that time, whereas Tories required 44,241 and Lib Dems 98,484. More recently, the system has begun favouring the Conservatives and punishing the Lib Dems even more than before. In 2015, the Tories won 51 per cent of all Commons constituencies on the strength of a 37 per cent voting share, with Labour winning 36 per cent of seats despite only mustering 30 per cent of votes cast, and the Lib Dems only gaining 1.2 per cent of all MPs from 8 per cent of the vote. According to a parliamentary question tabled by Lib Dem Lord Rennard the following month, the Tories needed only 34,244 votes to elect each MP, while Labour required 40,290 and his own party 301,986.

Historically, this imbalance between voting share and the distribution of Commons seats has produced some perverse outcomes. In February 1974, incumbent Prime Minister Ted Heath's Tories won 225,789 more votes than Labour, but secured four fewer seats. Heath's attempts to strike a survival deal with then Liberal leader Jeremy Thorpe failed—largely due to the Conservatives' unwillingness to countenance electoral reform. Within days, Wilson took office, consolidating his victory that October by securing a small working majority of three seats and one million more votes than the Tories, but this did little to defuse the initial sense of injustice. It was not always that way around, though: in 1951, Labour Prime Minister Clement Attlee was beaten by Winston Churchill's Tories, who won twenty-six more seats despite polling 250,000 fewer votes. Labour had polled a total of 13,948,385 votes—a colossal 48.8 per cent share and, at that point, the most votes ever cast for a single British political party. The huge combined Labour–Tory vote share in 1951 (amounting to nearly 97 per cent) was down to two principal factors: a (by today's standards) stratospheric turnout of 82.6 per cent, and the extreme weakness at the time of a residual Liberal Party, which won just 730,000 votes.

4.2.2 Tactical voting

Given the clear inequities of FPTP, it is hardly surprising that electors in certain constituencies increasingly vote *strategically*—backing candidates other than those they most want to see elected, but is more likely to win—with the aim of blocking those they like least. This method of casting votes is known as **tactical voting**.

An oft-cited example of this is when voters who strongly identify with Labour, but live in constituencies in which sitting MPs are Conservative, vote Lib Dem instead. If, at the previous election, the Labour candidates came third—behind not only the Tories, but also Lib Dems—on this basis votes for Labour would be 'wasted'. So, with the Lib Dems better placed to beat the Tories, the Labour supporter might be better voting tactically—backing the 'least worst option' over the one he or she genuinely favours.

Examples of MPs elected by tactical voting abound. Lib Dem Mark Oaten's decisive 1997 victory in the Winchester by-election prompted by an electoral petition from Tory Gerry Malone (see 4.3.1) is believed to have been secured by a wholesale tactical switch by Labour supporters to the Lib Dems. In 2001, meanwhile, singer Billy Bragg organized a national campaign to prevent Tories winning seats by encouraging fellow opponents of the party to 'trade' their tactical votes with electors elsewhere.

4.3 The election process

The sequence of events leading to a general election is outlined in Table 4.1.

Each candidate must pay a £500 **election deposit**, which is returned provided that he or she receives at least 5 per cent of votes cast in the relevant constituency. The deposit was introduced in 1918 to discourage 'frivolous' candidates—and, cynics suggest, to boost the Treasury's coffers (it made £773,000

Table 4.1 The general election process

Event	Condition
Election date announced	Elections called at least seventeen working days before polling.
Nominations for candidates—until recently, prospective parliamentary candidates (PPCs)—entered	Nomination process closes at 12 p.m. on nineteenth day before election (excluding Sundays and Bank Holidays).
Application for postal ballots closes	All applications for **postal votes** must be made by 5 p.m. on eleventh working day before poll.
Checking that nomination meets basic conditions for eligibility and registration	Each candidate must have his/her nomination proposed and seconded by two 'subscribing' local electors and signed by eight 'assenting' electors. Nomination includes brief description of candidate on ballot paper (six words, including name and political affiliation). Candidates not always backed by parties (i.e. can be 'independent'). Each allowed to post one 'election communication' to registered voters.
Disqualification of invalid nominations	Returning officers (see 4.3.1) may reject nomination papers deemed 'out of order'.

from forfeited deposits in 2015 alone). In many people's eyes it is something of an anachronism today, particularly given its relative affordability: the risk of losing a mere £500, critics argue, does little to put off more determined 'time-wasters'.

4.3.1 Voting procedure on the day—the role of the returning officer

Local administration of voting in general elections is tightly regulated. After polling closes, it culminates in an election-night 'count' at a chosen venue—normally a large council building somewhere near the constituency's geographical centre—overseen by a **returning officer**. In practice, the returning officer's role tends to be discharged by a senior officer in the local authority containing, coterminous with, or neighbouring the constituency—often its chief executive. But in theory it is the responsibility of the council's chairperson or mayor, except in 'county constituencies' (rural ones), in which the role now falls to 'acting returning officers' (electoral registration officers employed by nearby district councils). Electoral procedure on the day is outlined in Table 4.2.

Should results be especially close and it is felt that disallowed ballot papers might have produced a different result if included, dissatisfied candidates can apply to the High Court for an 'election petition' against the returning officer. This happened in 1997 when Mr Malone lost his Winchester seat by just two votes to Mr Oaten—the closest result since 1945. Mr Malone's petition succeeded, but when the election was rerun that November, he lost by a 21,566-vote landslide. The by-election result almost certainly reflected the electorate's original

Table 4.2 The electoral process on polling day

Event	Conditions
Polling stations open at 7 a.m. and close at 10 p.m.	Registered electors not voting by post or proxy may do so at stations based at schools, community centres, pubs, and supermarkets. Ballot papers issued to voters at polling stations by election staff (with official marks impressed).
Absent votes may be cast in advance	Those who cannot vote in person (e.g. are on holiday) can apply for 'absent votes', while people unable to vote because of disability or work routines can apply for 'indefinite absent votes'. Anyone entitled to absent vote can either vote by post or proxy. Postal ballot papers cannot be sent to addresses outside Britain.
Secrecy of ballot preserved—no interference with ballot boxes	Ballot boxes sealed at close of poll, before being taken to counting place to be counted.
Official count starts after close of poll—only valid papers counted	Count supervised by returning officer—observed by candidates, agents, media, and small number of 'scrutineers'. 'Spoilt' ballot papers—e.g. those defaced or with crosses beside more than one name—disallowed.
Deadline for voting—including receipt of postal votes	All votes must have been cast (and postal ballot papers received) by 10 p.m. on polling day.
Recount if result too close to call	If winner's victory is marginal, candidates can demand recount (occasionally, more than one—until returning officer decides result is clear).

wishes more than the knife-edge outcome of the general election poll, given that, on the earlier occasion, many voters had been confused by the candidacy of Richard Huggett, who listed himself on the official ballot paper as 'Liberal Democrat Top Choice for Parliament' (forcing Mr Oaten to have the words 'Liberal Democrat Leader Paddy Ashdown' written beside his name). Mr Huggett stood again in the ensuing by-election—under the label 'Literal Democrat'—but adverse publicity generated by his first campaign undermined his vote. The use of such deliberately confusing labels was subsequently banned by the Registration of Political Parties Act 1998, which established the Electoral Commission (see 4.4.1).

On exceptionally rare occasions when an election produces a dead heat—with multiple recounts confirming that two candidates have received exactly the same number of votes—it can fall to the returning officer to supervise the most primitive possible way of deciding the contest: asking the joint winners to draw lots. Most recently, 'sortition' (the name coined for the process in ancient Athens) was used in the 2011 local elections to determine political control of Bury. On this occasion, Joanne Columbine drew the longest straw to clinch the borough council for Labour from the Tories.

Disputes over close-run contests are not the only causes of election-night headaches. Occasionally, more serious administrative problems occur. Besides being the first election for thirty-six years to produce a hung Parliament, the 2010 poll was notable for widespread controversy over the number of electors unable to vote because of localized organizational hiccups. As early results were announced on the evening of 6 May, live reports about registered voters being denied their rights began flooding in from areas as disparate as Hackney, Liverpool, and Newcastle-upon-Tyne. Some had spent hours queuing, only to be locked out of polling stations when clocks struck 10 p.m. In Sheffield Hallam (Mr Clegg's constituency), the returning officer blamed a last-minute influx of students without polling cards for delays resulting in a number of people being denied votes. A swift investigation by the Electoral Commission found that 1,200 voters were barred from voting. The Commission's initial recommendation was for wholesale modernization of the voting process—which to date has relied largely on paper, rather than computerized, records. The 2010 election also saw a significant increase in postal voting—one of the main devices used by recent governments to boost otherwise dwindling turnouts (see 4.7). In some areas, the number of people voting by post soared by 60 per cent, but with this increase in apparent electoral engagement came a wave of allegations that people were abusing the system to fraudulently bolster their favoured candidates. In Oxfordshire, 667 postal ballot packs vanished a week before the election, by error or design, while some fifty separate investigations into alleged fraud were under way on the eve of polling. Notoriously, however, it can take years for police to bring successful prosecutions. It was not until September 2010—four months after that year's election—that two former councillors and three other men were jailed for an unsuccessful attempt at the 2005 poll to use fraudulent postal votes to swing the marginal seat of Bradford West behind then Tory candidate Haroon Rashid.

In addition to their procedural arrangements, election days witness curious conventions. Most notable is the 'blackout period' or 'election silence' on polling day, when most parties traditionally abide by a gentlemen's agreement to cease active campaigning to allow electors the opportunity to reflect before casting their votes. For the broadcast media, Ofcom rules stipulate that they must not air any material that might be capable of influencing voters while polls are still open.

4.3.2 Limits on election spending

Election spending is closely controlled by the Electoral Commission to stop any candidate or party 'buying' a significant advantage over competitors. Each candidate must appoint an election agent with a constituency-based office. The maximum sum that candidates may spend campaigning in their seats is fixed by law. At the time of writing, it was just under £7,150, plus 5 pence per voter in urban ('borough') constituencies and 7 pence in rural ('county') ones. At a central level, however, parties may also spend £30,000 fielding each candidate, though it is often argued that the legal distinctions between what counts as 'local' and 'national' expenditure are somewhat hazy.

These ambiguities sparked a controversy with potentially far-reaching repercussions in 2016, after *Channel 4 News* alleged the Conservative Party had broken spending rules in some thirty-three constituencies during a series of by-elections in 2014 and the ensuing 2015 election campaign—by falsely recording outgoings it incurred while campaigning at local level in its 'national' accounts.

Chief among these were costs (including overnight accommodation and subsistence) arising from visits by activists to target seats in the party's 'election battle bus', and leaflets that, while avoiding mentioning local candidates by name, urged people to vote Tory in specified areas. At one point, the Electoral Commission was forced to go to the High Court to demand that the party hand over documentation relating to the disputed claims, though this material was later disclosed without the need for a hearing. At time of writing, some twenty police forces were still understood to be investigating the fraud allegations, which related to at least as many sitting Tory MPs. If proven, they could potentially lead to criminal convictions and electoral re-runs in the affected seats—jeopardizing the Conservative government's hold on power, given the slender majority inherited by Mrs May.

In Labour's case, spending disputes have tended to revolve around the £500 caps imposed on 'recognized third parties', principally trades unions, when they campaign on behalf of individual candidates. Generally, though, unions have been permitted to spend much more supporting the party as a whole. For instance, one 'recognized third-party' Labour supporter, UNISON, was able to spend up to £793,500 in England, £108,000 in Scotland, £60,000 in Wales, and (if the party is fielding candidates) £27,000 in Northern Ireland at the time of the 2010 general election. Other 'non-party' organizations or individuals wishing to campaign on behalf of parties (rather than particular candidates), meanwhile, were legally limited to spending £10,000 in England or £5,000 elsewhere. These limits were sharply tightened, though, with the passage of the Transparency, Lobbying, Non-party Campaigning, and Trade Union Administration Act 2014. Though ostensibly introduced to 'clean up politics' by stopping wealthy individuals and organizations 'buying' political influence—among other measures, it introduced a new Registrar of Consultant Lobbyists to keep a list of legitimate lobbying interests—Labour argued that, by categorizing unions alongside multinational companies and billionaire businessmen, it represented an all-out assault on its core funding base (see 5.2). But critics of the so-called 'gagging bill' were not confined to Labour: new restrictions on campaigning by charities and pressure groups in the run-up to elections led to objections being lodged even by such normally pliable charities as the Royal British Legion and Salvation Army.

In referendums, meanwhile, 'permitted participants'—those registered to campaign for 'Yes' or 'No' votes—may spend up to £500,000 on a UK-wide poll, but only £10,000 may be spent by anyone *not* so permitted. The Commission may 'designate' specific permitted participants to campaign for a 'Yes' or 'No' vote to ensure order. It did this in the lead-up to the 2016 European Union referendum, by granting 'official' Brexit campaign status to 'Vote Leave', fronted by former London mayor Boris Johnson and Justice Secretary Michael Gove (much to the consternation of Nigel Farage, leader of the anti-EU UKIP and head of Vote Leave's main rival, 'Grassroots Out'). Such bodies may claim up to £600,000 to finance their campaigns and spend up to £5 million.

4.4 Before the event—how constituency boundaries are decided

There are currently 650 Commons constituencies in England, Wales, Scotland, and Northern Ireland. Historically, the number has fluctuated 'naturally' in line with population changes—aside from periods (like the present) when governments have consciously shaken up the system to distribute electors more fairly. Variations in population not only have an impact on the number of constituencies, however, but the size and shape of seats. In some cases, constituencies with falling populations are abolished or merged with neighbouring ones, while large localized increases in population can spawn additional seats or existing ones being split.

Regular reviews of parliamentary electoral boundaries occur on an eight to twelve-year cycle, to ensure they keep pace with demographic fluctuations. The task of conducting these reviews falls to four **Boundary Commissions**: one each for England, Scotland, Wales, and Northern Ireland. These are also responsible for periodically reviewing boundaries of constituencies for devolved assemblies.

Boundary changes have always been controversial. Abolishing constituencies, creating new ones, and subdividing or merging them can have a significant impact on the ability of particular parties to win seats at subsequent elections. Although Commissions are meant to be non-partisan, successive governments have been accused of influencing their decisions to ensure proposed changes are favourable to their own parties at election time. That said, New Labour's last boundary review was widely interpreted as a boost to the Tories, particularly given the eventual outcome of the 2010 election. Confirmed by the English and Welsh Commissions in April 2007, with new boundaries for constituencies in place for the National Assembly of Wales elections in May that year, it proved controversial in Labour heartlands, because all four new constituencies were in the south. The upcoming 2018 UK boundary changes are expected to create a number of new seats in southern England, raising the prospect that they might further damage Labour's prospects.

4.4.1 The Electoral Commission

The role of the Electoral Commission is to:

- register political parties (and prevent their names being used by others);
- ensure that people understand and follow rules on party and election finance;
- set standards for running elections and reporting on their implementation;
- ensure that people understand the importance of registering to vote and how to do so; and
- make sure that candidates fund their election campaigns legally and transparently.

In addition to overseeing election-related funding, the Commission also polices party finance as a whole, by vetting how parties raise money and declare donations (see 5.11).

4.4.2 How parties select candidates

Just as different political parties have their own membership policies, they also have preferences about how to select the candidates they field at elections. The workings of Britain's main political parties, and the internal procedures distinguishing one from the other, are the subject of Chapter 5, but it is worth considering here some significant developments in candidate selection procedures.

4.4.2.1 The Conservative Party

Historically, the Conservatives have favoured a centralized selection procedure, with lists of 'approved candidates' compiled by Conservative Campaign Headquarters. This initially involves staff from the party's Candidates' Department sifting through applicants' CVs and letters, and inviting a selection to attend a 'candidates' weekend', at which they face aptitude tests to ascertain their suitability. A central list is then drawn up and distributed to local Conservative constituency associations, which advertise vacancies for prospective local candidates as and when they arise (sitting MPs wishing to run again are normally automatically reselected, as in the other main parties). After several public meetings, at which between three and five competing applicants have the chance to prove their mettle in debates with rivals, a vote is held among party members on which individual should be adopted to fight the seat.

Mr Cameron's tenure saw contradictory moves towards greater centralization, on the one hand, and localization on the other. A controversial early move was his drawing up of an 'A-list' of aspiring Tory MPs prior to the 2010 election, including the likes of 'chick-lit' author Louise Bagshawe (now Louise Mensch) and Zac Goldsmith, editor of the *Ecologist* magazine and future London mayoral candidate. Both were elected, although Ms Mensch quit Parliament part way through her first term and Mr Goldsmith lost his seat in a by-election in December 2016, having quit the Conservatives to stand as an Independent in protest at the decision by Mrs May's government to approve the expansion of Heathrow Airport. Mr Cameron also pioneered 'open primaries' modelled on the US voting system. These give every elector in a constituency a chance to vote on which candidate should stand for the Conservatives at an election—irrespective of whether they are Tory members.

4.4.2.2 The Labour Party

Labour's selection process has traditionally been more democratic than that of the Conservatives. Under Mr Blair, however, it became increasingly centralized and it was only Ed Miliband who finally relented to trying out open primaries—five years behind the Tories.

Up to 31 January 2001, constituency Labour parties (equivalent to the Tories' constituency associations) and affiliated organizations, including unions, could each nominate up to two candidates from lists approved by local party leaderships. The general councils of Constituency Labour Party (CLP) branches then circulated shortlists among local members, and they voted either by postal ballot or at 'hustings'—public meetings involving debates between the rival candidates (as described in relation to the Conservative Party in 4.4.2.1).

Mr Blair introduced a streamlined version after 31 January 2001. To speed up initial vetting procedures, future candidate lists would be centrally approved by the party's 'ruling' National Executive Committee (NEC). Constituency Labour Party branches needing new candidates would be presented with these lists and asked to vote for one of the approved names. Mr Blair's critics saw this as an attempt to weed out left-wing candidates and impose a Blairite agenda on Labour's grassroots.

An earlier example of the centralizing tendency among recent Labour leaders was their adoption of all-women shortlists for parliamentary candidates in 1993. Positive discrimination was brought in to increase the number of women MPs, to better reflect the gender balance in the British population (which is 51 per cent female). In 1996, Labour's stand was judged unlawful, in a case brought under the Sex Discrimination Act 1975, but once in power the party introduced the Sex Discrimination (Election Candidates) Act 2002, which guaranteed the legality of all-women shortlists until 2015. In the run-up to the 2010 election, Mr Cameron became a convert to all-women shortlists and Labour continues to use them in many areas. Nonetheless, the policy still has its critics—notably some groups representing ethnic minorities, who argue that white women may get selected in some areas known for their racial diversity at the expense of strong male minority candidates.

4.4.2.3 The Liberal Democrat Party

Although they often claim to be more democratic than their rivals, the Lib Dems use a similarly centralized selection system. A list of approved names is drawn up centrally. Constituencies looking for new candidates must first advertise in *Liberal Democrat News*, the party's main publication, and individuals whose names are on that list may apply for vacancies. A selection committee then interviews them and a shortlist is put before local party members.

4.5 Quirks of the electoral system

Parliamentary candidates may stand, and even be elected, in more than one constituency. If returned in both, they must immediately choose which constituency they would like to represent and 'stand down' from the other. The seat forgone will pass to the second-choice candidate in that constituency. This follows rules set out in Erskine May (see 1.1.1.4) and laid down in Commons procedures.

Candidates may withdraw their nominations, provided that they do so in writing (with one witness attesting) by noon on the sixteenth day before polling. This throws up the intriguing possibility that an individual might one day be elected to Parliament, despite having decided against standing at the last minute.

The British electoral system produces a clear divide between 'marginal constituencies' (or 'marginals') and 'safe seats'. In marginals—key 'bellwether' battlegrounds on election-day—incumbent MPs have small majorities (in some cases, having won only a handful more votes than their nearest rivals at previous elections), so their seats are considered vulnerable and key targets for competitors. Candidates concentrate their energies on attracting the support of 'swing voters': individuals with no firm historical allegiance to particular parties. Safe seats, in contrast, are those in which sitting MPs have large majorities that (barring huge upsets) are unlikely to lose. These tend to be located in party political heartlands—traditionally, the north for Labour and Home Counties for the Tories. Such seats would require huge 'swings' from one candidate to another to change hands.

Other than local and European elections, one of the biggest litmus tests of public opinion is the by-election: a vote in a single constituency to replace a sitting MP who has either retired, been deselected (see 5.10), or died. Under Mr Major, by-elections frequently produced bruising results for the Tories, eating away at his tight twenty-one-seat majority until it all but evaporated. By 2008, it was Labour's turn to suffer repeated bloody noses: over one three-month period, it sustained several defeats, including two in previously safe seats: the Crewe and Nantwich constituency of veteran backbencher Gwyneth Dunwoody, whose 7,000-strong majority was overturned by the Conservatives in their first by-election victory over Labour for thirty years, and Glasgow

East, a dyed-in-the-wool Labour seat on Mr Brown's doorstep, which the Scottish Nationalists snatched on a 22.5 per cent swing (although Labour regained it, temporarily, in 2010). More recent by-elections have seen significant swings to UKIP, which gained two seats from the Tories in late 2014 and came second in twin polls in Labour heartlands in May 2016. One of the most unconventional, meanwhile, was that precipitated by the tragic June 2016 killing of Labour MP Jo Cox—a seat both the Conservatives and Lib Dems declined to contest out of respect for her.

4.5.1 How the Scottish and Welsh electoral systems work

Both the Scottish Parliament and Welsh Assembly have, since May 2011, been elected every five years (and previously on four-yearly cycles). Unlike Westminster MPs, MSPs and AMs are elected using the **additional member system (AMS)**. This widely used hybrid system—a fixture of states as diverse as Mexico and Italy—bears some resemblance to FPTP, but contains a 'proportional' element designed to ensure that parties which poll significant numbers of votes but would be poorly represented in the legislature if only the winning candidate in each constituency was allotted a seat still end up with a relatively 'fair' parliamentary presence. To ensure this happens, each elector has two votes: one for his or her constituency and a second for a regional 'top-up' list which can only be used to support a party, rather than a named candidate. Britain's most recent set of AMS elections, in May 2016, saw the regional vote prove a lifeline for Scottish Labour leader Kezia Dugdale, who only managed to scrape a seat at Holyrood this way, after losing her bid to capture the Edinburgh East constituency. The poor performance of Ms Dugdale's party was put down, in part, to the one significant difference between voting qualifications for Holyrood and those for both general elections and elections to the other devolved assemblies: since the Scottish Elections (Reduction of Voting Age) Act 2015, the voting age for Scottish Parliament polls has been permanently lowered to sixteen. The SNP presently enjoys strong youth support, on the back of its 2014 independence campaign (at which 16 and 17 year-olds were first allowed the vote). It is likely to only be a matter of time before voting ages are lowered in Wales and Northern Ireland, too. As long ago as 2012, a motion was passed in the Stormont assembly backing the extension of the franchise to 16 and 17 year-olds, should the power to do this be devolved in future. The government has previously agreed in principle to giving the Welsh Assembly authority to lower the voting age in Wales, and though this power has not yet been devolved it is likely to be by the 2021 election there.

4.5.2 How the Northern Irish electoral system works

Elections for the Northern Ireland Assembly (as in the neighbouring Irish republic) are decided by the single transferable vote (STV)—the system long favoured by electoral reform campaigners, including the Lib Dems, for Britain as a whole. Unlike in FPTP and other elections, STV uses multi-member constituencies: instead of a seat having just one MP, it will elect up to five, making it much more likely that most individual electors will end up with at least one representative they support.

Electors mark candidates in order of preference and, once one reaches a predetermined quota (e.g. one-fifth of votes cast if five seats available), he/she is elected. Second choices listed on all 'surplus' papers naming that candidate as 'first choice' are then treated as if they were first choices and distributed accordingly among the remaining candidates. The process of reallocating second and subsequent choices as 'first choices' continues until the required number of MLAs is elected. Given the relative complexity of this system, it is perhaps unsurprising that the results of Stormont elections tend to take much longer to be confirmed after polling day than those for Scotland, Wales or the UK Parliament. It is not usually until the following evening that final results are declared.

4.6 Arguments for proportional representation—and other PR systems

Such are the inequities of the Westminster electoral system that pro-democracy campaigners have long argued for its replacement by one that more accurately reflects the distribution of votes between rival candidates or parties. Pressure groups like the Electoral Reform Society and Unlock Democracy (until recently Charter 88) advocate **proportional representation (PR)**—an umbrella term referring to various alternative models, including AMS and STV (see Table 4.3). Such a switch has, for many years, been official policy for the Lib Dems, who have long suffered more than other parties under FPTP, owing to the wide geographical dispersal of their vote.

It has often been observed that, given the two main parties' vested interest in retaining the old system, the Lib Dems would need to achieve power to introduce it—but that this is unlikely to happen without it. Hardly surprising, then, that one of Mr Clegg's key demands before entering coalition with the Conservatives in 2010 was a referendum on this very issue. Though his wish was granted, when the poll came, on 5 May 2011, it was for a lesser prize than he might have hoped. This was the alternative vote (AV): a system, used in Australia, which retains the single-member constituency model familiar from FPTP elections while introducing an element of proportionality designed to weed out extremist candidates and produce end results that (however compromised) are acceptable to more constituents than straightforward 'knockout' contests based on simple majorities.

AV requires electors in each constituency to mark candidates in order of preference. Depending on how the system is implemented, a candidate will be

Table 4.3 Other forms of proportional representation (PR) and how they work

Name	How it works	Where used
Party list systems	Seats allocated to parties in direct proportion to their vote share. Candidates chosen by voters from lists supplied by their parties—meaning that they can theoretically opt for someone with local connection to area, even if 'constituency link' preserved by UK elections is more remote. In 'open' list systems, they vote for both party and individual: parties supply candidate lists; electors choose ones they want; party then allocates seats it wins to named candidates, according to those expressed preferences. In 'closed' list systems, parties have already decided which candidates they wish to take seats, if they win enough votes. All EU states, including Britain, use party list system to elect members of the European Parliament (MEPs).	European elections. Regional and national parliamentary elections in European states, including Sweden and Netherlands. Israel's Knesset.
Supplementary vote (SV)	Modified version of AV. If no candidate initially obtains absolute majority—more than half eligible voters—all but top two eliminated and their 'second choices' reallocated to produce winner.	English mayoral elections, including that for London Mayor.
Additional member system (AMS)	Hybrid system: some candidates elected in single-member constituencies (normally using FPTP) and second—'additional'—votes used to top up from regional lists, introducing measure of 'proportionality' between votes and parties. As with party list system, lists can be open or closed.	Elections for Scottish Parliament, Welsh Assembly, and London Assembly. Parliaments in Germany, Italy, Mexico, New Zealand, and Venezuela.

elected if he or she wins either a 'simple majority' (50 per cent plus one of all votes cast) or one that is 'absolute' (50 per cent plus one of all eligible voters). If (as commonly happens) no one reaches this based on first preferences alone, the lowest-placed candidate's name is struck off the ballot paper and his or her second preferences redistributed among the remaining contenders as if they were first choices (as with STV). This process continues until one candidate finally has a majority. In the event, after a lacklustre 'Yes' campaign, and amid fearsome opposition from a much better funded and organized 'No' lobby, the Lib Dems and their supporters (including then Labour leader Mr Miliband) lost the AV referendum—and, perhaps, a once-in-a-generation chance to improve

Table 4.4 Pros and cons of PR

For	Against
Governments elected under FPTP often win majority of seats despite securing only minority of votes.	PR produces more coalition governments. These can be less decisive or coordinated in policymaking. Extremist parties can sometimes hold balance of power because their support enables mainstream ones to form governments.
Many votes wasted under FPTP because numerous electors denied representation by MPs of same persuasion; PR produces overall results that better reflect distribution of votes cast.	Voters under PR are less able to hold particular governments responsible for actions by booting them out.
Alternating government between Left and Right can bring abrupt changes of policy direction—and lack of long-term continuity.	Some PR systems break constituency link between individual voters and MPs—a cornerstone of Britain's democracy.
FPTP denies voice to minority parties with significant support in country, but no elected MPs.	PR can lead to frequent elections and big policy compromises, because many coalitions are unstable. Firmer leadership or action is sometimes needed.

Britain's increasingly outmoded electoral system. On a nationwide turnout of just 42.2 per cent—ironically, a symbol of the disengagement with parliamentary politics that reformers had hoped to rectify—the 'No' vote triumphed by 68 to 32 per cent.

Key arguments used by advocates and opponents of the introduction of PR in the UK are outlined in Table 4.4.

4.7 The future of voting

Since 2001, electoral turnout has been consistently lower than at any time since the Second World War, although it rose by nearly 4 per cent in 2010—from 61.3 to 65.1 per cent—amid a period of political and economic upheaval following the recession and parliamentary expenses scandal. This has prompted an ongoing debate about voter disengagement—whether resulting from the widespread perception (particularly during the Blair–Brown years) that mainstream parties had become largely indistinguishable, or the perception that politicians say one thing in their manifestos and do another once elected. Others point to the increasing prominence of 'career politicians'—Oxbridge-educated academics who start out as bag-carrying political researchers before working their way up through the ranks of think-tanks and party policy units, and ultimately securing safe seats after two or three attempts at less winnable targets. A *Guardian* survey published in June 2014 found that 54 per cent of candidates selected by Labour to contest marginal seats in the 2015 election came from such backgrounds, compared to 46 per cent for the Lib Dems and only 17 per cent for the Tories (the bulk of whose candidates hailed from the worlds of business and finance). Mr Miliband, former Shadow Chancellor Ed Balls, and Mr Cameron all held Oxford degrees in philosophy, politics, and economics (PPE), and started their working lives in special adviser roles.

Although there remains a wide spectrum of different views on the merits and pitfalls of FPTP, there is a growing cross-party consensus that more needs to be done to encourage people to vote. One approach would be to make voting *easier*. The Representation of the People Act 2000 authorized various pilot schemes to see which worked best, including:

- electronic voting (via email, SMS text, the Internet);
- global postal voting;
- elections spread over several days or on Saturdays; and/or
- taking polling stations to the voter (that is, to supermarkets, doctors' surgeries, etc.).

Though Labour was a big advocate of postal voting, it continues to be seen as vulnerable to fraud. In multi-occupancy households, one resident could theoretically vote multiple times by filling in housemates' forms. Indeed, elections for Birmingham City Council in 2004 exposed systematic corruption after a number of Labour activists were implicated in fraudulently submitting multiple forms. At the time of writing, the question of how to increase voter turnout was back on the agenda following the 2014 local and European elections—both of which inspired barely a third of the electorate to turn out. In the wake of these results and the wildly contrasting 84.6 per cent showing for Scotland's independence vote—Britain's highest ever election turnout—16 and 17 year-olds have continued to be eligible to vote north of the border, and Labour has repeatedly pledged to extend this across the UK when it returns to power.

Topical feature idea

A recent poll in the main parliamentary constituency covered by your newspaper's catchment area found that at the time of the June 2016 EU referendum some 17 per cent of eligible voters had not registered. Some adults questioned were unaware that individual voter registration had even been introduced. Given the scale of the gap between eligible and registered voters, your editor wants you to write a background feature emphasizing the importance of registration—and how the system has changed. How would you research and write this article?

✷ Current issues

- **The Conservative election expenses scandal** At the time of writing, spending by the Conservative Party in 33-plus marginal constituencies in the run-up to the 2015 general election was under investigation by the police and Electoral Commission, amid allegations that significant sums spent at local level were incorrectly recorded as 'national' expenditure.
- **Controversy over individual voter registration** Since December 2015, it has no longer been possible for one member of a household to register all adults living at the same address to vote. Instead, it is each individual's responsibility to proactively register him or herself—a change some critics argue could favour the Conservatives over Labour, and skew future boundary changes that are based on the electoral roll. The deadline for voters to register for the 2016 EU referendum had to be extended for forty-eight hours after the online registration system crashed.
- **Restrictions on non-party election campaigning** The Transparency, Lobbying, Non-party Campaigning and Trade Union Administration Act 2014 introduced new curbs on campaigning by charities, pressure groups, and other non-party organizations—including trades unions. Labour has accused the Tories of using a supposed crack-down on political lobbying as cover for undermining its core funding base.

Key points

1. The House of Commons is elected using a first-past-the-post (FPTP) system. In each of 650 constituencies, the winner is the candidate achieving a relative majority of votes (more than anyone else).
2. Opponents of FPTP argue that it unfairly benefits parties with concentrations of support over those whose supporters are spread out geographically. This encourages people to vote for 'least worst options', rather than candidates whom they actually support (tactical voting).
3. Electoral systems that produce more equitable distributions of seats are collectively known as 'proportional representation' (PR). Forms of PR include the single transferrable vote (STV) and party lists.
4. To be eligible to vote in general elections, you must be aged at least 18 and a UK, Commonwealth, or Irish citizen living in Britain. Peers and convicted prisoners are among those barred.
5. To stand as an MP, you must be aged at least 18, a British, Commonwealth, or Irish citizen, and not disqualified for another reason—such as holding a peerage or serving a custodial sentence of twelve months or longer.

→ Further reading

Blais, A. (ed.) (2008) *To Keep or to Change First Past the Post? The Politics of Electoral Reform*, New York: Oxford University Press. **Expert analysis of the relative merits of 'first past the post' and other electoral systems, and critique of failures of the UK, United States, and other countries using FPTP to achieve reform.**

Cowley, P. and Ford, R. (2014) *Sex, Lies, and the Ballot Box: 50 Things You Need to Know about British Elections*, London: Biteback. **Collection of punchy and engaging essays by fifty-one leading political scientists on the qualities and quirks of the UK voting system.**

Denver, D., Carman, C., and Johns, R. (2012) *Elections and Voters in Britain*, 3rd edn, Basingstoke: Palgrave Macmillan. **Second edition of authoritative text focusing on UK voting patterns. Includes data from British Electoral Study (BES) surveys.**

Farrell, D. (2011) *Electoral Systems: A Comparative Introduction*, 2nd edn, Basingstoke: Palgrave Macmillan. **Illuminating comparative study of the six types of electoral system used in seventy of the world's most advanced democracies.**

Renwick, A. (2011) *A Citizen's Guide to Electoral Reform*, London: Biteback Publishing. **Expert and balanced analysis of pros and cons of various electoral systems used in Britain and other leading democracies.**

@ Online Resource Centre

www.oxfordtextbooks.co.uk/orc/Morrison5e/

Visit the Online Resource Centre that accompanies this book for web links and regular updates.

5

Political parties, party funding, and lobbying

The 'party system' has long been a cornerstone of British democracy. It derives from a series of nineteenth- and early twentieth-century works of political science, notably by James Bryce, Charles Merriam and William Nisbet Chambers—all focusing on the emergence of what was seen as a model democratic system in the United States. The notion of groups of like-minded individuals banding together to form 'parties' and campaigning collectively might have been relatively new in America, but in Britain the party was already a long-established institution, as was the country's own peculiar version of party politics: the 'two-party' (or, occasionally, 'three-party') system.

'First past the post' (FPTP) voting has always favoured candidates representing two or three mainstream parties. Given that British general elections produce 'winner takes all' outcomes at constituency level—with single representatives returned in each—it has tended to be those candidates most closely identified with the concerns of each area who have been elected (historically, social reformers in the industrial north and conservatives in the wealthier south). The formation of a coherent nationwide government is possible only if a number of elected representatives agree to share power and ascribe particular responsibilities to individuals from among them. It was this rationale that led to the emergence of Britain's party system.

From the point at which Parliament wrested sovereignty from the monarch in 1689 up to the emergence of the Liberal Party some 170 years later, the party system revolved around two political groupings: Whigs and Tories. The former are often crudely identified with the progressive tendencies later embodied by nineteenth-century Liberals and the latter with the modern-day Conservative Party. In truth, the distinction between the two was more nebulous. Both were associated, to a greater or lesser degree, with the moneyed classes and aristocracy. Their differences largely rested on Christian denominational grounds, with Whigs identifying more with non-Anglican believers ('dissenters' such as Scotland's emerging Presbyterian Church) and Tories the Church of England.

By the late eighteenth century, however, clearer party lines had emerged, with the ascendancy of Charles James Fox and William Pitt the Younger as Whig leader and Tory prime minister respectively. Within a few short decades, the Whigs would be advocating the abolition of slavery, the introduction of overseas free trade, and wider voting rights.

As this book's purpose is to give journalists a clear understanding of Britain's present-day political framework, the following sections will primarily focus on the internal structures and workings of the main parties as they are today, rather than their historical backgrounds. Moreover, while closest attention will be paid to what have traditionally been the three biggest parties—the Conservatives, Labour, and the Liberals (now Liberal Democrats)—it is important to recognize the significance of recent realignments in the party-political landscape, not only in Parliament but in local, devolved, and European Union legislatures. To this end, short sections are also included on the party that decisively supplanted the Lib Dems as second 'official' Opposition after the 2015 general election, the Scottish National Party (SNP), as well as its Welsh and Northern Irish equivalents, Plaid Cymru and Sinn Féin, the Green Party, the United Kingdom Independence Party (UKIP), and the Democratic Unionist Party (DUP).

5.1 Structure and organization of the modern Conservative Party

The Conservatives emerged in the early 1800s from one of two principal factions that had dominated Parliament since the late seventeenth century: Tories and Whigs (forerunners of the Liberal Party). Of the twenty-three politicians who have successfully scaled the 'greasy pole' to become British prime minister since 1900, fifteen have been Conservative, three Liberal, and five Labour. Including periods of coalition and 'national government' (such as during the First and Second World Wars), the Tories have held power for sixty-one years, the Liberals twenty-two, and Labour thirty-eight.

Many aspects of the Conservative Party's internal organization remain broadly the same today as when its then leader, Sir Robert Peel, coined its name in a founding constitutional document, the 1834 *The Tamworth Manifesto*. Tory members are connected to their national party through local constituency associations, which first began proliferating even earlier, with passage of the Reform Act 1832. Unlike Labour, in which membership activities have historically been centrally directed, these associations initially sprouted independently. They could, however, wield considerable clout: in affluent areas, they recruited candidates and financed their campaigns.

Table 5.1 The internal structure of the Conservative Party

Level	Party in the country	Party in Parliament
Top table	**Chairman of the Conservative Party** (head of Conservative Campaign Headquarters) and Conservative Party Board.	Leader
Middle tier	Constitutional college, incorporating National Conservative Convention (comprising MPs, MEPs, and other senior activists).	1922 Committee
Grass roots	Constituency associations	Individual backbenchers

Despite being gradually incorporated into the overall party structure, associations had considerable independence until 1998, when newly elected leader William Hague formalized their party status in an effort to discipline errant elements he controversially labelled 'out of touch' and 'racist'. To this end, he introduced the party's first codified constitutional document: *Fresh Future*. This imposed new conditions on associations, but gave them significant new rights. Their position in today's party hierarchy—beneath a constitutional college and **Conservative Campaign Headquarters** (formerly 'Conservative Central Office')—is explained in Table 5.1, while the way in which its various organizational components fit together is shown in table 5A to be found on the **Online Resource Centre (ORC)**.

The influence historically wielded by constituency associations extends to their role in party leadership elections (see 5.1.1), and is testament to the rule of thumb that leaders ignore the views of paid-up members at their peril. It is ordinary members who swell the party's coffers by paying annual subscriptions and raising funds to fight elections; troop out, unpaid, on cold winter nights to canvass support; and can (usually) be relied on to vote loyally for party candidates themselves on polling day. In return, it is incumbent on a party's leadership to give something back to its members—policies that they are happy to support and a sense of belonging. This can come through everything from participating in fundraising events to attending annual party conferences. Like those of Labour and the Lib Dems, the Tory conference is held towards the end of the summer recess, traditionally in a large coastal town such as Brighton, Bournemouth, or Blackpool.

Notwithstanding Labour's ties with the trades unions (see 5.2), the Tories used to boast the largest individual subscribing membership of any party—reaching an all-time high of 2.8 million in 1953. However, in recent decades, it has steeply declined, halving between 2005 and 2013—dropping from 253,000 to 134,000—before bouncing back to around 150,000 by 2015, according to the well-informed blog ConservativeHome.

Although the Tories traditionally perform poorly in Scottish and Welsh elections, they still contest some Northern Irish seats. This is a hangover from the party's strong historical ties to the province, as evidenced by its full official title: the Conservative and Unionist Party. In July 2008, David Cameron and the then leader of the Ulster Unionists, Sir Reg Empey, published a joint letter in *The Daily Telegraph* pledging to revive their parties' historic electoral alliance, which, though dating back to the 1880s, had been severed some thirty years earlier by factional fighting. More recently, the Conservative party has begun rebuilding itself in Scotland, where it overtook Labour for the first time in decades to become the official Opposition in the Scottish Parliament as of the May 2016 local elections—thanks largely to a campaign resting on the personal popularity of its Scottish leader, Ruth Davidson (whose literature, tellingly, made little or no mention of the Tories!).

5.1.1 How the Conservatives choose their leaders

From the mid-1960s until 1998, Conservative leaders were always elected by their parliamentary colleagues—with no formal input from rank-and-file members. Today, however, only the first stage of this process is handled exclusively by MPs and peers. Leadership contests normally occur either when an incumbent leader resigns (as Mr Cameron did immediately after the Brexit referendum—see 9.7) or because a rival decides to mount a challenge (as Michael Heseltine did to Margaret Thatcher in 1990). If only one candidate declares, he or she will effectively become leader without facing a ballot, whereas if only two emerge their names will immediately be put before ordinary members nationwide, on a 'one member, one vote' basis. However, if three or more candidates stand, as happened after Mr Cameron's resignation, a series of first-past-the-post (FPTP) ballots will then be called by the chairperson of the party's 1922 Committee (see next section), during which declared candidates will steadily be whittled down by MPs, with the contenders scoring the fewest votes in each successive ballot eliminated until two frontrunners emerge. The first of these ballots will take place on the Tuesday after the week in which nominations closed, with a second (if needed) on the subsequent Thursday, a third on the following Tuesday etc. Once there are only two candidates remaining, the final say rests with rank-and-file party members.

While the introduction of this huge extension of party democracy by former Tory leader William Hague signalled his seriousness about party modernization, it was not long before his fellow MPs were regretting having approved it. Following his defeat at the 2001 election, he resigned, to be replaced by little-known Iain Duncan Smith. Although widely perceived by both colleagues in Parliament and political commentators as uncharismatic, Mr Duncan Smith beat off dynamic challengers, including ex-ministers Kenneth Clarke and Michael Portillo, based on his solid support among party members in the country. An ex-Army officer, devoted family man, practising Christian, and Eurosceptic, he chimed far more than his rivals with typical Tory members—the average age of whom (despite Hague's reforms) was then sixty-four. In contrast, Clarke's pro-European views and Portillo's admission of a youthful homosexual relationship did little to endear them.

Mr Duncan Smith's later removal in a confidence vote instigated by disgruntled Tory MPs paved the way for another new leader: former Home Secretary Michael Howard. Recognizing the need to ensure that the party elected leaders more in touch with the wider public in future, after losing the May 2005 election Mr Howard tried to reverse the Hague reforms in his remaining months in office. His proposals were defeated, however, after failing to win the required two-thirds majority among Tory MPs and activists in the party's 1,141-strong constitutional college.

5.1.2 The 1922 Committee

Also known as the '1922 Backbench Committee', this comprises all Conservative MPs apart from the leader and can therefore number in the hundreds. It is often described as 'influential'—an understatement, given that it represents all elected Tory members and, as such, can claim to articulate the 'mood' of the parliamentary party like no other entity.

Far from being a talking shop, the 1922 Committee wields serious constitutional clout. It is headed by an eighteen-member executive committee, the chairperson of which is often referred to as the party's 'shop steward'. As detailed in the previous section, he or she is responsible for organizing leadership elections—and votes of confidence. These can be triggered by letters to the chairperson signed by 15 per cent of Tory MPs. The last time this happened was in 2003, when Mr Duncan Smith was deposed. The Committee also instigated the final twist of the knife that unseated Mrs Thatcher following Mr Heseltine's 1990 leadership challenge (see 3.1.3.4).

The Committee meets every week when Parliament is sitting and is governed by curious conventions. For its first eighty-eight years, frontbenchers were only permitted to attend meetings when the party was in opposition. Even then, the leader was barred—so his or her Shadow Cabinet colleagues had to act as intermediaries. When in government, neither leader nor Cabinet colleagues used to be able to attend, but today they may do so—though they may not vote on its motions.

Although the 1922 Committee is by far the most powerful Tory subgroup, MPs and peers may join a number of other such 'clubs', depending on where their views fall on the Conservative spectrum. These associations of like-minded left- or right-wingers—or members united over particular issues, like Europe—are customarily known as 'ginger groups', although many have recently morphed into semi-professional think tanks. Among the most active today are the Bow Group, which describes itself as Britain's 'oldest centre-right think tank', and the Thatcherite Conservative Way Forward. As befits the online age, however, the most influential is arguably a collaborative website—ConservativeHome—the editor of which, Tim Montgomerie, has cultivated a good relationship with both party rank-and-file and outspoken internal critics. An excellent source of news and gossip for political reporters, it is found online at http://conservativehome.blogs.com.

In addition to its various ginger groups, the Conservative Party has a long tradition of support from upmarket gentlemen's associations, including the Carlton Club.

5.2 Structure and organization of the Labour Party

Unlike the Conservative Party, which emerged in 'top-down' fashion from the moneyed classes, Labour was created in a 'bottom-up' way, as a membership-led movement formed through a coalition of establishment outsiders campaigning for greater parliamentary representation for the working classes: principally the trades unions, middle-class think tank the Fabian Society, and a loose body of aspiring parliamentary candidates and their supporters styling itself the Independent Labour Party (ILP). Its formation was therefore more 'deliberate', with several distinct groupings coalescing to establish it formally as the Labour Representation Committee (LRC) in 1900—initially with the primary aim of getting more working-class people elected. As such, Labour (unlike other parties) has had a codified constitution from the outset.

Undoubtedly the most symbolic sentence in Labour's constitution is (and always was) 'Clause 4'. Penned in 1917 by one of the intellectual architects of the party, Sidney Webb, it bore the imprint of the Marxist ideology on which its founding values were based—focusing on the need to take into public ownership the 'means of production' (industry and agriculture) and give workers a greater share in how their fruits were distributed. Webb's original wording was as follows:

> 'To secure for the workers by hand or by brain the full fruits of their industry and the most equitable distribution thereof that may be possible upon the basis of the common ownership of the means of production, distribution and exchange, and the best obtainable system of popular administration and control of each industry or service.'

In the context of a pre-war British society in which ownership of the country's assets and wealth was concentrated in the hands of very few individuals, and little or no 'public services' like healthcare or education were provided by the state, it is easy to see why these words originally carried such resonance. However, when Mr Blair became leader of the party, nearly eight decades later, he was determined to continue a process of 'modernization' begun some years earlier by his predecessor-but-one, Neil Kinnock, following a string of defeats by the Conservatives. To this end, one of his earliest actions was to rewrite

Clause 4 to better reflect the new, more business-friendly 'social democratic' (as opposed to socialist) policy direction in which he determined to take the party. Basing his own version of the sacred clause on a pamphlet that he had written for the Fabian Society, Mr Blair reworded Clause 4 as follows:

> 'The Labour Party is a democratic socialist party. It believes that by the strength of our common endeavour we achieve more than we achieve alone, so as to create for each of us the means to realise our true potential and for all of us a community in which power, wealth and opportunity are in the hands of the many, not the few, where the rights we enjoy reflect the duties we owe, and where we live together, freely, in a spirit of solidarity, tolerance and respect.'

The rewriting of Clause 4 proved a defining moment in the creation of Mr Blair's 'New Labour' brand—further softening the party's image following Mr Kinnock's decision to replace its Red-Flag-inspired logo (and conference anthem) with a red rose motif. Mr Blair also developed an affinity for media management—or 'spin'—designed to improve Labour's public image after years in the political wilderness. Soon terms such as 'third way', 'big tent politics', and 'triangulation' had entered the political lexicon to explain the tactics that he and his apparatchiks used to neutralize opponents, by bringing together people from different shades of progressive opinion in a new coalition against what he would later describe in a conference speech as the 'forces of conservatism'. Almost as totemic as Clause 4 is Labour's longstanding relationship with the union movement—and it was this that gave rise to a more recent leader's confrontation with his party rank-and-file over modernizing reforms. On top of its individual paying membership, Labour has long boasted de facto members, in the form of tens of thousands of workers historically co-opted into its ranks through their subscriptions to unions affiliated to the party—irrespective of whether they personally supported it. However, in a landmark change, at a special conference in March 2014, Mr Miliband controversially replaced the 'automatic affiliation' to Labour of union members with an 'opt-in' arrangement, under which they would be offered full participating party membership for a cut-price 'supporters' fee' of £3 (though, in a move apparently designed to deter 'entryists' from voting in a leadership election prompted by former Shadow Business Secretary Angela Eagle's decision to challenge leader Jeremy Corbyn in July 2016, an additional £25 fee was subsequently introduced by the party's National Executive Committee, not only for supporters but also full members who had signed up since 12 January that year). Mr Miliband's reforms—approved by 86.29 per cent of those who voted—had been portrayed by him as a way of transforming Labour back into a 'mass movement', by drawing in a new wave of fully participating members, in place of ranks of passive union ones who, in many cases, did not even support it. Party strategists, meanwhile, hoped the change might wrong-foot ongoing claims by Labour's political opponents that it was 'in the unions' pockets'. Indeed, the 'Corbyn surge' of summer 2015, in the run-up to that September's leadership contest, not to mention the spike in new members following the June 2016 'Brexit' vote (see 9.7), suggest that Mr Miliband's instincts about how best to encourage people to proactively join Labour were not as wide of the mark as sceptics (notably the unions) initially argued. Moreover, Mr Corbyn's election saw at least one major union that disaffiliated from the party during Mr Blair's tenure, the Fire Brigades Union (FBU), rejoin, while the left-wing general secretary of the Public and Commercial Services Union (PCS), Mark Serwotka, revived his own individual membership.

Today, Labour is Britain's biggest political party, and one of the largest in Europe. Having long since overtaken the Tories, in terms of membership, its numbers have surged sharply since the 2015 election—first in the run-up to the party's leadership contest that September, then in the immediate aftermath of veteran left-winger Mr Corbyn's landslide victory, the attempted coup by his own MPs the following summer, and his subsequent re-election. By offering an anti-austerity prospectus starkly at odds with the more centrist and pragmatic policies for which New Labour had been criticized by left-leaning voters, Mr Corbyn and his team were widely credited with galvanizing disaffected supporters to re-join Labour, and young people previously disengaged with British politics to do so for the first time. At the time of writing official figures showed the party's paid-up membership to be more than 500,000–100,000 higher than the previous record once achieved by Tony Blair. This was apparently boosted by 130,000 in a single fortnight after the Brexit referendum (see 9.7), during which Mr Corbyn had come under intense pressure from parliamentary colleagues to quit over what many viewed as his lacklustre contribution to the 'Remain' campaign.

Although it has traditionally had strongholds in Scotland, Wales, and northern England, Labour does not organize at all in Northern Ireland. Its closest equivalent there is the centre-left Social Democratic and Labour Party (SDLP). The party also has a longstanding relationship with the Cooperative Party—a related movement with similar working-class, communitarian roots. At present, some twenty-five of its MPs still sit in the Commons under a joint 'Labour and Cooperative Party' ticket. Conversely, as with the Conservative Party, recent years have seen Labour leaders in both Wales and Scotland attempt to distance themselves from the 'national' leadership, in an effort to carve out distinct identities for themselves. In Scotland, Labour's present leader, Kezia Dugdale, has rebranded the party 'Scottish Labour', in an effort to rebuild its support following years of being treated (in the words of her predecessor-but-one, Johann Lamont) as a 'branch office' of Westminster and its near-wipeout north of the border in 2015. This itself was blamed by many on the centralizing tendencies of the national party—as manifested, in this instance, by its willingness to join forces with the Tories to campaign for a 'No' vote in the independence referendum, rather than making its own distinct case for continued union.

The main constituent elements of the Labour Party today are outlined in table 5B to be found on the **Online Resource Centre**. Of its leadership bodies, the most significant is the **National Executive Committee (NEC) of the Labour**

Table 5.2 The main constitutional bodies of the Labour Party

Body	Role and composition	Notes
National Executive Committee of the Labour Party (NEC)	Labour's 'ruling' NEC is meant to represent all wings at national policymaking level, taking delegates from all affiliated groupings (see table 5B on the Online Resource Centre). Traditionally acts as counterweight to leadership, although its influence declined under Mr Blair, who formed the NPF. As of 2015, NEC had thirty-one members—not counting its two *ex officio* ones: party leader (Mr Corbyn) and deputy leader (Tom Watson). These included stalwart backbencher Dennis Skinner, and ex-London Mayor Ken Livingstone—though he had been suspended pending an independent inquiry into allegations of antisemitism within the party. It also enforces party discipline: in 2003, its 'constitutional committee' expelled then Labour MP George Galloway for bringing party into disrepute in speeches condemning Mr Blair's actions in Iraq.	Mr Blair's neutering of NEC followed his predecessors' run-ins over policy changes, such as party's abandonment of opposition to Britain's nuclear weapons, and repeated election to its membership of vocal leadership critics, including late left-winger Tony Benn.
National Policy Forum (NPF)	Formed by Mr Blair in 1997, this draws 184 members from all levels of the party. Meets two or three weekends a year to analyse proposal documents generated by six policy commissions, members of which include representatives of leadership, NEC, and NPF. Recommendations pass to conference for ratification.	Introduced officially as means of widening party democracy in Labour's ranks, but often perceived as leadership's instrument for quelling dissent.
Labour Party Conference	Unlike Conservative conference, traditionally a decision-making body rather than event. Presided over by Labour general-secretary.	Theoretically, conference still has final say on major policy/constitutional changes. Since 1997, leadership has made clear its willingness to overrule conference decisions. Mr Blair reduced weight of conference vote by affiliated organizations from 80% to 50% (four-fifths still wielded by unions).

Party. Its role in relation to two other key entities, the National Policy Forum (NPF) and the Labour Party Conference, is explained in Table 5.2.

5.2.1 How Labour chooses its leader

Labour's leadership election procedure has trodden a slow road towards democratization over recent decades. From 1922 to 1981, leaders were elected solely by the party's MPs. Annual contests were held at party conference, but leaders were normally re-elected unopposed, so these were formalities.

In 1981, Labour established an electoral college: in future, only three out of ten votes in leadership elections would be cast by Labour MPs, with 30 per cent going to Constituency Labour Parties (CLPs) and 40 per cent to the unions. Further reform followed in 1993, when the union block vote was scrapped and weighting equalized to give each grouping a one-third share of the vote. Inequities remained, however: individuals who were members of two or more affiliated organizations—for example a union and a CLP—could vote more than once. However, this discrepancy was addressed by Mr Miliband in 2014, and leadership elections have since conducted on a 'one member, one vote' basis—a key factor in helping veteran left-winger Mr Corbyn mobilize sufficient votes to win both the 2015 and 2016 contests.

To stand for the leadership, a sitting MP must be nominated by 15 per cent of his or her Commons colleagues. For challengers wishing to unseat an incumbent who does not wish to step down (a fate faced by Mr Corbyn after the Brexit referendum—see 9.7), the threshold is higher: with the support of one-fifth of all MPs and MEPs needed before a contest can commence. Once an election is called, however, it is instantly thrown open to all party members, rather than going through a ballot of MPs first. The electoral system used is the Alternative Vote (AV), which, in the end, requires the winning candidate to muster at least half of all votes cast (see 4.6).

While the process by which Labour elects its leader may now be more democratic, the disproportionate power he or she wields has been enhanced. In July 2011, Mr Miliband persuaded his backbenchers to abandon a decades-old tradition forcing frontbenchers to stand for re-election by the rest of the party's MPs every two years whenever Labour was in opposition—a move which effectively gives serving leaders executive authority to appoint, remove, or keep in place Shadow ministers. This and other powers swiftly became a source of simmering tension between Mr Corbyn and his MPs (only a handful of whom backed his candidacy)—leading to the humiliating spectacle of a vote of no confidence in his leadership after the Brexit debacle (see 9.7), which he lost by 172 votes to 40. At time of writing, debate in the party continued to rage about whether Shadow Cabinet elections should be reintroduced, to either reinstate MPs' say in its composition (an outcome favoured by Mr Corbyn's parliamentary critics) or, potentially, offer votes to ordinary party members (an option resisted by those same backbenchers, but favoured by the leader).

5.2.2 The Parliamentary Labour Party (PLP)

Like the Conservatives, Labour has a body that represents the views of rank-and-file MPs: the Parliamentary Labour Party (PLP). It too meets weekly in a room in Parliament and has a chairperson elected at the start of each parliamentary session.

Between 1921 and 1970, the chair of the PLP was the party leader. But since 1970 the two posts have been permanently split and the PLP has become (like the 1922 Committee) largely a means for backbenchers to hold leaders to account. Unlike the 1922 Committee, however, leaders have always been able to attend meetings, even when in government. Towards the end of his premiership, Mr Blair endured increasingly hostile receptions from the PLP, and Mr Corbyn has also been barracked repeatedly by outspoken backbenchers since becoming leader. Like the 1922 Committee, the PLP can instigate confidence votes in its leaders (though their constitutional significance is limited), but in practice Labour has generally refrained from doing so—with its June 2016 attempt to force out Mr Corbyn in this way being an exception. Even then, the sheer size of his mandate among party members in the country—he had won the AV ballot easily barely ten months earlier, with nearly 60 per cent of all 'first preference' votes—emboldened him to cling on beyond this, with qualified support from Labour's main union backers and local constituency parties.

As well as the PLP, Labour has within it several ginger groups. These include left-leaning factions like the Campaign Group, Compass, and Momentum—a grassroots pro-Corbyn group launched in the wake of his leadership victory. Blairite examples have included Progress and Demos.

5.3 Structure and organization of the Liberal Democrat Party

As the 'youngest' of Britain's major political parties, the Liberal Democrat Party—formed in March 1988 from the merger of the nineteenth-century Liberal Party of William Gladstone and the Social Democratic Party (SDP), a breakaway group launched in 1982 by four ex-Labour ministers concerned by that party's shift to the left—also has the newest constitution. Unlike either Labour or Conservatives, the party has a federal organization, comprising separate but conjoined parties for England, Scotland, and Wales. After years of declining membership, by September 2015 the Lib Dems had (according to then new leader Tim Farron) attracted 20,000 new sign-ups since their electoral collapse that May (while numbers under Mr Clegg were 47,000). Like Labour, the party encompasses several affiliated groupings, known as 'specified associated organizations' (SAOs). Each represents a particular section of its membership, such as women, ethnic minorities, lesbian, gay, bisexual, and transgender (LGBT) members, trade unionists, and youths and students.

As with the other major parties, the Lib Dems have their own parliamentary party to act as a voice for ordinary MPs; in fact, their federal structure means that they have three. The party also organizes in Northern Ireland, but rather than contesting elections under its own banner, it has a semi-official arrangement to support the Alliance Party of Northern Ireland.

5.3.1 How Liberal Democrats choose their leaders

The Lib Dems have long allowed every paid-up member an equal say in leadership elections. The various means by which these elections may be triggered, however, range from grass-roots-led (petitions backed by at least three-quarters of local parties sent to the party's president) to 'top-down' (no-confidence votes passed by a majority of Lib Dem MPs).

In recent years, the Lib Dems have been more than willing to depose leaders with whom they grow dissatisfied. Despite leading his troops to their highest tally of Commons seats in 2005 (sixty-two), the late Charles Kennedy was persuaded to resign in January 2007 following his public admission of a drink problem. Less than two years later, his successor, Menzies Campbell, also quit, after senior colleagues (including his deputy Vince Cable) briefed against him. Though he ultimately went of his own volition, Mr Clegg faced repeated calls for his resignation during the Coalition years, not least after his party's near-wipeout in the 2014 local and European elections (see 9.5).

5.3.2 The Lib Dem ideology: left, right, or somewhere in-between?

The question of where the Lib Dems fall on the left–right political spectrum is increasingly debatable. Like the Liberals before them, they have traditionally been seen as centrists: pro-state direction on one hand but advocates of free markets on the other. It is this that has arguably been their great electoral asset—enabling them to appeal to Labour voters in Tory-held marginals and Conservatives in Labour ones. Under Mr Kennedy, however, the Lib Dems often appeared more ideologically 'left-wing' than Labour—thanks in part to Mr Blair's rhetorical embrace of many Thatcherite economic reforms, marketization of public services, and an interventionist (some would argue 'neo-conservative') foreign policy. The Lib Dems also advocated a 50 per cent higher rate of income tax for many years before Labour Chancellor Alistair Darling finally introduced one in April 2010—and only then as a new 'top rate' pegged for people earning £150,000 a year or more. In addition, the Lib Dems long supported the principle of a local income tax to replace Council Tax, arguing that it would take more account of individuals' ability to pay.

Despite continuing to assert centre-left positions in relation to civil liberties and constitutional reform, under Mr Clegg there were clear signs of the party's return to a more 'classical liberal', free market approach to running the economy and public services. In 2004, Mr Clegg, along with several fellow leading lights (including the supposedly more left-leaning Mr Cable) had contributed to *The Orange Book*, a collection of essays advocating a return to a Gladstonian, nineteenth-century vision of liberalism. This 'laissez-faire' approach arguably characterized his time in government, with he and fellow Lib Dem ministers publicly endorsing—and at times initiating—market reforms that the party might have opposed under Mr Kennedy or even its more centrist founding leader, Paddy Ashdown. As Business Secretary, Mr Cable found himself in the invidious position of having to introduce a tripling of undergraduate tuition fees from the 2012–13 academic year (like most other Lib Dem MPs, he had signed a pledge before the 2010 election opposing fees in principle). He later steered through the controversial privatization of Royal Mail (see 7.5.1.1). Meanwhile, Chief Secretary to the Treasury Danny Alexander was made personally responsible for delivering the then Chancellor George Osborne's swingeing public spending cuts, while the entire parliamentary party was whipped into supporting controversial reforms of the NHS and welfare. However, Mr Clegg and colleagues repeatedly retorted that, despite being the 'junior coalition partner', the party succeeded in getting around three-quarters of its manifesto commitments onto the statute book—citing policies such as repeated rises in the personal income tax allowance (see Table 7.1).

As a testament to the unease of some party leading lights at their leadership's drift away from what they considered its founding principles, barely a week after the formal 'Coalition agreement' was signed, ex-leader Mr Kennedy outed himself as opposing it. (He had abstained when the parliamentary party voted to endorse it.) In an article for *The Guardian* on 15 May 2010, he warned that the Tories might try to absorb the Lib Dems over time, a fate that had effectively befallen the party on two previous occasions: first, when Joseph Chamberlain split it over Home Rule for Ireland in 1886 (ending up a Liberal Unionist); and second, when David Lloyd George, the architect of old-age pensions and a prototype welfare state, opted to continue in coalition with the Conservatives after the end of the First World War.

Unlike disaffected Tory or Labour members, though, disgruntled Lib Dems can console themselves with the knowledge that they have access to an unusual constitutional mechanism enabling them to prevent their leadership steering them in political directions with which they are uncomfortable. The 'triple lock' was originally agreed by the party's conference in 1998 amid growing concern among some members about increasingly close relations between the then Lib Dem leader Mr Ashdown and Labour. It is designed to be invoked whenever the leadership makes a 'substantial proposal that could affect the party's independence of political action'—for example, announcing its intention to join a coalition. To secure such a deal, leaders are required first to win support from at least three-quarters of members of both the parliamentary party and the Lib Dems' Federal Executive (an elected committee of thirty-five senior activists, MPs, and party officials). If no such backing is obtained, a special conference must be convened to decide the matter, mirroring the composition and voting rights of the standard annual party gathering. The triple lock was invoked for the first time on 12 May 2010, to approve the Lib Dems' entry into government.

5.4 The Scottish National Party (SNP)

The May 2015 general election saw the SNP leapfrog the Liberal Democrats to become the UK's second 'official' Opposition party, after winning fifty-six of the fifty-nine seats in Scotland. Indeed, during the chaos precipitated by Labour's backbench mutiny following the Brexit vote (see 7.6), its Westminster leader, Angus McNeill, unsuccessfully asked the Commons Speaker, John Bercow, to redesignate his party the *main* Opposition.

So comprehensive was the SNP's 2015 victory north of the border that it left just one seat apiece for the Lib Dems, Conservatives, and Labour (for long years, the biggest Scottish party). Described on its own website as a 'left of centre, social democratic, and progressive party', the SNP skilfully positioned itself to win over disaffected Labour voters throughout the Blair–Brown years, steadily eating away at that party's base as it stood accused of losing touch with its traditional working-class supporters and taking their votes for granted.

As befits a party with such an impressive recent campaigning record—the SNP also secured a third successive term in government at Holyrood in May 2016—as of February that year it had more than 115,000 members, which was equivalent to 2 per cent of the entire Scottish population.

The SNP's internal structure is something of a hybrid of Labour's and the Conservatives'. Like the Tory party, much of its local organization is left to its fifty-nine constituency associations: one each for every area represented by a seat in the Scottish Parliament. Like Labour, though, it has a National Executive Committee (elected at its annual National Conference), and conference itself is its main policymaking body. Delegates are drawn from all levels of the party, including every branch and constituency association, the whole of the NEC, and affiliated organizations, such as Young Scots for Independence and the SNP Trade Union Group. Every MP, MSP, and MEP, and a number of councillors also attend. Though all final policy decisions are subject to ratification (or veto) by the conference, in between meetings decisions are taken by another body—the National Council—which bears some resemblance to the role played by Labour's NEC. It also convenes regular meetings, open to all members, of a further body, the National Assembly, which—rather like Labour's National Policy Forum—is charged with debating potential policy changes.

The SNP holds leadership elections more often than almost any other UK party. Once a year both the leader (Nicola Sturgeon) and 'depute' leader (currently) must be formally re-elected in a ballot of all members, and to be eligible to stand in an election another candidate must be nominated by a minimum of 100 members, drawn from at least twenty branches.

5.5 United Kingdom Independence Party (UKIP)

Founded in 1991, originally as the Anti-Federalist League, UKIP is characterized by its strong opposition to Britain's continued membership of the European Union and its tough anti-immigration stance. UKIP's national profile has been dominated for many years by former Conservative Nigel Farage, who was first elected its leader in 2006. Perhaps surprisingly, Mr Farage enjoys one of the most democratic mandates of all major party leaders: serving UKIP leaders must submit themselves for formal re-election by postal ballot once every four years, and every paid-up member has an equal say in the outcome. In other respects, though, the party has a top-down hierarchical structure reminiscent of the Tory and Labour parties of old. Party policy is principally decided by a dedicated policy committee, but subject to approval by the National Executive Committee—and, if motions are passed by members at the party's annual conference calling for policy changes, these will only be considered 'advisory', with the NEC having the final say.

Despite winning nearly 3.9 million votes (or 13 per cent of all those cast) in the 2015 election, to date UKIP has only one Westminster MP: Conservative defector Douglas Carswell. However, it remains a strong force at local, devolved, and EU level, boasting some 498 councillors, seven AMs (as of May 2016), and twenty-four MEPs—more than any other UK party. And though UKIP's membership is thought to have declined since a high water-mark of 42,000 members prior to the 2015 poll, its unofficial 'Grassroots Out' campaign played a decisive role for the ultimately victorious 'Leave' side in the June 2016 Brexit referendum (see 9.7).

5.6 The Green Party

Since 1990, the Green Party in Britain—part of a worldwide network of sister parties—has been divided into three distinct, but connected, entities representing different portions of the UK. These are the Green Party of England and Wales; the Scottish Green Party; and the Green Party in Northern Ireland. Though, to date, the Greens have only ever returned one MP—Caroline Lucas, in Brighton Pavilion—the party's vote share rose by nearly 3 per cent in the 2015 election, to over 1 million, and it now boasts more than 60,000 members in

England and Wales alone. It performed strongly overall in the 2016 council and devolved assembly polls, winning six seats in Scotland, coming third in the London mayoral race—ahead of UKIP and the Lib Dems respectively—and solidifying its impressive 2012 showing in the Greater London Assembly poll by returning two members. However, despite this 'Green surge' (in the words of then leader Natalie Bennett), it failed to win any Welsh Assembly seats.

The party's leader and deputy leader (or co-leader) must stand for re-election in a postal ballot of all members every two years. And as a measure of the party's much-trumpeted diversity, its leadership can be held as a male/female 'job-share'—an eventuality which came about in September 2016, when Ms Lucas was re-elected to serve alongside its former Work and Pensions spokesman, Jonathan Bartley. Like the Lib Dems and (in earlier times) Labour, the Greens' annual conference remains its main policymaking body.

5.7 Plaid Cymru

Plaid Cymru (or 'Party of Wales', as its name translates) was formed in 1925—nine years ahead of its Scottish equivalent, the SNP. It currently boasts four MPs and one MEP, and secured twelve AMs at the 2016 Senedd election (an increase of one), with its leader, Ms Wood, depriving Labour of its previous majority by capturing the once dyed-in-the-wool red valley seat of the Rhondda.

Plaid Cymru's internal structure is among the most democratic of any British party. Above its local branches and district and parliamentary constituency committees perches a National Executive Committee in charge of day-to-day policy decisions, but ultimate policymaking authority rests with its annual conference, at which its relatively modest 10,000-strong membership have a direct say.

5.8 The Democratic Unionist Party (DUP)

As of the 2016 Stormont elections, Northern Ireland's main party of government remained the loyalist DUP. Formed in 1971, and long dominated by the late Reverend Iain Paisley, since 2007 it has been in (generally stable) coalition with its one-time arch-foe: republican party Sinn Féin.

Like the largely Roman Catholic Sinn Féin, the conservative DUP emerged out of a grassroots campaigning movement with strong historical links to (in its case, Protestant) paramilitary organizations involved in The Troubles (see 1.3.5). To this end, its constitution and internal organization remain in transition and, to date, changes of leadership have always occurred without any formal contest for the top job. Even if one did take place, it would only be open to elected parliamentarians (its thirty-eight Members of the Legislative Assembly (MLAs), eight MPs, and one MEP), rather than the rank-and-file membership. The most recent change of leadership at time of writing occurred in December 2015, when former Ulster Unionist Arlene Foster succeeded outgoing leader Peter Robinson, who stepped down for personal reasons.

5.9 Sinn Féin

Established in its present form in 1970, Sinn Féin has a leadership structure distinct from those of most other UK parties. Since 1983, its overall leader—or president—has been Gerry Adams, now a member of the Republic of Ireland parliament (the Dáil). However, its most prominent elected UK politician (and effective leader in Northern Ireland) has long been Martin McGuinness, who for a decade served under successive DUP leaders as Deputy First Minister until 2017. At time of writing, Sinn Féin—whose name translates as 'we ourselves'—had twenty-eight MLAs and four MPs. Historically, though, it declines to sit at Westminster (see 4.1.1). The party has a complex hierarchy, its lowest level being local branches (cumainn), above which are district and regional executives in turn. However, ordinary branch members do have a say in its political direction, in that they elect representatives to the supreme policymaking body: the Ardfheis (national delegate conference). Like other parties, Sinn Féin has a 'ruling' National Executive Committee, which nominates the Standing Committee responsible for its day-to-day running. Sinn Féin broadly styles itself as a democratic socialist party, but its ultimate aim is the reunification of the island of Ireland under a single parliament.

5.10 Deselection

Once parliamentary candidates have been selected by their constituency parties or associations and elected to Parliament, they usually serve until they retire or are voted out. Under certain circumstances, however, they may be 'deselected'—or sacked—by either their local parties or leaderships. The process by which this can happen varies from party to party, but in general terms follows much the same pattern.

A recent deselection was that of Tim Yeo, former Tory Minister and chairman of the Commons Energy and Climate Change Committee, who was removed by his local party in February 2014 for allegedly failing to devote enough time to constituency work while awaiting the outcome of an inquiry into claims he had abused Commons lobbying rules. Mr Yeo (later cleared by the inquiry) demanded a formal deselection vote by all members of his South Suffolk constituency association after its executive committee voted not to readopt him as a candidate. In exceptional circumstances, MPs can be 'sacked' in other ways: former Immigration Minister Phil Woolas was barred from standing again for Labour after a specially convened election court stripped him of his Oldham East and Saddleworth seat for lying about his Lib Dem rival during the 2010 election campaign.

Labour has recently been engulfed by a major debate on the issue of deselection, as tensions have grown between its MPs and many rank-and-file members over the former's mounting hostility towards Mr Corbyn. Before withdrawing her challenge to his leadership, in favour of 'unity candidate' Owen Smith, Angela Eagle faced the threat of deselection by her constituency party (which largely supported Mr Corbyn), while in a speech launching his bid to retain the leadership in July 2016, he raised the spectre of 'mandatory reselection' for all Labour MPs, to decide which ones should be allowed to contest seats in 2020 following the then imminent boundary review, in which a number of constituencies were expected to be abolished, merged, or otherwise altered in shape and size (see 4.4). If acted on, this would require all sitting MPs to be formally reselected by their constituency parties once their constituencies had been redrawn—potentially enabling 'Blairite' or 'moderate' incumbents critical of Mr Corbyn to be unseated by 'Cobynista' candidates on the left. Somewhat ironically, Mr Corbyn's words rebounded on him two months later, when draft proposals revealed his own Islington North constituency was among those scheduled for abolition. The plans—which envisaged reductions from 533 to 501 seats in England, 59 to 53 in Scotland, 49 to 29 in Wales, and 18 to 17 in Northern Ireland—would also spell the end of former Chancellor George Osborne's seat of Tatton in Cheshire.

Between general elections, an MP's deselection will normally lead to a **by-election**: an election in his or her constituency alone, in which another candidate drawn from his or her party is selected to defend the seat. However, this may not happen if the deselection occurs only a few weeks or months before a general election, added to which there are times when actions by MPs that would normally provoke deselection do not—including their decisions to voluntary 'deselect' themselves by switching parties. Notable examples of defectors who have *avoided* deselection include Emma Nicholson, Conservative MP for Torridge and West Devon, who 'crossed the floor' to the Lib Dems when John Major was prime minister, and fellow Tories Alan Howarth and Shaun Woodward, who both jumped ship to Labour shortly afterwards. All three clung on, avoiding by-elections, until the 1997 general election. More recently, Mr Carswell and fellow Tory Mark Reckless both switched membership to UKIP in 2014. Though both agreed to fight by-elections before the question of deselection could arise, each mustered sufficient support from his constituents to retain his seat (though Mr Reckless went on to lose his in May 2015).

5.11 Party funding now and in future

One endlessly debated issue surrounding the party system is funding. Because parties are intrinsic to British democracy, there has long been a vocal lobby calling for them to be financed, at least partly, by the state. At present, only Opposition parties receive state subsidies—a privilege known as 'Short Money', after Edward Short, the Leader of the House who first proposed it in Harold Wilson's 1974–6 government. Short Money is meant to counteract the advantage governing parties enjoy through the resources available to ministers. Introducing wholesale state funding would signal a major change. Without significantly increasing the tax burden, where would 'the public purse' find the extra cash needed to fund parties? And if state funding became an entitlement for all registered parties, it would not only be the larger and/or more mainstream ones that benefited: taxpayers could also expect some of their money to go to extremist ones like the British National Party (BNP).

For these and other reasons, successive governments have sidestepped the issue. But, in the absence of such grants, how should parties fund their campaigns? Because membership subscriptions provide only modest, if regular, revenue streams, parties have come to rely increasingly on bequests, loans, and donations from wealthy supporters. Naturally, this has given rise to charges of inequity: if one party attracts higher donations than another, it can mount bigger, more effective, campaigns.

The 1990s witnessed various controversies over party finance. During the Major years, there was growing unease about the Conservatives' use of anonymous multimillionaire donors and money originating in offshore tax havens—particularly the 'Ashcroft millions' funnelled away by the party's ex-pat treasurer, Lord Ashcroft. Labour promised to curtail the ability of 'non-domiciles' or 'non-doms'—individuals living or working in Britain, but registered for tax purposes in other countries—to finance parties. But, within months of his election, Mr Blair was embroiled in his own controversy when Formula One boss Sir Bernie Ecclestone was outed as the source of a £1 million donation to Labour. The fact that the racing mogul had been temporarily exempted from an impending ban on tobacco sponsorship fuelled suspicions he had bought influence.

Under the Political Parties, Elections, and Referendums Act 2000, registration of donations now rests with the Electoral Commission, which, in addition to overseeing election procedures, has the responsibilities laid out in table 5C to be found on the **Online Resource Centre**.

Thirteen years after the 1997 election, the Ashcroft saga resurfaced in the run-up to the 2010 poll, when it emerged that Lord Ashcroft—still a 'non-dom', despite having assured the then Tory leader Mr Hague a decade earlier that he intended to take up UK residency—was accused of pumping millions into target seats before the official campaign launch (thereby circumventing election spending limits). Two months after the election, with the Tories back in government, Lord Ashcroft finally dropped his non-dom status—agreeing to pay UK tax in return for keeping his peerage.

Figures published by the Commission in August 2010 found that overall donations made to Britain's political parties in the run-up to that year's election had been £6 million higher than before the 2005 poll—reaching a record £26.3 million. For the first time since 1997, the Conservatives trumped Labour, raising £12 million to its £11 million, although the two biggest single donations went to the latter (including £1 million from long-time supporter steel magnate Lakshmi Mittal). This trend has continued since, to the extent that a major investigation was mounted into whether the Tories spent too much at constituency level during the 2015 election campaign (see 4.3.2).

5.12 'Lobbygate', 'cash for honours', and other recent funding scandals

Mr Blair's government was frequently embroiled in controversies concerning alleged lack of financial transparency and underhand business links. By the time Mr Brown succeeded him, the tension between ministers' pledges to be 'whiter than white' financially while still raising enough money to keep the Labour machine afloat had reached breaking point. Successive scandals about undeclared (or, at best, under-declared) donations and loans had forced ministers into embarrassing admissions. The political initiative was consequently handed to Mr Cameron, who demanded a £50,000 cap on all individual payments, including its main lifeline: union donations. Whatever his political instincts, Mr Brown was hardly in a position to comply, arguing instead that union contributions should be viewed as comprising a number of smaller individual donations. Today, the two main parties remain at loggerheads over how best to reform the donation system and talks convened since 2010 have repeatedly broken down. One 'sop' to the Left in Mr Miliband's 2014 reforms of Labour's union links was his pledge to leave the level of donations that they could make to the party uncapped.

5.12.1 'Lobbygate'

Political lobbying is nothing new. The Conservatives have never hidden their links to business, while certain Labour constituencies have long been sponsored by unions. But the emergence of specialist lobbying companies purposely set up to help individuals and interest groups gain 'the ear' of ministers, in the hope of influencing government policy, was not widely witnessed until the 1990s.

The involvement of one such company, Ian Greer Associates, as an alleged intermediary in the 'cash for questions' affair (see 2.2.6) was, for many, the first they had heard of such practices. Labour promised to halt these activities, but within a year of regaining power senior ministers—including Mr Blair's right-hand man, Peter Mandelson—were being linked to lobbying firms boasting of their ability to buy access to ministers. One such firm was Lawson Lucas Mendelsohn, run by former Labour campaign strategist Neal Lawson, businessman Jon Mendelsohn, and Ben Lucas, one of Mr Blair's political briefers.

5.12.2 'Cash for honours'

If 'Lobbygate' and the Ecclestone affair were early shots across New Labour's bows, the various 'cash for honours' rows that followed showed the party was as capable of succumbing to the advances of big business as the Tories. Most damaging was the 'loans for peerages' scandal exposed by *The Independent on Sunday* in October 2005. Controversy erupted in earnest the following March, when the then new House of Lords Appointments Commission rejected several nominees Mr Blair had suggested for life peerages. It emerged that each of the men had anonymously given Labour substantial loans. A loophole in the 2000 Act meant that, though all £200-plus *donations* had to be declared, this did not apply to loans—provided they were taken out on commercial terms.

With the party in huge debt by the 2005 election, Mr Blair and his advisers appeared to have deliberately sidestepped a law his party had introduced on the pretext of wanting to make funding more transparent, by courting loans rather than donations. Although the revelation that the party had gone 'cap in hand' to anonymous lenders was embarrassing enough for the government, there was no suggestion the letter of election law had been breached, even if its spirit was. Though ultimately dropped, a criminal investigation followed—and with it the spectacle of Mr Blair becoming the first serving premier to be questioned by police (albeit as a witness), in response to SNP allegations that his aides had breached the Sale of Peerages Act 1925 by trying to sell honours.

To regain the political initiative, Mr Blair used his final months in office to launch an independent cross-party review of political funding. This duly recommended a cap of £50,000 on individual donations, though ongoing dissent between Labour and Tories means this has yet to be come about.

When the Coalition was formed, Mr Cameron described politicians' cosy relationship with lobbyists as Britain's 'next great political scandal', following then recent furores over MPs' expenses and the near collapse of the banking system. His words came back to haunt him, with the explosion of the *News of the World* phone-hacking saga, the prosecution of Mr Cameron's close friend and fellow Etonian Charlie Brooks and wife Rebekah (the paper's former editor), and the alleged collusion between senior ministers and then News International executives over the bid by the latter's parent company, News Corp, to take over BSkyB (see 3.1.3.2). A few weeks earlier, in a separate scandal, Mr Cameron had been forced to sack his party's treasurer, Peter Cruddas, after he was filmed in a 'sting' operation by *Sunday Times* journalists boasting that Tory donors could buy 'Premier League access' to the prime minister for as little as £250,000.

The Coalition finally made good on its pledge to 'crack down' on lobbying with the Transparency of Lobbying, Non-Party Campaigning, and Trade Union Administration Act 2014. It introduced:

- a US-style statutory register of consultant lobbyists;
- a register of lobbyists, to be enforced by a statutory registrar;
- tighter regulation of spending on political campaigns in election campaigns by those not registered for election or as political parties; and
- strengthened legal requirements on unions to keep their registered members' lists updated.

Although the principle of registering professional lobbyists was widely embraced, the 'Gagging Bill' (as its critics dubbed it) provoked heated parliamentary exchanges in its later stages, with key clauses repeatedly blocked by the Lords. The introduction of stricter spending rules for 'third parties' close to elections was greeted as an attempt to stifle dissent by organizations like 38 Degrees, www.opendemocracy.net, and others who had previously launched high-profile protests against the cuts programme—concerns echoed by more established, issue-specific groups like Friends of the Earth. Meanwhile, Labour accused the government of mounting a one-sided attack on its funding base, by explicitly applying these rules to its main donors, the unions.

Topical feature idea

Despite the barriers presented by Britain's 'first past the post' (FPTP) electoral system, recent elections at all levels have witnessed growing support for minority parties. Green MP Caroline Lucas retained her seat in 2015, while her party came third in the 2016 London assembly and mayoral elections. UKIP won the 2014 European Parliament elections—becoming the first party other than Labour and Conservatives to win a national poll since before the First World War—and went on to win 3.9 million votes in the 2015 general election and gain seven Welsh Assembly seats (from a previous base of zero) in the 2016 Welsh Assembly poll. Your editor asks you to carry out an online poll of your readers to crowd-source their current political allegiances. How strong is support for the main parties in your area? Are minority parties gaining ground and, if so, which ones—and why?

✷ Current issues

- **The rise and rise of the SNP** The Liberal Democrats' collapse at the 2015 general election, and Labour's disastrous performance in Scotland, has led to the SNP becoming the official Westminster Opposition for the first time—with the 2016 Holyrood poll returning them to power north of the border for a third consecutive term.
- **New curbs to political lobbying—and union influence** The ability of third-party groups to lobby governments and campaign politically has been reduced by the Transparency of Lobbying, Non-Party Campaigning, and Trade Union Administration Act 2014, which Labour sees as an assault on its longstanding links with the trade union movement.
- **Labour's resurgence as Britain's biggest party** The run-up and immediate aftermath of Jeremy Corbyn's election as Labour leader in September 2015 saw a huge increase in, first, affiliated supporters of the party and, in turn, full party membership. It now has around 380,000 registered members—more than twice as many as the Conservative Party.

Key points

1. Britain's democracy is characterized by a 'party system', which developed in tandem with its FPTP voting system. The two main parties are Labour and the Conservatives.
2. The Conservative and Lib Dems (formerly Liberals) emerged gradually from the landed and industrialist classes, but the Labour Party was formed deliberately by an alliance of trades unions and other organizations in the early twentieth century, with a mandate to promote working-class MPs.
3. The Conservatives are headed by a chairman and Conservative Party Board, and Labour by a National Executive Committee (NEC), comprising members from every branch of the party's organization, including Parliament and unions. The Lib Dems, Greens, and other parties, like Plaid Cymru, have federal structures, with no formal ruling bodies.
4. Members of Parliament in all three main parties have mechanisms to hold their leaders accountable and, in extreme cases, depose them. The Tories have a 1922 Backbench Committee, Labour a Parliamentary Labour Party, and the Lib Dems their own federal equivalents in England, Scotland, and Wales.
5. Local branches and constituency associations of most parties have powers to deselect their MPs if dissatisfied with their performance—and to choose alternative candidates.

➔ Further reading

Bale, T. (2016) *The Conservative Party: From Thatcher to Cameron*, 2nd edn, Cambridge: Polity Press. **Timely second edition of acclaimed book charting the Tories' long slide into unpopularity and 'reinvention' as an electable force under (now ex-premier) David Cameron.**

Clegg, N. (2016) *Politics: Between the Extremes*, London: Bodley Head. **Reflective insider account of the Coalition years and defence of the centre ground by the former Lib Dem Deputy Prime Minister.**

Driver, S. (2011) *Understanding British Party Politics*, Cambridge: Polity Press. **Thought-provoking, up-to-date examination of the British party system from a post-2010 perspective.**

Pugh, M. (2011) *Speak for Britain! A New History of the Labour Party*, London: Vintage. **Thoughtful, at times revisionist, history of Labour Party, from its origins to the election of Ed Miliband as leader.**

Seymour, R. (2016) *Corbyn: The Strange Rebirth of Radical Politics*, London: Verso Books. **Acclaimed diagnosis of the factors fuelling the nascent resurgence of the Left in Western parliamentary politics, focusing on the unlikely cult of Labour's veteran firebrand.**

@ Online Resource Centre

www.oxfordtextbooks.co.uk/orc/Morrison5e/

Visit the Online Resource Centre that accompanies this book for web links and regular updates.

6

The National Health Service

No British institution generates as many headlines as the National Health Service (NHS).

Founded in 1948, the NHS was designed to be exactly that: a *national* provider of high-quality medical treatment, 'free at the point of use' (or 'need'), offered to uniform standard the length and breadth of Britain. But subsequent decades—particularly the past thirty-five years—have witnessed the steady erosion of this idealized model of socialized healthcare. What was once a single, monolithic health service, run directly by central government, was transformed in the 1980s and 1990s—most noticeably in England—into an umbrella organization encompassing numerous connected, but increasingly autonomous, units. Much like individual companies in the commercial marketplace, most have acquired their own management boards and delegated budgets, and are expected to 'commission' services from (and 'sell' them to) one another. And with the rollout of concepts like hospital league tables and 'patient choice'—allowing people to shop around for hospital treatment like customers—today they effectively compete for business.

Under recent Conservative-led governments, market reforms initiated by Margaret Thatcher, and consolidated by John Major, then Tony Blair's Labour government, have been taken further than ever. As a result, the structure of today's NHS in England bears little resemblance to that of the original: local clinical commissioning groups (CCGs), led by general practitioners (GPs) and other community-based professionals, now 'commission' care for patients from NHS trusts (hospitals, mental health units, ambulance services, or groups of these), with a national body, NHS England, responsible for funding specialist services such as cardiac (heart) units, cancer care, and accident and emergency (A&E) units, to ensure that such provision is available in hospital settings nationwide.

This chapter explains how this complex NHS 'internal market' came about and how its various strands link together today.

6.1 The origins of the National Health Service (NHS)

Although not formally established until the National Health Service Act 1946, the NHS emerged from mounting concern about the ever-starker inequalities in personal well-being between the richest and poorest Britons. It had its roots in two key developments: the 'Beveridge Report' (of which more in a moment); and the introduction by Liberal Chancellor David Lloyd George in 1911 of a **National Insurance (NI)** scheme, which, in exchange for docking 4d a week from their wages, insured low-paid workers against sickness and unemployment (see 8.3.1).

When this modest measure was introduced, the concept of a comprehensive NHS was still a pipe dream. But in 1941, the wartime national government commissioned Liberal economist William Beveridge to chair an interdepartmental committee on social insurance and allied services. Its report, published a year later, would form the blueprint for the NHS and the all-encompassing 'welfare state' of which it became part.

The Health Minister entrusted with launching the NHS was Aneurin 'Nye' Bevan, whose vision was inspired by his memories of witnessing the suffering of steelworkers and miners in his native Tredegar, south-east Wales, as a younger man, and the work that voluntary societies and charity-funded cottage hospitals had done to care for such people. He reputedly modelled the NHS on the Tredegar Medical Aid Society, a community-run healthcare collective set up in 1874.

With no pre-existing national-level template for the NHS, Bevan initially had a fight on his hands persuading family doctors and consultants—previously used to setting their own pay and working conditions—to become involved. In the end, he did so by offering them generous contracts that, by his own admission, 'stuffed their mouths with gold'. When he triumphantly unveiled the new NHS at its inaugural outlet, Park Hospital in Manchester, on 5 July 1948, Bevan declared:

> ‘We now have the moral leadership of the world.’

Although Bevan's vision of a health service for all was largely fulfilled, the economics of providing universal healthcare on such a scale would soon start eating away at some of its guiding principles—notably that of universal free access to treatment, regardless of ability to pay. In May 1951, buffeted by global economic turbulence and its dependence on US loans to finance its social security programme, Labour reluctantly introduced the first NHS charges—for spectacles and dentures. Nominal general charges for prescriptions and dentistry followed a year later—much to the disgust of Bevan, who promptly resigned from the government.

6.1.1 How the NHS is funded

Although the proportion of Britain's gross domestic product (GDP) (see 7.1.5) ploughed into the NHS each year has varied wildly between governments

—with Labour traditionally investing more, even if not always wisely—the general breakdown of sources from which this investment derives has remained broadly the same since the early 1950s. Around 80 per cent comes from general taxation (income tax, VAT, duties on tobacco and alcohol) and the remaining 20 per cent from:

- an NHS element to NI contributions;
- charges to patients for drugs (prescriptions) and treatment;
- income from land sales and income-generation schemes; and
- funds raised from voluntary sources—for example local hospital appeals.

Given the current direction of health policy, this balance is likely to shift in future years, with substantially more coming from income-generation. One of many controversial measures included in the Health and Social Care Act 2012 was a clause allowing hospitals to earn up to 49 per cent of their future incomes by treating private patients, and within just two years there were indications that some had become so preoccupied with doing this that they were in danger of increasing waiting times for NHS patients requiring treatment. Between 2010–11 and 2013–14, according to *The Guardian*, the Royal Brompton and Harefield Trust alone boosted its private income from £613,000 to £1.5 million.

So politically sensitive is the NHS considered to be—former Tory Chancellor Nigel Lawson once dubbed it the 'nearest thing the English people have to a national religion'—that the Department of Health's annual budget has been consistently 'ring-fenced' since 2010, in defiance of cuts of up to 51 per cent weathered by other ministries. Despite this, critics argue that the estimated £3 billion cost of its most recent reorganization, in 2012–13, means that its actual working budget is slowly slipping behind those of other comparable health services overseas, and that a huge step-change increase in funding will be required in the coming years if it is to meet rising costs and growing demands for new treatments, while adapting to the needs of a rapidly ageing population. For the 2017–18 financial year, the total NHS budget in England is £106.4bn—up from £105bn the previous year. In Scotland, Wales, and Northern Ireland—where NHS spending is devolved—the 2016–17 budgets were approximately £13bn, £7bn, and £5bn respectively.

6.2 The end of the post-war consensus and the birth of NHS markets

For forty years or more, the NHS retained largely the same structure: it was funded centrally through taxation, with ministers and civil servants filtering money down to hospitals, surgeries, and ambulance services. Of the tens of thousands of nurses, doctors, paramedics, cleaners, and catering staff working across the health service, most were on the government's payroll.

But a series of institutional reforms since the late 1980s has transformed the NHS into a different organization altogether. Nowadays, most family doctors—or GPs—are self-employed; many specialists work as freelance locums, moving from hospital to hospital (and between public and private sectors) as demand arises; and junior doctors, nurses, and care workers are increasingly hired through private agencies, rather than as full-time NHS employees. Catering, cleaning, and security workers are routinely supplied by outside contractors, and even treatment itself is increasingly contracted out to external and/or commercial providers.

So how and why did this dramatic turnabout in the day-to-day running of the NHS arise, and who is responsible for running the modern-day health service?

It is impossible to understand the shape of the NHS today without first examining the emergence of the 'internal market'. As long ago as 1973, the National Health Service Reorganization Act, spearheaded by then Conservative Health and Social Security Secretary Keith Joseph (an architect of 'Thatcherism'), aimed to shake up the NHS by introducing a more efficient management structure, with 'generalist' managers joining existing clinical experts on hospital boards and incentives to generate revenue by letting out unused wards to private providers. These themes were revisited a decade later when, alarmed at the escalating cost of NHS treatment and wage bills, a more radical Tory administration led by Margaret Thatcher commissioned a series of reviews and inquiries by high-powered business leaders, which ultimately led to the creation of the 'internal market'.

The Act that finally established the internal market (and defined the term for the first time) was the National Health Service and Community Care Act 1990. It ushered in a phased reorganization resulting in the following **internal market** structure:

- Hospitals, mental health units, ambulance services, and other NHS 'providers' became **NHS trusts**—with their own management boards, incorporating both practitioners (consultants/other senior clinicians) and general managers charged with improving efficiency.
- GPs were invited to become *fund-holders*—'opting out' of control by *district health authorities (DHAs)* (the NHS administration 'on the ground') to manage their own budgets.
- GP fund-holding practices, DHAs, and *family health service authorities (FHSAs)* were redefined as 'purchasers' of NHS care on their patients' behalf. While GPs would now focus on *primary care*—providing 'first port of call' treatments such as diagnoses and vaccinations, and purchasing

Figure 6.1 How the Conservatives' NHS internal market was structured

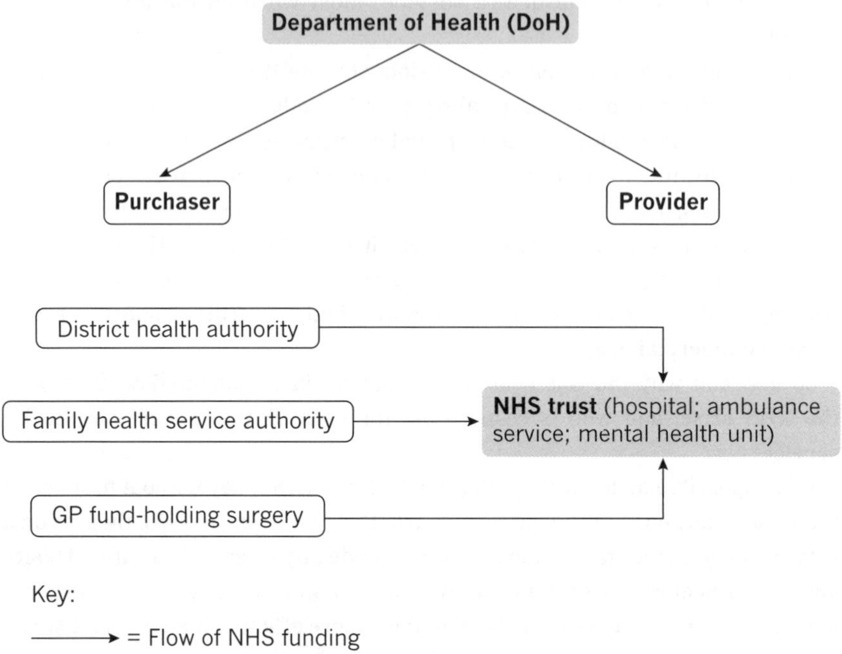

Source: Article courtesy of the BMA—British Medical Association.

BMA, (2014), Commissioning structure [ONLINE]. Available at: http://bma.org.uk/commissioning [Accessed 1 October 2014]

X-rays, tests, and small operations for their patients when needed—FHSAs would buy in other community-based services, with DHAs 'purchasing' acute hospital services like A&E facilities. Though these initial NHS market reforms never fully took off under the Thatcher or Major governments—and were repeatedly modified and reinvented by Labour under Tony Blair—they set the template for all subsequent structural realignments to date, especially in England. The original internal market structure is illustrated in Figure 6.1.

6.2.1 The Health and Social Care Act 2012 and today's NHS internal–external market

By the time the Conservatives returned to power, initially in coalition with the Liberal Democrats, an NHS internal market was firmly embedded in England (though not in Wales or Scotland, where variations of the old-style, more centralized, structure had been reintroduced since devolution—see 6.2.3). However, the original Tory concept of healthcare being 'purchased' by individual fund-holding GP practices had long been supplanted by a more collaborative approach to buying in services—a process Labour rebranded 'commissioning'. Under this system, organizations representing *all* practices in an area—*primary care trusts (PCTs)*—budgeted for and commissioned secondary services from NHS trusts collectively. Moreover, PCTs involved not only GPs themselves, but district nurses, midwives, health visitors, and other community-based professionals.

Shortly after the 2010 election, however, then Tory Health Secretary Andrew Lansley announced a sweeping NHS reorganization, under which GPs in England would assume more direct control of commissioning than ever. Although the individual fund-holder element of the original internal market remains a thing of the past, today's GP-led **clinical commissioning groups (CCGs)** wield more clout than either GP fund-holders or PCTs before them. Unlike fund-holding—an *optional* setup under which some practices chose to manage their own budgets but others did not—GPs' involvement in CCGs is mandatory. CCGs also commission the overwhelming majority of secondary services, rather than sharing purchasing duties with other local bodies, as fund-holders did with the long since defunct strategic health authorities (SHAs) responsible for allocating resources to practices that chose not to become fund-holders. Unlike Labour's PCTs, meanwhile, CCGs are also in charge of commissioning some *primary* as well as secondary services, creating the potential for conflicts of interest should GPs be seen to effectively commission themselves. This system—known as 'co-commissioning'—was introduced after the NHS Five-Year Forward View, published in October 2014. Mr Lansley's original plan to grant CCGs even greater freedom was watered down, however, during the Health and Social Care Act 2012's bumpy ride through Parliament (particularly in the House of Lords). As a result, in many respects today's CCGs face as much local scrutiny as PCTs did under Labour. The final shape of the present commissioning structure in England and the main bodies comprising the new healthcare hierarchy are as follows:

- **NHS England** (formerly the *NHS Commissioning Board*) is a national quango responsible for commissioning primary care—from GPs, dentists, pharmacists, etc.—and some specialist services, including maternity, cardiac, and A&E units, at both national and regional levels. It convenes *clinical senates* to provide medical advice on its commissioning plans and *clinical networks* to advise on service integration.
- **Clinical commissioning groups (CCGs)** replaced PCTs in April 2013 and receive the £65 billion-plus a year they spend on their patients' behalf via NHS England. Though primarily GP-led, the 211 CCGs now also involve other community-based professionals, including nurses.
- **Health and wellbeing boards (HWBs)** are local forums set up by all 130 'upper-tier' English local authorities (county councils and unitary

authorities—see Chapter 10) to bring together all commissioners of health and social care in each area, along with local Healthwatch branches (see 6.2.2), to promote integrated approaches to improving health. Boards include elected local councillors.

- **NHS trusts** remain the principal secondary care providers. All acute and/or emergency hospitals (or groups of hospitals), NHS mental health service providers, and ambulance services are NHS trusts. Under reforms introduced by Tony Blair's government, 152 NHS trusts have become 'self-governing' NHS **foundation trusts**, which, like CCGs, manage their own budgets, recruit their own staff, and have greater autonomy over their day-to-day decision-making.
- **Public Health England (PHE)** is an executive agency of the Department of Health launched to promote healthier lifestyles, funding £4 billion worth of public health initiatives across England each year. Public health services are now commissioned by councils from ring-fenced budgets (see 11.2.1.1) or the NHS at local level, using PHE finance.

The, at times, overlapping spheres of responsibility ushered in by this radically restructured NHS has led to significant tensions, rivalries—and buck-passing. In August 2016, a furious legal row erupted between NHS England and local authorities over which of them was statutorily required to finance a new HIV prevention drug called PrEP (pre-exposure prophylaxis). With both sides facing dwindling real-terms budgets, neither was keen to accept it was responsible, with the result that the High Court intervened to determine where authority lay to fund the treatment. In a case brought by the National AIDS Trust, it decided the buck stopped with NHS England (to the relief of town halls everywhere). In December 2016 NHS England reluctantly agreed to fund the new drugs after the ruling was upheld by the Court of Appeal.

The single most controversial innovation of the 2012 Act, however, is not immediately apparent from this outline structure. This is the fact that, unlike under previous reorganizations, secondary care today may be commissioned from 'any qualified provider'—a (to critics) catch-all term which has since allowed major commercial companies, such as US-based United Healthcare and Virgin Care, to compete for CCG contracts alongside NHS trusts and voluntary-sector bodies. Though opponents of the 2012 Act scored a symbolic victory by persuading ministers to rephrase this term from 'any *willing* provider'—as used in their original Bill—a number of concerns about questionable private-sector involvement in the English NHS have since arisen. As far back as September 2011, while the reforms were still battling their way through Parliament, *The Guardian* used the Freedom of Information Act (see Chapter 19) to obtain details of top-level talks that were already under way between the Department of Health (DoH), NHS managers, and overseas-based private health firms McKinsey and Helios about 'potential opportunities in London'. More disturbingly, a number of stories have since emerged of 'privatization' experiments that have proved highly costly and far from adequate in their outcomes: as recently as April 2016 *The Liverpool Echo* revealed that SSC Health, a private company contracted to run thirty GP practices across Liverpool and Sefton, had parted company with the NHS after charging it £26.7m. The firm's stewardship had provoked complaints from patients forced to queue in the street for appointments at one practice in Toxteth—one of several issues that led to the surgeries being placed in 'special measures' by the health service regulator, the Care Quality Commission (CQC) (**see** 6.2.2). Most controversial of all, however, was the ground-breaking public–private partnership (PPP) contract (see 7.6) signed in February 2012 (with ministerial approval) by Circle Partnership and Hinchingbrooke Hospital, Huntingdon (coincidentally, Mr Major's former constituency). Circle was tasked with introducing savings to turn around the trust's £40 million debt, in return for which it would keep the first £2 million of any 'profit' generated by the hospital, a quarter of all subsequent surpluses up to £6 million, and a third of those between £6 million and £10 million. Barely three years later, the deal collapsed after a CQC inspection rated Hinchingbrooke Health Care NHS Trust 'inadequate' and Circle boss Steve Melton was forced to admit that real-terms government spending cuts, combined with rising demand for treatments, had prevented his company from turning the hospital's finances around.

Leaving aside the lingering debate around the involvement of 'qualified' private providers, the structure of England's NHS has continued to be tweaked since the 2012 Act. Of greatest significance has been the granting of a previously undreamt-of level of devolution in management, budgetary control, and commissioning to metropolitan areas, beginning with Greater Manchester—which some see as yet another (even more radical) reorganization in all but name (*see 6.2.4*). On a more nationwide scale, 2015 saw the introduction of *vanguard sites*. These are individual NHS or voluntary-sector organizations, or partnerships of two or more, that are invited to pioneer new models of service delivery, including ones seeking to combine elements of healthcare and social care (the latter traditionally provided by local authorities, rather than the NHS—*see Chapter 17*). To date, fifty vanguard sites have been launched, charged with developing everything from more integrated primary and acute care services, to improved health provision in care homes, to new 'urgent care' support designed to ease the strain on hospital accident and emergency departments.

As of 1 April 2016, there has also been one further significant structural adjustment in the English NHS. This is the absorption of two organizations charged with overseeing the performance of, respectively, individual trusts and foundation trusts—the *NHS Trust Development Authority* and *Monitor*—into a single overarching body: **NHS Improvement**. In simple terms, the new body's role is to ensure that standards of secondary care and treatment are consistent in the health service, no matter which provider is delivering them: an NHS trust, foundation trust, private company, or charity. It has been introduced in response to mounting concerns about uneven, and at times woefully inadequate, standards of care offered by some public- and private-sector providers—as dramatically epitomized by the extreme neglect suffered by elderly patients at Stafford Hospital (see 6.2.2).

6.2.2 Regulation of the NHS in England

In addition to the oversight roles performed by bodies like Public Health England and NHS Improvement, today's English health service is regulated by a variety of organizations—including some devoted to highly specialist areas. These range from the Human Tissue Authority (HTA), which regulates how organs and tissue are used and stored in the NHS, to the Professional Standards Authority (PSA), which ensures that all medical staff working in the health service are fully registered and qualified to the required standards. The overarching regulatory system for healthcare providers, however, currently falls to three principal organizations:

- **The Care Quality Commission (CQC)**—this is the joint inspectorate for health and social care (two traditionally separate areas of policy which the present government is seeking to combine by 2020—see 6.2.4). It regularly visits GP surgeries, hospitals, care homes, dentists, and other community health providers to observe and grade the levels of service they are delivering. Like other inspection bodies, it publishes its findings, classifying providers as 'outstanding', 'good', 'requiring improvement', or 'inadequate'. The CQC's hospital inspection operation is headed up by a *Chief Inspector of Hospitals*, while regulation of GP and dental practices is ultimately the responsibility of a *Chief Inspector of General Practice*. The CQC may issue trusts, practices, or other errant providers with fines, fixed penalties, and enforcement notices for breaking the terms of their registrations. It can even withdraw NHS licences from acute hospitals, surgeries, and care homes that persistently fail cleanliness inspections.
- **Healthwatch England**—a statutory 'watchdog' with local branches based in all 152 upper-tier English local authority areas (unitary and county councils), this patient-led organization canvasses the views and experiences—and voices the complaints—of individuals who use the NHS, and can help hold health commissioners and providers to account by collecting performance data, liaising with the media, and through its presence on local HWBs (see 6.2.1). Healthwatch is the latest in a succession of

'patient-led' advocacy bodies in the NHS, ranging from the *community health councils (CHCs)*, which ran from the 1970s to 1990s, to the *local involvement networks* (*LINks*) established by Labour in 2008 but abolished in 2013.

- **The National Institute for Health and Care Excellence (NICE)**—initially designated a 'special health authority', NICE was made a non-departmental body (quango) by the Coalition government in 2013. Its main role is to approve drugs and treatments for use by the NHS and to publish national guidelines designed to improve and harmonize standards of health and social care across the country. Its name was changed from the National Institute for Health and *Clinical* Excellence in 2013, to reflect the widening of its remit to embrace social care as well as the NHS (see Chapter 17).

On entering office as Health Secretary in September 2012, Mr Lansley's successor, Jeremy Hunt, lost little time in styling his role as that of 'patient's advocate'—and, to that end, making reform of NHS regulation a driving mission. The first sign of his stamping a distinctive mark on the health service came in February 2013, following a damning report into institutionalized neglect and high mortality rates at Stafford Hospital between 2005 and 2008. The inquiry, led by Robert Francis QC, found that hundreds of patients (by some estimates, between 400 and 1,200) had been allowed to die unnecessarily because of a hospital culture obsessed with chasing tick-box targets at the expense of providing high-quality care. Among the lurid revelations to emerge from this and an earlier investigation by the CQC's precursor, the Healthcare Commission, was that some patients had been left for hours in their own urine and forced to drink water out of vases because they could not attract staff's attention. Ironically (as is so often the case in such circumstances), the resulting Francis Report made 290 recommendations for 'fundamental change'— each with the potential to lead to further box-ticking, if implemented on the ground by managers and front-line staff. The main ones were:

- the merger of regulation of both health and social care into a single body;
- introduction of a new code of conduct for senior managers, who would be disqualified if they failed to keep to it; and
- increased focus in staff recruitment on care and compassion, with a new 'aptitude test' to be completed by all recruits and regular checks introduced on doctors' competence.

Significantly, Mr Francis also condemned repeated NHS reorganizations as 'remote' and 'counterproductive'—a pointed aside at Mr Lansley's reforms on the eve of their rollout.

Mr Cameron's immediate response to the Francis Report was to apologize to affected families and announce a further five investigations of hospital trusts: in Colchester, Tameside, Blackpool, Basildon and Thurrock, and East Lancashire. Although at pains to avoid the 'elephant trap' of introducing yet more NHS regulation by formally implementing all of the Francis recommendations, Mr Hunt has since introduced a major shake-up of the routine hospital inspections regime, headed by new 'chief inspectors' modelled on the long-standing ones for schools and prisons. The first Chief Inspector for Hospitals (described by Mr Hunt as *primus inter pares* among NHS regulators) was leading cancer specialist Professor Sir Mike Richards, who wasted little time in sending a warning shot across the bows of NHS trusts by announcing that, like Ofsted (see 14.3.1), he would be holding both 'unannounced' and 'announced' inspections, and placing hospitals in need of drastic improvement into 'special measures', like failing schools (see Table 14.5). His new regime was initially introduced across eighteen hospital trusts—six regarded as 'high risk', six 'low risk', and the remainder 'mixed'—and has now been rolled out nationwide. The new, tougher CQC has since introduced a special measures regime for under-performing GP practices, and thirteen had already been placed in this category by mid-2015, after being rated 'inadequate' by inspectors (though, significantly, eight of these had made substantial improvements within six months). However, amid growing concern about mounting trust deficits (see 6.3.2), a minor respite from the 'stick' approach to improving performance was announced by NHS England in July 2016, when its head, Sir Mike Richards, opted to abandon fines for hospitals that fail to meet their waiting time targets for treating accident and emergency (A&E) patients, and replace them with a 'carrot-based' approach, under which those meeting or exceeding expectations would be rewarded with extra money.

The performance of local NHS services is further monitored by **health service scrutiny committees** set up by county councils and unitary authorities (see Chapter 10). These comprise around fifteen members, including chairpersons and vice-chairpersons. Membership is drawn not only from these authorities, but also from local districts or boroughs and relevant voluntary organizations, including Age Concern, the National Society for the Prevention of Cruelty to Children (NSPCC), and the National Association for Mental Health (Mind).

Introducing new regulatory and inspection regimes is symbolic of Mr Hunt's distinctive approach to running the DoH—which has seen him often openly castigate the NHS for its failings, as if from the position of a detached observer, rather than championing and defending it in the vein popularized by previous Health Secretaries. In March 2014, he unveiled yet another element of his drive to improve hospital performance, by asking NHS trust managers to join a 'Sign up to Safety' campaign to halve the risk of patients suffering 'avoidable harm'—such as medication errors, bedsores, and blood clots—by 2016–17. Three months later, he launched a new 'patient safety' section on the existing NHS Choices website, www.nhs.uk, on which the public can check levels of clinical competence at their local hospitals and compare them to those elsewhere. This came as figures revealed that one in five trusts were still failing to own up and/or adequately respond to breaches of patient safety.

Before appealing to the CQC (see 6.2.2), anyone dissatisfied with his or her NHS care may make a formal complaint, initially at local level, and his or her case may be referred to one of four ombudsmen—one each for England, Scotland, Wales, and Northern Ireland. In England, complaints are handled by the Parliamentary and Health Service Ombudsman; in Wales, the Public Services Ombudsman for Wales; in Scotland, the Scottish Public Services Ombudsman; and in Northern Ireland, the Northern Ireland Ombudsman.

Each ombudsman produces an annual report for consideration by its national assembly or parliament, and handles complaints in relation to:

- failure in NHS service standards;
- failure to provide a service 'to which a person is entitled';
- maladministration by an NHS body; and
- failure in the exercise of clinical judgment by hospitals or GPs.

Complaints are handled according to the sequence outlined in table 6A to be found on the **Online Resource Centre**.

6.2.3 From National Health Service to national health *services*: devolution in the NHS

The slow-burn fragmentation of the old centralized NHS structure in England into ever-evolving configurations of localized (if interdependent) sub-structures has not been replicated throughout the UK. Devolution in the nations has given Scotland, Wales, and Northern Ireland the freedom to depart from the English model—and they have largely rejected internal markets, instead reverting to their own variations on the original 'top-down' UK-wide approach. More significantly, in each of the three nations outside England, health and social care—that is, support and treatment given to the elderly, disabled, and those with mental health issues in the community or in care homes—have now been integrated, ending a longstanding apartheid between services traditionally provided by the NHS and those provided by local authorities (councils). As we shall see in 6.2.4, this is a major reform of the NHS in England to which the present UK government is committed.

When it comes to considering devolved NHS structures though, Scotland, Wales, and Northern Ireland are only part of the picture. To further complicate the overall 'NHS map', we could be on the cusp of seeing significant structural changes in some parts of England too, through the rollout of health service devolution in major metropolitan regions—starting with Greater Manchester, which gained control of its own £6bn health and social care budget from 1 April 2016. The following sub-sections give a brief overview of how NHS structures vary from one nation or region to another.

6.2.3.1 NHS Scotland

Responsibility for planning and coordinating health services in Scotland is down to fourteen *health boards (HBs)*, each covering a discrete geographical area. Although, as in England, the term 'commission' is used to describe the way in which the boards acquire services from GPs, dentists, opticians, and pharmacists—all independent contractors, as they always have been south of the border—in other respects, they are a throwback to the more centralized healthcare provision that existed UK-wide prior to the 1980s and 1990s reforms. Rather like the regional health authorities that existed in 1970s England, they not only commission from primary care providers but more or less directly control hospitals and other secondary care services: in other words, the levels of autonomy enjoyed by English NHS trusts, let alone foundation trusts (which have never existed in Scotland), are absent. Crucially, GPs and other primary care providers have no commissioning role—unlike in England. In addition, for all their independent status, primary care contractors are themselves incorporated into the NHS structure through the aegis of thirty-two *health and social care partnerships (HSCPs)* (one for each local authority area)—a term underlining the moves towards integrating health and social care, which HBs and councils were due to have completed by April 2015. At Scottish Government level, policymaking and implementation is shared between no fewer than eight Health and Social Care Directorates.

In terms of regulation, the picture in Scotland is, in some respects, more bureaucratic than in England—being a throwback to the times before the CQC brought together oversight of both health and social care services 'under one roof'. Since 1 April 2011, there have been two regulatory and inspection bodies: *Healthcare Improvement Scotland (HIS)*, which oversees health, and the *Care Inspectorate* (full name: Social Work and Social Care Improvement Scotland), in charge of social services. The latter's relevance to this chapter lies in the fact that, despite primarily being involved in regulating social care, it does have some limited healthcare responsibilities. For instance, both regulators work together to carry out joint inspections of all services for older people. Significantly, as in the Welsh system, regulation of health and social care providers is also more comprehensive than in England: whereas the English regulators only inspect private- and voluntary-sector providers if they are contracted to deliver services on behalf of the NHS or councils, in Scotland and

Wales the statutory regulators routinely inspect independent hospitals, clinics, and other providers.

6.2.3.2 NHS Wales

Of all the devolved nations, it is Wales that has adopted a model most closely resembling the old-style centralized structure which used to apply throughout Britain. In 2009 the pre-existing system based on the English internal market was replaced with a drastically simplified structure. Seven *health boards (HBs)* now plan and deliver NHS care in a unified way—in place of the twenty-two HBs and seven NHS trusts that preceded them and, together, preserved the distinction between commissioners and providers now embedded in England. The three surviving NHS trusts in Wales, rather than being locally or regionally based, have an 'all-Wales' focus and remits for overseeing specific aspects of health policy: they are *Public Health Wales* (an equivalent of the equally new Public Health England), a single Welsh Ambulance Services Trust, and Velindre NHS Trust, which specializes in cancer care and support services. Further recalling the old English system, patient oversight of Welsh health services is carried out by seven surviving *community health councils (CHCs)*, while the ministry responsible for health is the Department for Health and Social Services (DHSS)—an echo of the UK-wide Department of Health and Social *Security* which once administered both the NHS and welfare benefits. As in Scotland, the social services aspect of Wales' DHSS reflects the fact that health and social care are now closely integrated.

Also like Scotland, though health and social care are increasingly being brought under one roof, the Welsh regulatory system is bipartite: *Healthcare Inspectorate Wales (HIW)* covers health services, while the *Care and Social Services Inspectorate Wales (CSSIW)* handles social care.

6.2.3.3 The NHS in Northern Ireland

So closely integrated is health and social care provision in Northern Ireland that the NHS itself has a different name in the province: *Health and Social Care (HSC)*. In terms of its internal commissioning structure, HSC is something of a hybrid of the Scottish, Welsh, and English systems—though it is closer to the old UK-wide NHS than the more marketized system currently operating in England. As in all the other nations, health (and social) care on the ground is divided between primary (GPs, dentists, etc.) and secondary providers (in this case, five *health and social care trusts*, each covering a wide geographical area, as well as one ambulance trust). There is a single *Health and Social Care Board (HSCB)*, as opposed to the fifteen boards in Scotland and seven in Wales—but, while the board does not directly control hospitals or other providers (as they do in Scotland), it is responsible for commissioning *all* healthcare for the whole of Northern Ireland, whether secondary or primary. Although its work is divided internally between five *local commissioning groups (LCGs)* covering areas contiguous with the trusts, unlike in England GPs and other primary care providers only have limited commissioning powers, through the aegis of sub-sets of the LCGs called *primary care partnerships (PCPs)*. At present, these have no involvement in managing budgets—unlike in England. A recent innovation has been the move towards a further level of integration in health and social care: the effective 'merger' of some aspects of primary and secondary care by relocating some services from acute settings like hospitals into community ones like GP surgeries and clinics, where multidisciplinary teams of professionals work together in *integrated care partnerships (ICPs)*. As in the other nations, Northern Ireland has its own quango responsible for improving public health: the *Public Health Agency*.

Northern Ireland is unique among the three devolved nations in that it has rationalized its regulatory system to reflect the integration of health and social care, with a single body, *Regulation and Quality Improvement Authority (RQIA)*, responsible for both remits.

6.2.4 Towards a regional and integrated NHS in England?

By far the biggest recent 'twist' in the ongoing NHS revolution in England unfolded just weeks before the May 2015 general election. With Opposition parties preoccupied with campaigning, under the radar the Treasury reached an agreement with the Greater Manchester Combined Authority. This newly formed metropolitan council was seen by the then Chancellor George Osborne as an engine of his plan to shift Britain's centre of economic gravity away from the City of London by forging a 'northern powerhouse'. To this end, it was handed full control for planning and delivering health and social care in the north-west conurbation. This pioneering *regional* devolution in the NHS could matched by radically extended powers over other service areas in coming years, in return for Greater Manchester adopting a directly elected mayor modelled on those already established in London and other major cities.

On 1 April 2016, NHS devolution in Manchester came into effect, and the Greater Manchester authority now controls an annual budget of £6bn. Some thirty-seven separate NHS organizations have come together to develop a new, more integrated model of combined health and social care along the lines of those already in place in the devolved nations. The stated aim is twofold: to bring together aspects of primary and secondary care and treat more people in community settings rather than hospitals (as in Northern Ireland); and to develop a model for combined health and social care along the lines of those already in place in all three devolved nations, that might be adopted across the rest of England by the government's stated target date of 2020.

In terms of the structure it has adopted, the Greater Manchester authority has signalled a break with other recent NHS reorganizations, by resolving to create 'no extra bodies or layers of management'. Indeed, the shape of the health service across the conurbation is in the process of being rationalized, with an overarching *Health and Social Care Partnership Board* in charge of its overall management. Beneath this, a single *Joint Commissioning Board*—comprising representatives of CCGs, Manchester's ten local authorities, and NHS England—has effectively taken charge of all commissioning, replacing the more fragmented CCG-led system introduced nationwide in 2013. To this end, the twelve pre-existing CCGs in Greater Manchester have been reduced in number to just four, and charged with working more collaboratively in future.

The success or failure of these reforms is likely to set the template for NHS devolution to other combined authorities, as well as councils covering non-metropolitan areas. By March 2016, some thirty-four city-based and regional authorities had already submitted bids for enhanced devolved powers, under the terms of the Cities and Local Government Devolution Act 2016. Of these, nine had provisionally agreed deals with the government (all but Cornwall involving the introduction of elected mayors) and six were in the process of taking control of at least some aspects of their own NHS provision—from mental health services, in the case of the West Midlands Combined Authority, to more integrated models of health and social care in the cases of Cornwall County Council and the North East Combined Authority.

Devolving NHS services in such ways is all part of a bigger master plan which, if successful, could signal the culmination of several strands of the Conservatives' underlying strategy for government since 2010. One of these is the party's ongoing pursuit of an answer to the so-called 'English Question' (see 1.3.6). The tension arises from the fact that, while Scotland, Wales, and Northern Ireland each have their own parliamentary assemblies, empowered to take many decisions about how their countries are governed, the same does not apply in England. Another is its ongoing drive to roll out elected mayors and ever-greater devolution in public services (an aim viewed with scepticism by those who fear that devolving service commissioning and delivery can lead to privatization and widening postcode lotteries—see 6.3.1). Of most significance in the context of this particular chapter, though, is Mr Hunt's recent commitment to fully integrate NHS healthcare and social care across England by 2020, backed by Mr Osborne's decision in his 2015 Spending Review to relax his years-long freeze on council tax by introducing a 2 per cent 'social care precept' (see 11.2.4.3). Whether this will leave England with the kind of 'National Care Service' ex-Labour Health Secretary Andy Burnham often mooted—an issue explored in Chapter 16—remains unclear.

6.3 The future of the NHS: the big debates and issues

The emergence of sharp differences in the way the NHS is structured and administered in different parts of the UK has brought with it notable disparities in the way patients access and experience healthcare—as well as unintended consequences both for them and the organizations providing it. Most markedly, the ongoing drive towards more local autonomy and increased commissioning from private-sector providers in the English NHS has led to significant inequities opening up in the nature and quality of services available from one CCG area to another, let alone between England and its neighbouring countries. In this section, we will examine some of these key issues and tensions.

6.3.1 The 'postcode lottery' and treatment rationing

Despite disagreements over the wisdom of imposing an internal market on the English NHS, by the time it was introduced there was widespread agreement about one thing: reform of the original 'top-down' health service structure was long overdue, to cater for the changing needs of a society in which ever-clearer disparities existed between different areas, in terms of average income, age, healthcare needs, and other demographic factors. Nonetheless, the decision to grant increased autonomy to the bodies then charged with administering the NHS locally (*district health authorities* (*DHAs*) and individual fund-holding GPs) would have one early negative outcome: the steady emergence of significant variations in the level and/or nature of treatment available to people with the same conditions living in different locations. This ever-worsening trend—which has led many to question whether the NHS can any longer be described as a 'national' health service in terms of the consistency of the care it offers—has become known as the **postcode lottery**.

An early cause célèbre for those opposing delegation of funding decisions to local level was the case of beta interferon—an expensive drug that, according to some experts, dramatically decreases the number of relapses suffered by people with multiple sclerosis. In the early 1990s, it emerged that many DHAs were refusing to fund beta interferon on the NHS, arguing that the £10,000-a-year cost per patient would be better spent on other treatments, such as physiotherapy. Its supporters claimed that prescribing the medicine early could save the NHS money in the long run, by delaying the need for residential or palliative care. Other notorious postcode lotteries include the long-standing differential availability of fertility treatment for childless couples from one commissioning area to another, and the ever more variable patchwork of services available to patients whose 'lifestyle choices' are seen to be partly responsible for their medical needs—for example, those who smoke heavily or are obese. By way of example, in November 2005 it emerged that Ipswich Hospital NHS Trust and several Suffolk primary care trusts (PCTs) were rationing hip and knee replacement operations by refusing to offer them to obese patients, unless there were exceptional circumstances. Dr Brian Keeble, Director of Public Health for Ipswich PCT, justified the decision by telling the press it was for patients' own good, because overweight people 'do worse after operations' and hip replacements might fail. But critics of the move condemned it as discrimination against patients whose conditions were judged to be self-inflicted.

The postcode lottery is now such a political issue that ministers have increasingly been drawn into disputes over individual cases of patients denied treatment. So potentially damaging had the issue become by June 2008 that the then Health Secretary Alan Johnson pledged to ban PCTs from denying patients costly treatments approved by NICE. Despite this, inequities remain, and some fear that real-terms budget cuts, combined with the recent introduction of wholesale GP commissioning, could see widening disparities emerge in primary health provision from area to area. In June 2012, a Freedom of Information Act request by *GP Magazine* revealed that nine out of ten NHS trusts were already rationing certain operations—including tonsillectomies and cataract surgery (89 and 66 per cent of trusts respectively). While ministers maintained that rationing on grounds of cost (as opposed to clinical judgment) was unacceptable, David Stout, Deputy Chief Executive of the NHS Confederation, which represents PCTs, argued that restrictions were justified in some cases, because of the 'considerable financial pressures and scarce resources' engendered by the then Coalition's deficit-reduction programme (see 7.1.2).

6.3.1.1 The postcode lottery in NHS charges

It is not only NHS treatment that is subject to the vagaries of a postcode lottery. Devolution in the health service has also allowed huge disparities to open up between individual nations in terms of whether, and to what extent, they levy charges on patients. For instance, while adults visiting their dentist or optician for a check-up in England expect to pay £25 or more a time (aside from any treatment which may be judged necessary), in Scotland these charges do not apply. More significantly perhaps, in April 2007 the National Assembly for Wales became the first devolved chamber to scrap prescription charges, having previously halved them. The Northern Ireland Assembly followed suit in April 2010 and the Scottish Parliament a year later. As yet, English patients (other than children, pregnant and new mothers, some benefit claimants, and those with a handful of long-term conditions) still pay. Similarly, all three devolved administrations have abandoned parking charges at NHS hospitals, whereas these routinely apply in England.

6.3.2 Hospital closures, deficits, and the perils of market-centred thinking in the NHS

Pressure to balance the books like commercial companies has become an increasing issue for the constituent bodies in the NHS—particularly acute trusts (hospitals) with foundation status. As far back as the mid-2000s, NHS trusts had begun to accumulate substantial deficits, in their efforts to service rising debts caused, in large part, by interest payments on major building programmes for new hospitals and specialist units funded through private finance initiative (PFI) and PPP deals (see 7.6). Their problems had been exacerbated by the high costs associated with maintaining 'national levels' of care in key areas demanded by the (now defunct) *national service frameworks* introduced by the then Labour government to harmonize NHS provision nationwide. In 2006, then Health Secretary Patricia Hewitt responded to an escalating deficit crisis in some areas by giving debt-ridden trusts permission to borrow money from 'better performing' ones with financial surpluses. Yet still the deficit problem worsens: figures published in June 2014 showed that one in three acute NHS trusts was in debt by 2013–14, compared to one in ten at the time of the 2010 election.

More seriously, it is no longer unheard of for debt-ridden trusts, like struggling companies, to enter administration—a logical extension, argue critics, of the introduction of budgetary independence and the removal of the implicit safety net offered by the unified NHS of old. Symbolically, in mid-2012 South London Healthcare became the first NHS trust to go bankrupt after revealing it faced running up a deficit of between £30m and £75m a year over the following five years, due to cumulative PFI-related debt. This prompted Mr Hunt to swoop in to downgrade the A&E and maternity units at neighbouring Lewisham Hospital, south-east London, in an effort to save it. Indeed, the battle over South London Healthcare—one of at least twenty-three trusts revealed to be on the verge of administration due to multi-million pound debt mountains during 2012 alone—would lead to a controversial legal change with potentially sweeping long-term ramifications for overburdened trusts. After the High Court ruled in October 2013 that he had acted beyond his powers in his South London intervention, Mr Hunt inserted an amendment into the Care Act 2014 known as 'Clause 119'. In brief, this gives the Health Secretary, and **trust special administrators** appointed to act for him or her, executive powers to close or downgrade A&E departments, maternity units, and other hospital services within forty days, and with little public consultation, if neighbouring trusts are suffering financially. Although Clause 119 made it onto the statute book, it provoked storms of protest from an unlikely alliance of Tory backbenchers, Labour, and campaign group 38 Degrees. While in one sense it arguably represented the extreme end of what can transpire when a 'market-centred' approach to running the NHS fails—with financially struggling trusts creating a negative knock-on effect that sends ripples through other parts of the health service—in another it exemplified precisely the kind of direct state intervention that Conservative governments had eschewed for decades. By interfering with the NHS internal market, rather than allowing 'failing' trusts to fail (and potentially close), Mr Hunt sent out the message that a similar fate could befall any trust, however 'successful', should its neighbours be ailing.

6.3.3 Mr Hunt's 'seven-day NHS' and the junior doctors' dispute

One of the most explosive political sagas in the recent history of the NHS in England erupted in 2015, when, in an effort to implement what he dubbed a 'seven-day NHS', Mr Hunt announced plans to radically renegotiate the contracts of both GPs and hospital-based doctors. Although officially the NHS has *always* been a 24/7 health service, a succession of studies published since the 1990s had revealed that, in practice, hospital staffing levels were significantly lower at weekends, meaning that far fewer operations were carried out at weekends and in some cases trusts were offering little more than a glorified emergency service. Meanwhile, GP surgeries (as most people would testify) had long been closed at weekends. More worryingly, some research had shown an apparent correlation between skeleton staffing levels on the wards and higher death rates at weekends among patients admitted for surgery and urgent treatment. As a result, Mr Hunt resolved to persuade not only GPs and specialist consultants to sign up to a new seven-day NHS working routine but to reorganize junior doctors' rotas to incorporate Saturdays and Sundays—and, crucially, on the same rates of pay as weekdays (in other words, abolishing paid 'overtime'). Junior doctors' leaders retorted that, in the absence of a massive new recruitment and training drive, the only way the new arrangement could be made to work would be to force existing staff to work even longer hours than the ninety-plus hours a week said to be typical for many—thereby severely compromising patient safety.

Mr Hunt's no-nonsense proposition provoked the first strike by British doctors in forty years, after the normally temperate British Medical Association (BMA) rejected then prime minister David Cameron's plea to abandon threats of industrial action in January 2016. Although striking doctors initially agreed to maintain cover for emergency care, a fiercer confrontation came when, after the Health Secretary threatened to impose the new contract, regardless of their wishes, they mounted the first *all-out* strike (including withdrawing emergency care) in NHS history. Though a putative deal was agreed early in summer 2016, that July six out of ten junior doctors voted to reject a BMA committee's recommendation that they accept it. Committee chair Dr Johann Malawana, subsequently resigned—and the stage was set for a fresh wave of strikes. Another aspect of the seven-day NHS plans sparked criticism in January 2017, when Professor Helen Stokes-Lampard, chair of the Royal College of GPs, warned family doctors were spread 'far too thin' to open at weekends.

6.3.4 The row over data-sharing

Back in 2010, deficit reduction was also the motivation for Lib Dem and Tory manifesto promises to cut wasteful spending on consultants, managers, and IT projects in the NHS. Once in office, however, the Coalition quickly reneged on a related pledge: to scrap the Summary Care Record (SCR) database, commissioned by Labour to store all electronic patient records centrally so that they could be accessed by NHS professionals working anywhere in England. The Coalition's version of this database—which patients had to proactively 'opt out of' if they wanted their details kept private—began rolling out in April 2010, and by June 2014 more than half of all patients in England had their own summary care records. However, ministers' plans to extend the growing database further, by setting up a single centralized medical record system—and allowing access not only to NHS staff, but also to private companies and voluntary organizations involved in patient care—ran aground in February 2014 after privacy campaigners and consumer groups complained that it could compromise individuals' confidentiality. Amid a wave of negative media coverage, this embryonic system was shelved temporarily, but it has since been revived—under the new brand name 'care.data'. At the time of writing, GP practices in four areas of England (Blackburn with Darwen, Somerset, West Hampshire, and Leeds) were involved in piloting a prototype version that the Conservative government hoped to roll out nationally in the coming years.

Topical feature idea

The following article is taken from the *Torquay Herald Express* of 14 April 2016. It focuses on a furious row over proposals to close down a local community hospital due to local budget pressures. How would you develop this news story into a background feature on the wider implications for hospital services in the area? Who would you approach for interviews and what would you ask them?

Article published by *Torquay Herald Express*, 14 April 2016

'Slash and burn' claims over Paignton Hospital closure rejected

By Tina Crowson

WORRIED Paignton residents have been assured there would be a three-month consultation if health chiefs agree to consider proposals to close the town's hospital.

Patients, residents and union representatives have reacted angrily on social media after confirmation on Wednesday of a move to close the hospital. Unions claimed it was a case of 'slash and burn' hospital inpatient beds.

Torbay MP Kevin Foster said closure was 'not the right answer'.

A Facebook campaign has already been set up to 'save' the hospital.

Health leaders have said the move could increase investment in healthcare facilities closer to home and avoid the need for people to go into hospital.

The Trade Union Group for Torbay and South Devon Torbay Clinical Commissioning group said it had had no notification from the trust on the Paignton Hospital site being at risk of being 'culled'.

Spokesman Paul Raybould said: 'It was the same again with the Closure of St Kilda's in Brixham there was no mention of it at the Joint Negotiating Group of Unions and the integrated care organisation senior management on March 10 at Torbay Hospital.

'We fear other community hospitals may also be at risk with the CCG looking to save money.'

He added: 'The idea that the Clinical Commission Group for Torbay and South Devon have a plan to shut up to 150 beds in Community and Torbay Hospital is not attainable in the time allowed of six years, in fact it is impossible. The new model of care is being rushed through to meet financial pressures.

'It does appear to be slash and burn as far as inpatient beds are concerned and also the new model of care is merely out sourcing clients or residents into private sector providers who are already bursting to seams.'

A spokesman for South Devon and Torbay Clinical Commissioning Group said: 'The draft plans involve moving resources away from hospital beds and into more community support so as to meet rising demand and enable more people to be treated close to or in their own homes.

'The final draft proposals were only signed off last week and we have briefed staff and stakeholders, including the trust's staffside leaders, since then and ahead of the recommendations being published.

'If the proposals are agreed by the CCG Governing Body later this month we will be holding a 12-week consultation, when everyone will be able to comment on the suggested changes and make alternative proposals.'

✶ Current issues

- **The junior doctors' dispute, GP changes, and the pursuit of a 'seven-day NHS'**
  Health Secretary Jeremy Hunt has been embroiled in a bitter dispute with junior hospital doctors and GPs in England over his proposals to force them to accept new

contracts designed to ensure wards operate with the same staffing levels seven days a week and surgeries open at weekends. The row over junior doctors' hours has led to a wave of ongoing strikes.

- **Devolution of the health service to the regions** As of 1 April 2016, the Greater Manchester Combined Authority has taken over full control of the conurbation's £6bn NHS budget from central government, allowing it to potentially reshape local health services to a level never before seen. Other major city regions are also set to take over their NHS budgets in the coming years and months, potentially paving the way for more widespread devolution in the health service.
- **Moves towards integrating health and social care across the UK** Health and social care are now integrated (to a greater or less extent) in all British nations other than England—which Mr Hunt has set on a course to achieve integration by 2020 at the latest. The fullest integration to date exists in Northern Ireland, where the NHS itself is known as Health and Social Care (HSC).

Key points

1. The NHS operates on the principle that it is a 'universal' health service, which can be accessed by British residents 'free at the point of use'.
2. It is funded from a combination of general taxation and National Insurance, in an 80:20 per cent split. At least £60 billion of its annual £100 billion budget in England is under the control of clinical commissioning groups (CCGs).
3. These CCGs comprise GPs and other primary care professionals. They 'commission' secondary care from NHS trusts (hospitals, ambulance services, etc.) and 'any qualified provider' from the private or voluntary sectors. NHS England commissions specialist and A&E units.
4. The NHS internal market is regulated by NHS Improvement, but the quality of health and social care provided by CCGs, NHS trusts, GPs, and other providers is regulated by the Care Quality Commission (CQC).
5. The NHS is structured differently in Scotland, Wales, and Northern Ireland, where there are no foundation (fully autonomous) trusts, and health and social care are integrated.

→ Further reading

Exworthy, M., Mannion, R., and Powell, M. (2016) *Dismantling the NHS? Evaluating the Impact of Health Reforms*, Bristol: Policy Press. **Considered and objective analysis of the impact of the Coalition and Conservatives' market reforms to the NHS.**

Ham, C. (2009) *Health Policy in Britain: The Politics and Organisation of The National Health Service*, 6th edn, Basingstoke: Palgrave Macmillan. **Sixth edition of the**

leading text on the history of the NHS, including updates on Labour's reforms and developments in Scotland, Wales, and Northern Ireland.

Klein, R. (2013) *The New Politics of the NHS: From Creation to Reinvention*, 7th edn, Abingdon: Radcliffe Publishing. **Comprehensive overview of the evolution of the health service, encompassing recent market reforms.**

Leys, C. and Player, S. (2011) *The Plot Against the NHS*, Perth: Merlin Press. **Provocative interrogation of the political agenda underlying the Coalition's reform plans for the NHS, envisaging an emergence of a US-style insurance-based health system.**

Online Resource Centre

www.oxfordtextbooks.co.uk/orc/Morrison5e/

Visit the Online Resource Centre that accompanies this book for web links and regular updates.

7

The Treasury, industry, and the utilities

During the 1992 US presidential election race, James Carville, campaign strategist for the then aspiring Democratic nominee Bill Clinton, coined a phrase that would go down in political folklore. Identifying the issue he judged most crucial to persuading the electorate to back a candidate, he replied: 'The economy, stupid.' This was ever the case in Britain. Although political historians have observed that UK voters do not always switch horses at times of economic crisis (the deep recession of the early 1990s saw John Major return the Conservatives to power, albeit with a drastically reduced majority), perceived economic competence has proved the making of certain prime ministers (Margaret Thatcher, Tony Blair, David Cameron) and mismanagement the downfall of others (Ted Heath, James Callaghan, Gordon Brown).

This chapter explores the work of the two principal government departments charged with overseeing Britain's economy—HM Treasury and the Department for Business, Energy, and Industrial Strategy (BEIS) with particular emphasis on the former. It also examines the remit and composition of the main non-departmental bodies charged with managing specific areas of economic performance, and the structure and regulation of the utility markets.

7.1 The Treasury and Chancellor of the Exchequer

If the prime minister can be said to have a true 'number two', it is less the titular 'Deputy PM' of the day than the minister who holds the government's purse strings: the Chancellor of the Exchequer. Government would grind to a halt were it not for taxes and loans, and it is the Chancellor's job to raise this money. Even the name of the department he or she heads—the Treasury—testifies to his or her authority. And it is no coincidence that the prime minister's own official title is 'First Lord of the Treasury'.

The Chancellor is ultimately responsible for all of the following:

- overseeing government public spending commitments by managing fiscal policy—raising or lowering taxes and investing in public services (schools, hospitals, roads);
- managing national debt—the level of borrowing needed to top up tax revenues to finance government spending programmes;
- promoting economic growth at home and encouraging exports; and
- controlling domestic inflation (rises in the cost of living) and unemployment.

In recognition of the huge responsibility that comes with their post, Chancellors are assisted by the largest ministerial team of any Whitehall department. Unlike most ministries, the Treasury boasts at least three secretaries of state in addition to the Chancellor him or herself: the Chief Secretary to the Treasury, Financial Secretary to the Treasury, and Economic Secretary to the Treasury.

7.1.1 Fiscal policy and taxation

One of the principal means by which British governments attempt to control the economy is through 'tax and spend' tactics—or *fiscal policy*. Based on the writings of Liberal economist John Maynard Keynes, this involves raising or lowering taxation to influence consumer behaviour (and improve the health of the government's finances). A 'Keynesian' approach to tackling inflation might see the Chancellor raise income tax, for example, in order to cut individuals' take-home pay: in other words, spending power. In theory, this will reduce demand for goods and services, thereby curbing price rises. Increasing taxes also boosts government revenue for spending on schools, hospitals and so on, reducing the need to *borrow* money (which increases the UK's Budget deficit and, over time, 'national debt').

Until the 1980s, there was a broad post-war consensus in favour of managing the economy through fiscal policy—although, on balance, this approach tended to be favoured more by Labour than Conservative governments. Labour's enthusiasm arose largely out of its traditional emphasis on taxation as an instrument for redistributing income from higher to lower earners through 'transfer payments', or benefits (see 8.3.1). From the advent of the NHS onwards, Labour also gained a reputation as the 'high tax party' because of its ideological commitment to strong investment in state healthcare and education (which required substantial revenues). Before the Thatcher years, the party also favoured public ownership of many industries and these, too, required huge injections of money to maintain. The Conservatives, in contrast, have traditionally been the party of tax cuts or breaks (particularly for business)—favouring a 'supply side' approach to running the economy that leaves more money in individuals' pockets in the hope of boosting growth through private, rather than public, expenditure. The theory is that keeping taxes as low as possible for everyone (including the rich) can have a 'trickle down' effect on the wider economy, boosting investment and employment that benefits those lower down the scale.

There are two broad forms of taxation: **direct taxes** and **indirect taxes**. Direct taxes are 'up front'—explicitly taken from individuals or businesses as deductions from their basic earnings. The main types are outlined in Table 7.1.

The fact that direct taxation is charged at different rates, according to individuals' or companies' incomes, means that it is often referred to as 'progressive'. By taking into account people's ability to pay, it is seen as fairer than flat-rate charges—such as water bills or television licences—which cost everyone the same, regardless of their earnings. This has not stopped some campaigners arguing for a more once-size-fits-all approach, however. And in light of recent debates about the perceived need to simplify Britain's hideously complex 'tax code' (the rulebook governing how much each individual is charged, based on their precise financial circumstances), the notion of combining income tax with National Insurance (NI) has periodically been revived in Conservative circles, while UKIP has mooted replacing the current banded income tax structure with a 'flat rate' of 31 per cent for everyone earning £11,500 or more.

In contrast to direct taxes, indirect ones are often described as 'regressive'. Unlike income or corporation taxes, they are built into the prices of goods and services that consumers buy (including basic utilities like water and energy). Because these pay-as-you-spend charges—often described as 'hidden' or 'stealth' taxes—are levied at universal rates, they take no account of individuals' ability to pay. The most familiar—VAT, tobacco and alcohol duties, and fuel duty—are set out in Table 7.2.

The British tax system has long been notoriously complex, prompting Mr Osborne to establish a new Office for Tax Simplification in July 2010 to rationalize the then 11,000-page Exchequer Code, ending Britain's 'spaghetti bowl' of tax law. At the time of writing, though, the omens did not look good. A March 2016 report by the Centre for Policy Studies think tank revealed that the length of the code had actually almost doubled since 2009, largely on Mr Osborne's watch—taking it from 5 to 10 million words.

The Treasury's efforts to tackle its other great bugbears—tax evasion and avoidance, together estimated to cost Britain anything up to £120 billion a year—have also had mixed success, despite its frequent threats to scrutinize the accounts of high earners to ensure they are paying their fair share. The issue of 'tax-dodging' has steadily moved up the political agenda since the 2008 financial collapse (see 7.3.4)—not least thanks to campaigns by groups like UK Uncut, highlighting the fact that the annual cost to the Exchequer of those at the top of the pile abusing the tax system is many times greater than that of

Table 7.1 Types and rates of UK direct taxation

Tax	How administered	Rates (2017–18)	Notes
Income tax	Pay-as-you-earn (PAYE) contributions deducted from workers' gross salaries by employers, or retrospective 'self-assessment' payments to HM Revenue and Customs (HMRC) by self-employed.	Personal allowance for those aged under 65: £11,500 as of 2017–18. Personal allowance cut for those earning £100,000 or more by £1 for every £2 adjusted net income is above that level, so no personal allowance for those earning £122,000 or over. Standard rate for those earning up to £33,500 above the personal allowance—or £45,000: 20% (20p in £1) Higher rate for those earning over £45,000: 40% (40p in £1) Additional rate for those earning £150,000 or more: 45% (45p in £1).	'Personal allowance' (the amount a person can earn before paying tax) has risen incrementally each year since 2010, with all those earning less than £10,000 a year taken out of tax altogether (a Lib Dem manifesto pledge) by 2014–15 and further annual rises following since, with aim of hitting £12,500 by 2020 election. Additional age-related allowances for those aged 65–74 and 75 and over scrapped in April 2016. Level at which 40% higher rate kicks in has been lowered incrementally and had reached £31,866 by 2014–15, but is now rising again under the Tories. Additional rate lowered from 50% (50p in £1) in April 2013. Scottish Rate of Income Tax introduced in April 2016, but bands and rates have so far been set at same levels as those in rest of UK.
Corporation tax	Paid by companies on their profits—an 'income tax for companies'.	Rate: 19% (19p in £1) from April 2017—down from 26% (26p in £1) in 2010.	Previous small profits rate for companies with profits of £300,000 or less combined with main rate from 1 April 2015. New unified rate is due to fall to 18% (18p in £1) by April 2020.
Capital gains tax (CGT)	Paid by owners of financial assets, property, and other items, such as expensive jewellery or sports cars, sold for personal gain.	Entrepreneurs' rate: 10% (10p in £1) on first £5m made during lifetime General rate: 10% (10p in £1) Higher taxpayers' rate: 18% (18p in £1).	Debates rage about CGT, in light of mammoth profits made by 'private equity' investors—wealthy speculators who buy underperforming companies, improve their fortunes, and sell them for profit. Labour introduced 18% flat rate for anyone whose gains exceeded £1m (but with 10% 'entrepreneurs' rate' for gains of less than £1m).

(continued)

Table 7.1 *(continued)*

Tax	How administered	Rates (2017–18)	Notes
			George Osborne initially raised it to 28% for higher-rate taxpayers. At same time, entrepreneurs' rate was extended to apply to first £5m of individual's lifetime gains. But since 6 April 2016 general and higher rates have fallen to 10% and 18% respectively.
Inheritance tax (IHT)	'Death duty' paid on value of estates (including financial assets, property, and other valuable items) handed down from deceased to friends/family members by executors of their wills.	Legacies of over £325,000: 40% (40p in £1)—or 36% (36p in £1) for those leaving 10% or more of net estates to charity—since April 2012.	Until recently, IHT was charged at 40% on all estates worth £300,000 or more, but mounting controversy over this low threshold (average house prices were near that level by 2007) prompted Labour to introduce 'exempt transfers' for individuals who leave estates to a spouse, civil partner, or charity. In effect, this means recipients may use both their own and their deceased partners' allowances—doubling their thresholds to £650,000. Labour was widely criticized for 'stealing' Conservative policy. By 2020, total exemptions for married couples will be £1m, after Mr Osborne introduced *transferable main residence allowance* in 2015 allowing married people to leave their individual allowances to their partners/spouses on death. Levels of these transferable allowances will rise from £100,000 to £175,000 between 2017 and 2020.

NOTE: A regularly updated version of this table can be found on the **Online Resource Centre** that accompanies this book.

Table 7.2 Types and rates of UK indirect taxation

Name	How administered	Rates (2016–17)	Notes
Value added tax (VAT)	'Hidden tax' embedded in retail prices of consumer goods	20% (20p in £1)	Reduced rate of 5% for essential items, such as domestic fuel and power, while food, children's clothes, books, newspapers and magazines, and some disability equipment are exempt. During 'credit crunch', Labour cut rate for 13 months from 17.5% (17.5p in £1) to 15% (15p in £1). Coalition raised it in January 2011 to 20% (20p in £1).
Tobacco products duty and alcohol excise duties	Embedded in retail prices of items subject to excise duty	Cigarettes: 16.5% of the retail price of a packet of twenty, plus £196.42 per 1,000 as of 16 March 2016. General beer duty: £18.37 per hectolitre percentage (hect %) of alcohol, plus £8.10 per hect % for lower strength (1.2–2.8%) and £5.48 per hect % for high strength (over 7.5%). Still cider and perry: £38.87 per 100 litres (1.2–7.5%) and £58.75 per 100l (7.5–8.5%). Sparkling cider/perry: £38.87 (1.2–5.5%) and £268.99 (5.5–8.5%). Wine: £85.60 per 100l (1.2–4%), £117.72 (4–5.5%), £277.84 (5.5–15%), and £370.41 (15–22%). Sparkling wine: £268.99 per 100l (5.5–8.5%) and £355.87 (8.5–15%). Spirits: £27.66 per 1l of pure alcohol.	Always controversial among smokers and drinkers, these are higher in Britain than elsewhere in European Union (EU). Duties on alcohol products range widely. Mr Osborne froze tobacco and most alcohol duties in June 2010 Budget, but in March 2014 Budget announced tobacco duty would rise annually by minimum of 2% above retail price index (RPI) to end of parliament. Since 2015, though, most rates have fallen, in response to lobbying from licensing industry.

(continued)

Table 7.2 *(continued)*

Name	How administered	Rates (2016–17)	Notes
Fuel duty	Additional tax added to VAT on motor fuel	Unleaded petrol, diesel, biodiesel, and bioethanol: 58p in £1 per litre since 23 March 2011.	Petrol duties have long proved controversial due to long-running upward trend in underlying prices caused by global peak oil crisis. In 2000, Mr Brown angered farmers and lorry drivers by raising fuel duty—and introducing automatic annual 'fuel tax escalator'. In its last Budget, Labour announced that it was phasing in a proposed 'all-in-one-go' rise of nearly 3p a litre in three stages, but in June 2010 Mr Osborne announced no further rise in fuel duty. He later cut duty by 1p in £1 in his March 2011 Budget and scrapped the escalator, with later planned rises subsequently cancelled.

NOTE: A regularly updated version of this table can be found on the **Online Resource Centre** that accompanies this book.

'benefit fraud' (see 8.3.2.1). Tax evasion and avoidance returned to the top of the political agenda in March 2016, with the release of the so-called 'Panama Papers'. This dossier of 1.5 million confidential documents—leaked anonymously from the offices of offshore law firm Mossack Fonseca—revealed a labyrinthine trail of secretive funds and loopholes being used by some of the world's richest people, including twelve national leaders and a further 141 politicians, to avoid paying their fair share of tax. Those alleged to have taken advantage included Russian president Vladimir Putin, Petro Poroshenko, president of Ukraine, and David Cameron's late father, Ian, who set up a trust for this purpose called Blairmore Holdings. Though the then prime minister was forced to concede he himself had owned shares worth £31,500 in the trust, he used a defiant Commons statement to insist that he had disposed of them before becoming premier in 2010, and that his family would no longer benefit from his father's arrangements. Shortly after 'Panama-gate' erupted, the government confirmed the launch of a long-awaited *Central Register of Company Beneficiaries* in offshore funds held in territories including the British Virgin Islands and Cayman Islands—two Commonwealth countries (see 9.8.6) widely recognized as tax havens. However, his admission that the register would only be made available to tax authorities, rather than the general public (as originally promised in 2013) ensured that the issue of tax avoidance and evasion continued to dominate headlines. Soon after, *The Guardian* began running a series of investigations into the 'dirty money' being invested in London's high-end property market by overseas billionaires keen to avoid paying tax. It remains to be seen how long this pattern will continue, though, now that a new *Register of Beneficial Ownership* requiring overseas investors to declare their holdings in UK property has come into force.

While on this occasion government action was announced by Mr Cameron, major tax and public spending announcements are customarily reserved for the Budget (see 7.2.1). In 1997, though, Mr Brown introduced an innovation designed to set out his spending plans for up to three years at a time: the **spending review**. Although keen to create the appearance of greater financial transparency, he also sought to encourage individual spending departments dependent on Treasury handouts to plan in a long-term way, rather than year to year as previously. Reviews have generally been held on a three-yearly cycle ever since, with less frequent (but more far-reaching) *Comprehensive Spending Reviews (CSRs)* occurring so far on only four occasions (in 1998, 2007, 2010, and 2015).

7.1.2 Managing national debt

National debt—sometimes referred to as 'public', 'government', or 'sovereign' debt (see 9.4.3)—is the total of all credit owed at any one time by every level of government (or government-owned institution) in a given state. Other than raising taxes, governments' main tool for financing public spending is borrowing. On a month-by-month basis, Chancellors run a **public sector net cash requirement (PSNCR)**. Formerly the 'public sector borrowing requirement' (PSBR), this is effectively the difference between the total that ministers intend to spend on public services in a year and the amount available through taxation. To avoid unpopular tax rises or spending cuts, governments have historically favoured loans as a means of financing costly public expenditure. Usually, these are raised by selling bonds ('gilt-edged securities', or 'gilts') to the public. These are effectively government 'IOUs', which are considered safe investments and yield steady interest payments—though far less lucrative ones than those offered by riskier stocks and shares. By borrowing from investors to maintain or increase spending, governments often run up short-term debts—much like individuals using their bank overdrafts or credit cards. Overspends of this kind within a given financial year are known as **budget deficits**.

Since a more 'monetarist' approach to running the economy was adopted in the 1980s (see 7.1.4.1), successive governments have made a virtue of trying to 'balance the books' within overall *economic cycles* (periods, usually of a few years, during which economies 'naturally' fluctuate between bouts of expansion and contraction) by reining in taxation and controlling spending. But the impact of the 2008 global financial collapse, ensuing recessions, and the 'eurozone' sovereign debt crisis changed this. In 2009–10, the last tax year before the 2010 election, government borrowing reached a peacetime record of £163.4 billion—*excluding* the cost of aid to the banking sector.

The principal debate in Britain since 2010 has centred on the state of the country's 'structural', rather than 'cyclical', deficit. A **cyclical deficit**—a familiar concept in most market economies—is the *periodic* budgetary overspend most governments incur during bouts of short-term economic turbulence (e.g. recessions). A **structural deficit** is deeper-rooted. It results from what the *Financial Times* describes as a 'fundamental imbalance in a government's receipts and expenditure, as opposed to one-off or short-term factors'. In other words, structural deficits emerge after prolonged periods during which governments consistently spend more money than they raise through taxes and/or selling off assets—forcing them to borrow more (often at high commercial interest rates) to plug the gap.

When the Coalition took office, its ministers claimed that the true size of Britain's structural deficit 'black hole' was even worse than feared. In his last Budget, Labour Chancellor Alistair Darling said this overspend (estimated at around £77 billion of Britain's overall £167 billion deficit) had peaked at 8.4 per cent of gross domestic product (GDP) during 2009–10, and would fall to 2.5 per cent by 2014–15 on the back of a phased programme of £73 billion in spending cuts and tax rises. He repeated an earlier Labour pledge to halve the country's overall deficit within four years.

But neither Mr Darling's figures nor the speed of his response to Britain's debt crisis impressed the Conservatives. Delivering his own 'emergency' Budget barely two months later, Mr Osborne unveiled a swingeing package of austerity measures—principally a squeeze on social security benefits (see Chapter 8) and annual spending cuts of £40 billion by 2015, *in addition to* the billions earmarked by Labour. In so doing, he warned departments other than those with previously ring-fenced front-line budgets that their funding would fall by up to a quarter (later asking ministers to 'model' cuts of up to 40 per cent). By 2015–16, Mr Osborne predicted, the structural *current* deficit—the part of the structural deficit used to fund public sector running costs such as wages and maintenance, rather than capital investment—would enter a modest surplus, allowing him to start addressing Britain's overall national debt. Based on his Budget, the Office for Budget Responsibility (OBR) (see 7.1.3) predicted that this debt would peak at £70.3 billion in 2013–14—compared to the £74.9 billion anticipated for 2014–15 under Labour's plans. He was repeatedly forced to revise his timetable for eradicating the deficit, first until at least 2017, but more recently until 2019–20 at the earliest. He finally abandoned this target immediately after the 'out' vote in the June 2016 European Union referendum (see 9.7). This position has since been confirmed by Theresa May and her new Chancellor, Philip Hammond, who used his November 2016 Autumn Statement to (in his own words) 'reset' the government's fiscal policy somewhat, by announcing a string of modest but significant new capital investment projects, including a £2.3bn Housing Infrastructure Fund to deliver up to 100,000 news homes in high-demand areas, £1.1bn extra for local public transport, and £2bn a year for research and development by 2020–21. At the same time, he alarmed some commentators, and fellow Conservatives, by forecasting that by 2020–21—a decade after the Tories' return to power—the scale of the UK's cumulative debt is likely to have topped £1.9 trillion (more than 90 per cent of its national income), pushing it higher than during the 2008 financial crisis. More politically damaging, potentially, was the prognosis of the independent Institute for Fiscal Studies (IFS). It predicted that, by the next election, millions of workers will have endured "the worst decade for living standards since the last war and probably since the 1920s"—a prospect it lamented as 'dreadful'.

This slowdown, if not abandonment, of 'austerity' signalled a (to critics, belated) recognition of the fallout from seven years of cuts. Given his repeated public pronouncement that 'we are all in this together', Mr Osborne's contention that his Budgets had always been 'fair'—by, for example, repeatedly raising the personal income tax allowance, thereby taking millions of low-paid workers out of direct tax altogether—were consistently challenged not just by opposition parties and poverty charities but respected think-tanks like the IFS and Resolution Foundation. In an in-depth analysis of his first Budget, the IFS had branded it 'clearly regressive' and claimed the poorest tenth of households stood to lose 5 per cent of their incomes by 2014, while non-pensioner households without children in the richest tenth would sacrifice less than 1 per cent. Despite this warning, Mr Osborne's CSR later that year slashed £81bn from public expenditure—the biggest cut by a British government since the 1970s—with the Treasury itself estimating a loss of nearly 500,000 public sector jobs.

During acute economic crises, it has sometimes been necessary for governments to approach global financial institutions. In the mid-1970s, Mr Callaghan's Chancellor, Denis Healey, borrowed money from the International Monetary Fund (IMF)—a crisis bank that Britain had co-founded in the wake of the Second World War (see 9.4.3)—to stabilize the economy as it was buffeted by stagflation (simultaneous rises in inflation and unemployment). The IMF agreed only on condition that the government made substantial public spending cuts to save money. Documents released by the National Archive in December 2006 under the then 'thirty-year rule' (see 19.5)—a convention stipulating that all but the most sensitive government papers should be made public thirty years after being written (a gift for journalists!)—revealed that Britain nearly had to scrap its nuclear deterrent simply to balance the books.

More recently, it emerged that huge injections of extra funding into health and education under Tony Blair and Mr Brown's governments were financed largely by borrowing—meaning that even before they were forced into considering a multibillion-pound bailout for the banks, ministers were accumulating a mounting structural deficit. According to figures released in 2008, having initially dropped sharply after the party returned to power in 1997, national debt more than doubled between 2001–2 and 2007–8, leaping to £650 billion. It rose by £100bn in a single stroke when the government bailed out the Northern Rock bank in 2007, to save its customers' deposits and restore confidence in the financial sector following its near collapse. Northern Rock—which had overstretched itself by making high-risk home loans to customers who had no guaranteed means of repaying them—initially made an emergency plea for support to the Bank of England (reflecting trends in the US 'sub-prime market'—see 7.3.4). It was nationalized as a 'temporary measure', after months of talks to find a private buyer failed, but in January 2012 Mr Osborne sold it to Virgin Money, for a mere £747 million—barely half the £1.4bn Labour had spent taking it into public ownership.

By the time Northern Rock was nationalized, the bill for propping it up had topped £100 billion (equivalent to the total annual spend on the NHS), and repaying Britain's national debt was costing taxpayers £31 billion a year in interest alone—marginally less than the country's defence budget. In July 2008, Mr Darling conceded that he was reviewing Mr Brown's fiscal 'Golden Rule': the principle, adhered to for a decade or more, that government should borrow only for *investment*, rather than *current spending*. In a swift move designed to signify that ministers had learned lessons from the Northern Rock debacle, in September 2008 Mr Darling nationalized the assets of another bank, Bradford & Bingley, to avert its collapse (it would be eight years before his successor, Mr Osborne, felt emboldened to begin re-privatizing the lender, and even then only gradually). While some critics accused Labour of again using taxpayers' money to secure irresponsible loans made by a reckless bank at the height of the credit boom, ministers were widely praised for some innovations, including the creation of a new Financial Services Compensation Scheme (FSCS). This effectively forced the banking sector as a whole to absorb Bradford & Bingley's losses, while still guaranteeing protection to those with savings up to £31,700 (eventually £85,000).

Towards the end of its thirteen-year rule, Labour reverted to even more of a Keynesian approach to buoying up the economy. As the recession bit, it committed to a 'fiscal stimulus' designed to limit job losses by boosting growth through strategic tax cuts (including a short-term cut in VAT—see Table 7.2) and increased public investment. By bringing forward capital projects originally earmarked for future years, it tried to keep people in employment by offsetting the sharp decline in activity in the by then free-falling housing and small business sectors. Figures published by the Office for National Statistics (ONS) in July 2010 suggested that it might indeed have been the fiscal stimulus that hauled the British economy out of recession (growth reached 1.2 per cent in the second quarter).

To stimulate a recovery in property and small business, the government began using its stake in the part-nationalized banks to nudge them into lending more money (at affordable rates) to consumers and struggling companies. An Asset Protection Scheme was also introduced to insure major British banks against potential losses caused by previous 'toxic debt' (see 7.3.4). At the same time, in a move unseen for decades, the Bank of England opted to use its own device to encourage more lending, pumping liquidity into the system by increasing the supply of sterling by boosting its own bank balance electronically: a process known as **quantitative easing (QE)**.

Briefly, QE involves central banks purchasing bonds or equities from retail banks, in so doing increasing the prices of those assets and reducing the interest rates payable on them. The effect of this (at least theoretically) is to 'recapitalize' banks, lowering overall interest rates in the economy and passing on these cheaper borrowing costs to ordinary customers, including individuals and businesses seeking loans for investment they can then use to create jobs. With Britain's economic recovery stalling, and later slipping back into recession, QE has continued to be used periodically, but it remains unclear how effective it has been, with some economists arguing that it has done little more than enabling banks to shore up their own finances without passing on the benefits to their customers.

Another tactic introduced by Mr Osborne to help small businesses secure finance they need to expand was 'credit easing'—the practice of the Treasury lending money, via banks, to companies with turnovers of up to £50 million at cut-price interest rates designed to lessen repayment costs. Mr Osborne initially released £5 billion of taxpayers' money over a six-month period at a rate 1 per cent below that commonly available commercially, with another £15 billion following over the ensuing eighteen months. Participating banks included Royal Bank of Scotland (RBS), Lloyds, Barclays, Santander, and new specialist lender Aldermore.

7.1.2.1 Bond markets, borrowing costs, and the tyranny of 'credit ratings'

Just as individuals and companies must be 'creditworthy' to obtain loans from banks, so too do governments. An enduring principle underpinning Mr Osborne's fiscal squeeze was a conviction that Britain should rebalance the nation's books—and that only by doing so would it reassure the all-important bond markets (pension funds, venture capitalists, and other institutional or individual investors) that 'UK plc' remained a safe haven for their money.

In addition, today's Chancellors are mindful of the ominous influence on the markets of *credit rating agencies*, the pronouncements of which can have the power of life and death over a state's long-term financial health. For some time, three main agencies—Standard & Poor's, Fitch Ratings, and Moody's—continued to award Britain the maximum gold-starred 'triple-A' rating, ensuring that the interest rates the country was charged for borrowing remained low. However, in April 2013, Fitch caused a wobble in the markets by becoming the first agency to downgrade Britain's rating since 1978—reducing it to AA+ days after the IMF issued a pessimistic outlook for economic growth. Barely three years later, Standard & Poor's cut its UK rating even further, to AA, in the wake of even gloomier predictions arising from Britain's 'out' vote in its June 2016 European Union referendum (see 9.7).

7.1.3 The Office for Budget Responsibility (OBR)

In a symbolic move intended to take responsibility for making medium- to longer-term economic forecasts out of the hands of politically motivated Chancellors, Mr Osborne introduced the **Office for Budget Responsibility (OBR)** in 2010. While the OBR gave a broad thumbs-up to the cutbacks and tax changes that he introduced to tackle Britain's deficit in his maiden Budget, one of its earliest pronouncements was remarkably positive about the economic competence of his predecessor. Although it revised down Mr Darling's predicted growth rates of 3 per cent or more from 2011 onwards (instead predicting fluctuations between 2.6 and 2.8 per cent), it revealed that surprisingly buoyant tax receipts in early 2010—boosted by the introduction of a (since abandoned) 50p top income tax rate—meant that government borrowing over the following five years was likely to be £22 billion less than he had warned. The OBR has continued to be a mixed blessing for the Treasury—often intervening to describe its predictions about likely future economic growth as over-optimistic or suggesting alternatives to previously announced austerity measures, which might involve lowering its target budget surplus or being prepared to borrow more, rather than cut. Labour and other opposition parties have repeatedly offered to subject their own alternative budget plans to OBR scrutiny, to demonstrate that their own 'sums add up'. In April 2016, Shadow Chancellor John McDonnell outlined a putative 'fiscal credibility rule' which would require future Labour Chancellors to persuade the OBR at every Budget that they could 'balance the books' five years hence, albeit only in *current* spending (as opposed to investment). For a famously 'anti-austerity' MP with hard-left credentials, this was a bold move—representing, as it did, an emboldened reinvention of a 'Golden Rule' once championed by Mr Brown.

7.1.4 Controlling inflation and unemployment

When **inflation** is rising, unemployment tends to be low, and vice versa. Only usually at major crisis points—such as the 1930s Depression or late 1970s oil crash—do both rise noticeably at the same time. This is known as 'stagflation'.

The reasons for this trade-off relate to basic 'supply and demand' economics. When prices of goods and services rise, this usually means one of two things: either demand for them is high ('demand-pull inflation') or the cost of producing them is rising ('cost-push inflation'). Demand-pull inflation occurs when shops and manufacturers find they are able to charge more for goods and services, because rising disposable incomes mean people are willing and able to pay. Cost-push inflation results from increasing production costs, often (but not always) related to mounting wage bills: in other words, more workers have been hired to produce and deliver those goods and services, and/or their salaries have risen.

At times when consumer demand is falling, the first casualties tend to be workers employed to produce them. Employers lay off staff to cut running costs and stay in business, on a more manageable scale—reducing prices to attract more custom if necessary. When such redundancies become more widespread, overall unemployment rises. And, of course, at times of high unemployment, people have less money to spend—so prices will have to fall further if demand is to be sustained.

Therefore rising unemployment tends to lead to falling inflation. A knock-on effect of this is a reduction in economic **growth**—the expansion of the economy through rising demand for goods and services, and increased private sector investment, job creation, and exports. Theoretically, growth is a virtuous circle: more jobs should mean more people with money to buy things, more companies manufacturing goods, and higher employment. In practice, the promotion of free trade has meant that many products British people buy today are cheap imports from the Far East and elsewhere—meaning their purchases no longer necessarily help companies expand and create jobs in Britain.

Given the delicate relationship between inflation and unemployment—sometimes known as the 'inflation–unemployment see-saw'—governments find it hard to keep on top of both for very long. When Labour was elected in 1997, Mr Brown pledged to end 'boom and bust', but these words returned to haunt him years later. Despite the fact that Britain proceeded to enjoy a further decade of sustained growth under his stewardship, two years after he became prime minister the economy slumped into its first recession for nearly twenty years.

7.1.4.1 The Bank of England's role in monetary policy

If fiscal policy was the favoured approach to keeping Britain's economy afloat in the 1950s and 1960s, 'monetary policy' has been in vogue since the 1980s. Widely credited as the 'invention' of free market US economist Milton Friedman (a hero of Mrs Thatcher's), the contrasting approach to economic management favoured by monetarism involves using **interest rates**—the cost of borrowing money—to direct consumer behaviour and control inflation. Theoretically, if rates rise people will be more likely to *save* (banks and building societies should be offering them profitable returns for their investment) and less likely to borrow or spend (credit cards and loans cost more).

In Britain, inflation is calculated monthly, according to two measures: the **retail price index (RPI)** and **consumer price index (CPI)**. Both track movements in the cost of notional 'baskets' of 650-odd items bought regularly by 'typical' households—including food, clothing, and tobacco. The difference between the two is that CPI—the measure preferred by governments and the European Central Bank (see 9.4.2)—*excludes* housing costs such as Council Tax and mortgage rates, while 'core CPI' (also often quoted) omits day-to-day expenses, including food and energy bills. Both place more emphasis on goods that people buy only occasionally—for example DVD players and other electronic products. Given that routine purchases such as food and utilities are the costs that most burden households, critics view CPI as highly misleading. Nonetheless, the use of these statistics enabled Labour to maintain low rates of both 'headline' (CPI) and 'underlying' inflation (CPI adjusted to exclude volatile items, such as tax rises) on the whole, even when RPI figures cited by the Opposition and some economists rose.

Until 1997, responsibility for reviewing interest rates monthly rested with the Chancellor. Within days of taking that job, however, Mr Brown made the **Bank of England** independent—handing it the task of controlling inflation on his behalf. Decisions about interest rates have since rested with the **Monetary Policy Committee (MPC)**, composed of nine members, including the bank's chief economist, and chaired by its governor. The government sets an inflation target—currently 2 per cent—and if this is missed by more than one CPI percentage point, the governor must write to the Chancellor explaining why and setting out the action that the MPC intends to take to rectify this. In April 2007, Mervyn King became the first incumbent to have to do this, when headline inflation hit 3.1 per cent. For several years, until May 2012, when inflation finally fell back to 3 per cent for the first time in nine quarters, this would become a monthly ritual. More recently, a combination of anaemic consumption and falling fuel costs (in part, due to the global downturn in wholesale oil and gas prices) has forced the present governor, Mark Carney, to 'apologise' for an inflation rate a percentage point or more *below* the target.

7.1.4.2 The quest for full employment

Successive Chancellors have dreamed of the holy grail of 'full employment'—an ideal state in which everyone capable of work can find a sustainable job—and in April 2014 Mr Osborne became the latest to commit himself to this goal. In practice, full employment has always remained elusive.

At certain times, unemployment has reached levels that have been politically damaging for governments. In the early 1980s, Mrs Thatcher's mass closure of coal pits, steelworks, and shipyards in northern England, Wales, and Scotland, combined with her crackdown on trades union power (see 7.4), saw the national jobless total rise to between 3 and 4 million. While Labour largely maintained a much lower official unemployment rate—using a combination of 'carrot' and 'stick' policies, such as tax credits and its 'New Deal' to entice people into work—nationwide unemployment still hovered above 1.5 million, even before the recession pushed it nearer 2.5 million. Moreover, there has been huge criticism of the increasing 'casualization' of Britain's working environment, with many new jobs created since the early 1990s taking the form of part-time, short-term and/or 'zero-hours' contracts devoid of entitlements like pensions and holiday pay available to full-time, permanent staff.

Despite remaining stubbornly high for the first three years of the Coalition—not least because thousands of public sector jobs were axed as a result of cuts—officially, unemployment has since fallen. Although it had topped 2.65 million by April 2012, from that point it began to drop. By March 2014, the headline rate was down to 2.2 million—a five-year low and 133,000 down on the previous three months. However, the number of 16–24 year-olds out of work remains a cause for particular concern: while significantly lower than the symbolic 1 million mark—which it had reached for the first time in 2011—the youth unemployment rate remained alarmingly high, at 868,000. Overall levels continue to oscillate from one economic quarter (three-month period) to another, with April 2016 seeing the first rise (of 21,000) since the previous June, taking the headline figure to 1.7 million.

7.1.5 Promoting growth and UK exports

If one word strikes terror into the hearts of prime ministers and Chancellors it is **recession**—defined as two successive economic quarters in which the economy 'shrinks'. Such bouts of negative growth generally lead to less money being borrowed and spent by consumers, lower sales and profits for businesses, reduced production, and redundancies. Britain has lived through three recent recessions: in the early 1980s, early 1990s, and from April 2008 to December 2009. A further period of stalling or negative growth, in 2012, was for many months recorded as a slip into a second post-crash recession (dubbed a 'double-dip'), but in June 2013 revised figures showed the economy was actually flat, rather than falling, in the first three months of that year. By 2014, annual growth had bounced back to 2.9 per cent, making Britain's the fastest growing major economy, but it slowed down to 2.2 per cent in 2015, and only managed 0.4 per cent in the first quarter of 2016—a tail-off blamed by some in government on uncertainty over whether Britain would remain in the European Union following the then impending 'Brexit' referendum (see 9.7).

In light of the consequences of recessions (rising unemployment, and falling consumer spending and business investment), it is little wonder that governments are so obsessed with achieving growth. Indeed, a report published in June 2014 in the *British Journal of Psychiatry* suggested that the most recent recession was so detrimental to many individuals and families that up to 10,000 people committed suicide across Europe and North America because of its impact on their lives. Two engines are traditionally used to achieve growth: boosting employment and, by extension, domestic demand; and developing overseas export markets for products manufactured at home. In theory, each should lead to wealth creation.

This chapter has already examined the inflation–unemployment conundrum and how British governments try to boost the economy by juggling these 'twin evils'. But how do they promote Britain's exports abroad—and measure their success or failure in doing so? Taking the latter question first, there are two measures:

- **balance of trade**—the annual difference in value between the total of all goods and services bought by British residents from overseas (imports) and all UK-made products sold abroad (exports), encompassing 'visible' items (physical goods, such as food, clothes, and televisions) and 'invisible' ones (virtual goods, including legal and financial services); and
- **balance of payments**—the difference in value between the total of *all* payments flowing between Britain and other countries, including financial transfers and debt payments to foreigners.

If, in a given financial year, Britons purchase more imports than the country exports overseas, the current account (the balance between money coming into the country and going out) is in *deficit*. If it sells more abroad than it buys in, it is in *surplus*—a much healthier state.

Recent decades—particularly since Britain joined the EU (see Chapter 9)—have seen it importing disproportionate quantities of cheap foreign clothing, toys, electrical items, and motor vehicles. The slow decline of indigenous industries such as shipbuilding and coalmining, meanwhile, has seen the country's economic output switch to services including telecommunications, information technology (IT), and finance. As a result, while Britain has historically had a significant balance of trade deficit in visible items, its service sector often generates a surplus. Despite selling more aircraft abroad than ever before, and increasing its car exports, a dramatic fall in overseas sales of chemicals combined with the impact of a worldwide slump in one of its biggest sectors, oil and gas, saw the UK's overall trade deficit in physical goods hit a record high of £125bn in 2015, according to figures from the Office for National Statistics (ONS).

In addition to the balances of trade and payments, there are two other 'litmus tests' of economic growth:

- **gross domestic product (GDP)**—the market value of all goods and services produced within Britain annually, regardless of which country derives income from them (sometimes referred to as 'national output'); and
- **gross national product (GNP)**—the value of all goods and services produced by British-owned companies, labour, and property each year, irrespective of where those assets are based (sometimes referred to as 'national income').

It has become customary for governments to cite favourable GDP figures as evidence of strong economic performance. In reality, however, while high GDP should reduce unemployment (a foreign-owned company on UK soil is as likely to create jobs and consumer spending as a British one), this is only part of the picture. Most income generated by foreign-owned companies flows back to the countries in which they are headquartered, limiting the longer-term benefits to the British economy brought by overseas businesses that locate here. Therefore GNP may often give a truer indication of levels of wealth generation for 'UK plc': the numerous British-based banks and telecoms firms that have outsourced call centres to the Far East, where labour costs are cheaper, may do little to help Britain's employment figures, but much of their income returns to the Treasury.

7.2 The Budget

The highlight of the Treasury's calendar is the **Budget**. Traditionally an autumn event, Mr Brown switched it to the spring, with an annual Pre-Budget Report (or 'Autumn Statement') following it in November or December. This was initially intended simply to set the scene for prospective tax and spending announcements in the next Budget, acting as a 'health check' on the performance of Britain's economy over the preceding twelve months, but in time it became almost as big a media event as the Budget itself—with Chancellors using it to make increasingly firm policy commitments. It was this sense that it had become a 'second Budget' in all but name that moved Mr Hammond to use his inaugural Autumn Statement to announce its abolition. From 2017, the Budget was due to return to its traditional autumn slot, with a shorter and simpler Spring Statement preceding it (though it remains to be seen whether, over time, history would repeat itself by inflating this to a bigger annual diary event).

The Budget itself has two elements: the Budget Speech/Statement and the Finance Act.

7.2.1 The Budget Speech

The Budget Speech is designed to:

- forecast short- to medium-term movements in the economy (over one to three years) and review its performance in the preceding twelve months;
- announce changes in direct and indirect taxation and public spending, and prioritize particular areas over others (for example health or education);
- announce new taxes, tax breaks, and/or benefits to finance investment or help low-income groups (for example tax credits); and
- give the Chancellor a platform for political grandstanding—allowing him or her to boast about the country's economic performance.

The Speech—which regularly runs for about an hour—is immediately followed by a similarly lengthy retort from the Leader of the Opposition (the Shadow Chancellor has his or her chance the following evening on national television) and a debate in the Commons. More than 150 years after the event, William Gladstone holds the dubious honour of having delivered the longest ever Budget Speech: his 1853 address lasted four hours and 45 minutes.

7.2.2 The Finance Act

For measures announced in the Budget to be implemented, the Commons must legislate. Unlike most laws, however, the Bill needed to deliver the proposals is given swift passage and substantially passed on the same day as the Speech. Dubbed the 'Finance Bill', it is automatically designated a 'money Bill' by the Speaker—enabling it to bypass the usual stages that Bills must negotiate before receiving royal assent (see Table 2.7). The initial 'stages' are effectively gone through in one go, with the Speech itself treated as the first reading. The Commons must pass individual resolutions to approve each specific tax or duty change within ten sitting days, but, under the Collection of Taxes Act 1968, minor changes can be agreed immediately—enabling government business to continue in the interim. A second reading must be heard within thirty days, but the committee stage may be split, with more important resolutions heard by a committee of the whole house and remaining ones considered by a standing committee of thirty to forty members of Parliament (MPs). After this, the third reading is steamrollered through, usually on the second day of the report stage.

Since the confrontation between the Commons and House of Lords over Lloyd George's 1909 'People's Budget' (see 2.3.1), there has been no Lords stage to the Finance Bill. Nonetheless, even today there is scope for Budgets to fall at a late hurdle. The row over Labour's abolition of the 10p starting rate of income tax so raised the hackles of backbench rebels led by former Welfare Minister Frank Field that, before announcing a compensation package for low earners penalized by the change, it looked as if Mr Darling's first Budget (in 2008) might be defeated, forcing his resignation. In the event, he staved off this prospect by issuing an 'emergency Budget' designed to compensate the losers. If Labour's 2008 Budget proved a political minefield, Mr Osborne came close to having to rewrite large chunks of his at least twice. Over a period of three months or more after the 2012 Budget, several provisions in the accompanying Finance Bill unravelled—with ministers performing a succession of U-turns over controversial measures ranging from a tabloid-christened 'granny tax' (proposed cuts to the personal tax allowance for those aged over 65), to a 'pasty tax' on hot takeaway snacks. The slew of policy reversals led to the Budget memorably being dubbed an 'omnishambles' by then Labour leader Ed Miliband—a reference to a term coined by fictional spin doctor Malcolm Tucker in BBC sitcom *The Thick of It*. Four years later, an Osborne Budget threatened to dissolve again, amid a huge backlash against his plan to cut disability benefits—a measure which provided the pretext for the sudden and dramatic resignation of Work and Pensions Secretary Iain Duncan Smith.

7.2.3 Public spending outside England: the Barnett Formula

To ensure that Scotland, Wales, and Northern Ireland benefit fairly from central government tax revenues, public spending is allocated on a per capita basis across Britain, using a system called the 'Barnett Formula'. In theory, the formula—devised in the late 1970s by then Labour Chief Secretary to the Treasury Joel (the late Lord) Barnett—ensures that the amount given to each country corresponds to its population size (and, by definition, the extent to which its inhabitants contribute to taxes).

In practice, it remains controversial: successive recalculations have disproportionately benefited Scotland and the distribution of funding has moved increasingly out of step with levels of economic need in different parts of Britain. Resentment between Scotland and England, in particular, has escalated since devolution was introduced in 1998, largely because Holyrood continues to do disproportionately well out of taxes, on paper—with annual spending north of the border in 2014–15 at £10,374 per head, compared to £8,638 in England and £9,904 in Wales (though it was highest in Northern Ireland, at £11,106).

The formula returned to the forefront of political debate during the 2014 Scottish referendum campaign (see 1.3.3), when, spooked by late opinion polls suggesting independence supporters could be poised for victory, Westminster's main party leaders tacitly agreed to preserve it indefinitely (to the dismay of many English MPs and the Welsh Government).

7.3 The government's role in promoting industry and commerce

For the past thirty years, British governments have taken an increasingly laissez-faire approach to economic management. The mass privatization programme of the 1980s saw a swathe of industries sold into private ownership, from motor manufacturer British Leyland to British Airways, British Steel, all major utilities (gas, electricity, water), and ultimately the railways (see 7.5). In the decades since, the mantra has been one of 'consumer choice', with successive governments promoting competition between rival private sector providers over any state monopoly, and even importing this idea into the funding and organization of taxpayer-funded public services. In theory, this allows people to shop around for the best deals on virtually any product—with market forces (supply and demand) ensuring their quality and competitive pricing.

In practice, however, the government continues to play an interventionist role in promoting British industry and protecting it from the worst ravages of **globalization:** the process by which national economies are becoming increasingly interdependent. Recent decisions by ministers to shore up failing banks and broker rescue packages for car manufacturers, such as Nissan and Rover, not to mention the Indian-owned Tata Steel plants in the North East of England and Port Talbot in Wales have demonstrated this (if not always wholeheartedly). Moreover, the free market ideal of a private sector that, left alone, will 'regulate itself' fairly has proved elusive—forcing the state to introduce greater regulation.

7.3.1 The Department for Business, Energy, and Industrial Strategy (BEIS)

The department responsible for promoting and regulating British industry and commerce has been through numerous previous incarnations—from the archaic Board of Trade to the Department of Trade and Industry to (most recently) the Department for Business, Innovation, and Skills (BIS).

Along with its newly absorbed brief to oversee the energy sector (a responsibility previously held by the now-defunct Department for Energy and Climate Change), the reconstituted BEIS is responsible for:

- creating conditions for business investment and raising productivity in Britain;
- championing the interests of employees and employers;
- promoting consumer interests; and
- encouraging sustainable business development.

Although formal regulation of the business environment is delegated to various non-departmental bodies, recent Business Secretaries have, at times, played more hands-on roles than previously. Despite being widely criticized for its sluggish response to Tata Steel's sudden announcement in March 2016 that it planned to close its UK plants, with the loss of 15,000 jobs (then premier Mr Cameron was on holiday at the time and his Secretary of State Sajid Javid was attending a black-tie dinner in Australia), the Conservative government later intervened to broker a rescue deal—albeit one which meant sacrificing employee pension benefits to persuade the company to think again. Soon after the Brexit referendum (see 9.7), meanwhile, Nissan was persuaded to boost car production at its plant in Sunderland, despite its misgivings about Britain's long-term economic prospects—prompting speculation that ministers had secretly agreed a 'sweetheart deal' involving government-backed guarantees.

Back in January 2009, then Business Secretary Lord Mandelson had tried a tactic along these lines in the wake of the banking crisis, jump-starting the car industry by pledging £2.3 billion in loan guarantees—including £1.3 billion from the European Investment Bank—for motor firms prepared to invest in 'high technology' and green alternatives to conventional engines.

As well as overseeing the regulatory framework, it is the Business Secretary's job to liaise regularly with the main bodies representing employees and employers: the Trades Union Congress (TUC) (see 7.4) and the Confederation of British Industry (CBI), respectively.

7.3.2 Regulatory authorities

While DBEIS drafts laws governing competition, consumer protection, and business, these are policed by an independent regulator: the **Competition and Markets Authority (CMA)**.

7.3.2.1 The Competition and Markets Authority (CMA)

Established in 1973, the Office of Fair Trading (OFT) was charged with ensuring that the 'rules' of fair play—genuine choice and competition—were applied in practice. Its founding remit was to protect both consumers and companies, shielding small businesses from anti-competitive practices by larger, more established, rivals. Until 2003, it was headed by a Director General of Fair Trading (later replaced by a board and chairperson). The Competition Commission (CC—formerly the Monopolies and Mergers Commission) was less concerned with the day-to-day market practices preoccupying the OFT than with movements in company ownership that might affect *future* competition. Although most markets are now 'deregulated'—open to full free market competition—in practice this has led to consolidations of ownership, with bigger, more profitable, companies taking over or merging with smaller ones. As a result, markets that once offered dozens of alternatives from which consumers could choose are increasingly dominated by a handful of providers—and sometimes only one or two. High-profile interventions to prevent the emergence of 'monopolies'—defined as the point at which one company secures more than a 25 per cent market share in a particular market—include the Commission's decision to approve supermarket chain Morrisons' takeover of rival Safeway in 2003 only on condition that it first sold fifty-three stores in areas where local competition might otherwise suffer.

The remits of both CC and OFT have now been assumed by the Competition and Markets Authority (CMA), which vets prospective mergers or takeovers and polices companies' competitive behaviour on a daily basis.

With a mission statement to 'promote competition for the benefit of consumers, both inside and outside the UK', its duties are to:

- investigate mergers that could restrict competition;
- conduct market studies and investigations where there may be competition and consumer problems;

- investigate potential breaches of UK/EU prohibitions against anti-competitive agreements and abuses of dominant positions;
- bring criminal proceedings against individuals who commit cartel offences;
- enforce consumer protection legislation to tackle practices and market conditions that make it difficult for consumers to exercise choice;
- cooperate with other regulators and encourage them to use their powers; and
- consider regulatory references and appeals.

To take some recent examples of alleged market abuses, supermarket chains have repeatedly been accused of unfair trading in relation to the prices they pay their suppliers. Both Tesco and Asda have been accused of offering below-cost-price payment to producers in developing countries for everything from bananas to coffee, while British farmers have complained of similar treatment in relation to their meat and dairy products. The appalling press generated by such controversies has prompted retailers to embrace 'fair trade' goods and invest millions in corporate social responsibility (CSR) programmes.

Of course, it is not only business that is hurt by restrictive practices; it is often consumers who suffer most. In December 2007, following an OFT investigation, Asda and Sainsbury's admitted having conspired to fix the price of milk. The supermarkets charged inflated prices for the product—despite offering farmers minimal payment—and British consumers were left £270 million out of pocket.

It was in the spirit of acting as a 'consumer champion' that the CMA later mounted a full-scale competition inquiry into the provision of current and business accounts by the high-street banking sector, which was still taking submissions at time of writing.

7.3.2.2 Regulating the financial markets

In 1997, a separate regulator was set up to oversee the financial services sector—banks, building societies, and insurance companies—assuming responsibilities previously held by the Bank of England. But the effectiveness of this body, the Financial Services Authority (FSA), was questioned after its failure to act on the banking sector's increasingly cavalier mortgage lending policies prior to the collapse of Northern Rock and wider banking crisis (see 7.3.4). Following Labour's multibillion-pound bailout of the banks—and the soaring structural deficit that resulted—the party was condemned for such 'light touch' financial regulation. Another criticism concerned the 'tripartite' nature of the regulatory regime it had introduced—effectively splitting responsibilities for policing banking between the FSA, the Bank of England, and HM Treasury, and creating confusion over which should intervene (and when). In truth, introducing the FSA had slightly tightened the regulatory framework, compared to the laissez-faire regime ushered in by Margaret Thatcher's 'Big Bang' City deregulation in October 1986. Nonetheless, it fell to the Coalition to toughen up banking regulation for the future, by dividing the FSA's responsibilities between three new authorities. These bodies, which together replaced the FSA on 1 April 2013, are:

- the **Financial Conduct Authority (FCA)**, which polices the overall conduct of every financial company authorized to provide services to the public and maintains the overall integrity of UK money markets;
- the **Prudential Regulatory Authority (PRA)**, a subsidiary of the Bank of England set up to prevent financial companies—from banks and building societies, to insurers and brokers—taking imprudent risks with their investors' money; and
- the **Financial Policy Committee (FPC)**, another new division of the Bank of England, modelled in composition on the MPC. Charged with identifying potential financial and macroeconomic risks to the stability of Britain's economy and, where possible, taking pre-emptive action to avert them, it started work a year earlier than the other two, in March 2012.

7.3.3 The London Stock Exchange (LSE)

Shares in plcs are traded on global stock markets, one of the biggest being the London Stock Exchange (LSE). Established in 1760, when 150 brokers expelled from the Royal Exchange for rowdiness formed a spontaneous share-trading club at Jonathan's Coffee House, it registered as a private limited company in 1986, and finally as a public limited company (plc) in 2000. Like all plcs, the LSE is susceptible to potential takeover. In 2004, it became the first stock market to be targeted by a prospective purchaser when it faced an £822 million hostile bid from little-known Swedish company the OM Group, a technology manufacturer that runs the Swedish Stock Exchange. Four years later, LSE's shareholders rejected a £1.35 billion offer by its German rival, Deutsche Börse. In 2016, however, the company revived its takeover plans, and at the time of writing was engaged in an incipient bidding war with US-based Intercontinental Exchange.

Today, the LSE has regional bases in Belfast, Birmingham, Glasgow, Leeds, and Manchester. Some 2,600 UK and overseas companies are listed at any time, and shares are traded electronically via a computerized system called 'CREST'. Minute-by-minute movements in share prices of listed companies are tracked by a series of nine indices, collectively known as the 'Financial Times Stock Exchange' ('FTSE', or 'Footsie'). Most famous is the **FT100 Share Index**, which lists the 100 highest-valued companies in order of value and monitors movements in their share prices. The FT All-Share Index, meanwhile, lists all companies on the stock market, again in order of size/value.

Numerous factors can impact on company share prices. Mergers and takeovers—or the mere prospect of them—can send prices soaring or crashing, according to the market's assessment of how favourable such outcomes are for a firm's commercial fortunes. Shares in iconic high-street companies such as Tesco and Marks & Spencer, meanwhile, are notoriously prone to fluctuations, depending on the movements of senior personnel, and the state of their sales and profits, particularly at what is expected to be the height of their business cycle: Christmas time.

Often, companies' share prices suffer because of factors beyond their control. Amid growing suspicions among share traders that the 1980s stock market bubble was about to burst, 'Black Monday' on 1 October 1987 saw the biggest one-day crash in history. Within the month, LSE shares alone had plummeted by 26.4 per cent.

Linked to the LSE, London also boasts an Alternative Investment Market (AIM) Launched in 1995, it is a market for the trading of shares in smaller developing companies and/or those whose value has fallen so low that they have decided to 'delist' from the FTSE are traded. Today more than 3,600 companies trade on AIM, including a growing number of renewable energy companies and 'ethical' businesses.

7.3.4 The global banking crisis and its fallout

After years of unsustainable growth in the mortgage sector and the credit market as a whole, autumn 2008 witnessed the biggest global financial meltdown since the 1929 Wall Street Crash and the ensuing Great Depression. Eighteen months after the term 'sub-prime' had first seeped into the mainstream media—referring to 'toxic' loans made by US banks to people with limited means and poor credit records, many of whom subsequently defaulted—major financial institutions from Europe to the Far East were brought to their knees by the knock-on effects of these and similar practices elsewhere. In the end, the position of household-name banks, from Merrill Lynch to Barclays, became so perilous that governments in Britain, the United States, and mainland Europe were forced into doing what the long-standing 'neoliberal' consensus would previously have deemed unthinkable: pouring vast sums of money into the sector to shore up savings and pensions and keep the institutions afloat. But even this was not enough and, before long, Mr Brown was leading the way—by buying up controlling stakes in several major high-street banks. After decades of runaway privatization and deregulation, the term 'nationalization' re-entered the political lexicon.

The escalating financial crisis came to a head in late September 2008 when, in a single week, investment bank Lehman Brothers filed for bankruptcy, Merrill Lynch was taken over by the Bank of America, and the US Federal Reserve Bank (the US equivalent of the Bank of England) announced a US $85 billion rescue package and effective nationalization of the country's biggest insurance firm, AIG. Within a fortnight, an even bigger collapse occurred, when Washington Mutual—the largest US mortgage lender—was shut down by regulators and sold to JPMorgan Chase. To prevent other financial giants facing a similar fate, the White House administration was left battling to force a $700 billion rescue package for the country's entire banking sector through a Congress furious at the conduct of reckless bankers.

In Britain, even more dramatic state interventions followed. Barely a week after Lloyds TSB stepped in to announce a buyout of Halifax Bank of Scotland (HBOS), one of the biggest mortgage lenders, ministers nationalized the bulk of Bradford & Bingley's assets, while selling off its branches and savings operation to Spanish bank Santander. The Treasury then moved to guarantee all deposits in UK banks of up to an initial £31,700, to prevent a 'run'—that is, the mass withdrawal of savings by panicked investors worried about losing their money if institutions collapse.

Then, on 8 October, amid feverish rumours and jittery trading, Messrs Brown and Darling announced details of a £500 billion bailout for the UK's banking sector, which would see up to eight high-street banks and building societies part-nationalized in a last-ditch attempt to persuade institutions to resume lending to each other and—more importantly for the 'real economy'—their customers. While only Lloyds TSB, HBOS, and RBS initially accepted the government's offer—other major banks such as Barclays opting to retain their independence by raising capital on the open market—the price paid by these institutions for their cut of the 'final' £37 billion Treasury share offer was significant. First, the FSA ordered the government to acquire both 'preference shares' (which give shareholders priority in receiving dividends, but no voting rights) and 'ordinary' ones, allowing ministers a direct say in running the companies. Second, it emerged that the government would be appointing its own directors to the banks' boards and that no bonuses would be paid to senior staff for at least the first year. This latter measure went some way towards allaying mounting public outrage at the scale of the 'bonus culture' fostered during the boom years, with directors often pocketing multimillion-pound perks irrespective of how well their companies were performing. The government replaced several leading bankers at the helm of semi-nationalized institutions, including RBS chief executive Sir Fred 'the Shred' Goodwin, whose nickname derived from his reputation as a ruthless cost-cutter (and whose knighthood was rescinded in 2012). Royal Bank of Scotland was 60 per cent nationalized, while the state took a 41 per cent stake in Lloyds TSB and HBOS. It would be a number of years before these banks began their transfer back into private hands, under the Conservatives—amid criticisms from some quarters that they were being sold off on the cheap, rather than for prices that adequately compensated taxpayers for their earlier bailouts. In March 2016, the OBR reported that the Treasury's initial hopes of raising £29bn from share sales in RBS over the ensuing five years had been revised down by a quarter due to weakening share prices, at least partly caused by the ripple effect of slowing growth in China and other emerging markets. By contrast, an earlier series of share issues in Lloyds TSB—backed by a marketing campaign based on the successful 'Tell Sid' television adverts used to promote British Gas's 1980s privatization—did better, encouraging the Coalition to dispose of all but 10 per cent of its stake in the bank by October 2015. HBOS, meanwhile, has been owned by Lloyds TSB since January 2009.

The aftermath of the banking crisis, and its ongoing impact on Britain's public finances, saw Opposition politicians and media commentators pour scorn on City traders and demand firm action to ensure that there could be no repeat of the reckless practices that led to the near-collapse of so many institutions. Vocal critics included future Lib Dem Business Secretary Vince Cable, who ridiculed what he saw as Mr Darling's ineffectual response—a call for international action to impose strict new trading conditions on the banking sector and a one-off 50 per cent tax on bonuses of £25,000-plus that was levied only in April 2010 (although it raised £2.3 billion). However, once in office, the Coalition, in which Mr Cable served consistently, wavered over how to make the sector pay for its past errors: Mr Osborne initially imposed only a modest levy on the banks, based on their overall balance sheets rather than individuals' bonuses. Since then, debate has raged over how best to deter future rogue practices and ensure that the big banks saved by taxpayer-funded bailouts make fair reparations for wrongdoing. Agreement has also been elusive over various proposals for some form of levy on banking transactions, or 'Robin Hood Tax'. The EU came close to adopting a Union-wide financial transaction tax (FTT), modelled on an idea first proposed by Nobel Laureate James Tobin. Its sister plan for a European Fiscal Compact (see 9.4.3)—approved by all member states but Britain and the Czech Republic in March 2012—has required signatory countries to commit to maintaining national budget surpluses or balanced accounts since 1 January 2013. Mr Cameron's rationale for opting out of this deal was that it could have a disproportionate impact on the City, which, at a time of stubbornly high national debt and a widening trade deficit, remained the most likely engine of Britain's recovery.

In 2013, Mr Cable finally went some way to implementing the Lib Dems' pre-election pledge to 'break up' bigger banks into separate retail and investment arms, to stop ordinary customers ever again being exposed to the perils of high-stakes risk-taking. Following publication of a report by an Independent Commission on Banking (ICB), headed by economist Sir John Vickers, and a Treasury White Paper setting out concrete proposals for restructuring the sector, the Banking Reform Act 2013 enshrined in law three key principles relating to the future structure and governance of banking:

- high-street banks must be kept separate from investment banks;
- in the event of a bank's 'failure', its investors, rather than taxpayers, would be responsible for bailing it out; and

- the first compensation paid out to anyone in such circumstances would be full refunds of savers' deposits.

7.3.4.1 Short-selling, interest-rate 'fixes', and wider questions about banking

Another scandal that emerged at the height of the financial crisis was the widespread practice of 'short-selling'. This shady form of stock market speculation involves seasoned speculators gambling on the fortunes of ailing companies by 'borrowing' from third parties shares in those that they expect to fall in value, selling them on, and then buying them back after their price has plummeted—before returning them to their original owner for a profit. The FSA introduced a short-term ban on this practice at the height of the banking crisis and it was later unilaterally outlawed in Germany. This paved the way for the EU's European Securities and Markets Authority (ESMA) to ban short-selling across the Union as a whole, as of 1 November 2012. However, none of this deterred UK ministers from filing a lawsuit to the European Court of Justice (ECJ) in June that year, challenging the EU-wide plans—though this was subsequently rejected, in January 2014, making Britain's stock market subject to the ban.

Just when the spectre of 'casino banking' finally seemed to have been banished amid the moves to ban short-selling, a major new scandal erupted. This time, the initial culprit identified was Barclays, which in June 2012 was fined £291 million by the FSA and US Department of Justice for repeatedly lying about the twin interest rates that it paid to borrow money from other institutions: the so-called London Interbank Offered Rate (Libor) and the Euro Interbank Offered Rate (Euribor). The investigation found that, from 2005, individual traders working for Barclays Capital repeatedly lied for personal gain, by claiming that rates were higher than they actually were, while at the height of the 2008 crisis their managers ordered them to make out that the bank was paying *less* than it was (a tactic known as 'low-balling'), to improve its balance sheets and reduce the rates that it was charged elsewhere. It appeared to many that Barclays had deliberately misrepresented its borrowing rates to avert its collapse and/or nationalization by the then Labour government. The scandal claimed the scalp of, among others, Barclays' chief executive Bob Diamond, although he denied any knowledge of or involvement in the Libor deceptions. The Libor scandal continues to rumble, though, with Britain's Serious Fraud Office (SFO) having pursued a series of prosecutions of individual traders, albeit with mixed success. To date, former Citibank and UBS trader Tom Hayes has been the only culprit convicted of rigging Libor rates, and is currently serving an eleven-year sentence following his guilty verdict in August 2015. In January 2016, Darrell Read became the last of six defendants to be acquitted of aiding and abetting Hayes. However, at time of writing a further trial was under way, this time involving five former Barclays traders, and six other individuals were being pursued by the SFO in relation to allegations of fixing the European equivalent of Libor, Euribor.

Myriad inquiries and reviews into the rate-fixing have since been held, with each recommending significant reforms to clean up the system; but critics complain that little change has yet materialized. A (still ongoing) investigation by the FCA, has so far led to several traders being issued with life bans from financial trading, but it has been encumbered by dissembling, with some companies reportedly failing to cooperate with it, including Deutsche Bank. Moreover, as far back as August 2012 a review by FSA managing director Martin Wheatley sparked by the initial Barclays revelations described the existing Libor system as no longer being a 'viable option' and proposed the introduction of both formal regulation and the pegging of Libor rates to objective market data, rather than subjective submissions from banks that might be vulnerable to human error and corruption. Following a public consultation, the Coalition did act—amending the Financial Services Act to make manipulation of Libor a criminal offence and to bring Libor within the overall scope of UK financial regulation—but concerns persist that determined manipulators would still succeed. And still scandals continue to dog the banking sector: in June 2012, another dubious banking practice was exposed, when the FSA announced it had reached settlements with Barclays, HSBC, Lloyds, and RBS over its demands for 'redress' for their 'serious failings' in mis-selling specialist insurance to companies seeking to protect themselves against rising interest rates. Then, two years later, it transpired that 15 leading banks were being investigated over allegations that their employees had been involved in rigging prices on the foreign exchange market (Forex), on which banks buy and sell currencies to each other. It was alleged that traders from rival institutions had colluded to set benchmark exchange rates at 4 p.m. each day, rather than operating independently in a competitive market. In November 2014, six banks were fined a total of £2.6 billion by the British and US regulators for the actions of rogue currency dealers on their payrolls.

Despite all this, there have been a handful of more positive developments in the banking sector. The Coalition belatedly introduced a **Green Investment Bank**, originally announced in Mr Darling's last Budget. Based in Edinburgh, and backed by an initial capitalization fund of £3 billion, the bank opened for business in November 2012, its stated mission to invest in environmentally sustainable infrastructure projects, addressing private sector market failures and achieving a 'double bottom line' that will both innovate in green technologies and generate profits.

7.4 The government's role in industrial relations

In the 1960s and 1970s, when many industries were still state-owned, battles between government and trades unions over wages policy, working conditions, and taking industrial action frequently made the news. After years of struggle between unions and employers, and growing infighting in the Labour movement, tensions exploded during the 1978–79 'Winter of Discontent'—a prolonged period of wildcat action (sudden walk-outs).

Hand in hand with its mass privatization programme, Mrs Thatcher's government clamped down on the rights of workers to take industrial action. Legal barriers were introduced to block strikes, while the new generation of private sector employers with which unions were confronted no longer even had to 'recognize' their existence—let alone formally negotiate with them over job cuts or changing working practices. Mrs Thatcher also ended:

- 'the closed shop'—a rule forcing employees in certain trades or industries to join specific unions; and
- 'secondary picketing'—the ability of workers in trades *related* to others in dispute with their employers to take 'sympathy action'.

Although both the above remain illegal, when Labour returned to power in 1997 certain workers' rights were restored. Many of these—the right to sick pay, paid leave, and a maximum number of weekly working hours—were guaranteed under the European Social Chapter, signed by Mr Blair in 1998 (see 9.5). The new government also introduced a **national minimum wage (NMW)**, and extended some rights previously the preserve of full-time permanent employees to those on part-time and temporary contracts. Despite these early moves, it took nearly thirteen years before a more thoroughgoing equalization of the rights of temporary or agency workers and those with full-time contracts was introduced, in the Agency Workers Regulations, which were finally adopted by Britain shortly before the 2010 election. Derived from the EU's Agency Workers Directive, this came into force across the Union on 1 October 2011 and was formally (if grudgingly) introduced by the Coalition on Christmas Eve that year. Its principal achievement was to give temporary and agency employees the same rights as permanent staff after twelve weeks' continuous employment.

7.4.1 The role of unions

As discussed at 5.2, unions initially emerged in the eighteenth and nineteenth centuries. They were formed to provide representation for the large groups of workers recruited by the owners of Britain's emerging manufacturing industries. In time, dismayed by the lack of attention paid to their cause by politicians, they began seeking their own stake in power and joined with other bodies to form the Labour Party—to which many remain formally affiliated to this day (see Table 5.3).

Although most workers' rights are enshrined in British and/or EU law, unions have historically adhered to a self-help approach to representing their members' interests known as 'voluntarism'—a tradition that shies away from seeking legal intervention in workplace disputes, in favour of 'free collective bargaining'. In material terms, unions' aims are to:

- negotiate and protect a fair wage for given trades and professions;
- negotiate fair working conditions—hours, holiday entitlement, sick pay, and compensation for work-related injuries or illnesses; and
- provide members with training, educational and social opportunities, and a 'fighting fund' for living costs during prolonged industrial disputes.

In addition, unions offer legal and financial support in the event of disputes between individual employees and their employers. Unions have historically achieved many favourable settlements for aggrieved workers unfairly dismissed from their jobs, or bullied or harassed by colleagues or bosses. Sometimes, this is done on an out-of-court basis, but on other occasions unions represent workers at employment tribunals.

Over the past thirty years, the number of unions has declined by a third, with many pooling their resources to strengthen their voice at the negotiating table. The most recent amalgamation was that of the Transport and General Workers' Union (TGWU) and Amicus, Britain's biggest technical union, which merged to form Unite in 2007. As in the Labour Party, the senior officer of a trade union is usually called the 'general secretary', and has an elected national executive committee that debates changes of policy. Beneath this it will have regional and district organizations. It will also have branches (often based in individual workplaces) and houses, chapels, or shop stewards' committees, which act as focal points for negotiations between employees and employers.

The 'big three' British unions as of 2016 are set out in table 7A to be found on the **Online Resource Centre**.

Most unions are affiliated to a single representative body, the Trades Union Congress (TUC), which holds an annual conference like those organized by the main political parties to rally opinion from members and ratify changes in policy. The serving Labour leader is traditionally invited to give its keynote speech.

The TUC dates back to 1868 and its membership currently consists of fifty-two unions, representing around 5.8 million people (equivalent to eight out of ten union members). It has eight regional councils in England and one for Wales. Scotland has its own equivalent body: the Scottish Trades Union Congress (STUC).

7.4.2 Union recognition—and what it is worth

For unions to be able to negotiate with employers about working practices, pay, and conditions, they need to be 'recognized' by them. After years of having their rights diluted, unions were given a new impetus to recruit in the Employment Relations Act 1999, which introduced a statutory process through which they could demand recognition on meeting specific criteria.

If claims for recognition cannot be satisfied bilaterally between a union and relevant employers, it may apply for help from a central arbitration committee (CAC), which assigns a three-person panel to each case. There are two main ways for unions to achieve recognition—regardless of whether this is desired by the employers disputing it:

- *without* a ballot—a union is 'automatically' recognized if *more than 50 per cent* of its 'bargaining unit' (all employees entitled to join it) have done so; or
- *with* a ballot—if *at least 40 per cent* of the bargaining unit vote in favour of recognition in a ballot and this number amounts to a majority of those who vote (a worker in a bargaining unit does not need to have joined a union to vote).

Perhaps ironically, one of the most notorious industries for union recognition is journalism. There have been many cases in which the managers of larger regional newspapers and some nationals (including Express Newspapers, and Independent News and Media) have fought to prevent it. Prior to 1999, some regional newspaper groups disingenuously argued that, to achieve recognition, the unions representing their journalists would need to obtain the support of 40 per cent of their *overall* workforces—including advertising and sales staff, etc.—rather than simply the writers and subeditors who constituted the bargaining unit.

From the mid-1980s to late 1990s, unions were restricted from taking strike action, in the sense that any withdrawal of their labour over a dispute constituted a breach of contract. Theoretically, this entitled bosses either to sack striking workers or sue them for damages and loss of business. However, the 1999 Act entitles 'recognized' unions to be consulted formally over changes in working practices for employees whom they represent—for example, the movement of a British-based call centre to the Far East or a proposed organizational merger. It also gives unions immunity from prosecution for industrial action, provided that:

- the action is 'wholly or mainly in contemplation or furtherance of a trade dispute between workers and their employer' (that is, not secondary picketing); and
- the union goes through the correct procedures beforehand—a secret postal ballot, followed by a letter giving the employer seven days' notice of the intended action and details of the ballot result.

Restrictions remain, however, and these were significantly tightened by the controversial Trade Union Act 2016. In addition to being barred from secondary action, unions have long had to keep their 'picket lines' to negotiated levels to avoid intimidating colleagues not taking part and avoid the kinds of harassment to which 'strike-breaking' coalminers and other workers were allegedly subjected in the 1980s by picketers.

Following a coordinated strike of more than 1 million public sector workers on 10 July 2014—the latest in a succession of strikes protesting against the Coalition's imposition of wage freezes and job cuts—Mr Cameron's newly elected majority Tory government legislated to ban unions from striking unless at least half their membership turn out to vote one way or the other. In 'important public services'—a (to critics) catch-all category embracing everything from health, education, and border security to transport and the fire service—an 'additional threshold' was also introduced, to prevent industrial action taking place unless 40 per cent of a union's eligible members had voted for it. The Act also explicitly stop single ballots from sanctioning 'rolling programmes' of strikes, as had happened in 2014, by requiring fresh ballots authorizing action at least every six months. The issue of the 50 per cent turnout threshold was perhaps most hotly contested: while a vote authorizing a walkout by the National Union of Teachers (NUT) had been won on a mere 27 per cent turnout. Back in 2012, union leaders pointed out that if the legitimacy of *parliamentary* elections were predicated on remotely similar measures, many politicians would never have won sufficient votes to be elected.

Other recent changes have also angered the unions—not least the Coalition's introduction in some sectors of new regional pay scales to take account of variations in the cost of living from one part of England to another, which dispensed with decades of national wage agreements.

7.4.3 Avoiding strikes—the role of the Advisory, Conciliation, and Arbitration Service (ACAS)

When employer–employee negotiations break down, one or other party may seek impartial help to reach a settlement from the **Advisory, Conciliation, and Arbitration Service (ACAS)**. This quango's role is to:

- *advise* warring parties how to avoid industrial action;
- *conciliate* in disputes when invited to do so and try to encourage parties to reach agreement peacefully;
- *arbitrate* to restart negotiations in disputes resulting in industrial action; and
- *mediate* over grievances between individual employees and their employers—notably in relation to prospective tribunal cases (concerning unfair dismissal, gender, age, or racial discrimination, etc.).

ACAS has been involved in numerous recent disputes. In July 2007, its chair was called in by ministers to report on the issues arising from a strike by Royal Mail workers over the imposition of new modernization plans and a below-inflation 2.5 per cent pay deal. In May 2005, it was approached by the National Union of Journalists (NUJ) to mediate between it and then BBC director general Mark Thompson over his plans to slash 4,000 jobs.

More generally, as part of its drive to cut 'red tape' for business, the Coalition also speeded up employment tribunals, while also cutting the number of cases brought before them. Under the Enterprise and Regulatory Reform Act 2013, employees may bring unfair dismissal cases against their employers only after working for them for two years (as opposed to one year previously), unless their actions rest on alleged sacking because of their political opinions or affiliations. The Act also encourages parties to resolve their differences using a new 'early conciliation service', launched through ACAS from April 2014, and/or reach compromises known as 'settlement agreements'.

7.4.4 Workplace health and safety

Health and safety in the workplace is regulated by the Health and Safety at Work Act 1974, which covers the operation of work-based equipment, and various subsequent regulations and statutory instruments, including the Control of Substances Hazardous to Health (COSHH) Regulations 1999, relating to exposure to virtually all potentially dangerous substances.

Since April 2008, the job of both developing policy guidelines on workplace health and safety and enforcing these rules through inspections has fallen to the **Health and Safety Executive (HSE)**.

The HSE's day-to-day work is carried out by its Field Operations Directorate (which incorporates separate factory, agriculture, and quarries inspectorates) and regional officers of the Employment Medical Advisory Service. Its powers are set out in table 7B to be found on the **Online Resource Centre**.

In addition, some health and safety legislation (covering shops, offices, warehouses, restaurants, etc.) is enforced by council environmental health departments (see 18.2.1). In its drive to reduce red tape—particularly for small businesses—the Coalition appointed former Tory Trade Secretary Lord Young to review existing legislation, and he recommended sweeping rationalization of the 'bureaucracy' surrounding health and safety rules. Subsequent legislative proposals have focused on a perceived need to simplify regulations to 'ease the burden on business' and weed out 'rogue health and safety consultants'. The Coalition ultimately adopted a headline-grabbing 'one in, one out' policy towards introducing new health and safety rules, inviting the public to report irritating and unnecessary regulations that they think should be scrapped as part of a so-called 'red tape challenge'.

7.5 The utilities

A 'utility' is an organization—whether publicly or privately owned—that is responsible for maintaining and delivering reliable and affordable supplies of a commodity essential to the lives of a country's citizens. The main utilities are those charged with providing 'natural monopolies'—basic services needed to sustain a society, such as water and energy (gas and electricity). Traditionally, the railways, postal services, and telecommunications have also been grouped under the 'utilities' umbrella.

Recognizing the vital nature of water and power—and persuaded that everyone should have guaranteed, equitable access to them—the post-war Labour government nationalized all utilities in 1948. Until then, like schools and hospitals, they had been owned by an ad hoc medley of local corporations and charities, with the result that service standards and transparency varied wildly from place to place.

For forty years, the utilities remained in the public sector. While individuals still had to pay their own rail fares and electricity bills, the industries were hugely subsidized through general taxation and, at least in theory, everything spent on the services was ploughed back into improving their performance and reducing prices in the longer-term, rather than being top-sliced to pay dividends to private shareholders. Despite the fact that there was no outside competition from other suppliers to drive down prices, subsidies generally enabled utilities to keep charges at reasonable levels.

7.5.1 Privatization of the utilities

In the 1980s, the ethos governing the way in which state-owned utilities were perceived began to change, as free market economics infiltrated public services for the first time. Mrs Thatcher's government began a wholesale privatization, arguing that monolithic state-owned industries were inefficient, overly bureaucratic, and offered too little 'choice'. Arguments for and against privatization are set out in Table 7.3.

Privatization (examples of which are explored in more detail below) was the first step in Mrs Thatcher's mission to 'liberalize' Britain's utilities (which have included British Telecom, General Post Office, the British Gas Board, railways and Royal Mail). She initially moved tentatively—allowing minimal competition in privatized utilities to ensure the transition from public to private sectors had time to bed down before being opened to the ravages of the free market. But by the early 1990s gas, electricity, and telecommunications had been totally 'deregulated', allowing various different companies to compete for business in each sector for the first time. On the railways, travellers were redesignated as 'customers' rather than 'passengers'.

The onward march of deregulation continues to this day, even in the few sectors still dominated by major public sector providers, with British governments favouring 'light touch' regulation, to let market forces determine prices and services. That said, they continue to set certain minimum standards for each sector—for example BT (successor to British Telecom) is still required by its licence terms to maintain public telephone boxes to ensure that there is provision for people without mobile phones, particularly in isolated areas. Royal Mail, meanwhile, currently retains a 'universal service obligation' requiring it

Table 7.3 Arguments for and against utility privatization

For	Against
Privatization improves efficiency by introducing competition and helping providers woo managers with commercial expertise.	Introducing profits raises suspicions that providers' main priorities are boosting revenue and share dividends, rather than using savings to lower prices or improve services.
It enables them to respond to consumers' wishes by reacting to supply and demand with wider choice of services—rather than assuming the 'state knows best'.	Periods of intense competition between rival gas and electricity suppliers, and ineffective regulation, lead to consolidation under fewer companies. Old-style public monopolies are eventually replaced by *private* ones—and company boards (unlike governments) are not accountable to service users.
Privatization removes 'statist' philosophy imposed on publicly owned utilities, allowing them to cut waste and contract out ancillary services—cleaning, catering, etc.—to smaller specialist companies. Doing so cuts overheads, providing more cash for investment.	Some privatized utilities—particularly monopolies such as water companies—pass costs on to consumers, rather than bear them internally, to placate shareholders. Major infrastructural investment required by recent EU directives led to disproportionately high water bill increases, but dividends kept rising.
Privatization raises revenue for future government spending, while saving taxpayers' money by cutting the cost of maintaining infrastructure.	Privatization divests country of significant assets built up through prior investment of taxpayers' money, giving commercial companies 'something for nothing'. Former Tory Prime Minister Harold Macmillan called it 'selling off the family silver'.

to deliver to every home and business in Britain, however remote (although, since privatization, its chief executive, Moya Greene, has repeatedly warned that this will be threatened if industry regulator Ofcom fails to stop competitors not bound by the same condition from undercutting it by cherry-picking easy services in urban areas). In addition, each industry is overseen by at least one statutory regulator tasked with ensuring its customers receive value for money and appropriate access to essential services. The overall responsibilities of regulators include:

- setting limits on price increases;
- monitoring service quality; and
- ensuring that true competition is maintained.

Over the years, however, there has been considerable criticism of these regulators—often derided as 'watchdogs without teeth' because of their perceived reluctance to interfere in how utilities are managed.

7.5.1.1 Communications

British Telecom was privatized in 1984. Initially, only limited competition was allowed, with a single alternative provider, Mercury Communications Ltd, entering the market.

After a well-received trial, this 'duopoly' ended in 1991. Some 150 licensed telecommunications companies soon sprang up, including 125 cable and 19 regional and national public telecoms operators, although the market has since been rationalized through mergers and takeovers. Today, consumers can also choose from multiple mobile phone networks, the largest of which include Orange, O2, Vodafone, and T-Mobile, not to mention numerous Internet service providers, including BT Broadband and Virgin Media.

Confusingly, most telephone landlines are still provided by BT engineers, but customers are billed by the suppliers that deliver their services through those lines. A similar division, between the companies that own the physical infrastructure and those who use it, exists in most utilities.

In recognition of the growing convergence of telecommunications and broadcast media, since 2003 telecoms regulation has been regulated by the **Office of Communications (Ofcom)**, a 'super-regulator' that also oversees television, radio, and digital media services providers. As a media regulator, Ofcom is solely concerned with broadcast and digital or online platforms. In May 2016, following a lengthy review into the future of the BBC, a White Paper unveiled by Culture Secretary John Whittingdale confirmed that it, too, will be brought under Ofcom's oversight in future, with its internal BBC Trust replaced by a board with a much-reduced remit limited to the corporation's day-to-day running. Print media regulation, meanwhile, recently passed from the Press Complaints Commission (PCC) to a new **Independent Press Standards Organization (IPSO)** following the Leveson Inquiry (see 3.1.2.3). Unlike Ofcom, but like the PCC before it, IPSO is 'self-regulatory', with a governing board comprising media and non-media professionals (a slight break with its precursor, which had been dominated by major figures from the newspaper industry, raising questions about its independence). IPSO's responsibility is to ensure that newspapers and magazines comply with an editors' code of practice covering everything from respect for the privacy of the bereaved to protection of confidential sources.

Previously, telecoms were policed by the now-defunct Office of Telecommunications (Oftel), while broadcasting had been overseen by several disparate regulators.

Since 1 October 2011, with the abolition of Postcomm, the postal industry has also been under the ambit of Ofcom. The consumer-run body Consumer Focus, which channelled complaints from public to government in relation to most utilities, has also been scrapped, with its role franchised to the charity Citizens Advice.

Ofcom's role in relation to postal services, acquired from Postcomm, is to:

- protect a universal postal service;
- license postal operators;
- introduce competition into mail services;

- regulate Royal Mail; and
- advise the government on the Post Office network.

The road to privatization for Royal Mail began with a series of interventions by Postcomm highlighting its ailing business model. In May 2008, the regulator issued a report warning that unless it was part-privatized, allowing it to raise investment on the open market, it might have to axe Saturday postal deliveries to save money. Despite already having controversially abandoned twice-daily weekday deliveries, in the year to March 2010 the company made a pre-tax loss of £262 million, which it blamed on growing competition from private providers and consumer resistance to rising first-class mail prices during the recession.

When Royal Mail's stock market flotation finally occurred, however, it proved more modest than initially outlined by the Coalition, and bore some similarities to a 'part-privatization' plan proposed by Lord Mandelson in Labour's final months in office: only 70 per cent of the business was sold and shares were pegged at a cautiously low price of 266 pence apiece. Moreover, in a nod to the mutual model championed by Mr Cable for the future restructure of Royal Mail's counter service, the Post Office, 10 per cent of shares were reserved for its own employees. With ministers (for which read 'taxpayers') having already bought up Royal Mail's £9.5 billion pension deficit and its remaining £1 billion of debt written off, it was hardly surprising that investors were quick to buy up. By the time trading ended on day one, shares had already jumped by more than a third in value (to 455 pence each) and within five months they had risen to 72 per cent more than their sale price. At a time when the government was still pursuing a determined cuts programme, Labour and the unions condemned ministers for short-changing taxpayers, while the independent National Audit Office concluded that the sell-off was 'marked by deep caution, the price of which was borne by the taxpayer'. In July 2014, the Commons Business Committee went further—arguing that the public purse had lost out by as much as £1 billion.

7.5.1.2 Energy

In 1986, gas—then the preserve of the British Gas Board—was privatized. Although the newly rechristened 'British Gas' was initially a private monopoly, the industry swiftly became the first fully deregulated utility. At first, the emerging new generation of gas companies (like electricity suppliers later) were regionally based: households and businesses in south-east England, for example, were given a choice of only one alternative to British Gas, based in their regions. Today, most people can buy their gas from suppliers headquartered anywhere in Britain, or even abroad, and many companies, including British Gas, supply 'dual fuel' (both gas and electricity). Others, including high-street names such as Sainsbury's and Marks & Spencer, offer energy but subcontract the business of actually supplying it to British Gas or rival companies.

As with telecoms, there is a division between supply companies that bill customers and the single firm that owns the infrastructure used to 'transport' fuel to them. Both the network of pipes for gas and the cables or pylons used to transmit electricity are owned by National Grid plc, a monopoly. Suppliers pay it for using its network.

When electricity was privatized in 1990, it was originally split into three generating companies and twelve suppliers. Since then, the electricity supply chain has evolved into the three-stage process outlined in table 7C to be found on the **Online Resource Centre**.

While England and Wales are governed by this system, Scottish Power plc and Scottish Hydro-Electric generate, transmit, and distribute all electricity in Scotland.

The gas and electricity utilities used to have separate regulators, but are now overseen by the **Office of Gas and Electricity Markets (Ofgem)** and Director General of Gas and Electricity Markets. Following a number of controversies over double-digit rises in energy bills (blamed by companies on the rising price of crude oil—despite the fact that most have continued to report substantial profits), a succession of consumer watchdogs have also emerged. The first, Energywatch, was absorbed by Consumer Focus in 2008. Energy prices—and the often baffling complexity of customers' bills and the competing 'tariffs' they are offered—have become such a fraught issue in recent times that both government and Opposition have repeatedly threatened to introduce price freezes or new transparency rules. In March 2016, the CMA recommended a four-year cap for customers on pre-paid meters and a new central customer database to make it easier for people to switch suppliers in pursuit of better deals. Controversially, though, it called for the scrapping of Ofgem's then newly introduced stipulation that companies should only offer customers a maximum of four tariff choices, in order to make it easier for them to find the one best suited to their circumstances.

7.5.1.3 Water and sewerage

The most controversial utility privatization was that of water, in 1989. Given the essential nature of clean, safe water supplies, many critics of privatization (and some supporters) saw the idea of opening it up to market competition as a step too far.

There were also practical objections. Given the peculiar difficulties of 'subdividing' the industry's infrastructure—to use an extreme illustration, splitting stretches of a reservoir between different companies—it quickly became clear that conventional competition would be impossible. To this day, water is supplied to British consumers by companies that are local monopolies—making a mockery, critics argue, of the premise of privatization.

Table 7.4 Regulation of the water industry

Regulator	Remit
Water Services Regulatory Authority (Ofwat)	Regulates industry's structure and financial transparency (examining accounts and vetting mergers/takeovers).
Drinking Water Inspectorate	Regulates quality of water supplied to consumers.
Environment Agency	Monitors pollution and regulates water quality in inland, estuary, and coastal waters; also responsible for flood protection.

Initially, ten water and sewerage companies were formed. Each was given responsibility for supplying water, storing and recycling it, and treating and disposing of sewerage. Confusingly for consumers (and journalists), the industry today is regulated by not one, but three bodies, the roles of which are outlined in Table 7.4.

Industrial and commercial water users are metered nowadays, and households may be charged on the basis of Council Tax band or opt to be metered, depending on where they live. Consumers with a record of unpaid bills are often *forced* to install prepayment meters to avoid them slipping into future arrears and, in certain areas, including parts of the south east, companies have begun to roll out a compulsory meter programme with the stated aim of encouraging people to cut back on their usage, while also charging them for their *actual* consumption, rather than an estimated one as previously. As in the energy industry, there has been periodic controversy about meters, with campaigners arguing that they leave poor people vulnerable: if they do not have change available at a given time, their water supply is cut off. Moreover, companies have been criticized for charging higher rates per unit to customers with meters than to those who pay by conventional bill. These and other concerns prompted the emergence of another watchdog: the **Consumer Council for Water**.

In Scotland, water effectively remains a nationalized utility. Three regional water authorities, covering the north, east, and west of the country, were merged in April 2002 to form a single state-owned company: Scottish Water. Scottish Water is overseen by the Water Industry Commission for Scotland (WICS) and its accounts are audited by Audit Scotland. Pricing is also arguably more progressive, as customers are charged on the basis of their Council Tax bands (see 11.2.4).

7.5.1.4 Railways

Rail privatization took a different route from that of other utilities and today (albeit by default) the industry remains a public–private partnership (PPP). In 1993, following years of negotiation to sell franchises covering marginal and unprofitable lines, British Rail was finally privatized. It was initially fragmented under 100-plus private operators—companies that bought up engines and rolling stock to manage individual routes on renewable franchises. Meanwhile, ownership of the network (in this case, tracks, signals, and stations) was transferred from government to Railtrack: a private monopoly. Following a spate of controversies—including the 1999 Paddington train crash, in which thirty-one people died—in 2002 ministers replaced Railtrack with a not-for-dividend company: **Network Rail**. The infrastructure was therefore effectively taken back into qualified public ownership - until in December 2016 Transport Secretary Chris Grayling pledged to end Network Rail's monopoly over track maintenance by introducing 'joint management teams' through which they would share responsibility for repairs with operating companies.

Network Rail charges the remaining twenty-five operators for using its infrastructure, although in practice many operating companies run their local stations as subcontractors. Franchises are awarded by the government on the basis of a guaranteed 'minimum level of service' specific to each route, and companies tender for renewable terms of anything between seven and twenty years. The company that wins a franchise will usually be the one willing to run services with the lowest government subsidy—giving rise to concerns about underinvestment and price rises. Current franchisees include Southern, which runs the main London–Brighton line and manages stations for Network Rail along that route, and South West Trains, which operates various lines across southern England and greater London.

In some areas, two or more companies operate services in competition, but elsewhere local monopolies exist. Competition is arguably illusory in practice, because it is physically impossible for two companies to run directly competing services (after all, no two trains can use the same track between the same stations at the same time).

Huge increases in numbers of people commuting to work have put growing pressure on the rail network and fare prices have repeatedly risen well above inflation, even at times when service quality has deteriorated. Overcrowded carriages, broken-down engines, late arrivals, and cancellations—at a time when annual government subsidies to the rail network have remained significantly higher than those before privatization—make the railways an enduring ministerial headache. The Coalition's cuts to subsidies led to further dissatisfaction, as year-on-year price rises for commuters repeatedly soared well above wages, despite the fact the industry continued receiving upwards of £4 billion a year from the taxpayer. Indeed, the recent direction of government policy has arguably been to 'privatize' rail in another respect: by shifting the cost of investment in the railways disproportionately onto the shoulders of commuters and other regular users, rather than the general taxpayer, in a similar vein to the way in which undergraduate tuition fees are now used to fund higher education in England. However, attempts by the Tories to return the infrastructure to private hands, by privatizing Network Rail, have so far hit the buffers, with an independent review published in March 2016 recommending only a limited role for business in tracks and stations.

Rail regulation is split two ways in each UK nation. The **Office of Rail and Road** (formerly the Office of Rail Regulation) monitors the performance and safety of the infrastructure, by regulating Network Rail, and licenses train operating companies to use it, while ensuring that there they are given equitable access to tracks and routes. Regulation of train fares and operating companies themselves is, however, more centralized—with the Department for Transport (DfT) itself responsible for awarding and reviewing franchises and fining operators for repeated lateness, cancellations, and other aspects of poor performance in England, while Transport Scotland, the Welsh Government, and the Department of Regional Development, Northern Ireland, fulfil these roles in Scotland, Wales, and Northern Ireland respectively. Indeed, there have been some signs of a willingness by ministers to flex their muscles when services have been particularly poor. In 2009, then Transport Secretary Lord Adonis took the East Coast franchise back into public ownership after its then operator, National Express, ran into financial difficulties. The ensuing publicly run service was consistently rated the most comfortable and efficient in Britain by consumers, but this did not stop the Coalition re-privatizing it, in 2015. As with the other utilities, there is a watchdog to represent consumers: **Transport Focus** (formerly *Passenger Focus*).

7.6 Private finance initiatives (PFIs) and public–private partnerships (PPPs)

In common with major public building projects, the huge infrastructural investments required by utilities are often funded by **private finance initiatives (PFI)**—the system introduced by Mr Major's Conservative government in 1992, initially to pay for new prisons at a time of acute overcrowding and repeated breakouts (see 8.9.6.3). The classic PFI model sees a private company financing the bulk of initial capital investment (buildings and equipment), often along with some ancillary staff to man the facility, and effectively 'owning' it for years or decades afterwards. The taxpayer gradually 'buys it back' in a long-term leaseback arrangement resembling a mortgage.

Although initially sceptical, Labour embraced PFI as it moved to fund an extensive programme of new schools and hospitals, rechristening such projects **public–private partnerships (PPPs)**. Today virtually all new public capital investment is financed this way—and so too are some related to utilities. The proposed new generation of nuclear power stations approved in 2008 is

Table 7.5 Criticisms of PFI/PPP

Criticism	Explanation
Can generally be financed only through borrowing	Because government borrowing is better secured than that of the private sector, the interest rates faced by private investors are usually higher than those offered to states.
Companies put shareholders before public (or 'customers')	Private companies are legally obliged to earn profits for shareholders—so, whatever the short-term savings, the final costs to taxpayers might be greater than if the state had wholly financed the project.
PFI/PPP agreements are like credit card debt or 'hire purchase' agreements of 1960s	There is confusion over who 'owns' the project: hire purchase deals entail ministers using taxpayers' money to mortgage public assets on the 'never, never'.
Who is responsible if something goes wrong—private investor or taxpayer?	The closure of Railtrack increased pressure on the state to lure private sector investment by providing costly guarantees.

likely to be largely, if not wholly, privately financed when it eventually materializes.

One big advantage of using private finance to fund capital projects is that initial outlays do not appear on the Treasury's balance sheet—so they do not technically 'count' as public expenditure. In contrast to the huge start-up costs of some projects, the face values of contracts awarded to private businesses as incentives to carry out building work are relatively low. Critics argue, however, that PPPs have notable disadvantages—as outlined in Table 7.5—and recent difficulties encountered by NHS trusts in servicing their contracts testify to this. There has been mounting concern about the looming scale of public debt racked up by PFI/PPP contracts under successive governments. One NHS trust, South London Healthcare, entered administration at least partly because of its capital 'debt', and others have faced similar difficulties (see 6.3.2). Despite this, the success of the Coalition's and now Conservatives' incipient 'infrastructure plan' appears to rest on hybrid public–private funding arrangements resembling PFI/PPP in all but name.

Topical feature idea

The following is an extract from a story that appeared on *The Guardian* website on 13 June 2016. It concerned a report from Citizens Advice warning that nearly one in six working people are in insecure work—including 'zero-hours' contracts which offer no regular contractual hours or pay. How would you develop this into a lively backgrounder? How many of your readers are in this position, and what stories do they have to tell about their experiences?

Extract from an article published in *The Guardian*, 13 June 2016

Nearly one in six workers in England and Wales in insecure work

The Guardian

13 June 2016

Web link: **https://www.theguardian.com/money/2016/jun/13/england-wales-zero-hours-contracts-citizens-advice-insecure-work**

Four-and-a-half million people in England and Wales are in insecure work, according to research by Citizens Advice, which has warned too much focus on boosting pay risks ignoring the problem of unpredictable incomes for many households. The charity highlighted the debt problems and difficulties accessing in-work benefits for the millions of people who do not have fixed, regular working hours. Its analysis of official figures published on Monday has revealed more than 2.3 million people are working variable shift patterns, a further 1.1 million are on temporary contracts and 800,000 are on either zero-hour or agency contracts.

Zero-hours contracts, which are widely used in the retail industry and do not guarantee employees any work from week to week, have been back in the spotlight this month after the billionaire Sports Direct founder, Mike Ashley, admitted his company had broken the law by failing to pay staff the national minimum wage. Ashley's admission last week to MPs investigating his firm's treatment of its workers, confirmed the findings of a Guardian investigation last year in which undercover reporters exposed how the company was paying staff less than the legal minimum and subjected them to a harsh regime of surveillance and financial penalties for lateness.

Citizens Advice warned that many of the 4.5 million people it classes as being in insecure work—equivalent to about 14% of the working population—do not have regular hours or predictable shifts and so struggle to manage their budgets or plan for the future. 'While for some people working shifts or temporary contracts may provide the flexibility they want, many others struggle to balance the books in the face of such insecure employment', said the Citizens Advice chief executive, Gillian Guy.

The charity welcomed recent changes to boost working people's income—such as the introduction of the 'national living wage' and raising the personal tax allowance threshold—but it wants to see those urgently complemented by efforts to improve people's security at work.

© www.theguardian.com

✷ Current issues

- **The abandonment of Mr Osborne's budget surplus target** Mr Osborne originally promised to eliminate Britain's budget deficit before the end of the 2010–15 parliament. He entered the 2015 election promising to achieve a surplus in 'normal times' from 2020 onwards, but in July 2016 formally abandoned this pledge in the uncertain financial climate following the UK electorate's shock decision to leave the EU.
- **Britain's escalating steel crisis** Britain faces losing nearly 3,000 jobs in the steel industry, with Tata Steel threatening to axe 1,050 and the Caparo Group another

1,700. The slump is being blamed on global pressures, including rising energy bills, the imposition of tariffs in China, and cheap steel imports from the Far East.

- **New curbs on trade union power** The Trade Union Act 2016 has introduced a tough new 50 per cent threshold for voter turnout in ballots on industrial action, to make it harder for unions to muster enough votes in favour of future strikes. New ballots must also be called at least every six months to sanction action, preventing unions from running rolling programmes of strikes without gaining fresh mandates.

Key points

1. The ministry responsible for funding public spending through taxation and borrowing is HM Treasury, while British business interests are promoted by the Department for Business, Innovation, and Skills (BIS).
2. The senior minister who heads the Treasury, the Chancellor of the Exchequer, makes an annual Budget Statement—enshrined by the Finance Act—which raises and lowers taxes, increases or cuts public expenditure, and appraises the performance of Britain's economy.
3. Financial regulation is split four ways: the Bank of England's Monetary Policy Committee (MPC) controls inflation by raising or lowering interest rates; its Financial Policy Committee (FPC) identifies risks to the banking system; the Financial Conduct Authority (FCA) polices banks and other finance companies; and the Prudential Regulatory Authority (PRA) stops them acting irresponsibly.
4. Direct taxes are those paid 'up front' (for example income tax and corporation tax), while indirect ones are 'hidden' within prices of goods and services (for example value added tax, or VAT).
5. Utilities are organizations or companies providing those commodities or services that are considered essential to citizens' day-to-day lives. They include energy, water, and telecommunications.

→ Further reading

Colling, T. and Terry, M. (2010) *Industrial Relations: Theory and Practice (Industrial Revolutions)*, 3rd edn, Oxford: Wiley Blackwell. **Fully revised edition of acclaimed text focusing on the changing nature of worker–employer relations in Britain in the context of changing labour markets.**

Gumbrell-McCormick, R. and Hyman, R. (2013) *Trade Unions in Western Europe: Hard Times, Hard Choices*, Oxford: Oxford University Press. **Examination of the changing role and influence of trade unions in late-modern Britain and western Europe following recent labour market transformations.**

Michie, R. C. (2001) *The London Stock Exchange: A History*, Oxford: Oxford University Press. **Acclaimed history of Britain's biggest money market—one of the largest in the world—incorporating up-to-date explanations of the LSE and how FTSE works.**

Monbiot, G. (2001) *Captive State: The Corporate Takeover of Britain*, London: Pan Books. **Critically acclaimed exposé by a leading campaigning journalist of the creeping growth in influence of commercial companies in British public affairs.**

Smith, D. (2016) *Something Will Turn Up: Britain's Economy, Past, Present, and Future*, London: Profile Books. **Lively and engaging exploration of the major economic debates that have shaped Treasury and Stock Market activity past and present, by one of the UK's leading economics journalists.**

Stiglitz, J. (2010) *Freefall: Free Markets and the Sinking of the Global Economy*, London: Penguin. **Searing critique by a leading economist of the social and economic folly that led to the 2008 global banking collapse and contemporary crisis in capitalism.**

Online Resource Centre

www.oxfordtextbooks.co.uk/orc/Morrison5e/

Visit the Online Resource Centre that accompanies this book for web links and regular updates.

8

Social security and home affairs

The related briefs of 'social affairs' and 'home affairs' occupy more column inches, airtime, and web space than almost any other areas of British life. From government crackdowns on supposed 'welfare scroungers' to controversies about immigration levels to scare stories about rising terrorist threats, barely a week goes by without them generating screaming headlines.

The story of British citizenship in the modern age is one of 'carrot' and 'stick': the 'carrot' of rights, entitlements, and benefits for which UK citizens are eligible; and the 'stick' that threatens prosecution, punishment, and ultimately imprisonment to those who abuse the system by failing to meet their responsibilities.

8.1 The basis of the 'welfare state'

The primary purpose of the 'welfare state' initiated by Herbert Asquith's Liberal government and solidified by Clement Attlee's Labour administration was to provide a safety net for people who fell on hard times, whether temporarily (through losing their jobs or falling ill and being unable to work) or indefinitely (because of serious injury or long-term illness). Other than in exceptional situations, life 'on the social', 'on the sick', or 'on the dole' was never envisaged as a permanent state of affairs for anyone; rather, it was meant to protect those who found themselves unable to work, earning low wages, or otherwise impoverished. The concept of 'deserving' and 'undeserving' poor, culturally hardwired since Elizabethan times, was arguably enshrined even in the mind of William Beveridge (see 6.1).

The term 'welfare state' is widely attributed to William Temple, Archbishop of Canterbury during the Second World War. The *practical* foundations of a prototype welfare state, however, had been laid during David Lloyd George's time as, first, Chancellor of the Exchequer, then prime minister. His 1909

'People's Budget' (see 2.3.1) introduced both old-age pensions and National Insurance (NI)—the progressive tax that remains the bedrock of the benefits system. From the outset, the welfare state was to be based on both *need* and *entitlement*: the needy would be looked after, but their eligibility for this support derived from the presumption that if and when they were able to work and pay their way, they would do so. Today, more than ever, British citizens' ability to claim higher-rate benefits to help them through periods of sickness or unemployment is contingent on their making sufficient NI contributions and paying enough tax during periods of work.

Nonetheless, while a certain amount of 'responsibility' was always expected of those receiving welfare support, there has been a marked hardening of attitudes under recent governments. The early 1980s saw a huge increase in unemployment as entire industries like steel production, shipbuilding, and coal mining were effectively dismantled through Margaret Thatcher's radical market reforms. Few could argue that the hundreds of thousands of workers made redundant were to blame for their own predicament. Yet Mrs Thatcher's ministers did not take long to invoke the image of the jobless layabout. Shortly after the Handsworth and Brixton Riots of 1981, her Employment Secretary, Norman Tebbit, told a journalist:

> ‘I grew up in the 1930s with an unemployed father. He did not riot. He got on his bike and looked for work, and he went on looking until he found it.’

Mr Tebbit's reply went down in British political folklore and set the tone for future policy among not only the Conservatives, but also the Blair-Brown Labour governments, and subsequent Tory-led administations.

8.2 Social welfare services today

As Figure 8.1 illustrates, the social security bill represents the single largest area of government expenditure in Britain. Defined broadly as welfare provision allocated to guarantee 'a basic standard of living for those in financial need', between 2016–17 and 2020–1 it is expected to account for around 27.8 per cent of Britain's overall public spending budget. Yet, contrary to the accusatory headlines of countless media stories that would have us believe it is largely spent on work-shy 'scroungers', according to the independent Institute for Fiscal Studies (IFS), by far the biggest share of the overall £219.8 billion social security spend in 2015–16 (including tax credits—see 8.4)—£92.1bn or 41.8 per cent—was reserved for pensions. Moreover, additional welfare support, including free television licences for over 75-year-olds, pension credits, and Housing Benefit for the poorest, takes the annual total of *all* pensioner benefits to well over half the total welfare budget. It is these benefits primarily, rather than those paid to unemployed and

Figure 8.1 Projected breakdown of public sector spending by department: 2016–17 to 2020–1 (total £4 trillion)

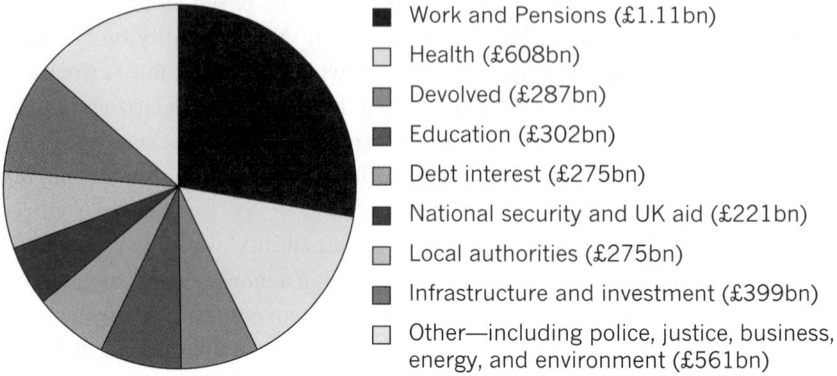

Source: www.gov.uk

low-paid working-age households, that are responsible (on the surface) for the disproportionately high percentage of public expenditure projected to be used for social security in the present parliament, as illustrated in Figure 8.1.

Over the years, social security has been administered by a succession of often overlapping and sometimes conflicting departments. Today, it is split between the Department for Work and Pensions (DWP), the Department for Education (DfE), the Department of Health (DoH), and Revenue & Customs (HMRC)—as illustrated in table 8A to be found on the **Online Resource Centre** that accompanies this book. At the time of writing, however, the bulk of the benefits system for Scotland was in the process of being devolved to Scotland, following a settlement agreed after the close-run 2014 independence referendum.

Because the first half of this chapter is primarily focused on social security—specifically, the benefits and tax incentives introduced by governments to promote welfare and employment—it concentrates on the work of the three biggest players involved: the DWP, the Treasury, and now the Scottish Government.

8.3 The Department for Work and Pensions (DWP)

The DWP has overall responsibility for promoting employment. When Labour returned to power in 1997, its immediate concern was to tackle the emerging problem of intergenerational unemployment—the perceived rise in the number of jobless 18–25 year-olds whose parents also suffered sustained periods of unemployment. The so-called 'New Deal' policies that followed were criticized as much for their narrow focus on these two target groups as for the stiff

Table 8.1 Executive agencies involved in social security

Agency	Role
Jobcentre Plus	Administers most state benefits, ranging from Child Benefit, maternity benefits, and widows' pensions, to Income Support, ESA, Personal Independence Payments (PIPs), and JSA. Council housing departments administer Housing Benefit/Local Housing Allowance (see 16.5) on its behalf.
Child Support Agency (CSA)	Assesses/collects maintenance payments for children from parents under arrangements made in family courts.
Pension Service	Helps older people navigate complex web of alternative pension options and related benefits/tax credits.

conditions that they imposed on those whom they were designed to help. Following the 2001 and 2005 Labour victories, the New Deal was extended to, in turn, over-25s, over-50s, lone parents, and people with disabilities.

The vast and complex benefits system over which the DWP presides is administered in practice by a range of executive agencies. Their roles are outlined in Table 8.1.

8.3.1 Types of benefit and their relationship to National Insurance

Although bedevilled by numerous delays, IT problems, and, in March 2016, the sudden resignation of its architect, long-running Work and Pensions Secretary Iain Duncan Smith, the benefits system is currently working through the most radical shake-up since its inception, with the phased introduction of Universal Credit (UC) (see 8.5). However, even under this new regime—and certainly for those who will remain under the existing one for now—there are two broad 'categories' of UK benefit. Whether a particular payment falls into one or the other depends on the extent of recipients' National Insurance (NI) records. The two categories are:

- **Contributory benefits**—available to people who have paid sufficient NI contributions during the previous two years. These include contributions-based Jobseeker's Allowance (JSA) (the higher rate), Employment and Support Allowance (ESA), and Incapacity Benefit (IB).
- **Non-contributory benefits**—not related to individuals' prior NI contributions. Most are 'needs-based' payments for anyone whose income falls below certain levels and/or who meets other criteria (such as disability). These include Income Support and basic JSA. Some, however, are 'universal' for those who meet other criteria—for example, being in the required age group. Winter Fuel Payment is a cold weather-related allowance paid to everyone over 60, irrespective of their personal financial circumstances.

There are five 'classes' of NI contribution. The most important is Class 1, which employed people pay in proportion to their earnings. One oft-cited advantage of working for someone else is that for every £1 invested in the Class 1 NI 'pot' entitling people to future benefits, should they need them, a further £1 at least is contributed by their employers. By contrast, self-employed people have sole responsibility for making their NI contributions (Class 2, paid weekly, and Class 4, which are profit-based).

8.3.2 Different types of benefit

At present, in addition to Universal Credit (see 8.5), there remain a wide variety of distinct benefits available, depending on whether people are unemployed, disabled, or low-paid.

8.3.2.1 Jobseeker's Allowance (JSA)

Paid to adults working fewer than sixteen hours a week and 'available for and actively seeking' full-time work, there are two levels of JSA: contributions-based and income-based (for those who satisfy financial means tests and the job-seeking criteria, regardless of NI contributions paid). People with savings of £16,000 or more are unlikely to be eligible, while those with between £6,000 and £16,000 receive reduced payments.

As with earlier unemployment-related benefits, JSA has not been immune to criticism. For decades, British governments have agonized over the benefits-related 'poverty trap': put crudely, the fear that giving too much money to the unemployed, or taking too much away from them too quickly if they find a job, acts as a disincentive for them to work. In taking up jobs, unemployed people instantly lose entitlement to out-of-work benefits, and even if they continue to qualify for certain other payments—for example Housing Benefit (HB) or Local Housing Allowance (LHA)—they will immediately be paying income tax and NI contributions out of their wages. For some, such as single parents, the option of taking up a low-paid, temporary, part-time, and/or 'zero-hours' job rather than remaining on JSA often seems impractical: the cost of childcare that they would otherwise not need, combined with an immediate loss of benefits and a delay in receiving any tax credits to which they may be entitled, can make the prospect of remaining unemployed (however unpalatable) the lesser of two evils. Few would dispute that out-of-work benefits should remain lower than pay rates to encourage people to work when they find suitable jobs. But for some campaigners, including social policy think tanks like the Joseph Rowntree Foundation, the poverty trap results less from overinflated benefits than from depressed wages. In the 2016–17 tax year, maximum weekly JSA rates stood at £57.90 for 18–24 year-olds and £73.10 for over-25s—hardly the stuff of which millionaires are made! Indeed, the relatively meagre level of JSA prompted an unusual intervention from the Council of Europe in January 2014, when it described the benefit as 'manifestly inadequate' and suggested that it be doubled. By contrast, for the first time since the mid-1970s, the Coalition's Benefits Uprating Bill 2013 removed the automatic annual increase of welfare payments in line with inflation, instead pegging them to the 1 per cent cap previously imposed by ministers on public-sector pay.

Labour tried to address the low pay issue by introducing Britain's first national minimum wage in 1997 (see 7.4). Yet many workers—particularly those in low-skilled jobs such as call-centre, security, and care work—have continued to receive poverty wages that take little account of local costs of living. Concern about the poverty trap led Labour to roll out tax credits (see 8.4. in this chapter)—a form of welfare top-up for people on low incomes, directed to those of working age through their pay packets, rather than the traditional giro cheque-based benefits system. More recently, former Conservative Chancellor George Osborne's oft-stated resolve to 'make work pay' has seen ministers place renewed emphasis on enforcing the minimum wage legislation and discouraging employers from using 'zero-hours' contracts—under which workers are expected to commit to erratic shift systems in insecure jobs, with no guaranteed weekly working hours (or wages). Most significantly, shortly after the 2015 general election Mr Osborne stole a march on Labour by introducing a higher level of minimum wage for over 25-year-olds and dubbing it the *national living wage*: a term referring to the growing gap between then 'minimum' pay levels and living costs, particularly in south-east England. Since 1 April 2016, those over 25 could have been entitled to at least £7.20 an hour (up from £6.70), though 18 to 24-year-olds remain on a lower 'minimum' wage of £6.70, with those aged 18 to 20 receiving £5.30. By the end of the 2015–20 parliament, the new 'living' wage rate is due to reach £9. Nonetheless, poverty pay campaigners continue to argue that the present levels set by ministers remain out of step with the true cost of modern life—with the Living Wage Foundation urging employers to voluntarily adopt an £8.25 hourly rate, as of October 2015, to keep pace with the rising real-world costs of private-sector rents, utility bills, transport, and food. Acknowledging this, London's then outgoing Tory Mayor, Boris Johnson, who had committed the Greater London Authority (GLA) to a voluntary 'London living wage' several years earlier, raised this from £9.15 to £9.40 an hour. At the same time, budget supermarket chain Lidl introduced a minimum hourly rate of £8.25 across England, Scotland, and Wales (£9.35 in London). Meanwhile, critics continue to condemn the exemption of under 25 year-olds from the mandatory living wage—pointing out that many young people forced to subsist on the lower minimum wage also face soaring rents and rising debt levels, not least thanks to the recent tripling of undergraduate tuition fees in England. Others, notably the Green Party, have argued for the issue of low incomes to be tackled more radically, through the introduction of an unconditional 'citizen's income'—which would give every individual, regardless of any other earnings or wealth, an annual state-funded payment pegged at a level that should cover their basic living costs, such as rent and energy bills. At the time of writing, Shadow Chancellor John McDonnell had recently committed Labour to considering this policy, arguing that, far from acting as a disincentive to work, the safety net it provided would encourage the poor to be participating members of society by offering them a stake by birthright in the fruits of economic growth. At the same time, the universal principle underpinning it would, he argued, encourage 'buy-in' by the better off (as with the NHS—see Chapter 6).

Moves to incentivize work by improving the lot of low-paid employees have, however, been tempered by continuing threats to make life harder for the minority of people whom successive governments accuse of 'refusing' to work, despite being able to do so. In February 2008, Labour launched a major welfare 'rethink', contracting out Jobcentre Plus-style job search advice and support services to the private sector. Companies were paid for successfully finding claimants work and keeping them in those jobs for six months, which was backed by penalties for those who failed to attend interviews or appointments with personal supervisors. The Coalition and now the Conservatives have taken an even tougher stance. One measure introduced by the former was a 'three strikes and you're out' sanctions policy for those who repeatedly refuse job offers. First-time 'offenders' today lose their benefits for three months, second-timers for six months, and third-timers for up to three years.

Unemployed people are also increasingly expected to work for their benefits, with the present government's overarching 'Work Programme' embracing a suite of schemes central to its efforts to help the young and long-term jobless to find (and stay in) work.

Among its various 'conditionality-based' initiatives—inspired by the 'Workfare' system long established in the United States—are several aimed primarily at 16–24-year-olds with little prior workplace experience. Most controversial has been the self-explanatory 'Mandatory Work Activity', which requires those judged to need extra help to engage (or re-engage) with employment to undertake unpaid four-week stints working on community projects for up to thirty hours a week. People who fail to turn up or see placements through to the end lose their benefits for three months for 'first offences' and six for the second. Equally unpopular with the unemployed have been new 'work experience' schemes aimed mainly at the young: although notionally voluntary, if participants leave part-way through 'without good reason', they lose up to two weeks' JSA. A national backlash against these measures began in early 2012, after Cait Reilly, a Birmingham University geology graduate, sued the Coalition under the Human Rights Act 1998 for forcing her to give up a sought-after museum placement that might have led to a professional career opportunity to undertake what she described as 'slave labour' in high-street discount chain Poundland. Amid the negative publicity that followed and a grass-roots protest mobilized by the 'Right to Work' campaign, several major companies withdrew from the scheme—including Sainsbury's, Waterstones, and Superdrug. One of the few prominent surviving participants, Tesco, offered all 1,500 people on placements in its stores and warehouses the choice of continuing on the government scheme or undertaking four-week *paid* internships, leading to guaranteed jobs if they performed well.

Similarly incendiary were the alleged malpractices of some private companies contracted to implement the Work Programme on an offshoot of Labour's 'payment-by-results' basis. In February 2012, it emerged that four employees of A4E ('Action for Employment')—a firm initially hired by Gordon Brown's government, and the biggest recipient of DWP contracts under the Coalition—had been arrested amid allegations of fraud at its office in Slough. Following further arrests and disclosures about an internal audit showing that company bosses were alerted as early as 2009 to potential irregular or criminal activities by employees across Britain, Mr Grayling (Minister of State for Employment at the time) cancelled A4E's contract to arrange placements in south-east England. Three months earlier, Emma Harrison, founder of A4E, had quit as both company chairwoman and the Coalition's 'Family Champion' and 'Back-to-Work Tsar'.

Even the performance of private contractors that have been honestly going about their business has been questioned. In February 2013, the Commons Public Accounts Committee (PAC) criticized their track record after it emerged that, during the first fourteen months of the government's flagship Work Programme, they had helped only 3.6 per cent of people into sustainable jobs—less than a third of the DWP's target number. The PAC concluded that fewer people had found jobs through the scheme than would have been expected to do so of their own accord.

8.3.2.2 Income Support

This flexible non-contributory benefit is available to 16–60 year-olds on low incomes who are not in full-time employment, and who satisfy various other criteria (for example being single parents, full-time carers, or registered blind). It comprises two elements: a basic 'personal allowance' and variable top-ups, or 'premiums', for those who tick certain other boxes (for example, having a partner who is a pensioner or being a full-time carer). As of summer 2016, the two rates for single people were:

- £57.90 for 16–24 year-olds; and
- £73.10 for those aged 25-plus.

As with other benefits, payments to couples take account of their ability to cut costs by shopping and cooking together, and paying joint utility bills. These combined payments are lower as a result—leading critics to argue that couples are unfairly penalized. The standard 2016–17 weekly rate for couples in which both partners were aged 18 or over was £114.85. Eligible single parents were entitled to £57.90 if aged 16 or 17, and £73.10 if aged 18 or over, but since 2008 incremental changes have been introduced to encourage parents to take up jobs once their children reach a certain age, by withdrawing Income Support at that point. Lone parents with children aged over 12 lost their entitlements in November 2008, followed by those with children aged over 10 in October 2009, and everyone with children due to reach the age of seven within the year from October 2010.

As with JSA, restrictions on individuals' ability to claim Income Support apply if they have savings of £6,000 or more.

8.3.2.3 Employment and Support Allowance (ESA) and Personal Independence Payments (PIPS)

Just as there are different levels and types of JSA, so too there is more than one form of benefit for sick and disabled people. Although still scheduled to be replaced eventually by the long-delayed Universal Credit, **Employment and Support Allowance (ESA)** recently supplanted the longstanding *Incapacity Benefit (IB)* as the main contributions-based payment for people judged incapable of working while under State Pension age, who are one or more of the following:

- recipients of Statutory Sick Pay (SSP) through their employer that has ended, although they remain incapable of working;
- self-employed or unemployed; and/or
- former recipients of Statutory Maternity Pay (SMP) who have not gone back to work because of sickness.

Since 31 January 2011, all new applicants for out-of-work benefits related to illness or disability have been assessed for ESA. Long-term IB claimants are currently having their eligibility reviewed incrementally—a process originally due to be completed by 2014, but which has repeatedly been delayed owing to mounting controversy over the number of people pronounced 'fit for work' who have successfully appealed these decisions. The rate at which ESA is paid initially depends on what stage someone's application is at. During the 'assessment phase'—the first thirteen weeks of a claim, when decisions should be made about the applicant's ability to return to work in the short, medium, or long term—the rates for 2016–17 were pegged at the same level as JSA, as follows:

- £57.90 for a single person under 25; and
- £73.10 for a single person aged 25-plus.

Then, if assessments confirm that they have limited ability to work due to illness or disability, claimants are placed in one of the following two groups and paid corresponding levels of benefit:

- the work-related activity group—claimants judged capable of undertaking structured activities designed to prepare them for returning to work receive up to £102.15; and
- the support group—those confirmed as being too sick or disabled to work for the foreseeable future, for whom the rate is up to £109. 30.

While income-based ESA is non-taxable, those who have paid sufficient NI contributions may receive a more generous rate. It is a little-known fact, though, that claimants receiving these higher payments may be liable for tax—depending on whether they have any other income.

Although there has been a widespread consensus around the need to reduce the bill for disability-related benefits—by 2008 there were 2.6 million IB claimants, costing taxpayers £12bn a year—serious questions have been raised about the conduct of the **work capability assessments (WCAs)** used to determine whether new applicants should be granted ESA and existing recipients allowed to continue with it. Subcontracted for some years to occupational health company Atos Healthcare (a branch of a French-owned information technology firm), the assessments have generally been carried out by healthcare professionals, but have long been criticized for lasting barely thirty minutes, involving no medical examination, and centring on 'tick box' questions on computer-based forms.

In May 2010, Mr Duncan Smith announced plans to roll out the tests to existing IB claimants from 2011. A report by Citizens Advice Scotland (where they were piloted) labelled them 'unfit for purpose' after finding that up to two-thirds of claimants put through them under Labour had been declared fit after their medicals—20 per cent more than anticipated. As a result, 8,000 appeals were being heard each month, with two out of five succeeding. A BBC investigation found that many general practitioners (GPs) involved in conducting the tests had strong reservations about their efficacy, particularly in relation to people with mental health problems and other less 'visible' illnesses or disabilities. And calls for them to be scrapped have continued ever since, starting with GPs' unanimous vote at the British Medical Association's 2012 conference condemning them as 'inadequate' and having 'little regard to the nature or complexity of the needs of long-term sick or disabled persons'. By this time, four out of ten appeals reaching tribunals were succeeding.

A more disturbing outcome of the WCA regime has been the mounting evidence of its impact on vulnerable claimants. In June 2012, *The Guardian* revealed the existence of an internal email from senior Jobcentre Plus managers urging staff to handle 'customers' with 'utmost care and sensitivity' to acclimatize them to 'difficult changes' to which they 'may take some time to accept and adjust'. The Black Triangle Campaign, a grass-roots group representing disabled people, had been established a year earlier, largely in response to the apparent suicide of Paul Reekie, a mentally ill man found dead beside two letters: one notifying him of a decision to cancel his Housing Benefit, the other his IB payments. Since then, it has been repeatedly claimed that a number of people have committed suicide after having their IB/ESA cancelled, while official government statistics show that, between December 2011 and February 2014, 2,650 people died within six weeks of being pronounced 'fit for work'. In total, 40,680 of the 2 million-plus people who had received a WCA decision one way or the other between 1 May 2010 and 28 February 2013 passed away within a year. In March 2014 Atos finally surrendered its contract, announcing that it would pull out six months prematurely, in early 2015 (it has since been replaced by another private company, US-based Maximus). Its decision to abandon the tests that it had initiated followed two years of negative publicity, beginning with the unedifying spectacle of disability campaigners occupying the company's London headquarters during the 2012 Paralympic Games.

Only marginally less controversial than ESA is the second principal sickness-related benefit: Disability Living Allowance (DLA), or (as it was recently renamed) **Personal Independence Payment (PIP)**. Eligibility for this non-contributory benefit is based purely on someone's verified mental or physical needs (regardless of income, savings, or ability to work). Those under 65 have traditionally been able to claim DLA if they are physically or mentally disabled. Because it covers both aspects, DLA/PIP comprises both 'care' ('daily living' under PIP) and 'mobility' components, with some individuals qualifying for both. Nonetheless (again ahead of the transfer to UC), since 2013 ministers have insisted that all new claimants undergo medical assessments. As of 2016–17, the 'enhanced' rate of PIP daily living component (the 'higher' rate of DLA care component) was £82.30, while the PIP 'standard' rate was £55.10—the same as the 'middle' rate for those still on DLA. A lower rate still available to DLA claimants of £21.80 does not exist for PIP. Comparisons between the DLA and PIP mobility components are simpler, because both have only higher and lower rates: £57.45 and £21.80 respectively.

8.4 HM Revenue & Customs (HMRC)

HMRC is integral to the welfare system in two respects: it raises taxes to fund benefits and makes discrete payments to families, pensioners, and others on limited incomes through tax credits. Tax credits are designed to encourage low earners to stay in employment and others to take up work, by rewarding them with modest 'rebates' through their pay packets. As the tax credit system has evolved, it has expanded to provide 'minimum income guarantees' (MIGs) for other vulnerable groups, including pensioners. The main types are outlined in table 8B to be found on the **Online Resource Centre** for this book.

Although criticized for its complexity, the tax credit system was initially welcomed by low pay campaigners. However, in recent times even Labour has questioned its unintended consequences, in light of research suggesting that one of its biggest effects has been to subsidize employers paying salaries at, or marginally above, the minimum wage (see 7.4).

8.5 Rationalizing welfare: Universal Credit and the great reform debate

Despite numerous delays and setbacks, the centrepiece of the Conservatives' 'welfare reform' programme remained, at the time of writing, **Universal Credit (UC)**—a putative all-in-one benefit-cum-tax credit designed to rationalize the fiendishly complex array of payment types outlined in this chapter into a single (variable) payment tailored to claimants' individual circumstances. The other stated aim of UC is to better incentivize unemployed claimants to enter work by supplanting an old system that effectively 'punished' people for taking up part-time or full-time work by immediately withdrawing all or most of their social security support. This sometimes left ex-claimants facing short-term 'marginal tax rates' of up to 95 per cent. In addition, those signing temporary contracts were forced to start their benefit claims again from scratch if they found themselves back on the unemployment register when a short-term post ended. The success or failure of UC will therefore rest on the ability of the computer system used to administer it to make accurate real-time calculations of entitlement for the individuals claiming it, taking account of sudden and/or periodic changes in their circumstances. It is hardly surprising, perhaps, that—as with all the best-laid government plans—UC has encountered various obstacles and that the planned mass rollout in October 2013 did not materialize. In fact, by the end of September that year, only 2,150 people in the whole country were receiving it—all in the initial pilot areas of Warrington, Wigan, Oldham, and Tameside. By spring 2016, UC had finally been rolled out to every jobcentre for all single jobseekers. For those living with partners and/or dependent children, however, it was still only available in around 110 areas. The introduction of UC has spawned other innovations designed to streamline the benefits system, including online accounts and monthly (rather than fortnightly) payments, which go direct into claimants' banks. Support with housing costs is also in the process of being incorporated into the benefit.

Although there has long been cross-party support for the *principle* of UC, and some other aspects of welfare reform, this broad consensus has lately broken down, with the election of left-wing Labour leader Jeremy Corbyn and the emergence of mounting evidence that the government's wider welfare reform agenda has contributed to increasing, rather than alleviating, poverty. One of Mr Osborne's driving missions as Chancellor was to force down the cost of 'welfare'. While he managed this feat to some extent (DWP's budget shrank by nearly 36 per cent overall between 2010 and 2016), it proved difficult for him to achieve dramatic cuts for many reasons. Despite a series of swingeing cuts to HB/LHA and the eligibility criteria for claiming them, the Centre for Cities think tank revealed that the overall 'Housing Benefit bill' rose from £20bn to £25bn between 2010 and 2015, due largely to soaring private rental costs and falling wages (average annual salaries dropped by £1,300 per person in that period). Mr Osborne also made his own job harder by insisting on a 'triple-lock' to protect the value of the State Pension: by far the single most costly social security benefit (see 8.2). As a result, the overwhelming weight of welfare cuts has fallen on working-age people, particularly the unemployed, younger claimants, and the sick and disabled—leading critics to condemn ministers for increasing intergenerational inequality and penalizing the most vulnerable. Controversial changes since 2010 have included the introduction of an initial £500-a-week or £26,000-a-year household 'benefit cap' (reduced from autumn 2016 to £23,000 a year for families living inside Greater London and just £20,000 for those elsewhere); the pegging of ESA levels for sick and disabled claimants in the 'work-related activity group' to the same level as JSA (equivalent to a 30 per cent benefit cut); the end to 'automatic' HB/LHA entitlement for low-earning or jobless 18 to 21-year-olds (a policy which has forced many to return to live with their parents—assuming they have them); and implementation of the 'bedroom tax' (see 16.5).

In practice, however, Mr Osborne was repeatedly forced to retreat from attempts to further extend the scope of cuts to working-age benefits. In November 2015, a dogged Labour-led rebellion in the House of Lords blocked ministers' attempts to force through a cut to working tax credits which would have left some 3 million low earners up to £1,700 a year worse off—blatantly contradicting the government's oft-repeated promise to reward 'hard-working families' who 'do the right thing' by 'making work pay'. In performing this U-turn, Mr Osborne had to breach a self-imposed cap (of £122bn in 2016–17) on the overall bill for benefits excluding pensions, JSA, and other unemployment-related payments—barely two years after introducing it. But greater humiliation was to come: within days of delivering his March 2016 Budget Speech, a chastened Mr Osborne returned to the Commons to confirm he was abandoning plans to cut PIP payments for 370,000 disabled people by up to £3,500 a year. This followed Mr Duncan Smith's resignation. Mr Smith branded the proposed cuts 'indefensible' at a time when high earners were set to gain from other Budget measures, including a rise in the threshold above which the higher rate of income tax is paid. Within days, a symbolic line in the sand appeared to have been reached, when Mr Duncan Smith's short-lived successor, Stephen Crabb, used his maiden Commons speech to state that the government had no plans for further welfare cuts before 2020. However, it remains to be seen how long this pledge will last, following the appointment in July 2016 of a new Welfare Secretary, Damian Green, by newly installed premier Theresa May.

8.5.1 'Universal benefits' versus 'means-testing': the future of welfare for parents and older people

In addition to some of the disability benefits outlined throughout this chapter, several other sources of support have continued to be available 'universally'. These **universal benefits** are paid to recipients who meet criteria *other than* financial need and, as such, have traditionally been available to rich and poor alike—like access to the NHS. In most (but not all) cases, these tend to be payments for children and the elderly.

Child Benefit has traditionally been paid to all mothers in respect of every child under the age of 18 (or 20 if they are in full-time education or training). But it has long been controversial, given that high-income families arguably have little need for it, yet until recently received the same amount per child as the poor. After initially being frozen by the Coalition, since January 2013 Child Benefit was removed from all families with at least one adult earning £60,000 or more. Parents on £50,000–£60,000 must repay a portion of the Child Benefit their household receives through tax, at a rate of 1 per cent for every £100 they earn over the lower threshold. Critics condemned the injustice of a move that enables households with two earners, each taking home £49,000, to retain their entitlements while single parents on just over that amount lose it. Yet Mr Osborne's original idea had been significantly harsher: removing it from any household in which one adult was a higher-rate taxpayer (at the time earning as little as £42,875). More recently, a long-mooted 'two-child' policy was introduced in relation to Child Tax Credits (see 8.4), meaning that from April 2017 all households with more than two children will only receive them for their first and second children. Although larger families already claiming for their third or subsequent offspring prior to this date will continue to do so, poverty campaigners argue that the change will plunge many poorer working households into penury. They also point out that the reform goes against the spirit of other policies designed to encourage work (however poorly paid), including increases in the income tax threshold (see 7.1.2).

The Child Benefit debate had its roots in two key issues: the historical context underpinning it, and the overarching concept of 'universalism'. To begin with the former, Child Benefit—paid directly to mothers—was long seen as a means of liberating women from dependency on their husbands or partners and giving them direct control over a 'household budget' (which, in times gone by, might have been their only income). More generally, universal benefits like this have long been defended, notably by politicians on the Left, because paying them to everyone, regardless of income, gives those who do not need benefits on financial grounds a 'stake' in the welfare system—thus promoting solidarity about the importance of maintaining it for those who do. Labour also long resisted **means-tested benefits**: payments targeted only at those who can prove they are on low incomes and have minimal savings. Their principal objection has been that requiring people to demonstrate their poverty was humiliating and might discourage many in urgent need of financial help from claiming money to which they were entitled.

A more pragmatic argument against means-testing is that it is too complex and costly, given the need to reassess households repeatedly whenever their incomes fluctuate. Yet, ironically, such real-time adjustments are precisely the principle on which UC was, from the outset, predicated (see 8.5).

The same principle of universality currently applies to certain forms of welfare targeted at the elderly—notably, free bus passes for use on local services anywhere in England and Wales (for those aged 60 and above) and the Winter Fuel Payment (which currently amounts to £200 for individuals living alone who were born on or before 5 May 1953, or £300 for those aged 80 or over in the qualifying week). As with other benefits, couples receive reduced sums (£100 and £200 each, respectively), but the poorest pensioners (those on Pension Credit, income-based JSA, or income-related ESA) receive £200 or, if over the age of 80, £300, irrespective of whether they live with another adult. In addition, means-tested Cold Weather Payments are paid to those who qualify for Pension Credit at times when the temperature has been, or is expected to be, at or below zero degrees Celsius for seven days in a row between 1 November and 31 March.

Two further universal benefits for those meeting the criteria based on their family situations are Statutory Maternity Pay (SMP) and Statutory Paternity Pay (SPP). These are paid via employers to parents of recently born children. Mothers are now entitled to up to fifty-two weeks' maternity leave, thirty-nine of them paid—albeit at 90 per cent of their average gross weekly earnings for the first six weeks and whichever is lowest of £139.58 a week or 90 per cent of gross earnings for the remaining thirty-three weeks. Fathers are eligible for two weeks' paid paternity leave, at either 90 per cent of their normal earnings or the £139.58 rate (whichever is lower)—and, since 3 April 2011, have been able to use up to six months of the maternity leave entitlement if the mother decides to return to work sooner. This arrangement is known as Shared Parental Leave (SPL) or Statutory Shared Parental Pay (SSPP), and fathers who take their wives' or partners' leave to enable them to work may use up their entitlement in 'blocks', separated by periods of employment, rather than having to take it all in one go—provided they claim it all within the child's first year.

Other entitlements include Statutory Sick Pay (SSP), available for up to twenty-eight weeks to full-time employees unable to work through ill health, and widows' pensions—lump sums paid to women whose husbands were below retirement age when they died. Payments begin from the date the husbands would have qualified for pensions had they lived.

Taken together, the sheer scope of universal benefits has led even some long-time defenders of universalism to reflect that the principle has had its day. Perhaps the most 'regressive' example of the contributory principle in action is the continued entitlement to Winter Fuel Payments of wealthy ex-patriot Britons who retire abroad. Others point out that resistance against means-testing is based on a false premise. With fewer and fewer elderly and disabled people entitled to automatic government help with social care costs (see 17.2.1), because their savings or incomes are judged too high, in many areas of life it already exists.

One longstanding form of welfare support that *was* targeted at those on low incomes was the one-off payment. This traditionally took one of several forms, the most common being budgeting and crisis loans—lump sums used, respectively, to smooth over gaps between pay packets or benefit payments, or to help out in the event of emergencies, such as floods or fires, or with urgent unforeseen expenses such as funeral costs. These were derived from a centrally held pot of money known as the Discretionary Social Fund. The Welfare Reform Act 2012 abolished both this and a centrally directed budget loans system from April 2013, replacing them with an initial £178 million-a-year spending pot from which councils could draw to offer those in severe financial need 'discretionary support'. But critics have consistently argued that this is far less than was previously spent nationally—and as the money has not generally been ring-fenced to *force* councils to spend it on the poor, in practice they have used it to plug funding gaps in other service areas caused by public spending cuts. The only part of Britain where discretionary money *has* been ring-fenced, to date, is Scotland, where devolved powers were used to formalize a Scottish Welfare Fund by statute as of 1 April 2016.

Indeed, the end of the Social Fund in most areas, combined with other recent aspects of welfare reform—including benefit cuts for the young, sick, and disabled, and the introduction of ever-harsher sanctions for those who miss job interviews or DWP appointments—has left many low-income households reliant on food banks run by churches and charities for basic essentials, in a throwback to the patchy support offered to 'deserving' paupers in the pre-welfare state era. According to leading food bank charity the Trussell Trust, which runs 420 such outlets, more than a million emergency food parcels were distributed between 2014 and 2015 alone—400,000 of them to children.

8.6 Pensions and the great retirement debate

Although there has been much consternation in recent years about its paltry size, Britons are still automatically entitled to a state retirement pension funded out of general taxation.

Retirement ages for men and women are gradually being equalized. At the time of writing, men born before 6 December 1953 were retiring at the age of 65, while women born after 5 April 1950, but before 6 December 1953, retired between 60 and 65. Following a review of existing retirement ages by an Independent Public Service Pensions Commission, the Pensions Act 2011 speeded up raising the retirement age for women to age 65, to be phased in between April 2016 and November 2018. The Act also stipulated that the state pension age for all women born on or after 6 April 1953 and all men born on or after 6 December 1953 will start rising to 66 between December 2018 and October 2020 and the pensionable age will rise further, to 67, between 2034 and 2036, and to 68 between 2044 and 2046.

The pension age increase has since been fast tracked, though, and by 2028 at the latest everyone will be retiring by 67. Moreover, in his March 2012 Budget,

Mr Osborne stated that, from that date onwards, the retirement age would be linked directly to changes in life expectancy.

The basic State Pension was one of the founding initiatives of the welfare state. Funded through NI contributions, this baseline provision was supplemented in 1978 with the introduction of the State Earnings-Related Pension Scheme (SERPS), championed by the late Baroness Castle, who, as Health and Social Security Secretary, was its main architect. SERPS—eventually replaced with the State Second Pension (S2P) by Labour itself in 2002—was seen by many as guaranteeing a civilized degree of comfort to people in retirement because of the principle underpinning it: that pensions should keep pace with average wages.

By the late 1970s, most working people were required by their employers to contribute to second, occupational pensions (normally through their wages). For some years, however, pension provision in Britain has been a patchwork, with many workers having neither the job security nor the income to pay into a scheme beyond the state one. Mrs Thatcher's government actively encouraged employees to opt out of SERPS and invest in potentially more lucrative (if riskier) personal pensions. However, the vulnerability of private schemes has repeatedly been exposed since—through scandals ranging from the mis-selling of pensions by Royal and Sun Alliance and Standard Life, to the fraudulent misuse of the Mirror Group pension fund by late newspaper tycoon Robert Maxwell, to the revelation that 11,000 BHS staff made redundant by the collapse of the high-street retail chain in May 2016 also faced uncertainty over their security in retirement as a result of a £571m pension fund deficit left by the company's former owners.

Since the mid-1990s, the pensions issue has become increasingly toxic. As more people are living longer, radical steps are needed to ensure that, in years to come, everyone can retire on liveable incomes. Although, in principle, individuals' entitlement to claim State Pension when they reach retirement age relates to the fact that they have part-funded their own pension (by 'paying into the pot' during their working lives), in practice the pensions of today are actually paid for by the working-age population. Given Britain's rapidly ageing population, no longer are there guaranteed to be enough working-age taxpayers to support the pensioners of tomorrow.

The Welfare Reform and Pensions Act 1999 paved the way for potentially radical pension changes. But ministers' attempts to move from this to a definitive framework for state-funded pensions stuttered for years afterwards. Following a 2006 report by Lord Turner's Pensions Commission, however, Labour proposed a radical shake-up designed to co-opt all workers into a new national pension savings scheme from 2012 and relink the State Pension to average earnings—for the first time since SERPS was abolished. Both these moves were eventually acted on by the Coalition. The earnings link was restored in Mr Osborne's 2011 Budget, while the Pensions Act 2011 introduced the principle of automatic enrolment ('auto-enrolment') for workers into occupational schemes their employers were obliged to set up, commencing from 1 October

2012. Then Pensions Minister Steve Webb initially set an 'earnings trigger' forcing bosses to enrol their staff in work-based schemes as soon as their salaries reached £7,475, later raising this to £10,000—in line with the then PAYE personal allowance threshold (see Table 7.1). Second, in the most ambitious rationalization of state pensions for generations, from 6 April 2016 all adults born on or before 6 April 1953 and 1951 respectively have qualified for 'single-tier' pensions equivalent to the existing basic and additional State Pension combined.

Less welcome (for some) was a second piece of legislation: the Public Sector Pensions Act 2013. This enshrined in law a requirement for state workers to retire later than previously and to pay more into their occupational pensions, but with lower incomes guaranteed in retirement. Its passage followed months of acrimonious negotiations between ministers and unions, and several strikes by public servants, including teachers, doctors, and council workers, in protest at ministers' earlier imposition of tougher pension terms (see 7.4.2).

There was also to be a late twist to the Coalition's overall pension settlement for workers when, in June 2016, Business Secretary Sajid Javid announced plans to relax obligations imposed on employers to link pension payouts to the retail price index (RPI) (typically the higher measure of inflation—see 7.1.4), rather than the consumer price index (CPI). This was done with the aim of attracting investors to buy up plants owned by Tata Steel UK, potentially saving up to 40,000 jobs. Mr Webb—by then an ex-MP, having lost his seat in the 2015 election—condemned the move, warning that it might set a precedent for other companies to demand comparable exemptions.

As of 6 April 2016, the three types of government-backed pension are as outlined in Table 8.2.

Table 8.2 The three types of government-backed pension

Type of pension	How it works
State Pension	Contributory benefit received by those reaching State Pension age before 6 April 2016 with minimum of thirty years' NI contributions. Currently linked to whichever is highest of average earnings, CPI inflation, or 2.5%. Those with insufficient NI contributions qualify for Income Support.
Stakeholder pension	For those without occupational pensions (e.g. self-employed), but earning enough to save for retirement. Distinct from most pension schemes operated by banks or building societies in being cheaper and more flexible (people can move them from job to job). Government pays monthly contributions in place of employers.
Single-tier pension	New single payment for people reaching State Pension age after 6 April 2016, based on thirty-five years' NI contributions (pro rata sums paid to others). Estimated introductory rate of £144 a week, rising annually in line with 'triple lock' (higher of inflation, average earnings, or 2.5%).

8.7 Reviews and appeals under the benefits system

If claimants are dissatisfied with decisions on their eligibility for benefits, or moves to withdraw them, they may appeal. Before appealing, however, they must go through a lengthy process, requiring them to file formal complaints with 'local decision-makers'. If dissatisfied with the outcomes of these, they may apply for 'reviews' by those decision-makers.

Finally, claimants have recourse to one last stab at 'justice': appeals handled by a branch of the Tribunals Service known as the Social Security and Child Support Tribunal (SSCS—formerly the Appeals Service). Incorporated into the Tribunals Service in 2006, this agency handles appeals about claims for all kinds of benefit, from DLA to SMP.

Once the SSCS has reached a decision, appeals can only ever be taken further on a 'point of law'. In such circumstances, they are dealt with by an independent ombudsman (either a Social Security Commissioner or Child Support Commissioner).

8.8 Devolving benefits: the future of welfare in Scotland

With the passage of the Scotland Act 2016, after months of 'parliamentary ping pong', Holyrood finally gained control of its first slate of devolved powers over social security. Although the UK Parliament retains 'reserved' powers to set the levels of all means-tested and contributory benefits in Scotland—collectively defined as 'excluded'—£2.7bn worth of benefits, including DLA, PIP, and various other needs-based payments relating to disability or illness, have been devolved. The Scottish Parliament also has authority to introduce new reliefs in these areas. Equally significantly, although JSA and UC will continue to be set at Westminster, Holyrood may now choose to top up these reserved benefits out of its own coffers—even going so far as to treble unemployment-related payments. Whether the new Scottish powers, for all their limitations, lead to pressure for social security devolution to Wales and Northern Ireland remains to be seen. In the run-up to the May 2016 Holyrood elections, First Minister Nicola Sturgeon confirmed her government would set up a distinct Scottish Benefits Agency in Scotland from 2017, committing it to taking a more 'compassionate' approach to administering welfare policy than its Whitehall equivalent, Jobcentre Plus. There were also plans to raise Carer's Allowance to the same level as JSA and revert to a fortnightly, rather than monthly, payment cycle for UC claimants, to make it easier for them to budget.

8.9 The changing face of home affairs

Officially the 'Home Department', the Home Office was split in two in spring 2007 by Mr Blair's final Home Secretary, John Reid, who declared it 'not fit for purpose' following a succession of public embarrassments over its handling of anti-terrorism and asylum policy, and a prison service creaking under the weight of too many inmates. Mr Reid went on to instigate one of the biggest shake-ups in this sprawling department's 225-year history. For some years, there had been an artificial 'Chinese Wall' between the responsibilities of the Home Office and the then Lord Chancellor's Department (briefly renamed the 'Department for Constitutional Affairs' in 2005) regarding crime and disorder. With the emergence of major new internal security issues in relation to the growing threat of Islamist terrorism, Mr Reid judged that the department needed to cede some criminal justice powers and focus more effectively on the many other policy areas in its ambit.

When Mr Brown arrived in Downing Street, he replaced the Department for Constitutional Affairs with a new Ministry of Justice (MoJ). Jack Straw became the first Lord Chancellor in more than 300 years to be a member of Parliament (MP) rather than a peer. This newly established 'tradition' has continued ever since, with the latest incumbent, Liz Truss, marking two other breaks with the past as both a woman and a non-lawyer. As 'commoners', today's Lord Chancellors also hold an additional title: Secretary of State for Justice. This better describes their powers, in light of the fact that the post has lost several of the Lord Chancellor's historical trappings, notably his or her chairmanship of debate in the Lords, now undertaken by Lord Speaker (see 1.1.1.3). The division of responsibilities between the dual departments resulting from these reforms is now as outlined in Table 8.3.

To aid the Home Office in its new counterterrorism responsibilities, has gained a new 'sub-department': the Office for Security and Counter Terrorism. A National Security Board (NSB)—a weekly forum chaired by the Home Secretary—was also formed to discuss security threats when they occurred, with a National Criminal Justice Board (NCJB) promoting 'joined-up government' between the two departments responsible for different aspects of criminal justice policy (chaired jointly by the Home Secretary, Justice Secretary, and Attorney General).

Table 8.3 Breakdown of responsibilities of the Home Office and Ministry of Justice

Home Office	Ministry of Justice
Policing and crime prevention	Court system and sentencing policy
Security and counterterrorism	Prisons
Human Rights Act (HRA) 1998	Probation and prevention of reoffending

8.9.1 Policing and crime prevention

The role of Her Majesty's Constabulary is explored in depth in Chapter 10. In examining the work of the Home Office, however, it is important to outline the extent to which English and Welsh police forces remain under the department's authority.

The Home Office is responsible for recruitment, training, and remuneration of the police. Responsibility for organizing policing on the ground, however, is delegated to local police and crime commissioners (see 10.7.1.1), who, in turn, hire and fire chief constables. In practice, even today the Home Secretary must endorse these appointments, and if there is a perception of declining confidence in either chief constables or commissioners, he or she may intervene to remove them. In June 2001, the then Home Secretary David Blunkett publicly urged Sussex Police Authority to sack local chief constable Paul Whitehouse over his handling of an inquiry into the fatal shooting by a police marksman of an unarmed alleged drug dealer several years earlier. Mr Whitehouse, who had promoted two of the officers involved, subsequently resigned.

The Home Secretary's traditional responsibility for overseeing policing in London, through the Metropolitan Police Commissioner, was formally handed to a newly created police authority answerable to the Greater London Authority (GLA) in 2000—and the GLA has not been afraid to use these powers. In November 2007, it passed a vote of 'no confidence' in the then Commissioner Sir Ian Blair following the Met's conviction for breaching health and safety legislation when anti-terror officers mistakenly shot dead Jean Charles De Menezes, an innocent Brazilian man, at Stockwell Tube station in July 2005. An inquest jury subsequently returned an open verdict into his death in December 2008—pointedly disbelieving testimony by police officers who insisted they had shouted a warning to him before opening fire—and it was only a matter of time before Sir Ian was forced out (effectively by London Mayor Boris Johnson).

Recent governments have also had periodic run-ins with the police as a whole—usually over pay, recruitment, and/or pensions. As the age of austerity bit, the then Conservative Home Secretary Theresa May repeatedly received glacial receptions at conferences of the Police Federation of England and Wales—the national body representing front-line officers and the police service's closest equivalent to a union. In May 2012, she was heckled while addressing the Federation against the backdrop of 20 per cent budget cuts, a tough new pensions settlement, and mass government-backed outsourcing of policing functions to the private sector. But two years later, she delivered a steely speech in which she ordered the police service to reform or face enforced changes imposed 'by statute'. She also withdrew state funding for the Federation with immediate effect. To place this clash in context, it came against the backdrop of a succession of high-profile embarrassments for the police. For example, a long-awaited report was published into South Yorkshire Police's mishandling of the 1989 Hillsborough Stadium disaster (ultimately leading to a belated inquest verdict, in April 2016, that the ninety-six Liverpool fans who perished in it had been 'unlawfully killed' as a result of the failings of the emergency services) and allegations surfaced of unlawful payments passing between News International journalists and serving officers in the Metropolitan Police. On a more 'personal' level for the Conservatives, there was lingering distrust between ministers and the Met following the bizarre 'Plebgate' row. In December 2012 former Cabinet Secretary Andrew Mitchell was forced to resign amid accusations that he had grumpily called two police officers 'plebs' after they asked him to dismount from his bicycle when exiting through the gates of Downing Street. CCTV footage, leaked emails, and the imprisonment of one officer, PC Keith Wallis, for misconduct in public office appeared for a time to support Mr Mitchell's denials, but in November 2014 he lost a libel action against News Group Newspapers over the article which first raised the 'plebgate' allegations. The judge in the case, Mr Justice Mitting, ruled that he probably had used 'the politically toxic word pleb'.

In policy terms, the most significant ongoing disagreement between the police and government relates to the pace and nature of reform. Although ministers initially insisted that only 'back office' police work would be franchised out to the private sector—leaving front-line policing to officers employed by the state—by March 2012 this plan had stalled. That month, West Midlands and Surrey police forces (apparently with ministerial approval, and on behalf of all English and Welsh forces) invited bids from private companies—including the world's biggest security firm, G4S—to take over day-to-day running of a wide range of duties, including criminal investigations and detaining suspects. Earlier in the year, Lincolnshire Police had signed a £200 million contract with G4S to 'privatize' its civilian staff by transferring them to the company, which also confirmed plans to build and run England's first private police station. By November 2015, G4S' managing director for public services, John Shaw, claimed to have saved the force £6m.

Like hospitals, schools, and care homes, police forces are independently inspected. The body responsible, Her Majesty's Inspectorate of Constabulary (HMIC), is the oldest organization of its kind—dating back to the County and Borough Police Act 1856. Its remit covers England, Wales, and Northern Ireland—there is a separate inspectorate for Scotland—and it is headed by a Chief Inspector of Constabulary.

Like Ofsted, the Inspectorate can be outspoken. In July 2012, it warned that three regional forces—the Met, Devon and Cornwall, and Lincolnshire—were on the verge of being unable 'to provide a sufficiently efficient or effective service' because of the negative impact of budget cuts. Contrary to ministerial assurances, it estimated that there would be 5,800 fewer front-line officers across England and Wales' forty-three forces by 2015, with 26,600 other personnel losing their jobs.

8.9.2 Security and counterterrorism

When fifty-two commuters were killed in coordinated suicide bombings in central London on 7 July 2005, ministers decided that security policy must be at the heart of their future policy agenda. Ever since the attacks on New York's World Trade Center on 11 September 2001, and Britain's subsequent support for US-led military action in Afghanistan and Iraq, the country had been periodically threatened with its own atrocity—both covertly, through tip-offs gathered by intelligence services, and overtly, by the increasingly bellicose online proclamations of the late Osama bin Laden, his chief 'lieutenant' Ayman Al Zawahiri, and others.

Because of these threats—real and perceived—Mr Blair's government had already passed several 'anti-terror' laws long before the 7 July bombings. In fact, so proactive had it been that critics argued that, far from preventing further attacks, it risked provoking them.

Of all these anti-terror policies, the most controversial and far-reaching were those relating to the detention of terrorist suspects. At the heart of the controversy was ministers' readiness to dispense with more than 800 years of due legal process by detaining people for prolonged periods without charge. Civil liberties campaigners saw moves such as the internment in Belmarsh Prison of individuals suspected of (but not immediately tried for) terror offences as a breach of the sacrosanct constitutional principle of habeas corpus—the right to a fair trial before one's peers—introduced under Magna Carta. Signed by King John in 1215 (see 1.1.1.1), this mammoth document stipulated that:

> 'No free man shall be seized or imprisoned ... except by the lawful judgement of his equals or by the law of the land.'

The policy of detaining 'terror suspects' summarily (before trial) at Belmarsh began in late 2001, shortly after the 11 September attacks. It was not long before the government—which had opted out of the section of the Human Rights Act 1998 barring it from taking such action—faced significant challenges. As early as July 2002, the Special Immigration Appeals Commission (SIAC), a Home Office quango, ruled that four detainees imprisoned under the Anti-Terrorism, Crime, and Security Act 2001 had been unjustifiably discriminated against as foreign nationals. Although this ruling was later overturned by the Court of Appeal, worse was to come for ministers. Most significantly, in December 2004 the Law Lords ruled that continued detention of the twelve individuals still in custody was incompatible with human rights legislation.

Despite an initial show of defiance, the then Home Secretary Charles Clarke was forced to release the suspects early in 2005, replacing indefinite detention with 'control orders'—sweeping powers to confine suspects in the community using electronic tagging, curfews, and even house arrest. But this 'guilty until proved innocent' approach to security policing only managed to go so far: in

November 2005, Mr Blair suffered his first Commons defeat in eight years by staking his authority on a vote to increase the period of time for which police could detain terror suspects for questioning, from an existing fourteen-day limit to ninety days. Mr Blair—who claimed senior police officers had presented a 'compelling' case for extending their detention powers—had to accept a compromise of twenty-eight days.

His successor, Mr Brown, later tried to raise this to forty-two days by offering rebellious backbenchers a series of sweeteners and railroading the measure through on a three-line whip. But he and the then Home Secretary Jacqui Smith shelved the plans after being defeated in the Lords by a 191-vote majority.

Having fought the 2010 election on pro-civil liberties platforms, the Tories and Lib Dems launched a wholesale review of anti-terrorism policies on entering government. In January 2011, they confirmed that 'Section 44' police stop-and-search powers (allowing officers to stop people without reasonable grounds for suspicion) would in future be sanctioned only with the permission of very senior officers and in circumstances in which a terrorist attack was believed imminent, while the twenty-eight-day detention period would be halved to fourteen days. Ministers' move to scrap control orders was widely mocked, however, when they did little more than 'rebrand' them—as **terrorism prevention and investigation measures (TPims)**, lasting up to two years. Meanwhile, the ability of the authorities to impose sixteen-hour curfews on tagged suspects was reduced to a maximum of ten hours—with curfews themselves redefined as **overnight residency requirements**. In July 2012, the first Tpim breach was confirmed when an alleged al-Qaeda sympathizer, identified only as 'CF', was repeatedly intercepted crossing through the Olympic Park in Stratford, east London.

8.9.3 Asylum, immigration, and citizenship

Another of the biggest home affairs issues of recent years has been immigration. The term 'asylum seeker' entered the media lexicon around the time that war broke out in the Balkans in the early 1990s. The media was quick to focus on this new 'threat' to Britain's borders, and by 2002 the red-tops were filled with scare stories about impending invasions of 'asylum seekers' lured by a supposedly 'soft touch' benefits system. Their agitated prose was fuelled by the French government's initially laissez-faire attitude towards a burgeoning refugee camp at Sangatte, near Calais, from which 1,600 asylum seekers were apparently planning to sneak into England.

Enlargement of the European Union (EU), ultimately to twenty-eight countries, has led to significant influxes of *economic* migrants from other countries—particularly those in the former Eastern Bloc—in pursuit of paid work. This, too, has been controversial, with more right-leaning newspapers pandering to the concerns of local communities in some areas that foreign workers were 'stealing' jobs from longstanding residents and putting pressure on already overstretched public services, such as social housing, schools, and healthcare. There have also been numerous headlines blaming immigrants for rises in crime. More recently, attention has switched to the supposed problem of 'benefit tourists'—specifically, migrants from poorer EU countries (see 9.6). Ongoing debate about the perceived strain placed by migrants on welfare and public services has seen not only anti-EU parties like the British National Party (BNP) and UKIP, but all the 'mainstream' ones adopt increasingly harsh (to some, borderline racist) rhetoric and policy positions. One outcome has been the Conservative government's introduction of a ban on EU migrants receiving UC, HB/LHA, or other means-tested benefits until they have started work in Britain first, and the then prime minister David Cameron's pursuit of an 'emergency brake' depriving them of working tax credits until they have worked in the country (and paid National Insurance contributions) for four years (see 9.3.4). Although this creates the bizarre anomaly that two adults working alongside each other in identical jobs, on identical rates of low pay, could have different entitlements to state support, the Tories (and, until Mr Corbyn's election as leader, Labour) have justified this approach on the grounds that it ends any expectation among migrants that they can receive 'something for nothing'. Restrictions to migrants' entitlements have also been imposed in the NHS, though with the focus primarily on those from outside the European Economic Area (EEA)—the EU member states plus Iceland, Norway, and Lichtenstein. Non-EEA migrants intending to stay in the country for more than six months have had to pay annual £200 surcharges (£150 for students) for NHS cover since 6 April 2015. Meanwhile, an NHS (Overseas Visitors Charging) Bill listed in the 2016 Queen's Speech promises to restrict free NHS access for foreigners even further, introducing charges for tourists and other visitors to the UK for the first time, though its precise details had not been published at the time of writing.

And yet, according to numerous studies, migrants and immigrants have had not had anywhere near as much impact on either crime or demand for public services and benefits as tabloid headlines would suggest. In April 2008, the Association of Chief Police Officers (ACPO) found that offending rates in the Polish, Romanian, and Bulgarian communities (the report's focus, owing to the influx of migrants from those countries following their then recent accession to the EU) were proportionate to those in Britain's population as a whole. The same month, a joint study by the Equality and Human Rights Commission (EHRC) and Local Government Association (LGA) dismissed the idea that migrants were queue-jumping to obtain social housing; in fact, 60 per cent of those who had moved to Britain in the previous five years were in private rented accommodation. And, in October 2013, the European Commission found 'little evidence' that the 'main motivation' of migrants moving to Britain was the pursuit of benefits, stressing that they were more likely than native people to be in paid work. Moreover, according to the EU's statistics service, Eurostats, as of 2011 (shortly before annual benefits uprating was frozen at 1 per cent by the Coalition) levels of UK 'social assistance' were only just above the overall EU average—and below those of Germany, France, Italy, and the eurozone countries. The highest rates were paid in Luxembourg, followed by Denmark and the Netherlands.

But not every survey paints a rosy picture of immigration: in December 2007, analysis of employment data by the Statistics Commission found that eight out of ten new jobs created in Britain since 1997 (1.4 million out of 1.7 million) had gone to foreign-born workers. Around the same time, Ms Smith admitted that as many as 11,000 non-EU nationals licensed to work in the security sector might be illegal immigrants. One had been involved in repairing Mr Blair's car; another was working as a cleaner in the Commons in February 2008. Despite widespread perceptions, asylum seekers, illegal immigrants, and economic migrants often have a far from cushy time when they arrive in Britain. In 1999, newspapers across southern England were filled with reports about the appalling housing conditions some families endured while their applications were processed and they awaited 'dispersal' around the country. Meanwhile, an emerging black market in cheap foreign labour at the hands of unscrupulous people-traffickers has led to high-profile tragedies. Most infamously, in February 2004, twenty-one Chinese refugees were drowned in Morecambe Bay, Lancashire, while illegally working as cockle-pickers. Meanwhile, in February 2016, amid an escalating refugee crisis involving large-scale population movements from Syria, Iraq, Libya, and other war-torn Middle Eastern and North African states, the National Crime Agency (NCA) revealed that the scale of human trafficking had surged by 40 per cent in a year—with 3,266 people from 102 countries being illegally shipped to the UK.

Sensationalism aside, Britain's population is rising fast: according to the Office for National Statistics (ONS), it had reached 64.9 million by January 2016—an increase of a million in three years—while the 2011 census recorded a 3.7 million rise in England and Wales alone in the previous decade (up to 56.1 million), with 55 per cent of this attributed to net migration. By 2027, it is expected to top 70 million. The decision by aspiring immigrants/migrants to relocate to Britain can also have negative knock-on effects for their countries of origin. The migration of large numbers of skilled Polish workers, such as plumbers and electricians, produced as many negative newspaper headlines in Poland as in Britain. In some media, whole towns were depicted as being 'drained' of their most highly trained artisans by Britain and other western European countries. Meanwhile, the backlash among some sections of the electorate over the perceived impact of inward migration on the availability of job opportunities for native Britons led to the UK imposing temporary restrictions on incomers from Bulgaria and Romania (both of which joined the EU in January 2007), which were only lifted in 2014.

Asylum policy has, since 2008, been overseen by the UK Border Agency (UKBA)—a Home Office agency. However, in March 2012, the then Home Secretary Mrs May split it into two following a high-profile public row with Brodie Clark, head of its front-line arm, the UK Border Force, over the suspension of routine checks on overseas visitors with biometric passports the previous year. The then Immigration Minister Damian Green had given the go-ahead for checks to be halted temporarily over Easter 2011 to cope with lengthy queues at Heathrow and other ports, but according to an inquiry published in February 2012 by UKBA Chief Inspector John Vince, Mr Clark had unilaterally continued to waive them. Following his forced resignation, the Tories effectively revived their pre-election pledge to introduce a new dedicated 'border police force' by announcing the formal separation of its back office and front-line functions.

The question of whether to grant asylum does not arise in the case of Irish Republic or Commonwealth citizens who had the right of abode in Britain before January 1983, or other EU citizens, and applies only marginally to EEA nationals. But nationals of most countries outside these areas, including many African and Asian nations, require visas before entering Britain. Some also need 'entry clearance'.

An annual cap on migrants from outside the EU was promised in the Conservatives' 2010 election manifesto and, on 19 July that year, Mrs May introduced a temporary cap on entry into the UK by non-EU citizens (of 24,100 between then and April 2011) to avoid a rush of people trying to migrate before the permanent limit came into force.

The Home Office has also introduced tough new measures to make it harder for foreigners to claim asylum. These are explained in table 8C on the **Online Resource Centre**. In addition, successful applicants for British citizenship must now sign up to a number of 'responsibilities' in order to claim the 'rights' that go with it. These are outlined in table 8D on the **Online Resource Centre**.

8.9.4 The great 'Big Brother' debate

If one issue during the Blair-Brown era exercised civil liberties campaigners more even than detention without trial it was the perceived 'Big Brother' approach that ministers took towards detection and prevention of crime and terrorism. This tactic was symbolized for many by two signature Blairite policies: national identity (ID) cards and the National DNA Database (NDNAD).

Between 2009 and 2010, British citizens applying for or renewing adult passports were offered a choice between ID cards containing both their specific personal details (name, age, address, etc.) and biometric data (fingerprints, facial characteristics, irises), or 'biometric passports' bearing more limited information. The aim of the 'biographical footprint' held on ID cards was to enable certain accredited organizations to use it—with the cardholders' permission—to confirm their identities. Foreign nationals living and working in the UK began being issued with biometric ID cards in 2008. Although having a card was not initially compulsory, Labour sought to make it so.

Opponents of ID cards broadly fell into two camps: pragmatists and idealists. Pragmatists like former Conservative Shadow Home Secretary David Davis argued that questions over the reliability of technology used to produce the cards, combined with the fact that owning one would not initially be compulsory, threatened to make the scheme ineffective. Idealists, such as campaign group Liberty, saw the cards as a dangerous next step on the road to turning Britain into a paranoid surveillance society. The (for now) historical ID card debate has continued to play out in the context of other 'Big Brother' moves since, notably the expansion of the NDNAD—a sprawling electronic record of genetic samples taken from crime scenes and individuals held in custody, which by 2010 contained material from 5.1 million people (nearly one in ten of the population). Since 2004, anyone penalized for an arrestable offence—even those given a simple police caution—have had their samples added to the database. Although, in its maiden Queen's Speech, the Coalition announced plans to restrict the future use and growth of the database, while also regulating CCTV cameras, easing existing limitations on peaceful protest, and reducing the state's ability to monitor individuals' email and Internet records (another crime prevention measure introduced by Mr Brown), in practice it has largely continued on the same trajectory as 'New' Labour. Defying initial ministerial pledges to remove from the database the DNA of people subsequently found to be innocent, police have been allowed to retain their genetic profiles in anonymized form—leaving open the option of linking these to named individuals in future.

More explosively, to the dismay of civil liberties groups and some Lib Dems, Mrs May published a draft Communications Data Bill—swiftly dubbed a 'snoopers' charter'—which, if passed, would require communications companies to store records of all UK citizens' email conversations, Internet phone calls, games, and other social networking activities for a year, and allow police and intelligence services to access the material in pursuit of terrorists and fraudsters. At the time of writing, the renamed Investigatory Powers Bill had been revived in the wake of the growing terrorist threat posed by self-styled Islamic State (IS), as demonstrated by a series of deadly attacks in other European countries, including France and Belgium. The revised Bill, published in March 2016 and finally passed into law later that year, included a number of privacy safeguards in response to the three parliamentary committee reports published into it beforehand. These included proposals for six new codes of practice to regulate the levels of access security services would be permitted to individuals' mobile phone records and Internet browsing histories, with an additional protection for journalists: namely that their communications data could not be divulged to intelligence agencies without a senior judge's prior permission. The latter measure was particularly welcome in light of revelations that the existing Regulation of Investigatory Powers Act (RIPA) had repeatedly been misused by both police and security services for the purpose of monitoring journalists. None of these measures were sufficient to stop a petition calling for the new Act's immediate repeal reaching 100,000 signatures by the end of November 2016.

The jury is still out on 'snooper's charter mark 2', given the backdrop of continuing concern about the scale of the National Security Agency (NSA) scandal in America. This arose from a 2013 *Guardian* exposé based on testimony from former CIA systems administrator Edward Snowden about a covert surveillance programme, codenamed 'Tempora', enabling both NSA and Government Communication Headquarters (GCHQ) to tap into the network of fibre-optic cables transmitting the world's phone calls, emails, and social media exchanges. Amid accusations by civil liberties groups that this represented an unethical, if not illegal, invasion of privacy, Charles Farr, director general of Britain's Office for Security and Counter Terrorism, admitted in June 2014 that searches on Google, Facebook, Twitter, and YouTube, and emails to and from non-British citizens abroad were considered suitable for monitoring on the basis that they were 'external communications'. It was hardly surprising, then, to hear Snowden himself brand the powers in the fledgling Act 'the most extreme surveillance in the history of western democracy' and worse than 'many autocracies'.

8.9.5 Safeguarding human rights for British citizens

Despite recent governments' predilection for vigilance, the Human Rights Act 1998 (see Table 1.1) marked the beginning of a sustained championing of equality of opportunity and other basic freedoms for British citizens, which led to everything from the equalization of the age of consent for gay and heterosexual sex, to civil partnerships for homosexual couples. The latter right was extended by the Coalition, with the Same Sex Marriage Act 2013 letting gay couples marry for the first time.

To spearhead the government's drive to guarantee British citizens equal opportunities—regardless of age, gender, race, or disability—Labour established three new quangos on entering office in 1997, and in 2007 these were merged to form a single Commission for Equality and Human Rights, also known as the **Equality and Human Rights Commission (EHRC)**. The Commission's remit was extended to cover sexual orientation and religious beliefs, in addition to the areas overseen by the previous bodies, and it was also expected to enforce the law relating to equal opportunities and rights, to influence the development of the law and government policy, to promote good practice, and to foster better relations between communities.

8.9.6 The Ministry of Justice (MoJ)

Britain's criminal justice system has two core elements—the court system and the treatment of offenders—both of which are now the Justice Secretary's responsibility.

8.9.6.1 The court system and civil law

The day-to-day running of Britain's courts is overseen by an MoJ executive agency, Her Majesty's Courts Service. The Justice Secretary is personally responsible for promoting more general reforms of civil law and the legal aid system.

The government's principal legal advisers are the Attorney General and Solicitor General—both either MPs or peers. In Scotland, their roles are performed by the Advocate General for Scotland (who assumed the roles previously held by the Lord Advocate and the Solicitor General for Scotland).

Subordinate to the Attorney General are the Director of Public Prosecutions (DPP), who runs the Crown Prosecution Service (CPS)—the state-owned legal service that brings prosecutions on behalf of the Crown—and the DPP for Northern Ireland, along with the Director of the Serious Fraud Office (SFO).

8.9.6.2 Criminal law

The Justice Secretary has overall responsibility for criminal law and introducing Bills to change it. This work is delegated to two principal agencies: the National Probation Service (NPS) and the **National Offender Management Service (NOMS)**.

Briefly, the NPS has traditionally supervised all individuals serving community-based sentences for criminal offences or prison terms during which they are permitted to live in the community. Historically, the NPS has overseen some 175,000 offenders a year—90 per cent male and a quarter aged 16–20. However, in June 2014, the NPS was part-privatized, with supervision of 'medium to low-risk offenders' (the overwhelming majority) transferred to twenty-one new area-based *community rehabilitation companies*, which replaced thirty-five longstanding 'probation trusts'. As if privatizing probation was not contentious enough, in December 2014 it emerged that just two businesses—oil industry contractor Sodexo and construction firm Interserve—had been chosen as preferred bidders for the initial seven-year contracts to run eleven of the twenty-one new services. Interserve subsequently teamed up with three other organizations, social enterprise P3, third-sector management company 3SC, and housing charity Shelter, to form a partnership called Purple Futures. The remaining 30,000 'high-risk' convicts have remained the responsibility of a slimmed-down NPS. Since 2001, the NPS has been overseen by the Home Office's National Probation Directorate and has been supervised by an independent HM Inspectorate of Probation.

NOMS runs all 123 English and Welsh prisons—whether publicly or privately funded/owned—with HM Prison Service (one part of NOMS) responsible only for the 109 that are in the public sector. In Scotland, a dedicated Scottish Prison Service is responsible for all thirteen publicly run and two privately managed jails, while the Northern Ireland Prison Service oversees a further three. Formed in April 2008, NOMS has a chief executive, responsible for administrative mistakes arising from its conduct.

8.9.6.3 Recent and future developments in the prison system

NOMS employs the 50,000-plus wardens, officers, and governors who administer prisons on the ground. Since the Criminal Justice Act 1991, management of many prisons has been contracted out to private firms, as has transportation of defendants in custody to and from court.

The first four newly built prisons handed over to private managers were the Wolds (Humberside), Blakenhurst (Worcestershire), Doncaster, and Buckley Hall (Rochdale). By April 2012, there were fourteen privately managed jails, run by major independent security providers including G4S Justice Services, Serco, and Sodexo Justice Services. And, despite the then Coalition Justice Secretary Kenneth Clarke's determination to launch the biggest mass privatization of prisons in British history—putting nine jails out to tender and closing two others (the Latchmere House resettlement unit in Richmond, west London, and Brockhill Prison, Redditch) in a drive to save £4.9 million upfront from the MoJ budget and £11.4 million a year thereafter—the number of independently run jails has since stalled. The cause of prison privatization has hardly been helped by growing concerns about inadequate training and staff conduct at some private detention facilities. In April 2016, an undercover investigation by BBC1's *Panorama* into allegations of violence against ten young offenders at Medway Secure Training Centre, Rochester, prompted a succession of arrests of employees of security firm G4S on suspicion of offences including child neglect, assault, and misconduct in public office. G4S—a FTSE-listed company—is one of the biggest private contractors in the system, running three youth facilities and five adult prisons.

Complaints about prisons and probation services are handled by the Prisons and Probation Ombudsman for England and Wales (PPO), the Northern Ireland Prisoner Ombudsman (NIPO), and an overarching Scottish Public Services Ombudsman (SPSO). HM Prison Inspectorates—one for each of England, Scotland, and Wales—are charged with inspecting prisons every three years, with Criminal Justice Inspection Northern Ireland (CJINI) fulfilling a similar role in the province. Individual prisons and young offenders' institutions also have 'boards of visitors'—groups of locals appointed by the Home Secretary to relay complaints from prisoners in the same way as Healthwatch groups operate in the NHS (see 6.2.2).

Since the early 1990s, prisons have seldom been out of the news. Typically, stories tend to be negative, focusing on overcrowding, riots, and breakouts. To provide spare capacity, successive governments have done everything from adapting military camps to act as temporary prisons, to commissioning a 'prison ship', *HMP Weare*, moored off Portland, Dorset. During his time as a tough-talking Home Secretary in the 1990s, later Tory leader Michael Howard famously declared 'Prison works!'—a statement that set him on a collision course with the then director general of the Prisons Service, Derek Lewis, who warned of dangerous overcrowding. In January 1995, the simmering prisons crisis came to a head during a succession of riots and breakouts, first at Everthorpe Jail, Humberside, then at Parkhurst. A damning report into the state of the system saw Mr Howard sack Mr Lewis that October—but not without facing tough questioning from Jeremy Paxman in a now legendary interview for BBC2's *Newsnight*, during which he was asked twelve times if he had 'threatened to overrule' Mr Lewis.

Overcrowding remains a serious concern today. In May 2007, the prison population reached 80,500—within a whisker of its maximum capacity—prompting Lord Falconer, then Justice Secretary, to appeal to the courts to limit their use of custodial sentences for people convicted of minor offences. To add to the then Labour government's embarrassment, Lord Phillips, the Lord Chief Justice, declared the country's jails 'full', warning that the rate of prison sentencing would soon 'outstrip the capacity of the prisons'. By the end of 2015 the prison population had reached a record high of 85,641—nearly twice its level under Mr Howard's 'prisons work' regime. More recently, former Justice Secretary Michael Gove signalled a softening of the main parties' customary position on prison policy, recalling a pledge by his predecessor-but-one, Mr Clarke, to orchestrate a 'rehabilitation revolution'. A draft Prison Reform Bill published in March 2016 began the process of putting renewed emphasis on tackling Britain's high rates of reoffending—70 per cent of prisoners have at least seven previous offences—primarily through improved education and training in prisons, and discouraging courts from jailing minor offenders. Mr Gove announced plans for six 'reform prisons' (modelled on academy schools—see 14.2.2), whose governors would have increased autonomy. As with schools and hospital trusts, their performance would be tracked through league tables, with 'failing' prisons taken over by successful ones. Mr Gove also took steps to address the high rates of suicide and self-harm among prisoners, by setting out plans to improve mental health provision in jails and roll out the introduction of 'safer cells' for vulnerable inmates. In November 2016, Ms Truss signalled her intention to pursue this renewed emphasis on rehabilitation and reform, after the annual report of chief inspector Peter Clarke highlighted growing concerns among prison governors about the poor conditions endured by both officers and inmates; drug-taking and general indiscipline in more overcrowded jails; and high rates of reoffending among recently released offenders. In a further echo of the past, several riots by inmates followed in subsequent weeks.

In Scotland, prison reform has stolen a march on the rest of the UK. June 2010 saw the Scottish Parliament unilaterally cut prisoner numbers, introducing a Criminal Justice and Licensing Bill that enshrined a presumption against sentences of three months or less, alongside a commitment to tougher community sentences. The Bill also raised the age of criminal responsibility in Scotland from 8 to 12—two years higher than that in England and Wales.

8.9.6.4 Rehabilitation in the community

Convicted offenders receive sentences that are either *custodial* (imprisonment) or *non-custodial* (for example conditional discharge, community service, probation, fines, or compensation orders). The latter are supervised in England and Wales by the NPS, and in Scotland by council-employed social workers.

Other than in the exceptional cases in which royal pardons are issued on the advice of the Justice Secretary (see 1.2.2.2), prisoners are generally granted early release only in recognition of 'good behaviour'. This is known as **parole**. Although the application process is relatively simple, parole itself is complex, in that prisoners' eligibility depends on various factors—notably the nature and severity of their offences.

Concerns about prison overcrowding have led to parole becoming all but automatic for most offenders. Though it stipulated that prisoners serving less than one year should normally be released halfway through their sentences, the Criminal Justice Act 1991 toughened the terms for those jailed for one to four years, who are only now released at this stage on licence.

Inmates other than the most serious offenders (rapists and murderers) serving *four years or more* should be released on Parole Board recommendation after serving half their sentences, and normally automatically after serving two-thirds. The Act's most severe rules related to the life sentences handed down for certain kinds of murder—murder of police officers, terrorism, and child killings—which now tend to automatically last at least twenty years. Early release of such 'mandatory life prisoners' can be authorized only by the Justice Secretary, in consultation with the Board and judiciary.

While those sentenced to life for offences *other than* murder are normally released by the Justice Secretary after a period set by the judge at their trial, the Board still has authority to order continued confinement if this is judged necessary for public protection. Such 'indeterminate sentences for public protection' (IPP) have since been used with increasing frequency, causing political headaches for recent governments. In February 2008, three Court of Appeal judges and the Lord Chief Justice ruled that the Board was not sufficiently independent of ministers to approve IPPs, and accused the then Justice Secretary Mr Straw of acting 'unlawfully' in his prior treatment of such prisoners. Among the high-profile inmates repeatedly refused release on grounds of public safety were the late Moors murderer Myra Hindley and serial killer Rose West. Peter Sutcliffe, the 'Yorkshire Ripper', was told by a High Court judge in July 2010 that he would never be released. Others awarded 'indefinite' sentences have actually been released after relatively short terms: Tracey Connelly, mother of child abuse victim Peter Connelly ('Baby P'), was jailed in May 2009, supposedly for a minimum of five years, but released on licence in October 2013 (although, less than eighteen months later, she was returned to prison on the grounds that she still posed a potential danger to society, after being accused of selling pornographic pictures of herself to people obsessed with her notoriety).

In addition to the 1991 Act, the Crime (Sentences) Act 1997 further toughened the sentencing regime by putting greater emphasis on the idea of prisoners *earning* parole—restyling them 'early release days' and introducing the idea that they could be 'gained' and 'lost'. It also introduced:

- automatic life sentences for those convicted twice of serious sexual or violent crimes; and
- mandatory minimum prison sentences for drug dealers and serial burglars.

Until 2006, Scottish parole policy was more lenient than those elsewhere in Britain—with prisoners serving between four and ten years released on the Board's say-so after serving half their sentences, and only those incarcerated for more than ten years needing the Home Secretary's consent. But under the Custodial Sentences and Weapons Act 2007, conditions for early release were toughened. Automatic early release without conditions for prisoners serving fewer than four years was replaced with a new licensing system. Anyone released early who breaches a licence is now returned to jail. In addition, sentencing judges who consider a defendant to be of particular public risk can stipulate that he or she waits longer than the usual halfway mark before qualifying for parole. The Board also has powers to increase this custodial period at a later date, should the circumstances arise. The Management of Offenders (Scotland) Act 2005, meanwhile, ended unconditional early release for sex offenders sentenced to between six months and four years, subjecting them to a new licence and supervision system.

In Northern Ireland, special circumstances apply in terrorism cases, reflecting the unique history of 'The Troubles'. Until 1995, terrorists sentenced to five years or more were usually paroled only after serving two-thirds of their terms, but this has since been harmonized with the rest of Britain—that is, they are eligible after serving half a sentence. Terrorists convicted of another offence before the end of their original sentence must complete the original sentence before the next starts.

Topical feature idea

Since spring 2016, Universal Credit (UC)—the government's flagship welfare reform—has finally been rolled out to all jobcentre areas for new unemployed claimants who are single. UC is meant to simplify the previous maze of benefits available to jobseekers, while also offering a bigger incentive for people to work, by removing state support less steeply and quickly once they find a job. How many jobseekers are now claiming UC, rather than JSA, in your area? Visit a local jobcentre to meet some of them and find out how well the UC system is working out in practice.

Current issues

- **The end of benefit cuts?** Following the then Chancellor George Osborne's U-turns over cuts to working tax credits and PIPs and the resignation of Welfare Secretary Iain Duncan Smith, Stephen Crabb, the latter's replacement, confirmed that no further benefit curbs were planned before 2020.
- **Introduction of the national living wage** As of April 2016, a step-change increase to the national minimum wage has been introduced for over 25 year-olds, who now earn a 'living' wage of at least £7.20 an hour (younger adults are still reliant on lower existing 'minimum' pay levels). The national living wage is due to rise to £9 an hour by the 2020 election.
- **A 'rehabilitation revolution' in prisons?** Former Justice Secretary Michael Gove published a draft Prison Reform Bill in 2016 setting out plans for six new, self-governing 'reform prisons', modelled on academy schools, to deliver enhanced educational and training programmes. It proposed putting failing jails into 'special measures' and allowing them to be taken over by successful ones.

Key points

1. The 'welfare state' is the overarching term for the social security system administered by the Department for Work and Pensions (DWP).
2. There are two main categories of social security payment: contributory and non-contributory. Non-contributory benefits are purely needs-based, while contributory ones are awarded to people based on both qualifying criteria and their prior National Insurance (NI) contributions record.
3. Benefits can also be divided into universal and means-tested. The former are paid to everyone who meets particular qualifying criteria, irrespective of income/wealth (for example Statutory Maternity Pay, or SMP), while the latter are available only to those on low incomes.

4. The Conservatives' flagship welfare reform is Universal Credit—a new 'all in one' benefit set to replace JSA for the unemployed, ESA for the sick and disabled, Income Support, and various tax credits.
5. Home affairs are the responsibility of two government departments: the Home Office and Ministry of Justice (MoJ). The former is in charge of immigration and asylum policy, national security, and the police; the latter is responsible for the courts and legal system.

→ Further reading

Bartholomew, J. (2014) *The Welfare State We're In*, London: Biteback Publishing. **Openly one-sided, provocative, but intriguing critique of Britain's social security system, arguing that it has fostered a dependency culture.**

Bochell, H., Powell, M., and Bochell, H. M. (eds) (2016) *The Coalition Government and Social Policy: Restructuring the Welfare State*, Bristol: Policy Press. **Critical examination of the welfare reform agenda of the Lib Dem–Conservative Coalition and the impact of benefit changes and cutbacks.**

Golding, P. and Middleton, S. (1982) *Images of Welfare*, Oxford: Mark Robertson. **Classic historical overview of the evolution of welfare policy and public attitudes towards claimants, backed by authoritative analysis of media portrayals.**

Hansen, R. S. (2001) *Citizenship and Immigration in Post-war Britain: The Institutional Origins of a Multicultural Nation*, Oxford: Oxford University Press. **Accomplished evaluation of the socio-economic and cultural impact of immigration since 1945.**

Reiner, R. (2010) *The Politics of the Police*, 4th edn, Oxford: Oxford University Press. **Fully revised fourth edition of standard text on the origins, history, and present-day make-up of the British police. Includes detailed analysis of current issues, including those arising from the Macpherson Report into the Stephen Lawrence case.**

Sanders, A. (2010) *Criminal Justice*, 4th edn, London: LexisNexis UK. **Critical analysis of the British criminal justice system, focusing on all aspects of crime and punishment, including habeas corpus, the penal system, and sentencing procedures.**

Online Resource Centre

www.oxfordtextbooks.co.uk/orc/Morrison5e/

Visit the Online Resource Centre that accompanies this book for web links and regular updates.

9

The European Union and other international institutions

For more than forty-four years, Britain has been a member of one of the world's most powerful supranational trading and political alliances: the European Union (EU). But, in a seismic turn of events which was greeted with a mix of irritation and incomprehension by its twenty-seven fellow member states, on 23 June 2016 the country's electorate voted by a 52 to 48 per cent margin to leave the Union, in a national referendum which is certain to have long-lasting repercussions for its standing in the world.

The immediate background to (and fallout from) 'Brexit'—shorthand for 'British exit'—is examined in detail later in this chapter. For now, though, the UK remains a full participating member of the EU, until such time as it formally acts on Article 50 of the 2007 Treaty of Lisbon and leaves (see 9.1). Invoking this clause in its membership contract - an action prime minister Theresa May pledged to perform by the end of March 2017—will set the stopwatch ticking on the two-year period departing states are given to prepare for the exit doors. But with some senior politicians—notably Jeremy Corbyn's unsuccessful challenger for the Labour leadership, Owen Smith, and Liberal Democrat leader Tim Farron—arguing that a second referendum will be warranted to sanction Britain's final withdrawal, once negotiations on the terms of its future relationship with the EU are concluded, there remains the slim possibility that it could still be a member for years to come. For the time being, then, the obligations and opportunities arising from EU membership continue to have a direct impact on the day-to-day lives of British citizens—making a knowledge of the Union, and its component institutions, as essential for journalists as ever.

What, then, *does* EU membership mean for Britain, and how did it originally come about?

9.1 Britain's twisty path to EU membership

The European 'Common Market' (as it was widely known in Britain until the 1970s) began slowly emerging in the post-war period, as the continent struggled to rebuild itself. But although it shared many of the same economic interests as its neighbours, for a long time Britain's attitude towards them was lukewarm. Buffered by the existence of its Commonwealth of dependent nations, on the one hand (see 9.8.6) and its nascent 'special relationship' with the United States on the other, it was reluctant to be too tied to the activities of its Continental cousins.

By 1961, however, the positive economic impact membership of the then European Economic Community (EEC) appeared to be having for its member states encouraged the UK, under Conservative Prime Minister Harold Macmillan, to apply for membership alongside Denmark, Ireland, and Norway. At the time, its application was blocked by France's, President Charles de Gaulle, who twice obstructed it (in 1963 and 1967), but following his resignation in 1969, negotiations began in earnest for Britain's accession. It was duly admitted under Edward Heath's Conservative government in 1973. Ireland and Denmark joined at the same time.

Yet any hopes that the UK's entry would put an end to its years of squabbling with its European neighbours—not to mention infighting over the European Community (EC) within the UK's main political parties—were short-lived. By the time Heath was succeeded by Labour's Harold Wilson, in 1974, divisions were so marked that the stage was set for Britain's first referendum on the subject. In a then unprecedented move that would be replicated four decades later by Tory premier David Cameron, Wilson waived the decades-old convention of collective responsibility (see 3.2.2) to let members of his government opposed to his pro-EC stance actively campaign against the country's continued membership. His opponents at the Cabinet table included then Industry Secretary Tony Benn and Employment Secretary Michael Foot, who argued that free trade between Britain and its Continental neighbours was allowing cheap imports to flood high-street shops, undermining the profits of British-based manufacturers and leading to job cuts.

Despite the efforts of the 'no' lobby, Wilson got his way decisively enough to lay to rest the EC membership debate for a generation: his 'Yes' campaign clinched more than two-thirds of votes in the referendum, on a 64 per cent turnout. His triumph was, however, pyrrhic: Britain's admission into the EU marked the beginning of what would continue to be a troubled and deeply conflicted relationship with the Union. At various points during its membership, the country has refused to toe the line—negotiating 'opt-outs' from clauses to treaties that bind most, if not all, of its peers (for example John Major's refusal to sign the Social Chapter of the 'Maastricht Treaty' and David Cameron's rejection of the Fiscal Compact approved by all other member states save the Czech Republic in December 2011) and struggling to win parliamentary approval for various others. In 1992, Mr Major's government was almost felled by its own backbenchers over 'Maastricht'—an episode explored in depth later in this chapter—while Tony Blair and Gordon Brown both resisted the clamour for a referendum on the 'Lisbon Treaty', a similarly controversial agreement that many 'Eurosceptics' (and some 'Europhiles', such as Tory Kenneth Clarke) argued was essentially the same document as the ill-fated 'EU Constitution' (see 9.5). Hardly surprising, perhaps, that, despite vowing more than a decade earlier to stop his party 'banging on about Europe', by the time of the 2015 general election Mr Cameron was leader of a party still so riven with splits over the EU that he was forced to promise a decisive 'in-out referendum' in the event of being returned to government. Aside from Sweden and Denmark, Britain is the only pre-1990s EU state to have held out against joining the euro (see 9.4.2), while its refusal to sign the Schengen Agreement (see Table 9.1) is the reason Britons are still expected to show their national passports when crossing internal EU borders—and citizens of other member states to do likewise when entering the UK—while freedom of movement brings with it no such obligations elsewhere.

9.2 Evolution of the European Union (EU)

So how did today's EU come about? And how was it transformed from a loose confederation of states cooperating over trade in core post-war raw materials (principally steel and coal) into a sprawling supranational alliance exercising a degree of control—often contentiously—over everything from employment rights to economic migration?

The EU's evolution can best be charted with reference to the treaties and summits that paved the way for it to become the hugely influential entity it is today. The most significant stages in the EU's evolution are outlined in Table 9.1.

Of all treaties listed, the British government found it most difficult to ratify 'Maastricht' (see later in this chapter). It was not alone: in its own 1992 national referendum, Danish citizens rejected it and their government only squeaked it through eleven months later, after negotiating 'opt-outs' from two of its key provisions: economic and monetary union (EMU) and then moves towards a common European defence policy.

Table 9.1 Chronology of main EU treaties

Agreement	Year signed	Main provisions
Treaty of Paris	1951	Established European Coal and Steel Community (ECSC), to initiate joint production of two materials most central to war effort (coal and steel) and fledgling European assembly, which met for first time in Strasbourg in September 1952.
Treaties of Rome	1957	These twin treaties spawned two organizations later to coalesce: European Economic Community (EEC) and European Atomic Energy Community (EURATOM). Joint aim was to foster trade between member states by ending tariffs and other distortions in market and: 1. introducing Common Agricultural Policy (CAP)—encouraging free trade in agricultural products, while guaranteeing farmers' incomes in relation to competition from third-party countries through subsidies; and 2. creating 'common market' for free movement of goods, services, and capital between member states (in practice, only free trade in goods followed until Single European Act 1986).
Merger of three European Unions	1965	Led to 1967 merger of ECSC, EURATOM, and EEC into single European Community (EC), framed around four core institutions: European Commission; European Assembly (later renamed European Parliament (EP)); European Court of Justice (ECJ); and future Council of Ministers.
Launch of European Monetary System (EMS)	1979	Relaxed exchange rates between member states leading to launch of euro.
Enlargement	1981	Greece admitted into EC.
Single European Act and further enlargement	1986	First full-scale revision of original 1957 European Treaties, defining structure of new-look EC, and paving way for following extensions of community: 1. greater economic integration; 2. strengthened supranational institutions; and 3. practical moves towards single European currency and linked exchange rates in form of economic and monetary union (EMU). In same year, Spain and Portugal entered EC.
Treaty on the European Union ('Maastricht Treaty')	1992	EC formally renamed 'European Union' (EU), adding new areas of responsibility. Although signed in February 1992, had to be formally ratified by each state and passage was far from smooth in Britain. It: 1. introduced EU-wide commitment to move towards full EMU—and eventual single currency or 'common' one (native currencies retained, in parallel with EU one); 2. established single European Union from existing communities; 3. set up framework for potential common foreign and security policy; 4. increased cooperation on domestic issues, particularly criminal justice;

(continued)

Table 9.1 (*Continued*)

Agreement	Year signed	Main provisions
		5. established principle of subsidiarity—system defining EU institutions as 'subsidiary to' those of individual member states and safeguarding their ability to run own internal affairs without consulting EU unless unable to achieve national objectives unilaterally; and 6. introduced concept of 'EU citizenship'.
Corfu Treaty	1994	Allowed Austria, Finland, and Sweden to join EU in January 1995, and paved way for Norway's accession (though it has never joined).
Amsterdam Treaty	1997	Arose out of 1996 Intergovernmental Conference (IGC) convened by heads of EU states. Extended rights of EU citizens in relation to: 1. consumer protection; 2. fight against crime and drugs; and 3. environmental protection. Treaty also introduced Charter on Fundamental Workers' Rights. Britain, Ireland, and Denmark opted out of common EU immigration/asylum policy, leaving rest to form Schengen Group, which UK declined to join in 2000. Its name referred to the **Schengen Agreement**—signed in two stages, in 1985 and 1990—abolishing border controls between participating nations.
Helsinki Summit	1999	Removed existing system under which notional target dates set for accession of specific countries to EU membership. From now on, any country meeting conditions would be eligible for swift entry.
Agenda 2000, *For a Stronger and Wider Europe*	2000	Document proposing blueprint for onward development of Community in twenty-first century. Many provisions intended to prevent future disagreements between members like those provoked by discussion of EMU, proposed common defence policy, and CAP. Also signalled attempt to set firm rules for acceptance of new countries. Among its stipulations were: 1. any new country wishing to join EU must meet economic and political criteria for membership and adopt *acquis communitaire*—laws and policies of EU—before being accepted; 2. redefining CAP and 'structural funds' used to ensure equitable socio-economic infrastructure across Europe; 3. expressing then Commission's view on proposed accession to EU of central/eastern European states; and 4. proposing new budgetary framework for EU, with initial proposals for Community-wide budget 'not exceeding 1.27% of EU's GNP'.

Table 9.1 *(Continued)*

Agreement	Year signed	Main provisions
Nice Treaty	2000	'Proclaimed' EU Charter of Fundamental Rights (conflation of principles outlined in preceding European Convention on Human Rights—see 1.1.1.1). Charter's 53 'Articles' not legally binding, but expressed shared set of aims, including: 1. equality between men and women; 2. fair and just working conditions; 3. workers' rights to collective bargaining and industrial action; 4. public rights to access EU documents; and 5. right of elderly to life of 'dignity'. Consensus emerged that EU's main governing institutions would have to change over time for following reasons: 1. arrival of twelve potential new members meant they needed votes in Council of Ministers, own EU commissioners, seats in EP, and judges; 2. reunification of Germany, following 1990 fall of Berlin Wall; and 3. impact of EU enlargement on asylum, immigration, and economic migration.
Göteborg Summit	2001	Focused on perceived conflict between EU membership and Irish Constitution, particularly regarding province's neutrality. Around same time, Ireland voted 'No' in referendum on EU membership. Another controversy stemmed from realization of larger member states that enlargement might result in reductions in funds they received from EU.
Enlargement of the Union	2004	Czech Republic, Estonia, Hungary, Latvia, Lithuania, Poland, Slovakia, Slovenia, Malta, and Greek Cyprus joined EU.
Enlargement	2007	Romania and Bulgaria joined.
European Union Reform Treaty ('Treaty of Lisbon')	2007	Succeeded short-lived 'EU Constitution'—abandoned after being rejected in French and Dutch referendums. 'Lisbon Treaty' also rejected by Ireland (initially), but eventually came into force in December 2009. Main provisions were to: 1. make Charter of Fundamental Rights legally binding; 2. extend role of directly elected European Parliament; 3. introduce permanent president of European Council to replace 'rotating presidency' and formally recognize Council as fifth EU governing institution; and 4. give EU legal status as single entity capable of signing international treaties with other institutions or bodies.
Enlargement	2013	Croatia joined.

9.3 The main EU institutions

As with almost any subject, the most newsworthy EU stories have tended to arise out of conflict and division. Notwithstanding ongoing wrangles over the Union's future direction and scope, many contentious issues have emerged from day-to-day deliberations of the EU's five principal governing institutions:

- European Commission (EC);
- European Parliament (EP);
- Council of the European Union (Council of Ministers);
- Court of Justice of the European Union (CJEU); and
- European Council.

Each institution is chaired by its own president, elected or appointed in a distinct way.

9.3.1 The European Commission

Formed in 1951 and based in Brussels, the **European Commission** is the EU's civil service and executive rolled into one. It employs 25,000 staff working at various levels across more than thirty 'departments and services', known as *Directorates-General*.

Each Directorate-General is headed by one of twenty-eight commissioners (one from each member state, appointed for a five-year period). Meetings are chaired by one of their number, elected president by the European Parliament (on the recommendation of the European Council, or Summit). The president chairs meetings of the Commission much as a prime minister sitting in Cabinet. Although the Council of Ministers, composed of representatives from each member state's government, takes most final decisions on major political developments and structural changes in the EU, the Commission is responsible for *initiating* policy. It does this in much the same way as national policy is originated through Cabinet government, with commissioners sitting around a table developing ideas for prospective legislation.

What makes the Commission more controversial is that none of its members is elected; rather, all are 'proposed' (nominated) by the governments of their native countries. The fact that they are chosen by democratically elected politicians arguably gives them some degree of legitimacy, but they are not directly answerable to the European citizens whose lives their proposals affect. This perceived lack of accountability was famously described in a 1980s pamphlet as a 'democratic deficit' by Liberal Democrat MEP Bill Newton Dunn.

The Commission issues its policy proposals in three broad guises: regulations, decisions, and directives. Both regulations and directives must be scrutinized by the European Parliament and Council of Ministers before they can be enacted, but this is where any similarity between them ends. Regulations are EU-wide laws similar to British primary legislation, which, once passed in Council, will automatically apply in all member states. Directives are broader 'end results' that must be achieved in each state, but it is left up to individual members to decide how to implement them. Decisions, meanwhile, are binding laws (akin to private Bills in the UK—see 2.4.1.1) used to impose conditions or confer rights on individuals or authorities in a particular state: e.g. forcing a government department to issue new guidelines to local authorities on road signage or recycling.

Not that policies devised by the Commission are automatically a done deal: contrary to popular myths about 'Brussels diktats', elected MEPs have ample opportunity to scrutinize and even reject them, and the final say on new regulations rests with the Council of Ministers. Moreover, although it has far greater political clout than the British Civil Service—which is merely tasked with implementing government policy 'on the ground' once Parliament has approved it—the Commission also fulfils this basic administrative function.

In addition, the European Parliament may dismiss the Commission in exceptional circumstances—although, curiously, it is prevented from removing individual commissioners and must instead sack *all* of them. This scenario has arisen more than once. In March 1999, the Commission, under then President Jacques Santer, resigned en masse following publication of a damning report into its alleged nepotism. Although it stopped short of suggesting that any commissioner was directly involved in corrupt practices, the 144-page report, by five independent 'wise persons', singled out former French Prime Minister Edith Cresson for her 'dysfunctional' organization and favouritism in staff appointments.

Although unelected, commissioners are invariably experienced politicians or public figures who have previously served in senior positions in their home countries. Until the EU's membership expanded from fifteen to twenty-five states in 2004, the countries with the biggest populations—Britain, Germany, France, and Italy—had two each, with smaller states having just one. Among those who served in this capacity were former Labour leader Neil Kinnock, who was Commissioner for Transport, and the late Sir Leon Brittan, an ex-Conservative Home Secretary. Former Northern Ireland Secretary Lord Mandelson became Britain's first single Commissioner in 2004 (overseeing trade), but after being recalled to the British Cabinet in Mr Brown's second reshuffle he was replaced by Baroness Ashton of Upholland four years into his term. Following implementation of the Lisbon Treaty in December 2009, the Commission was dissolved and reconstituted, and Lady Ashton was elevated to the newly created role of **High Representative for Foreign Affairs and Security Policy** (and one of seven vice-presidential positions). Her swift promotion was interpreted by some in the media as a consolation prize for Britain in the wake of the EU's 'snub' to former Prime Minister Mr Blair's designs on the first permanent 'EU presidency'. At time of writing, Mr Cameron's appointee, Lord Hill, had recently quit as Baroness Ashton's successor, in response to the outcome of the June 2016 'Brexit' referendum. Lord Hill, who had held the then newly created brief overseeing financial stability, financial services, and capital markets, was replaced by Sir Julian King, Britain's former ambassador to France, in one of Mr Cameron's final acts in office. While there may have been a sense of déjà vu about some aspects of Sir Julian's new role—he was put in charge of organized crime and counter-terrorism (an echo of Baroness Ashton's responsibilities)—a pointed 'mission letter' by EC president Jean-Claude Juncker emphasized that none of the powers of existing commissioners would be handed to the new incumbent. This means that overarching authority over security policy remains with the home affairs commissioner (currently Dimitris Avramopoulos), who continues to represent the Commission in the European Parliament and Council of Ministers.

Enduring controversy over the Commission's composition, powers, and privileges has led to repeated attempts to reform it. Its mammoth expenses bill is often cited as a concern for EU taxpayers, and terms like 'Brussels bureaucrats' and 'gravy train' are staple clichés in Britain's tabloids. Expenses were somewhat addressed in the 1999 report and subsequent reforms, and in proposals for several further changes in early drafts of the 'Lisbon Treaty'. These were to have included a reduction in the number of commissioners, with only two-thirds of member states being represented at any one time from 2014 and seats distributed fairly on a rotating basis. However, Ireland's initial rejection of Lisbon in its 2008 referendum prompted the European Council to take the executive decision to retain the existing 'one member, one commissioner' system for the foreseeable future, by way of a peace offering to it and other smaller nations. The European Council's ability to do this was itself formalized by Lisbon, which gives it the right to alter the number of commissioners unilaterally at any time, subject to unanimous approval by its members.

The Commission's present composition is outlined in table 9A to be found on the **Online Resource Centre** that accompanies this book.

9.3.2 The European Parliament

Although the **European Parliament** is the one directly elected EU institution, until recently it had considerably less influence on law-making than either Commission or Council of Ministers. Traditionally, it has tended to be *consulted* on decisions, rather than taking them itself, rather like a giant House of Commons select committee, rather than a legislative assembly per se. For this reason, it has often been caricatured as a supine talking shop. However, Maastricht gave it the ability to *reject* legislation it disliked, according it 'joint' legislative status with the Council of Ministers in certain areas, under a process known as 'co-decision'. Briefly, this works as follows: the Commission will pass a proposal for a new regulation or directive to the Parliament, which then expresses its opinion at a 'first reading'. If the Council approves of this opinion, the 'law' is passed; if not, it will deliver its own verdict to the EP, together with an accompanying explanation. The Parliament then enters a 'second reading' stage, at which it can either approve the Council's changes (in which case the law is passed), amend them, or reject the law outright. All the while, the Commission will also be giving its opinions on suggested amendments and, if it rejects any, the Council must vote to approve the amended law unanimously, rather than by a majority. If, on the other hand, a stalemate between the Parliament and Council lasts more than three months, the presidents of the two institutions may convene a conciliation committee, made up of equal numbers of MEPs and Council members, to broker a compromise.

This drawn-out, to some overly bureaucratic, approach to law-making—renamed the 'ordinary legislative procedure' (OLP) under Lisbon—used to exist in relation to only a few areas, such as health, culture, science, sport, and some aspects of asylum policy. But Lisbon extended it to most others—including agriculture, transport, and decisions over how to allocate European structural funds. The Parliament also has powers to legislate in relation to the smooth operation of the 'eurozone' and, crucially, veto the EU budget. And (subject to agreement with the Council of Ministers) it may take action over other aspects of economic policy: in July 2010, the Parliament passed legislation capping bankers' bonuses. Since January 2011, upfront cash bonuses have been limited to a quarter of the total (or 20 per cent for 'particularly large' bonuses), with 40–60 per cent deferred. In a move designed to deter excessive risk-taking by bankers, the rules also stipulated that at least half the total bonus should be paid as 'contingent capital'—meaning that it would be the first money to be called upon in the case of future debt or liquidity problems. On 1 January 2014, new rules were also introduced to cap bonuses at no more than 100 per cent of bankers' annual salaries, or twice that level if shareholders explicitly approved after being approved by the Parliament.

Despite its title, when originally christened in 1958, the EP's representatives were not elected at all, but appointed—one by each member country. But, since 1979, it has been fully elected. By the time of its first election, the number of representatives—today known as **members of the European Parliament (MEPs)**—had increased from 142 to 410.

The current membership numbers 751. Elections are held every five years and, prior to 1999, were conducted on a 'first-past-the-post' (FPTP) system analogous to that used in UK general elections (see 4.2.1). The European Parliament Act 1999 changed this by introducing proportional representation (PR), generally based on the party list system. Parties are now awarded a number of seats proportional to their share of the vote.

Britain is currently divided into twelve European electoral regions (including Northern Ireland, which uses the Single Transferrable Vote/STV—see 4.5.2). Each region returns between three and ten MEPs, depending on its population. There are seventy-two British MEPs altogether (down from seventy-eight since the recent enlargements): fifty-nine in England, six in Scotland, four in Wales, and three in Northern Ireland.

Like the Commission, the European Parliament has its own president, elected by absolute majority in a secret ballot of members for renewable two-and-a-half-year terms, and its principal base is in Brussels, where it sits for three weeks a month. For the other week, its members travel to Strasbourg in France, convening in an identical chamber (a long-time cause of controversy, given the relocation costs involved).

As in Britain's Parliament, MEPs sit in political groupings reflecting their ideological affiliations, rather than regional or national delegations.

Following the June 2015 formation of a new alliance of right-wing parties, the Europe of Nations and Freedom (ENF), led by Marine le Pen's Front National, there are currently eight political groupings. At the time of writing, though, fifteen MEPs remained 'non-attached' ('non-inscrit').

The groupings sit at designated points around the 'hemispherical' (semi-circular) parliamentary chamber, according to their notional position on the Left–Right political spectrum. Communist MEPs will therefore sit to the far left of the central seat occupied by the Parliament's president, while fascists and extreme Right parties occupy seats on the far right.

To be recognized as a legitimate grouping (and, since 2011, entitled to additional funding), an interparty alliance needs to number at least twenty-five MEPs from a minimum of seven member states. The current political groupings are:

- European People's Party (EPP)—215 members;
- Progressive Alliance of Socialists and Democrats (S&D)—189 members;
- Alliance of Liberals and Democrats for Europe (ALDE)—67 members;
- The Greens/European Free Alliance (Greens/EFA)—50 members;
- European Conservatives and Reformists (ECR)—74 members;
- European United Left/Nordic Green Left (EUL/NGL)—52 members;
- Europe of Freedom and Direct Democracy (EFDD)—46 members; and
- Europe of Nations and Freedom (ENF)—39 members.

While Britain's Labour Party has long been part of the socialist grouping, after much internal debate the Conservatives acted on a long-standing promise to pull out of the centre-right EPP after the June 2009 European elections. Mr Cameron, who had made this pledge a central plank of his 2005 campaign for the party's leadership, announced the formation of the European

Conservatives and Reformists (ECR): a Eurosceptic alliance including several 'extremist' parties, among them Poland's Law and Justice Party (which draws much of its support from ultra-conservative Catholics) and Latvia's Fatherland and Freedom Party, which counts among its members former recruits to Hitler's Waffen SS. The Tories' decision to quit the EPP earned it barbs from centre-right European leaders including then French President Nicolas Sarkozy and German Chancellor Angela Merkel.

EP administrative functions are overseen by yet another layer of EU bureaucracy: a 'bureau' run by the president, fourteen vice-presidents, and five 'quaestors' (civil servants responsible for accounting matters directly affecting MEPs themselves). All these officials are elected, like the president, for two-and-a-half years at a time.

9.3.3 The Council of Ministers

The **Council of the European Union** (or **Council of Ministers**) is the single most powerful EU institution. Comprising departmental ministers from each of the twenty-eight member states, its precise composition varies according to the issue being debated on a given day. If the Council is debating health policy, a health minister from each member state will attend, while discussions about crime, policing, and security will involve interior ministers (in Britain's case, the Home Secretary or another Home Office minister).

The Council has ten 'configurations', reflecting the broad policy areas under its jurisdiction:

- General Affairs;
- Foreign Affairs;
- Economic and Financial Affairs;
- Justice and Home Affairs;
- Employment, Social Policy, Health, and Consumer Affairs;
- Competitiveness;
- Transport, Telecommunications, and Energy;
- Agriculture and Fisheries;
- Environment; and
- Education, Youth, Culture, and Sport.

Although policy ideas are often proactively proposed by the Commission, all but the most minor must be formally approved by the Council to make them 'law'. To this end, it is supported by a related institution, the Committee of Permanent Representatives (COREPER), comprising civil servants or ambassadors seconded from each member state (and itself backed by another 150 committees and working groups).

All Council meetings are chaired by a senior politician (normally the president or prime minister) from the country currently holding the rotating EU presidency. Britain last held the presidency in 2005. In view of the need for continuity emphasized by this rota, the Council has its own dedicated civil service: the General Secretariat of the Council.

9.3.3.1 Qualified majority voting (QMV)

The voting system used in the Council is complex and, as such, warrants its own section, given its importance in determining the direction of EU policy.

Unanimous approval by member states is normally required to pass major decisions with implications for the future of the EU—such as whether to admit additional countries into the Union. The annual confirmation of the EU's Budget also traditionally requires unanimity. Since Maastricht, however, an increasing number of (often significant) decisions have been agreed through a process known as **qualified majority voting (QMV).** As its name suggests, the premise of QMV is for policy agreements to be reached without the need for every member state's approval—that is, on a majority basis. This majority system is 'qualified', however, in two respects:

- Member states are not accorded an equal say in the Council; rather, the number of votes allocated to each is weighted to reflect its population size, giving some countries greater clout than others.
- A simple majority system (like that which determines whether Acts are passed in the UK Parliament) used to require only one more 'Yes' vote than the total number of 'No' votes, but this system was later amended to stipulate that decisions needed the backing of 74.8 per cent of weighted votes in the Council (258 out of 345), representing 62 per cent of the EU's population (on the request of a member state). As of 1 November 2014, the bar has been raised even higher, though, and today a 'qualified majority', requires a 'double majority' to be achieved for a motion to be carried. In other words, at least 55 per cent of member states (fifteen countries), representing 65 per cent or more of the EU's population, must have approved it—with a minimum of four states needing to join forces to block it. The rationale behind this new variant of QMV is that it is 'fairer' both to larger and smaller countries: by weighting decisions to take account of both states with large populations and the sovereign voting rights of *individual* countries, no matter how small. Although this system is now firmly established, between 2014 and 31 March 2017 any member state was still within its rights to request that the old system be used.

Of the bigger states, France, Britain, Germany, and Italy presently have the most votes, with twenty-nine apiece. The least populated country, Malta, has just three. The overall breakdown of vote allocations under QMV is spelt out in table 9B to be found on the **Online Resource Centre**.

Perhaps unsurprisingly, QMV remains divisive. Some smaller states continue to complain of having policies foisted on them—regardless of their views—by more heavily populated ones. Eurosceptics, meanwhile, see the absence of a 'one member, one vote' system as evidence that individual countries are increasingly being subsumed within an embryonic 'European superstate', rather than treated as a confederation of independent (and equal) countries.

9.3.4 The Court of Justice of the European Union (CJEU)

Established in 1952, the **Court of Justice of the European Union**—formerly the European Court of Justice—is the EU's supreme legal institution. Unlike other bodies, it is based in Luxembourg City, but like them it has its own president (appointed by fellow judges on a renewable three-year term).

Again like the other key EU institutions, the Court comprises twenty-eight members: one judge per member state. For practical reasons, a maximum of fifteen judges will usually hear a case at any one time, sitting as a 'grand chamber'. The judges are assisted by eleven *advocates-general*: lawyers tasked with presenting to them impartial 'opinions' on individual cases. Judgments are made in a collegiate way and must be unanimous.

Judges are nominated by the member states from which they hail, on renewable six-year terms. Six advocates-general are nominated by the biggest EU member states—Britain, France, Germany, Italy, Spain, and Poland—with the others rotating in alphabetical order between the remaining twenty-two. Under Lisbon, it is possible for eleven advocates-general to be enlisted, if the Court requests this.

The Court may be required to pass judgment in a variety of circumstances—for example, if there is evidence that a member state has not implemented a treaty or directive or if a complainant alleges that a governmental institution, non-government organization (NGO), or commercial business has in some other way broken EU law.

Areas of EU law covered include:

- free trade and the movement of goods and services in the EU single market;
- employment law and the European Social Chapter;
- competition law (cartels, monopolies, mergers, and acquisitions); and
- public sector regulation.

In practice, it is unusual for a case involving an individual or small group of individuals to go before the Court of Justice itself. And even when a case *is* heard in this way, this will often be by a smaller chamber of three or five judges. Only in exceptional cases (such as when an EU commissioner is alleged to have seriously failed to fulfil his or her obligations) will it ever sit as a grand chamber, and even then only as a quorum of fifteen judges—rather than the full complement of twenty-eight.

In lesser cases, hearings are convened by a junior body established in 1988 to deal with the growing number of routine complaints being generated as the EU extended its influence: the General Court (until Lisbon, the 'Court of First Instance'). Today this boasts thirty-eight judges (at least one from each member state) and a president appointed by them for renewable three-year terms. Again, cases may either be heard by smaller chambers (of one, three, or five judges) or, if legally complex, a grand chamber of fifteen. Unlike the main Court of Justice, however, the General Court has no advocates-general, so a judge from among its own number is sometimes nominated to this role. A 'judge-rapporteur' will also be appointed to oversee proceedings and draft a provisional judgment—to be deliberated on by the judges—after hearing representations from complainant and respondent.

The General Court's responsibilities encompass the following policy areas:

- agriculture;
- state aid;
- competition;
- commercial policy;
- regional policy;
- social policy;
- institutional law;
- trademark law; and
- transport.

It has the authority to impose various penalties, as outlined in table 9C to be found on the **Online Resource Centre**.

Judgments by the General Court are subject to appeals to the Court of Justice. In addition to the General Court, two further courts exist to deal with more specific cases: the Civil Service Tribunal, which handles complaints about maladministration by EU employees, and the Court of Auditors, which oversees its accounts.

For individual member states, the extent to which European law can be said to take precedence over national legislatures, judiciaries, and (where relevant) constitutions has been a subject of intense interest and ongoing debate. In recent years, however, a series of landmark Court judgments have pointed towards a growing sense that the EU holds supreme. In 1999, Mr Blair's government faced a compensation bill of up to £100 million after the ECJ ruled that Margaret Thatcher had broken European law by passing a 1988 Act intended to ban Spanish trawlermen from using UK-registered boats to fish in UK waters—a practice known as 'quota-hopping'. The final judgment in this case, known as *Factortame* (after the name of one of the 100-plus Spanish fishing companies that brought the original action), came only after a decade of legal ping-pong between London and Luxembourg.

Several 'test case' rulings have focused on the scope of EU employment law—in particular, the extent to which commercial companies and other non-government organizations can be bound by it. In the 1986 case *M. H. Marshall v. Southampton and South-West Hampshire Area Health Authority*, Ms Marshall sued her employer after being dismissed from her job on reaching the then State Pension age for women (sixty). She argued that this contravened the 1976 Equal Treatment Directive, because men were not expected to retire before the age of sixty-five and the Directive created rights that could be enforced 'horizontally' between individuals. The then ECJ ruled against this interpretation—stipulating that directives generally applied only 'vertically' (that is, through the aegis of the specific individuals or organizations at whom they were directed). However, there was a silver lining for Ms Marshall: because the health authority employing her was 'an organ of the state' (meaning that it was bound by the Directive on a vertical basis), she still won her case.

Some judgments have proved so momentous that new legal concepts have been named after them: in 1991, a group of Italian workers who lost their jobs when their employer became insolvent successfully sued the country's government for failing to implement the 1980 Insolvency Protection Directive, which would have guaranteed them compensation. The ECJ's ruling in favour of the workers established the principle of member states being liable for compliance with EU law by all bodies based on their soil, including private companies. This has been christened the '*Frankovich* principle' (after the surname of one victor).

But not all ECJ rulings have gone the claimant's way, and some outcomes suggest a rather less clear-cut balance of power between UK courts and the EU. In the 1974 case *Van Duyn v. Home Office*, the ECJ found in favour of Britain after a Dutch national, Yvonne Van Duyn, sued under the Treaty of Rome for being denied entry to the country because she was a practising Scientologist. The Court ruled that member states could bar individuals on the basis of their 'personal conduct' if this conflicted with national 'public policy' objectives—and UK policy was to prevent the spread of Scientology. More significantly, in 1993, the German judicial system successfully asserted its supremacy over the EU in internal constitutional matters. In *Brunner v. the European Union Treaty*, the German Constitutional Court ruled that it was for it alone to determine whether European laws, and the powers conferred on individual Union institutions, were compatible with Germany's constitution. And, in a warning similar to Mr Cameron's refusal to cede any further powers to the EU without consulting the British public first, it ruled that the country would not be bound by any interpretation of the Treaty that extended the Union's overall remit (or *kompetenz*), or any laws subsequently adopted by the EU that increased its existing powers—unless German law decided such laws should apply.

9.3.5 The European Council

For many years referred to as the 'European Summit' (to avoid confusion with the Council of Ministers), the **European Council** finally gained official status as an EU governing institution in the Lisbon Treaty. Composed of heads of state or government of all member states, it meets up to four times a year, usually in the Justus Lipsius Building in Brussels: headquarters of the Council of Ministers.

The Council is today chaired by a full-time, 'permanent' **president of the European Council** selected by members for up two terms of two-and-a-half years. The present incumbent, former Polish prime minister Donald Tusk, was due to end his first term on 31 May 2017.

Under new rules, presidents must now reflect the political complexion of the European Parliament at any given time. Previously, chairmanship of the Council rotated between member states, with individual heads of government taking it in turns to hold it for six months at a time, in tandem with their parallel presidency of the Council of Ministers. While the European Council has no legislative power (unlike its near-namesake), a member state may complain formally to it if it disputes a decision taken in the Council of Ministers, under 'emergency brake' procedures. The Council may then choose to settle the matter by holding its own vote—giving it what some observers see as the ultimate veto over disputed EU policy. Since Lisbon, it has also been charged officially with mapping the EU's overall future strategic direction.

In February 2016, Mr Cameron negotiated a partial 'emergency brake' for Britain, in his frantic efforts to appease Eurosceptics over one of the most contentious aspect of EU policy, ahead of the then impending referendum (see 9.7): the 'free movement' of people (and, specifically, mobility of labour) between member states. Right-wing critics, including the United Kingdom Independence Party (UKIP), elements of the press, and many of his Tory colleagues, had long argued that the influx of economic migrants from poorer EU states over previous years had been motivated, in part, by the supposed generosity of Britain's welfare system (see Chapter 8). To allay concerns about 'benefit tourism', Mr Cameron secured permission to restrict access to in-work benefits for new migrant workers for up to four years—but only in circumstances when inward migration had been of 'exceptional magnitude' and 'over an extended period of time'. His attempt to portray the deal as a breakthrough was further undermined by other caveats—including the fact that the new arrangements apply to *all* EU states (not just Britain) and can only be invoked at times when a sustained inflow of foreign workers is shown to have damaged 'essential aspects' of a country's social security system; put 'exceptional pressure' on its public services; or caused problems in its employment market.

9.4 Evolution of the euro

Moves towards some form of single European currency quietly fermented for decades. But what started out as the seed of an idea in the minds of European commissioners in the late 1960s took some thirty years to reach fruition.

9.4.1 The exchange rate mechanism (ERM) debacle and 'Black Wednesday'

The first tentative moves towards economic and monetary union (EMU) in the EU began in 1979, when, in an effort to curb inflation, encourage trade, and stabilize exchange rates between individual member states, it introduced the *exchange rate mechanism (ERM)*. The ERM was based on the idea of fixing narrower margins between which the relative values of individual states' currencies would be permitted to fluctuate—effectively 'pegging' one country's exchange rate to another's. Before the ERM, bilateral exchange rates between EU states were based on the European currency unit (ecu), a 'virtual' European currency traded in stock markets. As a condition of EU membership, states were required to contain fluctuations in the value of their currencies within a 2.25 per cent margin either side of their bilateral exchange rates (except Italy, which was allowed a variance of up to 6 per cent).

The Maastricht Treaty envisaged the European monetary system (EMS) moving towards full monetary union in three stages, as set out in table 9D to be found on the **Online Resource Centre**.

As with many EU innovations, Britain was slow to sign up. It finally did so in 1990, when Mr Major was Chancellor, but his successor, Norman Lamont, pulled out dramatically on 16 September 1992, after a panic-stricken day of stock market speculation and interest rate hikes.

'Black Wednesday'—as it came to be known—arose out of the unsustainable position of the British currency (the pound sterling) during the months after the country signed up to the ERM. Throughout much of the 1980s, Margaret Thatcher's Chancellor Nigel Lawson had 'shadowed' the German Deutschmark when deciding whether to raise or lower interest rates to maintain sterling's value. By September 1992, this had had the effect of valuing sterling unrealistically high compared to the US dollar. Because many British exports were valued in dollars, not sterling, the UK was potentially losing considerable income from overseas markets by allowing the gap between dollar and pound to widen. But with Britain pegged to the ecu in the ERM, there was limited room for the Chancellor to 'devalue' sterling (as he otherwise might have done) to remedy this.

The approaching crisis reached its tipping point when US speculators, including billionaire George Soros, began frenziedly borrowing pounds and selling them for Deutschmarks in mid-September, in the belief that sterling was about to be devalued and that they could therefore profit by repaying their loans at deflated prices. This prompted Mr Lamont to raise interest rates from 10 to 12 per cent on 16 September alone (with the 'promise' of a further increase, to 15 per cent, later the same day), to stop sterling's value falling too far by tempting speculators to buy pounds. But, apparently disbelieving him, speculators continued selling pounds in anticipation of a slump in value.

With sterling plummeting as a consequence, at 7 p.m. Mr Lamont withdrew Britain from the ERM: freezing temporarily interest rates at 12 per cent, rather than raising them to the promised 15 per cent. During the course of a single day, he had spent billions of pounds of foreign currency reserves propping up the pound. By the time the Conservatives lost to Labour five years later, the ultimate cost to the taxpayer of 'Black Wednesday' was £3.3 billion, according to Treasury papers released in 2005. The Tories' previous reputation for economic competence was dealt a body blow by the events of that day, from which it took years to recover.

9.4.2 The launch of the euro and growth of the eurozone

The **euro** (€) has existed in 'non-physical' form—in the guise of travellers' cheques, electronic transfers, etc.—since 1 January 1999, but it officially came into being on 1 January 2002, when the **European Central Bank (ECB)** in Frankfurt began issuing notes and coins in the twelve EU member states that had signed up to join. At the time, there were only fifteen EU states, and membership of the euro has since been extended to include seven of the additional thirteen countries admitted through enlargement: Malta, Cyprus, Slovenia, Estonia, Slovakia, Latvia, and Lithuania (the newest member, having joined on 1 January 2015). Of the 'original' fifteen EU members, Britain, Sweden, and Denmark are the only three to have resisted joining. Both Swedish and Danish populations have rejected the single currency in national referendums (the latter twice), and the former has since circumvented any pressure from 'eurozone' states to make a fresh attempt to join them by failing to adhere to the 'convergence criteria' that countries are expected to meet before being accepted into the euro.

The main convergence criteria, designed to promote price stability across participating states, require an applicant to achieve the following:

- an inflation rate no more than 1.5 per cent higher than that of the three lowest-inflation member states of the EU;
- a ratio of no more than 3 per cent between annual government deficit and gross domestic product (GDP) at the end of the preceding tax year;
- a ratio of gross government debt to GDP no greater than 60 per cent at the end of the preceding tax year (although it is sometimes acceptable to approach this target);

- membership of the successor to the original ERM—'ERM II'—for at least two consecutive years without at any point simultaneously devaluing the applicant's currency; and
- nominal long-term interest rates no more than 2 per cent higher than that of the three lowest-inflation EU member states.

At time of writing, the nineteen countries in the eurozone were (in alphabetical order): Austria, Belgium, Cyprus, Estonia, Finland, France, Germany, Greece, Ireland, Italy, Latvia, Lithuania, Luxembourg, Malta, the Netherlands, Portugal, Slovakia, Slovenia, and Spain. In addition, several European states outside the EU are now using the euro—Monaco, San Marino, and Vatican City—have all signed formal agreements allowing them to issue their own euro coinage, while Andorra has a monetary agreement with the Union allowing it to do so, and aspiring EU members Kosovo and Montenegro have adopted it as their official currency, but without any formal recognition allowing them to mint coins.

Britain has always remained a refusenik. Mr Major's government negotiated an 'opt-out protocol' before belatedly signing Maastricht—removing any obligation on its part to move from stage two to stage three of EMU. Mr Blair repeatedly promised to hold a referendum before committing the UK to the single currency (of which it was thought to be broadly in favour). In practice, however, any hope of doing so was thwarted by the insistence of his Chancellor, Mr Brown, that Britain would have to meet five (somewhat nebulous) 'economic tests' before it was safe to sacrifice the strength of sterling to the untested vagaries of the euro.

9.4.3 The 'sovereign debt crisis'

Because several EU member states have yet to join the single currency, the Union has often been described as a 'two-speed' Europe. Until recently, many observers argued that (whatever their preferences) a time would one day come when Britain and all other member states outside the euro would be forced to join—if only to retain their influence at the negotiating table over other issues affecting the Union.

However, tumultuous recent events in the eurozone sparked by sovereign debt crises in several member states—notably the dismissively termed 'PIGS' economies of Portugal, Ireland, Greece, and Spain—only sharpened opposition to joining within Britain's political establishment. Sparked, in part, by the 2008–9 banking collapse (see 7.3.4), there have been so many twists in this escalating emergency that it is impossible to give a definitive account of it here. Nonetheless, it would be remiss not to include a broad overview of the origins of the crisis and its most immediate ramifications.

In May 2010, the euro was plunged into the biggest slump in its short history after first Greece, then several other EU states using the single currency, became the subject of intense concern over the extent of their 'sovereign debt': the individual budget deficits they had accumulated following the global financial meltdown and (in some cases) their previous levels of borrowing.

Trouble began in Greece, where a package of austerity measures unveiled by the then government provoked a wave of wildcat public sector strikes and violent demonstrations. Financial ratings agency Standard & Poor's swiftly reduced the status of the country's government bonds to 'junk'. To contain Greece's downturn—preventing it from having a knock-on effect on the euro and, by extension, other states' economies—on 2 May the eurozone countries teamed up with the International Monetary Fund (IMF) to offer the country an unprecedented €110 billion (£93 billion) loan bailout, on condition that it imposed harsh domestic spending cuts. Within a week, though, a further massive cash injection was required to stabilize the euro. This saw Europe's finance ministers collectively approve a loans package worth £624 billion aimed at ensuring financial stability across Europe by shoring up the sixteen states by that point struggling to service their debts. In one of his last actions as Chancellor, Labour's Alistair Darling signed off the deal—committing Britain to providing between £9.6 billion and £13 billion to support a new £95 billion 'stabilization mechanism' designed to stop individual countries' economies collapsing.

In ensuing weeks, governments in a succession of other eurozone states, including Spain, Portugal, and Italy, began implementing similar austerity. But as international money markets indicated a new wariness towards the previously unassailable euro, the crisis came closer to home, as Ireland had to accept a joint €85 billion (£71 billion) bailout by the IMF and the eurozone countries.

The following two years saw more bailouts—and further waves of painful austerity in states forced to accept them. In unprecedented scenes, two countries paralysed by their deepening debt problems, Greece and Italy, formed temporary governments led by so-called 'technocrats': unelected officials with extensive professional experience of working in the financial sector, but no democratic mandate. Central to the often fraught negotiations among member states—including Britain and others outside the euro—was the question of how far the country with the strongest economy, Germany, was willing to 'prop up' those in crisis to avoid collapse of the eurozone. At various stages, the idea was mooted that Greece (the state in the weakest financial position) might be forced to 'default' on its debt, or even withdraw from the euro and/or EU altogether. This would allow it to devalue in the hope of boosting export areas, such as tourism and shipping, in which it had a 'comparative advantage' (defined in economics as goods or services that a country can afford to produce at lower marginal costs than its competitors).

At the height of the sovereign debt storm, in December 2011, eurozone members led by Germany and France proposed a twin-pronged strategy for limiting the likelihood of future financial crises on the scale of that which had begun three years earlier. The first element was a new **Fiscal Compact**, which (although boycotted by Britain and the Czech Republic) now effectively allows the ECB to vet individual member states' national budget plans. Officially entitled the 'Treaty on Stability, Coordination, and Governance in the Economic and Monetary Union', the Compact requires all signatories to introduce into their domestic laws formal requirements that future governments keep their annual budgets in balance or surplus. Any state breaking this pledge will be fined 0.1 per cent of its GDP by the ECJ. The Compact was eventually ratified by sixteen signatories (four more than the required twelve) and came into force in those states on 1 January 2013. The second element of this eurozone 'firewall' would be a EU 'financial transaction tax' (FTT), which, if enacted according to the EC's proposals, will see a charge of 0.1 per cent imposed against the exchange of shares and bonds, and 0.01 per cent against derivatives contracts transacted between financial institutions in all signatory states. The FTT has, however, been the subject of protracted, and ever more tortuous, negotiations and legal challenges—notably from the UK, whose financial centre in the City of London, critics argue, could be disproportionately affected by it, despite Britain's refusal to sign up to the levy. It was the proposal to raise some €57 billion a year through the FTT, more than the planned Compact, that prompted Mr Cameron to stage his equally celebrated and derided 'walkout' from negotiations in December 2011. At time of writing, agreement appeared to be as elusive as ever on the timetable for implementing a FTT, or indeed what form it would finally take, following repeated postponements of its introduction—the latest taking it to at least September 2016. Nearly seven years down the line, meanwhile, the underlying sovereign debt crisis is far from over. Though it is widely agreed that a certain amount of stability has finally returned to the eurozone, one long-term reform still favoured by some member states (but viewed cautiously by Germany) is for an additional bulwark against future financial collapse to be introduced, in the form of a eurozone-wide 'banking union' to supplement the extant financial one. This would offer centralized deposit insurance guarantees, bank regulation, and mechanisms allowing for future failing banks to be recapitalized, if necessary, from joint eurozone funds.

9.5 Towards an EU 'superstate'?

The EU-related concern that has preoccupied Britain's political classes more than any other over the years has been the perceived shift over time from what was once little more than a trading alliance between fully independent nation states towards a closer, more all-embracing 'political' union akin to the United States of America. By the late 1980s, the perception that many mainland European countries (particularly France and Germany) wanted to create a

'European superstate' or 'United States of Europe' was meeting staunch resistance from Mrs Thatcher and other Eurosceptic ministers to almost any prospect of further UK involvement. Famously, during a 1990 Commons debate on then EC President Jacques Delors' plans to accelerate EU integration, she declared 'No, no, no'.

Although, as leader of the Opposition, Mrs Thatcher had supported the 'Yes' campaign for Britain to remain in the then EEC, by the end of her premiership she saw things differently. Not only had the pace of integration accelerated by that point, but the likes of Mr Delors and German Chancellor Helmut Kohl were championing ever-closer ties between member states, with the contents of the Maastricht Treaty a particular concern. High-profile resignations by pro-European Cabinet colleagues, such as Chancellor Nigel Lawson and Foreign Secretary Sir Geoffrey Howe, did little to dent her resolve. It was the Tories' growing internal rift over Europe as much as the Poll Tax riots that led to her ultimate downfall (see 3.1.3.4).

Despite producing a more mild-mannered replacement, the ensuing leadership election failed to heal party wounds. Mr Major did much to placate his Eurosceptic colleagues: in particular, negotiating British opt-outs to various clauses in Maastricht, notably the Social Chapter enshrining new rights for EU workers, including the Working Time Directive barring employers from forcing staff to work more than forty-eight hours a week (later signed by Mr Blair).

But such fillips to the Right could only delay an inevitable confrontation over Maastricht (which effectively *had* to be signed if Britain were to remain in the EU). By May 1992, having just secured a narrow fourth successive Tory victory, Mr Major was effectively held to ransom by a hard core of Eurosceptic backbenchers, known collectively as the 'Maastricht rebels'. Only by temporarily withdrawing the whip from these MPs, forging a fractious alliance with the Ulster Unionists and Democratic Unionists, and threatening his party with a further election (which it would almost certainly have lost) did he force through the European Communities (Amendment) Bill on a wafer-thin majority. Among those actively rebelling from the backbenches were bullish former Employment Secretary Lord Tebbit and one Mrs Thatcher. In addition to the usual suspects, such as stalwart Eurosceptic Bill Cash, the rebels included no fewer than three future Coalition ministers: David Willetts, Liam Fox, and Iain Duncan Smith.

It was to be a dozen years or more before the furore over Maastricht came close to being matched: this time over another supposedly 'red-line' proposal, the draft 2004 Constitutional Treaty (dubbed the 'EU Constitution' by critics). Though ultimately supplanted by the Lisbon Treaty, of all EU agreements this putative deal was the one that most clearly enshrined the concept of **subsidiarity**: the *antithesis* of **federalism**, the US-style multi-state system of government so feared by the defenders of British sovereignty. The EU definition of subsidiarity defines member states as paramount and the Union as only a 'last port of call' should individual countries' self-determination falter. The Constitutional Treaty also set out, for the first time, practical exit strategies for states keen to withdraw from the EU altogether. Nonetheless, under mounting pressure from the Tories and his own backbenchers, Mr Blair promised a referendum on it if he were to win a third term in the 2005 election (although, by then, his pledge was redundant, as both France and the Netherlands had, by then, already rejected it).

Lisbon (to all intents and purposes a rewrite of the ill-fated 'Constitution') also proved divisive. Yet, after months of pressure from his own backbenchers and a Commons debate lasting twelve days, Mr Blair's successor, Mr Brown, formally settled the issue in February 2008 with a slim victory approving ratification on a three-line whip. With twenty-nine Labour MPs defying the party whip by backing a referendum, it was only then Liberal Democrat leader Nick Clegg's decision to whip his MPs into abstaining (rather than opposing the government) that carried the day for the prime minister. In doing so, he angered some in his own ranks: three frontbenchers resigned and fifteen voted for a referendum, despite his using a three-line whip to discipline them. While Lisbon ultimately had a smoother passage than the abortive Constitution, Britain was not the only country to have trouble ratifying it. On 13 June 2008, the only EU nation granted a referendum, Ireland, rejected it by 53.4 to 46.6 per cent (paving the way for a failed last-ditch attempt by Tory peers to delay it in the Lords). Facing the threat of isolation or, worse, expulsion from the EU, Ireland finally approved the treaty in October 2009. But it was not until December that year—eighteen months after it had been signed by EU leaders—that it came into force.

9.6 Other issues facing the EU

Before turning to the question of the UK's decision to leave the EU, it is worth giving some space to a brief consideration of some of the contentious issues relating to its membership—aside from those, like monetary union, we have already examined. The most significant are summarized in Table 9.2.

9.7 Brexit

In hindsight, Britain's impending departure from the EU has been a long time coming. As much of this chapter has demonstrated, UK governments—representing an island state located on the far north-western fringes of the European

Table 9.2 Major issues facing Britain's membership of the EU

Issue	Explanation
Common Agricultural Policy (CAP) and the British rebate	CAP takes biggest annual chunk of EU Budget—equivalent to 44% of spending each year. Mrs Thatcher negotiated generous yearly rebate for Britain from CAP and other subsidies in late 1980s, because UK receives less than more farming-dependent states. In December 2005, Mr Blair accepted £1bn annual cut in Britain's £3.6bn rebate following row with French President Mr Chirac that briefly paralysed EU Budget negotiations. His opponents argued that increased subsidies from richer western European countries were needed to help new members: e.g. ex-Soviet countries.
Common Fisheries Policy (CFP)	Long-standing protection of European fish and seafood stocks using 'quota' system for fishing rights, allocated among relevant member states. In mid-1990s, frequent confrontations occurred between Britain and Spain over 'quota-hopping': Spanish trawlers' alleged practice of fishing in British waters using boats registered under third-country 'flags of convenience', so they could exceed Spain's quota. Many UK trawlermen scrapped boats because of strict quotas introduced in British waters.
Common Defence Policy	Concept of greater cooperation over defence formally introduced in Maastricht. Idea of EU 'Rapid Reaction Force' designed to intervene swiftly if member state threatened or invaded still on table.
Economic migration	EU expansion to encompass former Eastern Bloc countries led to more economic migration from poorer to richer countries, fostered by free movement of labour enshrined in various treaties. Community relations and public services strained in some areas—creating tensions between migrants and indigenous peoples. In 2007, Britain became first member state to introduce new restrictions on migrant workers from two newest EU entrants: Bulgaria and Romania (removed in 2014). Curbs on free access to NHS and 'emergency brake' allowing government to limit in-work benefits for new migrants negotiated by Britain.
Transatlantic Trade and Investment Partnership (TTIP)	Modelled on existing Trans-Pacific Trade Partnership (TPTC) between United States and twelve Pacific Rim countries, this proposed deal would introduce new US/EU-wide free trade zone. Still under prolonged negotiation, it would cover three broad areas: access to markets for US and EU firms; regulation; and other rules and principles underpinning trade within and between the two blocs. Critics warn TTIP could prioritize profit and economic growth over environmental protection, and some fear it could promote further privatization of public services, like the NHS (see Chapter 6), by forcing them to operate like other free markets and enabling firms to sue for loss of contracts and access to those restricted to government and/or charitable providers.

continent—have generally been lukewarm, if not decidedly frosty, in their dealings with the Union. And this ambivalence is hardly unreciprocated. Decades after those infamous tussles between Macmillan and de Gaulle, and Mrs Thatcher's run-ins with Mr Delores, member states' collective response to the 2016 referendum result was most memorably symbolized by EC president

Mr Juncker's quip that, while Britain's exit was unlikely to be 'an amicable divorce', the years of its membership had hardly been a 'tight love affair'.

But how and why did the referendum come about in the first place—and what does the short- to medium-term hold for Britain, now that the country has voted to go it alone? Though it is impossible to give any kind of definitive account of the origins of 'Brexit' in a book of this nature, it would be fair to attribute it, in large part, to the longstanding divisions within the Conservative Party over the pace and trajectory of EU integration in recent decades. Back in the 1990s, at the time of the Maastricht debacle (see 9.5), these divisions had been framed primarily around questions of sovereignty: specifically, the perceived erosion of the primacy of the Westminster Parliament by increasingly assertive EU institutions. But by the time the Tories returned to power in 2010, after thirteen years of Labour government, this issue had been eclipsed by another factor which, if anything, proved even more of an influence on the eventual outcome of the European 'debate': immigration or, to put it correctly, economic migration (otherwise known as freedom of movement/mobility of labour). During the intervening years, Conservative Eurosceptics had been emboldened by the growing fear of losing ground to Nigel Farage's UKIP. By gradually insinuating itself into the political mainstream, UKIP had successfully mobilized an unholy alliance of flag-waving 'little Englanders' from the Tory shires and disaffected white, working-class voters (many of them former Labour loyalists) who had come to feel buffeted by a toxic mix of global market forces and competition from migrant workers for the same (often scarce) jobs and public services. In short, UKIP's time had come. What had started out as an anti-EU protest movement redolent of the short-lived Referendum Party that helped send several prominent Tories packing in 1997 had, by 2010, transformed itself into a formidable (if often unruly and outrageous) electoral force.

While in coalition with the Europhile Lib Dems, it proved impossible for Mr Cameron to stage the 'in-out referendum' he had long mooted as a means of silencing his party's Eurosceptics (whatever the result). Having pledged to do so in his 2015 manifesto, however, no such get-out clause awaited him when the Tories unexpectedly clawed their way to a slim parliamentary majority that May. Although it only managed to secure a single seat in the general election itself (for Douglas Carswell, one of two ex-Tory MPs who had defected the previous year), UKIP was by this point Britain's biggest party in the European Parliament, having surged from third place in 2009 to win twenty-four seats to Labour's twenty and the Tories' nineteen in 2014. Not only that: its Westminster candidates had come second to Labour in a string of formerly solid northern strongholds and, within a year, it would boast a total of 488 local councillors and seven Assembly members (AMs) in the Welsh Assembly (including the Tories' own disgraced ex-minister, Neil Hamilton—see 1.1.1.1).

By May 2015, then, the die was cast, and all that remained was for the government, under the watchful eye of the Electoral Commission (see 4.4.1), to set a date and ground rules for the now-unavoidable vote. Yet, if anyone naively hoped this might be a smooth and uncontroversial process, they were sorely mistaken. From the moment the starter pistol was fired on the (initially informal) referendum campaign, deep divisions began to be exposed not only in Tory ranks, but also in Labour's and even UKIP's—both about the question of Britain's continued EU membership itself and the manner in which campaigning should be conducted. Even after the Commission finally decided on two 'official' camps—'Remain' (fronted by Mr Cameron himself) and 'Vote Leave' (led by his supposed friends, ex-London Mayor Boris Johnson and then Justice Secretary Michael Gove)—the field was cluttered by a torrent of competing, and conflicting, voices. Anxious to avoid a repeat of its electorally disastrous decision to share the podium with prominent Tories in the run-up to the 2014 Scottish referendum (see 1.3.3), Labour launched a separate 'In' campaign of its own, chaired by former Cabinet minister Alan Johnson: the clunkily titled 'Labour In for Britain'. Its efforts were somewhat undermined, however, by the decision of fellow former party bigwigs Harriet Harman and Ed Balls to break ranks by appearing on the campaign trail alongside Mr Cameron and Mr Osborne respectively. To add to the confusion, a handful of Labour *Eurosceptics*, including Vauxhall MP Kate Hoey, unveiled an opposing faction, 'Labour Leave'—even as her parliamentary colleague, Gisela Stewart, was hosting joint press conferences with Messrs Johnson and Gove. Meanwhile, the long-term architect of the whole exercise, Mr Farage, had to play second fiddle to the *official* 'Out' campaign by launching his own 'anti-establishment' effort: 'Grassroots Out'.

The bewildering, and ill-disciplined, nature of the rival/opposing alignments was reflected in the equally befuddling (and frequently bad-tempered) tone and content of the referendum 'debate'. With 'In' campaigners warning of dire peril for Britain's economic stability if it left the EU single market, 'Outers' sloganized about the need to 'take back control' of the country's destiny, while cautioning about the risk of its being swamped with migrants should it opt to stay. If truth be told, *neither* side distinguished itself with a very positive vision of the country's future should their campaign succeed.

The rest, as they say, is history—at least to the extent that, on 23 June 2016, in a 72 per cent turnout, the British electorate voted to leave the Union, by a margin of 51.9 to 42.1 per cent; Mr Cameron resigned as prime minister, to be swiftly replaced by Theresa May; and Labour descended into a bitter internal feud, sparked by allegations about its leader's half-hearted contribution to the 'In' cause, that may well resurface in future. But, though the immediate decision has been taken, so many questions remain about the precise timing (and nature) of the UK's departure from the EU that the shape of its ongoing relationship with Europe (and the wider world) seems far from certain. Indeed, by November the road to departure looked more thorny than ever, thanks to a High Court judgment upholding a demand by investment manager Gina

Miller, London-based hairdresser Deir Dos Santos, and the crowd-funded People's Challenge group that Parliament must be consulted in a formal vote before ministers are authorized to invoke Article 50. The ruling was a constitutional milestone, in that it upheld the principle that parliamentary sovereignty, in the end, trumps the Executive's exercise of prerogative powers (see 1.1.1.1). Although ministers' immediate reaction was to set in train an appeal to the UK Supreme Court, at time of writing a January 2017 judgment upholding the original High Court decision was widely expected. To compound the complexities of this constitutional tussle, the appeal hearing had heard representations from Scotland and Wales's most senior law officers, the Lord Advocate and Counsel General for Wales respectively. Also involved were campaigners for victims of paramilitary violence in Northern Ireland and an unlikely further party: the Independent Workers' Union of Great Britain, which represents freelance, agency, and low-paid migrant workers. At time of writing, ministers were preparing a simple, three-line Bill to authorize the Article 50 process if all else failed. Given the constitutional quagmire they would otherwise face, this looked the most viable option—particularly after a further lawsuit was launched, weeks after the first, by a group of lawyers going under the name British Influence. They argued that, by including only a single question on the referendum ballot paper, ministers had failed to give voters a say on the UK's future in the single market itself.

Assuming all finally goes to plan, Mrs May has said she will introduce a 'Great Repeal Bill' during the 2017–18 parliamentary session, to formally end the Union's authority over the UK in one fell swoop on the day Brexit finally occurs, by converting all EU provisions into British law. The 1972 European Communities Act, which originally paved the way for Britain's accession, would be repealed at the same time. Beyond this, though no one can predict exactly how 'Brexit' will turn out in the end, it is possible to sketch out some broad alternative scenarios—and it is to these that we now turn.

9.7.1 Britain joins the European Economic Area (EEA) and retains access to the single market

For all her clarity on entering Downing Street that 'Brexit means Brexit', and her stated determination to invoke Article 50 by the end of March 2017, Mrs May has since faltered in setting out how she will achieve an exit deal that preserves as many of the economic benefits of EU membership as possible, while somehow sidestepping the UK's previous obligations. Central to this conundrum is the long-cherished ideal of so-called 'soft' Brexiteers that Britain might be allowed to opt out of the free movement of peoples (thus curbing inward migration), while retaining full or partial access to the 'single market': tariff-free reciprocal trade of goods and services between states.

Opinion is divided, however, about whether this is an option: while Mrs May's new 'Brexit Secretary', David Davis, has suggested a 'generous settlement' along these lines can be negotiated, her Chancellor, Philip Hammond, has repeatedly stated that Britain will be forced out of the single market, even if it can subsequently negotiate more or less equitable access to the trading bloc as a partner in the **European Economic Area (EEA)**. Established by the European Economic Area Agreement in 1992, the EEA is effectively an extension of the single-market region, and currently encompasses three countries that are members of the European Free Trade Association (EFTA), rather than EU: Liechtenstein, Iceland, and Norway. The fourth member of the EFTA, Switzerland, has a unique relationship with the EU, enjoying access to the single market while also restricting incoming migrants, following a 2014 referendum in which its population rejected free movement (though it has repeatedly been told to re-stage this vote, as the result breaches the terms of its deal).

Although forging a relationship along these lines should theoretically be a formality, the sticking-point (as with Switzerland) is likely to be whether it agrees to the *quid pro quo* for renewed single-market access: continued acceptance of EU free movement rules, but without the ability to any longer *influence* those rules, as a non-member. Given that the scale of immigration from fellow member states was a decisive factor in the referendum result (net EU migration to Britain was 184,000 in 2015), this would prove a difficult deal to 'sell' to a wary public. Yet Switzerland and Norway's dealings with the EU—for long years held up by Eurosceptics as a model of how Britain might forge a rosy European future outside the Union—have been predicated on such arrangements. Moreover, 2014 figures produced by independent think tank Open Europe show that net inward EU migration to Switzerland has been much higher than that to Britain in recent years (hence that year's referendum). As of 2013, EU citizens accounted for 15.6 per cent of the Swiss population—nearly four times as many as the 4.2 per cent of Britain's populace made up of non-UK EU nationals. Moreover, the price of retaining single-market access could be high: contrary to repeated claims by 'leave' campaigners that quitting the EU would save Britons billions of pounds each year, as the UK will no longer need to contribute to its budget, EEA states in fact pay substantial annuities to the Union. Analysis published by Open Europe in October 2015 showed that Norway makes a net per capita contribution to the EU of 107.4 Euros, compared to 139 Euros for each UK citizen.

9.7.2 Britain leaves both EU and single market and enters new bilateral trade partnerships

Were the prospect of securing ongoing single-market access only in return for continued acceptance of large-scale EU migration to prove too politically unpalatable for ministers, the other obvious alternative would be for Britain to broker what has come to be known as a 'hard Brexit' option: i.e. forging its own bilateral, or multilateral, trade deals. Given its comparative advantage in some specialist hi-tech industries and, especially, financial services, in theory this should be feasible. Indeed, within days of his appointment, Mrs May's International Trade Secretary, Liam Fox, told the *Sunday Times* in July 2016 that he was already 'scoping out' up to a dozen potential agreements. Among Britain's most likely prospective partners, given the countries' long-touted 'special relationship', would be the USA, while the so-called 'Osborne Doctrine' pursued by Mr Hammond's predecessor saw the UK forge ever-closer ties with China—to the dismay of human rights campaigners and some in the security lobby. In September 2013, Mr Osborne announced plans to make China Britain's second biggest trading partner (after the US) by 2025, while one of his final actions, in July 2016, was to sign a deal ensuring future UK nuclear power plants will be part-funded by Chinese investors. Though relations between Britain and Russia remain frosty following the latter's 2014 invasion of Ukraine, there is also scope for other deals with individual 'BRIC' states (the acronym often used for the fast-developing economies of Brazil, Russia, India, and China).

9.7.3 Britain holds a second referendum—and votes to stay

Though the 'spirit' of the statute that paved the way for the 2016 referendum, the European Referendum Act 2015, suggested it would be legally binding, lawyers and campaigners on either side continue to dispute whether the 'letter' of the law actually *states* this—with prominent voices on the 'In' side arguing it should be treated only as 'advisory'. A handful, including Labour backbencher David Lammy, have even suggested that Parliament should simply ignore the will of the people and resist pressure to invoke Article 50, in the 'best interests' of the country. Others, like fellow Opposition MP Owen Smith and former prime ministers Mr Blair and Sir John Major, have steered a middle way—arguing it would be legitimate to hold a second referendum, to re-confirm the 'out' vote, as soon as Britain has sight of a final 'deal' outlining what it will gain (and lose) on leaving the EU. Mr Farron even pledged that the Lib Dems would campaign on a 'second referendum' ticket at the 2020 election. If Britons declared they had changed their minds at that time, he argued, so be it.

9.7.4 Britain leaves the EU (in whatever form)—but Scotland and/or Northern Ireland stay

If, as expected, the UK does withdraw from the EU in due course, a question mark remains over whether the slim overall 'Out' vote is automatically binding on the two nations that voted to remain: Scotland and Northern Ireland. Several Scottish Nationalist Party politicians, including depute leadership hopeful

Tommy Sheppard, have repeatedly mooted the idea of helping an alliance of pro-EU MPs block any government attempt to obtain formal backing from the Commons to invoke Article 50, if ministers fail to offer 'special arrangements' for Scotland. More seriously, perhaps, SNP First Minister Nicola Sturgeon has raised the prospect of the Scottish Parliament using its devolved powers to veto 'Brexit'—though it is unlikely that the courts would regard this as constitutionally legitimate. More realistic, arguably, is the prospect of a further Scottish independence referendum in the event that ministers activate Article 50 without first trying to persuade the European Commission to let Scotland remain (as six out of ten Scots voters had hoped).

Though such a deal might sound far-fetched to some, in fact it has clear precedents: although the British protectorate of Gibraltar stands to leave the EU, having been consulted in the referendum, several other UK territories (notably Jersey, Guernsey, and the Isle of Man) have never been in the Union, while Greenland, part of the state of Denmark, voted to leave the then EEC in 1985, though the rest of the country remained. Perhaps unsurprisingly, Northern Ireland's vote to stay in the EU (by 56 to 44 per cent) has also reopened thorny constitutional questions across the Irish Sea. Although its First Minister, Democratic Unionist leader Arlene Foster (a 'leave' supporter), was quick to embrace the UK-wide result, her then Sinn Féin deputy, Martin McGuinness, used Brexit as an opportunity to renew his call for the reunification of Ireland as a whole, citing concerns that Northern Ireland's departure would otherwise lead to new border controls between the province and the Republic of Ireland in the south, undermining tenets of the 'Good Friday Agreement' (see 1.3.5).

9.8 Other international institutions

Though the EU is by far the most influential supranational organization of which Britain is (for now) a member, it would be remiss to conclude this chapter without briefly mentioning the other significant alliances in which it is involved.

9.8.1 The United Nations (UN)

The **United Nations (UN)** is a global body set up after the Second World War with the stated aim of promoting peace, preventing future conflicts, and achieving international cooperation on economic, social, cultural, and humanitarian issues. Committed to solving disputes between nations by peaceful means, when it sends troops into countries this tends to be in a 'peacekeeping' capacity—to police borders, refugees, or aid routes, rather than engage in active hostilities.

Formally established in October 1945 and based in New York, the UN set out to avoid the perceived errors of its precursor, the League of Nations. The League—born out of the First World War—had imposed crippling reparations on Germany, in so doing contributing to the dire economic woes that fostered the popularity of Nazism. Initially founded by fifty-one states, today the UN embraces 193—with the then newly created state of South Sudan welcomed into its fold in July 2011. The most senior UN official is its Secretary-General (until 31 December 2016, Ban Ki-Moon), and its main governing bodies are the *UN Security Council (UNSC)* and the *UN General Assembly*. The former is (as its name suggests) in charge of the security/military aspects of the UN's role. Decisions are taken by five permanent members—the UK, France, China, the US and Russia—and a further ten rotating members, elected by the UN's 'parliament', the General Assembly, every other year. As a mark of its seniority, each permanent member has the right to veto prospective UN actions. It was this fact that presented the biggest stumbling block to the Anglo–American campaign to win support for invading Iraq in 2003. Both then French President Jacques Chirac and his Russian counterpart, Vladimir Putin, refused to back any further resolution authorizing military strikes without conclusive proof that Saddam was stockpiling weapons of mass destruction (WMDs): the ostensible pretext for action. The General Assembly's primary purpose is to approve the UN's annual budget and drive collective policymaking by member states on areas requiring global cooperation, such as international aid and climate change. The UN also has a number of agencies, brief outlines of which are given in table 9E to be found on the **Online Resource Centre**.

9.8.2 NATO

Founded in 1949 and based in Brussels, the **North Atlantic Treaty Organization (NATO)** is a *military* alliance, established against the backdrop of the Cold War between East and West. NATO comprises twenty-eight members—the United States, Canada, and several western European states—although since the Soviet Union's collapse it has also embraced several former Eastern Bloc nations.

The foundation-stone of NATO was the North Atlantic Treaty, the most oft-cited clause of which is Article V, which sets down the principle of 'collective defence'. Its opening sentence reads:

> 'The Parties of NATO agreed that an armed attack against one or more of them in Europe or North America shall be considered an attack against them all.'

Article V was invoked in the aftermath of the 11 September attacks on New York, when the US government argued that the terrorist strikes on the World Trade Center amounted to a military attack on the country and therefore required a joint response from NATO members. There was some dispute about whether the usual rules applied, given that precise nationalities of some of the terrorists were not immediately known—making any decision to target a specific country in retaliation problematic. Having asserted an Al-Qaeda link, the United States argued that the Taliban in Afghanistan was principally answerable, since its then leader, the late Mullah Omar, was believed to be harbouring Al-Qaeda's leader, Osama bin Laden. In the event, action in defence of the United States was authorized on 4 October 2001 (despite rowdy scenes in some meetings) and the alliance participated in two further related operations. Whether the US itself continues to abide by the rules of 'collective defence' in response to threats to its NATO allies over coming years remains to be seen, following US President Donald Trump's recent criticisms of states that failed to pay their 'fair share' of its budget. NATO's main governing body is the *North Atlantic Council (NAC)* and it, too, has a Secretary-General (since October 2014, former Norwegian Prime Minister Jens Stoltenberg). Operational decisions are taken by senior Armed Forces representatives on its *Military Committee*.

9.8.3 The Council of Europe

Founded in 1949, the **Council of Europe** pre-dates the EU (with which it and its institutions are often confused) by two years. As such, it is the longest-running organization dedicated to promoting European integration and cooperation. It has forty-seven member states and aims to foster members' adoption of common legal standards and human rights. To this end its most famous institution is the **European Court of Human Rights (ECtHR)** in Strasbourg, and its most celebrated (if often disputed) achievement the European Convention on Human Rights (ECHR) (see 1.1.1.1).

9.8.4 The G8 and G20

The **G8**—or 'Group of Eight'—is not a formal body like many others in this list, but rather a forum comprising the world's biggest industrialized nations and military superpowers. Its membership is as follows: Canada, France, Germany, Italy, Japan, Russia, the UK, and the US. Even today, the group sometimes convenes in Russia's absence (as the 'Group of Seven' or G7)—and this has happened several times during the West's ongoing dispute with President Putin over his decision to annex the Crimea from Ukraine in 2014, following a referendum in the region supporting its return to Russian rule. The G7/8's origins date back to the economic turmoil created in Europe by the 1973 oil crisis—pitting the United States, Japan, Britain, and other western European countries against Arab nations aligned to the Organization of the

Petroleum Exporting Countries (OPEC). And, aptly, it was another international economic crisis, the 2008–9 banking collapse, that saw it eclipsed in influence (and media coverage) by the then newly convened **G20** ('Group of 20'). Though the G20's material achievements have since been patchy, in the aftermath of the 'crash' it established an international *Financial Stability Board (FSB)*, charged with introducing a raft of measures to guard against future crises. Many of its proposals—including a global crackdown on 'tax havens' and the regulation of hedge funds and private equity firms—have, however, yet to materialize.

9.8.5 Global financial institutions

Long pre-dating the FSB, the *International Monetary Fund (IMF)* is tasked with maintaining/restoring stability in the global financial sector and preventing widespread recessions, using mechanisms like exchange-rate agreements and short-term financial aid. One of its key roles since its formation in 1945 has been to loan money to countries experiencing temporary economic blips—borrowing funds from a pool contributed to by member states. The IMF today boasts 189 members, comprising all UN states bar North Korea, Cuba, Andorra, Monaco, and Liechtenstein.

Based, like the IMF, in Washington DC, *The World Bank* (or, to use its full title, International Bank for Reconstruction and Development) was set up on 27 December 1945. Its remit now mainly revolves around globally agreed 'Millennium Development Goals' to end child poverty and improve education and human rights for the poorest nations, yet it has encountered increasing hostility from some development charities because of the 'conditionalities' it imposes before agreeing to assist struggling states. Some see its criteria, typically involving market deregulation and/or privatization of state assets, as an attempt to impose a Western-influenced neoliberal economic model on nations whose indigenous institutions and sociocultural make-up do not sit easily with it.

Other noteworthy bodies include the *World Trade Organization (WTO)*, which promotes free and fair trade between nations, and the Paris-based *Organization for Economic Co-operation and Development (OECD)*, which allies a similar focus on global free trade with promoting human rights.

9.8.6 The Commonwealth of Nations

The vestiges of the one-time British Empire, today's residual Commonwealth comprises fifty-three countries—most (but not all) former British colonies. Its current membership is outlined in table 9F to be found on the **Online Resource Centre**.

Topical feature idea

Britain's impending departure from the European Union has sparked concerns among EU economic migrants already living and working in the UK that they might be asked to leave the country once it has formally left. These fears have been stoked by Mrs May's refusal to confirm their long-term status and Brexit Secretary Mr Davis's suggestion that some could be deported. Mindful that there is a large Polish population in your paper's catchment area, your editor wants you to write a balanced backgrounder on this subject. How would you find firm statistics on the numbers of migrants living locally, and which sources would you go to for both sides of the migration debate?

Current issues

- **Negotiating Brexit** With the UK having opted out of the EU, Theresa May's government faces having to negotiate a deal on its future partnership with the Union (and other states) that will give British companies and consumers favourable access to markets without forcing the country to accept conditions that undermine its decision to leave (e.g. free movement).
- **Further EU enlargement** Negotiations over Turkey's accession to the EU began seriously in 2004, but its questionable human rights record, particularly after President Erdogan's 2016 crackdown following a failed military coup, have slowed progress. Kosovo is currently lobbying for entry and looks set to be accepted before Turkey.
- **Controversy over TTIP** The EU and the United States are currently locked in ongoing negotiations over the terms of a putative Transatlantic Trade and Investment Partnership (TTIP), which would liberalize trade between the two economic blocs. Critics argue that one consequence of the deregulation it envisages would be to allow private firms to force taxpayer-funded public services, like the NHS, to offer more contracts to commercial firms.

Key points

1. The European Union (EU) is a community of states initially formed to promote free trade, but which has developed cooperative policies on employment rights, asylum and immigration, and security and policing. It currently comprises twenty-eight (soon to be twenty-seven) members.
2. Eighteen EU member states share a joint currency: the euro. This is issued by the European Central Bank (ECB), based in Frankfurt.
3. There are four main governing EU institutions, each with a permanent president: the European Council; the European Commission; European Parliament; and the Council of the European Union (Council of Ministers). The last is the most powerful.

4 Membership of the Council of Ministers varies, depending on which issue is being debated (for example finance ministers attend if it is debating the economy). It votes using a system called qualified majority voting (QMV), weighted to give the biggest say to states with the largest populations.

5 Prosecutions under EU law may be brought to the Court of Justice of the European Union (CJEU), based in Strasbourg. Cases are normally held by its lower court, the General Court.

→ Further reading

Bennett, O. (2016) *The Brexit Club: The Inside Story of the Leave Campaign's Shock Victory*, London: Biteback Publishing. **Political journalist Owen Bennett's engrossing 'insider's account' of the tactics UKIP and other Leave campaigners used to swing the 2016 referendum.**

Geddes, A. (2013) *Britain and the European Union*, Basingstoke: Palgrave Macmillan. **Candid analysis of Britain's chequered history as a member of the EU.**

Kenealey, D., Peterson, J., and Corbett, R. (eds) (2015) *The European Union: How Does it Work?*, 4th edn, Oxford: Oxford University Press. **Fully revised edition of this invaluable introductory text for demystifying key EU institutions and their sometimes byzantine governing procedures.**

McCormick, J. (2014) *Understanding the European Union: A Concise Introduction*, 6th edn, Basingstoke: Palgrave Macmillan. **Leading introductory text to the history, institutions, and treaties of the EU. Latest edition includes a comprehensive assessment of the Lisbon Treaty and impact of EU enlargement.**

Online Resource Centre

www.oxfordtextbooks.co.uk/orc/Morrison5e/

Visit the Online Resource Centre that accompanies this book for web links and regular updates.

10

The origins and structure of local government

The evolution of government in Britain can be rationalized into two phases: gradual unification beneath first a single monarch, then a centralized Parliament; followed by the incremental devolution of many powers accrued at the centre to local and, more recently, regional administrations.

When the process of nation-building first began, competing kings vied with each other to extend their realms to encompass first England, then Wales, Scotland, and in due course Ireland. Ironically, by the time these countries were formally consolidated into a single 'United Kingdom', in the 1707 Acts of Union, the monarchy's power was already waning, and it was not long before Parliament would begin ceding considerable powers of self-determination to the provinces.

That said, the evolution of local government has been as much a bottom-up as a top-down process. Medieval monarchs needed to appoint locally based courts, and created titled landowners to maintain loyalty among their subjects. Conversely, pressure for jurisdiction over issues as diverse as public health, road maintenance, and refuse collection to be handed to locally based individuals, guilds, and eventually elected councils came from the artisans, manufacturers, and merchants whose trade and enterprise depended on them. Over time, these early moves towards local government became increasingly sophisticated.

Since May 2015, there have been 418 'principal' UK local authorities (councils)—down from 433 previously. In England there are 353, in Scotland thirty-two, and in Wales twenty-two. The latter tally had been due to fall to eight or nine after the May 2016 Welsh Assembly elections, but at the time of writing newly re-elected Labour First Minister Carwyn Jones appeared to have abandoned this plan. Following tortuous negotiations, Northern Ireland's total was cut from twenty-six to eleven at the May 2014 local elections, though for the first year the new 'super-councils' operated in 'shadow' alongside their precursors.

In England, the range of council types is particularly baffling. Many people living outside London and other metropolitan areas come under a 'two-tier' system, in which local services are split between 'lower-tier' district/borough and 'upper-tier' county councils, while others have a single (unitary) authority—including residents of the capital and other major cities such as Birmingham, Manchester, and Sheffield (where those councils are styled London borough and metropolitan borough councils respectively). The recent introduction of new 'super-councils' known as combined authorities in six conurbations—with more to come, including in non-metropolitan areas—has added further complexity to this picture (see 10.2.4).

10.1 The first British local authorities

Long before the emergence of anything that could be described as a 'council'—the term by which we refer to local authorities today—it suited those at the top of British society to maintain a rudimentary 'local government'. To this end, Saxon kings set up 'shire courts' across the countryside and their Norman successors established a feudal system based on this.

By the twelfth century, with urbanization taking root, individuals and groups whose activities provided the bedrock of their local economies began to see the virtue of establishing a strengthened form of local autonomy. Their pleas were rewarded with the granting of the first 'letters patent' and 'royal charters', conferring the status of 'incorporated bodies' (self-governing entities) on cities and 'municipal boroughs' (smaller towns recognized as having legitimate claims to run their own commercial and legal affairs). These areas were run by nominally elected 'municipal corporations'.

Both cities and boroughs exist to this day—albeit largely in name, as their powers have been brought into line with those of other forms of council. In rural areas, however, shire courts were short-lived and were eventually replaced by a new regime overseen by individuals who, in many ways, can be viewed as antecedents of today's elected mayors and police and crime commissioners (see 12.3 and 10.7 respectively): Justices of the Peace (JPs). Their authority derived from Acts of Parliament rather than common law, and over time they were assisted in their work by their local 'parishes'. These bodies were effectively embryonic councils—based initially around ecclesiastical parish boundaries, but ultimately evolving into the civil parishes (see 10.4).

10.1.1 The emergence of modern local authorities

It was during the Industrial Revolution that a combination of commercial, political, and simple logistical pressures combined to promote the first true councils.

By the early nineteenth century, there were 800 boroughs, most governed by majors (mayors) and councils elected exclusively from among the wealthiest merchants, industrialists, and landowners. The electorate (to the extent that it existed) was limited to other equally moneyed individuals and a handful of marginally less affluent tradesmen. Early public services—street lighting and road maintenance, for example—were delivered largely to make conditions better for commerce.

No new charters were granted in the eighteenth century, so major emerging industrial towns and cities like Manchester and Birmingham had limited autonomy, in the form of 'improvement commissioners' approved by Parliament. In rural areas, the established JP/parish combination continued to hold sway. Justices and parish councils met four times a year in 'quarter sessions', which generally took place in public houses. Their core officials (parish constables, highway surveyors, and overseers of the poor) were funded by 'rates' they collected from local households—taxes based on the 'rateable' (or rental) value of land and property, which continued in one form or another until 1990.

The origins of today's local government system lie in the key Acts listed in table 10A to be found on the **Online Resource Centre** that accompanies this book.

By 1894, five types of local authority existed outside London: county councils, county borough councils, municipal borough councils, urban district councils, and rural district councils. This would remain the framework for English local government for the best part of eighty years.

10.2 The rolling reorganization of local government

Since the 1970s, there have been five significant local government reorganizations:

- 1974—the introduction of a 'two-tier' structure in England and Wales;
- 1986—the abolition of metropolitan counties in major urban areas;
- 1990s onwards—the phased introduction of unitary authorities;
- 2000 onwards—the gradual introduction of directly elected mayors in major towns and cities; and
- 2011 onwards—the incremental reintroduction of metropolitan/regional local government through the emergence of combined authorities.

The following section examines each of these developments in detail.

Because the evolution of local government in London and Scotland followed different trajectories from the rest of Britain, they are considered separately.

10.2.1 The 1974 reorganization

The largest-scale restructuring of the council framework in England and Wales (excluding London), this originated in the conclusions of a Royal Commission on Local Government, which in its 1969 report recommended that the 1,000 existing councils should be replaced by a rationalized system of sixty-one 'local authority areas', of which fifty-eight would be 'all-purpose'. These would effectively be unitary authorities (see 10.2.3), taking responsibility for all local services. Conurbations (major urban centres where two or more towns and cities had merged to form single built-up areas), such as Greater Manchester and the West Midlands, would have their own two-tier *metropolitan* authorities, in recognition of their greater populations and community needs.

The Labour government which had set up the inquiry lost the 1970 election and the Commission's recommendations were deemed too revolutionary by Ted Heath's incoming Conservatives. In the event, it was not until the tenure of (ironically) another Tory, John Major, in the 1990s that unitary authorities finally appeared. However, Heath's government recognized the need for some reform and duly instituted this in the guise of the Local Government Act 1972, which took effect in 1974. This introduced the following:

- A **two-tier structure** of counties and districts, which remained the norm until the mid-1990s and still exists in many areas. Numerous districts subsequently applied for Royal Charters, entitling them to call themselves 'borough' or 'city' councils (like the boroughs and cities of old). This move led to some districts and counties amalgamating—reducing the overall number of councils to thirty-nine counties and 296 districts in England, with an eight/thirty-seven split in Wales.
- An alternative two-tier metropolitan county structure in six pilot conurbations: West Midlands, Merseyside, Greater Manchester, West Yorkshire, South Yorkshire, and Tyne and Wear. Each conurbation was split, for administrative purposes, into several *metropolitan borough councils*, charged with financing and running most day-to-day local services—for example rubbish collection, housing, and environmental health. Conurbations were each overseen by single *metropolitan county councils*, in charge of services affecting their whole areas, such as strategic town and country planning, main roads linking neighbouring towns, public transport, emergency services, and civil protection. (A breakdown of towns and cities encompassed by each is contained in table 10B to be found on the **Online Resource Centre**.)

The new two-tier structure saw the end of longstanding counties like Cumberland, Westmorland, and the three different parts of Lincolnshire, and the introduction of new ones, including Avon, Cleveland, Cumbria, Humberside, Clwyd, Dyfed, and Gwent. Some were never wholly accepted by local people

Table 10.1 Breakdown of council services offered by different types of local authority

District councils, borough councils, metropolitan borough councils, and unitary authorities	County councils and unitary authorities
Environmental health (sanitation, drainage, pollution, food hygiene)	Education (schools and further education)
Development control (planning permission)	Social services (care for elderly, mentally ill, and vulnerable children)
Housing and the homeless	Highways (road-building, maintenance, and on-street parking)
Refuse collection (now including waste for recycling)	Refuse disposal (landfill sites)
Car parks	Emergency planning
Council Tax and Uniform Business Rates (UBR) collection	Cultural and leisure services (libraries, museums, sports centres)
Local strategic planning	Countywide strategic planning
Licensing	Passenger transport (buses, trams)

and subsequently vanished (for instance, Avon was merged with neighbouring Somerset in the post-1992 unitary settlement). The reorganization also saw certain cities stripped of their 'municipal borough' status. These included Nottingham, Bristol, Leicester, and Norwich—although as compensation they were allowed to retain the nomenclature 'city', not to mention 'lord mayors' (councillors who take it in turn to spend a year carrying out ceremonial duties and in other towns are simply called **mayors**).

Under the rationalized two-tier structure, **district councils**, **borough councils**, and the new metropolitan borough councils were equivalent to each other, and were each given the same responsibilities—largely providing localized, 'door-to-door' services like refuse collection. Conversely, **county councils** and metropolitan county councils became responsible for providing countywide services, with social care and education the biggest spending areas. A full breakdown of current council responsibilities is outlined in Table 10.1, and a list of the central government departments at Whitehall responsible for overseeing each service area is given in table 10C to be found on the **Online Resource Centre**.

Northern Ireland's council reorganization took a different form, and happened more swiftly. In 1973, twenty-six districts emerged, but many functions were transferred from local to central government.

10.2.2 The 1986 reorganization

The Conservatives' 1983 election manifesto described the six metropolitan county councils that it inherited on regaining power in 1979—alongside the then Greater London Council (GLC), under the leadership of Ken Livingstone—as a 'wasteful and unnecessary tier of government'. The party went on to abolish them, returning their functions to the second-tier metropolitan borough councils that still existed 'beneath' them (confusingly, redesignated 'metropolitan *districts*' for administrative purposes), while at the same time establishing new police authorities in each of these areas. Tyne and Wear was unusual, in that its police provision fell under the Northumbria Police Authority. Metropolitan areas also gained their own fire and civil defence and passenger transport authorities, and some acquired joint boards responsible for handling waste disposal services. This happened in Merseyside and Greater Manchester (except Wigan), for example.

Other than introducing these new, service-specific types of local authority, in all other respects the effect of the 1986 changes was to replace the previous metropolitan two-tier structure with what were effectively the first unitary authorities—all-purpose councils, responsible for fulfilling the roles split in other areas between districts/boroughs and counties. Opponents of the move saw in it a clear attempt by the Conservatives to diminish metropolitan councils' authority by reducing them to lower-level administrations, on the one hand, and hiving off responsibilities formerly overseen by the scrapped metropolitan counties to new bodies with limited scope, on the other. Mr Livingstone and other left-wing council leaders, including Sheffield City Council and South Yorkshire County Council's David Blunkett (a future Labour Home Secretary), saw the diluted powers as an assault on their socialist policies by a right-wing government fearful of major populated areas becoming 'states within states'. Referring to this notion explicitly at one point in the late 1980s, Sir Cyril Irvine Patnick, Tory member of Parliament (MP) for Sheffield Hallam, famously described Mr Blunkett's domain as 'the People's Republic of South Yorkshire'.

Curiously, though, it was to be a future Tory-led government that would revive this 'super-council' approach in metropolitan areas, as section 10.2.4 explains.

10.2.3 The 1990s introduction of unitary authorities

The most significant council restructure since 1974 began in 1992, in a phased process designed to rationalize local government across England and Wales. The stated aim of introducing a **unitary structure** was to improve the efficiency and transparency of local administration by reducing service duplication, slashing bureaucracy, and establishing a simplified, uniform council structure across the two countries. By way of a simple definition, unitary authorities are defined as 'any authority which is the sole principal council for its local government area'. Excluding the thirty-two London and thirty-six metropolitan boroughs (which are unitary authorities in all but name), there are presently fifty-seven in England, thirty-two in Scotland (where they are simply called 'councils'), twenty-two in Wales (where they are known as 'principal areas'), and eleven in Northern Ireland (where they are designated 'districts' and have no powers over education, road-building, or housing). Though they go by different labels in each of the devolved nations, unitary authorities are now the norm everywhere in Britain except England: in other words, it is only the English system that retains two-tier structures in some areas.

Contrary to bold claims favouring the unitary system, critics argue that it has only added to the overall level of confusion about local government, by creating a patchwork landscape of council structures, with unitaries in many areas sitting directly alongside councils retaining the two-tier structure. Counties in which both unitary and two-tier systems coexist are defined as having a **hybrid structure**. A classic example would be the geographical county of East Sussex, in which Brighton and Hove City Council (a unitary) exists alongside a two-tier structure topped by East Sussex County Council, beneath which sit several lower-tier authorities, including Eastbourne Borough Council and Lewes District Council. The evolution of unitary authorities is outlined in table 10D to be found on the **Online Resource Centre**.

In addition to hybrid counties, the unitary system produces other quirks. Several unitary councils encompass entire counties—notably the Isle of Wight, Rutland, County Durham, and Cornwall. The Isles of Scilly, meanwhile, have a unique form of council that was long treated as *sui generis* (meaning 'in a class of its own'), but is now seen as a unitary.

10.2.4 The emergence of combined authorities

Initially with little fanfare, the Local Democracy, Economic Development, and Construction Act 2009 ushered in the beginnings of the most radical shake-up of English local democracy since 1974. The Act heralded the birth of a new tier of government which, over time, may go some way towards answering calls for England to be granted levels of autonomy comparable to those being devolved to national assemblies in Scotland, Wales, and Northern Ireland (see 1.3). More than three years before the close-run referendum on Scottish independence that would bring these calls to a head (see 1.3.3), April 2011 saw the establishment of the first of these entities: the Greater Manchester Combined Authority. A further six **combined authorities (CAs)** have so far followed, four in April 2014 alone—covering Liverpool City Region, the North East, Sheffield City Region, and West Yorkshire—another (Tees Valley) in April 2016, and a sixth (West Midlands) two months later.

Combined authorities—so far largely clustered in northern England—are designed to address a number of political objectives favoured by first the Coalition and now the present Conservative government. In addition to addressing the 'English Question' (see 1.3.6), it is hoped that it will successfully revive the faltering drive towards rolling out US-style directly elected mayors (see 12.3), while also acting as an engine for the much-touted 'northern powerhouse' project—an economic 'rebalancing act' designed to edge Britain away from its customary over-reliance on the profitability of the City of London. Each authority 'combines' (or pools the resources of) anything between four and (in Greater Manchester's case) ten existing metropolitan district, district, county, and unitary authorities, which continue to exist beneath. In material terms, the powers of a combined authority are potentially significant: in addition to being legally designated as the *integrated transport authority* and *economic prosperity board* for its area/region, it may levy precepts (see 11.2.4.2) on its constituent councils and borrow money on the open market (subject to certain restrictions). To illustrate, Greater Manchester had already agreed loans worth more than £1 million from the European Investment Bank by 2015. The scope of combined authorities' powers was defined most clearly by the Cities and Local Government Devolution Act 2016, which, in addition to formalizing the requirement for them to adopt elected mayors, conferred on them autonomy over planning, transport, housing, and policing. In addition, the trailblazing Greater Manchester authority has now assumed control of its £6bn NHS budget—a service area previously beyond the scope of local authorities (see Chapter 6)—and, following his or her election in May 2017, its elected mayor will also take control of policing and fire services from the Greater Manchester Police and Crime Commissioner and Greater Manchester Fire and Rescue Authority.

For as long as the Tories remain in power, the combined authority 'principle' is likely to roll out much further—with distinctly *non*-metropolitan areas also getting in on the act. Among the authority groupings already involved in talks with the Treasury about the possibility of setting up their own combined authorities are the neighbouring 'home counties' of Oxfordshire, Buckinghamshire, and Northamptonshire, and a consortium of twenty-four councils in eastern England keen to collectively form the East Anglia Combined Authority. Moreover, the Act potentially allows for various other radical reconfigurations. These range from the formation of combined authorities by groups of councils that are not immediate neighbours, to arrangements under which county councils share or delegate powers to CAs over districts/boroughs whose geographical boundaries fall in their areas.

10.3 City councils and 'city status'

Historically, cities were synonymous with ecclesiastical centres and, more specifically, the presence of Church of England cathedrals and diocesan bishops. But even centuries ago this was not always true: in the Tudor period, city status was sometimes conferred by sovereigns through letters patent (legal instruments issued by monarchs), the granting of a town's royal charter, or even, over time, accepted custom and practice.

In the nineteenth century, the Church of England actively sought to multiply its urban dioceses, creating more cities in the process. Not all towns designated as cities had previously had royal borough status, and by the end of the 1800s cities were springing up in places without cathedrals. Around this time, Scotland gained its first cities by letters patent and royal charter; prior to 1889, major medieval towns like Edinburgh were often referred to as 'civitas' and, although the word 'city' had been coined by the eighteenth century, their status remained unofficial.

Today, 'city status' no longer depends on the presence of a cathedral or any significant ecclesiastical influence. Neither are cities always major population centres: with a mere 2,000 inhabitants, Britain's smallest city, St David's in Pembrokeshire, has a populace much smaller than most towns.

For much of the twentieth century, it was Home Secretaries' responsibility to advise monarchs on which towns should be designated cities. This happened to Lancaster in 1937, Swansea in 1969, and Sunderland in 1992. More recently, however, the rules have been bent. In December 2000, three new cities were created, in Brighton and Hove, Wolverhampton, and Inverness, as part of a 'Millennium City' competition launched by the then Labour government. The Queen created five more in 2002 to mark her Golden Jubilee: Stirling, Preston, Newport, Lisburn, and Newry. She repeated this for three more—Chelmsford, Perth, and St Asaph in north Wales, which boasts Britain's smallest cathedral—in the run-up to her Diamond Jubilee. This brought the overall number of cities to sixty-nine.

Just as the criteria used to determine whether a town qualifies for city status are nebulous, so is the degree to which becoming one has any tangible impact. A **city council**—the moniker adopted by authorities covering places with official city designation—is not a *type* of council or administration, but little more than an honorary title. In terms of their 'functions', city councils tend to be unitary authorities (Brighton and Hove, York, and Stoke-on-Trent), metropolitan boroughs/districts (Birmingham, Wolverhampton), or simple district/borough councils.

There are some curious exceptions. Confusingly, seven English cities—Chichester, Ely, Hereford, Lichfield, Ripon, Truro, and Wells—are lowly civil parishes, in terms of their administrative status. This means that technically they fall within the remit of parish councils: the lowest tier of local government (see 10.4). Similarly, in three Welsh cities (Bangor, St David's, and St Asaph), the city status applies to community councils (equivalent to parish councils). In two English cities (Bath and Salisbury), meanwhile, city status is the preserve of so-called 'charter trustees'—an arcane form of local administration intended to be a temporary stopgap for towns when their borough status was removed by the Crown prior to their 'conversion' into parish councils. A full rundown of designated cities, together with details of the type of authority in each place, is listed in table 10E to be found on the **Online Resource Centre**.

10.4 Parish, town, and community councils

The lowest tier of local government is represented by parish councils in England and community councils in Wales and Scotland. Civil parish councils—not to be confused with pre-existing *ecclesiastical* parishes established by the Church—were created in 1894 to oversee social welfare and basic civic duties in villages and small towns, and act as the 'voices' of these communities. Historically, some parish and community councils in larger villages and small towns came to call themselves 'town councils'. Those that still do so tend to have their own town mayors—not to be confused with the more official (if also largely ceremonial) mayors of borough and city councils, let alone the directly elected mayors now found in some towns and cities (see 12.3.6). Councillors take turns to spend a year as mayor, on rotation, with formal 'mayor-making ceremonies' held in town halls to mark the handover from one to another. Mayors' roles are largely ceremonial (opening church fetes, switching on Christmas lights), although they also often chair full council meetings.

Under the 1972 Act, all parishes with more than 150 inhabitants were compelled to establish parish councils—a stipulation that has significantly increased their number. Those with smaller populations, however, were required only to hold **parish meetings**—regular gatherings open to all local electors. Unlike meetings held in towns and villages with formal parish councils, those convened in lesser populated parishes have statutory powers to act as de facto councils. In such circumstances, a clerk and chairman are elected to preside over business.

Today, many of the limited day-to-day powers once exercised by parish, community, and town councils are wielded by higher-level authorities. But parish councils are still allocated budgets by those authorities ('parish precepts'), which, unlike revenue raised for their own use, cannot be capped by central government. Therefore, in areas in which parishes are more proactive, precepts can be high: Thurston Parish Council in Suffolk, for example, raised its Council Tax share by 214 per cent in 2008–9. In most areas, however, the precept is sufficient only to rent the buildings in which it holds monthly meetings and fund minor local improvements, such as replacement street lights, park benches, or new goalposts for the village football pitch.

Parish councils, however, remain significant. They have a statutory right to be formally consulted by, and represented on, public inquiries into major planning applications affecting their areas. In fact, often the first time a reporter—and, by extension, his or her news organization—hears of a potentially controversial planning proposal will be at a parish council meeting. For a time, this lowest tier of government looked to have a bright and influential future under David Cameron's drive to replace many traditionally state- or council-run services with a more *community*-directed approach that he dubbed the 'Big Society' (see 12.1.4), but a lack of political clarity combined with lukewarm enthusiasm at grass-roots level has, to date, left this ambition largely unfulfilled.

10.5 The evolution of London local government

London's autonomy has always been exercised in a distinct way from the rest of Britain, although its local government structure continues to resemble that of the metropolitan areas described earlier. Today, London operates under a unique two-tier system, with responsibilities for service provision split between the **Greater London Authority (GLA)**, headed by an elected mayor, and thirty-three second-tier councils (a system akin to the pre-1986 metropolitan county and borough structure abolished by Margaret Thatcher's government).

Of these thirty-three councils, thirty-two are London boroughs, elected in similar fashion to those in metropolitan areas, but the last is a unique entity run by an unreformed medieval-style 'old boys' network': the City of London Corporation (officially, the 'Mayor and Commonalty and Citizens of the City of London'). Britain's oldest surviving council, this covers the 'Square Mile' containing the capital's central financial district and, although democratically accountable like other authorities, has long attracted criticism for the anachronistic nature of its electoral processes and peculiar customs. As the only corporation to escape the axe when the Municipal Corporations Act 1835 abolished all others, the City continues to be presided over by a non-partisan administration of a kind once more widespread before the emergence of formal political parties: a Court of Common Council, with a range of committees overseeing specific policy areas, and overseen by a Lord Mayor of London and his attendant aldermen. Again uniquely, the Corporation was allowed to retain a system of *non-residential voting* (widely dubbed the 'business vote') after this was abolished elsewhere in 1969. This concession was, in part, a recognition of its tiny resident population (just 7,400 as of the 2011 census). Vocal critics of the Corporation—which many see as a self-perpetuating, privileged cabal—include Shadow Chancellor John McDonnell, who memorably dismissed it in 2002 as 'a group of hangers-on, who create what is known as the best dining club in the City ... a rotten borough'. A timeline of the evolution of London's local government is presented in table10F to be found on the **Online Resource Centre**.

10.5.1 London's modern-day local government structure

In tandem with its prospectus for introducing devolution in Scotland, Wales, and Northern Ireland, Labour's 1997 manifesto pledged to introduce a new form of 'elected city government' in London, topped by a US- or European-style elected mayor. A year after regaining power, the promised poll was held, and 72 per cent of London's electorate voted in favour of the proposed GLA. Twelve months later, the Greater London Authority Act 1999 formalized the new authority and, with more than a hint of déjà vu, Mr Livingstone was duly elected the first London Mayor in March 2000.

Although the GLA has become a model for certain other towns and cities that have since adopted elected mayors (see 12.3.6), initially its method of conducting business was unique among councils. In a manner akin to the US president's power-sharing with that country's parliament (Congress), London's mayor is elected separately to the twenty-five-strong London Assembly with which he or she shares power over the GLA. Like the US president, the mayor is responsible for initiating policies and drawing up annual budgets to finance services that he or she hopes to provide in coming years. The Assembly must then approve or amend these proposals (much like Congress) and its committees and subcommittees may scrutinize the mayor's actions and the performance of services provided by the GLA. The parallels between the London mayoral and US parliamentary systems have gone further in recent years, in light of changes to the political composition of both. Just as President Barack Obama (a Democrat) spent much of his time in the White House fighting to get the more contentious aspects of his legislative programme through a Republican-dominated House of Representatives, both Mr Livingstone and his successor, the Conservative Boris Johnson, were forced to negotiate delicate compromises with their political opponents during their second terms.

The GLA is the top tier of London local government, with individual boroughs continuing to provide day-to-day services. The division between the roles of the GLA and boroughs is explained in Table 10.2; of the major roles fulfilled by the GLA, the majority are overseen by the agencies listed in Table 10.3.

Table 10.2 Breakdown of local authority responsibilities in London

Greater London Authority (GLA)	London boroughs
Transport	Schools and further education (FE)
Policing	Social services
Fire and rescue	Waste collection
Congestion charging	Highways repair and maintenance
Environmental policy	Libraries, and local leisure and cultural services (museums, theatres)
Strategic development and planning	Development control

Table 10.3 Main agencies of the Greater London Authority (GLA)

Agency	Responsibilities
Transport for London (TfL)	Manages most aspects of London's transport system, including London Underground, Docklands Light Railway, London buses, main roads, and traffic management (incorporating the congestion charge zone)
Metropolitan Police Authority (MPA)	Oversees Metropolitan Police Service
London Fire and Emergency Planning Authority (LFEPA)	Administers London Fire Brigade and coordinates emergency planning

10.6 Local government in Scotland

As with several other aspects of public affairs—notably its legal and education systems—Scotland has a different local government framework from the rest of Britain's.

Between the Local Government (Scotland) Act 1973 and the mid-1990s, a more or less universal two-tier system existed north of the border, with pre-existing lower-tier district councils joined by 'new' upper-tier regional councils (with the exception of the Western Isles, Shetland, and Orkney, which were allowed to retain the single-tier system that had prevailed across the country previously).

All this changed, though, when in 1996 Mr Major's government decided against the 'phased' approach to introducing unitary authorities applied elsewhere in Britain, and to adopt a 'big bang' strategy, co-opting the whole of Scotland into the new framework in one go. While it had the benefit of rationalizing the patchwork that preceded it, this 'one size fits all' strategy caused controversy in some areas—not least because of the wildly varying population sizes covered by individual councils. The unitary authority for Inverclyde (an area with relatively few inhabitants) followed the same boundaries as the extant district council, while Clackmannanshire embraced the whole of that county plus Highland, a sprawling 30,650 km swathe of north-west Scotland, encompassing chunks of the former counties of Inverness-shire, Ross and Cromarty, Caithness and Nairnshire, and all Sutherland.

Today, there are thirty-two unitary 'council areas'. In May 2012, a report by the Reform Scotland think tank recommended reducing the number of councils to nineteen and merging them with existing health and police boards to create a more integrated approach to local public services, but such a change has yet to materialize.

10.7 Emergency services at the local level

While ambulance services are today part of the NHS (see Chapter 6), with trust status akin to that accorded to hospitals, other core emergency services are overseen by discrete local or regional authorities.

10.7.1 The origins of the British police force

Until the early nineteenth century, Britain had no countrywide police force; instead, it fell to town magistrates to maintain local law and order. Perhaps unsurprisingly, London was the first UK city to adopt its own police force, and in 1749 author Henry Fielding and his brother, Sir John, set up a group of semi-professional law enforcers known as 'The Bow Street Runners'. These early police officers wore civilian clothes and did not patrol the streets routinely like today's counterparts, but acted to intercept criminals and bring them before the courts on magistrates' authority.

Shortly afterwards, an embryonic Thames Police was formed, but it was not until some eighty years later, when Sir Robert Peel was Home Secretary, that the first true constabulary was set up, in the guise of the Metropolitan Police, based at Scotland Yard. Established in 1829, and variously dubbed 'Bobbies' and 'Peelers' after their founder, the 'Met' were funded by a local tax—'the police rate'—which citizens had to pay on top of the 'poor rate'. In due course, similar innovations followed in emerging borough council areas.

Today, the UK Police Service, although notionally a nationwide organization, is divided into thirty-nine local forces in England and four in Wales. Scotland had eight regional forces between 1967 and the Police and Fire Reform (Scotland) Act 2012, when they were replaced by a single Scottish service, Police Scotland. Northern Ireland, too, has its own dedicated police force, dubbed the Police Service of Northern Ireland (PSNI), which replaced the erstwhile Royal Ulster Constabulary (RUC) in November 2001.

Most forces in England and Wales still respect county boundaries, although there are increasing exceptions: a single force, Sussex Police, covers both East and West Sussex, while the south-westernmost force is Devon and Cornwall Police. In 2006, the then Home Secretary Charles Clarke proposed merging several forces (among them, the five forces in the East Midlands, which would have become a unified 'super-force'), reducing the total in England and Wales to just twenty-four, in an effort to streamline the service and better equip the country to fight terrorism. Although his plans were shelved, more recently individual police forces in certain regions have voluntarily entered negotiations about possible mergers, with Durham and Northumbria among those still mooting amalgamation. In August 2015, the National Police Chiefs' Council (NPCC) formally approved the principle of mergers, in light of the government's moves towards devolving control of policing to combined authorities (see 10.2.4).

10.7.1.1 Police force accountability: from authorities to commissioners

Other than in Greater Manchester (as of May 2017) and London, where the Metropolitan Police Authority was handed executive control over the Met by ministers in the Greater London Authority Act 1999, UK police forces all come under the overarching control of the Home Secretary (or, in Scotland, the Deputy First Minister). Until 1995, forces were regulated by police committees answerable to county councils or unitary authorities, but the Police and Magistrates' Court Act 1994 saw these replaced by a new second tier: the police authority. The change, consolidated by the Police Act 1996, reduced the involvement of councillors from relevant local authorities in favour of a mixed membership intended to better represent local residents and the business community.

Police authorities raised revenue by levying precepts (annual budget requests) on their billing authorities, which were then included explicitly in local Council Tax bills (see 11.2.4). Their responsibilities included: maintaining effective and efficient forces for their areas (with the Home Secretary or Home Office Inspectorate empowered to 'act in default' if they failed); appointing, holding to account, and occasionally dismissing their local chief constables and assistant chief constables; and convening regular open public meetings along the lines of those held by councils, at which their members were expected to answer questions on their activities.

On 15 November 2012, all former police authority responsibilities were assumed in England and Wales by new US-style directly elected **police and crime commissioners (PCCs)**, in a highly contentious move condemned by some, including Sir Hugh Orde, president of the Association of Chief Police Officers (ACPO), as 'politicizing' the police. In Scotland, the eight preceding police authorities were replaced with one *Scottish Police Authority*, mirroring the country's single force—Police Scotland—while the *Northern Ireland Policing Board* fulfils the same role in that province.

The following further duties of PCCs in England and Wales were set out under the Police Reform and Social Responsibility Act 2011 as:

- setting the strategic accountability and direction for policing;
- working with partners to prevent and tackle crime;
- invoking the voice of the public, the vulnerable, and victims;
- contributing to resourcing of policing response to regional and national threats; and
- ensuring value for money.

The initial PCC elections, when finally held, proved contentious: amid accusations that ministers had failed to notify electors adequately of the fact a vote was even coming (let alone explain what PCCs were), they suffered the ignominy of recording Britain's lowest ever turnouts, hovering between 10 and 20 per cent. Mandates were considerably stronger three and a half years later, however, when the second set of PCC elections was purposely aligned with the date of the 2016 (and, thereafter, 2020, 2024 etc.) local elections. At the time of writing, the political affiliations of incumbent PCCs were as follows: Conservatives (twenty), Labour (fifteen), Plaid Cymru (two). The remaining three of the forty re-elected in May 2016 were independent, with the forty-first PCC area, Greater Manchester, postponing its election pending the assumption of policing powers by the conurbation's putative elected mayor in 2017. Though mayors of combined authorities, like Manchester's, will increasingly be appointed as their PCCs as well, in practice the day-to-day duties of commissioners are expected to be carried out by deputy PCCs.

The new commissioners were only ever established in forty-one of the forty-three English and Welsh police force areas because the City of London (as with so many special liberties) was exempted on historical grounds, while the role of overall commissioner for the capital was automatically assumed by the Mayor of London, Mr Johnson. Since their election, PCCs have continued courting controversy—not least for their generous salaries, lack of transparency, and, in some cases, perceived low calibre. In May 2014, Ann Barnes, PCC for Kent, faced calls to resign from her £85,000-a-year post after appearing in a Channel 4 *Cutting Edge* documentary in which she was shown struggling to explain her policing strategy, bringing her dogs into her office, and writing her own job title incorrectly on a whiteboard. Ms Barnes had previously faced criticism after Paris Brown, the 17 year-old whom she had appointed as Britain's first 'youth PCC', was forced to resign over allegedly racist and homophobic tweets she had posted as a younger teenager.

In terms of day-to-day accountability, the actions of PCCs are scrutinized by *police and crime panels*, comprising a minimum of ten local councillors—at least one from each local authority covered by the corresponding force area, plus two co-opted lay members.

10.7.1.2 The role of chief constables

The statutory responsibilities of **chief constables** have always been separate from those of their governing committees, authorities, or PCCs. Primarily, it is their role to deliver policy 'on the ground'—appointing all officers below the rank of assistant chief constable, producing annual reports on their performance in the preceding twelve months (covering specific categories of offence, along with other areas highlighted as being of local concern, such as violent crime), and disciplining officers for misconduct.

In operational terms, it is the chief constable and his or her assistants' role to manage the force's budget, hire and fire other officers, and ensure that personnel are suitably allocated to maintain adequate patrols across the force area. But over the past twenty years, as both population levels and the range of policing responsibilities have increased out of proportion with rises in numbers of officers, successive governments have tried to reduce the burden of police professionals' more mundane patrol duties by bolstering them with semi-trained back-up officers recruited from the local community. Today these include part-time volunteers known as 'special constables', or 'specials', and semi-trained policemen and women called **police community support officers (PCSOs)**.

As at 31 March 2011, when the last definitive survey was conducted, 15,820 PCSOs were employed across England and Wales—down from a peak of 16,814 in 2009. Around a quarter were based in London, with Manchester having the second largest contingent. In November 2007, they received enhanced powers—partly in response to complaints from senior police officers that trained staff were overstretched because of increased paperwork generated by legislation designed to make stop-and-search and arrest procedures more transparent. Although they have always been entitled to paid overtime, a minimum of twenty-one days' annual leave, and various other benefits, PCSOs used to earn significantly less than fully trained officers. However, since starting salaries for professional police constables (PCs)—the lowest rank—were reduced by £4,000 to £19,000 in 2013, to cut costs, the differential between them and PCSOs has been negligible. The powers of PCSOs are largely limited to dealing with low-level 'offences' relating to so-called antisocial behaviour (ASB), defined by the Crime and Disorder Act 1998 as conduct that:

> ‘caused or was likely to cause alarm, harassment or distress to one or more persons not of the same household as him or herself and where an ASBO is seen as necessary to protect relevant persons from further anti-social acts by the defendant.’

To this end, PCSOs can remove alcohol from people under the age of 18 and issue summary fixed-penalty notices to those who commit infringements ranging from littering and cycling on footpaths to failing to keep dogs under control. Under authority deriving from New Labour's 'Respect' agenda, they may also require names and addresses from people apprehended for other forms of ASB—for example fighting or swearing in the street. These details may subsequently be used by police or councils to apply to magistrates' courts for permission to issue individuals with summary penalties for various levels of antisocial behaviour—principally *antisocial behaviour orders* (ASBOs) until their replacement with several new measures by the Coalition (described later in this section). ASBOs were civil penalties in the first instance, but individuals who breached their conditions—by, for instance, failing to respect curfews or by remaining resident at prohibited addresses—could be prosecuted for criminal offences.

In addition to being able to impose orders and contracts on named individuals, PCSOs may (like ordinary police officers) apply to councils for *dispersal orders* to cover locations judged to be antisocial behaviour 'black spots'. Groups of two or more people alleged to be causing 'harassment, alarm, or distress' may be forcibly broken up and/or moved on from a location under these orders. Failure to comply can lead to prosecution and fines of up to £2,500.

Police can also obtain and enforce *designated public place orders* (DPPOs)—a variation on the dispersal order concept designed to clear specific streets, squares, or alleyways of drink-related antisocial behaviour. Anyone caught drinking in these locations who refuses to surrender his or her alcohol is liable for a £50 fixed penalty, or for arrest and a fine of up to £500.

Despite the widespread ridicule with which news of some ASBOs was greeted in the media (a man was banned from his own home after being given an

ASBO for playing his music too loudly, while several have been imposed on grumpy pensioners for relatively minor 'offences' such as cursing at their neighbours), they proved hugely popular among law enforcement agencies and many communities blighted by unruly behaviour. According to Home Office figures, 18,566 ASBOs were issued between their introduction in April 1999 and January 2011. Embarrassingly for ministers, though, 10,380 of these were breached by their recipients at least once. Despite this, Labour used their popularity as a springboard to expand the scope of its antisocial behaviour crackdown, by increasing the range of 'misdemeanours' for which summary penalties could be issued by police and local authorities, and giving parish and community councils powers to impose them. The Coalition replaced ASBOs with three principal orders, introduced by the Antisocial Behaviour, Crime, and Policing Act 2014, which continued to embody most of their abiding principles:

- the **criminal behaviour order (CBO)**—a 'ban' on forms of antisocial behaviour, with the ability to 'force' people to undertake programmes, such as drug or alcohol rehabilitation courses, to improve their conduct;
- the **crime prevention injunction (CPI)**—a 'fast-track' ASBO for lower-level antisocial behaviour, which can be imposed more quickly (within days or hours of an 'offence' being committed) while requiring a lower standard of proof than the ASBO; and
- the **community protection notice (CPN)**—an order requiring people to do or stop doing a specified thing, e.g. graffiti, dropping litter, or leaving excess refuse in gardens or driveways.

A further proposed order—included in the original Bill as an 'injunction to prevent nuisance or annoyance' (IPNA)—was withdrawn by the time it received royal assent, after a defeat in the Lords. This was lampooned in the media as something that would, theoretically, have given police a licence to penalize hawkers, buskers, screaming children, people wearing headphones, or anyone else subjectively deemed a 'nuisance' by others. The ill-fated idea was later revived, however, in the form of *public spaces protection orders (PSPOs)*, under which councils can impose spot fines or prosecute any behaviour judged a 'persistent nuisance'. Notoriously, Oxford City Council has used a PSPO to target beggars 'perceived to be intimidating or aggressive', while Bassetlaw District Council banned under 16-year-olds from gathering in groups of three or more, if 'causing annoyance'.

10.7.1.3 The police complaints process

Allegations of misconduct initially follow the same process as other complaints about the local police force. This process is outlined in Figure 10.1.

All cases involving deaths in police custody or at the hands of officers in the community—for example the shooting of a suspect—are automatically passed

Figure 10.1 Flow chart outlining the police complaints process

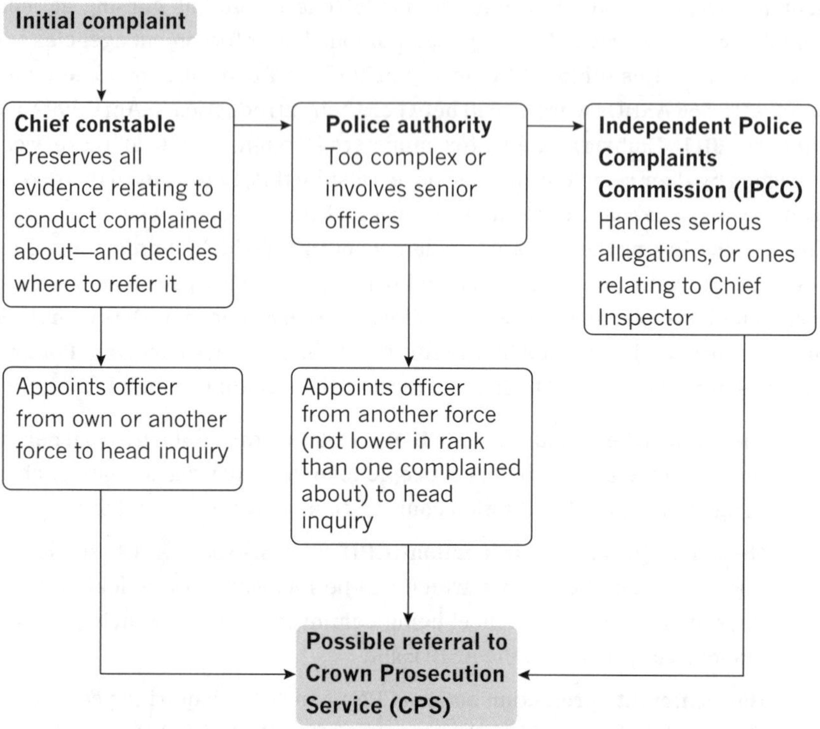

to the **Independent Police Complaints Commission (IPCC)**. Even when matters are handled locally by the chief constable or PCC, the IPCC may intervene if dissatisfied with the choice of investigating officer. Alternatively, it will approve his or her appointment by issuing an 'appropriate statement'.

Formal disciplinary action is a matter for the local commissioner in relation to most senior officers (including chief constables), or the chief constable himself or herself with others. If a chief constable indicates that he or she is *unwilling* to take action where the IPCC has become involved, the Commission can *direct* him or her to do so. Disciplinary charges imposed on officers are heard by chief constables (unless they or an assistant chief constable are the accused) and punishment can include cautions, demotions, or even dismissal. There is a right of appeal from the chief constable's decision, which must go to a police disciplinary appeals tribunal. In the last resort, complainants unhappy at how a complaint has been dealt with may apply to the courts for a private summons to prosecute the officers concerned (as attempted unsuccessfully by the family of Mr de Menezes, prior to their successful private prosecution of the Met for breaching health and safety legislation).

In recent years, there has been some controversy over the stringent 'standard of proof' required before disciplinary charges may be brought. This is illustrated by the stark contrast between the wording of the 'civil' standard—which applies in most employment-related situations—and the 'police' standard. The former is worded thus:

> 'Is it more likely than not, on the balance of probabilities, that the police officer committed the disciplinary offence?'

The latter reads:

> 'Did the police officer commit the disciplinary offence, beyond all reasonable doubt?'

10.7.2 Fire and rescue authorities

In contrast to the police (which, although divided into local forces, all fall under national police services), fire and rescue services—or 'fire brigades' as they once were—are entirely locally based. In common with the police, they are managed by separate authorities, but unlike them they have not, up to now, had their own discrete controlling bodies. Instead, in two-tier council areas, the 'fire and rescue authorities' are usually county councils, but for fire services based in unitary and hybrid areas, 'combined' fire authorities exist. With the soon-to-be exception of Greater Manchester, fire services in metropolitan areas (as in London) are overseen by separate fire and civil defence authorities.

Despite the longstanding separation of the individual emergency services and, to date, the lack of dedicated entities responsible for managing fire brigades, the Police and Crime Bill 2016 proposes extending the powers of PCCs to oversee fire services as well as police forces. This proposed change—part of the same ministerial drive to integrate related public services that is informing their ongoing moves to combine health services with social care (see 6.2.3)—would also allow PCCs to set up joint 'police and fire services', and potentially even extend their ambits still further in future years to absorb ambulance trusts as well. The history of Britain's fire services is outlined in table 10G to be found on the **Online Resource Centre**.

An important distinction between fire services currently falling under county councils and combined fire (or fire and civil defence) authorities is that the former are supervised and managed financially by county council committees, while the latter two determine their own budgets, like PCCs. They are all, however, answerable to the Secretary of State for Communities and Local Government.

It is the Communities Secretary's role to check each year the establishment schemes in place in each fire service area—that is, the level and precise nature of the provision that it makes available to local people. In law, all fire services must:

- equip and train a firefighting force;
- make arrangements for dealing with calls for help;

- gather information about local 'risk' buildings—for example high-rises, timber-framed structures, or ones housing large numbers of elderly or disabled people;
- give advice on fire protection to businesses, schools, etc.;
- ensure that local water companies maintain adequate supplies of water at pressures suitable for firefighting; and
- draw up mutually beneficial 'reinforcement schemes' with neighbouring fire services to help them deal with major fires.

Fire services are also called on to respond to other emergencies. These 'special services' are divided into two broad categories: humanitarian (for example serious road accidents and floods) and non-humanitarian (less urgent calls, such as requests to help residents gain access to their homes after losing their keys). Whereas firefighters would once willingly answer calls to scale trees in pursuit of errant cats, it has become increasingly commonplace for today's services to charge for such 'non-essential' operations.

Under the Fire Precautions Act 1971, various premises are now barred from operating without official fire service seals of approval in the form of fire certificates. These are issued, following inspections, by fire authorities. The types of premises affected include:

- offices;
- sports grounds;
- hotels; and
- theatres.

Other Acts passed to increase fire safety include:

- the Public Health Act 1936, which stipulated that fire escapes must be provided in buildings such as hotels and theatres; and
- the Fire Safety and Safety of Places of Sport Act 1987, which introduced tough new seating standards following the 1985 Bradford City Football Club tragedy (including a cut in attendance limits at football grounds).

10.7.3 Emergency planning and civil defence

The aspect of 'emergency services' provision in which councils have historically been most directly involved is contingency planning and civil defence. The notion of 'civil defence' in particular—protection of citizens against enemy attack or other forms of security emergency—arose after the Second World War. As a policy, it was initiated by the post-war Labour government, but has remained largely a notional peacetime responsibility—its most tangible application being plans for a hypothetical nuclear attack that councils were expected to update at various junctures during the Cold War. Notable exceptions included strategies employed to safeguard London's population from terrorist bombs during The Troubles and measures implemented following the Real IRA's attack on a Manchester shopping centre in 1996. In this age of increased security threats, however, it is not hard to imagine a time when renewed importance may be attached to civil defence departments.

As recently as 2004, a new Civil Contingencies Act effectively replaced the entire body of existing emergency planning legislation on the statute book. The most significant aspect of the shake-up, ordered by the then Secretary of State for Transport, Local Government, and the Regions John Prescott, was the new requirement placed on so-called 'responder' organizations in each area to appoint a full-time **emergency planning officer** (sometimes known as a 'civil contingencies officer', 'civil protection officer', or 'resilience officer') to coordinate measures that would be implemented in the event of a civil emergency. As well as security threats, civil emergencies might include any number of natural or man-made disasters—for example floods, major fires, landslides, or nuclear accidents. Responder organizations are divided into 'Category 1' and 'Category 2'. The list of bodies in each category is outlined in table 10H to be found on the **Online Resource Centre**.

The history of local government's involvement with civil defence began with the passage of the Civil Defence Act 1948, under which the Home Secretary was empowered to direct councils to take 'appropriate measures' to ensure that their population was adequately protected. These were further defined by the Civil Defence (Planning) Regulations 1974, which gave county councils powers to 'make plans to deal with hostile attacks' and, in certain circumstances, to prepare for war, in consultation with boroughs or districts. It was only in the 1990s, after the Cold War ended, that the term 'emergency' was explicitly redefined to cover peacetime disasters such as floods—an issue that has returned to the fore in recent times, following the devastating 2013–14 winter storms that left thousands of families isolated, without power, and, in areas such as the Somerset levels, homeless. Finally, in 2001, responsibility for civil defence shifted from the Home Secretary to a Cabinet Office coordination unit.

Another type of agency involved in preparing for civil emergencies is the recently formed 'regional resilience board'. Sometimes referred to as 'regional control and resilience boards', these are joint bodies drawing together representatives from police forces, fire authorities, and council civil defence departments to oversee overall emergency planning for entire regions. The 2004 Act also required responder organizations to form more localized versions of the regional boards—'local resilience forums' (LRFs)—based in each police area. These are expected to produce community risk registers specific to their localities, outlining particular locations, buildings, businesses, or residential areas seen to be particularly vulnerable. They are overseen at national level by a Cabinet Office executive agency: the Civil Contingencies Secretariat.

The Labour government's much-vaunted 'resilience' strategy for the country was prompted, in large part, by the 11 September 2001 terrorist attacks and the

2004 Madrid bombings (not to mention persistent fears of outbreaks of avian flu and various other pandemics, which have been periodically publicized by the media since 2003). But this new state of preparedness failed to prevent the 7 July 2005 attacks on London. And more embarrassing for ministers has been the repeated organizational chaos and buck-passing between local authorities, the Environment Agency, and central government that has greeted the widespread winter floods that have devastated parts of Britain in recent years—most recently towards the end of 2015 and in the early months of 2016.

At the top of the chain of command for emergency planning is an ad hoc government committee, code-named 'Cobra' and headed by the prime minister, which meets in the Cabinet Office whenever there is a major incident. In recent years it has been convened in the wake of everything from the aforementioned floods to outbreaks of foot-and-mouth disease to the 2015 and 2016 terrorist attacks in Paris and Belgium respectively. The committee's James Bond-style name is actually an acronym standing for something altogether more banal: 'Cabinet Office Briefing Room A'.

10.8 Empowering local authorities in the post-Cameron age?

While community groups and lower-tier authorities now have enhanced powers to hold upper-tier ones to account—and even to take over running services if dissatisfied with those they are receiving—a 'flip side' of Mr Cameron's first-term 'Big Society' drive was to bestow greater freedoms on local government itself. The Localism Act 2011 introduced a 'general power of competence' for all councils—from towns and parishes, through districts, counties, and unitaries, to fire and rescue authorities. To cut 'red tape' and encourage more entrepreneurial thinking by officers and councillors at a time of harsh budget cuts, ministers aimed to move away from what they saw as a 'can't do' culture, in which councils 'can only do what the law says they can', to a 'can do' one that frees them up to 'do anything—provided that they do not break other laws'. As an example, the Act spelt out its hope that councils would develop innovative ways of working together to 'drive down costs' and to do 'creative, innovative things to meet local people's needs'.

10.9 Local government associations

The Local Government Association (LGA) was established in 1997 to provide a collective voice in Whitehall policymaking for all 353 English local authorities. A self-styled 'voluntary lobbying organization' (rather than a trade union or association), it is based close to Parliament, at Smith Square, in the former Transport House: historic headquarters of the Labour Party. In addition to representing districts and boroughs, counties, metropolitan boroughs, and unitaries, the LGA also speaks on behalf of subscribing police, fire, national park, and passenger transport authorities. Councils in Wales are represented by a Welsh Local Government Association (WLGA), a subset of the LGA, while there is a separate Northern Ireland Local Government Association. Scotland has a Convention of Scottish Local Authorities (COSLA).

In 2007–8, the LGA published strategic objectives, which are summarized in table 10I to be found on the **Online Resource Centre**.

In addition to the central LGA, there are thirteen regional **local government associations**, the remits of which broadly follow the boundaries of the government's English regions.

Topical feature idea

The Conservative government is encouraging councils up and down England to join forces to become combined authorities in the mould of Greater Manchester, which took over running its own NHS services in May 2016 and is due to gain power over policing and fire and rescue (among other areas) in 2017. What plans, if any, do the local authorities in your area have to join forces with other councils? How, if at all, would this transform the way services were delivered—and what do local people think about this idea?

✱ Current issues

- **Reduction in the number of local authorities** In May 2014, the total number of UK councils was cut from 433 to 418, following a reduction in Northern Ireland from twenty-nine to eleven. Plans to scale back the number in Wales from twenty-two to eight or nine were put on hold after the May 2016 Welsh Assembly election.
- **Police and crime commissioners (PCCs) to gain control of fire services** The Police and Crime Bill 2016 proposes putting PCCs in charge of their local fire and rescue budgets, as well as policing, potentially allowing them to also merge the two emergency services on the ground. Meanwhile, the existing Greater Manchester PCC will be replaced by an 'all-powerful' elected mayor in May 2017.
- **The rollout of combined authorities** In the wake of recent extensions to the powers of the Greater Manchester Combined Authority, six other major urban areas in England now have combined authorities. Several other groups of councils—not all covering large towns or cities—are in talks with ministers about following their lead.

Key points

1. Local authorities (councils) first emerged in the nineteenth century to promote public health and maintain trade routes. Today, there are 418 councils: 353 in England, twenty-two in Wales, thirty-two in Scotland, and eleven in Northern Ireland. In addition, in seven areas of England a number of councils have united to form new overarching combined authorities, and these are likely to multiply in coming years.
2. Outside London and the six metropolitan areas, council structures in England are either 'two-tier', unitary, or hybrid. In two-tier areas, each citizen is covered by two councils: a county and district or borough. Counties in which unitary and two-tier systems coexist have hybrid structures.
3. In two-tier areas, services are divided between the two different types of council: counties are responsible for schools, waste disposal, highways and transport, social care, and libraries, while districts or boroughs oversee housing, waste collection, planning decisions, and Council Tax collection.
4. Local police forces are led by senior officers called chief constables, but appointed and funded by elected police and crime commissioners (PCCs).
5. Fire services are governed by their own local fire authorities, though PCCs may take responsibility for them in future. At present, in two-tier areas they come under county councils, but in unitary and hybrid ones, there are separate 'combined' fire authorities.

→ Further reading

Caless, B. and Owens, J. (2016) *Police and Crime Commissioners: The Transformation of Police Accountability*, Bristol: Policy Press. **Timely empirical analysis and critique of the impact, to date, of the introduction of PCCs in England.**

Newman, I. (2014) *Reclaiming Local Democracy: A Progressive Future for Local Government*, Bristol: Policy Press. **Up-to-date examination of the challenges and opportunities facing local government in the age of austerity.**

Norman, J. (2010) *The Big Society: The Anatomy of the New Politics*, Buckingham: University of Buckingham Press. **One-sided, but illuminating, manifesto for the concept of David Cameron's 'Big Society' written by a loyalist Conservative MP.**

Stevens, A. (2006) *Politico's Guide to Local Government*, 2nd edn, London: Politico's Publishing. **Fully updated second edition of the comprehensive guide to every aspect of local government, including the interplay between local and central administrations.**

Wilson, D., Ashton, J., and Sharpe, D. (2001) *What Everyone in Britain Should Know about the Police*, 2nd edn, London: Blackstone Press. **Fully revised second edition of the informative core text charting developments in the UK police service, from its origins in the early nineteenth century up to the present day, with a focus on recent**

changes from the idea of the traditional 'Bobby on the beat' to today's target-led—and frequently armed—officers.

Wilson, D. and Game, C. (2011) *Local Government in the United Kingdom*, 5th edn, Basingstoke: Palgrave Macmillan. **Revised fourth edition of the standard text on contemporary local government in Britain. Covers all of the major recent developments, including the introduction of unitary authorities and elected mayors.**

Online Resource Centre

www.oxfordtextbooks.co.uk/orc/Morrison5e/

Visit the Online Resource Centre that accompanies this book for web links and regular updates.

11

Financing local government

Some of the most newsworthy local government stories arise from the way in which it is financed—and how this funding is spent. Above-inflation rises in councillor allowances, all-expenses-paid 'fact-finding' junkets for members and officers, hikes in Council Tax bills, and the impact of government cuts on the delivery of grass-roots services have become staples of today's local press.

11.1 Revenue versus capital finance

Councils need money for two types of spending: to build infrastructure (offices, roads, traffic crossings, schools, and housing); and to operate and maintain these facilities on a day-to-day basis. The cost of building things falls under **capital expenditure**, while that of staffing, lighting, heating, and repairing them is defined as **revenue expenditure**.

11.2 Revenue expenditure and how it is financed

In simple terms, revenue spending is financed through councils' *income*: grants that they receive from central government, taxes they raise locally, and any upfront fees or penalties they charge for services (for example parking permits and library fines). The main sources of revenue income today are as follows:

- central government grants;
- Council Tax;

- Uniform Business Rates (UBR); and
- fees, charges, and reserves.

Each of these income streams is examined in detail below.

11.2.1 The reformed government grant system

Around three-quarters of local authority revenue finance has customarily derived from government grants, but in 2016–17 this dropped dramatically, to 57.4 per cent. The bulk of this reduction was compensated for, though, by an increase in the income councils were allowed to 'retain' from their own tax-raising—part of a longer-term trend engineered by ministers to 'repatriate' uniform business rates (UBR) paid by companies to the areas in which they are generated (see 11.2.5).

For many years, the single biggest government grant was the **revenue support grant (RSG)** or **general block grant**, which individual councils were left to spend at their own discretion, focusing on particular local funding needs. Under New Labour, however, the process by which central grants were allocated to councils became more complex, as ministers increasingly micro-managed their budgets by prescribing precisely where and how councils were allowed to spend the money given to them. Although the Coalition began the process of reversing this trend and restored local financial autonomy to councils, this was against a backdrop of significant real-terms cuts in overall local government funding. As a result, initial rises after 2010 in the proportion of grant money allotted to the RSG, as opposed to targeted grants, have been tempered by ever-steeper declines in the overall revenue grant pot—and the Conservatives' November 2016 Comprehensive Spending Review (CSR—see 7.1.1) projected dramatically dwindling RSG settlements for the years up to 2020.

As of the 2016–17 tax year, Coalition ministers had yet to banish every 'ring-fenced' grant, although they continued to relax the system of 'passporting' Labour ministers used to control precisely how cash was spent at local level. More significantly, in his CSR speech, then Chancellor George Osborne set out plans to slash central government grants to local authorities by at least half by 2020, while allowing councils to keep 100 per cent of the money they generated themselves through UBR—the bulk of which, at time of writing, was still being siphoned off and redistributed elsewhere by the Treasury (see 11.2.5). Following Mr Osborne's replacement by Philip Hammond in July 2016, it was unclear how rigidly these changes would be pursued—particularly given the new Chancellor's stated intention to 'reset' the government's approach to fiscal policy should the impact of the 'Brexit' referendum negatively affect Britain's economic prospects (see 7.1.2). However, it seemed reasonable to assume that the overall direction of travel—to a world in which local authorities generally raise and retain much of their own funding—would stay much the same.

11.2.1.1 Types of revenue grant

At present, central government calculates annually how much money it thinks individual councils need to provide services for their communities, up to a standard 'national level'. Under Labour, grants allocated on this basis became collectively known as 'formula grants'. In addition to RSG, there was also a principal formula police grant (PFPG) and a grant derived from the redistributed UBR (otherwise known as **national non-domestic rates**, or **NNDR**), also calculated by a formula.

Although the precise ways in which these three different grants were worked out differed, the principle underpinning them all was that a substantial proportion of the government's overall revenue funding pot should be directed to councils on the basis of their comparative 'needs'. In other words, more money would be distributed to councils covering areas with high levels of socio-economic deprivation and/or facing particular demographic challenges, such as disproportionately elderly and/or infirm populations. This approach to funding supplanted the earlier system, which had adopted a more straightforward 'per capita' ('per head') model for funding councils—allocating grants broadly on the basis of the relative *size* (rather than *nature*) of local populations.

In addition to formula grants, Tony Blair's government introduced two types of *non-formula* grants, which had the effect of tying councils' hands by forcing them to spend money on particular services and/or geographical areas that ministers judged high priority. The two main categories were *area-based grants (ABGs)*—payments set aside, as the name suggests, for specific localities within each council's ambit—and **specific grants**. It is the latter to which we will pay closest attention here because, despite the Conservatives' rejection of Labour's 'top-down' approach to funding local government, as of 2016–17, nearly £5 out of every £10 in revenue income received by English councils still came in the form of specific grants.

Labour divided specific grants into two subcategories: *ring-fenced* and *unfenced* (or 'targeted'). The former—as their name suggested—were 'hived off' for very particular ends. One of the most famous ring-fenced payments (still present today) is the **dedicated schools grant (DSG)**, which councils were forbidden from spending on anything other than staffing and maintaining schools or providing related services like special needs teaching. Under Labour, as well as being reserved for schools generally, the DSG was at times prescribed further—with ministers stipulating that it must go towards specific running costs, such as buying textbooks or improving extracurricular activities. By contrast, councils could spend 'unfenced' grants however they saw fit—albeit within certain parameters dictated by ministers. Unlike RSG, they were not calculated on the basis of formulae related to local demographic and socio-economic factors; rather, they were residual pots of money to be spent on services judged equally worthy of central government funding nationwide. An example of a long-standing unfenced specific grant was the Housing and Planning

Delivery Grant (HPDG). Although councils could spend it only on services related to housing or planning, in practice they used them in various different ways.

By the time Labour left office, the lion's share of local government revenue grants were passported and there was a bewildering array of individual payments—many targeted for highly specific purposes. The lack of manoeuvre councils had to determine for themselves how best to spend the resources at their disposal spurred Coalition Communities Secretary Eric Pickles to introduce a radically simplified system, although he nominally retained the ring-fenced/unfenced distinction. The new breakdown of revenue grants is as follows:

(a) Formula:
  - Revenue support grant (RSG)
  - Principal formula police grant (PFPG)

(b) Non-formula:
  - Local services support grant (LSSG)
  - Specific grants:
    (i) **Ring-fenced grants**—DSG and a **public health grant (PHG)**
    (ii) **Unfenced grants**—including **early intervention grant (EIG)**

Of the specific grants introduced since 2010, EIG has already proved the most contentious—largely because of the huge expectations placed on it. Former Education Secretary Michael Gove specified that it was to be used to fund multiple costly, complex, and politically sensitive services, ranging from the (previously ring-fenced) Sure Start budget (see 14.8.1), through free preschool education for disadvantaged 2-year-olds, to drug and alcohol misuse prevention projects for teenagers. The other most notable non-formula grant is the **local services support grant (LSSG)**—effectively a replacement for Labour's area-based grant—which councils now receive in twelve monthly instalments. To give some idea of the impact of this one reform, LSSG currently draws from seven 'funding streams' (sources), whereas, by the time it ended in 2010–11, ABG drew on sixty-one. But while councils may welcome simplification of their notoriously complex revenue settlements, LSSG does not amount to much as yet: in 2014–15, it totalled just £33 million in England, which barely registered at all as a portion of the overall £98.8 billion revenue budget (see Figure 11.1).

11.2.2 Calculating core grants: how the revenue support grant (RSG) and principal formula police grant (PFPG) are decided

Since 2006–7, levels of both RSG and PFPG awarded to individual authorities have been calculated by subtracting the relative resource amount for each area from its relative needs formula. The **relative needs formula (RNF)** is a calculation based on detailed information about the population size, social structure,

Figure 11.1 Breakdown of regular local authority revenue income in England for 2016–17

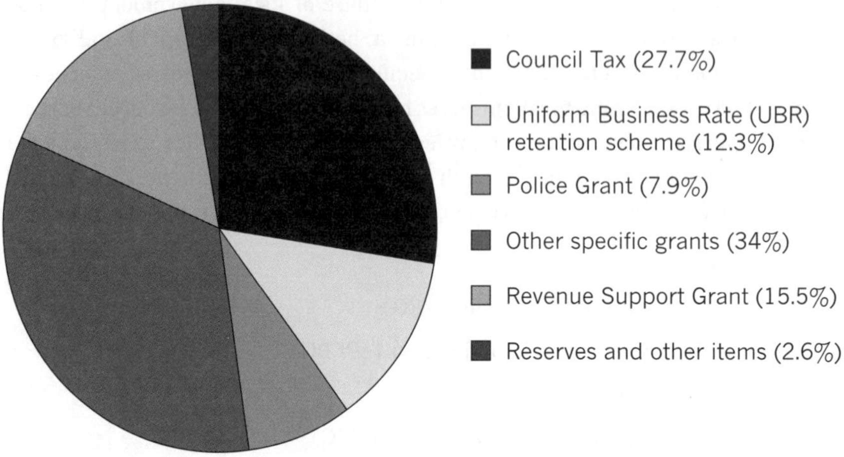

Source: Department of Communities and Local Government (DCLG) © Crown Copyright 2016

and other characteristics of a council area. By quantifying precise local factors, such as the number of pensioners and school-aged children living in an area and its relative economic prosperity, ministers have aimed to allocate funds that fairly and accurately reflect the cost of servicing its needs. Within the RNF, separate formulae determine how much should be allocated to individual councils to cover likely expenses associated with each 'major service area': education, adult social services, children's services, police, fire, highways maintenance, environmental, protective and cultural services (EPCS), and capital financing. The **relative resource amount (RRA)**, by contrast, is a *negative* figure. It has been based on the logical assumption that areas with many Council Tax-paying households—particularly those in higher tax bands, indicative of relatively affluent populations—need less financial help from central government than poorer ones. The RRA is subtracted from RNF to give a figure more accurately reflecting what individual areas require in formula grants.

Resulting grants have been shared between councils in proportion to their levels of responsibility—with 'upper-tier' counties and unitaries gaining more than 'lower-tier' districts or boroughs, and police and crime commissioners (PCCs) or fire authorities.

Over and above the core chunk of formula grants allocated in this way, a small percentage has tended to remain in an overall 'formula pot', to be distributed between council areas on a purely per capita basis. Known as 'central allocation', this is traditionally the same for all councils delivering the same services: that is, all districts or boroughs receive identical per capita amounts. In addition, Labour introduced so-called 'floor-damping' to ensure that every council—no matter how relatively well it fared from a grant settlement—received at least a *minimum* annual increase in formula grant. With real-terms cuts now the order of the day, though, this quaintly named concept is a distant memory. The total value of all grants allocated by the government to English councils for 2016–17 was £54 billion—down from £77.5 billion three years previously—with those outside London expected to draw on their reserves to the tune of £2.4bn to compensate for budget shortfalls.

11.2.3 The end of passporting—and return of virement?

Labour's efforts to constrain councils' ability to spend revenue income where they pleased did not end with specific grants. It was once commonplace for authorities faced with unexpected shortfalls in one spending department during a financial year to transfer surpluses from another budget: a process known as **virement**. But under Labour, repeated extensions of the passporting regime rendered all but the most modest shuffling of books impossible. Mr Osborne signalled the return of virement by abolishing all but two ring-fenced grants in his October 2010 Comprehensive Spending Review (CSR) (see 7.1.2). The astute political timing of his gesture (ahead of the announcement of swingeing spending cuts) was not lost on the BBC's political editor, Nick Robinson, who evoked the following 'old Whitehall saying' on his blog:

> Governments with money centralize and claim the credit; those without decentralize and spread the blame.

Figure 11.1 gives a full breakdown of the sources of local government revenue finance in England in 2016–17—at which point the Conservatives' repatriation of locally generated income remained a work in progress. Figure 11.2 summarizes

Figure 11.2 Breakdown of annual local authority revenue spending patterns for 2016–17

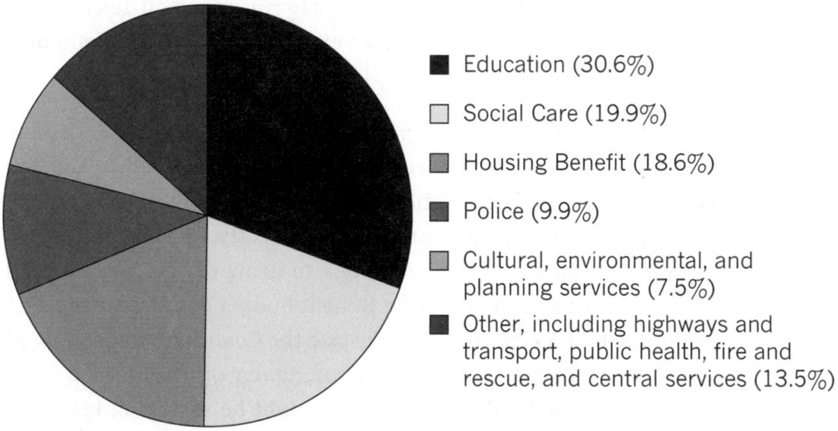

Source: Department of Communities and Local Government (DCLG) © Crown Copyright 2016

the overall percentages of English local authority revenue spending that year in each service area.

Particular aspects of the 2016–17 revenue funding breakdown are worthy of comment. Defying the Coalition's moves towards localizing spending decisions, specific grants still presently comprise the biggest chunk of council income (at £39.4bn, or over 70 per cent of the overall grant pot). Although the RSG now stands at around 15.5 per cent of the overall budget—up from just 0.6 per cent back in 2012–13—it fell by nearly a quarter on the previous financial year. This was due to a particular change introduced by ministers in finalizing the overall 2016–17 funding settlement, which sought to reduce councils' 'core spending power' (including RSG) in line with an *anticipated* rise in Council Tax income, comparable to increases seen in 2013–14 and 2015–16. Critics, notably the Local Government Association, described this expectation as 'ambitious' and noted how the erosion of grants—ultimately driven by pressure on the Department for Communities and Local Government to implement ongoing Treasury-imposed cuts to its own budget—has only been partly compensated for by other financial adjustments announced by ministers at the same time. These adjustments—some applicable for 2016–17 only—included:

- A 'transitional grant' fund of £150m for both 2016–17 and 2017–18 to help smooth the passage to a reduced RSG for councils disproportionately affected by this change.
- 'One-off' annual pots amounting to a further £28m of 'negative grant' money to ameliorate the effects of expecting councils to 'top up' their previous core funding levels.
- Increases of £60.5bn and £30bn in 2016–17 and 2017–18 respectively to the *Rural Services Delivery Grant*—a fund which tops up grant money paid to sparsely populated rural areas to take account of the disproportionate costs of service delivery in remote places.
- Permission for all district/borough councils to raise Council Tax by up to £5 per year or 2 per cent a year (whichever is greater), without holding a local referendum first (see 11.2.4.3).

Figure 11.2 also shows some intriguing patterns—notably the gradual decline of education as the dominant area of revenue spending. This fell to £34.2bn from £38.8bn three years earlier, as more state schools convert to academy status (see 14.2.2), under which they are funded directly by central government. Net spending on public health continues to grow (by 5.7 per cent on 2015–16), while, interestingly, the Housing Benefit budget has risen from 17.1 to 18.6 per cent of the total since 2012–13—despite the Coalition's imposition of a £26,000-a-year benefit cap and the 'bedroom tax', among other cuts (see 16.5). This suggests that, while individual households might be receiving less than previously to help them with the rental costs, the overall number of people whose incomes have fallen to a level at which they are eligible to claim it (including many workers) is increasing.

While the way in which the overall revenue 'cake' is divided to prioritize particular service areas tends to be fairly uniform across Britain, devolution has yielded widening disparities between different administrations' approaches to funding councils in individual nations. In 2016–17, nearly 33 per cent of the Welsh local government budget was earmarked for education (a level maintained for the previous four years), 21.2 per cent for social services, and 8.5 per cent for policing—broadly on a par with spending allocations in England. However, while the percentages of income Welsh authorities derived from Council Tax was comparable to that received by English ones (at 26.9 to 27.7 per cent), 16 per cent of revenue money in Wales continued to derive from business rates (based on redistribution from central government, rather than councils raising and retaining rates locally—see 11.2.5) and the remaining 53.5 per cent was made up not of passported grants but old-style RSG. In March 2016, an Independent Commission on Local Government Finance in Wales recommended a number of significant changes to the revenue funding system for Welsh councils, including the replacement of UBR with a fully localized business tax, which could be subsidized with a small additional tariff in city regions like Cardiff and Swansea, to fund major transport projects in a manner reminiscent of new arrangements being introduced for major metropolitan areas in England (see 10.2.4). The Commission also proposed a reduction in the number of central grants and that funding settlements be made three years ahead in future, to enable councils to plan more effectively. Since the May 2016 Welsh Assembly elections, though, there has been little news on the progress of these recommendations, and at the time of writing they remained just that.

11.2.4 Local taxation and the evolution of the Council Tax

The idea of local taxation dates back to the tithes that medieval parishioners paid their churches for renting their land and the taxes levied on peasant farmers by feudal lords of the manor. But as early as 1601 it began to become more systematic, with the emergence of 'rates'—a property tax based on the 'rateable' (rental) values of individual's homes. This would remain in place (with modifications) for four centuries.

Rates were a tax levied on domestic properties, rather than those occupying them—the broad assumption being that the bigger a property, the wealthier its occupants were likely to be. But, over time, the rating system produced peculiar anomalies that led to growing calls for reform. Before its eventual abolition by Margaret Thatcher's government in 1990 (1989 in Scotland), the most oft-cited illustration of its unfairness was that an elderly pensioner living alone, on a fixed income, in a house for which he or she had spent a lifetime paying, might be charged exactly the same as several sharing professionals living next door, with much greater combined and/or individual incomes. Although there was widespread agreement that rates needed reforming, their immediate successor was short-lived: the Community Charge (dubbed the 'Poll Tax' by opponents) sought to address the grievances of ratepayers 'punished' for living alone by shifting the onus from property onto people. In future, individual residents would be billed for using local services—forcing everyone to pay their way. But while this may sound fairer in theory, in practice the new 'head tax' rapidly became even more unpopular than rates. While the unemployed were exempt, working people living in the same area ended up paying identical sums—regardless of differences in their incomes. A multimillionaire tycoon might be charged exactly the same as his or her cleaner. In addition, some low-income groups previously excluded from local taxation altogether were suddenly included. Full-time students, for example, became liable (albeit with a 75 per cent discount).

Such was the furore over the Community Charge that it became the tipping point that ultimately led to Mrs Thatcher's resignation (see 3.1.3.4). The tax also proved extremely costly to administer, partly because many refuseniks seemed prepared to forgo their place on the electoral register rather than be tracked down by billing authorities. Others openly refused to pay, leading to costly litigation by councils (much of which never bore fruit). Following the biggest peacetime protests ever seen in Britain at that time, Mrs Thatcher's successor, John Major, abandoned the charge—replacing it with **Council Tax**. This 'hybrid' tax reinstated the property link, but unlike rates related it to *capital* values, rather than rateable ones. To placate critics of rates, it also retained an element of the individual liability introduced by the Community Charge. Each household was billed on the assumption that it comprised two adults (meaning that bills did not increase for three or more). But to avoid returning to a time when households occupying identical properties paid exactly the same—regardless of how many working adults lived in each—a range of reductions and exemptions for single people and low-income groups was introduced to make the system fairer, such as a 25 per cent 'single person discount' for those living alone or with one other person of whom they were the carer. Those existing today are outlined in table 11A to be found on the **Online Resource Centre** that accompanies this book. Although designed to deal with many anomalies and inequities preserved by previous local taxes, the new benefits and exemptions system produced its own.

Full-time students might have been exempt from Council Tax theoretically, but in practice those renting from private landlords invariably found themselves having to pay it on the homeowner's behalf—or having their rents artificially inflated to cover the cost. Students sharing houses with one or more employed adults also lost their exemptions by default, as such households automatically became liable.

Perhaps most controversial has been the 50 per cent reduction traditionally available to households owning two or more properties. In Wales and south-west

England, in particular, 'ghost towns' created in picturesque areas favoured by wealthy city-dwellers as holiday home locations were exacerbated by the relative cheapness of keeping such properties unoccupied for long periods, given the Council Tax discounts that they receive. Under Labour, councils in certain areas blighted by this trend were given limited discretion to charge more than 50 per cent, to deter property owners from leaving homes unoccupied. In 2003, unoccupied (but furnished) properties—those most likely to be used as second homes—became liable for reduced discounts of 10 per cent, while some long-term empty homes faced losing their reductions altogether. In April 2008, Newcastle City Council used this new power to scrap discounts for unfurnished and uninhabitable homes.

The Coalition went further in some respects to address what it has described as the 'national scandal' of empty homes. The Local Government Finance Act 2012 dispensed with the long-running 'empty dwelling exemption'—a provision entirely exempting, for up to twelve months, homes undergoing or requiring major repairs to make them habitable—in favour of locally determined discounts. More significantly, from 1 April 2013, it introduced an 'empty homes premium', enabling councils to charge owners of dwellings left empty for two years or more up to one-and-a-half times as much as other homeowners.

For all these changes, Council Tax is still seen by many as regressive. Newspapers frequently feature stories about financial problems caused to pensioners and others on low or modest fixed incomes who do not fall into convenient categories making them eligible for reductions—for example people on Employment and Support Allowance (ESA—see 8.3.2.3). Some have even been fined or jailed for 'refusing' to pay. In September 2005, Sylvia Hardy, a 73 year-old retired social worker from Exeter, was imprisoned for refusing to pay £53.71 in 'unjust' Council Tax arrears on time. The Scottish Parliament has the power to alter local tax regimes and the ruling Scottish National Party have long pledged to introduce a local income tax, though this has yet to materialize. Before the September 2014 independence referendum, then First Minister Alex Salmond confirmed plans to do so in the event of a 'Yes' vote, but since Scotland's decision to remain in the UK this has failed to transpire. Table 11.1 outlines arguments for and against a property-based (rather than people-based) local tax.

11.2.4.1 Council Tax banding

Council Tax bills in England, Scotland, and Wales are based on a system that divides domestic properties into one of eight 'bands' (nine in Wales)—A–H (A–I), respectively—according to their notional capital values. In Wales, these bands were revised in 2005, to take account of changes in property prices in the fourteen years that had elapsed since the original ones were set on 1 April 1991. Controversially, however, neither England nor Scotland has had its bands changed since they were originally set—meaning they remain exactly the same

Table 11.1 Arguments for and against property-based and people-based local taxes

Property-based tax	People-based tax
Cheap to administer and collect, and provides predictable income source.	Boosts local finances because number of bills sent out increases to reflect fact all adults—rather than households—charged.
Difficult for people to avoid paying rates or Council Tax because property, unlike people, is immobile.	Some argue it is fairer, because the burden of paying for services is spread across *all* adults—including those otherwise 'invisible' to taxes based on property values. 'Head tax' does not need to be 'one size fits all': local income tax would reflect ability to pay.
Simple, clearly understood system.	Fosters greater council accountability, because all adults charged and can voice views at elections on how money is spent.
Fair in theory, in that people occupying larger dwellings are likely to be better off.	Because individuals have to complete forms accepting liability for taxes like Community Charge, there is a disincentive to register. When introduced in Britain, many councils collected barely half what they were owed—and those unable/unwilling to pay lost voting rights by dropping off the electoral roll.
Property taxes can be a disincentive to home improvement, because major refurbishment/extension is likely to hike bills.	Straight head taxes mean that low-income groups such as students, pensioners, and working people on modest wages pay same as vastly richer ones—unless explicit exemptions and reductions introduced.

as on 1 April 1993 (by which time even original valuations were outdated). Despite pledging in its 2005 election manifesto to revise the bands if re-elected, Labour dropped the policy on returning to power. Cynics saw its reluctance to tackle the issue anywhere but in Wales as an example of political back-pedalling, motivated by a fear that it would lose future votes in marginal constituencies where people whose house prices had significantly risen since the early 1990s. In fact, according to Local Government Association (LGA) research, the number of households likely to lose out in a revaluation was the same as the number that would have benefited (around 4 million).

Whatever the merits of retaining existing bands, the property values to which they pertain are undeniably anachronistic today, in light of substantial rises in house prices seen across much of Britain. In England, the highest Council Tax band (H) currently applies to all homes valued at more than £320,000 in 1991, while in Scotland (where bands are set by Scottish assessors) the top rate starts at just over £212,000. As stated previously, only in Wales has there been any re-banding since 1993: as of 1 April 2005, a top band (I) has applied there for properties worth more than £424,000. Homes built since the dates on which bands were set are given nominal values based on what they would have been worth had they existed on 1 April 1991 (1 April 2003 in Wales). The lowest Council Tax band (A) is set for homes worth £40,000 or less in

England, £44,000 in Wales, and £27,000 or less in Scotland, while the 'average band' (D) applies to those worth between £68,000 and £88,000 in England, £91,000 and £123,000 in Wales, and £45,000 and £58,000 in Scotland.

The introduction of revised banding in Wales led to complaints that the country was no longer on an equal footing with the rest of Britain. Moreover, despite the fact that the price ranges covered by each Welsh band were all adjusted upwards to reflect the general surge in property values since 1993, the revaluation was not simply a question of mapping properties in the old Band A into the new one: it produced clear winners and losers. Because values in some areas had risen significantly further than others—with some previously cheaper homes overtaking in value those that were once more expensive—around a third of households found themselves moving into higher bands than before. Most jumped at least one band, while some leapfrogged three or more. Only 8 per cent of homes moved down.

Around one in four homes currently fall into the lowest bands in England and Scotland, although in north-east England this proportion rises to six out of ten. Current Council Tax bandings in England, Scotland, and Wales are outlined in Table 11.2.

11.2.4.2 How individual bills are calculated—and who collects the money

So who actually puts properties in bands, and determines the nominal 1991/2003 values of homes built in the years since they were originally set?

Responsibility for valuing homes rests with the Valuation Office Agency (VOA), an executive agency of HM Revenue and Customs (HMRC)—and, ultimately, HM Treasury—but it is for individual billing authorities to maintain lists of valuations. The VOA's day-to-day work is undertaken by regional *listing officers*, who compile and update lists of banded properties grouped in their areas. Overall responsibility for running district offices falls to local *valuation officers* (sometimes known as 'district valuers'). It is their job to

Table 11.2 Current Council Tax bands and values in England, Scotland, and Wales

Band	England	Scotland	Wales
A	Up to £40,000	Up to £27,000	Up to £44,000
B	£40,001–£52,000	£27,001–£35,000	£44,001–£65,000
C	£52,001–£68,000	£35,001–£45,000	£65,001–£91,000
D	£68,001–£88,000	£45,001–£58,000	£91,001–£123,000
E	£88,001–£120,000	£58,001–£80,000	£123,001–£162,000
F	£120,001–£160,000	£80,001–£106,000	£162,001–£223,000
G	£160,001–£320,000	£106,001–£212,000	£223,001–£324,000
H	£320,001 and above	£212,001 and above	£324,001–£424,000
I	N/a	N/a	£424,001 and above

hear formal appeals initiated by households unhappy with their property valuations.

Although Council Tax banding has never been reset in England and Scotland, homes can still move into different bands: they might go up or down for any of the reasons outlined in table 11B to be found on the **Online Resource Centre**.

Over the years, considerable vitriol has been aimed at the VOA, not least by those with homes in higher bands. When valuations were initially set in 1991, an urban myth circulated that its agents 'valued' homes by simply driving past and awarding them notional market values based on their locations and outer appearances—so-called 'second-gear valuations'.

Local authorities fall into two broad categories in relation to their involvement with Council Tax, depending on their degree of involvement in collecting the money, as follows:

- **Billing authorities**, or collection authorities, are councils that send out bills to households, and collect the proceeds to be distributed between themselves and neighbouring authorities. In two-tier areas, billing authorities are districts or boroughs.
- **Precepting authorities** are all types of council entitled to issue 'precepts' (instructions or orders) to their billing authorities asking for shares of Council Tax proceeds. In two-tier areas, this applies to billing authorities themselves, counties (in their roles as both top-tier councils and fire authorities), and PCCs (see 10.7.1.1). In unitary areas, there are still three precepting authorities: unitary and fire authorities, and PCCs. Council Tax bills received by paying households should include breakdowns of the chunks allocated to each precepting authority. The largest portions go to top-tier councils. Parishes also issue precepts for the modest local services they provide, so precepting authorities are grouped into 'major' (county/district/unitary) and 'minor' (parish/town/community).

When Council Tax bills for the coming tax year have been determined by local precepting authorities, they express their precepts publicly in terms of 'average rates' of Council Tax and 'average rises' in compared to previous years. As indicated earlier, the 'average rate' is that applying to a Band D property. It is determined by the formula:

$$\frac{\text{Total amount the authority intends to spend—Total non-Council Tax revenue}}{\text{Council Tax base (number of eligible households)}}$$

11.2.4.3 How central government 'controls' Council Tax bills

Ministers have powers to prevent excessive Council Tax rises by introducing formal ceilings to stop bills topping specified levels. This process—known as **capping**—was introduced by the Tories in the Rates Act 1984, and used increasingly in the 1980s and 1990s to restrict bill increases by supposed high-spending councils (often Labour ones in poorer areas, which argued that they faced above-average costs in housing, education, and social care). Labour proved reluctant to cap, although it retained reserve powers allowing it to do so and increasingly brandished these towards the end of its thirteen-year term.

Such examples aside, Labour's approach to holding down Council Tax bills largely remained that of using reserve powers to target specific authorities, rather than favouring the across-the-board capping previously used by the Conservatives. Since returning to power, that party has adopted a more indirect way of holding down Council Tax bills—forcing councils wishing to raise them above an annually reviewed threshold first to obtain local electors' permission in a referendum. For 2016–17 (as for the previous three years), this applies to any authority hoping to increase Council Tax by 2 per cent or more, although the November 2015 CSR gave non-metropolitan district and borough councils permission to increase bills by the higher rate of £5 per household annually or 2 per cent without holding a vote, as partial compensation for the step-change cut in RSG it introduced at the same time.

One unintended consequence of the 'referendum lock' is that councils often now raise bills to just below the 2 per cent threshold, thereby just avoiding referendums while still significantly increasing their tax incomes (a practice former minister Grant Shapps condemned as a 'democratic dodge'). In February 2014, Brighton and Hove City Council's then Green administration proposed raising Council Tax by 4.75 per cent—a policy that, if backed by a vote in full council, would have triggered a referendum. Its plans were later blocked by an alliance of Labour and Tory opposition councillors, but the former subsequently supported the Greens in raising bills by 1.99 per cent (just below the trigger threshold).

A similarly rebellious response greeted Mr Osborne's announcement in June 2010 that he was 'freezing' Council Tax rates across England for two years. Although the Coalition repeatedly cited the 'freeze' as an example of how it was working to restrict the impact of financial pressures on hard-pressed households at a time of falling real wages and rising household bills, its claim to have prevented rises across the board was disingenuous. Because the freeze was not imposed as a formal cap, in practice authorities remained at liberty to raise Council Tax if they wished—provided they respected the referendum lock.

Since their re-election in 2015, the Conservatives have sent mixed signals about whether they intend to continue limiting authorities' ability to raise Council Tax in the longer term. In a curious reversal of his party's previous aversion to ring-fencing in local government finance (see 11.2.4.2), Mr Osborne's 2015 CSR introduced a 'social care precept' allowing councils to increase Council Tax by up to 2 per cent without seeking their electorates' permission first—provided the extra money was spent specifically on adult social care (a growing priority, as Britain's population continues to age—see 17.2.2). This accompanies a £3.5bn-a-year 'Better Care Fund' (see 17.2.1) introduced in the

2013 spending round, which provides pooled pots of money for health and social care providers to use collaboratively for new community-based services aimed at older and/or disabled adults—another retread of Labour's more targeted approach. Furthermore, as of 2015 ministers have begun allocating BCF funds in such a way that areas capable of generating more social care money through Council Tax rises (for example, because there is a high proportion of tax-paying households) receive less from the central pot, particularly if the relative social care needs of other areas are greater.

In terms of Council Tax itself, mayors elected to run the new breed of combined authorities covering metropolitan areas of England (see 10.2.4) will potentially be allowed to levy additional precepts on the tax bills of their constituent councils, subject to permission being granted through a formal order enacted by the Secretary of State. A template of sorts may have now been set for this in Scotland, where the Scottish Parliament voted in November 2016 to raise bills in coming years, with all homes in Bands E and above facing significant rises from April the following year.

11.2.4.4 The gearing effect

Notwithstanding central government's ability to 'cap' bills, Council Tax has traditionally been the one device available to authorities to generate significant income to finance costly expenditure. Therefore any decision by ministers to *reduce* a council's grants (either by cutting or freezing them) has tended to push them into increasing bills significantly to address resulting shortfalls. Similarly, if councils suddenly face unforeseen revenue demands, but their contributions from government are already set, they will again turn to Council Tax. The disproportionate rise in bills that can result is known as the *gearing effect*.

Speaking hypothetically, if a council raises a total revenue income for the coming year of £100 million—approximately £25 million from Council Tax—but ends up needing £101 million to meet its final spending demands, it will need to raise Council Tax by significantly more than the 1 per cent shortfall to achieve this, in the absence of other funding streams. In fact, its average Council Tax bills would have to rise by 4 per cent:

$$\text{Projected Council Tax increase} = \frac{\text{£1 million}}{\text{£25 million}} = 4\%$$

11.2.5 Uniform Business Rates (UBR)

In addition to their responsibilities for valuing domestic properties, listing and valuation officers are also charged with administering the 'equivalent' tax for businesses. While this may sound straightforward, **Uniform Business Rates (UBR)** have proved almost as controversial as Council Tax. Introduced alongside the Community Charge in 1990, the initial tax bands for UBR were based on a revaluation instigated at the time (aligned to rateable values in 1991), but have since been revalued every five years. The most recent revaluation was back in 2010, however, as the Coalition took the decision to postpone the uprating due in 2015 until 2017, to (in its own words) 'protect businesses from any increase' while the economy was 'still coming out of recession' and 'enable them to budget with certainty' for the then coming five years.

11.2.5.1 How UBR has traditionally worked—and why it is unpopular

Like both the long-standing domestic rates system and the preceding local business tax, UBR is based not on a property's capital value, but its **rateable value**. Listing officers keep rating lists covering all business premises in their area. When first introduced in 1990, UBR caused uproar among many occupants of commercial and industrial land or buildings because of the huge increases in the values of those premises that had occurred since 1973, when the previous business tax—the 'general rate'—had been set.

UBR has customarily worked as follows. Business premises are valued by local listing officers (in Scotland, assessors), based on how much they could be let for on a relevant date. The amount businesses are actually charged in UBR annually will then depend on a centrally determined calculation made by the Communities Secretary, known as the 'national multiplier' ('poundage' in Scotland). The multiplier is the number of pence in each pound of the rateable value ascribed to a given premises that its owner is liable to pay that year. It is set at two levels: a 'standard' rate for middle-range or bigger companies and a 'small business' rate for those meeting necessary criteria to be defined as such by ministers (for example, operating out of property with a relatively low rateable value). Whichever category it falls into, the multiplier is normally held below the level of inflation for business properties with 'average' values.

The UBR is therefore determined by the following formula:

$$\text{Rateable value of property} \times \text{National multiplier}$$

For example, a business with premises that have a rateable value of £50,000 would be expected to pay £25,000 in a year when the multiplier was 50 pence.

As of April 2008, empty business premises became liable for UBR—although, as with all bills, companies may appeal against their ratings.

Separate multipliers are currently set for England and Wales. Scotland, in contrast, retains a different system of business rates, which is largely the same as that which first came into existence there in 1854. Although the 1988 Act amended the existing Scottish system as it did elsewhere in Britain, it remains distinct to this day. Until recently, when the Scottish Government began 'pooling' business rate revenue and redistributing it from the centre, one of its primary differences from the English and Welsh UBR was the fact it was still a 'local tax'—that is, one both collected and spent in each area.

Indeed, this was long the single most contentious aspect of UBR. Until recently, all money raised by the tax was collected by councils, but then gathered up by central government and redistributed around the country on the basis of perceived need, with poorer areas and/or those facing particular financial challenges for demographic reasons receiving larger slices of the pie than more affluent ones. For decades, this bred resentment among some businesses that the rates they paid were used to subsidize other areas, rather than invested in their own communities. The Local Government Finance Act 2012 partially ended this, though, by beginning the process of 'repatriating' UBR to the areas in which it was generated, and the current plan is for 100 per cent of it to be retained in this way by 2020. Indeed, in an effort to encourage planning authorities to approve hydraulic fracturing (fracking) projects designed to mine shale gas, councils may already keep up to 100 per cent of UBR generated by drilling companies (see 15.3.5). More broadly, the Coalition's distaste for 'one of the most centralized' council funding regimes 'in the world' was initially matched by its awareness of an increasingly urgent need to promote growth in Britain's stalling economy—and the pursuit of jobs and industrial expansion is now being used as justification for localizing UBR. By allowing councils to keep more and more of the UBR paid in their areas and the same proportion of any increases in UBR takings that they generate over time, the government hopes to incentivize them to proactively push for local business investment—taking advantage of other 'Big Society' changes introduced by ministers to foster partnerships and fast track planning applications (see 15.1). In various consultation and briefing papers issued by Mr Pickles' office prior to the Act, he argued that, if anything, councils previously had a *disincentive* to 'go for growth'—encumbered as they were by planning red tape and a lack of investment finance for infrastructure.

To allay the fears of those concerned about authorities with 'weak business rate bases' losing out—many covering relatively deprived areas in need of greater investment than those able to generate more UBR—a new system of central government 'top-ups' has been introduced to compensate them for losses. Over time, this short-term safety net is due to be replaced with money redistributed to poorer areas from a new levy on the proceeds of additional UBR income received by more prosperous authorities. But not everyone is convinced that this will be enough to compensate 'losers' for their losses. In its official response to the CSR announcement confirming the impending end to redistribution of business rates from richer to poorer authority areas, the LGA described as 'essential' the continued use of 'top-ups and tariffs' to redistribute revenue 'between authorities'. To date, though, question-marks remain over the generosity of future compensation payments, or precisely how (and by whom) they will be calculated and administered.

Moves towards 'localizing' UBR are not all about raising *more* money for authorities allowed to retain their revenues, however. The Localism Act 2011 also empowered councils to offer UBR 'discounts'. This would *cut* the sums from UBR coming back into localities—'deficits' that councils would have to then make up from other resources. In addition, the Act watered down the generally unpopular Business Rates Supplement Act 2009, introduced by Labour to give counties and unitaries a measure of local determination over income generated from local businesses by allowing them to impose additional levies on companies, provided the proceeds were directly used to promote economic development. Since 2011, supplements can be levied only if local business communities first approve them in formal ballots (effectively referendums).

The means used to distribute UBR proceeds is far from its only controversial aspect. Another long-standing debate has revolved around how it is calculated—a system that, at the time of writing, ministers appeared happy to maintain. The practice of charging businesses according to the rateable values of their premises, rather than profits, is seen to penalize unfairly companies operating large factories or warehouses, which pay significantly more than businesses based in single offices—irrespective of which generates the most revenue. Many businesses offering IT support or legal and financial advice (the 'service sector') generate huge profits, despite being run from modest premises, with low overheads. By contrast, the decline of the manufacturing sector has seen turnovers plummet for old-style industries producing large consumer goods using expensive plants and machinery. In his final Budget, however, Mr Osborne introduced a series of measures to address the inequities arising from this system, including exempting 600,000 of the smallest businesses, such as corner shops, newsagents, and hairdressers, from UBR altogether from April 2017. At the same time, he eased the burden on a further 250,000 small companies by increasing the existing small business rate relief from 50 to up to 100 per cent for companies with property of rateable values of £12,000 or less, and raising the threshold above which firms pay the higher rate of UBR from £18,000 to £51,000.

These examples aside, like Council Tax, UBR offers reductions and exemptions for certain kinds of property. In addition to those left unoccupied for prolonged periods, exemptions include:

- agricultural land and buildings;
- places of public worship—for example churches and mosques;
- properties used by the disabled;
- fish farms;
- sewers;
- public parks;
- road crossings over watercourses—that is, traffic bridges;
- properties built in specified 'enterprise zones'—designations intended to rejuvenate deprived areas; and
- properties occupied by visiting Armed Forces.

11.2.6 Other sources of local authority revenue income

In addition to Council Tax, UBR, and grants, authorities derive income from:

- leisure service use—for example swimming pools, sports centres, library fines, etc.;
- the collection of trade refuse;
- car parking tickets, fines, etc.;
- income from private contractors; and
- European Social Fund (ESF) grants to companies, voluntary groups, and communities in deprived areas to improve training and employment prospects.

11.2.7 The annual budget timetable at local level

As with most other organizations, the financial year for councils runs from 1 April to 31 March. While capital expenditure (see 11.3) has traditionally been planned on three- to five-year cycles, only recently have ministers sought to move revenue expenditure onto the same footing by introducing three-year grant settlements.

The timetable by which local revenue budgets are set—a useful calendar for journalists looking to tease out stories at the appropriate times—is outlined in Table 11.3.

Table 11.3 Local authority budget-setting timetable

Time	Stage
April	Council holds provisional meeting early in financial year to decide overall 'budget strategy' for next one.
Late April/ early May	Follow-up meeting to decide Council Tax levels needed to finance coming year's expenditure.
Late May/ early June	Full council meeting follows earlier meetings of main financial committee or cabinet (see 12.3). Council leader/elected mayor must obtain formal cabinet endorsement for major budgetary decisions.
July–September	Once overall budget strategy determined, broad revenue estimates for following years must be finalized.
October–December	Government announces following year's grant allocations, forcing authorities to adjust budgeting for coming financial year. Usually last stage at which individual departments can increase requests for revenue funding from authority's 'pot'. To do so, they must submit **supplementary estimates**, outlining reasons for higher-than-expected outgoings.
January–February	Council usually confirms and publishes final draft estimates for revenue spending.
February	Full council has 'final say' at special meeting, deciding spending and Council Tax levels for next financial year (approximate budgets normally approved, subject to later modifications).

Stories about councils being forced to slash jobs and budgets for essential services because of real-terms cuts in government grants have long been a staple of British newspapers. But in October 2008, the LGA revealed that up to £1 billion of taxpayers' money had been collectively invested by councils and police authorities in Icelandic banks that had collapsed as a result of the global banking crisis (see 7.3.4). Kent County Council had invested £50 million, Transport for London (TfL) £40 million, and the Metropolitan Police £30 million, while Winchester City Council had invested £1 million in Heritable, a subsidiary of Iceland's national bank Landsbanki barely a fortnight before its parent company's collapse.

In March 2009, the (now-defunct) Audit Commission published a report criticizing seven councils for 'negligently' ignoring official warnings by continuing to invest in Icelandic banks even after their credit ratings had been downgraded below acceptable levels. It found that £32.8 million had been deposited between the reclassification of the Landsbanki and Glitnir banks as 'adequate' on 30 September 2008 and their collapse barely a week later.

Although not directly related to the issue of investment in banks, the Coalition's wide-ranging review of local finance has led to a loosening of the rules concerning councils' ability to acquire corporate bonds. While the 2003 regulations that introduced prudential borrowing (see Table 11.4) also allowed authorities to invest surplus funds in bonds and shares (albeit at their own risk), it also stipulated that if they were to invest in individual companies, these transactions would be treated as 'capital expenditure' for accounting purposes. This rule—intended to discourage 'speculative' investments—has now been amended explicitly to allow councils to invest in corporate bonds (although not shares). Justifying the change, ministers argued that bonds issued by firms with 'triple-A' credit ratings were often 'a safer investment option than a collective scheme with a lower rating'. The rule change also altered the definition of *income* generated through the sale or redemption of bonds—specifying that only those acquired before 1 April 2012 would be treated as 'capital receipts' (see 11.3) on being sold or reaching maturity.

11.3 The local authority capital budget

The main sources of local government capital finance are outlined in Table 11.4.

11.3.1 Capital borrowing

Although capital projects are funded in discrete ways significantly different from those used to finance revenue spending, they do incur costs to Council Tax payers. One regular outgoing that councils are compelled to factor into their

Table 11.4 Main sources of capital finance available to local authorities

Source	How it works
Prudential borrowing	Introduced in Local Government Act 2003 to replace previous 'credit approvals'—limits agreed by government. Today's prudential borrowing is determined in three ways: 1. Each council may borrow up to 'affordable' figure in line with Prudential Code endorsed by Chartered Institute of Public Finance and Accountancy (CIPFA). 2. Low-interest loans for specific projects from central government, through **Public Works Loan Board (PWLB)**—body operating within UK Debt Management Office (a Treasury executive agency). Councils repay borrowings from own resources without government support. They calculate how much they can afford to borrow according to CIPFA Code. 3. US-inspired **tax-increment financing (TIF)** introduced in England and Wales in 2013–14—allows councils to borrow money for infrastructural capital investment against future income expected to be generated through UBR from companies benefiting from investment. Also being developed in Scotland.
Supported capital expenditure (supported borrowing in Scotland)	Councils may borrow to finance capital spending with central government support—with funds available to help them to repay loan and interest. Most finance comes from Department of Communities and Local Government (DCLG), but other departments also contribute, including Department for Education (DfE), Department of Health (DoH), and Home Office.
Capital receipts	Money raised through councils' sales of capital (land and buildings). Divided into *usable* and *reserve* parts. Council must set latter aside for specified uses, including repaying existing debts. Former can be used to supplement prudential borrowing for new infrastructure. Communities Secretary determines percentage of usable capital receipts at any time. In 1998, agreed percentage was 50 per cent—except receipts from council home sales, only 25 per cent of which could be used for capital spending. A 2003 Act revoked stipulation that proportion of housing receipts must be set aside by councils for debt reduction, introducing centralized 'pooling' arrangement under which 75 per cent of capital receipts from council home sales under 'Right to Buy' scheme (see 16.3.1) and 50 per cent of other housing-related receipts are redistributed from authorities with less housing shortage to needier ones. Authorities in 'demonstrable financial difficulty' may apply to DCLG for 'direction' allowing them to use capital receipts for 'specified revenue expenditure'. Items such as redundancy payments, equal pay awards, and pension fund contributions have previously been redefined as capital expenditure.

Table 11.4 *(continued)*

Source	How it works
Capital grants	Traditionally come from government departments, public bodies distributing National Lottery money, or hybrid arrangements combining borrowing with grants (e.g. Transport Supplementary Grant, Single Regeneration Budget, New Deal for Communities, City Challenge, etc.). Coalition moving to 'less bureaucratic' approach, with limited grants drawn from supported capital expenditure budget.
European Union (EU) grants and loans	Money from EU, including: European Regional Development Fund (ERDF—for infrastructure projects and industrial development, usually in deprived areas); European Social Fund (ESF—training/employment initiatives aimed at young people); and structural funds. Currently, EU 'Convergence' funds available to areas, such as Cornwall, where gross domestic product (GDP) less than 75 per cent of Union's average.
Private sector investment	Often 'in kind' offers, such as development land, and/or funding for capital works, such as road access/traffic management, from private company in exchange for ability to recoup investment at later date by running profit-based business related to land concerned (*planning gain*—see 15.3.1). Favourite means of encouraging private capital investment today involves private finance initiative (PFI)/public–private partnership (PPP) deals (see 7.6). These see private companies footing much of upfront costs, enabling projects to progress more quickly than if reliant solely on public funds. In return, companies are paid back—with interest—over period of years, in arrangements similar to mortgages. Final costs to taxpayers significantly higher than if projects were funded by councils.
Local lotteries	Councils can run lotteries under conditions outlined in National Lottery Act 1993.
Local strategic partnerships (LSPs)	Labour's £36m Community Empowerment Fund to encourage community/voluntary organizations to cooperate in LSPs to tackle social deprivation supplanted by Coalition's *Total Place*—'Big Society' scheme to boost cooperation between councils and agencies over wider geographical areas, to avoid duplicating services by adopting 'whole area' approach. Councils may invest up to 15% of money that they save to pay employees' pensions in infrastructure projects such as roads and housing (equivalent to £22.5bn of the £150bn collectively held by them in this way). Thirteen councils involved in pilot, with potential future pot of £45bn.

annual revenue budgets is a 'minimum revenue provision' to cover systematic repayment of outstanding debt. This is usually equivalent to 2 per cent of housing debt and 4 per cent of that incurred for other capital purposes in a given year. In addition to repaying debt itself, councils must also provide for any interest on their long-term capital borrowing—the 'revenue implications of the capital programme'. These repayments of capital interest from the revenue account are known as a **debt charge**.

Despite the fact that it incurs interest and can take years to pay off, borrowing to invest is often seen as politically desirable by both central and local government. The rationale is that, by taking out loans, authorities are 'spreading the costs' of their spending over a number of years—meaning that it is not only local taxpayers living in an area at the time that a borrowing decision is taken who shoulder the burden, but anyone benefiting from the resulting investment during its lifetime. In addition, borrowing avoids authorities having to fund expensive projects entirely up front, enabling them to fast track construction of schools, libraries, and other amenities that they would otherwise take decades to afford.

Similar arguments have been made by recent governments in favour of councils forming co-funding alliances with the private sector—public–private partnerships (PPPs) or private finance initiatives (PFIs)—to enable capital projects that would otherwise take years to realize through public funds alone (see 7.6).

11.4 Financial transparency at local level

For journalists, some of the best (and most accessible) stories can be found in councils' publicly available accounts. Under section 15 of the Audit Commission Act 1998, press and public have the right both to inspect and copy these accounts, and all books, deeds, contracts, bills, vouchers, and receipts relating to them. On completing their audited accounts for the previous tax year (usually by June), all authorities with budgets of £6.5 million or more must open them to public inspection for twenty working days, advertising this in advance both in the local press and on their websites. The publication threshold was raised from £1 million in new regulations issued in 2011, to balance the Coalition's push for greater transparency with its desire to protect smaller bodies, such as parish councils, from punitive publishing costs.

Several notable court judgments have flowed from the 1998 Act, which introduced the twenty-day inspection system—most upholding the public's right to disclosure. In December 2009, *Veolia ES Nottinghamshire Ltd v. Nottinghamshire County Council* saw the High Court uphold the council's decision to open the files on confidential documents relating to its signing of a commercial waste management contract. Citing a line in the Act compelling authorities to disclose 'all the financial movements or items of account of the council's funds', it confirmed the Act did not exempt commercially confidential information (unlike the law on access to council meetings—see 13.3).

The Act also redressed the balance in previous legislation towards a particular aspect of local financial transparency: local electors' right to access details of council payrolls under section 17(1) of the Local Government Finance Act 1982. Prompted by the 1985 case *Oliver v. Northampton Borough Council*, the Act precluded public access to accounts or documents containing personal information about authority employees.

The Coalition embarked on a push to promote more financial transparency by councils—forcing them to publish online everything from senior staff salaries to all items of spending and contracts worth £500-plus (see 13.2.2.1).

Topical feature idea

The following is an extract from a briefing note published by the independent Institute for Fiscal Studies (IFS) ahead of the 2015 general election, outlining the relative impact of the Coalition government's cuts on local authority budgets and spending in different parts of England in the previous parliament. What are the most newsworthy points made here and, on the whole, is this a 'positive' or 'negative' story about the way in which councils have coped with the cuts?

Executive summary

- Local authorities have had to cut spending in the face of falls in their main sources of revenue. Grants from central government to local government (excluding housing benefit grant and those specifically for education, public health, police, and fire and rescue services and the housing benefit grant) have been cut by 36.3% overall (and by 38.7% per person) in real terms between 2009–10 and 2014–15. Total council tax revenues have grown slightly in real terms over this period (3.2%), although this still represents a decline of 0.7% per person. Taking grants and council tax revenues together, local authorities' total revenues have fallen by 19.9% overall (or 22.9% per person) in real terms. Council tax revenues funded just over half of local government spending in 2014-15, up from 41% in 2009–10.
- Even though revenues have fallen significantly, on average local authorities have spent less than they received from grants and council tax over the last five years, meaning that on average they have increased their reserves rather than drawn from them. The average increase in reserves across local authorities in England was an increase equal to 5% of annual spending in 2009–10.
- While the average cut to local authority net service spending per person (excluding education, public health, police, and fire and rescue) was 23.4%, the change seen by individual local authorities ranged from a maximum reduction of 46.3% per person (in Westminster) to a reduction of 6.2% per person (in North East Lincolnshire).
- Cuts to net service spending have tended to be larger in those areas that were initially more reliant on central government grants (as opposed to locally-raised revenues) to fund spending—these are areas that have, historically, been deemed

to have a high level of spending need relative to their local revenue-raising capacity. The cuts to spending per person were also higher on average in areas that saw faster population growth.

- As a result, London boroughs, the North East and the North West have seen the largest average cuts to spending per person. Since these regions initially had the highest level of spending per person, there has been some equalisation in the average level of local authority spending per person across regions over the last five years. In 2009–10, spending per person was on average 80.1% higher in London than in the South East; by 2014–15—with London having seen spending cuts that were nearly twice as deep as those seen in the South East—this differential had fallen to 48.0%.
- Since central government grants were cut much more deeply than council tax revenues, it is perhaps not surprising that those authorities for which grants made up a larger share of income saw larger cuts to their overall spending power.

✶ Current issues

- **The phasing out of government grants?** In his 2015 Comprehensive Spending Review (CSR), then Chancellor George Osborne unveiled plans to cut central government grants to local authorities by up to half by 2020. After initially rising as a proportion of the grant pot under the Coalition, the revenue support grant (RSG) has already started dwindling.
- **New freedoms to top up Council Tax** After years of being forced to hold local referendums before raising Council Tax any higher than 1.99 per cent, councils may now add a 2 per cent precept, provided they use all the extra money to fund adult social care.
- **Full 'repatriation' and other reforms to Uniform Business Rates (UBR)** The Local Government Finance Act 2012 allows councils to 'repatriate' up to half of business rates raised locally, and the CSR confirmed all UBR would be retained in the areas where it is generated by 2020. Rates for the smallest companies have since been abolished and the threshold for paying the higher rate more than doubled (as of 2017).

Key points

1. Council budgets are divided into revenue and capital accounts. Revenue finances day-to-day spending (staff, maintenance, etc.) and capital builds new roads, schools, etc.
2. Around three-quarters of councils' revenue budgets derive from government grants, the biggest being the revenue support grant (RSG), which they may spend as they wish. Specific grants must be spent in particular areas—for example the dedicated schools grant (DSG) for school repairs.
3. Council Tax—a tax on households—makes up about a quarter of councils' revenue incomes. All authorities set precepts and the combined total makes up the bill.

4. Commercial companies also pay a local tax, Uniform Business Rates (UBR), based on a national multiplier set by ministers. Some of this is pooled centrally but a growing proportion now stays in the area where it is raised.
5. The main sources of capital finance for councils include public–private partnerships (PPPs), capital receipts from property sales, prudential borrowing, and European or government loans.

→ Further reading

Betty, S. (2011) *The PFI; 'Teething Problems or Fundamentally Flawed?': A Critical Analysis of the UK's Private Finance Initiative*, Bury St Edmunds: Lambert Academic Publishing. **Critical overview of the impact, positive and negative, of the PFI revolution in UK capital financing.**

Fischel, W. A. (2005) *The Homevoter Hypothesis: How Home Values Influence Local Government Taxation, School Finance, and Land-Use Policies*, Cambridge, MA: Harvard University Press. **Globe-spanning sociological text examining the impact of homeowners on the concentration and quality of local services, and the emergence of 'stakeholder-led localism'.**

Hollis, G., Davies, H., Plokker, K., and Sutherland, M. (1994) *Local Government Finance: An International Comparative Study*, London: LGC Communications. **Again targeted at local professionals, this offers useful comparisons between Britain's system of local government finance and those applied elsewhere, primarily in mainland Europe.**

Midwinter, A. F. and Monaghan, C. (1993) *From Rates to the Poll Tax: Local Government Finance in the Thatcher Era*, Edinburgh: Edinburgh University Press. **Thoughtful exploration of the turbulent Thatcherite reforms of local government finance, focusing on the replacement of rates by the Community Charge.**

Online Resource Centre

www.oxfordtextbooks.co.uk/orc/Morrison5e/

Visit the Online Resource Centre that accompanies this book for web links and regular updates.

12

Local government decision-making

The previous two chapters examined the nature of councils, how they evolved, and the funding systems underpinning them. But how are they structured internally and how do they take decisions?

12.1 Councillors and officers: who's who?

Local authorities' work is divided between two sets of individuals: councillors and officers. Like central government, councils comprise a series of spending departments. These departments—covering areas like education and housing—are administered by paid civil servants who are meant to be politically neutral. Appointed on merit, they are known as **officers**.

While officers are concerned with process, decisions to put money into one service rather than another—and precise choices about how services are run—are based on political judgments taken by elected **councillors**, whose role is to 'govern' authorities, similar to how members of Parliament (MPs) take decisions affecting Britain or members of the Scottish Parliament (MSPs), Welsh Assembly members (AMs), and members of the Legislative Assembly in Northern Ireland (MLAs) vote on devolved legislation. Like MPs, councillors (or 'members') each represent a constituency. And, depending on the arrangements adopted by individual authorities, policymaking rests either with Westminster-style cabinets, led by senior councillors in the ruling group, or committees, comprising members drawn from all parties on the council.

12.1.1 What kind of person becomes a councillor?

The seminal 1972 Bains Report defined councillors' duties as:

- directing and controlling the affairs of the authority;
- taking key policy decisions defining the council's objectives and allocating resources required to attain them; and
- continually reviewing the progress and performance of local services.

This vision of local governance was echoed fourteen years later by the 1986 Widdicombe Report, which stressed the importance of 'part-time councillors' having a 'complementary relationship' with 'full-time officers with professional expertise'.

Although councillors may be likened to MPs in their democratic accountability, there is a fundamental difference between the two: unlike MPs, councillors are unsalaried. Their work is therefore voluntary and, for those trying to juggle it alongside day jobs or childcare, necessarily 'part-time'.

The fact that councillors are unpaid has given rise to considerable controversy, not least because it leads to many councils being dominated by the retired and/or wealthy: in essence, those with time and money to spend on unpaid community work. Because most councils and committees customarily meet for business during normal working days, employed people able to stand as councillors have tended to be in managerial posts or running their own businesses. In other words, only those free to set their own hours or negotiate time off for meetings have been in a position to stand.

This combination of militating factors discriminates against women, fewer of whom have historically held such senior posts. Ethnic minorities also continue to be under-represented—even in areas with multicultural or cosmopolitan populations. It is hardly surprising, perhaps, that the media so often portrays town halls (with some justification) as the preserve of pushy pensioners and white, middle-aged, middle-class men. Recent moves to introduce evening sittings—particularly in and around London, where many people work unsocial hours and commute long distances—have done something to address these issues, but not enough to satisfy critics.

In 1986, the Widdicombe Committee found that eight out of ten councillors were male and 59 per cent hailed from one of three socio-economic groups—professionals, employers and managers, and 'intermediate non-manual' jobs—together representative of only 23 per cent of the overall population. The average councillor at the time was aged 45, with none aged under 24. The oldest was 85. The Committee made eighty-eight recommendations—although most concerned moves to democratize the *political* composition of councils and committees. Many were implemented by the Local Government and Housing Act 1989.

A succession of surveys by the Local Government Association (LGA) and Improvement and Development Agency (IDeA) suggest that little has improved since. The 2013 survey in England (the most recent to date) revealed that while the proportion of women councillors had risen by more than half—from 19 per cent in 1986 to 32.7 per cent in 2013—the average age of councillors had continued stubbornly to *increase*—rising marginally to 60.2 from 59.7 in 2010. Ethnic minorities also continued to fare poorly: only 4 per cent were non-white (compared to 8.4 per cent of Britain's population). In Scotland, the picture was more encouraging, with 3.4 per cent of councillors hailing from ethnic minority backgrounds—broadly reflective of the balance in its population—while the least representative nation appears to be Wales, where the most recent census (dating back to 2004) recorded a 99.2 to 0.8 per cent split between white and non-white councillors.

Almost as contentious as the question of how to make councillors more representative of multicultural twenty-first-century Britain is the issue of how much work should be expected of them, given their 'unpaid' status. Various attempts have been made to quantify exactly how many hours the average member spends on council duties, both inside and outside 'official hours' (principally meetings). Widdicombe compared his own research with that contained in a 1964 study. At that time, the average amount of time that councillors spent on duties was fifty-two hours a month, but by 1986 this had risen to seventy-four hours (a finding confirmed in a more comprehensive survey, carried out by the Joseph Rowntree Foundation in 1994). According to the 2013 findings, this had increased to more than 100 hours (or 25.1 hours per week), including seventeen hours a month spent on party or group business.

12.1.2 Councillors' allowances and expenses

Introducing 'flexible' working hours is not the only device that councils have used to increase participation by younger working people, women, and minorities. In a radical attempt to widen participation, some have bent the rules to offer more generous allowances in lieu of formal 'wages'. A recognized system of allowances and expenses has existed for some time. Allowances are designed to give elected members modest payments for attending meetings, while they may also claim reimbursements for the cost of return travel to meetings by car, bicycle, or public transport. Expenses are also available to cover other outgoings arising from their official duties, such as paying for overnight accommodation, subsistence, and subsidizing postal costs and domestic telephone bills for phone calls relating to pastoral work with electors. Councillors aged under 70 are also eligible to join the generous Local Government Pension Scheme. There are two main types of allowance:

- **basic allowance**—a flat-rate annual payment, usually paid monthly, for *all* councillors representing a specific authority; and

- **special responsibility allowance**—an additional payment received by councillors who hold posts of greater responsibility, the size of which varies according to how much responsibility a councillor has (council leaders receive the biggest, while committee or subcommittee members are paid much smaller allowances).

Those with dependent children or other relations may also claim carers' or dependants' allowances.

Each English council is free to set its own allowance levels, subject to certain restrictions. Since the Local Government Act 2000 (LGA 2000), every council has been required by law to establish an **independent remuneration panel** comprising at least three individuals (none of whom are themselves councillors). It is the panel's task to review and adjudicate on applications by authorities to increase or otherwise amend their allowances—the reverse of the system now adopted at Westminster, under which MPs' salaries are *set* by an independent body, the Independent Parliamentary Standards Authority (IPSA) (see 2.2.1). Intriguingly, though, while councillors can choose to reject remuneration panels' recommendations, MPs are bound by the decisions of IPSA. In Scotland, Wales, and Northern Ireland, the system is administered centrally, with councillors' allowances in each devolved country set by a single independent panel. The powers of the panels are limited, however—for example councillors are not legally obliged to accept panel recommendations to cut or freeze allowances.

Recent surveys point to wide disparities in the generosity of allowances paid by different councils—with some offering payments comparable to full-time salaries. According to figures published in March 2011, a number of council leaders earned £50,000 or more in the 2010–11 tax year, while average annual allowances for other councillors topped £10,000 in many areas and £20,000 in London—defying pay caps and cuts endured by most council employees. The district of Rochford, Essex, had seen the biggest increase in the previous five years—surging by 158 per cent. But such cases tend to be exceptions: as of 2013, the LGA estimated that average basic allowances were around £7,000, while a report published in January that year by the Commons Communities and Local Government Committee, entitled *Councillors on the Front Line*, mooted the idea of introducing a standardized national framework to ensure that they were consistent nationwide—and adequately rewarded councillors for hours they put in. As Robert Gordon, leader of Hertfordshire County Council, put it when addressing the Committee's inquiry:

> ‘Allowances now for front-line councillors, certainly for leading councillors, are high enough to offend the public but not high enough to encourage any sane person to give up their career and earning capacity to take it on.’

Devolved administrations have proved considerably more generous with allowance settlements: in 2010, the Independent Remuneration Panel for Wales recommended a rise in basic allowances from the £11,000-plus that many councillors had previously received to £13,868, with council leaders (many already 'earning' £40,000 or more) licensed to claim up to £57,785. Alive to public disquiet about the then recent MPs' expenses scandal—not to mention the pay cuts and freezes that many workers had endured under the Coalition's austerity drive—some authorities, including Cardiff City Council, refrained from claiming their full entitlements. Meanwhile, in January 2010, the Convention of Scottish Local Authorities (COSLA) voted to back a one-year freeze on basic allowances (which already averaged £15,000—twice the level in England at the time). In Northern Ireland—where, by August 2010, around two-thirds of members of the Legislative Assembly (MLAs), each earning at least £42,000, also retained seats as local councillors—controversy has focused less on the size of members' allowances, which averaged £9,500 in 2009, than on their (still unresolved) 'double-jobbing' status and the fact that they have been able to continue claiming for council duties while sitting at Stormont.

12.1.3 **Meet the experts: the role of local government officers**

The number of officers employed by councils varies widely and is ultimately decided by the level of resources that councillors allocate to finance them. Every council is obliged to provide certain statutory services and its administration is therefore split, like Whitehall's, into different departments—each run by an expert professional.

There are two main types of council spending department:

- *service departments*—responsible for delivering housing, education, etc.; and
- *central departments*—responsible for *administering* the council's functions, principally its legal and financial departments, and overseeing its corporate activities, such as public relations (PR) and marketing.

Council officers, like Whitehall civil servants, must be *politically neutral*—whatever their levels of seniority. Those in senior grades are also *politically restricted* (see 3.3.1). Despite being required to avoid political bias, however, officers are expected to provide councillors with policy advice based on their knowledge and experience. Their roles are to:

- *advise*—defined by the Widdicombe Report as giving 'politically impartial' information and support to aid councillors in their decision-making; and
- *support* the executive, non-executive, and scrutiny arms of the council—helping *all* councillors, not only the most senior ones.

Each department is headed by the equivalent of a Whitehall permanent secretary. Among the most influential are the leading civil servants in the biggest spending areas: directors of social services and chief planning officers.

Higher up still are three officials whose roles are to oversee the workings of the council as a whole, as follows.

- The **chief executive** (or '**head of the paid service**') is the council's main policy adviser, manager, and coordinator. Chief executives or their deputies often perform the role of 'acting returning officer' at elections, on behalf of the official returning officer—normally the council chairperson or mayor (see 4.3.1).
- The **monitoring officer** reports to members any acts of maladministration or failures by officers or councillors to uphold the council's **code of conduct**. They are normally also their councils' chief legal officers, so should be trained lawyers, and must ensure that their councils act within their statutory remits at all times (that is, not ultra vires).
- The chief financial officer (or 'treasurer', or 'director of finance') oversees administration of a council's finances and must be a member of a recognized accountancy body. He or she may also be referred to as 'director of central services' or 'section 151 officer' (referring to the statutory provision from which his or her authority derives).

Under the LGA 2000, chief executives are formally barred from being appointed as monitoring officers. In addition, like any other officer, chief executives, monitoring officers, and chief financial officers are all subject to statutory disciplinary procedures, and ultimately dismissal, for alleged misconduct.

To streamline administration, improve efficiency, and avoid duplication, councils now have 'chief officers' management teams'. These are groups of senior officers, headed by chief executives, which meet weekly or fortnightly to discuss policy ideas to be put forward for councillors' consideration at meetings and/or issues relevant to more than one department.

Despite largely sidestepping the 'politics' of local government, officers are far from immune to controversy. Recent years have witnessed numerous negative news stories about the eye-watering salaries that it is possible for senior council figures to earn—and, like heads of NHS trusts, it is not uncommon for chief executives to earn more than prime ministers. Partly in response to these furores, former Communities Secretary Eric Pickles introduced a new rule requiring councillors to vote on and publish formal policy statements on pay scales for their officers. In addition to publicizing details of the allowances and expenses claimed by their members, all councils must also now do the same in relation to senior managers. And, following a 2011 ruling by the Information Commissioner (see 19.1.5), Mr Pickles ordered them to go further—by publishing the names and salaries of all staff earning £58,200 or more. Following his criticism of some councils for paying salaries that would make Premiership football managers blush, some groups of neighbouring councils now 'share' chief executives to cut managerial wage bills and protect front-line services.

12.1.4 New models for service delivery: subcontracting and outsourcing

Until the 1980s, most local services—from refuse collection and street cleaning to building, equipping, and maintaining schools and care homes—were delivered directly by council employees. But over the past thirty years there has been a fundamental shift in the role of councils from being *providers* to becoming *commissioners*. Whereas everyone from local parking attendants to account clerks would once have been council employees, today they are as likely to be on the payrolls of private companies, voluntary organizations, or agencies. Rather than delivering services through their own officers and departments, councils increasingly coordinate and 'commission' them—and the private and voluntary sectors have as much chance of winning contracts as authorities themselves. In the Coalition's short-lived 'Big Society' era, this trend was accelerated—with local taxpayers given the chance to take over running their services directly, under 'community rights' to 'bid' and 'challenge', and some councils experimenting with wholesale outsourcing (see 12.1.5).

The system that originally ushered in this contract-based approach to service delivery was 'compulsory competitive tendering' (CCT). Introduced under the Local Government, Planning, and Land Act 1980, this forced councils to put services out to tender, inviting competing bids from public, voluntary, and/or private organizations. The idea was that the most 'cost-effective' bid would win—cutting waste and bureaucracy and giving local people better value for money.

The CCT system initially applied largely to 'blue collar' areas of service provision, such as building maintenance and construction work, but was extended by the Local Government Act 1988 to include refuse collection, street cleaning, and school catering, and by the Local Government Act 1992 to cover 'professional' and/or 'support services', such as information technology (IT), marketing, and PR. Councils wishing to continue providing services in-house had to form arm's-length 'companies' to compete for contracts against the private and voluntary sectors. When Labour returned to power in 1997, it scrapped CCT, replacing it with its own system of procurement, dubbed 'Best Value' (BV). A statutory obligation was introduced requiring councils to hire the 'most suitable' provider (whether public, private, or voluntary), choosing those best placed to deliver 'economic, efficient, and effective' services (the '3 Es')—rather than, for example, simply outsourcing work to cut costs. Yet Labour still expected councils to franchise services out and, although price was no longer the biggest factor in determining successful bids, many argued that 'BV' amounted to CCT in all but name.

12.1.5 The legacy of Cameron's 'Big Society': what role for councillors and officers now?

A central plank of the Conservatives' 2010 election campaign was the (to many) nebulous concept of the 'Big Society'. Although derided by critics for lacking tangibility, the philosophy underpinning David Cameron's approach to government was an appetite for devolving as much power as possible from Whitehall (and, indeed, from councils) to citizens themselves—in many respects, a logical extension of the direction of public service reform since the Thatcher era. This delegation of power, and responsibility, to communities manifested itself in several ways in the early days of the Coalition: in the loosening of 'red tape' Mr Cameron saw as stymieing business investment and the planning process; the 'freeing' of schools and hospitals from direct government control (see 14.2.2); and new opportunities for ordinary people, working alone, in groups, or in partnership with charities or private companies, to set up and run their own local services.

The idea of community-run buses or road-sweeping patrols may sound fanciful, but in a speech in July 2010 Mr Cameron signalled his hope of returning to a (to some, imagined) golden era of active 'volunteerism'. He talked of transforming the 'third sector' (charities and voluntary organizations) into the 'first', and 'turning government upside-down'. While Opposition MPs dismissed this rhetoric as a smokescreen for further cuts and/or a buck-passing exercise enabling ministers to shift the blame for service reduction onto councils, Mr Cameron went on to launch a new Big Society bank (subsequently launched as Big Society Capital—see later in this section), to which people could apply for start-up funding—financed by money held in dormant British bank accounts. He also named four council areas as trailblazing 'Big Society communities': Liverpool, Eden Valley in Cumbria, Windsor and Maidenhead, and Sutton in Greater London.

Among the (largely Conservative-led) authorities keen to take its 'licence to contract out' to a logical conclusion was the London Borough of Barnet, which, after rebranding itself 'One Barnet', began preparing to shed a swathe of services. This bold experiment—which saw the authority dubbed 'easyCouncil' (a reference to budget airline easyJet)—encountered the first of a series of hurdles when, in June 2011, local bloggers exposed the fact it had spent £1.3 million buying in services from private security firm MetPro without first conducting basic financial or security tests, or even putting contracts out to tender. That same month, Barnet even went so far as to mimic the government, by setting up its own Big Society Innovation Bank (initially with a three-year lifespan) to kick-start community-led initiatives. But the council's plans finally came to fruition eighteen months later, when it agreed a contract worth hundreds of millions of pounds with Capita—outsourcing 70 per cent of its services in one go, including its entire highways, finance, and human resources departments, and those involved in administering benefits. Capita's immediate response was to relocate several of the departments hundreds of miles away from the London borough, to Northern Ireland, and south-west and northern England, with the loss of 200 local jobs. Though its heyday has arguably passed, One Barnet continues to attract vocal and organized opposition from local activists representing the communities affected by the cutbacks imposed in its name. And such 'blue-sky Big Society thinking' has caused problems for others, too. In

May 2011, Suffolk County Council was forced into a 'period of reflection' over radical plans to reduce itself to the status of a 'virtual' council by outsourcing almost all local services, after backbench councillors uncomfortable with the plans rebelled. Officially these plans have since been shelved indefinitely, though in practice many services previously provided directly by the authority are now being managed by community groups, including an industrial and provident society (IPS) set up to run its libraries.

Despite its conspicuous absence from the Conservatives' 2015 manifesto, and Mr Cameron's recent resignation as prime minister, today the 'Big Society' concept lives on, through a series of 'rights' introduced in the Localism Act 2011. These are the:

- 'community right to build'—a right for citizen groups to bypass the normal planning process to construct small-scale, site-specific capital projects like community centres, libraries, or pubs;
- 'community right to challenge'—the right for community groups, voluntary organizations, parish councils, or council employees to take over running services they feel they can deliver more effectively than their councils;
- 'community right to bid'—the right of such groups to bid to purchase and take over council-owned assets they judge important for their areas;
- 'community right to reclaim land'—the right of community groups to request that unused or underused publicly owned land is brought back into 'beneficial use'; and
- neighbourhood planning—a right for communities to decide what developments should be built in their areas, rather than leaving this to councils (see 15.1).

Of these, community rights to bid and challenge are most relevant in the context of local service delivery. They are open to everyone—from groups of interested residents or existing council employees who wish to form their own mutuals or social enterprises, to charities, voluntary groups, and parish councils (an echo of enhanced powers previously conferred on 'quality parish councils' by Mr Blair's government—see 10.4). The right to challenge allows 'relevant bodies' like these to confront councils proactively at any time about services they regard as inadequate and would like to take over. In one sense, the right to bid is a more straightforward extension of the existing process used to outsource services, which allows communities to compete with other organizations for contracts. Where it differs is in allowing 'neighbourhood forums' (citizens themselves) or other community bodies not only to take over responsibility for running services, but also to acquire associated capital assets. In considering bids, councils are expected to give such bodies fair, even preferential, hearings. However, if several bids are received from rival groups, the normal procurement process must be followed.

Sceptics have long argued that, during a period of severe austerity and with many people struggling to find paid work to make ends meet themselves, citizen-run services, manned by volunteers, were unlikely to take off. But by May 2012, so confident was the then Communities Minister Andrew Stunell that citizens would be eager to do so that he launched a new 'Communities in Action' map to flag up examples of 'local projects that are making a real difference' for all to see (and, where suitable, emulate). To buoy such projects, around the same time the government launched **Big Society Capital**—a state-sponsored, but independently run, financial institution designed to 'develop and shape a sustainable social investment market', by giving charities, community groups, and other voluntary organizations the funds required to tackle 'major social issues'. By lending money to a range of recognized social investment finance intermediaries (SIFIs)—banks, trusts, and other bodies with track records of financing social enterprises—the fund directs low-interest loans and grants to groups and individuals working at the coalface. Take-up of the various 'community rights' was initially sluggish, but it later appeared to pick up pace, with the government's mycommunity.org.uk website—an increasingly good source of human interest stories for local journalists—showcasing a wide variety of successful projects at the time of writing. These included everything from the Ivy House pub in Nunhead, South London—the first UK property to be listed as an 'asset of community value'—to Hastings Pier in East Sussex. The latter was salvaged from years of neglect by its offshore owners, Panama-based company Ravenclaw, thanks to the determined pursuit of a successful £11.4 million Heritage Lottery Fund bid by Hastings Borough Council and the Hastings Pier and White Rock Trust.

In terms of its wider application to large-scale public services, however, opinions on the practicability of the 'Big Society' ideal remain deeply divided. In his book, *Faith in the Public Square*, former Archbishop of Canterbury Rowan Williams criticized the concept as 'aspirational waffle designed to conceal a deeply damaging withdrawal of the state from its responsibilities to the most vulnerable'.

12.1.6 The politicization of council officers: the rise of political assistants

While officers are expected to be politically neutral, as early as the Widdicombe Report it was recognized that senior councillors might benefit from access to professional political advice from central government-style special advisers (see 3.3.6). It envisaged 'political assistants' being hired by councils with chief executives who were 'by disposition' managers rather than politicians, or where authorities were 'hung', with three parties sharing the balance of power.

The terms under which such assistants were to be employed are listed in table 12A to be found on the **Online Resource Centre**.

In addition, elected mayors are entitled to appoint their own political assistants. Successive Mayors of London have hired several 'spin doctors', in addition to policy gurus such as US public transport expert Bob Kiley, who advised the first holder of this office, Ken Livingstone, on the part-privatization of the London Underground. Although many such individuals are effectively independent consultants, journalists should be wary when dealing with councils or their leaderships through advisers, rather than press officers. As political appointees, they are not expected to give objective views of their paymasters' policies and achievements.

12.2 Local government hierarchies before the LGA 2000 and under 'alternative arrangements'

Before the LGA 2000, one fundamental truth applied to all councillors, irrespective of whether the parties to which they were affiliated held overall power locally: they each had a *direct say* in most policy decisions that their councils took. Proposals were initially referred to specialist subcommittees or committees of councillors covering relevant subject areas and had to be 'recommended' by them before ever being presented for final approval to the full council. If rejected at these early stages, full councils would never get to discuss them. If reworded, diluted, consolidated, or otherwise amended, the versions of policies voted on by full councils had usually been substantially shaped by committees and/or subcommittees.

Because every councillor (whatever his or her party) sat on at least one committee, he or she had a direct input, however minor, into the policymaking process. Committee decisions were formally couched as 'recommendations'—that is, subject to final full council approval. Councils also reserved the right to reject their rulings or **refer back** items for further reconsideration. Committees therefore constituted an important part of the day-to-day policymaking function of their councils—a 'bottom-up' approach to policymaking, as illustrated by the flow chart in Figure 12.1.

In addition to giving all councillors a direct (on paper, equal) say in decisions, the setup pre-LGA 2000 preserved a simple hierarchy not dissimilar to that seen among MPs. A party that won sufficient seats in a local election to secure an 'overall majority' on the council would become 'the government' in all but name, and its leader would automatically be appointed **leader of the council**—rather like a local 'prime minister'. Beyond this, there were no visible divisions in 'status' between members of the ruling party (or group) and other councillors. The pre-LGA 2000 model remains relevant to this day, because it still applies to local authorities covering populations of 85,000 or fewer—where it is referred

Figure 12.1 The decision-making process in 'old-style' local authorities and district/borough councils operating under 'alternative arrangements'

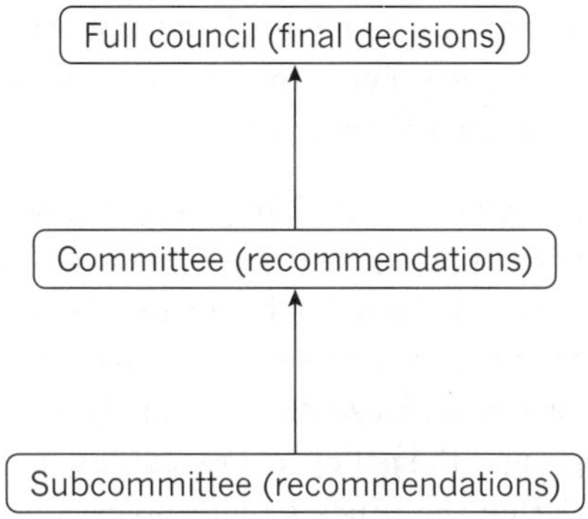

to as 'alternative arrangements'—and is slowly becoming more widespread again, following the Coalition's decision to allow councils with cabinets to readopt it if they so wish.

This old-style model includes three types of committee:

- *standing (statutory) permanent committees*—these discharge specific functions (for example taking decisions on education or environmental policy);
- *ad hoc committees*—often given briefs directly related to the above, these are set up to consider specific issues in greater detail than is possible on standing committees; and
- *area-based committees*—formed to look at policy governing specific geographical areas under a council's control, these sometimes contain members of the local community in addition to councillors, and even hold delegated budgets.

As in Parliament, the political composition of committees and subcommittees generally reflects the balance of power on the full council. If the Conservatives are in overall control, most committee chairpersons will be Tories, with overall membership broadly proportional to the distribution of seats between parties. Where no political group has overall control, standing committees may have no permanent chair; instead, different chairpersons are elected to serve on a meeting-by-meeting basis.

Other conventions governing old-style committees include the following.

- Non-councillors can be 'co-opted' to serve on them, either temporarily or indefinitely. These de facto members do not have voting rights—unless they are church representatives sitting on education-related committees.
- Mayors, council chairpersons, and leaders are *ex officio* members of *all* committees. Significantly, this gives them rights both to attend *and* vote on committees.

- Councils must avoid perceived or real conflicts of interest by ensuring that committees with related functions have different memberships.
- In addition to committees, councils often form working parties comprising both councillors and officers to consider detailed policy options, and their proceedings are not always public.

Despite the influence of committees, like governing parties at Westminster, ruling groups tend to devise many of the policy ideas debated in full council. Indeed, assuming they have big enough majorities, they normally muster sufficient votes to drive through their proposals—whatever the relevant committee thinks of them. Leaders also usually appoint the chairperson of the most powerful council subgroup—the **policy and resources committee**—and in practice many of them take up these posts themselves. Because this committee controls the council's purse strings, it has to approve major policy decisions likely to involve significant resources, and can veto those that it considers too costly. Many smaller councils have now abolished these committees, but some have retained equivalent 'boards' or 'panels'.

In other ways, ruling groups on 'pre-LGA 2000 councils' have little real executive power, in the sense that the government and prime minister do nationally—a clear contrast to their position in councils with cabinets (see 12.3). Although leaders can effectively appoint cabinets even under the old model, these have no authority to make executive policy decisions behind closed doors, as commonly occurs both at Westminster and in councils that have adopted post-LGA 2000 executive arrangements. Moreover, in practice, the limited majorities attained by ruling groups in many local elections make coalitions commonplace—forcing largest parties to compromise their policy ideas.

Besides districts or boroughs covering fewer than 85,000 people, the only authorities permitted to retain 'alternative arrangements' until recently were those, like Brighton and Hove City Council, that had held unsuccessful referendums to introduce directly elected mayors. Even then, this was on condition that they adopted committee-based systems with sufficient scrutiny powers to carry out the same functions competently. Under Labour, there was a tacit recognition in these areas that it was only a matter of time before they would be forced to adopt a post-LGA 2000 executive model.

12.3 Local government hierarchies since the LGA 2000

The main difference between the 'old-style' system and its principal replacements is that, under post-LGA 2000 structures, the balance of power between 'ordinary' councillors and those in ruling groups has shifted radically towards the latter. Whereas all councillors were once active participants in the local legislative process, today's council leaders—or, where adopted, elected mayors—hold disproportionate power. Their cabinets, too, have moved from being largely nominal entities to become ones that take executive decisions that the rest of the council has little chance of overturning.

The three types of executive management introduced by the LGA 2000 were:

- leader of the council and cabinet/executive;
- directly elected mayor (DEM) and cabinet/executive; and
- DEM and council manager.

The third option was formally scrapped by Labour in the 2007 Act, after the experience of the only council to adopt it—Stoke-on-Trent—became an object lesson for disproportionate powers that could be accrued by some individuals. Under this system, executive decision-making powers were vested in only one person other than the elected mayor: the council manager (an officer). Following repeated claims that this model was leading to a culture of secrecy in Stoke, in October 2008 local electors voted to replace it with a leader and cabinet model.

Nonetheless, until the Localism Act 2011, councils continued to be encouraged by ministers to adopt one of the other LGA 2000-style models. Before doing so, authorities must go through the following two-stage consultation process.

1. They must issue an explanation to the public of the three models of executive structure.
2. They must carry out a more detailed formal consultation among local people.

Once a decision has been taken to adopt a particular model, the council must agree the wording of a formal constitution with the Communities Secretary. Any subsequent attempt to change it requires the constitution to be rewritten in consultation with ministers.

Under both surviving LGA 2000 models, the leader or mayor's position is paramount. All councils adopting either system are further divided hierarchically into the following functions: executive, non-executive, and scrutiny. As is the case nationally, the term 'executive' refers to powers exercised by senior councillors—cabinet members plus the leader or mayor. Like the prime minister and his or her Cabinet, these individuals may initiate policy privately (going so far as to take final decisions on some matters) without needing to consult committees or subcommittees, as happened under the old-style system.

The terms 'scrutiny' and 'non-executive' both apply to committees and subcommittees. Each describes one of the two roles undertaken by committees under the post-LGA 2000 regimes.

12.3.1 Non-executive committees

Committees overseeing regulatory matters such as planning and licensing have delegated powers to take some decisions, rejecting or approving matters brought before them. The range of matters referred to non-executive committees is limited, however, compared to those deliberated over by old-style ones. A planning subcommittee or committee, for example, might decide to reject or approve an application brought before it without the need to refer it to a full council or cabinet for final approval—but this would apply only to *minor* applications (for example those relating to an extension to someone's house). The outcome of such applications will already largely have been dictated by the authority's existing planning rules, as previously agreed by the full council and set by higher tiers of government. Major applications—for example a bid by Tesco to open an out-of-town superstore—must still be approved by the full council.

12.3.2 Scrutiny committees

'Overview and scrutiny' (or simply 'scrutiny') refers to the function accorded to committees and subcommittees charged with examining specific council policy proposals and the workings of individual spending departments—for example children's services, education, or transport. Their powers, then, are more akin to those of Westminster-style select committees (see 2.2.3.1) than old-style council ones: like parliamentary committees, they can propose policy amendments, call witnesses, and publish reports, but have little power to reject or overturn executive decisions. All authorities—including those operating under alternative arrangements—are required to establish an overarching **overview and scrutiny committee** comprising councillors drawn from parties in proportion to the distribution of seats on the council. In practice, most split their scrutiny function among several subject-specific subcommittees or panels, with some even referring to these as 'select committees' in reference to their parliamentary equivalents.

12.3.3 Criticisms of the 'new' systems

One of the Blair government's principal arguments for the new-style hierarchies was a desire to speed up council decision-making, by reducing committees' tendency to delay final policy decisions. But the stark division between the influence on policymaking exerted today by cabinet members, compared to 'ordinary' councillors, for many years sparked severe criticism of these reforms—not least from veteran councillors who, often after decades of public service, found themselves with less direct say than previously in running their councils. The new-style models were seen to have introduced two 'tiers' of councillors, as at Westminster: a powerful 'front bench' and a sometimes vocal, but often toothless, 'back bench'.

Some criticisms of the post-2000 committee changes are arguably justified—not least those levelled by frustrated journalists who yearn for a return to the more knockabout meetings and policy standoffs of old. However, many scrutiny committees have had tangible input into councils' policy initiatives. In July 2009, the London Borough of Hounslow's children and young people scrutiny panel was awarded £90,000 by the Department of Health (DoH) to commission new services to tackle speech and language difficulties among poor children in its area. More recently, October 2015 saw Birmingham City Council launch a new refuse collection 'dashboard' in Sutton Coldfield and Erdington, after residents' complaints about missed wheelie bin collections were relayed to the authority's Community Services Scrutiny Committee by two local councillors.

Table 12.1 gives an overview of arguments for and against the LGA 2000 hierarchical models.

Since the Localism Act 2011 came into force in 2012, councils have been permitted to bypass or abandon the LGA 2000 systems for good—with authorities that previously switched from the old system allowed to 'move away from an executive form of governance'. In order to do so, they must first pass majority resolutions favouring the moves; revise their constitutions to incorporate the proposed changes; and publicize the proposals, including in one or more local newspapers. On 23 May 2012, South Gloucestershire Council became one of the first authorities to revert to a committee-led system, after its ruling Conservative group was outvoted by a

Table 12.1 Arguments for and against the LGA 2000 management models

For	Against
Allowing leaders, elected mayors, and cabinets to take some executive decisions unilaterally makes the local legislative process faster/more efficient than when committees had to approve everything.	New models create 'two-tier' councils, with frontbenchers having more influence on policymaking than backbenchers.
Introducing elected mayors engages the public more with local democracy—giving it a direct say in decisions over council leadership. It is more democratic and councils are more accountable than under the old system.	By giving small groups of individuals executive powers, 'elective dictatorships' can form, making councils *less* democratically accountable.
The LGA 2000 laid down a process by which local electorates could demand referendums on the introduction of elected mayors—bottom-up local democracy in action.	Introducing three alternative models for council leadership has led to a patchwork landscape of local authority hierarchies. This confuses voters and can lead to inconsistent local representation.

coalition of Labour and Lib Dem members approving the move. Before losing control of Barnet Council in May 2014, the Tory-led group announced plans to abandon the cabinet system, while Fylde Borough Council in Lancashire returned to a committee-led setup after a local referendum prompted by a petition signed by more than 5 per cent of local electors voted 57.8 to 42.2 per cent in favour.

The dominant decision-making setup in Wales is the leader and cabinet model, but in Scotland most councils continue to operate old-style committee systems. Some, however, have adopted more hierarchical, cabinet-style, setups (albeit with notably less executive power accruing to their leaders than in England). Meanwhile, under changes proposed by the Draft Local Government (Executive Arrangements) Regulations (Northern Ireland) 2014, the eleven recently formed single-tier Northern Irish councils can choose either to continue with the longstanding committee-based system, adopting a bespoke 'prescribed arrangement' negotiated with the province's assembly, or switch to a strict executive-style model, under which most operational decisions are delegated to one or more committees made up of between six and ten councillors, with no full council involvement.

12.3.4 Types and levels of council decision

Under post-LGA 2000 executive models, where they still apply, the full council is now concerned with formally approving only the most significant decisions. Proposals affecting two or more wards or electoral divisions and likely to incur 'significant' expenditure are called **key decisions**. An example might be the approval of a Council Tax rise or a planning application by developers keen to build a new road (which, by definition, will affect several wards). Each month, in the interests of transparency to local electors, every authority must publish a **forward plan** of all key decisions it intends to take over the coming four weeks, with its cabinet or executive agreeing its own.

Whatever internal decision-making frameworks they favour, certain other terms are common to the proceedings of all councils, as follows.

- The specific roles or powers delegated to them by statute—and by them to committees, subcommittees, and cabinets—are known as **prescribed functions**.
- Whenever final decisions are taken on matters before committees, full councils, or cabinets and executives, these are known as **resolved items**. Scrutiny committees or panels may, however, 'call in' items resolved in cabinet and/or refer them back for rethinks (as with old-style committees).

Figure 12.2 illustrates the top-down chain of command in post-LGA councils.

Figure 12.2 The decision-making process in post-LGA 2000 councils

12.3.5 The 'leader and cabinet' model

Of the three executive management options introduced by the LGA 2000, the one with most similarities to the pre-existing system is the 'leader and cabinet' model. As under the old-style council hierarchy, the leader is normally head of his or her party—usually that with the most councillors. He or she heads a **cabinet** or 'executive' comprising close confidantes on the council, normally drawn from his or her own party or a coalition (where no single party has overall control).

But this is where any similarities between pre- and post-LGA 2000 leader and cabinet systems end. 'New-style' cabinets or executives are much more like those formed by prime ministers than the earlier, more informal, ones. Until December 2010, it was left to individual councils' discretion to decide whether they wanted 'weak' or 'strong' leaders. Under the former approach, the council as a whole selected its leader and individual cabinet members, and all executive decisions had to be taken *collectively* by cabinet. The 'strong leader' approach, in contrast, allowed the leader (once elected by fellow councillors) to choose cabinet members—delegating Westminster-style policy portfolios to each. Today this approach is mandatory for all councils with leaders and cabinets—with county councils, London boroughs, metropolitan districts, non-metropolitan districts or boroughs, and unitary authorities introducing them successively in a programme of phased reform ushered in by the Local Government and Public Involvement in Health Act 2007. This Act also stipulated that executive leaders should serve automatic terms of four years—an approach dubbed 'strong leader-plus'—whereas the 2000 changes had allowed councils to appoint them for one year at a time.

Controversially, although individual cabinet members are generally expected to consult with frontbench colleagues, in some cases they may take executive action on their own. The same applies to leaders. Of still greater concern to critics is the fact that, although most cabinets now meet publicly at least some of the time, they are *obliged* to do so only in relation to policy matters that they have agreed to resolve collectively. In other words, decisions delegated to individual cabinet members (or, in some cases, unelected officers) may be taken in secret. Under the Localism Act 2011, cabinets retain their ability to meet privately.

Committees have therefore gone from being *proactive* agents in policymaking to largely *reactive* ones. Meanwhile, full council meetings—which still nominally have the final say over whether policies are approved—can resemble 'rubber stamps' for decisions already finalized behind closed doors in cabinet. Similar charges are made of the second model.

12.3.6 The 'directly elected mayor and cabinet' model

As explained in 10.1.1, there is a longstanding tradition among districts/boroughs and metropolitan districts of appointing mayors. The office of mayor (known in Scotland as the 'convenor' or 'provost') has customarily been ceremonial—with elected councillors taking turns to spend a year in the role, before passing on their chain of office to a colleague. Incumbent mayors adopt the role of returning officer in the event of local, general, or European elections, officiate over civic duties (opening fetes, visiting schools, etc.), and (usually) chair meetings of full council. Like Commons Speakers, mayors drop party allegiances and voting rights for the duration of their office. Some authorities, however, choose to divest mayors of their council chairmanships by electing separate speakers to perform this duty. In May 2012, Sylvia Gillard was elected by Bedford Borough Council.

Directly elected mayors (DEMs) occupy different positions entirely. First, unlike both council leaders and old-style mayors, they are not themselves councillors; instead, they are voted in by local electorates in separate ballots run *alongside* council elections. When Mr Johnson thwarted Mr Livingstone's bid for a London mayoral comeback in 2012, the separate election for the London Assembly saw Labour increase its grip on City Hall—securing twelve members to the Tories' nine. In this respect, elected mayors bear more similarity to local presidents than prime ministers. While no Labour premier could remain in post long after an election in which the Tories won more seats, the same is not true of presidents: for six of his eight years in the White House, US president Barack Obama had to horse-trade with a Republican-dominated House of Representatives and (after his 2014 mid-term elections) Senate.

London's mayor occupies a uniquely powerful position, compared to those of other towns and cities: he or she enjoys sweeping executive powers over strategic planning, transport, fire and emergency planning, policing and crime, and economic development, with the Greater London Authority (GLA) exercising little more than a glorified scrutiny function. Nonetheless, the powers of DEMs generally should not be underestimated, even if they are subject to the constraints of normal cabinet government. Hardly surprising, then, that ministers eager to spread the model outside the capital initially proceeded with caution. Between the passage of the LGA 2000 and the Local Government and Public Involvement in Health Act 2007, councils generally had to call (and win) local referendums before being permitted to introduce DEMs. Conversely, if 5 per cent of a local electorate signed a petition in favour of a mayoral system, it could *demand* a referendum—whatever the council's view on the matter.

Over time, though, the sluggish take-up of elected mayors outside London has encouraged successive governments to try all manner of tactics to roll out the system more widely. With eight out of ten English councils stubbornly sticking with the leader and cabinet model, and only one Welsh authority ever having held a referendum (Ceredigion County Council, whose voters decisively rejected the idea of a mayor), the 2007 Act modified the law to allow councils to bypass the need for a public vote before introducing elected mayors, provided two-thirds of their councillors approved the change. The Coalition later mounted its own drive to persuade cities to adopt elected mayors. On 3 May 2012, Liverpool elected its first DEM (former Labour council leader Joe Anderson) and the ten other biggest cities outside London were forced to hold referendums. In the event, any 'Big Bang' hopes backfired: nine out ten referendum cities, including Birmingham and Nottingham, rejected the idea, with only Bristol approving it. As an exercise in direct democracy, the referendums hardly set electorates on fire either: average turnouts for the polls, held on the same day as English local elections, were below 29 per cent.

In the end, the most decisive reboot of the mayoral principle was to come in the dying days of the Coalition, when the then Chancellor George Osborne finalized a deal with the Greater Manchester Combined Authority to devolve to it control over a swathe of local services, including its own NHS budget, in return for its adoption of an elected mayor (see 12.3). The Cities and Local Government Devolution Act 2016 has since formalized this arrangement, with the result that, as of April 2017, a Greater Manchester mayor is due to join the seventeen existing mayoralties. Among those to announce his early candidacy for the post was former Labour minister and Shadow Home Secretary Andy Burnham. Though further DEM elections in combined authority areas had still to be finalized at the time of writing, Greater Manchester was widely expected to be joined by at least half a dozen other regions in coming months: Liverpool City

Region, the North East, Sheffield City Region, the Tees Valley, the West Midlands, and the North Midlands.

Though the DEM principle might soon have a new lease of life, the concept has failed to endure even in some areas initially enthused by it. At least four local campaigns have so far been launched to abolish mayoral posts: successfully in Stoke-on-Trent and Hartlepool (where, in 2009, Hartlepool United Football Club mascot 'H'Angus the Monkey'—alias Stuart Drummond—had earlier become the first DEM to win a third term), but also in Doncaster and Lewisham. The seventeen councils operating an elected mayoral system as of 2016 (including London) are listed in table 12B to be found on the **Online Resource Centre**.

Topical feature idea

Five years after the Coalition introduced new 'community rights' for citizens and third-sector groups to take over the running of 'failing' council services or threatened community resources, such as pubs and libraries, the government's map of such 'Big Society' projects suggests that a growing number of initiatives are finally being launched. Are there any community-led projects in your area that are examples of the 'Big Society' in action? If so, what are they and who is behind them? What government resources are available to local people, including readers of your paper, who might be interested in starting one?

Current issues

- **The 'resurgence' of directly elected mayors** As of April 2017, the number of DEMs in England will increase, with the Greater Manchester Combined Authority expected to be the first of several metropolitan councils to adopt a mayor and cabinet model in exchange for extensive new devolved powers as part of ex-Chancellor George Osborne's 'northern powerhouse' initiative.
- **Improving the demographic profile of councillors?** A 2013 report by the Commons Communities and Local Government Committee concluded that 'low pay' was a barrier to more working-aged people and women standing for election as councillors. It found that, contrary to media reports, the average basic allowance was £7,000—far too low to persuade people to sacrifice paid jobs to take part in local democracy. The average age of councillors remained stubbornly high, at 60.2, with only 32.7 per cent women and 4 per cent from ethnic minorities.
- **The end of the 'Big Society'?** An end to the wholesale outsourcing of local services in areas from Barnet to East Anglia, combined with a growing tide of 'anti-austerity' sentiment and Mr Cameron's recent departure from Downing Street, has raised questions over the future of his once-cherished 'Big Society' vision for future service delivery.

Key points

1. Local authorities are run by two groups of people: officers and councillors (members). Officers are civil servants, paid salaries to administer council departments; councillors are elected to decide councils' policies and receive only allowances.
2. The Local Government Act 2000 (LGA 2000) replaced the 'old-style' way in which councillors used to take decisions with one of two new hierarchies: a 'leader and cabinet' or 'directly elected mayor and cabinet' model. Under these models, policies are devised by 'frontbench' councillors in cabinet, then scrutinized by committees and voted on by full council.
3. Before the LGA 2000, all councillors took part in policy decisions. Policies were initially recommended by subcommittees or committees focusing on specific issues (e.g. education), then approved or rejected by full council. Although smaller councils still use this model, other councils may also now readopt it.
4. At present, there are seventeen directly elected mayors, with at least one more due in 2017—all in England. Prior to adopting or abandoning elected mayors, councils must hold local referendums or receive petitions signed by at least 5 per cent of their local electorates. Alternatively, if two-thirds of councillors approve a DEM, no referendum is needed.
5. Rather than being directly provided by councils, many local services today are delivered by private companies and voluntary organizations. Citizens may now take over services themselves, or set up their own, under new 'community rights'.

→ Further reading

Cooper, K. and Macfarland, C. (2012) *Clubbing Together: The Hidden Wealth of Communities*, London: ResPublica. **Report by 'Red Tory' think tank ResPublica on how community-based social activities, clubs, and societies can foster Big Society-style projects delivering public benefits.**

Leach, S. (2010) *Managing in a Political World: The Life Cycle of Local Authority Chief Executives*, Basingstoke: Palgrave Macmillan. **Thoughtful and up-to-date overview of the role and importance of chief executives, and the levels of scrutiny to which they and their salaries are subjected.**

Newman, I. (2014) *Renewing Local Democracy: A Progressive Future for Local Government*, Bristol: Policy Press. **Reflective analysis of the impact of years of austerity on UK councils' ability to govern effectively and a manifesto for reclaiming the civic purpose of local government.**

Online Resource Centre

www.oxfordtextbooks.co.uk/orc/Morrison5e/

Visit the Online Resource Centre that accompanies this book for web links and regular updates.

13

Local government accountability and elections

British local authorities are responsible for spending more than £65 billion a year in taxpayers' money, so it's perhaps only right that their decisions are subject to considerable scrutiny.

Councils are accountable to local citizens by:

- publishing their own standing orders, codes of conduct, and constitutions;
- submitting their accounts to independent audits and publishing performance data;
- allowing press and public to attend meetings and access agendas and reports; and
- giving local people a direct say through elections.

This chapter focuses on the ways in which today's councillors (and officers) are held to account.

13.1 Local government post-Nolan: the new era of transparency

As with central government, councils have long been expected to adhere to systems, rules, and procedures in conducting their business. But the extent to which they were required to *demonstrate* their integrity underwent a profound shift following the succession of high-profile parliamentary scandals that led to the Nolan Inquiry (see 2.2.6).

The immediate effect of Lord Nolan's recommendations, published in 1996, was to compel all public officials—starting with members of Parliament (MPs), but extending to local councillors and officers—to uphold '*Seven Principles of Public Life*': selflessness, integrity, objectivity, accountability, openness, honesty, and leadership. But Lord Nolan and the prime minister who commissioned him, John Major, wanted to go further, and their determination was shared by the latter's successor, Tony Blair, who consolidated the reforms in the Local Government Act 2000 (LGA 2000). Today, the processes introduced to police the behaviour of MPs and peers (see 2.2.6) also underpin accountability in local government.

13.2 The emergence of council constitutions

Under the LGA 2000, every council is now obliged to draw up—and agree with the Communities Secretary—its own **council constitution**. Within reason, this constitution can take any number of forms: from a broad mission statement to a more detailed breakdown of the council's responsibilities and services. Indeed, the very fact that individual councils are free, in theory, to devise their own wording reflects an acknowledgement by government that the particular issues different councils face in running their affairs vary. Since 19 December 2000, however, *all* constitutions have had to contain all of the components listed in Table 13.1.

Table 13.1 Compulsory components of a council constitution

	Component
1.	Summary and explanation of purpose and content.
2.	Description of council's composition, scheme of ordinary elections, and terms of office.
3.	Breakdown of principal roles and functions of councillors, including rights and duties of individual members.
4.	Scheme of allowances for councillors.
5.	Description of local inhabitants' rights and responsibilities, including their rights to vote in elections and access information about local services and council, committee, subcommittee, and cabinet/executive meetings.
6.	Description of council's roles.
7.	Rules governing conduct and proceedings of council meetings.
8.	Description of roles/functions of council chairperson/mayor, leader/directly elected mayor (DEM), cabinet/executive, individual cabinet members, and officers with delegated executive powers.
9.	Description of operational arrangements, terms of reference, membership, and rules for overview and scrutiny committees.

(continued)

Table 13.1 *(continued)*

10.	Provisions in council's executive arrangements with respect to appointment of committees of executive.
11.	Membership, terms of reference, and functions of committees and subcommittees, and any rules governing conduct of their meetings.
12.	Description of roles and membership of standards committee and any parish council subcommittee thereof.
13.	Description of roles and membership of any area committees of authority.
14.	Description of any joint arrangements made with other councils.
15.	Description of officers' roles, including those of senior management.
16.	Roles and functions of chief executive, monitoring officer, and chief finance officer.
17.	Code of conduct for officers issued under Act, plus any details governing their recruitment, disciplinary procedures, etc.
18.	Any protocol established by authority in respect of relationships between its members and officers.
19.	Description of arrangements for public access to members, and officers to meetings of full council, cabinet/executive, committees, subcommittees, and joint committees.
20.	Description of arrangements for public access to members, and officers to information about decisions made—or to be made—by any of above meetings.
21.	Register of names/addresses of executive members, their wards/divisions, and names of every executive committee member.
22.	Description of rules/procedures for management of authority's financial, contractual, and legal affairs, including procedures for auditing.
23.	Authority's financial rules and regulations, and those governing procedures regarding contracts and procurement (including authentication of documents).
24.	Rules and procedures for legal proceedings brought by and against authority.
25.	Description of register of members' interests of all full and co-opted councillors, and procedures for publicizing, maintaining, and updating it.
26.	Description of rules and procedures for reviewing/revising authority's constitution and management structure.
27.	Copy of authority's standing orders and code of conduct.

Section 37 of the LGA 2000 specifies that copies of councils' constitutions must be available for inspection by the public 'at their principal offices' within 'all reasonable hours'. Personal copies must also be supplied on request (albeit for a 'reasonable fee').

13.2.1 The foundation stones of council constitutions

What, then, of the various technical terms highlighted in the government's criteria for constitutions? The concept of **standing orders** should be familiar to anyone who has worked for an organization of any size, whether in the public, private, or voluntary sectors. It refers to the overall system of rules and guidelines governing the day-to-day conduct of that organization's official business. Like their constitution as a whole, individual councils set their own standing orders—and, again, these can be as detailed or indicative as they wish. Some incorporate into them rules governing the propriety of councillors and officers—for example the requirement that those with financial interests in matters due to be discussed by a committee on which they sit must declare this fact and remove themselves from its meetings. Others confine their standing orders to mundane procedural issues (as a bare minimum, most contain breakdowns of the customary order of business at council, committee, and cabinet meetings).

The LGA 2000 also emphasized that constitutions must address the post-Nolan preoccupation with enforcing national standards of ethical conduct by public officials. Most councils have long had agreed codes of conduct specifying lists of 'dos and don'ts' by which members must abide. Following the sleaze allegations of the 1990s, however, a new onus was placed on those in all levels of public life to clean up their acts—in particular, to keep 'outside interests' separate from duties performed on the public's behalf.

Given that councillors are unpaid and many juggle their duties with earning livings elsewhere, the potential conflicts of interest in local government are more multifarious than those faced by MPs. The councillor who sits on a planning committee as well as the board of a company with local development interests poses an all-too-familiar conundrum—and for this reason most councils have long had clear rules compelling any member with potentially conflicting pecuniary interests to make a **declaration of interest**. There has also been some criticism that councillors in this position are relegated to weaker positions than others—particularly those standing for election on 'independent' tickets related to particular causes, such as defending local services from closure, rather than conventional party-political platforms. It was partly in response to this concern that Coalition Communities Secretary Eric Pickles inserted a clause into the Localism Act 2011 to 'clarify' rules on 'predetermination': the notion that, whatever their personal interests in particular local matters, individual councillors should come to council discussions demonstrating 'an open mind'. While any councillor henceforth exposed for withholding details of (or otherwise misrepresenting) financial interests would be liable for criminal prosecution, the rewritten rulebook would generally allow him or her greater freedom to 'play an active part' in local debate, free from the threat of 'legal challenge'. Journalists had previously complained of councillors' reluctance to speak to them ahead of meetings for fear of 'fettering' their discretion—that is, breaching their code of conduct or prejudicing potential future judicial reviews of council decisions.

The Local Government Act 1972 introduced local registers of interests, but because these were voluntary, councils were not obliged to comply. It was the LGA 2000 that standardized the process, requiring *every* council to publish a reworded constitution reflecting Lord Nolan's '*Seven Principles*'. Declarations of interest, meanwhile, must now be made at the point at which someone first stands for election. As with MPs and peers, they are required to enter all interests on registers of members' interests (see 2.2.6) within twenty-eight days of being elected. The register must be updated within twenty-eight days of any subsequent interests emerging. Councillors must also declare relevant interests at the start of meetings in which they are participants if they have personal involvement in any **agenda** item. They should also remove themselves from those meetings for the duration of any discussion about that item. Handily for journalists (and curious members of the public) a one-stop shop for looking up the registered interests of individual councillors in England is now available via the website local.direct.gov.uk.

The main types of interest defined by law are:

- employment or business interests;
- contributions to election expenses;
- shareholdings of £25,000 or more, or ownership of more than 1 per cent of issued share capital, in a company based in the council's area;
- a business interest in contracts between the council and any other;
- land owned, leased, or held under licence for more than twenty-eight days in the council's area; and
- membership or management of a public authority, company, charity, trade union, or professional association.

Beyond this, it is the precise 'nature and extent' of a councillor's interest that determines whether it falls into one of two categories that might affect his or her ability to act impartially. Relevant interests were once defined as either 'pecuniary' or 'non-pecuniary', with the LGA 2000 redefining them as 'personal' (financial) or 'prejudicial' (likely to cloud a councillor's judgement of an issue before him or her). However, in England the rules changed again with the 2011 Act and 2012 Regulations, which replaced these definitions with:

- 'disclosable pecuniary interest'—any matter, the outcome of which might reasonably be seen as affecting the financial position of the councillor or his or her civil partner or spouse, which might include any employment, trade, profession, or vocation carried out for profit or gain, or involvement in sponsorship, contracts, land interests or licences, or corporate tenancies, or the holding of securities in parties related to matters due for decision; and
- 'sensitive interest'—any personal interest (whether or not pecuniary) of which the monitoring office feels disclosure could lead to the councillor being subject to violence or intimidation.

The LGA 2000 system continues to apply in Wales.

13.2.2 Regulating standards

Who, then, polices these rules? As explained in Chapter 12 (see 12.1.3), each council has a designated monitoring officer, whose job is to ensure that it acts within the law and does not overreach its powers. The introduction of codes of conduct and registers of interests—coupled with the onus placed on officers, as well as councillors, to act accountably—was initially accompanied by a greater emphasis on objective scrutiny. To this end, the LGA 2000 required each council to appoint its own Westminster-style **standards committee** to monitor its officials' actions and to raise concerns about unethical conduct. Its independence was theoretically assured by the fact that, in addition to two or more councillors, it must include at least one individual who was neither a member nor an officer of that or 'any other relevant' authority.

Standards committees were expected to:

- promote and maintain high standards of conduct by members and co-opted members;
- assist members and co-opted members of the authority to observe its code of conduct;
- advise the authority on the adoption or revision of a code of conduct;
- monitor the operation of the code of conduct; and
- advise, train, or arrange to train councillors and co-opted members on matters relating to the code of conduct.

On a day-to-day basis, they often devolved functions to subcommittees, but their compositions and precise remits must be formally agreed with the involvement of local parish councils.

For more than a decade, the conduct of councillors was further overseen by a quango, Standards for England (formerly the Standards Board for England), until its abolition in the Localism Act 2011. The Act also removed the statutory requirement for councils to have standards committees, although in practice many continue to do so. Since then, each authority has had to draw up a new code governing members' conduct, using the full force of criminal law to prosecute them for wrongdoing on the rare occasions when such action becomes necessary. In the absence of a more independently policed standards framework, however, it remains to be seen how future breaches will come to light in the first place.

In Wales, allegations of councillor misconduct continue to be handled by the overarching Public Services Ombudsman for Wales, while errant members of Scottish authorities may be disciplined by the Standards Commission for Scotland. Following prolonged negotiations, a new 'ethical standards framework' for local government in Northern Ireland came into force on 28 May 2014, coinciding with the elections for the province's eleven new 'super-councils'. This is policed by the Northern Ireland Local Government Commissioner for Standards, who works within the overarching Office of the Northern Ireland Ombudsman.

While the various standards regulators have only minimal legal powers, helpfully for the media they normally disclose the fact that a complaint has been made, as well as issuing full details of their eventual decisions and any sanctions imposed.

13.2.2.1 From 'performance targets and league tables' to 'armchair auditing'

Renewed emphasis on promoting high ethical standards among public officials corresponded with what critics of Tony Blair's Labour government, in particular, decried as a spiralling government obsession with centrally directed performance targets, league tables, and ratings systems to grade the quality of their work. Before long, taxpayers could visit the website of Labour's (now-defunct) Audit Commission to access their councils' performance 'scorecards', while annual reports would 'name and shame' the best and worst performers of the previous year, judging them not only on their absolute star ratings, but also against value-added criteria, known as 'direction of travel'.

The Coalition scrapped all such measures in 2010, but in a move seen by some as contradictory Mr Pickles made good on another of the Conservatives' stated aims—to make councils more accountable for their spending decisions—by stipulating that they publish everything from waste disposal and recycling rates to food hygiene reports and pub licensing decisions online. Today they must also post details of all items of expenditure, contracts, and tenders worth £500 or more, all payments to councillors, and all staff salaries of £58,200 and over (see 11.4). Then Communities Secretary Eric Pickles repeatedly claimed to be ushering in an era of 'armchair auditing'—empowering ordinary citizens to keep tabs on their councils' profligacy from the comfort of their own living rooms. To this end, he also abolished the Commission (ironically, the brainchild of Thatcher's Tory government) in favour of a network of independent providers. When the first tranche of contracts for this work were awarded in March 2012, critics of this 'privatization' of public sector auditing claimed that their warnings had been vindicated: DA Partnership, an employee-owned offshoot of the Commission touted by ministers as an example of the new forms of community-based company that they wanted to promote as part of the 'Big Society', secured only one of ten regional franchises available. The rest were carved up by private consultancy firms Ernst & Young, KPMG, and Grant Thornton. The latter—which won four five-year contracts, with a combined value of £41.3 million—had pledged to take on 300 of the Commission's existing 2,000-strong staff, but even this proved controversial, with 500 employees taking industrial action in February that year over concerns about their pension rights being eroded. The Commission's auditing role ended on 1 November 2012, at which point 700 of its auditors were transferred to the new providers. It was formally abolished by the Local Audit and Accountability Act 2014.

In theory, any 'armchair auditing' revolution may sound like a boon to journalists, but in practice it can be difficult to sift through the sea of data routinely 'info-dumped' on councils' websites under ministers' newly enforced 'transparency' policy. Authorities are inconsistent in where they place details of their spending, councillor allowances, and senior officer salaries online—and details are often presented in all-but impenetrable form, with lengthy spreadsheets in place of user-friendly graphs or tables. Not for nothing did the Commons Public Accounts Committee (PAC) brand councils' early efforts to throw open their books 'not fit for purpose' in a scathing report in July 2012.

So how should journalists make sense of the data? A useful tactic is to utilize one of a number of online data visualization programs that can now be downloaded, free of charge, as open-source software, the most well-known being Datawrapper, available online at **www.datawrapper.de**. More proactive councils, like Poole, Cherwell, and Cumbria, also use the government's favoured program, Spotlightonspend, which allows easy spending comparisons to be made between comparable authorities covering similar-sized populations. Even where councils do not present data in this way, journalists and the public can access graphs and charts illustrating their spending on the website **whatis.spotlightonspend.org.uk**. Beyond all of this, the growing availability of open data from public bodies has spawned something of a new cottage industry in 'data journalism'—with *The Guardian* now having a dedicated 'data blog' adjunct to its main website, and collaborative amateur sites such as (the now-defunct) **www.openlylocal.com** springing up to collate and compare councils' spending statistics with the help of online 'dashboards'.

13.2.3 The last resort: the role of Local Government Ombudsman

Of course, targets, league tables, and publication of performance data can deliver only so much accountability. What should people do if they feel that they have suffered an injustice at the hands of their councils—or that they have lost out because of, say, incorrect decisions by officers about their eligibility for services?

In relation to English authorities, for nearly forty years the answer has been to lodge a formal complaint with the **Local Government Ombudsman (LGO)**. The remit of the two ombudsmen employed by the service is to investigate allegations of maladministration—negligent or incompetent running of local services. They are not there simply to consider complaints relating to decisions about which people are unhappy, *unless* those decisions show evidence of maladministration. Since 1988, complainants have been able to take their cases direct to the Ombudsmen—each responsible for a roughly equal-sized patchwork of English councils—without needing to use councillors as intermediaries (a principle enshrined in the Local Government Act 1974, which first established the service). This change had an immediate impact on the number of complaints made: in the first year alone, they soared by 44 per cent.

Handily for journalists (and the public), 'annual reviews' of individual councils' overall performance in dealing with Ombudsman complaints are published online at **http://www.lgo.org.uk/information-centre/councils-performance**.

In Wales, since 2006 local government maladministration has been policed by the overarching Public Services Ombudsman for Wales; in Scotland, a Scottish Public Services Ombudsman (SPSO) was introduced in 2003; while the Northern Ireland Public Services Ombudsman, again located in the overall Office of the Northern Ireland Ombudsman, fulfils the same function there.

Complaints processes to these bodies are subject to various conditions. Those applying in England are outlined in table 13A to be found on the **Online Resource Centre** that accompanies this book.

As more people become aware of the role of their 'Ombudsmen', so the number of complaints investigated each year rises. The powers of these services have also been extended, allowing the ombudsmen to handle two new categories of complaint: those made by adults arranging and/or funding their own social care (see 17.2.3); and criticisms by pupils and parents about school performance in fourteen local education authority areas in England. Recent years have also seen notable increases in the number of complaints about local administration of the benefits system—significantly, at a time of major cuts to housing and Council Tax benefits (see 16.5). Understandably, journalists are always keen to learn about upcoming cases, because they tend to concern major complaints with significant human impact, thereby making them highly newsworthy. At times, however, these stories can be frustrating: while final adjudications are always publicized, because the identities of those involved are usually kept anonymous, resulting reports are rarely as revealing as press or public might like.

13.2.4 Punishing errant councillors and officers

In exceptional circumstances, individual councillors and senior officers found culpable of major financial or managerial irregularities used to be personally *surcharged* by the Audit Commission. The most infamous example of wilful misconduct of this kind was the 'homes for votes' scandal of July 1987, which saw then Conservative leader of Westminster City Council Dame Shirley Porter and her colleague, David Weeks, conspire to sell 500 council houses a year to potential Tory voters living in marginal wards, apparently to engineer victories for the party in forthcoming elections, in an abuse of the Thatcher government's 'Right to Buy' scheme (see 16.3.1). Eventually, Dame Shirley, a Tesco heiress, was ordered to repay the council £27 million, plus interest and legal costs—and she finally settled by reimbursing it £12 million in 2004. Surcharging powers were repealed by the LGA 2000 but, like MPs, councillors and officers can be prosecuted for fraud.

13.3 Access to council meetings and business: the 'old' system

Until recently, the rights of press and public to attend meetings of councils, committees, and subcommittees were straightforward. Although authorities often refer to the Local Government Act 1972 in their published papers, it was the Local Government (Access to Information) Act 1985—arising out of a private member's Bill introduced by Conservative backbencher Robin Squire—that enshrined their right to attend *all* such meetings, unless information due for discussion was classified as 'confidential' or 'exempt'. The former category refers to specified classes of information supplied by government departments or matters disclosure of which is prohibited under statute or by the courts. An example might be details relating to national security or crime prevention prohibited by either the Official Secrets Act or anti-terror laws. 'Exempt' information includes:

- details judged 'personal' and/or 'commercially sensitive'—for example those relating to terms of contracts, disclosure of which might have a negative impact on the council's future ability to negotiate value for money;
- matters 'in the process of being negotiated'—for example details of contractual negotiations with competing companies that the council is considering hiring to provide services; and
- issues 'protected by legal privilege'—for example when members are discussing confidential legal advice received in relation to litigation by or against the council, or contractual matters that they are seeking to resolve through the courts.

Under these arrangements, councils tend to use one of two methods for excluding press and public from meetings (or *sections* of meetings). Most commonly, councils divide their meetings into 'part ones' and 'part twos'—with all confidential and/or exempt items (known as 'below the line' items) discussed in the second halves. Alternatively, they might hold votes to exclude press and public during single, specified agenda items. Such votes must be formally proposed, seconded, and carried by members at the meeting—and *reasons* must be given to those excluded (usually citing the Schedule to the 1985 Act under which the exclusion was being sought). If a motion fails, the matter must be heard publicly, and copies of supporting reports must be instantly circulated to members of the press and public present.

Table 13.2 Access-to-meetings requirements expected of local authorities

Requirement	What it means
Public registers	Councils must keep lists of councillors' names and addresses, and details of committees on which they serve. Powers delegated to individual officers must be listed.
Copies of agenda papers	Orders of business and all reports prepared by officers—and submitted during open parts of meetings—must be available on the day. No matters must be heard unless listed on agendas three days beforehand—unless urgent issues arise that could not be predicted. These should be mentioned during 'matters arising', towards end of the agenda.
Access to **background papers**	All reports presented for public inspection should list background papers used to draft them. Press and public may also examine these (although they may be charged 'reasonable fee').
Minutes of previous meetings	Copies of minutes of open meetings should be available automatically to press and local electors on request. Minutes are records of proceedings that *actually* take place—including items debated, but not on original agenda—and all decisions taken. They normally resemble detailed 'summing up' of what each person said, rather than a verbatim record. Minutes of council meetings usually sent to journalists, along with agendas for subsequent meetings.
'Reasonable accommodation'	This must be provided for both press and public, and normally means that there should be sufficient numbers of seats and/or press benches. At meetings expected to be unusually popular, 'overflow rooms' should be provided. If oversubscribed, audio/video feeds of proceedings should be available to those forced to sit/stand outside the meeting room, so that they can see/hear proceedings.

In addition to granting press and public automatic access to meetings themselves, councils are also required to provide information both *before* proceedings and afterwards, to publicize upcoming votes and debates and their outcomes. During meetings, clerks have to ensure that they go further, in the interests of accessibility, than simply unlocking the doors to the press and public galleries. Most of these access provisions are listed in Table 13.2.

In the past, councils were frequently accused of going against the spirit (if not letter) of these access requirements. The not uncommon practice of holding meetings on controversial issues in small rooms—and barring entry because of 'overcrowding'—was once famously condemned as 'bad faith' by then Lord Chief Justice Lord Widgery. Admission for press and public to meetings of other bodies, including NHS trusts and non-principal authorities (parish or town councils), are guaranteed by the Public Bodies (Admissions to Meetings) Act 1960.

Other measures that councils have long been encouraged to take to improve their communication with—and accountability to—press and public include appointing public relations (PR) or press officers (a move suggested in the Bains Report). The remit of such paid PR people would be strictly to promote *council* initiatives and policies, rather than generate positive publicity for specific *political groupings*. Councils were also expected to give journalists access to individual councillors—particularly committee chairmen or cabinet members—to obtain quotes justifying political decisions, and senior officers, where technical explanations were required.

In practice, by the late 1990s many councils still had no press offices, although today journalists commonly complain that they place *too much* emphasis on proactive media management, to deflect criticism of their actions and promote council policies, and too little on serving news organizations' needs. Controversy has also surrounded the plethora of taxpayer-funded newspapers, magazines, and newsletters published by councils, ostensibly to inform residents about their services. Editors of commercial newspapers have accused some authorities of undercutting them by courting paid external advertising, and professionalizing their publications by recruiting experienced journalists on generous salaries and broadening their coverage to encompass non-council-related stories. By 2010, *East End Life*, a weekly published by the London Borough of Tower Hamlets, was being posted free of charge through the letterboxes of 81,000 homes, while its long-established independent rival, the *East London Advertiser*, was selling just 6,800 copies at a 50 pence cover price.

In their defence, some councils argue that they have no option but to publish their own news-sheets because of their local media's reluctance to run positive stories, or ones concerning worthy (if dull) information that they need to relay to local people. However, mounting concern about the use of public money for such purposes has prompted successive Communities Secretaries to liken council publications to the Soviet-era state-owned newspaper *Pravda* and 'propaganda sheets'. In 2011, Mr Pickles clamped down on the practice by introducing a new 'publicity code' banning councils from directly competing with the local press, producing papers more often than once a quarter, or including in their pages anything unrelated to services that they provided or commissioned.

13.4 Access to local authority business: the 'new' system

The LGA 2000 introduced significant new limitations on the extent to which press and public would be allowed access to meetings of councils adopting one of the 'new-style' executive arrangements (see 12.2). While full council, committee, and subcommittee meetings remained as public as ever, access to others became restricted. Because many final decisions were now effectively taken by cabinets or related bodies with delegated powers, critics argued that (contrary to their rhetoric) councils had become *less* transparent than before.

Table 13.3 Changes to access-to-meetings criteria following recent legislation

	Change
1.	Executives/cabinets, full councils, committees, subcommittees, including overview and scrutiny committees/panels, to meet in public, subject to 'access to information' requirements under 1985 Act.
2.	Executives/cabinets may meet in private only if presence of public 'likely to result in council breaching legal obligation to third parties about keeping of confidential information' or 'lawful power used to exclude public to maintain orderly conduct or prevent misbehaviour at meeting'.
3.	Decisions of mayors/executive politicians and senior officers subject to 1985 Act—but 'written records' of their decisions must be published on council's website and at its offices.

Initially, cabinets were not obliged to meet publicly at all, but the LGA 2000 was modified by government guidance issued in 2002 requiring them to convene openly whenever discussing key decisions (see 12.3.4) taken by their members collectively. Controversially, however, key decisions delegated to individual cabinet members, or even officers, could still be taken in private.

Transparency has since been increased, through new regulations introduced in the 2011 Act, which now compel councils to hold *all* meetings in public, including those of cabinets or executives, other than in exceptional cases. The main requirements for openness in council decision-making under the LGA 2000 (as modified by the Local Government and Public Involvement in Health Act 2007 and the 2012 Regulations) are listed in Table 13.3.

To journalists and engaged local citizens, the need for the recent relaxation of privacy rules were self-evident. Because many significant policy-related decisions have been taken in cabinet in recent years—or even individually, by elected mayors, leaders, or cabinet members (and sometimes officers) with delegated powers—by holding such meetings privately, councils could stop the public finding out about plans until after the event. In February 2010, Woking Borough Council finalized the £68 million purchase of a shopping centre in a closed meeting—only revealing the fact in a statement afterwards on its website. The buyout relied on a loan from the Public Works Loan Board (PWLB) that would take the borough's taxpayers some fifty years to repay. Such practices are occurring, say critics, at a time when meetings that *are* still held in public—those of subcommittees, committees, and even the full councils—are being reduced to talking shops.

Under the revised rules, press and public also have rights to the following:

- three days' notice of open meetings;
- 'at least twenty-eight clear days' notice' of any matter to be heard in private, to be published on the council's website and at its offices and confirmation of this intention at least five days before the meeting;

- agendas, minutes, and 'written statements' outlining key outcomes of meetings;
- registers of planning applications;
- records of payments to councillors;
- the council constitution, code of conduct, and standing orders;
- a statutory register of members' interests;
- copies of any reports into allegations of maladministration by the Local Government Commissioner (Ombudsman);
- the council's annual accounts, annual audit (including the right to inspect certain items), performance indicators, and future performance plans;
- general financial information; and
- the council's full annual report (including comparative data indicating how well it has performed as against 'similar authorities').

13.4.1 The order of business in local authority meetings

All meetings of councillors—whether committee, full council, or executive—follow the same format as the old system, as outlined in Table 13.4.

Table 13.4 Order of business in council, committee, and subcommittee meetings

Order of business	What happens
Publication of agenda	Agenda—document outlining matters to be discussed and proposed order of business—prepared by council's chief executive, secretary, or director of administration and publicized in advance.
Approval of minutes	Meeting opens with formal approval of record of previous meeting.
Questions	Usually written down in advance by specific councillors, these are put to committee chairpersons. At full meetings of councils that have adopted a post-LGA 2000 constitution, questions are put to elected mayor, leader, or relevant cabinet member.
Public questions	Observers on public benches given chance to question committee chairpersons (optional).
Petitions	Any petitions from electors (e.g. over planning issue) presented to full council by councillors representing relevant ward or electoral division. Actual debates held at relevant later committee meetings.
Consideration of reports	In full council, reports from committees considered, while committees consider those of subcommittees. Debates often arise over 'political' matters: councillors with strong objections to given proposal may ask for it to be amended or 'referred back' to committee/cabinet.
Notices of motion	Individual councillors should table these in advance. They usually cover issues not formally listed on agenda. In LGA 2000-style councils, any notices impinging on executive issues must be referred to executive/cabinet for final decision.

Several recent innovations have been introduced to make council meetings more transparent and accessible—many by individual authorities. It is now commonplace for councils to stream key meetings live, either on their own websites or (increasingly) a dedicated YouTube channel, while also providing archives of previous ones, to be watched (or re-watched) by journalists and the public at leisure. On Mr Pickles' watch, town halls were also dragged into the social media age (under duress, in some cases) with a guide published in June 2013 ordering them to allow press and public to tweet and blog from meetings, and film or record proceedings for their own purposes. Mr Pickles's decision to issue the guide followed repeated complaints from news organizations that councils struggling to adjust to the arrival of social media were denying them these freedoms, despite their formal introduction in the Local Authorities (Executive Arrangements) (Meetings and Access to Information) (England) Regulations 2012. Wrexham Borough Council had reportedly banned the local *Daily Post* newspaper and bloggers from using Twitter in meetings, while Wirral Council tried to stop its pensions committee being filmed on 'health and safety' grounds—citing rules that the Health and Safety Executive (see 7.4.4) swiftly dismissed as spurious. In the most extreme case, blogger Jacqui Thompson was handcuffed by police for filming a meeting of Carmarthenshire Council on her Smartphone.

13.5 Local elections

Until 1974, local elections were held throughout the first week in May, but the Local Government Act 1972 stipulated that they occur on the first Thursday in that month (unless the Home Secretary of the day fixed an alternative, for example to avoid a clash with a general election). The Act also clarified that *all* councillors must be directly elected (until this point, archaic offices had remained in certain areas—for example 'aldermen', who were elected only by other councillors).

Each individual councillor is now elected for four years—except if voted in, mid-term, at a by-election resulting from the death of a sitting member or his or her resignation/disqualification. Councillors elected in by-elections sit for the remaining terms of those they replace and stand for re-election at the same time as their colleagues. If a councillor dies or otherwise leaves office after the September of a year preceding an election, however, his or her seat remains vacant until the next general polling day.

13.5.1 Local authority constituencies

Councillors, like MPs, have their own constituencies (albeit covering far smaller geographical areas than parliamentary ones). Unlike Commons seats, however, those used in council elections have up to three representatives at a time.

The terms used to refer to these constituencies differ from one council type to another, as follows.

- 'County divisions'—or **electoral divisions**—are constituencies in county council elections in England and Wales. Some unitary authorities also use electoral divisions. They tend to be geographically bigger (and represent more people) than those for other types of council.
- **Wards** are constituencies in districts or boroughs, metropolitan districts, London boroughs, and most unitaries. All Scottish councils have wards.

Whether wards or electoral divisions are represented by one, two, or three councillors is determined by the sizes of their populations. Most urban wards contain roughly the same number of electors and, being based in towns, have fairly high populations. They are generally represented by three councillors. In rural electoral divisions and wards in mixed rural/urban areas, population levels can be significantly more varied—meaning that some have only one councillor, while others are designated 'multimember' divisions/wards, with up to three.

Since 31 December 2010, there have been 9,434 wards and electoral divisions in the UK, each covering an average population of 5,500. Table 13B, to be found on the **Online Resource Centre**, gives an overview of the number of wards and electoral divisions in each of the four countries of England, Wales, Scotland, and Northern Ireland.

13.5.2 Local authority election cycles

The precise election cycle followed by a council—that is, the years during which it holds its elections—depends on which 'type' of authority it is. In Wales, Scotland, and Northern Ireland—where single-tier authorities hold sway—other than in exceptional circumstances, all councillors stand for re-election at the same time, once every four years. The most recent exception to this was the one-off five-year term granted to Welsh, Scottish, and Northern Irish members elected in 2012, in order to avoid a clash with the 2016 Cardiff and Holyrood elections. Due to the varied local government structures prevalent in England, cycles here are far more complex. The present system in the country is as listed in Table 13.5.

English local election cycles have been known to baffle electors. This is especially true for those living in two-tier areas, who face them more often than most, given that they are covered by not one but two councils: a district/borough council and a county council. In some areas, where district or borough and county elections are occasionally held in the same year, the process can be even more confusing.

Among its many innovations, the LGA 2000 envisaged councils' patchwork election cycles gradually being rationalized. But, since it was left up to individual councils to decide whether to reform (let alone when), like many centrally

Table 13.5 Electoral cycles for different types of English council

Type of local authority	Electoral cycle
County council	Every four years, with whole council retiring at same time. Elections last held in 2013, and due in 2017, 2021, etc.
London borough councils	Every four years—with whole council retiring simultaneously. To avoid conflicting with county polls, London boroughs hold elections in different years. Last held in 2014.
Metropolitan borough councils	Three out of every four years—one-third of councillors retire each time (usually one per ward). Elections never take place here in same year as county polls. Current cycle began in 2010.
District/borough councils	Choice of elections *either* three out of every four years, in which case, one-third of council retires each time, *or* every four years, for all councillors in one go. If districts/boroughs opt for former, electoral calendar is same as that for metropolitan districts. If they opt for latter, these are held midway between those of counties—in 2015, 2019, etc.
Unitary authorities	Choice of elections *either* three out of every four years *or* all in one go—with special arrangements in hybrid counties (see 10.2.3). When new unitary authority is created by amalgamating pre-existing district and county, statutory order may be passed stating that new council should initially sit for *less than four years*—to stop elections clashing with future county ones.
Parish, town, and community councils	Every four years—whole council retires at same time, in 2015, 2019, etc. Each parish must have at least five councillors—but actual numbers are fixed by local district. Some follow ward-based system (like their parent authorities).

directed proposals the recommendation ended up a casualty of localism. In January 2004, following a lengthy consultation, the Electoral Commission warned that public confusion about electoral cycles was contributing to the general malaise afflicting local democracy, by further eroding turnouts already dwindling as a result of widespread political apathy. It cited research conducted in April 2003 by MORI, which found that a quarter of British people did not know whether elections were due to be held in their areas that May and only one in six could say how often they were asked to vote. The findings prompted the Commission to make the following (as yet unimplemented) recommendations:

- all English councils should hold whole-council elections every four years; and
- counties and the Greater London Authority (GLA) should hold elections in different years from boroughs or districts, unitaries, metropolitan districts, and London boroughs.

Quite apart from their complexity, England's electoral cycles have produced curious quirks. Because individual districts or boroughs can choose whether to follow a whole-council election model or one in which votes are held in three out of four years, there are some counties in which elections may be held for a borough, district, county, and potentially even neighbouring unitary in a single year. By the same token, adjacent districts or boroughs may choose different cycles, meaning that (despite having the same responsibilities) they hold elections on the same day as each other at most once every four years.

13.5.3 Who can stand as a councillor?

As at general elections (see 4.2), any UK, Irish, or Commonwealth citizen normally resident in Britain and aged over 18 on the day he or she is nominated may stand—provided that he or she can prove one of a range of verifiable connections with the local area and is not legally disqualified for any of the reasons listed in Table 13.6. There is no requirement for an election deposit.

Unlike at general elections, candidature is also open to European Union (EU) citizens meeting the same criteria. To be nominated, prospective councillors must obtain signatures from both *proposers* and *seconders* who are registered to vote in the relevant election. Candidates must also prove *at least one* of these statuses:

- legitimate listing on their local electoral registers (see 4.1.1);
- local residency for twelve months before the nomination process;
- location of their 'principal or only' places of work in the local area for the whole preceding year; or
- ownership of local property for the whole preceding year.

The eligibility of EU citizens to stand as councillors and the rather fluid test of 'residency' in a council's area make the qualifications for council candidates seem less stringent than those for prospective MPs. Unlike in general elections,

Table 13.6 Disqualifications for candidacy as a councillor

Category of person	Details of disqualification
Some bankrupts	Prospective candidates barred if subject to bankruptcy restriction orders made by Insolvency Service. This means they have acted dishonestly or in other 'blameworthy' way. In Northern Ireland, bar extends to all bankrupts; in Scotland, to anyone whose estate is sequestered.
Certain recent convicts	Those convicted of criminal offences with minimum three-month prison term during five years before election.
Electoral fraudster	Anyone convicted of corrupt/illegal election practice in previous five years.
Politically restricted officials	Those working for council for which they intend to stand or holding politically restricted post with another authority (see 3.3.1). Whitehall civil servants above 'Grade 7' may stand only with permission of employers (most senior ones banned).

this liberal attitude extends to peers with seats in the Lords, who (though barred from standing for the Commons) may become councillors. Lord Bassam, the Opposition Chief Whip in the Lords, was once leader of Brighton and Hove Council.

13.5.4 Who can vote in local elections?

Only people whose names are on the local **electoral register** may vote. To be eligible, a person must be:

- at least 18 or due to turn 18 during the twelve-month period that the register covers (provided that this is by polling day);
- a UK, Commonwealth, Irish, or other EU citizen;
- normally resident in Britain, serving in the Armed Forces or as a merchant seaman, or a declared voluntary mental patient; and
- not barred because he or she is a non-EU or Commonwealth foreign national, a convict detained in prison or a mental institution, or has been convicted within the previous five years of corrupt or illegal practices.

As with general elections, it is the electoral registration officer's responsibility to ensure that electoral registration forms are completed and, since summer 2014, each adult has been expected to register individually—replacing the pre-existing household registration system (see 4.1.1). Anyone moving from one council area to another may have his or her name added to the register at the start of a given month under a 'rolling registration' system introduced in 2000.

13.5.5 The local election process

The procedure governing local elections is very similar to that relating to general elections, and is as summarized in table 13C to be found on the **Online Resource Centre** accompanying this book.

Of the various other rules governing conduct of elections, most notable are those limiting the sums that candidates are allowed to spend on campaigning. The spending cap for those standing as councillors in England and Wales is currently £740, plus 6 pence per eligible registered elector. In Northern Ireland, the limit is £600 plus 5p per eligible voter, while in Scotland it is £705 plus 6p per voter. To ensure that limits are not exceeded, agents must send inventories of their candidates' expenses to their returning officer after the poll.

13.5.6 Moves towards improving local election turnout

Dwindling engagement in local elections has long concerned UK governments. Compared to many EU countries, the turnout in Britain's local polls can seem pitifully low: in a 2000 survey by the then Office of the Deputy Prime Minister (ODPM), it came bottom of the European league, with an average turnout of just two out of five electors (a drop of 37 per cent since 1987). Between 2 million and 6 million people are estimated to be unregistered at any one time—whether intentionally (to avoid Council Tax) or out of apathy. Since the Coalition introduced individual voter registration, some estimates suggest this has increased to nearer 7.5 million, with first-time voters and transient groups, like students and benefit claimants, most likely to not be on the electoral roll (prompting Labour to complain that its potential voter base had been disproportionately undermined—see 4.1.1).

New Labour, aided by the Commission, mooted several changes to boost turnout, but with the exception of universal entitlement to postal voting, up to now these have been implemented in only a piecemeal way. The other proposed innovations included:

- introducing anonymous registration for those reluctant to have their names listed;
- opening polling stations at supermarkets, workplaces, colleges, doctors' surgeries, etc.;
- allowing voting over a period of days, rather than only one;
- electronic voting—via email, the Internet, text messaging, etc.; and/or
- holding annual elections for at least a portion of each council, to make councils more accountable to electors by forcing them to campaign for votes continually.

The most 'successful' local elections—such as the 2016 vote for London Mayor, which recorded a turnout of 45 per cent (up 7 per cent on 2012)—are often viewed through the prism of national and global political events, rather than as true tests of public opinion about the merits of local candidates and parties. Results of 'mid-term' local elections—those held partway through Parliaments, by which time voters are often disenchanted with serving governments—are often interpreted as 'protest votes' by political commentators and pollsters. The 2008 local elections were an object lesson in protest voting: a week after the then prime minister Gordon Brown's government had meekly pledged to compensate low-earners hit by the abolition of the 10 pence starting rate of income tax (including many of its own grass-roots voters), Labour polled its worst result for more than forty years. It scored barely 24 per cent, coming one point behind the Lib Dems and 20 per cent shy of the Tories—a share that would have sent it to a crushing general election defeat. The success of the UK Independence Party (UKIP) in recent town-hall elections also signifies, to many, a generalized 'protest' against more mainstream political parties and mounting disaffection with the democratic process. Most recently, the May 2016 local elections—which came mere weeks before the party's triumph in the

'Brexit' referendum (see 9.7)—saw it make a net gain of twenty-five councillors in England, and come within a whisker of taking overall control of its first local authority: Thurrock Council. It also gained two seats on the GLA, coming fourth (ahead of the Liberal Democrats) with its strongest performance in the capital for many years. As at national and European level, UKIP has increasingly capitalized on the disaffection of traditional white, working-class former Labour voters, as well as the right-wing ex-Conservative supporters with whose anti-European, free market views its policies might be seen to more naturally chime.

The task of reviewing English councils' electoral arrangements—and overall structures or boundaries—was until recently the responsibility of a committee of the Boundary Committee for England, but in 2010 it was a replaced by a new dedicated **Local Government Boundary Commission for England (LGBCE)**. This carries out electoral reviews of all councils every few years to ensure that the numbers of electors represented by each councillor are broadly the same nationwide. It may also undertake discrete reviews for individual councils, such as newly established unitaries. There are separate local boundary commissions for Scotland and Wales, and a Local Government Boundaries Commissioner for Northern Ireland.

Topical feature idea

Below is an edited extract from Grant Thornton's annual audit letter for Worcestershire County Council to year end 31 March 2015. What questions are raised by the 'key messages' listed here? What potential news angles might you tease out of these brief comments and how would you research the detail needed to back them up?

Extract from Grant Thornton's annual audit letter for Worcestershire County Council to year end 31 March 2015:

Financial statements audit (including audit opinion)	We reported our findings arising from the audit of the financial statements in our Audit Findings Report on 26 June 2015 to the Audit and Governance Committee. The most significant findings were related to accounting for schools. While the authority had considered the changes required as a result of the amendments to the accounting requirements, limited evidence was available initially to support the accounting decisions made. Additional work was necessary by both officers and audit staff to ensure the decisions made were fully justified and documented. Following discussion of the initial treatment of school assets within the accounts, it was agreed that rather than accounting for the policy change in year, a prior period adjustment was required. We worked with officers to ensure that this change was made to the final set of financial statements. While the adjustment of £97.8m was significant, this did not impact on the Council's overall reported financial position.

	In addition to these issues, our other main findings were: • Substantive testing identified errors in both employee remuneration and operating expenditure. In both cases this led to additional sampling being undertaken, plus more detailed quantification work to ensure that the results of the testing did not indicate a material error within the financial statements. We recognise that the need to produce the financial statements earlier will mean a greater level of estimation is needed in the accounts, and as such it's likely that in future years we will meet similar problems when undertaking detailed testing. We need to work with officers to ensure appropriate mechanisms are in place to evaluate any issues identified and their impact on the financial statements. • While the draft accounts were presented for audit in line with the timetable agreed, we experienced some difficulties with both the quality of working papers and the speed of response to queries. This was particularly evident in relation to the capital accounting entries, but also where information was provided from departments beyond the central finance team. We have discussed the issues arising from this year's audit extensively with the Chief Financial Officer and his team and have received a positive and constructive response to our concerns. We will continue to work closely with officers to ensure that similar issues do not occur in 2015/16.
Value for Money (VfM) conclusion	We issued an unqualified VfM conclusion for 2014/15 on 21 September 2015. Overall, our work highlighted that the Council, like many others nationally, continues to face challenges in how to balance its budget. The authority delivered its savings target in 2014/15 although some of this was achieved through one off alternative funding. Pressures remain in key areas, particularly in looked after children. However, appropriate arrangements are in place to monitor and respond to these pressures. The ambition of becoming a 'Commissioning Authority' is still a strong theme in all that the Council does, with an increasing proportion of services now being commissioned from outside organizations. On the basis of our work, and having regard to the guidance on the specified criteria published by the Audit Commission, we are satisfied that in all significant respects the Council put in place proper arrangements to secure economy, efficiency and effectiveness in its use of resources for the year ending 31 March 2015.

✷ Current issues

- **Continuing decline in voter registration** In the run-up to the May 2016 local elections and ensuing referendum on Britain's European Union membership, the Electoral Commission estimated that at least 7.5 million eligible voters had failed to register under the new individual registration system introduced by the Coalition.

- **UKIP's ongoing increase in council representation** The United Kingdom Independence Party's status as a growing force in local government shows little sign of diminishing, after a steady increase in support in recent elections. The party scored a net increase of twenty-five councillors in the 2016 local elections, winning two members of the Greater London Authority and coming close to taking control of Thurrock Council from Labour.
- **Privatization of local government auditing** The Coalition scrapped the Audit Commission, replacing it with independent oversight of councils' accounts by private contractors. Ten regional franchises have since been awarded to four companies.

Key points

1. Councillors are elected for four-year terms, whatever the type of authority on which they serve, but electoral cycles vary from one council to another. Counties hold elections once every four years, but districts or boroughs and unitaries may choose between this system or one in which a third of councillors are replaced in three out of every four years.
2. British, Commonwealth, Irish, or European Union citizens aged over 18 may stand for council elections, provided they are not disqualified and can prove one of the following 'local connections': residency for the previous twelve months, a main or only place of work, ownership of property in the area, and/or registration on the electoral roll.
3. The media and public must be given 'reasonable accommodation' and allowed into council meetings unless they are dealing with information classed as 'confidential' or 'exempt', or a 'lawful order' is used to maintain order and prevent misbehaviour at the meeting. 'Confidential' covers details supplied by government relating to security and crime prevention, while 'exempt' usually relates to commercially sensitive information.
4. Councils must also routinely make other information public. This includes agendas and background papers for upcoming meetings, minutes of previous ones, information on councillors' allowances and expenses and senior officer pay, and monthly online disclosures of all spending and contracts put out to tender worth £500 or more.
5. Local citizens who believe that they may have a case against their council for maladministration can appeal to their Commissioner for Local Administration (Local Government Ombudsman).

→ Further reading

Atkinson, H. (2012) *Local Democracy, Civic Engagement and Community: From New Labour to the Big Society*, Manchester: Manchester University Press.

Forward-looking assessment of the potential for improved democratic participation and civic engagement in the new age of localism.

Bowles, N., Hamilton, J., and Levy, D. A. L. (2013) *Transparency in Politics and the Media: Accountability and Open Government*, London: I. B. Tauris. **Examination of the growing trend towards 'open government' and publication of data online by British and other Western governments.**

Johnston, R. and Pattie, C. (2006) *Putting Voters in Their Place: Geography and Elections in Great Britain*, Oxford: Oxford University Press. **Thoughtful examination of the geographical differences in voting and turnout patterns in local, national, and European elections. Examines the emergence of safe seats, and the roles of marginal wards and constituencies in winning polls.**

Pratchett, L. (2000) *Renewing Local Democracy? The Modernisation Agenda in British Local Government*, London: Frank Cass. **Still relevant assessment of the impact of 'New Labour' reform agenda, focusing on attempts to increase public participation in local democracy through mayoral elections and new forms of voting.**

Online Resource Centre

www.oxfordtextbooks.co.uk/orc/Morrison5e/

Visit the Online Resource Centre that accompanies this book for web links and regular updates.

14

Education

If one policy area can compete for the emotions with the NHS it is education. Whether it is local unrest over changes to school catchment areas, anger over disruption caused by striking teachers, reports about soaring undergraduate student debt, or the frantic scramble for university places through the clearing system each summer, the trials and tribulations of parents and pupils are seldom far from the media spotlight.

Although diluted in recent years, the involvement of local education authorities (LEAs) in this huge policy area stretches across all four 'phases' of the education process beyond preschool level: primary, secondary, further (or 'tertiary') education (FE), and higher education (HE). These are explained in Table 14.1.

In addition, LEAs are responsible for ensuring that suitable preschool education is available across their areas, through nurseries, registered childminders, and other recognized early years childcare providers. This chapter examines each layer of state education in detail, beginning with perhaps the most important (and certainly the most controversial): schools.

14.1 The origins and evolution of LEA schools

For the uninitiated, today's school landscape is a complex and mind-boggling thing. State-funded schools can be run by local councils, jointly overseen by LEAs and their own governors, or (as is increasingly the case) entirely 'self-governing'. Moreover, each of these categories embraces more than one type of state school. While those run by LEAs tend to be designated county, community, or 'comprehensive' schools, some areas also retain academically selective grammars. Elsewhere, there are foundation and trust schools, which, although largely independently run, are still partly overseen by councils. Even fully

Table 14.1 Structure of the British education system

Phase	Structure
Primary	Education in 'primary' subjects (e.g. English language, maths, basic history, science). Takes place in primary schools (ages 5–11) or infant (5–7) and junior schools (7–11). In some areas, children attend first schools (5–8/9), then middle schools (8/9–12/13).
Secondary	Education for 11–16 year-olds (or 13–16 year-olds in some areas) in core subjects such as English and maths, with increasing specialization in other areas after children take 'options' at age 13/14. Compulsory secondary education in England, Wales, and Northern Ireland leads to final assessment between ages of 14 and 16, through GCSEs and/or vocational diplomas. GCSEs awarded through mix of exams and coursework across eight grade bands: A*–G. In England, GCSEs in English, maths, and sciences to be replaced by new English Baccalaureate Certificate (EBac) from 2017. Scotland's GCSE equivalent is Standard Grade (levels 1–7). Standard Grades take up first half of four-year National Qualification (NQ) programme, encompassing Scottish equivalent of gold standard pre-degree qualification in rest of UK, A levels (Scottish Highers). School-age qualifications and most qualifications taught in sixth forms/at FE level in England regulated by **Office of the Qualifications and Examinations Regulator (Ofqual)**, which also oversees vocational qualifications in Northern Ireland. These qualifications accorded a 'level' on National Qualifications Framework (NQF)—a form of 'credit transfer' system for accredited UK courses/exams. In Northern Ireland, school-age qualifications regulated by Council for the Curriculum, Examinations, and Assessment (CCEA); in Wales, in-house by Department for Children, Education, Lifelong Learning, and Skills (DCELLS); in Scotland, by Scottish Qualifications Authority (SQA).
Further education (FE)	'Sixth-form' education in chosen subjects to A level in England, Wales, and Northern Ireland, Advanced Subsidiary (AS) level (taken during first year of standard two-year A level course), vocational diploma, or International Baccalaureate (IB) (qualification widely taught outside UK). In Scotland, pupils study for intermediate-level certificates, followed by Scottish Highers. 'Catch-up' tuition for less academic/those retaking GCSEs/Standard Grades also offered. BTEC National Diplomas, foundation degrees, and other practical, trade-based post-GCSE certificates often taught in school sixth forms, and at further education (FE), technical, or tertiary colleges.
Higher education (HE)	University education to degree—Bachelor of Arts (BA) and Bachelor of Science (BSc)—and postgraduate—Master of Arts (MA), Master of Science (MSc), Doctor of Philosophy (PhD)—level for those with requisite A levels or equivalent qualifications.

self-governing schools come in different varieties—embracing academies, free schools, and city technology colleges (CTCs).

Until Victorian times, things were much simpler—if wholly inadequate, in terms of providing an education for Britain's children. While the aristocracy and burgeoning middle class fostered a blossoming private education system for those who could afford it, there was little or no formal schooling for the offspring of the poor.

By the late nineteenth century, however, there was a growing clamour for government to provide basic schooling for all children. The foundation stone of the modern 'state school' system—or 'maintained sector'—was the Elementary Education Act 1870, which introduced nationwide *elementary schools*. The term 'elementary' is key: even at this stage, poorer children were offered only the most basic level of teaching and only up to the age of 13. Neither was this guaranteed to be within the grasp of all families: local school boards still charged a fee. While boards had discretion to waive their fees for the poorest households, they could do so only for limited periods. It was only with the Education Act 1891 that elementary education became free for most pupils, and not until 1918 that the last fees were abolished. This reform was initiated by county councils—which, as of 1901, were designated LEAs.

The path towards introducing secondary schools was even more protracted: not until the Education Act 1944 was there a nationwide system open to all children, regardless of parents' ability to pay. When the 1870 Act was passed, the compulsory school age ended at 10 (despite the fact that elementary schools taught up to the age of 13). The leaving age was increased incrementally—first to 11, then 13, then 14—by three subsequent Acts, in 1893, 1899, and 1918. But it was only Tory Education Minister Rab Butler's 1944 Act that introduced secondary schooling for all in England and Wales (a provision extended to Northern Ireland in 1947).

Despite the widespread welcome given to the new universal free secondaries, the Butler Act proved contentious. Its most controversial innovation was the introduction of not one, but three types of secondary school:

- **grammar schools**—for the most academically gifted;
- secondary modern schools—a more standard alternative for the less able; and
- technical schools—offering a vocational, rather than academic, education.

Whether a child was admitted into one or other would depend on his or her performance in a new exam sat at elementary school leaving age: the '11-plus'. This system came to be known as **selection**. A chronology of key Education Acts can be found in table 14A to be found on the **Online Resource Centre** that accompanies this book.

Despite having introduced selection, Labour became increasingly opposed to it over time. One of its administrations—Harold Wilson's first, elected in

1964—came close to scrapping grammar schools altogether. Under the Conservative governments of the late 1950s and early 1960s, the number of non-selective secondary schools had gradually increased to cater for the post-war 'baby boomer' generation. These schools, focusing on a broad-based academic education, eventually came to be known as **comprehensive schools**, high schools, community schools, in Northern Ireland controlled schools, and in Scotland academies (not to be confused with their modern-day namesakes—see 14.2.2).

The number of grammar schools later fell dramatically, thanks to a slow attrition beginning in the late 1960s. Between then and the late 1970s, successive Labour and Conservative governments engaged in a game of educational ping-pong over the future of grammars—with Labour instructing councils to abolish them whenever it returned to power and the Tories repeatedly countermanding these orders. By the time Mrs Thatcher became prime minister in 1979, a significant number still remained.

In their mid-1960s heyday, there had been several hundred grammars, including 179 'direct grant' schools—fee-paying ones that agreed to take between a quarter and half of their pupils from poorer families in return for state subsidies. Today, there are 164 grammars in England, spread over ten LEA areas, including Devon, Kent, and Lincolnshire, and sixty-eight in Northern Ireland. The Conservatives' traditional support for selection gave grammars a reprieve in the 1980s, although few new ones were set up at that time.

And the 11-plus continued into New Labour's reign, thanks to the more consensual way in which Tony Blair broached the issue of grammar schools after his party's 1997 election landslide. Though the creation of new grammars was banned in the School Standards and Framework Act 1998, rather than abolishing all existing ones, Labour instead gave parents in areas where they remained a ballot on whether the English grammars then still open should be kept or scrapped. The party's failure to make good on its longstanding pledge to abolish grammars infuriated many of its backbenchers, as did ministers' subsequent decision to *introduce* a degree of selection in academies and specialist schools (see 14.2.2).

On returning to government in 2010, the Conservatives began to slowly extend the scope of grammars again—subtly at first, but later dramatically, with the then newly installed prime minister Theresa May's confirmation, in September 2016, that she intended to revive them on such a scale that selective schools could soon become the norm, rather than the exception. This policy would, she argued, boost social mobility by reintroducing the concept of selecting by academic ability, rather than 'house price' (a reference to the prevailing system, in which only wealthier families, she argued, could afford to move into the catchment areas of the best state schools).

The first tentative sign of the Tories' hope of reviving selection had come with the then Education Secretary Michael Gove's 2012 decision to reword the School Admissions Code (the rulebook governing the allocation of school places to children in the state sector) to approve the first expansion of an existing grammar in fifty years. The rewritten Code contained a clause allowing oversubscribed state schools (whatever their category) to expand beyond their existing boundaries, and prompted Kent councillors to approve a new 'satellite school' in Sevenoaks as an overflow for oversubscribed grammars elsewhere in the area. This so-called 'annexe' was due to open in 2017.

But this modest move was as nothing to Mrs May's dramatic decision to formally revive the selection ideal, in a speech denouncing the 'dogma and ideology' that had long barred the creation of new grammars. Amid widespread opprobrium—Labour argued the plans would 'entrench inequality' by consigning many poorer children to substandard comprehensives, while the government's outgoing Chief Inspector of Schools, Sir Michael Wilshaw, described her claim that they would increase social mobility as 'tosh'—she went even further than earlier rumours had predicted, by announcing that all English secondary schools would be allowed to apply for permission to select some or all of their pupils by ability. By opening up the option of partial (as well as full) selection to comprehensives, not just self-governing schools like academies, the government would potentially be normalizing a 'bilateral school' model already followed by a small number of state secondaries, which select between 13 and 35 per cent of their pupils. However, she offered an olive branch to critics by floating a range of options to modify the way existing selection worked, including a new requirement for grammars to take fixed proportions of their pupils from lower-income households; introducing further tests after the 11-plus, to allow admission for late developers; and ensuring that new grammars were set up in deprived, as well as prosperous, areas.

Philosophical and pedagogic debates about selection, then, continue to rage. Fans of selection, like Mrs May, have long argued it is an engine for social mobility—giving 'bright' pupils from poorer families a leg up, when they might otherwise have been consigned to substandard, mixed-ability comprehensives. Yet official Department for Education (DfE) figures suggest that poorer pupils are simply not gaining entry to existing grammars in anything like the numbers necessary to substantiate this claim: in 2016, only 3 per cent of grammar school entrants were eligible for free school meals, compared to 14.3 per cent of those attending state schools generally. Moreover, an academic study published in May 2014 found strong evidence that former grammar school pupils consistently earned significantly more than their bright peers from comprehensives in working life, and concluded that academic selection contributed to making society *less*, not more, equal. Such concerns have failed to sway Mrs May, though—or, indeed, Northern Ireland's Education Minister, Peter Weir, who overturned a ban on 11-plus tests introduced by his predecessor, Martin McGuinness, just days before the prime minister's intervention.

In terms of the other main forms of LEA-run school in England and Wales, the largest category is **community schools**: an all-embracing term covering 'ordinary' state primaries and comprehensives. LEAs own and maintain their infrastructure, determine their admissions policies, and recruit and pay their staff. Prior to the 1998 Education Act, many of these standard primary and comprehensive (or 'high') schools had for some time been known as 'county schools'. In addition, some community schools have, over time, been redesignated community *colleges*, to reflect the fact that, in addition to teaching the National Curriculum (**see** 14.2), they also offer adult education and training like that provided by FE and tertiary colleges (normally through evening classes).

The other key grouping of schools overseen (to one degree or other) by LEAs is **voluntary schools**. As the term suggests, these are stalwarts of earlier times, normally linked to either the Church of England or Roman Catholic (RC) Church. They are divided into two types: *voluntary aided schools* and *voluntary controlled schools*. The former operate from premises owned by either a church or charitable foundation, but receive all of their revenue funding and up to half their capital outlay from central government, in return for teaching the National Curriculum and offering free school places. As with foundation schools, however, their governing boards may determine their admissions and staffing policies. The principal difference between aided and controlled schools is that, in the latter case, the LEA controls admissions and staffing procedures in return for providing all of the funding. Although the term 'voluntary school' is not generally used in Scotland, since the Education Act 1918 it has been commonplace for secondary schools to specify a denominational bias, with a number labelling themselves 'RC schools'.

In Scotland, where all schools are council-run, they are designated either primaries or academies (at secondary level), while those in Northern Ireland managed by LEAs (known there simply as education authorities or EAs) are termed *controlled schools*. Though voluntary schools are common, there they are subdivided into denominational 'maintained' or 'non-maintained', with an additional category of joint Roman Catholic and Protestant—or 'integrated'—schools designed to bring these communities together in recognition of the decades of sectarian tensions in Northern Ireland (**see** 1.3.5).

14.2 The 1988 Act—and the rise of the 'mixed market' in state schools

Just as it turned its back on four decades of consensus over health policy by introducing the NHS internal market (see 6.2), in 1988 Mrs Thatcher's Conservative government initiated the most profound change in the state education system since the dawn of comprehensives. The Education Reform Act 1988 introduced the concept of 'parent choice' by ushering in various new models of state school and revolutionizing the management of primaries and secondaries by liberating them from LEA control. In so doing, it polarized political opinion between people who viewed the transfer of power from councils to parents and teachers—in effect, 'citizens' themselves—as a triumph of localism over bureaucratic interference, and those who saw in it a recipe for postcode lotteries and fragmenting the universal ideal. The so-called 'Great Debate' over how far to increase school autonomy continues to dominate the education agenda in England to this day (see 14.2.2).

Until 1988, the designation 'independent schools' was used as an umbrella term for private sector fee-paying schools: 'private schools' and older, more exclusive, 'public schools' like Eton. What the 1988 Act did was introduce the concept of independent *governance* to schools in the *state* sector. Schools would be offered the opportunity to 'opt out' of LEA control—in much the same way as general practitioners (GPs) could at the time become independent fund-holders (see 6.2). Schools opting out would become 'grant-maintained' (GM): autonomous in terms of admissions, staffing, and spending, and funded by direct grants from central government. The Tories were handing them de facto independent status (albeit without the freedom to charge fees) in the name of a new form of localism directly aimed at ordinary citizens, rather than councillors elected to discharge it on their behalf. The underpinning philosophy—a foretaste of Mr Cameron's 'Big Society' (see 12.1.5)—was that decisions on running vital public services such as education, health, and social care should be placed in the hands of the individuals who *used* or staffed them, rather than politicians or bureaucrats. The main provisions of the 1988 Act—still the bedrock of all later school reforms—are outlined in Table 14.2.

The Local Management of Schools (LMS) scheme that supported GM schools proved divisive. The element of selection introduced by some popular schools to simplify their admissions procedures and cherry-pick 'academic' applicants was seen to favour children with educated, professional parents—and those who could afford top-up home tuition—while discriminating against those from disadvantaged backgrounds, and critics argued that it would worsen existing inequalities between schools. The ability of head teachers and governors to set their own pay scales and headhunt the 'best' staff was seen to compound this problem: by poaching high-performing teachers from LEA-run schools, or ones with poorer results, they were able to make their own schools yet more 'successful' while further impoverishing those that were already struggling. To top it all, government money followed high-performing schools—rewarding them with bonuses and extra freedoms, and fast tracking grant allocations for GM head teachers.

Although it would adopt its own version of LMS after regaining power, Labour initially opposed the 1988 reforms. All the more embarrassing for Mr Blair, then, when it emerged in 1995 that his son attended the London Oratory, a Roman Catholic GM school—while Harriet Harman, Labour's then health spokesperson, was sending one of her sons to the same school and her other to a grammar.

To some opponents, the idea of introducing 'parent choice' into the GM schools equation set the final seal on an emerging two-tier state system. If

Table 14.2 Main provisions of the Education Reform Act 1988

Reform	Effect
Introduction of grant-maintained (GM) schools	Primary and secondary schools with 300-plus pupils could 'opt out' of LEA control, becoming GM schools. Initially, entitlement was a 'reward' for high-performing schools (those with high numbers of pupils attaining five or more A–C GCSEs). GM schools could set staff pay/conditions and decide admissions policies. They received direct grants and could apply for capital funding for new equipment/buildings and repairs.
Local Management of Schools (LMS)	Day-to-day financial decisions and full autonomy over staff recruitment delegated to GM heads, working with governors. LEA-run schools also given greater leeway than before, with heads redefined more as managers than educators, and governors given shared autonomy to hire and fire staff (although LEA remained employer).
Introduction of **National Curriculum (NC)**	Dictated not only key subjects that all schoolchildren must be taught/offered, but also core skills/content covered (e.g. basic spelling and punctuation). Curriculum to cover broadly same content throughout England and Wales, including GCSEs, with exams at 'Key Stages' 1, 2, and 3 (ages 7, 11, and 14), through NC assessments or **Standard Attainment Tests (Sats)**. Welsh Assembly has authority to make adjustments in Wales—with Welsh language compulsory in all state schools, alongside English.
Launch of Key Stages (KS)	Formal stages introduced by which each pupil expected to attain objectives ('key stages'). Normally established through testing/continuous assessment.
Emergence of parent choice	First signs of 'choice' introduced in school admissions process, with parents allowed to specify which local school they wanted children to attend.
First school league tables	Publication of school exam results—intended to provide 'objective' information on school performance for parents considering where to send children. Attention today focuses on comparative data relating to truancy, exclusions, and performance in external exams—primarily GCSEs, to benchmark how many children achieve five 'good' passes (A*–C). Since 2007, A*–C grades recorded by all schools for league table purposes—excluding academies—have had to include English language and maths, following criticism that many top grades were obtained by children studying 'easier' subjects.
Introduction of city technology colleges (CTCs)	New generation of specialist schools established, geared to needs of industry and technology sector, with private companies invited to sponsor them. Most later became academies.

Table 14.3 Arguments for and against state schools being allowed to 'opt out'

For	Against
Parents know what is best for their children. Giving them direct input into running schools enables them to customize teaching to suit individual children's needs, replacing a bureaucratic 'one size fits all' approach.	Allowing schools to become self-governing worsens inequalities in state system. Given budgetary control, schools poach 'best' teachers/pupils from elsewhere—widening gap between 'successful' and 'failing' schools.
Giving head teachers and governors (parents, teachers, and members of community) more power gives them a sense of 'ownership' of the school. Ownership increases determination to drive up standards.	Giving schools control of own disciplinary procedures, staff recruitment, and budget decisions breeds huge inconsistencies in nature/quality of provision across sector. How long before they can select brightest pupils—or use 'social selection' to do so by back door?
LEAs are unwieldy and bureaucratic, and slow to take decisions. Empowering governors and head teachers speeds up decision-making by 'cutting out middleman'.	LEAs are run by elected councillors and therefore accountable to community at ballot box. School governors accountable to no one but parents of children already attending those schools, and 'responsible' only to those families. Who will stop them taking decisions that adversely affect other schools?

parents could choose between rival local schools, who in their right mind would opt for the one with worse results and fewer resources? As high-performing schools became richer and yet *more* successful, less popular ones were likely to fall further behind and become 'poorer'. Moreover, successful schools had only limited ability to expand to take in growing numbers of applicants and their vested interest in favouring those most likely to succeed might tempt them to become more selective. A summary of arguments for and against schools opting out of LEA control can be found in Table 14.3.

The first school to gain GM status was Skegness Grammar School, in 1988. By the time GM schools were abolished (in name at least) in 1998, there were nearly 1,100 nationwide—three out of five at secondary level.

14.2.1 City technology colleges (CTCs) and other specialist schools

Although pedants might point to post-war technical schools as early examples of secondaries specializing in specific disciplines (in their cases, practical subjects such as carpentry), **specialist schools** per se came decades later. Reviving the notion that some children are more predisposed towards vocational subjects than academic ones, the 1988 Act saw the Conservatives introduce a new generation of 'technical schools' called **city technology colleges (CTCs)**.

From the outset, these secondary schools-cum-sixth-form-colleges were distinct from anything before them. Inspired by US 'charter schools', CTCs saw private companies become involved not only in funding buildings and equipment, but also, controversially, in day-to-day decisions about their governance. Rather than focusing entirely on teaching practical subjects, they still offered under 16 year-olds all the usual subjects. *In addition* to this, however, they were equipped with particular specialisms in science, maths, information technology (IT), and other disciplines.

But the defining characteristic was the extent of private sector involvement. In capital terms, private sponsors financed up front the expansion and refurbishment of existing schools—and the construction of new ones—in return for long-term leaseback agreements that would make their investments profitable over time. This was one of the first tangible manifestations of the Tories' new 'big idea' for funding expensive public projects, the private finance initiative (PFI—see 7.6). But the sponsorship arrangements went deeper than this: companies investing in CTCs were given seats on their governing boards. To the horror of some, certain schools even incorporated the names of sponsoring companies into their official titles and logos. The first CTCs were set up in Kingshurst (Birmingham) and Nottingham. But the most controversial early opening—and the first to incorporate its sponsor's name so brazenly—was Dixons Bradford CTC, funded by the high-street electrical retailer. The college, which opened in 1990, later converted into an academy. Today only three CTCs remain: BRIT School, Croydon, Emmanuel CTC, Gateshead, and Thomas Telford School, Telford and Wrekin.

The purpose of CTCs was not solely to provide an education geared to the changing demands of industry. By granting them a degree of independence commensurate with that offered to GM schools, ministers were giving head teachers a decisive say in running their schools—with their governors gaining enhanced powers to hold heads to account for underperformance. Governing boards—far from being old-style talking shops, there for LEAs to 'consult', but otherwise ignore—gave parents, teachers, local residents, and businesspeople a direct say in school management for the first time. This model of governance, in time, became the norm.

In a further echo of the old post-war school system, the Coalition revived the CTC idea by introducing **university technical colleges (UTCs)** aimed at children aged 14 and over. Again privately sponsored, their aim is to train future generations of plumbers, electricians, and mechanics—ending what ministers decried as 'dead-end' vocational courses in favour of hard skills better suited to reviving Britain's flagging industrial fortunes. To inculcate a work ethic among students, UTCs generally eschew the customary 9 a.m. to 3 p.m. school day in favour of 'business hours'—holding classes for an extra two weeks a year beyond the length of the usual school calendar. Each UTC focuses on one or two technical specialisms, and is expected to work alongside local businesses and a local university, dedicating at least 40 per cent of its time to activities related to its specialism(s), involving design and building, teamwork, and problem-solving. By September 2016, there were already thirty-nine UTCs in place, with at least another eleven expected to open by 2018.

14.2.2 The growth of school autonomy: foundation schools, free schools, and academies

Mr Blair's election in 1997 owed much to his rallying cry of 'education, education, education'—and an accompanying pledge to improve school standards and opportunities for children from all backgrounds. Labour had opposed both CTCs and the principle of schools 'opting out' of LEA control while in opposition. But, as with the NHS, it was not long before it was converted into championing specialist schools, PFI (which it renamed public–private partnerships (PPPs))—and the concept of school autonomy.

In the end, the Blair and Brown governments left the state school landscape more fragmented than they found it. The School Standards and Framework Act 1998 converted all existing GM schools into **foundation schools**. The immediate effect of this was to bring them back under some measure of LEA control—to the extent that, rather than continuing to be funded directly by government, they would receive grants channelled through councils. In practice, however, the sums allocated to each foundation school would largely be determined by Whitehall, and in many respects they retained an independence akin to that earlier wielded by GM schools. The land and buildings occupied by foundation schools are owned by their governing boards (unless ownership has been handed, or the school has historically belonged, to a charitable foundation), and although banned from selecting pupils, they control their own admissions policies. They can also hire their own staff, rather than relying on councils to recruit for them.

The most controversial extension of autonomy was the second: if schools were to be allowed to decide which pupils to admit and exclude, critics argued, would this not reintroduce selection by the back door? A layer of complication was added to the debate when, in Mr Blair's final months in office, the Education and Inspections Act 2006 introduced **trust schools**. Trust status—a term borrowed, like 'foundation', from the NHS—has since been offered to foundation schools that set up charitable trusts to manage their affairs. These trusts employ their own staff, manage their own assets, and set their own admissions policies. Within a year, 300 foundation schools were in the process of converting into trusts, and a number have since been formed through the merger of two or more schools, or takeovers of 'failing' schools by more successful ones. Trust schools were not generally offered any additional funding as incentives to convert—nor were they allowed to 'opt out' of local authority control any further than foundation schools—but in December 2007 the then Schools Secretary Ed Balls offered 'sweeteners' to encourage high-performing schools to team up with less successful ones, including the promise of £300,000 cash injections to smooth over this process. The idea of multiple schools 'clubbing together' under a single head teacher and board was later extended by Labour, through the introduction of 'federations'—a form of shared governance, like trust status, open to both primary and secondary schools.

14.2.2.1 Academies

The most significant additional change to state school designations under Labour was its conversion to the twin ideas of specialization and independent management. The Learning and Skills Act 2000 introduced 'city academies'—schools with state-of-the-art buildings and facilities, part-funded by private sponsors, targeted at poorer postcode areas. They were allowed both to specialize in key subjects geared to the demands of their local communities and to manage their own affairs (including admissions). Some traditionalists saw in this policy a direct contradiction of the party's initial opposition to CTCs, and a betrayal of the ideals of state schooling being entirely funded and managed both within and *by* the public sector. Pragmatists like Mr Blair and the then Education Secretary David Blunkett saw it as a way of pumping much needed resources into deprived areas more quickly than if government were to finance the investment single-handedly, while equipping previously disadvantaged youngsters with the skills demanded by modern industry.

In their early years, **academies** (as they were later renamed) strongly resembled CTCs. Buildings and amenities received significant boosts from private capital, in return for complex PFI/PPP leaseback arrangements and often a stake in the running of the schools for sponsoring companies. For some, this was to be an 'arm's-length' arrangement—a presence on the governing board and consultation over expansions or mergers—but for others it became more hands-on. Towards the end of Labour's tenure, private investors often became directly involved in the day-to-day staffing of ancillary functions like administration, security, maintenance, and/or catering at academies such as William Hulme's Grammar School in Manchester. Pupils attending academies (as with CTCs) often work longer days than children in other schools and/or between different term dates. Unlike CTCs, however, they have not tended to specialize in scientific, business, or technological subjects: if their local communities lack adequate sports facilities, or there is demand for people with specific skills, these factors have generally determined their specialisms.

Perhaps the most controversial 'privilege' granted to academies under Labour was their qualified exemption from a cornerstone of the party's traditional education policy: its opposition to selection. From the outset, academies were permitted to select one in ten pupils on the basis of 'aptitude' in their specialist subjects. The choice of this word—tortuously distinguished from 'ability' by ministers—caused considerable controversy (not to say confusion). Labour appeared to be walking a tightrope between offering some head teachers the autonomy that they craved to introduce limited selection and distancing itself from the Conservatives' customary support for selective schools. In drawing what many saw as an artificial distinction between a pupil's *potential* to do well in a subject (his or her 'aptitude') and 'ability', however, ministers left many head teachers nursing headaches. In 2003, the House of Commons Education and Skills Select Committee recommended tests be scrapped, arguing that the government had failed to clearly define 'aptitude'. Ministers countered that the aim of introducing limited selection was to identify pupils who 'would benefit from' accessing a specialism.

Arguments about autonomy aside, the rise and fall of CTCs, and their later metamorphosis into academies, was in many ways the latest manifestation of a decades-old debate about the wisdom of dividing pupils into 'academic' and 'practical', and gearing education towards the needs of industry as well as the aspirations of young people keen to develop their intellects more widely. In earlier times, this debate had led to the schism between Left and Right over grammar schools; more recently, it has been played out in arguments over the introduction of new qualifications covering vocational disciplines. Since September 2008, 14–19 year-olds have had the option of studying for vocational diplomas covering subjects as varied as health and social care, creative media, and engineering, in addition to—or instead of—GCSEs and/or A levels.

Indeed, the specialization reintroduced under the academies programme is far from confined to those schools today. During the second and third Labour terms, it became so prevalent in the state sector that 3,000 secondary schools (nearly nine out of ten) now specialize in one or more subjects—meaning the oft-used label 'specialist school' is less a separate *category* than a catch-all term embracing each and every school with a specialism. A council-run community school (see 14.2.2.2) today is just as likely to specialize as an academy or one managed by a trust. Achieving specialist status under Labour earned schools significant injections of capital and revenue to support the development of their curriculums (up to an extra £100,000 or more each year in capital grants, plus an additional £130 per pupil). In return, specialist schools were expected to make their improved amenities available to neighbouring schools and community groups. Like academies, many specialist schools were permitted to select one in ten pupils based on their aptitude in a relevant subject, but only if they specialized in languages, performing and visual arts, or sport. Schools that could, over time, demonstrate improvements in academic performance in their specialist subjects were able to apply for 'high-performing specialist school' status. By the time Labour left office, three out of ten specialist schools had achieved this status. Though the Coalition ended the process of recognizing new specialisms, many old ones continue to operate.

14.2.2.2 Mr Gove's self-governing schools 'revolution'

Labour's original academies programme prioritized 'failing' comprehensives—principally those in deprived areas—using PPP investment to funnel capital into rejuvenating their existing facilities or building new schools from scratch. After a sluggish start, the number of academies grew steadily—rising to 203 by 2010. In Labour's third term, academies' greatest advocate, the then Education Minister Lord Adonis, invited private schools struggling to meet recruitment targets as a result of growing competition to consider converting into academies. Several, including Belvedere School in Liverpool and Bristol Cathedral School, subsequently did so. Meanwhile, applications for academy status were increasingly being granted to less obviously 'struggling' schools and/or those in more affluent areas.

But the arrival of Conservative Education Secretary Mr Gove heralded both a dramatic acceleration in the rollout of academies and a significantly more liberal attitude towards the kinds of school that qualified. Almost immediately, he wrote to the head teachers of every English primary and secondary, inviting them to convert. Under the ensuing Academies Act, rushed through the Commons before the 2010 summer recess, schools rated 'outstanding' by Ofsted could be 'fast-tracked' by that September—although any currently falling under the auspices of a foundation, trust, charity, church, or other faith group would need their consent before converting. In the event, only around thirty-two new academies were ready to open by the autumn term.

If take-up initially appeared slow, this soon changed dramatically. In a pincer movement designed to massively boost the number of academies, Mr Gove reiterated that all 'outstanding' schools should consider themselves 'pre-approved' for academy status, while the 2010 Act gave him new powers effectively to *force* 'failing' schools (those placed in 'special measures' by Ofsted—see 14.3.1) to convert, without consulting their governing LEAs. A further liberty granted to 'outstanding' schools (and 'good' schools with 'outstanding' features) was an exemption from the customary requirement for prospective academies to first secure sponsors. An explicit distinction was thus made between old-style *sponsored academies*—a status still accorded to 'failing' schools required to adopt academy status—and 'successful' *converter academies* that proactively opt out of LEA control in pursuit of greater independence.

Mr Gove's reforms had the desired effect. With heads of outstanding schools required to demonstrate only a commitment to work with 'struggling' providers to raise standards across the board, and those floundering at the bottom left with no option but to find sponsors and convert, the result was an unprecedented surge in academy numbers. By May 2016, 2,075 out of 3,381 secondary schools had converted to academies, though only 2,440 out of 16,766 primaries (fewer than 15 per cent) had done likewise. At the time of writing, it was unclear how enthusiastically the newly appointed Education Secretary Justine Greening would take up Mr Gove's passion for 'academization'—particularly given the embarrassing climbdown her immediate predecessor, Ms Morgan, had been forced into only a few months previously, when a backlash from parents' groups and teachers' unions persuaded her to downscale a post-election pledge to force all remaining LEA schools to become academies. For now, only council-run schools in areas where LEAs are judged to be 'underperforming' or no longer 'viable' are expected to be forced to convert wholesale into academies.

Nevertheless, the mass rollout of academies up to this point remains contentious. Among the most disputed aspects of the 2010 Act was a provision enabling academies to boost their revenue budgets by acquiring direct access to the 10 per cent of central government funding for each state school (academies included) currently still spent by LEAs collectively on their behalf. This provoked immediate criticisms from LEAs and unions, who argued that it would dilute the communal 'pools' of funding reserved for council-wide school services, including help for pupils with special educational needs (SENs) not attending academies.

There has also been resistance from some 'failing' schools that the government has ordered to convert. Downhills Primary School in Haringey, north London, became a media cause célèbre early in 2012 after teachers, parents, and local MP David Lammy (a former pupil) united in protest against Mr Gove's instruction for it to become an academy, following a critical 2010 Ofsted report in which it was ordered to make 'significant improvement'. Under pressure from Mr Gove, the school reluctantly agreed to a further Ofsted inspection, but when it was subsequently placed in 'special measures', its head, Leslie Church, resigned and the school relented.

Making good on his promise to allow heads of newly established academies significant additional freedoms, Mr Gove allowed them to partner other public- and private-sector organizations, and (like those already established) lengthen their school days and terms, and set their own pay and working conditions. Perhaps most contentious, however, was his decision to 'disapply' the National Curriculum that his own party introduced in the 1980s for these new converts—exempting them from teaching the same core subjects, in broadly the same ways and stages, as all other state schools. Significantly, the academies established under Labour, although given some freedom to deliver the Curriculum as they saw fit, still had to broadly frame their teaching around it.

A further controversy surrounds the fact that, unlike LEA-run schools, academies are automatically designated charities—a status conferring various privileges, including generous tax breaks. Unlike other charities, they also enjoy 'exempt' charity status, meaning they are not overseen by the Charity Commission regulator.

More seriously, nearly fifteen years after academies first appeared, evidence that they perform any better academically than other types of schools remains patchy. In September 2009, at the end of his final academic year as Schools Secretary, Mr Balls announced that GCSE results for academies had improved by more than twice the national average rate in the preceding twelve months. Critics pointed to less rosy examples and the fact that Labour's academies were exempt from the Freedom of Information Act 2000 until January 2011 (September 2010 in the case of those established by the Coalition), making it impossible to judge how well they had performed compared to other secondary schools, because their pupils might have been achieving top grades in 'easier' subjects (see 19.1.1.3). Proof that self-governing status does not necessarily beget improved performance came in November 2013, when the DfE sent thirty-four academies 'pre-warning' letters, threatening to 'sack' their existing sponsors if they failed to improve the schools' 'stubbornly low' results.

Table 14.4 outlines the main types of state school at the time of writing.

Table 14.4 Main types of state school

School type	Description
Community school/ college	Primary and secondary ('comprehensive') schools run directly by LEAs; community colleges offer evening classes for adults, as well as daytime teaching
Foundation school	Largely self-governing, but funds directed via LEA
Trust school	Foundation schools with independent trusts managing finances/policies at 'arm's length'
Free school	Fully self-governing, charitable primary/secondary providers set up by parents/teachers/communities in locations without sufficient 'good quality' schools
Academy	Fully 'independent' state schools, sponsored by business/ charity/other school; have charity status; can deviate from National Curriculum; can select up to 10 per cent of pupils based on 'aptitude'
Special school	Dedicated to children with 'special educational needs' (SENs)
Voluntary aided/ controlled school	Schools operating from church/charity-owned premises; 'aided' schools set own policies and employ own staff, but 'controlled' schools part-run by LEAs
Faith	Overall term for schools established by faith groups, including non-Christian ones such as Muslim, Hindu, and Jewish

14.2.2.3 Free schools

Creating new academies was but one element of the Coalition's mission to reshape the school system. Shortly after inviting all state schools in England and Wales to apply for academy status in 2010, Mr Gove wrote a second letter—this time to LEA chief executives and children's services directors—detailing how charities, universities, and other interested parties (including groups of teachers, governors, and/or parents) could found *their own* schools from scratch in areas lacking 'good quality' extant provision. Like academies, these **free schools** would be run independently of LEAs and allowed to decide their own curriculums. They would also have to admit children of all abilities and be non-selective. The resulting programme, a hybrid of a profit-based 'free school' model that originated in Sweden and the US charter school approach that originally inspired academies, aimed to:

- respond to parental demand in areas where few 'good quality' schools exist, by making it easier or quicker to establish new ones; and
- promote hands-on involvement by parents, teachers, and local businesspeople in developing the ethos, teaching methods, and outcomes of their schools, to foster greater community involvement in place of direct state intervention.

Mindful of early scepticism about the logistical hurdles that busy parents might face with the nitty-gritty of setting up their own schools, Mr Gove hired project managers to offer professional guidance through the New Schools Network—a charity established to promote social mobility by means of flexible models of state education. The Coalition also relaxed council planning policies to enable school-building programmes to be fast-tracked, with £50 million immediately diverted from Labour's Harnessing Technology Grant fund to provide upfront capital finance for free schools.

While Mr Gove himself modestly predicted he would be lucky to see sixteen free schools launched in the first year, demand quickly picked up, with twenty-four start-ups opening their doors in September 2011. In February 2014, he controversially relaxed the rules governing new school start-ups, to allow proposers of free schools up to three attempts a year (rather than only one) to apply for funding successfully. By August 2016, the number of free schools open or approved had risen to 438—embracing a wider mix of models than ever before, from straightforward primary and secondary schools to those offering an 'all-through' education (i.e. from reception to GCSE or A level stage) to those aimed purely at 16–19 year-olds.

Among the most high-profile free schools is the West London Free School, Hammersmith—brainchild of a 400-strong consortium of parents headed by journalist Toby Young, whose father, the late Labour peer Lord Young, had ironically been an architect of the comprehensive system that critics accused Mr Gove of dismantling. By summer 2012, the school was able to boast of receiving nine applications for each of the 120 places available in that September's intake.

Opponents of the scheme, initially including Labour, continue to warn that it contributes to a two-tier system—with 'pushy middle-class parents' exploiting new freedoms to set up schools dominated by children from similar households, while families in poorer areas (where new and better schools may well be needed) lack the skills, confidence, or time to do so. Others have condemned the folly of establishing free schools in areas where there was no shortage of 'good' providers already, when their introduction might generate surplus places and jeopardize existing providers. In April 2012, the National Union of Teachers (NUT) warned that, contrary to ministerial assurances, in practice free schools were increasingly being approved in areas with no shortage of places—and having a 'negative impact on existing good or outstanding local schools'. Among the towns and cities adversely affected was Bristol, where the opening of a free school left four head teachers struggling to fill 300 empty places, at a cost to the LEA of £450 a year per place. And in a counterproductive step even by ministers' own standards, academies were also said to be suffering—with one in Beccles, Suffolk, facing a 15 per cent budget cut because of the loss of potential pupils to a neighbouring free school.

Another criticism of free schools has concerned their freedom to employ teachers without formal qualifications—a liberty Mr Gove also extended to academies. By April 2014, 6 per cent (or 8,000) of the 141,000-strong teaching staff working in free schools or academies did not have qualified teaching status (QTS), prompting accusations from teaching unions that staff were being hired 'on the cheap'. Thorniest of all, however, is the ongoing question of whether free schools should be allowed to operate *more* 'freely'—in essence, like fully fledged private companies. They are already permitted to employ US-style 'educational management organizations' (EMOs) to oversee their day-to-day management—and these may operate for profit. Both Mr Gove and Sir David Bell, a former chief schools inspector and permanent secretary at the DfE, floated the idea of allowing free schools to become profit-making over time, though this has yet to happen. Questions also remain about the long-term academic effectiveness of the free school model, even in Sweden (where they were pioneered in the early 1990s). A report by the Organisation for Economic Co-operation and Development (OECD), published in December 2010—just as Mr Gove was inviting the first round of British free school bids—found that between 2000 and 2009 Swedish schoolchildren had dropped from ninth to nineteenth for literacy, and from seventeenth to twenty-fourth in maths, in a league table of fifty-seven countries. Critics claimed that part of the reason for the decline was cost-cutting by commercially run free schools, which often employed unqualified teachers.

14.2.3 Reviewing the curriculum: the future of teaching

In June 2012, Mr Gove announced a wide-ranging review of the primary curriculum, placing renewed emphasis on teaching traditional subjects, primarily the 'three Rs'—'reading, writing, and (a)rithmetic'—and rote-learned facts and figures about British history and culture. His back-to-basics approach brought him into conflict with the Tories' Lib Dem Coalition partners later that month, when the *Daily Mail* leaked plans for GCSEs to be supplanted in England by old-style exam-based qualifications modelled loosely on the 'Ordinary Level' (O level) regime that had preceded them (before one of Mr Gove's idols, Mrs Thatcher, abolished them).

Later that year, firmer proposals emerged, with the news that GCSEs in 'core subjects'—later defined as English, maths, the sciences, a language, and history or geography—would effectively be replaced by a new, Continental-style English Baccalaureate Certificate (EBacc) from 2017. The timetable for its rollout was later revised, and it will now be introduced in 2020 for all pupils who started Year 7 of their schooling in September 2015. In a separate, but related, move, the Coalition raised the school leaving age to 17 in 2013, and since 2015 children have had to stay in some form of formal education or training until the age of 18. Though baccalaureate qualifications also exist in all three devolved nations (all modelled on systems widely used in other European countries), as yet they have not been universally adopted anywhere outside England. A qualifications review board recommended they should ultimately be rolled out across Wales when it reported in 2012, but this has yet to happen, while Northern Ireland has also resisted wholesale conversion. Scotland, meanwhile, was always exempted from the English changes, having its own long-established alternatives to both GCSEs and A levels: Standard Grades and Highers respectively.

14.2.4 Faith schools

Another debate that has periodically resurfaced in recent years concerns **faith schools**—an umbrella term used to describe schools run by particular religious communities. The term 'faith school' has traditionally been used interchangeably with 'voluntary school' (see 14.2). In this context, it also denotes schools run by non-Christian faith groups, including Muslim, Sikh, Hindu, and Jewish communities. There are some 7,000 faith schools in England, Wales, and Northern Ireland, and a growing number in Scotland.

Faith schools were championed by Mr Blair (whose son attended one). He and other advocates argued they had above average attendance rates and high levels of achievement. They were also praised for instilling firm discipline and respect among pupils. Mr Blunkett said he wanted to 'bottle' their essence as a template for reform elsewhere. Yet faith schools have generated vocal opposition. Although most are subsidized by the state, non-fee-charging, and obliged to follow the National Curriculum, critics like the National Secular Society regard the idea of children being educated at schools with prescriptive underlying world views as a form of brainwashing incompatible with one of state education's primary roles: fostering freedom of thought and expression. Others, including some politicians and unions, argue that maintaining single-faith schools—whether inside or outside the state system—promotes ghettoization and undermines efforts elsewhere to promote multiculturalism. Some also object to their being allowed to exercise limited selection (albeit faith-based rather than academic), unlike most state schools. In March 2008, the NUT proposed requiring *all* state schools to become 'multi-faith' institutions, offering faith-based instruction, a choice of religious holidays, and varied prayer facilities.

Alleged self-segregation is not the only criticism levelled against faith schools: the ability of academies to vary their curriculums has, say some, enabled those sponsored by religious groups to introduce unconventional approaches to teaching certain subjects. Concern that some Christian schools were minded to teach 'intelligent design' or 'creationism'—the idea that the natural world was created by God, rather than being the product of evolution—as valid theory in science lessons prompted the DfE to threaten to withdraw funding from those attempting to do so in 2012. Among those who had campaigned for a crackdown on creationist teaching were the biologist Richard Dawkins, naturalist Sir David Attenborough, and the British Humanist Association.

But an even bigger row over the potential risks posed by 'faith-based' teaching erupted in March 2014, particularly in relation to academies. This concerned the so-called 'Operation Trojan Horse' plot, which emerged when a letter, allegedly written by Islamist extremists, outlined plans to infiltrate schools across Birmingham and other British towns and cities. Within weeks, it emerged that Birmingham City Council had received 200 or more complaints from parents alleging that their schools were in danger of being hijacked by fundamentalist orthodoxy. Subsequent investigations into twenty-one schools across the city by Ofsted and the Education Funding Trust identified five (including four academies) in which insufficient work had been done to protect children from exposure to extremist teachings. All five were subsequently placed in special measures (see 14.3.1). The ensuing scandal led to a feverish national debate, with Mr Gove at one point embroiled in an unseemly tussle with the then Home Secretary Mrs May, who accused his department of being too slow to tackle Islamic radicalization in schools. Meanwhile, critics of academies saw in it a vindication of their long-held concerns about lack of transparency in self-governing schools. Ex-Labour Education Secretary Mr Blunkett—a staunch advocate of academies—suggested a new Independent Director of School Standards was needed to closely monitor academies and free schools.

14.2.5 Specialist versus special schools: avoiding confusion

Despite their similar-sounding names, specialist schools are not to be confused with **special schools**. Special schools specialize not in particular *disciplines*, but in teaching children with learning difficulties, such as dyslexia or autism, or mental or physical disabilities. Before 1997, these were commonly known as 'special needs schools'.

To be judged eligible to attend a special school, children must be 'statemented'—that is, awarded a 'statement of special education need'—by their LEAs, following diagnosis by a GP or specialist and/or formal academic tests. Recent years have seen a growing trend towards integrating such pupils in mainstream schools, to avoid segregating them socially from their peers and, where possible, to help them attain skills and qualifications comparable to those of other children. Some mainstream primaries and secondaries have their own 'special units', while others integrate statemented children into general classes. However, the disparate approach adopted by different LEAs has created a widening postcode lottery.

The question of 'integration versus segregation' remains politically sensitive. During the 2010 election campaign, Mr Cameron was barracked in front of television cameras by future Green Party co-leader Jonathan Bartley, whose son has spina bifida. He accused the Tories of planning to 'segregate' disabled children by promoting a return to separate schools. Mr Cameron, whose late son, Ivan, had suffered from cerebral palsy and epilepsy, had used his party's manifesto to condemn Labour's 'ideologically driven closure of special schools' and propose ending the 'bias' towards pushing them into mainstream ones.

14.3 The continuing decline of LEAs

LEAs have had their powers progressively eroded—caught between the pincer movement of growing school self-determination and direct intervention in cases of underperformance by successive Education Secretaries. But the single most significant recent reform of local schooling occurred in the Children Act 2004, passed in response to the Victoria Climbié child abuse case (see 17.1.2). The media inquest into this gruesome tragedy led to a sweeping reorganization, under the 'Every Child Matters' agenda. This saw old-style education departments hand oversight of schools to across-the-board children's services departments (see 17.1), and chief education officers replaced by all-encompassing directors of children's services in each LEA area. The aim was to join up a range of previously fragmented services affecting children, to better safeguard child welfare and to make it less likely that warning signs of abuse would be missed in future.

Although they played an overarching role in implementing the 2004 Act, LEAs have seen even more significant reductions in their educational powers, as earlier sections in this chapter illustrate. Today, most are less the principal state schooling *providers* in their areas than enablers or coordinators, although their influence has periodically looked to be on the increase again—with Labour keen to give them a stake in running academies, should they return to office, and even the Conservatives flirting with the idea of letting councils set up their own academy chains—or 'multi-academy trusts' (MATs)—in order to drive through their (currently shelved) plans to 'academize' all remaining LEA-run schools. Indeed, Mr Gove was seen by some critics not as a 'localizer'—freeing schools from local bureaucrats to run their own affairs unimpeded—but a 'centralizer', happy to micromanage academies and free schools from Whitehall.

A full list of the powers retained and lost by LEAs in recent years is contained in table 14B to be found on the **Online Resource Centre**.

Despite the gradual erosion of their status, LEAs remain responsible for ensuring that each child in their area has access to schooling. In addition, they still have an input into many of the areas examined next—notably, monitoring school admissions policies and drawing up catchment boundaries.

14.3.1 Monitoring school standards—and the 'parent choice' debate today

The other great issue to have dominated debate about state schooling, besides selection, is the concept of 'parent choice'. This is the longstanding notion that families should be free to send their children to whichever local school they choose. Dividing lines were sharpened in the 1980s and 1990s, with the introduction of two key innovations designed to inform parents better about the relative academic merits of different schools: league tables and a national inspectorate, the Office for Standards in Education, now the **Office for Standards in Education, Children's Services, and Skills (Ofsted)**.

League tables of school exam results were introduced under the 1988 Act, but took a while to catch on with parents. The more decisive agent of choice was arguably the introduction of systematic school inspections four years later. The Education (Schools) Act 1992 and School Inspections Act 1996 established Ofsted in England and Estyn (formally Her Majesty's Inspectorate for Education and Training) in Wales, providing more consistent nationwide frameworks. Northern Ireland has an Education Training Inspectorate (ETI), while Scotland's inspections are undertaken by a Scottish Government executive agency, Education Scotland (see also 17.1.4.1).

Ofsted is headed by a Chief Inspector of Schools and has traditionally been tasked with conducting regular inspections of all English state schools. Its first visits to each school were carried out within four years of its inception, but thereafter they became six-yearly until Labour made them more frequent, giving shorter notice periods to allow schools less scope to 'clean up their acts' at the last minute.

Today, Ofsted inspects the following providers:

- nursery and primary schools;
- secondary schools;
- special schools;
- service children's education—for the offspring of those in the Armed Forces;
- pupil referral units—for children 'who cannot attend' normal schools, such as pregnant teenagers, those with specific medical problems, and pupils excluded from mainstream schools for problematic behaviour; and
- some independent schools—excluding members of the Independent Schools Council (ISC) and Focus Learning Trust, which are inspected by the Independent Schools Inspectorate (ISI) and School Inspection Services (SIS).

Ofsted has traditionally rated schools 'outstanding', 'good', 'satisfactory', or 'inadequate'. However, in pursuit of a situation in which most state schools could be described as 'good' or 'outstanding', Mr Gove significantly hardened Ofsted's remit. A new inspection framework was introduced in 2012 focusing on previously 'coasting' and underperforming schools by exempting those judged outstanding in their most recent reports from regular inspections—unless the need for one was 'triggered' by letter to Ofsted from teachers and/or parents raising concerns about deteriorating standards. For schools still subject to routine inspection, though, the system is now far tougher: in January 2014, then Chief Inspector Sir Michael Wilshaw introduced 'no notice' inspections for schools blighted by unruly pupil behaviour, later abandoning the long-standing 'satisfactory' label entirely, in favour of a new threefold rating system which recognized schools only as 'outstanding', 'good', or 'requiring improvement'. The inference that schools previously rated 'satisfactory' were effectively being redefined as 'unsatisfactory' angered many head teachers. And Chris Keates, general secretary of Britain's largest teaching union, the National Association of Schoolmasters Union of Women Teachers (NASUWT), condemned the change for 'trashing the reputation of Ofsted and removing anything that parents can rely on by which to judge a school'.

Whatever the outcome of an inspection, a school is expected to act on any recommendations that the report contains, as outlined in table 14C to be found on the **Online Resource Centre**.

Perhaps unsurprisingly, the arrival of league tables and Ofsted, and the ever-toughening performance regimes of recent years, has intensified competition for places at high-performing schools. By highlighting the 'best'—and 'worst'—they created a thriving, sometimes ruthless, market for places at successful providers and an exodus of middle-class families from those deemed 'failing'. There was no starker illustration of this pattern than the East Brighton Centre of Media Arts (COMART)—a struggling comprehensive that went through not one, but two name changes, and a costly PFI building programme, before finally closing in summer 2005. Based in a deprived ward identified as among the 5 per cent poorest by the government's own Indices of Multiple Deprivation, the school consistently had the worst local GCSE and truancy rates. Better-off parents voted with their feet—reducing its social mix and overall pupil numbers, and sending its standards plummeting further.

Critics claim that 'parent choice' has parallels with 'patient choice' in the NHS, which has seen successful hospitals oversubscribed and failing ones avoided. While more and more 'failing' schools are closing, 'successful' ones gain greater financial rewards and freedoms—enabling them to headhunt the most skilled and experienced staff and improve still further. Devoid of these privileges, underperforming schools can become locked in a downward spiral. For the media, particularly local journalists, Ofsted reports provide 'easy hit', newsworthy stories that can usefully fill space or air time. As inspections have become more frequent and the process better understood, however, the regulator has sent out fewer reports proactively to newspapers and television or radio stations, so it is usually up to vigilant reporters to chase them. They should also be wary of relying on schools' own accounts of their inspections: as with most things, it is best to go straight to the horse's mouth for the full story. Handily, though, all Ofsted's reports are available in downloadable PDF form on its website (just as those produced by the Welsh, Northern Irish, and Scottish inspectorates are on theirs).

Another controversy related to the growing national obsession with league tables concerns testing. Ministers have consistently clashed with head teachers' unions over the sheer volume of assessment that schoolchildren now face, and the pressure that this piles on both pupils and teachers. Opposition to testing intensified in summer 2008 when ETS Europe, a commercial company contracted to oversee marking of the Key Stage 2 and 3 tests for 11 and 14 year-olds, presided over a marking fiasco. Results for some schools suffered severe delays and there were reports of exam papers lying uncollected (and unmarked) weeks after the exams had been sat. The company subsequently had its contract terminated, but not before costing the taxpayer £39.6m for that year alone.

In October 2008, Mr Balls scrapped Standard Attainment Tests (Sats) for 14 year-olds, promising new US-style 'report cards' for each primary and secondary school child from 2011, giving an overall grade A–F covering not only exam results and performance, but also attendance and truancy, behaviour, and health. But in July 2011 Mr Gove confirmed that he was implementing the recommendations of an independent review into Sats by Lord Brew, a professor of politics at Queen's University, Belfast, by introducing more rigorous testing of core skills such as maths, grammar, and spelling, and improving assessments of children's creativity. These changes have not come in without resistance, though, and some schools, and teachers, boycott them to this day.

14.4 The future of school catchment areas

The flip side of 'failing' schools becoming unpopular is that 'successful' ones are oversubscribed. Trends in school applications fostered by extending 'parent choice' have had an inevitable impact on catchment areas—the geographical patches within which families need to live to be eligible to send their children to particular schools. Pressure on popular schools to admit more pupils—potentially at the expense of maintaining high standards—has seen some councils take drastic steps to 'ration' places, to keep their numbers sustainable and improve the social mix and performance of other schools.

In 2008, Brighton and Hove Council began allocating places for oversubscribed secondary schools in the city's 'Golden Triangle' by lottery ('random allocation'). Many local families had paid premium prices for their homes, expecting their children to be automatically entitled to attend one of these high-performing schools. Under the lottery, the schools' catchments were extended to cover areas until now devoid of comprehensives, and children from outlying districts became as likely to be admitted as those living nearby. Once applications to attend one of the affected schools exceeded the number of places available, a lottery was used as a tie-breaker. Brighton's experiment was soon emulated elsewhere and, after Labour introduced a new admissions code allowing town halls and head teachers of oversubscribed schools to determine who should be offered places by drawing names from a hat, lotteries of one kind or other were gradually adopted by one in three English LEAs. The government's guidelines—meant to stamp out 'selection by mortgage'—also banned schools from interviewing parents, considering their backgrounds, or excluding people financially by, for example, stipulating that they buy uniforms from expensive suppliers. However, a report published by the British Educational Research Association in September 2010 found that, contrary to expectations, Brighton's experiment had failed to produce any visible improvement in 'social mix' at the schools concerned. The report did not criticize the lottery system per se, but rather the fact that the council had redrawn catchments in such a way that even the enlarged area from which applications had since been accepted principally embraced other middle-class neighbourhoods, with poorer ones in peripheral areas still excluded.

Amid the inevitable backlash from potential Conservative voters, Mr Gove banned LEAs from using lotteries, but instead permitted academies and free schools (but not other state providers) to reserve places for children entitled to free school meals and those whose families earned less than £16,190 a year. Schools now also had to prioritize children in care and those whose parents were in the Armed Forces, and ensure that twins and triplets were taught in the same class—although, controversially, today's code also allows class sizes to rise above the notional thirty-pupil limit that Mr Gove inherited (already too high for some). In practice, many academies have used their freedoms to set their own admissions criteria to introduce lotteries, with others adopting a system known as 'banding' to ensure that each intake offers places to children across the range of abilities. By February 2014, according to the Sutton Trust, 121 self-governing schools were using banding and forty-two used lotteries—a riposte to critics who feared that their independence would encourage them to adopt more conventional forms of academic selection.

14.5 Bridging the educational divide: other recent developments

One tactic favoured by Labour's last prime minister to date, Gordon Brown, for bolstering the state sector (and breaking the perceived state/independent school divide) was to instruct the Charity Commission—the quango responsible for regulating registered charities—to impose new conditions on independent schools seeking to retain their charitable status. Having a charity label entitles organizations to significant tax breaks not enjoyed by companies. The biggest condition was a requirement to earn this privilege by opening up their playing fields and other facilities to state schools and community groups. Labour ministers also began a trend for inviting independent schools to sponsor academies and share amenities and expertise with the new trusts.

An innovation introduced by the Coalition (and retained, to date, by the Conservative-only government) was the **pupil premium**: a pot of money reserved for one-to-one tuition for disadvantaged children, to intercept potential educational inequalities early in their schooling. Starting in April 2011, £488 was allotted to each pupil who received free school meals, out of an initial £625 million budget (rising to £1.25 billion in year two). The money was distributed to schools to spend on these pupils' behalf as they saw fit, with LEAs controlling the purse strings for those taught in 'non-mainstream' settings. From 2012–13, it was extended to pupils who had received free school meals at any point during the previous six years. All infant school pupils throughout the UK (children up to the age of 8) are also now entitled to free school meals—a recent 'universal' initiative introduced at a time when most, including Child Benefit itself, were being cut (see 8.5.1).

Despite such innovations, the Coalition was frequently accused of placing roadblocks in the way of children from lower-income households. Among their most controversial decisions was the abolition of the Education Maintenance Allowance (EMA): a £30 weekly allowance introduced by Labour for 16 to 18 year-olds in continuing education, which academic studies credited with enhancing the career prospects of those from poorer households by incentivizing them to attain further qualifications or training. More explosive still was the Lib Dems' wholesale abandonment of a pre-election 'pledge' to the National Union of Students (NUS) to move towards scrapping undergraduate tuition fees, in favour of a Conservative-driven policy allowing universities to raise their annual fees from a £3,290 limit to £9,000 in England and Wales (though tuition fees do not currently apply for Scottish students attending universities in that country, and in Northern Ireland their maximum level is £3,925). By September 2014, nine out of ten universities were charging the new 'top rate' for some or all of their courses, prompting critics to argue that many talented prospective students from poorer households would either be forced to abandon hopes of studying for anything other than strictly vocational courses (that is, those better placed to 'guarantee' them employment) or deterred from applying altogether. Any deterrent effect is only likely to worsen in coming years, as, in his post-election 2015 Budget, Mr Osborne not only announced the scrapping of maintenance grants from September 2016, but also gave universities permission to further raise tuition fees in line with inflation from 2017–18.

14.5.1 Ensuring fairness: the role of schools adjudicators

Ofsted was not the only body introduced in the 1990s to police the state school system. The 1998 Act saw the establishment of a second: the **Office of the Schools Adjudicator (OSA)**. The office has ten adjudicators led by a chief adjudicator.

Table 14.5 Modern-day powers of the Education Secretary

Power	Effect
Intervention 'in default'	Prevents unreasonable uses of power by LEAs and 'acts in default' when they fail.
Managing the availability of school places	Directs LEAs to reduce surplus places in schools, by merging/ closing unpopular schools, or increasing provision where there is high demand.
Intervening in 'failing schools'	Places 'failing' schools under 'special measures' (two-year period during which Education Secretary closely observes their progress) and instigates 'Fresh Start' if they fail to improve—replacing head teacher and other teaching staff. In 2000, Mr Blunkett introduced 'fresh starts' for schools at which fewer than 15 per cent of pupils achieved five or more A–C GCSE passes. When Labour left office, schools at which fewer than 30 per cent of pupils achieved five A–Cs were judged 'underperforming', but Mr Gove raised bar to 35 per cent.
Tackling inequalities of educational opportunity	Intervenes, if necessary, to improve educational opportunities for poorer children. In 2007, Alan Johnson ordered LEAs to ensure good social mixes in their schools.

There are many misconceptions about OSA—the most common being that it is there to rule on complaints by parents about their children's failure to get into their chosen school. In fact, that role is taken by independent appeal panels. In contrast, OSA has to:

- determine objections to admission arrangements and appeals from schools against directions from the LEA to admit a pupil;
- resolve local disputes on statutory proposals for school reorganizations, or on the transfer and disposal of non-playing-field land and assets;
- decide on competitions to set up new schools where the LEA has entered the contest with its own proposals; and
- decide on requests to vary already agreed admission arrangements.

In the last resort, deciding individual cases still in dispute after OSA has made its judgment falls to the Education Secretary. It is one of many forms of direct intervention by the Education Secretary, as outlined in Table 14.5.

14.6 The role of LEAs in further education

Councils have long had an on–off relationship with the FE sector. Like schools, FE colleges—or 'technical colleges'—were both managed and financed by county councils until 1988. But the sweeping reforms under the 1988 Act included liberating FE and sixth-form colleges from LEA control, giving them 'semi-independent' status *within* the state sector, analogous to that granted first to GM schools and CTCs, then foundation and trust schools, academies, and free schools.

Labour initially did little to challenge FE colleges' new-found autonomy, but in the Learning and Skills Act 2000 it extended Ofsted's scope to include FE. From September 2001, Ofsted began inspecting all FE and sixth-form colleges on four-year cycles. This decision was, in part, an attempt to address growing concerns about lack of transparency and accountability in the management of some colleges, now they were shorn of direct LEA scrutiny. For example, in 1998, Stoke-on-Trent College received a bottom grade for management from government inspectors following a succession of scandals that led to an £8 million deficit, and the dismissal of a principal accused of bullying staff and running a pub in Wales while on extended sick leave.

Under Mr Brown, the tone of FE policy began shifting away from college autonomy. By the time Labour left office, ministers had drawn up plans to return the UK's 385 English and Welsh FE colleges to some form of LEA control, but the Coalition has reversed this again, with FE colleges' governing bodies—'boards' or 'corporations'—regaining primary autonomy over their day-to-day management and LEAs providing only a *strategic* role, as with a growing number of schools. Similarly, 'outstanding' FE colleges are now exempt from automatic Ofsted inspections in the same way as top-rated schools. In a rare example of a real-terms spending increase at a time of swingeing cutbacks, in May 2010 the then Chancellor George Osborne announced a modest £50 million boost for investment in FE building projects. Shortly afterwards, Business Secretary Vince Cable used a speech at London South Bank University to call for an end to artificial distinctions between further and higher education—signalling his intention to increase funds for technical, part-time, and adult courses in FE, and to have more HE-level courses taught in tertiary colleges.

14.7 The role of LEAs in higher education

The LEAs play an increasingly limited role in higher education (HE), though they have remained responsible for providing education maintenance grants to students from lower-income households undertaking full-time degree courses at universities or other HE institutions. As of September 2016, however, these grants were scrapped for new undergraduates in England and Wales, though continuing students (those who had started full-time HE courses before August that year) whose parents had a joint income of £25,000 or less were entitled to 'full' grants of £3,387 a year (the same level as in the previous two academic years) and to have their tuition fees paid for them. Those with parents earning up to £42,620 (down from £50,000 previously and, before that, £60,000) still received partial grants, but had to take out loans to cover the short-term cost of

their tuition fees—repaying these as and when their own incomes rose to £21,000 or higher. In general, maintenance grants have now been replaced with additional loans, although, in ending the decades-old grant system, the government introduced a special support grant for certain categories of undergraduate, such as lone parents and those with disabilities who qualified for Housing Benefit, the housing element of Universal Credit, Income Support, or income-related Employment Support Allowance (ESA) (see 8.3.2.3).

In Northern Ireland, grants still exist at present, though their level has recently been frozen and eligibility for them stops at a lower household income level than previously, and a significantly lower one than those that used to apply in England and Wales (£41,065). Full grants are, however, marginally higher for the poorest students than those that applied elsewhere—reaching £3,475 for students from families with joint incomes of £19,203 or less. Despite having also now lost their maintenance grants, arrangements for those on lower incomes remain noticeably more generous in Wales, with those attending the country's universities entitled to either Welsh Government Learning Grant of up to £5,161 a year, depending on their household incomes, or Special Support Grants up to the same level if they are single parents, have certain disabilities, and/or are receiving particular needs-related benefits. But by far the best deal—a source of resentment for some living elsewhere in Britain—is that offered to Scottish students taking first degrees in Scotland. Their tuition fees are paid by the Scottish Government, with variable bursaries available to those from households earning up to £16,999.

Over and above the mandatory undergraduate grants for students from poorer backgrounds, LEAs also still have the power to make discretionary awards to students following courses that do not benefit from this system—for example vocational postgraduate degrees—though, after years of austerity, the funds allowing them to do so are severely depleted.

14.7.1 Funding and monitoring fairness in higher education

Funding for HE in England is the responsibility of the **Higher Education Funding Council for England (HEFCE)**. There is a separate Higher Education Funding Council for Wales (HEFCW), while both FE and HE in Scotland are the province of the Scottish Funding Council (SFC). In Northern Ireland, funding is now delivered by Student Finance NI—a partnership set up by the province's Department for the Economy, Education Authority, and the Student Loans Company.

The principal roles and purpose of HEFCE are to:

- distribute public money for teaching and research to universities and FE colleges delivering HE courses;
- promote high-quality education and research in a 'financially healthy' sector; and
- play 'a key role' in ensuring accountability and promoting good practice.

To this end, HEFCE has its own board and committees with the following remits:

- quality assessment, learning, and teaching;
- widening participation;
- research;
- business and the community; and
- leadership, governance, and management.

The task of ensuring that HE institutions operate 'fairly'—particularly in relation to admissions policies—falls to the **Office for Fair Access (OFFA)**, led by a Director of Fair Access to Higher Education (currently Les Ebdon).

OFFA's primary job is to ensure that institutions that charge tuition fees above the 'standard level' produce 'access agreements' detailing how they are ensuring that they are accessible to people from disadvantaged backgrounds. In practice, many universities have done this voluntarily, by offering bursaries and scholarships targeted at high achievers from low-income households, those with disabilities, and people from under-represented minority groups.

The body was set up, in part, as a response to the perceived continuing bias of some 'top' universities towards young people from independent school backgrounds. Concern about this issue has been rumbling since Mr Brown publicly condemned Magdalen College, Oxford, in 2000, for failing to offer Laura Spence, a pupil at Monkseaton Community High School in Whitley Bay, North Tyneside, a place to read medicine—despite the fact that she had achieved ten A* passes at GCSE and was predicted to gain five As at A level. In the event, Ms Spence (who went on to secure straight As) won a £65,000 scholarship to Harvard.

As recently as August 2013, however, it emerged that private school pupils achieving three A* A levels or more were 9 per cent more likely to be offered places at Oxford than state school pupils with the same grades. Two years earlier, it had emerged that five schools were sending more pupils to Oxbridge each year between them than 2,000 others combined. These included just one state provider, Hills Road Sixth Form College, Cambridge, and four top public schools—among them Eton (attended by Mr Cameron), Westminster (where Nick Clegg was educated), and St Paul's (Mr Osborne's alma mater).

14.8 The growth of free preschool education

Today, LEAs have limited direct involvement in providing preschool or nursery education. Before 1997, the Conservatives left it up to individual councils whether to fund free nursery education for children from lower-income backgrounds. Given the choice between squeezing more money out of already tight budgets and leaving it to 'the market' to provide where there was sufficient demand, many voted with their feet. A 1986 audit found that free provision ranged from zero to a maximum of 27.5 places per 100 children—hardly a ringing endorsement of council investment. Many LEAs today run at least some nurseries, but most are provided by the private and voluntary sectors. In addition, money directed to enable children from poorer backgrounds to access preschool education tends to come directly from central government, rather than councils.

In the early 1990s, the Conservatives made limited inroads into funding free nursery care for preschool children. 'Nursery vouchers'—virtual money used to 'buy' access for children aged 4 and over to preschool education and/or childcare worth up to £1,100—were introduced in 1996, but abandoned by Labour. Vouchers had baffled many parents: although billed as an extension of 'parent choice', they could not compensate for the fact that—however willingly families shopped around for desirable nurseries—in many areas there simply were not enough places available.

Labour's solution was to launch its first National Childcare Strategy, focusing on two immediate priorities:

- increasing the number of childcare places available; and
- guaranteeing all 4 year-olds a nursery place from April 1998 onwards.

Provision has been gradually extended. From April 2004, LEAs were obliged to guarantee free nursery places to all 3 and 4 year-olds for up to twelve and a half hours a week, for thirty-three weeks a year. Since September 2010, 3 and 4 year-olds have been entitled to up to fifteen hours' free nursery provision for thirty-eight weeks a year, while the Coalition extended this to 2 year-olds from families receiving Income Support or income-based Jobseeker's Allowance (JSA) or Employment Support Allowance (ESA), and those claiming child tax credits and earning £16,190 or less. From autumn 2016 in some places and 2017 across the rest of England, the number of weekly funded hours during term-time was due to be extended to thirty hours—but questions remained about the viability of this scheme after repeated warnings from the National Day Nurseries Association, which represents providers, that its implementation had been underfunded.

14.8.1 Improving access and accountability in preschool education

While responsibility for 'early years education' rests with the devolved administrations in Scotland, Wales, and Northern Ireland, in England a new programme was established in 1999 to drive through the government's aims of guaranteeing high-quality provision for children from low-income households: **Sure Start**. Although its primary focus is welfare and educational development, Sure Start has extended its support to the whole of a child's family.

Sure Start arose out of New Labour's conviction that early years education was crucial to a child's social and emotional well-being, and that families prevented from accessing it were missing out on vital development tools. Ministers' decision that preschool teaching should be a core entitlement, rather than an optional 'add-on' accessible only to the middle classes, was based on research into its impact in later life and the outcomes of experiments in similar schemes pioneered in Scandinavia.

Sure Start aimed to:

- increase the availability of childcare for all children;
- improve health and emotional development for young children; and
- support parents as parents and in their aspirations towards employment.

Where it still exists, Sure Start operates through a network of children's centres, often based in community centres and church halls. Staffed by multidisciplinary teams comprising health visitors, teachers, and social workers, they are focal points for liaison between families and other support services, such as Jobcentre Plus, and antenatal and postnatal advice for new parents.

Where Sure Start ensures that everyone has *access* to preschool education, Ofsted monitors the *standard* of that provision. Its remit was recently increased to cover nurseries, nursery schools, playgroups, and childminders. While the Coalition nominally retained Sure Start, by de-ring-fencing its funding it was accused of giving councils struggling to balance their books the option of scrapping it to save money.

Topical feature idea

Despite having retreated on plans to force all remaining council-run state schools to become academies, ministers are pushing ahead (for now) with proposals to 'academize' all schools managed by 'underperforming' LEAs. The county council area covered by your newspaper's catchment area is one such authority, so your news editor has asked you to prepare a background feature outlining the possible implications of this policy for local families. How many non-academy schools in your area will be affected by this change, and what do their parents and teachers think about it?

✶ Current issues

- **The revival of grammar schools** Prime minister Theresa May has announced sweeping plans to allow all English secondary schools to apply for permission to select by ability.

- **The end of higher education maintenance grants in England** The decades-old eligibility of undergraduates from lower-income households for maintenance grants ended for new students from September 2016, to be replaced by a system of enhanced loans. Universities may also now raise their tuition fees above the previous £9,000 maximum, in line with increases in inflation.
- **Funding problems with the doubling of free preschool childcare for over 3 year-olds** The Conservative government is in the process of doubling the number of free weekly childcare hours for 3 and 4 year-olds in England from fifteen to thirty, but nursery providers and LEAs say the funds provided are too low to cover the cost of sufficient additional spaces.

Key points

1. Education in Britain is divided into five key phases: preschool, primary, secondary, further, and higher.
2. State schools in England and Wales can broadly be divided into those run by local education authorities (LEAs)—unitaries, counties, London boroughs, and metropolitan districts—and 'self-governing' ones, run by their head teachers and governors. LEA-run schools are generally known as 'community' schools/colleges, while the main self-governing ones are academies. There are also free schools (set up by parents and teachers) and semi-independent foundation and trust schools.
3. The main roles of LEAs (in addition to running community schools) is to ensure all children have school places, to decide catchment areas, and to propose new schools or to close existing ones if there are too many or too few places available.
4. All state schools other than fully self-governing academies and free schools must teach the same core subjects, to the same levels, under the National Curriculum.
5. All state schools are inspected by the Office for Standards in Education and Schools (Ofsted), led by the Chief Inspector of Schools. Regular inspections only occur at 'outstanding' schools if requested by teachers or parents, but 'no notice' inspections occur at schools with persistent behavioural issues.

→ Further reading

Adonis, A. (2012) *Education, Education, Education: Reforming England's Schools*, Kindle edn, London: Biteback Publishing. **Acclaimed analysis by former Labour Education Minister of the challenges and opportunities facing British schooling in the twenty-first century.**

Birbalsingh, K., Gove, M., Hill, S., Hunter, M., Johnson, D., Martin, J., Lewis, O., Womersley, D., Woodhead, C., and Young, T. (2013) *The Gove Revolution: Transforming England's Schools*, Kindle edn, London: Standpoint. Series of essays written by supporters and standard-bearers of the Coalition's free school and academy revolution. **Best read as a companion and partial retort to Adonis.**

Cribb, J., Jesson, D., Sibieta, L., Skipp, A., and Vignoles, A. (2013) *Poor Grammar: Entry into Grammar Schools for Disadvantaged Pupils in England*. Available online at www.suttontrust.com/researcharchive/poor-grammar-entry-grammar-schools-disadvantaged-pupils-england/. **Evidence-based critique of the negative impact of the grammar school system on children from deprived backgrounds.**

Phillips, R. and Furlong, J. (2001) *Education, Reform and the State: Twenty-Five Years of Politics, Policy and Practice*, London: Routledge Falmer. **Critical overview of the major trends and debates in educational reform in the UK over the past quarter-century.**

Online Resource Centre

www.oxfordtextbooks.co.uk/orc/Morrison5e/

Visit the Online Resource Centre that accompanies this book for web links and regular updates.

15

Planning policy and environmental protection

If there's one subject guaranteed to agitate the great British public as much as rising prices, train delays, or uncollected bins it is dodgy planning decisions. The media teems with such controversies on a daily basis: from rows about 'parasitical' out-of-town retail parks to objections about proposed wind farms or 'fracking' projects to protests against the building of 'unsympathetic' developments in Areas of Outstanding Natural Beauty (AONBs).

But away from the placard-waving and alarmist headlines, planning is a serious (if, at times, underappreciated and humdrum) business. Without it, there would be no schools, hospitals, offices, care homes, supermarkets, or village stores. Before businesses, schools, or NHS trusts get anywhere near commissioning, let alone opening, new premises (or altering existing ones), planning consent must be obtained. And councils' decisions about whether to grant it are dictated by overarching guidelines—some set by central government, others by themselves—that seek to balance a desire to provide infrastructure and promote economic growth with appropriate respect for our historic natural environment.

Compared to other council responsibilities—particularly highways, transport, and public health—town and country planning emerged relatively recently. Its three underlying principles are to ensure that:

- all development is supported by appropriate infrastructure—roads, traffic crossings, bus routes, leisure facilities, etc.;
- any environmental impact is sustainable; and
- development is steered towards land unlikely to be affected by factors like flooding.

For many years, a single Town and Country Planning Code governed all forms of development in England and Wales. It was established by nine principal Acts:

- Town and Country Planning Act 1947;
- Town and Country Planning Act 1968;
- four separate Acts passed in 1990;
- Planning and Compensation Act 1991;
- Planning and Compulsory Purchase Act 2004; and
- Planning Act 2008.

However, in recent years, there have been significant modifications to how the Code applies to the two countries. The Welsh Government gained significant devolved powers under the Government of Wales Act 2006, which places an onus on it to promote 'sustainable' development, while a contentious national framework introduced by the Liberal Democrat–Conservative Coalition in 2012 represented a major relaxation of previous restrictions.

Nevertheless, the planning process in both England and Wales remains divided into the following two levels:

1. *Forward planning*—the drawing up of strategic development plans by planning authorities (districts/boroughs and unitaries), with long-term strategies mapped out for each area to guide councils' day-to-day decisions.
2. *Development control*—day-to-day decisions on whether to approve individual applications to undertake material changes to existing land or buildings or build new developments.

The Communities Secretary's role in relation to planning is outlined in Table 15.1.

Table 15.1 Planning role of the Communities Secretary

Role	Responsibilities
Guidance	Publishes 'planning policy statements' (PPSs) telling planning authorities how to discharge their responsibilities. Overarching regional strategies used by Labour replaced by more localized planning under Coalition.
Setting ground rules	Draws up fixed rules about suitable development land.
Arbitration	Acts as final arbiter in disputes between individuals and councils, appointing independent inspectors to conduct inquiries to determine disputed applications.
Ruling in last resort	'Calls in' most controversial planning applications to give final rulings where inquiries fail to resolve issues.

15.1 Forward planning: from region to community and back again?

Between 1991 and 2008, there were several types of council development plan, the names of which varied according to which kind of authority drew them up. Under Labour, these were eventually replaced by a *regional* approach to development planning with the Planning and Compulsory Purchase Act 2004 beginning the process of simplifying the existing local patchwork, to speed up and harmonize forward planning. It gave eight (now-defunct) regional assemblies the power to take strategic decisions for swathes of the country by publishing *regional spatial strategies* (RSSs), which themselves were supplanted in 2010 when *regional development agencies* (RDAs) briefly took over the 'regional planning body' role and began publishing regional plans. As of March 2012, however, regional planning for most of the country formally ceased, following the Coalition's Localism Act 2011, and the stage was set for a new era of grassroots planning driven not by central government targets but community needs (and demands). In abolishing RSSs—which he dismissed as 'Soviet-style top-down planning targets'—and the unelected RDAs that had long been a bête noire of councillors, the then Communities Secretary Eric Pickles confirmed his intention to make councils' strategic plans less 'bureaucratic' and more 'bottom-up', in an echo of prime minister David Cameron's first-term 'Big Society' agenda.

To this end, from 2010 communities have been able to propose their own long-term **neighbourhood plans**. If approved by 51 per cent of locals in a referendum, these (in theory) have to be implemented by their councils in the same way as if they had been devised by councillors. Theoretically, neighbourhood plans allow small numbers of engaged citizens to determine for themselves where (and whether) they want new homes, shops, and offices built; what approved developments will look like; and which firms will build them. In the first year of the new policy, four waves of 'vanguard' council areas piloted it, including Exmoor in Devon and Milton Keynes. Inevitably, perhaps, it wasn't long before conflicts emerged between councillors' and citizens' planning priorities: in 2015, a row erupted after Milton Keynes Council approved a £70 million shopping-centre expansion which (according to objectors) openly flouted a then newly agreed neighbourhood plan.

Hot on the heels of neighbourhood plans came the 'community right to build' (see 12.1.5), launched in 2012. This entitles local citizens and other community groups to build their own amenities—shops, housing, community halls, playgrounds—where a demonstrable 'need for development' exists. Its virtue, theoretically, is that it circumvents the need for communities in desperate need of basic infrastructure, such as low-cost homes for key workers or school crossings, to follow the normal planning process—thereby fast tracking their applications (see 15.1.1). As with neighbourhood plans, however, development can only take place if the rest of the local electorate first approves it in a referendum and the council, too, gives it final approval. Money enabling community groups across England to build in this way was initially drawn from a fund administered by the Homes and Communities Agency (see 16.3), worth £175 million over three years, with separate arrangements applying in London.

The abrupt switch from regional to hyper-local planning under the Coalition was further underscored by its abandonment of Labour's centrally determined *national policy statements* (NPSs) and, with them, top-down 'housing quotas' and other targets that ministers had previously used to parachute developments into particular areas (see 16.3.2).

Abolishing RDAs and NPSs initially left a vacuum in terms of channelling rejuvenation funds to areas facing particular economic challenges, however. To answer concerns about this, Mr Pickles established **local enterprise partnerships (LEPs)**, which, like the groups responsible for drawing up neighbourhood plans, would be staunchly 'local' alliances of councils and businesses. In so doing, though, he left open the option for councils and business leaders to form regional alliances if these were justified or necessary. To facilitate this renewed emphasis on local (as opposed to regional) planning, the Coalition actually held on to some of Labour's innovations, to enable councils and, more particularly, community groups to have a bigger say in future development decisions. To this end, the principal planning strategies produced by individual councils remain **local development documents (LDDs)**—which today have arguably even more traction than under Labour, which gave councils little freedom to deviate from regionally set guidelines. Confusingly, some planning authorities prefer to use the simpler term 'local plan' for their LDDs (a throwback to how forward plans produced by districts/boroughs were designated under an even earlier system).

For all their sound and fury about the evils of 'top-down' planning, however, in practice Coalition ministers backtracked on initial promises to abandon it. Indeed, full-blooded regional planning is currently undergoing a steady revival, in relation to the growing autonomy of combined authorities—and, in time, could once more embrace not only major conurbations, like Greater Manchester, but large swathes of England, such as East Anglia, as they, too, are brought beneath the ambit of overarching 'combined' council structures (see 10.2.4). Regional planning also remains a feature of London's unique governmental framework: the capital, like the individual devolved nations, retains its own overarching spatial strategy. Moreover, as development pressures on land continue to intensify across Britain, recent years have seen the emergence of an additional aspect of regional planning: focusing not on the development of land, but of sea. As the UK is an island, an increasingly crucial resource, both for industry and energy generation, is its extensive coastal waters. A significant proportion of its gross domestic product (GDP) (see 7.1.5) has long derived from income generated from its exploitation of North Sea oil, particularly around Scotland, while that nation's long-term energy strategy under devolution involves developing a self-sufficient electricity supply based on the sustained expansion of both onshore and offshore wind farms. The first formal **marine plans** were ushered in by the Coalition in 2014, to set out priorities for sustainable future offshore development across eleven marine plan areas around England. Each area was charged with having a twenty-year plan in place by 2020, and reviewing it every three years. Overseen by a new quango, the *Marine Management Organization (MMO)*, the aims of marine plans are to:

- encourage local community involvement in offshore planning;
- make the most of growth and job opportunities;
- enable sustainable development with consideration of environmental factors;
- integrate marine planning with that taking place on land;
- save time and money for investors and developers by giving clear planning guidance;
- encourage shared use of busy offshore areas to benefit multiple industries; and
- encourage developments that consider wildlife and the natural environment.

Scotland's relatively higher dependency on the effective management of offshore resources led it to adopt marine planning earlier than the rest of the UK, in 2010. Since then, it has had a single *national marine plan*, in addition to regional plans for each of eleven Scottish marine regions, which are managed by *marine planning partnerships* and overseen by *Marine Scotland*: a directorate of the Scottish Government. In order to avoid potential conflict between Scottish and UK legislation in relation to marine development, the two governments signed a Joint Marine Planning Statement in 2009. Both the Welsh Government and a Northern Ireland Marine Taskforce began drawing up national marine plans in 2016.

15.1.1 The future of large-scale developments

It isn't only in relation to tensions between council planners and newly empowered, 'rights-asserting' citizens that contradictions have been exposed in the planning policies of recent Conservative-led governments. One of the Coalition's first apparent shifts in development policy under the Coalition came with its 2011 abolition of the Infrastructure Planning Commission Labour had introduced after the 2008 banking collapse to fast track major construction projects, including nuclear power stations and wind farms—potentially even on greenfield and greenbelt sites (see 15.3.2). It was not long, however, before the then new administration also stood accused of overriding the concerns of local decision makers by imposing major developments on them. A new National Planning Policy Framework announced by Coalition ministers in June 2011 introduced a 'presumption in favour of sustainable development'. Billed as a way of boosting economic output by fast tracking construction of new homes and business premises by removing obstructive 'red tape', this sparked immediate outcries from interest groups as varied as *The Daily Telegraph* (a long-time Conservative Party cheerleader) and the National Trust. To placate the environmental lobby, which raised the spectre of large tracts of English countryside being bulldozed, ministers emphasized the word 'sustainable'. However, critics argued that, however green they might be, any 'presumption' that major projects should be approved would severely blunt the ability of councils (let alone community groups) to obstruct developments judged commercially desirable. Examples of such projects include the upcoming London to Midlands high-speed rail link (dubbed 'HS2'), and hotly debated proposals for a third Heathrow Airport runway—approval for which was finally given (pending public consultation on a draft national policy statement) in October 2016.

More significantly, on the eve of her entry to Downing Street, Theresa May announced a shift back towards central government intervention to kick-start infrastructural investment—vowing to use Treasury-backed bonds to fast track large-scale projects, including major housebuilding programmes, in an effort to avert a potential 'post-Brexit' recession in the construction sector and boost the affordable housing stock (see 16.3.2). These proposals were a centrepiece of Chancellor Philip Hammond's November 2016 Autumn Statement.

15.2 Development control

Although long-term development plans impact significantly on British families and businesses, it is specific planning applications that typically arouse the strongest emotions. This is invariably reflected in the nature of press coverage about planning issues: while most people would struggle to remember details of their council's overall planning strategy, many will recall local rows about new sewage works, rubbish dumps, and high-rise tower-blocks.

The procedure used by councils to determine planning applications is termed 'development control', while the right to build on sites from scratch or make structural alterations to existing developments is known as **planning permission**. Minor building alterations require no permission, or only 'one-stop' decisions from councils to give consent, but most 'new-build' applications (however minor) require permission in two stages:

1. *Outline planning permission* (or consent 'in principle')—often used by major developers to 'test the water' with proposals they may not pursue

once they have investigated further to gauge their commercial and practical viability (e.g. proposed shopping malls). Plots of land are often sold to prospective developers with outline permission already in place. This lasts five years from the date granted, but if developers have not proceeded to the next stage within three, it lapses.

2. *Detailed planning permission*—applied for once outline permission is obtained and a developer decides to proceed. With major schemes, the outline planning process will usually have highlighted 'gaps' in detail the developer needs to fill—for example, detailed proposals for out-of-town retail parks need to address concerns about transport, access, and environmental impact. They must also specify the exact locations, dimensions, and make-up of proposed developments, including how many shops and parking spaces they will comprise. Like outline permission, detailed consent lapses if not acted on within five years.

When considering planning permission, authorities have three options:

- *unconditional consent*—approving the application with no alterations;
- *conditional consent*—approving it subject to provisos (for example better site access or improved traffic crossings), in which event developers will often be given outline permission with attached conditions and expected to satisfy these before gaining detailed consent; or
- *refusal* (outright rejection).

Before councils can decide whether to grant a proposed development permission, they are expected to follow a detailed process designed to give every 'interested party' (those most directly affected by its approval) a chance to air their views. This procedure is detailed in Table 15.2.

15.2.1 Small-scale planning applications—and changes of use

While a tight rein is kept on more ambitious plans because of their potential to affect large numbers of people, formal permission is not needed for many minor alterations to land or buildings. Under the Town and Country Planning (Use Classes) Orders 1987 and 1995, land and property are split into 'classes', and material changes of use 'within the same class' normally needs no consent. Neither will certain changes between 'related' classes, provided they do not entail major building work.

For example, a greengrocer's shop may be changed to a newsagent's with no need for permission, because both are class A1 business premises and therefore considered sufficiently similar. Restaurants, meanwhile, can be changed into shops without consent, because both are within the same overall 'class order' (the former A3 and the latter A1). The same is not always true in reverse,

Table 15.2 Stages of the development control application process

Stage	Process
Completing an application	Official forms obtained from planning authority (district/borough, unitary, or metropolitan district/London borough).
Entering on the register	Application appears in formal register of applicants, is published on councils' websites, and immediate neighbours notified. Parish/town/community councils fully consulted.
Advertising application	Major applications advertised in local press so others who 'may be affected' can comment.
Public consultation and exhibition stage (major applications only)	Public exhibitions organized for major developments, often involving detailed plans/models, at council offices or local libraries.
Subcommittee, committee, and full council decisions	Detailed reports on plans drawn up by officers, with recommendations to reject or approve (with or without conditions), to be presented to councillors. Routine/small-scale applications (e.g. domestic extensions) normally determined at subcommittee/committee level, based on published regulations. Major applications affecting two or more wards, or likely to incur 'significant' cost, treated as key decisions (see 12.3.4), and determined by both cabinet and full council.
Appealing	If application refused, applicant has six months to appeal to Communities Secretary. Each stage of application must be determined within two months (unless granted extension). If not, applicant may apply for central government ruling on 'non-determination' grounds.
'Calling in'	Communities Secretary may 'call in' controversial applications for final decision—normally when bid raises 'unusual issues' or ones of national/regional importance, or arouses 'more than local opposition', or it becomes 'unreasonable' for council to adjudicate alone.

however: changing a shop into a restaurant may also involve making further applications, including obtaining a liquor licence. Table 15A, to be found on the **Online Resource Centre** that accompanies this book, outlines changes currently allowed without formal permission.

In addition to permitted changes of commercial use, the 1995 Order allows home extensions to proceed without planning consent—provided they comply with specified conditions. Councils have discretion, however, to pass 'Article 4 directions' removing some of these permitted rights—particularly if extensions will negatively affect the view or quality of light of a neighbouring property.

Planning consent is not usually required to lop or fell a tree—provided it is not subject to a tree preservation order (TPO) or in a conservation area. If the former is violated, the council may prosecute.

Planning applications are *always* required for material changes of use involving amusement centres, theatres, scrapyards, petrol filling stations, car showrooms, taxi firms, car hire businesses, and youth hostels—all of which are categorized as *sui generis* (in a class of its own).

15.2.2 Planning appeals and inquiries

It is possible for either unsuccessful applicants or their executors to appeal to the Planning Inspectorate over councils' rejection of applications—but only within six months of the dates on decision letters. If permissions are refused, or only conditional consent granted, applicants may lodge free appeals. There is one inspectorate each for England and Wales.

Appeals are decided in one of three ways:

- by means of a planning inspector's consideration of written representations by both parties, alongside a brief site visit;
- by formal hearing, with both parties present; or
- after a full **planning inquiry**—by far the lengthiest and most costly option.

Four out of five appeals are determined by the 'written method', 16 per cent by hearings, and 4 per cent after inquiries. Although third-party objectors have no right of appeal against successful applications, they may mount legal challenges—sometimes resulting in inquiries (or even court cases). For example, plans to build nine wind turbines in west Devon, approved after an initial inquiry in 2006, were later subjected to a second after an alliance of local residents calling itself the 'Den Brook Judicial Review Group' persuaded the Secretary of State to overturn the decision owing to fears about noise pollution.

In Scotland, planning appeals are made to the Scottish Government's Planning and Environmental Appeals Division, while in Northern Ireland they are the responsibility of a Planning Appeals Commission.

The most high-profile planning inquiries are invariably those concerning applications that provoke strong opposition. Stansted Airport was the subject of two inquiries related to the expansion plans of its owner, the British Airports Authority (BAA)—forcibly abandoned after the High Court upheld a Competition Commission ruling in February 2012 that BAA must sell Stansted. The company's plans for a fifth terminal at Heathrow—finally realized in 2008—were subject to an inquiry lasting nearly four years, starting in May 1995.

Even after an inquiry, the Secretary of State occasionally intervenes with final rulings, based on inspectors' recommendations. This was the case in the decade-long debacle over Brighton and Hove Albion Football Club's ultimately successful application to build a new 22,000-seater stadium near the village of Falmer, East Sussex, which prompted two inquiries.

The only way in which the Secretary of State's 'final decision' in these exceptional cases may be challenged is by judicial review in the High Court, based on a point of law. Both appellant and council may apply to the inspector for the other side to pay its costs should the judgment favour them. In the Brighton case, then Secretary of State John Prescott's decision to back the proposal in October 2005 led to a pledge by its main opponents—Lewes District Council, Falmer Parish Council, and the South Downs Joint Committee—to challenge him. But after his successor, Hazel Blears, reaffirmed his verdict in July 2007, they reluctantly dropped their resistance.

The procedure surrounding planning inquiries is outlined in table 15B to be found on the **Online Resource Centre**.

Inquiries can be a fertile source of stories, often providing high drama during hearings and numerous follow-up angles. If reporters attend evidence sessions and register as interested parties, they should automatically receive copies of inspectors' full reports when they are published—ensuring they are kept abreast of final decisions.

15.3 Other issues affecting major developments

Although notionally rigorous, the convoluted consultation procedure surrounding planning applications has often been dismissed as a paper exercise. Despite its supposed transparency, councils (and developers acting under their instructions) are frequently criticized for doing too little to publicize such consultations—nailing poorly photocopied notices to trees and lamp posts, rather than proactively leafleting homes. The planning process was memorably lampooned in the Douglas Adams' book *The Hitchhiker's Guide to the Galaxy*, in which the hero, Arthur Dent, awoke to find a bulldozer demolishing his house to make way for a bypass, about which he had only found out by taking a torch into a disused toilet bearing a sign with the legend: 'Beware of the Leopard!'

In real life, if a proposed development is lawful, the odds are stacked in favour of major projects—especially where they are likely to generate jobs and other economic benefits.

15.3.1 Planning contribution/gain

Developers have increasingly sought to persuade councils to look kindly on their applications by offering 'sweeteners', such as additional infrastructure they would otherwise struggle to afford. For example, a company seeking permission to build a new luxury apartment complex might offer to build social housing elsewhere at a reduced price, to incentivize councillors to back its main project. This offer of a 'benefit in kind' is known variously as **planning contribution** or **planning gain**. Gain is also intended to avoid major new developments placing unnecessary strain on existing infrastructure, by ensuring that developers make the changes necessary to accommodate them.

Although it had operated informally for some years beforehand, planning gain was legally recognized only in the early 1990s. Until then, it had been the convention for developers to provide only infrastructure—roads, crossings, and community amenities—*within* the precincts of their developments. All external roads, access points, traffic crossings, etc., tended to be financed by councils. Since 1991, it has become commonplace for developers to provide both 'on-site' *and* 'off-site' gain to enable proposed developments to function properly—for example, giving people access to the site and/or transporting them there. Although this saves councils money and 'penalizes' developers, the quid pro quo is that applicants can use the incentive of off-site planning gain as a 'carrot' to wave before planners. In this sense, planning contribution is a 'gain' for both developer and council.

In England and Wales, planning gain was formalized by the 1990 and 1991 Acts, in the guise of 'section 106 agreements'. The Scottish equivalent is the 'section 75 agreement'. These rules specify that, having already granted outline permission, councils can subsequently require developers to sign legally binding contracts obliging them to provide community infrastructure, avoid damaging existing facilities, or even transfer ownership of development land to the authority or another body for 'safe keeping'. Examples might include handing over areas of woodland to a council, backed by a future maintenance budget; being required to plant a specified number of trees and/or reserve some land for amenity purposes; or demanding that the developer builds a given number of social homes, together with the necessary infrastructure.

Though developers cannot be *forced* to sign such agreements, in practice they often happily do so—especially in relation to controversial developments otherwise likely to become the subject of protracted legal challenges by disgruntled locals. In such contexts, the deals arguably offer the developer as much protection as the planning authority.

Planning gain has undeniably helped to finance many worthwhile projects. Examples have included the £2.5 million invested by London's Canary Wharf (a privately owned estate) in the Tower Hamlets Further and Higher Education Trust: a grant-giving body designed to provide educational opportunities for people from deprived backgrounds. Indeed, ministers have looked for even more imaginative ways of helping councils profit from commercial development. Towards the end of the most recent Labour tenure, various legal incentives were introduced to boost the rates of affordable house-building, while the succeeding Conservative-led governments have introduced various sweeteners to promote hydraulic fracturing, or 'fracking', as a source of energy efficiency and economic growth (see 11.2.5.1).

15.3.2 Greenfield versus brownfield sites—and the decline of the greenbelt

An enduring conflict facing councils is their struggle to balance the need for certain developments—homes, schools, hospitals, etc.—with their legal and ethical obligations to protect the environment. At a basic level, they must take daily decisions about whether to approve applications to build on **greenfield sites**—locations that have either never been developed or which have remained 'fallow' for long periods. Obvious examples of greenfield land include agricultural fields, parks, and public gardens. The alternative is to build on **brownfield sites**: plots of land (normally in town centres or suburbs) which were *previously* developed. These might include abandoned office blocks or car parks, or derelict scraps of wasteland.

Between the 1960s and 1980s, successive governments liberalized planning laws, making it easier for developers to build on 'out-of-town' or 'edge-of-town' greenfield sites, to ease pressure on tightly developed town centres—many of which had grown up in unplanned, organic ways ill-suited to coping with the rapid population (and traffic) growth of the late twentieth century. By the mid-1990s, however, a backlash had begun against such developments, with town centre businesses complaining of losing custom to out-of-town superstores, and growing social and infrastructural problems afflicting housing estates in peripheral areas—many the preserve of the poor and unemployed.

In its first few years in office, Tony Blair's government sought to redress the balance, introducing guidelines to encourage councils to lure developers into town centres. Its stated aim was twofold: to regenerate eyesore urban sites, while providing homes and amenities in the hearts of communities (integrating previously marginalized groups and helping them to obtain work or training).

But times (and government priorities) changed. Soaring house prices in the 1990s and 'Noughties' boom years saw many British people—including modestly paid 'key workers', such as nurses and teachers—unable to climb onto even the lowest rung of the property ladder. The limited space offered by brownfield sites for development on the scale necessary to tackle the national shortage of affordable homes led to sweeping quotas being imposed on many regions (and councils). This trend saw more developments targeted at rural areas, including the **greenbelt**: 'unspoilt' land formally preserved around towns and cities, to prevent urban sprawl and protect wildlife.

Introduced in 1935 by the then Greater London Regional Planning Committee, the notion of a ring of land indefinitely protected from urbanization quickly became fashionable in smaller centres. It was eventually formalized by central government: first, in the Town and Country Planning Act 1947, and then, Planning Policy Guidance Note 2 (PPG2, introduced in 1995). By 1993, around 13 per cent of the English countryside was designated greenbelt, covering 14 discrete areas.

Planning Policy Guidance Note 2 specifies that greenbelts should:

- check the unrestricted sprawl of large built-up areas;
- prevent neighbouring towns merging;
- assist in safeguarding countryside from encroachment;
- preserve the setting and special character of historic towns; and
- assist in urban regeneration, by 'recycling' derelict and other urban land.

Once an area has been designated greenbelt, that designation is expected to safeguard:

- opportunities for access to open countryside for the urban population;
- opportunities for outdoor sport or recreation near urban areas;
- attractive landscapes and enhanced landscape near people's homes;
- the improvement of damaged or derelict land around towns;
- secure nature conservation areas; and
- land in agricultural, forestry, and related uses.

For many years, greenbelts were treated as sacrosanct, but under pressure to meet Labour's targets councils increasingly compromised their long-held resistance to expansion into these zones. Between 1996 and 2010, developers proposing to build new supermarkets on the outskirts of towns, or within easy reach of them, were forced first to satisfy both 'needs tests' and 'impact tests'. The former required them to prove that new stores were 'needed' in these locations, given lack of choice for consumers elsewhere, while the latter was meant to limit negative impact on trade in nearby town centres. Towards the end of Gordon Brown's premiership, however, a new planning policy statement was issued, scrapping the needs test—a move that, according to the Association of Convenience Stores, had led to a notable rise in the number of out-of-town stores when adopted in Scotland. Though the Tories opposed this relaxation while in Opposition, once in power, the Coalition declined to reintroduce the needs test.

Greenbelts are not the only designation used to protect land from development. Some rural and coastal areas are regarded as so exceptional that they qualify for designation under the National Parks and Access to the Countryside Act 1949 as:

- an **area of outstanding natural beauty (AONB)**—a locality deserving special protection to conserve and enhance its natural beauty; meet the public's need for quiet enjoyment of the countryside; and protect the interests of those living and working there;
- a **national park**—an area with additional statutory protection against development, commercial exploitation, and habitation; or

- a **site of special scientific interest (SSSI)**—an area judged to have special or unique natural features, further subdivided into *biological SSSIs* (those with rare or unusual flora or fauna) and *geological SSSIs* (those of particular physiographic interest).

English AONBs, national parks, and SSSIs are today designated by a quango called **Natural England**. This role is fulfilled by *Natural Resources Wales*, Scottish Natural Heritage, and an overarching Northern Ireland Environment Agency (NIEA) in the devolved nations. Each body is expected to 'conserve, protect, and manage the natural environment for the benefit of current and future generations' and promote:

- a healthy natural environment;
- enjoyment of the natural environment;
- sustainable use of the natural environment; and
- a secure environmental future.

Despite its ecological remit, Natural England has been prepared to challenge some 'sacred cows' since its inception in October 2006. In 2007, the then chairman, Sir Martin Doughty, used his speech marking its first anniversary to argue that 'the sanctity of greenbelt land should be questioned' in light of perceived need to find space for 3 million more homes by 2020.

There are currently thirty-eight English and Welsh AONBs: thirty-three wholly in England, four entirely in Wales, and one straddling the border. Eight exist in Northern Ireland. The smallest is the Isles of Scilly (designated in 1976), which is just 16 km^2, and the largest, the Cotswolds (covering 2,038 km^2). Although they notionally qualify for greater protection than mere greenbelts, in practice councils are not required to preserve AONBs and have little power to do so, other than by applying standard planning controls more rigorously.

Perhaps because of this, significant development has continued on or alongside AONBs, prompting vociferous protests from countryside pressure groups such as the Campaign to Protect Rural England (CPRE). In 2006, it highlighted the plight of Dorset AONB, threatened by major road plans, and the Kent Downs, which faced the encroachment of thousands of new homes and offices proposed by Imperial College, London. Brighton's stadium debacle (see 15.2.2), meanwhile, was particularly sensitive because of the scheme's proximity to the Sussex Downs AONB (now a national park).

National parks are a higher form of designation afforded greater statutory protection than AONBs. Protected by their own national park authorities, there are fifteen in total: ten in England, three in Wales, and two in Scotland, where AONBs do not exist (the nearest equivalent being national scenic areas, or NSAs). The existing national parks are listed in Table 15.3.

Table 15.3 National parks

National park	Year established
Peak District	1951
Lake District	1951
Snowdonia (Welsh: *Eryri*)	1951
Dartmoor	1951
Pembrokeshire Coast (Welsh: *Arfordir Penfro*)	1952
North York Moors	1952
Yorkshire Dales	1954
Exmoor	1954
Northumberland	1956
Brecon Beacons (Welsh: *Bannau Brycheiniog*)	1957
The Broads	1988
Loch Lomond and the Trossachs	2002
Cairngorms	2003
New Forest	2005
South Downs	2008

In addition to AONBs, national parks, SSSIs, and greenbelts, successive governments have tried to protect Britain's ancient woodlands from ever-increasing development demands. The quango responsible for preserving woods for public benefit is the Forestry Commission, headed by a chairman and ten regional commissioners. The freedom that people have long enjoyed to ramble through forests unimpeded is so prized that woe betide any government that interferes with it. The Coalition found this out to its cost when its short-lived Environment Secretary, Caroline Spelman, proposed privatizing 258,000 hectares of woodland to promote a new 'mixed model' of ownership between public, private, charitable, and community sectors. Visions of 'no entry' signs and ticket booths springing up along public footpaths and bridleways achieved the seemingly impossible by uniting in opposition everyone from the Labour Party to *The Daily Telegraph* and moneyed middle-class activists in 'true blue' Tory heartlands. By February 2011, the policy had been dropped—forcing a humiliated Ms Spelman to concede she had 'got this one wrong'.

15.3.3 Land banks and the great supermarket stranglehold

A planning issue that has come to growing prominence in the context of wider controversy over out-of-town developments is the trend for some big developers to accumulate 'land banks'. This term refers to the practice of buying up pockets of land—and often securing outline planning permission to develop them—and then 'sitting' on them for long periods without developing them. Land banks are viewed as unscrupulous by many: although developers argue that they are merely guaranteeing themselves 'first refusal' to build on sites, the habit of 'land-banking' is seen as anti-competitive behaviour, because it stops others from doing so. In some cases, land banks have proved even more controversial, with developers or their clients buying up land only to sell it on to third parties—writing clauses into the sales agreements preventing it from being developed by rival companies.

Of all alleged 'land-bankers', the most notorious has been supermarket giant Tesco. Perceived threats to the historic town-centre marketplace of St Albans posed by a dormant land bank purchased by the company prompted the formation of a media-savvy 'St Albans Stop Tesco Group', and captured national headlines in 2007.

15.3.4 Traveller and gypsy sites

During the 1990s, local newspapers were full of disputes between traveller and gypsy communities looking for land on which to camp—often temporarily, but sometimes for longer periods—and sedentary households concerned about mess, noise, and damage to their own property prices caused by neighbouring encampments. Labour responded by introducing clear rules requiring councils to provide adequate land for camps. Over time, they received £150 million in grants to facilitate the construction of designated traveller sites.

In May 2010, the Coalition scrapped the £30 million set aside by Labour for new sites that year, before announcing a major revision of existing rules for establishing encampments. However, in describing most travellers as 'law-abiding', Mr Pickles announced that councils would be allowed to use some money from the New Homes Bonus scheme introduced to encourage affordable house-building to establish additional authorized traveller sites in suitable locations.

Otherwise, the Coalition's approach to accommodating travellers was ill-defined—with councils required only to 'make their own assessment' of need in their areas, to plan for necessary sites 'over a reasonable timescale', while protecting greenbelt from 'inappropriate development'. While councils were urged to promote 'private traveller site provision', wherever possible—encouraging travelling communities to buy their own land, instead of 'squatting' on other people's—ministers increased their powers to block or remove 'unauthorized' encampments. A vivid illustration of this no-nonsense approach to camps was Basildon Council's successful eviction of a 1,000-strong commune from Dale Farm, which made international headlines in late 2011/early 2012. Although the travellers had purchased the six-acre plot on which they were camped, it was located within a greenbelt, and they had built up their settlement extensively without obtaining prior planning permission (despite having secured consent for a camp comprising thirty-four legal pitches at neighbouring Oak Lane). After a decade-long legal battle, culminating in several High Court hearings and interventions by both the United Nations and Council of Europe in defence of the travellers' human rights, the council won its case, and the community was forcibly removed amid scenes of violence on both sides.

15.3.5 From wind farms to 'fracking': the rise of middle-class planning protests

Back in the 1990s, pressure for development in rural areas led to mounting opposition among previously passive elements of the middle classes, with major protests against the building of new roads, in particular. Recently, middle-class protestors have been on the march once again—opposing everything from the proposed North–South high-speed rail link to onshore wind farms (for which government subsidies have now largely ended, other than in exceptional locations such as the Scottish islands).

The bête noire of the moment for Britain's rural classes, however, is the Conservative-approved practice of 'fracking'. This involves mining companies injecting high-pressure liquid into rocks through drill-holes in pursuit of shale gas: a fuel recently embraced by HM Treasury as a future source of cheap energy to boost the country's self-sufficiency and temper the UK's increasing reliance on imported gas from volatile overseas markets (see 7.5.1.2). Concerns about the safety of shale gas exploration were first aired in Britain after a November 2011 study confirmed that two earth tremors recorded earlier that year in Lancashire were likely to have been caused by the drilling activity of fracking company Cuadrilla. Opposition to fracking later intensified, with e-petitions and social media campaigns drawing together local communities, international organizations such as 38 Degrees and Avaaz, and single-issue protest groups like the combatively named 'Frack Off'.

In terms of visible protest, things first came to a head when, in July 2013, an unlikely mix of colourfully dressed environmental campaigners and landed locals set up camp to stop Cuadrilla carrying out exploratory drilling operations in the deeply conservative village of Balcombe, West Sussex. The protest became a media circus, but from a public affairs perspective it was interesting in several respects—not least because permission for Cuadrilla to commence its operation was given by Balcombe Parish Council (one of whose members, Simon Greenwood, managed Balcombe Estate, where it was due to take place).

Despite Cuadrilla's retreat from Balcombe, fracking continues to be a live issue. The many recent relaxations ministers have introduced to liberalize planning law include various incentives to persuade councils to look favourably on applications for shale gas exploration. Committing Britain to 'going all out for shale', in January 2014 Mr Cameron told councils that they could keep 100 per cent of their Uniform Business Rate (UBR) receipts (see 11.2.5) from companies involved in fracking (compared to the 50 per cent limit in place up to that point). He had already declared that mining prospectors must pay local communities £100,000 ahead of any test-drilling and hand over a further 1 per cent of any revenues they generated on finding shale gas. Critics immediately retorted that such sweeteners placed austerity-hit councils in invidious positions: leaving them duty-bound to act as responsible planning authorities, but tantalizing them with handouts that they could ill afford to turn down. Undeterred, Mr Cameron went even further in championing the fracking cause in his 2014 Queen's Speech—confirming plans to change the laws on trespass to allow firms to drill beneath private land, including people's homes, without first seeking planning permission. This came to pass under the Infrastructure Act 2015, with a subsequent statutory instrument permitting fracking companies to encroach into national parks and SSSIs, provided they are drilling from outside their boundaries and at a depth of at least 1,200 metres underground. Ministers had already abolished regulations requiring prospectors to tell local residents individually of impending fracking activity. On the day of Mr Cameron's original announcement, Greenpeace campaigners in hard hats and high-visibility jackets sealed off his Oxfordshire cottage with security fencing—and planted a sign proclaiming, 'We apologize for any inconvenience we may cause while we frack under your home.'

Since then, the combined ministerial and big-business push for shale gas has continued unabated, with individual energy firms such as Ineos offering to pay affected homeowners up to 6 per cent of the proceeds from successful drilling operations and Theresa May's government launching a consultation in August 2016 on the creation of a £1 billion Shale Wealth Fund to funnel up to one-tenth of tax revenues generated by fracking firms back into local communities over an initial twenty-five-year period. Critics, including the Green Party, have, however, condemned such moves as 'bribery'—an accusation fuelled by a May 2014 investigation in *The Independent*, which reported that some planning authorities had vested interests in fracking going ahead, because their pension funds had invested millions of pounds in companies involved in the 'dash for shale gas'. Lincolnshire County Council alone had £1.9 million invested in Total, the first major oil firm to get involved in UK fracking, while West Sussex County Council (the authority that oversees Balcombe) had indirect holdings in Cuadrilla.

15.3.6 Compulsory purchase orders (CPOs) and planning blight

Sometimes, plans are approved for such mammoth developments—or ones with such a potentially huge impact on surrounding environments—that it is necessary for land or buildings that might otherwise stand in their way to be demolished before work proceeds. Examples of such projects include airport runways, roads, canals (waterways), or harbours. In such cases, councils sometimes seek to 'force' homeowners and businesses to move, so that their premises can be bulldozed. A **compulsory purchase order (CPO)** must therefore be served.

The CPO is not the only means by which councils can incur compensation claims from property owners because of planning decisions. Should a property's value drop because of a controversial application, it might be regarded as 'blighted'. In such cases, owners can effectively force councils to buy their properties—a 'CPO in reverse'.

15.4 Other quirks of the planning system

Authorities may decline to consider planning applications on grounds that the Secretary of State has refused a 'similar' one, on appeal, within the preceding two years. In addition, there are various ways of *enforcing* planning controls, as well as monitoring to ensure that developments granted are lawful, as listed in table 15C to be found on the **Online Resource Centre**.

15.4.1 Building regulations

Even when formal permission is not required for 'new builds' or to adapt existing structures, **building permission** (or compliance with **building regulations**) invariably will be. The reason for such regulations is to ensure that buildings are structurally sound. An inspector (normally from the council) will visit the property during work to ensure that it meets specified safety standards.

Other than in inner London (which has its own system), the standard of regulations is the same across England. It derives from the Public Health Act 1961—which stopped councils making their own building by-laws, returning this power to ministers—and the Health and Safety at Work Act 1974. The process for applying is as follows:

- plans for the building work must be submitted to the council; and
- if they comply with basic regulations and are not defective, prima facie they must be approved—but if not, they must be rejected.

Building regulation cases are usually overseen by trained inspectors, rather than councillors, because of their technical complexity. Councils can order buildings without consent to be demolished or remedial work to be undertaken by owners. Alternatively, they can carry out the work themselves—at the owners' cost.

15.4.2 Listed buildings and conservation areas

Although buildings of historic or architectural interest are not immune to demolition if they fall into severe disrepair, their owners can obtain substantial help with their upkeep by having them 'listed'.

Buildings are listed in England on the advice of **Historic England** (formerly English Heritage), a quango funded by the Department for Culture, Media, and Sport (DCMS). Listing is usually approved for buildings with:

- 'architectural interest'—for example the Grade II* Morecambe Bay Hotel in Lancashire, regarded as a classic example of Art Deco;
- 'historical interest'—reflective of a particular period or movement;
- links to nationally important people or events—for example Charleston, the Grade II listed country home of the Bloomsbury Set, near Lewes, East Sussex; or
- 'group value' as an architectural or historical unit, or a fine example of planning—for example the Regency Brunswick Square in Hove.

There are three 'grades' of **listed building**:

- *Grade I*—buildings judged 'exceptional';
- *Grade II**—fractionally lower down the pecking order than Grade I, these include the Shakespeare Memorial Theatre in Stratford-upon-Avon; and
- *Grade II*—buildings judged 'particularly important'.

Decisions to list buildings must be approved by the Culture Secretary under the Listed Buildings Act 1990. Although there was long reluctance to list post-war buildings, in 1988 a rolling 'thirty-year rule' was introduced, stipulating that any qualifying structure that is at least three decades old can be listed.

When buildings are listed, the lists themselves must be published and notified to councils, their owners, and occupiers. Once listing is confirmed, any alteration or addition to a building entails the owner obtaining listed building consent as well as other permissions. New constraints will include limitations on the types of material that they may use—and obligations to keep the property in a good and characteristic state of repair. Unauthorized work on listed buildings may see councils issue enforcement notices, requiring the work to be reversed.

If councils wish to protect 'non-listed' buildings threatened with demolition or serious alteration, they may serve building protection notices—a process referred to as 'spot-listing'. This covers the building for six months, during which time the Culture Secretary must decide whether to list it formally.

One further way of protecting groups of buildings—or whole areas of a village or town deemed of 'special architectural or historic interest'—is to designate **conservation areas**. Introduced by the Civic Amenities Act 1967, these offer particular protection for buildings from unsympathetic or inappropriate cosmetic alterations. Special attention is paid to conservation areas whenever planning applications arise within them. 'Permitted development rights', allowing changes of use of buildings without the need for planning permission, do not apply to those in conservation areas. Planners can also make 'Article 4 directives' to increase their control over the insertion of replacement doors and windows.

Councils must advertise in local papers all applications in conservation areas that might affect their 'character or appearance'—giving the public twenty-one days to object. It is a criminal offence to lop or fell trees in conservation areas.

In the devolved nations, listing is the preserve of three equivalent quangos: Historic Environment Scotland, Cadw (a Welsh word meaning 'to protect'), and the NIEA.

Topical feature idea

The chairwoman of a local green campaign group has written a letter to your newspaper to alert fellow readers to a consultation document the district council has just posted on its website in relation to its forthcoming draft local plan. In it, the council is proposing to proactively invite hydraulic fracturing ('fracking') companies to carry out test-drilling across the local authority area—including, potentially, under people's homes—with a view to generating increased revenues from uniform business rate retention and profit shares in successful operations over the next fifteen to twenty years. Your news editor has asked you to write a splash for tomorrow morning's edition based on the information in this letter, which was brought to his attention by the letters editor. Who should you contact for details and comments on this story—and what potential angles do you most need to explore?

Current issues

- **The ongoing 'shale rush'** Mrs May's government is consulting on the introduction of a £1bn Shale Wealth Fund, first mooted by ex-Chancellor Mr Osborne, to offer communities affected by fracking up to 10 per cent of tax revenues raised by drilling companies over twenty-five years.
- **The return of centralized and regionalized planning policy?** Conservative prime minister Theresa May has mooted introducing Treasury-backed bonds to encourage large-scale infrastructure projects, while regional strategic planning is returning under the aegis of emerging combined authorities.
- **A new era of marine planning** With pressure on land resources more intense than ever, each UK nation has launched a mixture of national and regional 'marine plans' paving the way for sustainable development of offshore sites around the coast.

Key points

1. Planning policy is implemented in two ways: long-term forward planning, involving all types of council; and development control, focusing on whether individual applications should be approved.
2. Planning authorities (districts or boroughs, unitaries, metropolitan districts, and London boroughs) may make one of three decisions when considering applications: approval with conditions, approval without conditions, or refusal.
3. Larger-scale applications, such as major housing or retail developments, require two levels of consent: outline permission and detailed permission.
4. Developers may offer 'sweeteners' to persuade councils to approve applications—including improvements to local infrastructure or 'off-site' benefits, such as schools and playgrounds. This is known as 'planning contribution/gain'.
5. Buildings of historical or architectural interest are often 'listed' to give them greater protection. Developing them entails obtaining both planning permission and listed building consent.

→ Further reading

Cullingworth, B., Nadin, V., Hart, T., Navoudi, S., Pendlebury, J., Vigar, G., Webb, D., and Townshend, T. (2014) *Town and Country Planning in the UK*, 15th edn, Abingdon: Routledge. **Indispensable fifteenth edition of classic 'bible' of planning law from the origins of local government to the present day.**

Dillon, D. and Fanning, B. (2012) *Lessons for the Big Society: Planning, Regeneration, and the Politics of Community Participation*, Kindle edn, Farnham: Ashgate. **Intriguing case study of planning and regeneration in the London Borough of Haringey as a litmus test for Coalition neighbourhood plans.**

Gallent, N. and Robinson, S. (2013) *Neighbourhood Planning: Communities, Networks, and Governance*, Bristol: Policy Press. **Illuminating and timely evaluation of the new trend towards 'bottom-up' planning policy introduced by the Coalition's neighbourhood plans.**

Ricketts, S. (2012) *Localism and Planning*, Haywards Heath: Bloomsbury Professional. **Indispensible overview and assessment of recent moves towards localizing town and country planning.**

@ Online Resource Centre

www.oxfordtextbooks.co.uk/orc/Morrison5e/

Visit the Online Resource Centre that accompanies this book for web links and regular updates.

16

Housing

Councils have traditionally been responsible for the following aspects of housing policy:

- building and maintaining housing stock;
- liaising with charities, including housing associations and private companies to bring low-cost or social housing to their local rented sector and affordable homes to the private market;
- granting planning permission for public, private, and voluntary housing schemes in locations best suited to meet demand;
- providing night shelters, temporary accommodation, and longer-term support for homeless people; and
- assessing claims for Housing Benefit or Local Housing Allowance (LHA) and administering them locally.

Until the mid-1980s, councils played a direct role in providing social housing for the poor and unemployed, by building flats and houses for rent at subsidized rates. But during Margaret Thatcher's premiership the council housing stock steadily diminished, as long-term tenants were given the right to buy their homes at discounted prices and councils' ability to build more to replace them was curbed in favour of an expanded role for the voluntary and private sectors.

According to the National Office for Statistics (ONS), around 2.2 million of the UK's 28.1 million homes remained in council ownership nationwide (7.7 per cent of the country's overall housing stock). Just under 2.8 million (one in ten) are owned by **housing associations (HAs)**: not-for-profit organizations that have gradually taken over the management of most or all social housing in many areas (see 16.1). What this means in human terms is that around 8 per cent of today's Britons live in council homes—a world away from the picture in 1980, as the Thatcher government contemplated its home-owning revolution, when more than four out of ten households rented direct from their local authorities.

In stark contrast, 17.7 million dwellings are now owner-occupied (63 per cent of the total) and 4.6 million (16 per cent) rented from private-sector landlords. This represents an 8 per cent rise in home ownership since 1980, with the private rented market (11 per cent in that year) seeing little change, compared to the drastically reduced size of the council housing sector.

Today's housing market is, then, a patchwork—and this chapter will start by explaining how this patchwork came about. To begin with some context, though, perhaps the biggest single political concern around housing today is one of capacity: in some areas of the UK (notably London and the south-east) there are now such shortages of 'affordable' homes to buy that it has become common for parties of all persuasions to speak of a 'housing crisis'. At the same time, in many areas the number of surviving 'council homes', in the strict sense of the term, is piecemeal to non-existent. Moreover, with much of the rented accommodation currently available to low-income tenants now managed and/or owned by private letting agencies, professional and semi-professional landlords, and a new generation of amateur 'buy-to-let' property developers, the many people forced to remain tenants are at the mercy of a distorted, largely unregulated 'sellers' market', in which unscrupulous landlords can get away with hiking rents well beyond a level with which wages can keep pace. It is the broader task of this chapter to unpick some of these highly sensitive and newsworthy issues.

16.1 From prefab to new town: a potted history of social housing

Providing fit and proper public housing has been one of the prime purposes of local government since embryonic councils first emerged (see 10.1). Eliminating overcrowded and poorly constructed housing—and introducing proper sanitation and sewerage systems to improve hygiene—was a vital part of the fight against diseases like cholera, dysentery, and typhoid fever undertaken by early public health authorities.

16.1.1 Public housing and the prefab

During the interwar years, there was a period of major public housing activity. A campaign dubbed 'Homes Fit for Heroes' arose out of concern about the poor physical health of many young servicemen from lowly backgrounds recruited to bolster the troops and, under the Housing Act 1919, a start was made on clearing the worst slums. Planned estates were constructed in their place, largely in existing urban areas. But it was not until after the Second World War that a proper house-building boom began, as the struggle to provide shelter for people rendered homeless by Hitler's bombing campaigns became a national emergency.

Large areas of wasteland created by the bombings of Britain's major cities offered ample scope for extensive housing projects, and soon cheap, functional homes for those returning from the battlefront and the many families left dispossessed by air raids were built.

Displaced families needed housing at a time when materials were in short supply, so 'prefabs' were developed: literally, prefabricated, single-storey compact houses, made not out of conventional bricks and mortar, but out of anything from shipping containers to surplus aluminium aircraft parts. Prefabs could be manufactured off-site and erected quickly. Their lifespan was intended to be limited, but they fared so well that they survived into the 1970s in many areas.

Prefabs were not the only weapon in the post-war Labour government's bid to provide new housing. In October 1945, Lord Reith was appointed chairman of a 'new town housing committee' charged with devising a workable solution to the growing problem of city overspill. His suggested solution was to draw inspiration from the British New Town movement of Victorian philanthropist Ebenezer Howard, who had created the Hertfordshire garden cities of Letchworth and Welwyn: government-backed development corporations would acquire land for construction within 'designated areas'. The resulting New Town Act 1946 designated Stevenage (again in Hertfordshire) as Britain's first official 'new town' and within a decade there were ten more.

16.1.2 The rise of high-rise living

The 1950s 'baby boom' inevitably led to increasing demand for housing, and by the end of the decade ministers had empowered councils to clear away jerry-built prefabs, demolish remaining inner-city slums, and commence a mammoth house-building programme.

Under a series of Acts, beginning with the Housing Act 1957, councils embarked on extensive slum-clearance schemes, using compulsory purchase orders (CPOs—see 15.3.6) to obtain enough land sufficiently quickly to allow the construction of suitable alternative housing. But no sooner had they done so than they faced an immediate dilemma that echoes to this day in the decision-making of urban planners: how were they to accommodate a rapidly rising population without resorting to similar tactics to their forebears, by cramming homes together in high-density Victorian-style terraces or overcrowded estates? Their solution was to build upwards, rather than laterally—creating the first high-rise tower blocks.

Although a number of multistorey blocks still exist in and around major towns, there has been a growing backlash against them since the 1970s by planners, politicians, and public. Tight terraces and sink estates might have been shoddily built and poorly served by infrastructure, but at least many such homes had their own backyards or small gardens, facilitating neighbourly interaction. Neither were residents forced to share the entrances into their blocks or to take temperamental lifts up ten or twenty floors to reach home.

Many tower blocks were initially of sturdier construction than social housing that preceded them, but over time their sheer scale led to structural weaknesses. The lack of accessible shared social spaces and amenities—especially for those living on higher levels—contributed to serious problems such as drug-taking, vandalism, violent crime, and general isolation. Today, like the sprawling slums they replaced, tower blocks are viewed by many as ghettoes for a forgotten 'underclass', cut off from mainstream society.

Some tower blocks witnessed particularly ugly scenes. Broadwater Farm in Tottenham, north London, was depicted as one of the worst places to live in Britain in Alice Coleman's influential 1985 book *Utopia on Trial*. Later that year, it witnessed one of the most notorious riots of the 1980s and, in an echo of that time, was the starting point for a protest march prompted by the police shooting of local man Mark Duggan, which in turn sparked the 2011 'riots'.

16.1.3 The great 'new town' boom

Given the limited capacity of tower blocks to cater for rapidly rising populations and the social deprivation increasingly associated with them, by the 1960s both central and local government were looking for alternative ways to provide mass low-cost housing for those unable to buy their own homes.

A consensus quickly emerged that there should be a further new towns roll-out, and ten more were founded in the 1960s. By far the most famous was Milton Keynes in the Midlands—founded from scratch in 1967. In other cases, the term 'new town' proved a misnomer: the ancient Cambridgeshire cathedral city of Peterborough was designated one in 1967, with Northampton acquiring this status a year later. In effect, these designations gave the towns—along with Warrington—a licence to expand on a scale out of step with towns elsewhere.

The advantages of new towns over other housing solutions were manifold. By starting with blank slates, urban planners could freely design roads, estates, and other infrastructure in 'human-centred' ways—maximizing space and integrating vital community facilities to enhance residents' quality of life. Housing itself was built on a domestic scale, with two- to three-storey homes arranged along clear street patterns, backed and fronted by individual gardens and focal spaces.

But, like all house-building programmes before them, new towns had their downsides: established urban areas rarely provided enough space for them, so they tended to develop in largely rural locations, becoming satellite or dormitory towns from which residents had to commute to established urban centres for work. They were made as self-sufficient as possible, though—with shops, sports and leisure centres, cinemas, and, in time, employment opportunities—and, over time, became so populated that new local authorities had to be established to provide their services.

Despite their demonstrable benefits for families on modest incomes who were previously excluded from the home-owning market, in practice new towns brought limited gains for those at the bottom. During the 1970s and 1980s, a growing divide opened up between poorer households living in new towns, in which there had been sufficient investment in council housing, and the large number of council tenants still confined to tower blocks elsewhere.

Between 1947 and 1970, twenty-one new towns were established in England and the new town experiment has since been extended to the rest of Britain, with Scotland acquiring six, and Wales and Northern Ireland two each. The thirty-two existing new towns to date, in alphabetical order, are as follows: Bracknell, Basildon, Central Lancashire (Preston, Chorley, and Leyland), Corby, Craigavon, Crawley, Cumbernauld, Cwmbran, Dawley, Derry, East Kilbride, Glenrothes, Harlow, Hemel Hempstead, Irvine, Letchworth, Livingston, Milton Keynes, Newton Aycliffe, Newtown, Northampton, Peterborough, Peterlee, Redditch, Runcorn, Skelmersdale, Stevenage, Telford, Warrington, Washington, Welwyn Garden City, and Hatfield.

After years of debate about Britain's worsening affordable housing situation, all the main parties entered the 2015 general election campaign pledging to found further new towns if elected. Sure enough, the newly elected Conservative government swiftly announced the first 'new' new towns in nearly half a century, to be established through a ground-breaking initiative led not by the Department for Communities and Local Government but by NHS England. Dubbed 'Healthy New Towns', the scheme aims to help address the need (identified in a succession of recent independent reports) for at least 200,000 new homes to be built in England each year, while also forming part of the government's wider strategy to begin the process of integrating health and social care (see 6.2.4) by (quite literally) building healthier, better designed, communities. This Utopian objective was entering its first phase at time of writing, with the announcement in March 2016 of ten 'Healthy New Towns demonstrator sites', including 10,800 new homes at Barking Riverside (London's largest brownfield site); 3,350 on the site of a former Army barracks at Whitehill and Bordon, Hampshire; and 15,000 in Britain's first garden city for 100 years, located at Ebbsfleet in Kent. Chancellor Philip Hammond went some way towards building on this legacy in his inaugural (and, as it transpired, final) Autumn Statement in November 2016, when he relaxed grant restrictions for developers to boost stocks of affordable rent and low-cost ownership homes by 40,000 by 2020–21.

16.2 The Housing Revenue Account (HRA)

All 170 local authorities that still hold housing stock are required by law to record their income and expenditure relating to it on a separate balance sheet from that used for their general revenue funds (see 11.2). This 'Housing Revenue Account' (HRA) is split into two halves: one covering revenue income and spending, and the other capital costs. Most income generated by HRAs is from rent, but councils may also charge one-off fees for arrears or property damage, and accounts accrue interest. The primary purpose of an HRA's capital component is to record all income generated from 'Right to Buy' (RTB) sales (see 16.3.1).

April 2012 heralded a radical change to the way the HRA system operates both locally and nationally. Prior to then, HRAs were part of a nationwide 'subsidy' framework, under which rents received locally were pooled nationally, with 'allowances' to *spend* money (including on new house-building) allocated by the Treasury to each local authority area on the basis of their relative needs—in a similar vein to how uniform business rates (UBR) used to operate (see 11.2.5). In effect, councils that raised more than their designated allowances through rent paid this surplus back into the global pot (thereby receiving 'negative subsidies'), while those unable to do so but with challenging housing needs stood to gain substantially higher (positive) subsidies. As with UBR, however, this longstanding HRA system has now been replaced by one of 'self-financing': today councils keep all the rental income they raise in their areas, but are responsible for taking future decisions locally about when, where, and how much to invest in council house-building themselves, in consultation with their tenants and other local residents. In order to set all housing authorities off on as level footing as possible at the outset, a one-off financial adjustment was made by the government on 28 March 2016, under which councils regularly in receipt of positive subsidies were given single payments to compensate them for the loss of further subsidy, while those used to 'paying back' money to the Treasury 'bought themselves out' of future contributions, by effectively pledging to pay the government back from future rental streams in their areas (in a manner akin to a private finance initiative/PFI arrangement—see 7.6). Recent indicators have pointed towards some worrying financial trends for authorities affected by these changes, though: a joint report by the Chartered Institute of Housing and Chartered Institute of Public Finance and Accounting (CIPFA), published in July 2016, revealed that the new arrangements had left many councils with falling incomes and mounting debt, hampering their ability to build new homes (a key aim of the reform).

16.2.1 Council tenants' rights and how they qualify

Council tenancies have traditionally boasted significant advantages over standard assured short-hold tenancies available when renting in the private sector, including:

- secure tenure;
- no deposit;
- rent set at levels substantially below market averages; and
- the tenants' right to buy the home at a discount.

Unsurprisingly, social housing is much prized among those on low incomes. To ensure that they allocated their limited housing stock as fairly and equitably as possible, councils traditionally kept 'housing registers' (or 'waiting lists'). Anyone over the age of 16 who met certain eligibility criteria could apply, with certain applicants prioritized—for example minors, the elderly, and those with longstanding local connections. This system was changed by the Homelessness Act 2002, which introduced a 'points system' to prioritize applicants. It stipulated that 'reasonable preference' should be given to anyone falling into a set of specified categories, although other longstanding factors favouring certain households over others must also be considered. These are outlined in table 16A to be found on the **Online Resource Centre**. Those granted council homes have customarily begun with one-year 'introductory tenancies'. Assuming that they 'pass' these probation periods, they would then be awarded 'secure tenancies', *unless* evicted for:

- not paying rent;
- causing nuisance to neighbours;
- using the property for illegal activities such as drug dealing; or
- leaving or subletting their homes.

The continuation of tenancies 'for life', although for many years seen as a justified perk of council housing, has become increasingly controversial as home shortages have worsened, particularly in oversubscribed areas of the south-east, where private accommodation is disproportionately pricey. Recent governments have faced growing pressure to prioritize Britain's limited social housing stock, if necessary by terminating tenancies for people whose financial positions significantly improve during their occupancy (enabling lower-income households to replace them). Finally, in 2010, the then Chancellor George Osborne scrapped secure tenancies for new social tenants in favour of fixed-term contracts. This followed David Cameron's earlier pledge to introduce greater 'flexibility' to encourage unemployed tenants to move around in pursuit of work and to move those whose incomes increased over time into private renting—freeing up housing for the neediest. Ministers also launched a 'Freedom Pass' scheme, allowing English social housing tenants to swap homes with those in other areas, to facilitate economic mobility. 'Social rents' have also undergone a transformation: at the same time as Housing Benefit was being capped, the Coalition introduced a new 'affordable rent' initiative, allowing registered housing providers to charge up to 80 per cent of local market rent levels for accommodation aimed at those on low incomes. By giving suppliers (including councils now managing their own HRA budgets—see 16.2) the flexibility to push rents higher than they were under traditional models of social housing, ministers hoped that they would incentivize them to invest more in relatively low-cost homes. In his 2013 Budget, Mr Osborne shifted the emphasis of housing policy further away from 'social' and more towards 'affordable' (see 16.3.2) by launching an 'affordable housing guarantee', with the government agreeing to underwrite money borrowed by private providers and housing associations (HAs—see 16.3), provided they used it to build cheaper homes.

Councils can also impose extra conditions to determine which people qualify for social housing. Some use their discretion to explicitly *disqualify* those who have left a previous tenancy owing money. Others introduce harsh sanctions for those judged in breach of their social housing contracts: Burnley Borough Council, Lancashire, has written clauses into tenancy agreements allowing social housing providers to evict tenants for antisocial behaviour (a sanction authorized by the Housing Act 1996). The concept of 'earned' tenancies was embedded by the Coalition, with individual councils given greater licence to distinguish between more and less 'deserving' cases. In December 2011, *The Guardian* reported plans by Westminster City Council to require unemployed people hoping to qualify for social housing and related benefits to sign, as a precondition, 'civic contracts' pledging to undertake local voluntary work. The idea (since replicated elsewhere) was one of several proposals that the Tory-run council said it was introducing to end the 'something-for-nothing culture' and better reward those who 'play by the rules'—language that could have been lifted from speeches by Coalition ministers. Among the other ways in which Westminster is now rationing the points that it allocates to prospective social tenants is to give more to nurses, volunteer police officers, Territorial Army members, ex-service personnel, and those who foster or adopt children—while deducting them from adults whose children persistently skip school and those penalized for antisocial behaviour.

However brutal these measures may seem, there have been signs of an emerging consensus on the need for tougher rationing of social housing. In June 2012, ministers published new guidelines pressing councils to move employed people looking for social homes higher up their housing lists. Significantly, Westminster Council's Labour opposition also abstained in the crucial vote on whether to introduce the Tory-instigated housing qualifications described above.

As with so many public services today, the availability of council housing, and how it is prioritized, varies greatly from place to place—something of a postcode lottery (see 6.3.1). While some councils use points-based systems to allocate homes, other prefer a broader 'banding' approach. In addition, prospective council tenants on the housing register (waiting list) in some areas can shop around for the most suitable home, in a favoured location, under a new system called 'choice-based letting', which mimics the way house buyers search for homes through commercial estate agents.

16.2.2 Other local authority housing responsibilities

In addition to building and maintaining their own housing, councils have duties to monitor the state of private accommodation in their areas. Many have now combined their housing and environmental health departments, following several court actions brought against landlords under various Public Health Acts. The 1990 Act outlined councils' duty to inspect existing buildings in their areas to detect and, if necessary, 'eliminate' smoke, dust, fumes, rubbish, noise pollution, and other 'statutory nuisances'.

Councils may also take action over any houses deemed 'unfit for human habitation'. When assessing if somewhere is 'unfit', they consider its state of repair, freedom from damp, natural lighting, ventilation, water supply, drainage, and sanitation. The Housing Act 1985 gave councils powers to serve 'repair notices' on owners of unfit homes. Alternatively, they may carry out specified repairs to bring dwellings up to habitable standards, sending owners the bill. In exceptional circumstances, they can serve 'closure notices' (ordering owners to cease using dwellings for that purpose) or 'demolition notices'—or even buy unfit houses outright and absorb them into their own stock. Sometimes, it is necessary to act against an entire 'area', requiring or undertaking improvements or demolition. Demolished areas are known as 'clearance areas'. Before a clearance order can be made, the authority must arrange rehousing for all tenants and finance the work. The Housing, Grants, Construction, and Regeneration Act 1996 enables councils to pay discretionary relocation grants to displaced people to help them to buy at least a part-share in a new home in the same area.

The Local Government and Housing Act 1989 also empowered councils to declare whole districts *renewal areas* for up to ten years. These normally encompass at least 300 dwellings, 75 per cent privately owned, and are areas in which a third of inhabitants receive benefits. Once renewal areas are designated, councils may acquire the land by agreement or by CPO, providing new housing, improving existing stock, and disposing of property to suitable third parties.

Private accommodation can also benefit from council help. The Housing Act 1996 introduced means-tested, mostly discretionary, grants to help homeowners who are unable to afford essential adaptations themselves. More recently, various new 'green' grants—funded by central government—have been introduced to help tenants and homeowners improve their energy efficiency, to reduce both their fuel bills and carbon footprints. The main types of grant are listed in table 16B to be found on the **Online Resource Centre**.

16.3 Thatcherite housing policy and the decline of council housing

As with many other areas of policy, the Thatcher government had a profound effect on the availability of social housing in Britain. Less than a year after gaining office in 1979, the Conservatives embarked on a radical overhaul of the extant council house framework—giving longstanding tenants the chance to buy their homes at knock-down prices and forcing authorities to sell to them. Within the decade, responsibility for building and maintaining social housing had moved decisively away from councils, towards HAs, overseen by a similarly unaccountable national quango, the Housing Corporation.

The change in law which formalized the effective handover of primary social housing provider status from councils to HAs was the Housing Act 1985 (which supplanted the Housing Act 1957 as 'principal' Act). Coming at the same time as Mrs Thatcher's government was confronting the Greater London Council, metropolitan borough councils, and 'loony Left' authorities elsewhere, the decision to dilute the powers of local housing departments was viewed by some as another assault on the autonomy of elected councillors. Long known as the 'third arm of housing', Britain's 1,700 HAs—today known as 'registered providers'—are regulated and funded by the Homes and Communities Agency (HCA). In Scotland, HAs are regulated directly by the Scottish Government, in Wales by the Welsh Assembly, and in Northern Ireland by the Northern Ireland Housing Executive. Most HAs are also registered as industrial and provident societies, and all have volunteer management committees elected by their membership. Some have no professional staff, while others, including Sovereign and Thames Valley, employ their own substantial workforces.

The primacy of HAs was cemented by the introduction of 'Tenants' Choice' in the Housing Act 1988, under which councils were pressurized to promote them as alternative social housing providers (a move consolidated in the Local Government and Housing Act 1989, which explicitly freed councils from any obligation to retain their own housing stock). Moreover, rather than simply giving tenants the right to move into HA properties, the 1988 Act sought to transfer housing stock itself into the associations' hands. In truth, even some Labour-run authorities (whatever their ideological objections) relished offloading homes, given the high running costs and other complexities associated with repairs and maintenance. Sure enough, by July 1996, fifty-one councils had transferred their entire stocks to HAs—totalling 220,000 properties.

Further emasculation of councils followed. The 1993 Act and detailed regulations flowing from it introduced the concept of 'tenant management organizations' (TMOs). Groups of council tenants living in designated areas were permitted to set up TMOs to take over day-to-day management of their housing and its finances—effectively *replacing* councils and forming de facto HAs. The National Federation of Tenant Management Organizations had more than 130 member TMOs by September 2016. And more was still to come, with the Housing Act 1996 introducing the label 'social landlord' to embrace not only HAs and TMOs but a variety of other models of shared social housing management, including not-for-profit 'housing companies' and 'housing cooperatives': in short, just the kind of 'pluralist and more market-oriented system' the Conservatives had long wanted.

16.3.1 'Right to Buy' and the privatization of council housing

One of the defining election-winning policies of the Thatcher era was the 'Right to Buy' (RTB) programme ushered in by the Housing Act 1980 in England and Wales and the Tenants' Rights (Scotland) Act 1980. Under this scheme, some 5 million 'long-term' council tenants were offered the chance to purchase their homes at a discount on the price that the houses were estimated to be worth on the open market.

Eligible tenants could initially claim the following discounts:

- Households who had occupied their homes for at least three years could buy at discounts of 33 per cent for houses or 44 per cent for flats.
- Those who had rented from councils for more than twenty years received 50 per cent discounts on either houses or flats.

The Housing Act 1985 increased the value of discounts significantly, as follows:

- Tenants living in houses for more than two years could claim 32 per cent discounts *plus* 1 per cent for each complete year by which the qualifying period exceeded two years (up to 60 per cent).
- Those resident for two years or more in flats could claim 44 per cent *plus* 2 per cent for each complete year by which the qualifying period exceeded two years (up to 70 per cent).

Between 1980 and 1995, 2.1 million homes previously in the council, HA, or new town social sectors were transferred to private ownership. Since then, social housing has continued to be privatized at a rate of 60,000 a year—with the result that some areas, including Leicester and parts of Argyll and Bute in Scotland, now have little or no council-owned stock left.

Right to Buy—lauded in the Tories' 1983 election manifesto as the 'the biggest single step towards a home-owning democracy ever taken'—was understandably popular with aspirational working-class voters. By the time of the party's 1987 election victory, even Labour had dropped its formal opposition. On the face of it, the policy also provided a welcome boon to hard-pressed councils, liberating them from maintaining often aged and creaky accommodation, and raising millions in capital receipts that (theoretically) could be spent elsewhere. According to social policy think tank the Joseph Rowntree Foundation, proceeds from council home sales between 1987–8 and 1989–90 generated £33 billion—more than the windfalls from privatizing BP, British Telecom, British Gas, British Airways, and Rolls Royce combined.

But many critics believe RTB has had a devastating impact on the ability of councils and HAs to provide homes for future generations without the financial means to rent privately or buy. Perhaps its most controversial feature was the strict controls that ministers imposed on councils' ability to spend receipts generated by sales on improving or increasing their remaining housing stock. Initially, they were limited to spending only one-fifth of this income on housing, rising to a quarter after the Housing Act 1989. But what the 1989 Act gave with one hand, it took with the other: the three-quarters of receipts remaining had to be spent not on building schools, care homes, or roads, but debt repayment. Similar rules continued for many years.

The Coalition re-embraced RTB—with the nominal guarantee that, this time round, councils would not only be permitted but required to spend income generated from selling homes on building new ones for those in need of them. Former Housing Minister Grant Shapps pledged that, for each additional council home sold, a new one must be provided at 'affordable rent'. The catch, however, was that councils selling off homes would be allowed to use only 30 per cent of their RTB receipts to fund new homes—forcing them to find the balance from a combination of the 'affordable rent' (of up to 80 per cent of market value) they charged on other properties, borrowing, and 'cross-subsidy' from their 'own resources'. Most controversially, RTB has now been extended, for the first time, beyond the scope of local authorities to gradually embrace homes owned by *all* 'public-sector landlords': a broad sweep encompassing everything from NHS trusts and armed services that rent out flats to their employees to housing associations. Initially, the only HA tenants eligible for RTB were those living in their homes at the time they were transferred from local authority to HA ownership—giving them a 'preserved right to buy'. But this was rapidly followed by a large-scale rollout: firstly, through the launch of pilot schemes involving five major HAs and twenty-four local authority areas, under which those who had spent ten years or more as public-sector tenants could apply for a 'voluntary right to buy', and latterly a version of the classic RTB model known as 'Right to Acquire', under which most public-sector tenants of three-plus years can purchase their properties, albeit at a smaller discount than under RTB.

To be eligible for RTB today, households must have held secure tenancies with public-sector landlords on self-contained dwellings that are their only homes for at least three years (though these do not have to have been consecutive). Since 6 April 2015, eligible English tenants may buy their homes at £77,900 below the market price (£103,900 in London)—a numerical reduction that effectively trebles the discount cap previously available. In Wales and Northern Ireland (where RTB is known as the House Sales Scheme) the discounts are significantly lower, at £8,000 and £24,000 respectively. Perhaps unsurprisingly, more than 33,000 households have taken up the right to buy their council homes in England since discounts were increased, and at the time of writing demand showed no sign of waning under Theresa May's Conservative government.

The ongoing mass sell-off of council homes continues to be blamed by some for reducing picturesque villages and coastal resorts to 'ghost towns'. The lack

Table 16.1 Arguments for and against 'Right to Buy'

For	Against
Offers low-income households chance to buy own homes—a progressive policy promoting opportunity, aspiration, and ownership among the poor.	Councils historically allowed to spend only fraction of capital receipts from RTB sales on building more. This has left fewer available for those in future need. Also, many homes sold were those in best condition, leaving councils with less attractive stock facing higher maintenance demands.
Council tenants traditionally relied on local authorities for repairs—often waiting months or years. Enabling them to buy their homes liberates them from local bureaucracy—giving them flexibility to pay for maintenance when needed and motivating them to keep properties to high standards.	Distribution of council housing has historically been unequal, with some more proactive about promoting RTB than others. Tenants' ability to buy their homes is subject to 'postcode lottery'—with those on low incomes forced to rent privately because of lack of social housing.
Raises significant revenue for local government to repay debts. Less debt means healthier finances, because more money left for essential services—and savings may lead to lower Council Tax.	Selling housing enables councils to offload repair costs onto (former) tenants. While initial sale prices may be attractive, disrepair of some homes leaves those purchasing them with high ongoing costs.

of social housing in such areas has priced many locals out of the property market, with buy-to-let and absentee holiday home buyers pushing up both private rents and sale prices way beyond the means of local people employed in traditional rural and seaside jobs. In Tenby, Pembrokeshire, the average house price had risen to £200,000 by 2010 and four out of ten were second homes. However, as of July that year, the Welsh Assembly Government was granted devolved powers to ban RTB purchases in situations in which allowing them would have detrimental knock-on effects on overall housing stock. At a wider national level, the Conservatives' favoured solution to shortages of affordable housing is for local communities to take it into their own hands to promote development—by allowing them to fast track applications for small-scale housing projects.

Following a lengthy review of RTB north of the border, the Scottish Parliament voted to scrap the policy in June 2014 and the ban came into effect in July 2016. Arguments for and against 'Right to Buy' are explored in Table 16.1.

In addition to RTB itself, over time ministers have introduced other subsidized schemes designed to boost home ownership among tenants, notably 'rent-to-mortgage' arrangements (under the Leasehold Reform, Housing, and Urban Development Act 1993). Under these arrangements, the price fixed for a house or flat comprised two elements:

- an *initial capital payment*—a part-mortgage paid in regular instalments at the same or a similar level to the rent for which they were previously liable; and

- a *deferred financial commitment*—a lump sum that accrued no interest, but was repayable on the property's sale, purchaser's death, or by voluntary payments at any time.

These models were forerunners of the shared ownership schemes commonplace today, under which 'tenants' buy shares in properties from HAs, using normal home loans, and rent the remainder.

16.3.2 The rise of owner-occupancy and the 'affordable housing' debate

Recent surveys—produced separately for England, Scotland, Wales, and Northern Ireland—suggest that, despite years of spiralling house prices and the well-reported financial obstacles faced by first-time buyers, Britain is close to becoming that great 'home-owning democracy' heralded by Mrs Thatcher back in 1983. Figures 16.1 and 16.2 contrast the breakdown of dwelling types in England in 1961 (the year in which records began) and 2014–15 (the most recent year for which data is available). Information from the 31 March 1961 census revealed that, of the 13.83 million dwellings in which English people then lived, 6.1 million (44 per cent) were owner-occupied houses and flats, with 4.4 million (32 per cent) rented from private landlords or as part of the residents' job or business, and 3.38 million (24 per cent) council housing. Some fifty-three years later, the United Kingdom Statistics Authority's English Housing Survey 2014–15 found that, of a total of 22.5 million dwellings, the number of owner-occupied properties had soared to 64 per cent (14.3 million). Although this had fallen from 17.5 million six years earlier, partly due to ongoing restraints on mortgage lending following the 2008 financial collapse (see 7.3.4), significantly, the proportion of people owning their own homes outright had clearly outstripped those paying off mortgages (by 33 to 30 per cent): a reflection of a growing wealth divide between ordinary 'home-owners' (and renters) and large-scale property investors and landlords. The percentage renting from councils or other social landlords had dropped by more than a third over the half-century—with the effect that the private rented sector had overtaken social housing for the first time since the 1960s. While 4.3 million households (a growing proportion of 19 per cent) were renting privately, only 3.9 million (17 per cent) were living in social homes. And the renewed dominance of private landlords is not just emerging in areas where one might expect home ownership to be unaffordable, such as London and the south-east: an August 2016 report by the Resolution Foundation revealed that northern conurbations like Greater Manchester and South Yorkshire were experiencing the most dramatic shift back towards private renting since the 1980s.

Despite the growth in home ownership, many—particularly those on low incomes and single people in south-east England—found it next to impossible to

Figure 16.1 Where English residents were living, 31 March 1961

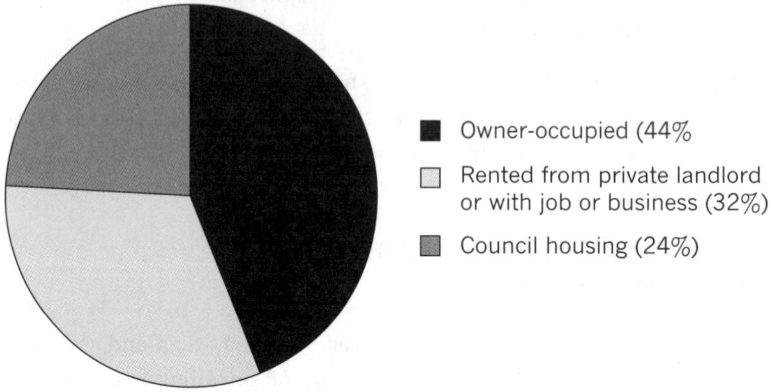

Source: Department for Communities and Local Government (DCLG) © Crown Copyright 2012

Figure 16.2 Where English residents were living, 2014–15

Source: Department for Communities and Local Government (DCLG) © Crown Copyright 2016

enter the property market during the Noughties housing boom. As a consequence, recent years have seen numerous policy initiatives geared towards helping out those who neither qualify for conventional social housing nor can afford their own homes. Particular emphasis has been placed on the plight of 'key workers'—public servants such as teachers and nurses, especially those living in areas such as inner London, where prices are disproportionately high.

To guarantee that the market provided more 'affordable' houses, the Blair–Brown governments set out to build 3 million new homes by 2020, at a projected cost of £8 billion. In theory, by targeting them at areas with shortages of affordable private-sector homes, this would have both provided bricks and mortar up front and forced prices down across the board. The sheer scale of development proposed for some areas, however, generated fierce opposition.

In the south-east, where 200,000 new houses were due to be built, councils and existing residents alike objected to the 'quotas' imposed on them by ministers. The newly designated South Downs National Park was targeted for thousands of homes (many in flood plains), to the fury of parish councils and environmental campaigners. There was also considerable controversy over ministers' pledge to give preferential permission to sustainable housing developments, or 'eco-towns'. Criticisms have included the fact that, to establish these supposed paragons of environmental friendliness, large tracts of as-yet-undeveloped countryside would need to be surrendered to house-building. Green campaigners also argued that some sites earmarked for such developments were in rural areas bereft of public transport infrastructure—a factor likely to lead to above average levels of car ownership among those who ended up living there, making a mockery of their 'eco' credentials. Campaigns against the mass house-building programme were launched from the south-west to the north-east, although some experts claimed that the government's plans were too modest: in October 2007, the National Housing and Planning Advice Unit predicted that typical UK house prices would spiral to nine-and-a-half times the average salary by 2026 unless ministers were to increase supply by 270,000 homes a year.

Whatever the true picture, Labour's top-down housing targets were abandoned in July 2010 by the Coalition. Since then, individual councils, and the communities they serve, have been responsible for deciding what former Communities Secretary Eric Pickles termed 'the right level of local housing provision in their area'. To allay fears that abolishing quotas might leave a short-term policy vacuum while councils worked out their ongoing approaches to strategic planning, Mr Pickles urged them to decide swiftly whether to abandon or retain targets previously imposed on them, so that 'communities and landowners know where they stand'. The following month, a New Homes Bonus scheme was launched, to incentivize councils to build affordable housing by offering them extra funding for doing so. For every new home built, the government would match Council Tax raised on the premises for the following six years. More recently, the government has tacitly accepted that some house-building targets are necessary. In September 2015, the then Housing Minister Brandon Lewis confirmed plans to build a million new homes by 2020, in the face of a National Housing Federation (NHF) survey claiming that the Coalition had built fewer than half as many homes in England as it should have done to meet demand between 2011 and 2014. Boosting housing supply is, in any case, only one part of the equation. A major obstacle facing many first-time buyers since the financial crash has been the reluctance of banks and building societies to grant them mortgages without demanding hefty deposits. In London and the south-east, even professional earners have been unable to borrow sufficient multiples of their salaries to afford the most modest homes available. The Coalition's response was a 'Help to Buy' scheme designed to enable households to purchase homes worth up to £600,000 with deposits of as little as 5 per cent of their value. By offering mortgage lenders taxpayer-backed guarantees on loans to eligible customers, between the scheme's October 2013 launch and the following May the government enabled 7,313 applicants to each borrow up to 85–90 per cent of their homes' values. At the time of writing, there were signs that Britain's volatile housing market was once more overheating, stoked in part by 'Help to Buy', with the Nationwide Building Society index revealing in July 2016 that, after years of positive growth, there had been a further year-on-year increase of 5.2 per cent (or £10,094) in average UK property prices over the previous twelve months—putting many homes further beyond the reach of those not benefiting from ministerial initiatives.

16.4 The homeless

Councils have a statutory duty to house the 'unintentionally homeless' and those threatened with homelessness 'within 28 days of being made aware of their predicament' under the Housing (Homeless Persons) Act 1977 and Homelessness Act 2002. Under the Housing Act 1996, however, the ambit of 'homelessness' was narrowed to allow councils to take into account available accommodation across Britain and even 'elsewhere'. The reform's aim was to help out councils presented with disproportionately high numbers of homeless people (particularly asylum seekers) because it would be unreasonable for them to have to house all applicants in their own areas. Ensuing regulations also tightened the law regarding asylum seekers' eligibility for housing assistance: anyone who did not claim this status at the port of their arrival was rendered ineligible (barring refugees and those granted 'exceptional or unconditional leave to remain' in Britain). The Act also introduced a two-year limit on provision of accommodation in certain cases and a review of all cases after that.

The types of homeless people treated as priority cases are those:

- with dependent children;
- made homeless by emergencies or disasters (flood, fire, etc.);
- vulnerable because of old age, or mental or physical disability; and
- who are pregnant.

When assessing applications from homeless people for permanent housing and while waiting for flats to become available, councils often use short-stay, hostel, and/or 'bed and breakfast' accommodation (in reality, seldom more than dingy bedsits or studio flats in multi-occupancy dwellings).

The overriding controversy around councils' responsibilities to the homeless, however, relates to the Act's wide-ranging definition of 'intentional homelessness'. Under the law, the 'intentionally homeless' include people evicted from private-sector accommodation for falling behind with rent and even those fleeing home 'voluntarily' to escape domestic abuse. Nonetheless, if 'intentionally homeless' people fit into priority categories, councils must provide them with advice, assistance, and temporary accommodation. The Coalition further diluted councils' responsibility towards the homeless—allowing them to abandon their 'duty of care' once they had successfully steered people into private accommodation for a year.

Homelessness returned to media prominence following recent cuts not only to social security benefits (see Chapter 8 and 16.5) but also to funding for beds in night hostels and entitlement to free legal housing advice (much of which has now been privatized, under Ministry of Justice reforms to legal aid). According to ONS figures, a 2015 spot survey in England found 3,659 people sleeping rough on the streets—more than double the number recorded in 2010. The number of people 'accepted as homeless' rose by 6 per cent, to 57,750, between 2014–15 and 2015–16, but the Homelessness Monitor, a collaboration between charity Crisis, the Joseph Rowntree Foundation, and Heriot-Watt University, argues that official statistics mask an iceberg-sized problem of 'hidden homelessness', with some 275,000 people having approached their councils for help in 2015–16.

16.5 Local authorities, Housing Benefit, and Local Housing Allowance (LHA)

Councils are responsible for administering Housing Benefit on behalf of the Department for Work and Pensions (DWP—see 8.3). Since April 2008, Housing Benefit (HB)—a payment equivalent to all or part of the rent charged to low-income tenants living in private, public, or voluntary-sector accommodation—has been calculated using a **Local Housing Allowance (LHA)** formula.

For many years, there were two types of HB, depending on individuals' circumstances:

- *standard*—for low-waged workers; and
- *certificated*—for those on out-of-work benefits such as Jobseeker's Allowance (JSA), or Incapacity Benefit or Employment and Support Allowance (ESA).

These distinctions have been supplanted by simplified eligibility criteria based purely on individuals' status as tenants, their low incomes, and that they do not have more than £16,000 in savings.

The principal difference between the new and old ways of calculating HB relates to the method used to assess how much claimants receive. The benefit used to involve individual properties being inspected by housing officers to determine their (notional) rental values, with successful claimants receiving payments commensurate with what their council felt the accommodation was worth. But LHA has simplified this process by offering claimants blanket rates for different levels of property (from one-bedroom flats to four-bedroom houses) based on 'middle of the range' (median) market rents for each category in their neighbourhoods (known as 'broad market rental areas', or BMRAs).

Anti-poverty campaigners argued that the LHA calculation method, introduced by Labour, meant that the sums received by even those granted full help with rental costs and living in modest properties often fall well short of what landlords actually charge. Disability groups, meanwhile, complain that the LHA discriminates against severely disabled people who require two-bedroom homes to accommodate live-in carers. In November 2009, a benefits tribunal found against Walsall Council in a case brought by the mother of a severely disabled woman, who argued that the reforms had unfairly left her with a weekly £70–75 rent shortfall on the two-bedroom home that they shared.

Discontent over cutbacks to Housing Benefit and the LHA escalated following the Welfare Reform Act 2012, which paved the way for them to be absorbed into an all-encompassing Universal Credit (UC—see 8.5), and the introduction of benefit capping. As well as bringing in a £280 weekly limit for a one-bedroom flat and one of £400 a week for a four-bedroom house, the Act formalized an across-the-board annual benefits cap for households of £26,000, including Housing Benefit—putting paid to the type of story, beloved of the *Daily Mail*, about welfare-dependent families receiving tens of thousands of pounds a year to live in palatial London homes that most wage-earners could never afford. The way in which the LHA itself is calculated has also become less generous: Labour set payments at 50 per cent of the BMRA, but the Coalition reduced this to 30 per cent. But most explosive of all was the introduction of the 'spare room subsidy'—dubbed the 'bedroom tax' by critics—which removed £40 a month from social tenants living in properties with additional bedrooms not used for sleeping, and £70 from those with two extra rooms. The move was designed to 'free up spare capacity' for those on waiting lists, but led to warnings from housing charities that vulnerable people would be forced out of their homes, and perhaps made homeless. Despite the offer of discretionary payments for the most needy, to be channelled through councils, the 'tax' was heavily opposed by disability campaigners, who argued that it would disproportionately penalize those whose 'spare' rooms were needed to store specialist equipment or to accommodate short-term carers. Within months of the subsidy's introduction, various reports testified to its negative impact: in February 2014, the NHF revealed that two-thirds of the 523,000 tenants affected had fallen into arrears (many for the first time)—with 72,000 HA renters attributing this directly to the new 'tax'. Of these, 15 per cent had already received eviction risk letters from their landlords. So serious were shortfalls in some households' budgets—and so limited their options, in terms of moving to smaller properties—that numerous councils opted to introduce 'no eviction' policies to protect rent-defaulters. Official DWP figures confirmed a similar picture that July, finding that six out of ten affected households had been unable to meet shortfalls of £14–£22 caused by the introduction of the 'tax', forcing them to borrow from high-interest payday loan companies and make invidious 'heat or eat' decisions. So stark were the findings that, ten months before the 2015 election, they prompted Lib Dem Deputy Prime Minister Nick Clegg to call for the policy to be overhauled, arguing that the market's failure to provide smaller homes for those affected meant it was 'not working'. Meanwhile, the Scottish Government pledged to find money centrally to cover the subsidy's £50 million cost in 2014–15.

Criticism of the Coalition's Housing Benefit reforms has come from an even wider range of voices. Before the 2012 Act even received royal assent, some London boroughs revealed that they were already seeking 'bed and breakfast' accommodation in cheaper outlying suburbs in anticipation of a rise in evictions—prompting Labour frontbencher Chris Bryant to condemn the government's reforms as 'social cleansing' and then Conservative Mayor of London Boris Johnson to tell a radio presenter that he would not allow poor people to be shunted out of the capital 'on my watch'. Although ministers retorted that such claims were scaremongering—arguing that benefit cuts would merely induce claimants to move into more modest rented properties and/or landlords to charge less, as the private market 'corrected' itself—since the Act came into force, this does not appear to have happened. Investigations by *The Guardian* and BBC Radio 4's *Today* programme have demonstrated that, in London and Oxford (the second most competitive rental market in England) respectively, there remain severe shortages of surplus private rented properties priced at or below LHA level, where benefit claimants are accepted. Given these findings, it came as little surprise to critics of the government's reforms when, in April 2012, *The Guardian* reported that Westminster and Hammersmith councils had begun shipping social tenants priced out of their homes elsewhere, while Labour-run Newham Council had approached a Stoke-based HA asking it to accommodate 500 families forced to leave the London borough as a result of the HB cap. Newham's move prompted ministers to accuse Labour of 'playing politics' with social tenants, but responding to their insistence that there were more than 1,000 affordable rental properties within a five-mile radius of Newham available on the Rightmove lettings website in April 2012, *Guardian* journalist Polly Curtis conducted her own experimental search. While she found 339 four-bedroom houses available in the area at or below the £400 cap level, not one of the half-dozen agents she called randomly about the properties were willing to accommodate benefit claimants.

Similar issues have surrounded the 'bedroom tax': in June 2012, *The Guardian* reported a warning by England's HAs of a chronic lack of space in social homes for the estimated 100,000 people who had already received letters telling them they needed to find smaller properties to continue receiving benefits. Iain Sim, chief executive of Coast & Country, one of north-east England's largest providers, told the paper that while he had 2,500 properties with at least one 'spare' room that could be freed up if 'underoccupiers' moved out, he only had sixteen one-bedroom flats available to house those who did. Around the same time, a government-commissioned study by the Centre for Regional Economic and Social Research at Sheffield Hallam University found that four out of ten private landlords in London, and a third of those elsewhere in England, planned to stop accepting claimants within the year.

Others have cast doubt on the entire premise of recent reforms: principally, the idea that workless benefit claimants are being unfairly subsidized by 'hard-working families' struggling to pay their own way unaided. In a 2010 article in *Inside Housing*, trade journal of the social housing sector, Helen Williams, assistant director of the NHF, argued that, far from being a mass of work-shy scroungers, three-quarters of the 4.7 million claiming HB were either retired, disabled, or full-time carers. Of the remaining 24 per cent, half were working. Figures from homelessness charity Shelter and the DWP itself backed up this assertion—the former demonstrating that fewer than one in eight Housing Benefit claimants were unemployed.

Although the administration of housing-related benefits has begun a process of change with the slow rollout of Universal Credit (UC—see 8.5), delays in implementing UC in most areas mean that, in many areas, it remains (for now) with local authorities. Alongside LHA, councils have traditionally administered Council Tax Benefit, which used to equate to full Council Tax rebates for LHA claimants. But in April 2013 this was scrapped for everyone other than pensioners, to be replaced by a new, more localized, system known as Council Tax Reduction, administered according to criteria determined by each council. Critics condemned the new scheme as another recipe for post-code lotteries, adding that numerous low-income households never previously charged Council Tax would be billed for the first time, because the budget set aside to implement the new policy was 10 per cent (£414 million) lower than that preceding it. Sure enough, in January 2014, the Institute for Fiscal Studies (IFS) think tank reported that 2.5 million working households had already lost £160 on average in 2013–14. Seven out of ten councils had asked households that previously qualified for Council Tax Benefit for a minimum payment, with only one in five managing to maintain existing levels of support.

16.6 Forcing down market rents: the case for 'rent controls'

Controversy about housing shortages and benefit cuts has revived debate about a longstanding policy for protecting low-income tenants, abandoned by the Thatcher government nearly a quarter of a century ago: 'rent controls'. Between 1915 and 1988, council-employed rent officers could intervene directly in their areas to limit rental costs for the unemployed and low-paid. The axing of controls was accompanied by the introduction of six-month 'assured short-hold' tenancies for both landlords and renters. Ministers argued that, however noble the intention behind them, controls had the effect of stifling investment in private rented housing, encouraging 'slum landlords' to let out substandard accommodation at bargain-basement rents to the poor. The reintroduction of rent controls was one of the signature policies to which Labour's Ken Livingstone shackled his ultimately unsuccessful campaign to be reinstated as London Mayor in May 2012, but this did not stop the party campaigning on a manifesto promising to cap private-sector rents in its also unsuccessful 2015 election campaign.

Topical feature idea

The local authority covered by your newspaper's catchment area has complained to the Communities Secretary about a sharp drop in its funding for new social house-building programmes, caused by recent changes to Right to Buy and the way Housing Revenue Accounts (HRAs) work. It now has to 'self-finance' its own housing schemes while making annual payments to the Treasury from its rent receipts to replace the contributions it used to make under the old 'pooled' system. At the same time, it claims it is being forced to sell off good-quality existing council housing, from which it would otherwise have continued generating rent, to tenants keen to exercise their rights to buy. Your editor is demanding a background feature on this complex topic, written in 'plain English' and with a strong 'human interest' angle. Who should you contact, and how else will you research the piece?

Current issues

- **The 'new town' renaissance** NHS England is piloting a 'Healthy New Towns' initiative in ten areas, with the aim of making a substantial contribution to the 200,000 new homes a year that independent estimates suggest are needed to plug Britain's affordable housing gap while fostering 'healthier' communities as part of the government's move to integrate health and social care.

- **Extension of Right to Buy to all 'public-sector' tenants** RTB is now available not only to long-term council tenants, but also to many of those renting from housing associations (HAs), NHS trusts, and the armed services. Discounts on market prices for RTB purchases in England have also been raised to £77,900 (£103,900 in London).
- **The return of large-scale homelessness** Government figures confirmed a 6 per cent year-on-year rise in street homelessness in 2015–16, and the most recent Homelessness Monitor survey found that 275,000 people had approached councils for help that year. The rise is attributed to a blizzard of cuts—to welfare benefits, funding for night shelters and hostels, and free legal housing advice.

Key points

1. 'Social housing' is the generic term for houses or flats available at reduced rents to those on low incomes. Traditionally provided by councils, it is now largely managed by housing associations (HAs).
2. The term 'affordable housing' applies to houses or flats available to purchase at prices below the market average. It is often targeted at first-time buyers and 'key workers' (essential professionals such as nurses and teachers).
3. The Housing Revenue Account (HRA) is a dedicated budget used to manage and maintain councils' housing stock. It is separate from the general revenue account and its principal income is rent received from tenants.
4. The main welfare support available to low-income tenants is Housing Benefit (HB), now generally known as Local Housing Allowance (LHA). The maximum that can be claimed in most areas is 30 per cent of median rents in tenants' postcode areas.
5. Councils are legally obliged to house the 'unintentionally homeless'—a category excluding those evicted for rent arrears or leaving home voluntarily. They must also provide emergency accommodation for pregnant women, adults with dependants, elderly people, and those left homeless by fire, flood, or other disaster.

→ Further reading

Hanley, L. (2013) *Estates: An Intimate History*, London: Granta Books. **Critical, but affectionate, first-hand evaluation of the life and culture of post-war housing estates by a former resident, set against the evolving policy landscape of recent decades.**

Lund, B. (2011) *Understanding Housing Policy*, 2nd edn, Bristol: Policy Press. **Up-to-date appraisal of issues in social and low-cost housing, focusing on the decline of local authority housing, and growth in the involvement of housing associations, cooperatives, and other providers.**

Malpass, P. (2005) *Housing and the Welfare State: The Development of Housing Policy in Britain*, Basingstoke: Palgrave Macmillan. **In-depth historical critique of the evolution of housing policy in Britain since the Second World War.**

Murie, A. (2016) *The Right to Buy? Selling off Public and Social Housing*, Bristol: Policy Press. **Critical exploration of the impact of RTB housing policies from the 1980s to the present day.**

Online Resource Centre

www.oxfordtextbooks.co.uk/orc/Morrison5e/

Visit the Online Resource Centre that accompanies this book for web links and regular updates.

17

Children's services and adult social care

One of the most intricate, sensitive, and (occasionally) explosive aspects of local policy delivery is 'social services' or social care—interchangeable umbrella terms referring to the provision of everything from foster care and adoptive parents for vulnerable children, to residential and nursing homes for the elderly and disabled. Today, 1.5 million people in England rely on support from social services, including 400,000 children.

Although the term 'social services' may not appear in the media as often as 'NHS' or 'welfare', stories relating to its successes—and, more usually, failings—are seldom far from the agenda. Controversies have ranged from complaints about errant social workers failing to uncover child abuse until it is too late, to screaming headlines about prematurely discharged mental patients running amok.

Most of these stories, however, have arisen out of atypical circumstances and, excepting specialist sections such as *Society Guardian* and the online magazine *www.communitycare.co.uk*, Britain's media is often accused of neglecting the complexities of this 'difficult' policy area in favour of sensationalism. But given some of the UK's current demographic and social trends—the liberalization of adoption laws, a rapidly ageing population, and increasing moves towards integrating social care provision into the NHS (see 6.2.4)—only a foolish editor would ignore the underlying issues that determine policy (and occasionally contribute to the more dramatic situations about which we often hear).

Until the early twentieth century, social services were provided on an ad hoc basis by charities and voluntary foundations, or in workhouses or infirmaries funded by parishes under the Poor Law. But social reform under the modernizing governments of David Lloyd George and Clement Attlee brought more coordinated social care provision, paralleling the nationwide establishment of the NHS and welfare state. The main landmarks included a seminal report by the 1968 Inter-Departmental Committee on Local Authority and Allied Personal Services (the 'Seebohm Report'), leading to the decision, two years later, to form discrete social services departments by merging pre-existing health and welfare and children's departments under the Local Authorities Social Services Act 1970. The new departments, run by county councils, worked closely with district or borough housing departments and the NHS.

Until 2004, when children gained their own dedicated departments following the Victoria Climbié case (see 17.1.2), social services departments were responsible for three broad policy areas:

- child protection;
- domiciliary and residential care for the elderly and disabled; and
- care for those with mental health problems.

17.1 Child protection

Historically, child protection was overseen collaboratively by social services departments, in partnership with:

- local education departments (normally within the same authority);
- police child protection units;
- NHS trusts and primary care trusts (PCTs), now clinical commissioning groups (CCGs—see 6.2.1);
- the National Society for the Prevention of Cruelty to Children (NSPCC); and
- registered adoption agencies.

Until 2004, these various bodies liaised through area review committees (ARCs), which determined the child protection procedures that each should follow and conducted reviews of cases in which those processes failed to prevent 'non-accidental injury' taking place. Information on vulnerable children was shared between them through local child protection registers maintained by the ARC.

The Children Act 2004, a response to the Climbié case, abandoned ARCs in favour of **children's trusts**: all-in-one bodies comprising representatives of every statutory agency involved in promoting child welfare in multidisciplinary teams of social workers, health visitors, paediatricians, and child psychologists. Local child protection registers were replaced by individual **child protection plans**, drawn up by professionals following initial conferences to assess a child's degree of risk.

The sweeping changes, ushered in under the 'Every Child Matters' banner (see 17.1.2), saw all services relating to children in England—from schooling to social care—combined under new *children's services* departments, headed by directors of children's services. In Wales, these departments retain the name children's social services, while in Northern Ireland, where health and social care are already more integrated than elsewhere in Britain, the dedicated departments are known as *gateway services for child protection* (or children's social work) and exist as discrete units within health and social care trusts (see 6.2.3.3). Child protection is the responsibility of children's social work teams in Scotland. In addition, in each Scottish local authority area there is a *reporter*: an independent official whose job is to judge whether legal interventions are needed to protect children reported to them.

Children's social services are required to:

- promote children's general welfare;
- encourage children's upbringing by their families (wherever possible);
- pay regard to children's wishes and feelings;
- work in partnership with parents in children's best interests;
- provide accommodation for children for whom no one has 'parental responsibility'—taking on a 'corporate parent' role if a child is lost or abandoned, or if the person responsible is unable to provide care; and
- advise, assist, and befriend children who leave local authority care—and provide financial assistance and support to find accommodation.

The following two sections primarily focus on the web of regulations and guidelines governing child protection policy in England and Wales, as derived from two key Acts: the Children Acts 1989 and 2004.

17.1.1 The Children Act 1989 and the definition of 'parental responsibility'

The 1989 Act synthesized existing public and private law on the care, protection, and safe upbringing of children, making it more cohesive. It came into force in England and Wales in 1991, and in Northern Ireland in 1996.

The Act implicitly presumed that the best place for children to be brought up was at home with their parents or guardians—unless there were serious concerns for their welfare in these environments. Councils were given a 'general duty' to 'keep a child safe and well' and provide suitable support services to help them to remain with their families. The Act's definition of 'family' was quite fluid—referring to any adult(s) with legal 'parental responsibility' for a child. It defined 'parental responsibility' as 'all the rights, duties, powers, responsibilities and authority which by law a parent of a child has in relation to the child and his property'.

The Act defines 'children in need' as those who are:

- disabled—blind, deaf, dumb, or with a mental disorder or physical impairment;
- unlikely to have—or have the opportunity to have—'a reasonable standard of health or development' without the help of services from a local authority; and/or
- unlikely to progress in health or development without the help of local authority services.

Under the Act, parents, guardians, or carers whose children might be eligible for services are entitled to contact councils for 'needs assessments'. Carried out by qualified social workers, these should take into account not only *children's* needs, but also those of their parent(s) or guardian(s). For example, the child might require remedial educational support or therapy, but the adult with parental responsibility might qualify for financial assistance, counselling, or respite care (a short break from caring, perhaps even a holiday, while the child is looked after by professionals). Since 2000, assessments have been conducted in a 'multi-agency' way, under the Framework for the Assessment of Children in Need and their Families of the Department of Health (DoH). In addition to providing for a child's immediate physical, mental, and emotional needs, a more holistic plan must be drafted—catering for ongoing specialist social, financial, or educational requirements.

The range of services available under the 1989 Act includes:

- short breaks;
- holiday play schemes;
- care at home—including help with washing, dressing, and mobility;
- some aids and adaptations—for example stair lifts, hoists, and wheelchairs; and
- financial help—for example, to pay for fares to hospital visits.

Services can be arranged by councils on behalf of families, with some provided in-house and outside agencies or charities contracted to deliver others. Alternatively, parents or guardians may request *direct payment* schemes. These involve families receiving cash payments, so that they can 'shop around' for services of their choice rather than being offered the 'one size fits all' provision traditionally offered by councils. Direct payments (or 'self-directed support')—based on a similar principle to 'patient choice' in the NHS—were piloted in the context of care packages for the elderly as early as 1996, but have since been extended, controversially, to severely mentally impaired adults (see 17.2.3).

As well as setting out the day-to-day services available for children in need, the 1989 Act attempts to address the thorny issue of councils' role in wider child welfare. In particular, it defines circumstances in which children's services should intervene to ask family courts to decide where (and with whom) a child 'at risk' of neglect or abuse by parents or guardians should live. It sets out four types of court order—collectively known as 'section 8 orders'—which are explained in table 17A to be found on the **Online Resource Centre** that accompanies this book.

Sometimes, the level of intervention that councils are permitted is insufficient to deal with children's care needs; at other times, orders may be breached, again putting children at unacceptable risk. In such circumstances, councils will need to consider taking children 'into care'—that is, away from those with parental responsibility. The procedure for doing this and the range of care options available to children once removed from home is discussed in the sections 17.1.3, 17.1.4.2, and 17.1.5.

The 1989 Act applies only to England and Wales, although most of its provisions are reflected in the Children (Scotland) Act 1995. The one significant difference is that, under Scottish law, legal proceedings surrounding child welfare follow a distinct 'children's hearings system', established in the early 1970s, which determines any compulsory supervision measures that a minor may need. The one notable strengthening of existing procedures under the 1995 Act was its emphasis on the role of 'safeguarders': individuals with relevant professional backgrounds (normally lawyers, social workers, or teachers) appointed as the 'voice of the child'.

17.1.2 The Children Act 2004 and the 'Every Child Matters' agenda

The 2004 Act focused less on introducing additional duties of care or legal powers for councils and courts than on radically shaking up child protection 'culture'. Its main emphasis was on improving early intervention and communication between professionals, following the horrific case of Victoria Climbié. In 2000, the 8 year-old died of hypothermia, with 128 separate injuries to her body, after two years of systematic torture and abuse by her great aunt, Marie Thérèse Kouao, and the latter's boyfriend, Carl Manning, in their London bedsit. Victoria's parents, both living on the Ivory Coast, had sent her to Britain in the hope of a better life. In the months before her death, Victoria was systematically beaten, burnt with cigarettes and scalding water, tied up, and forced to sleep in a bath with only a bin liner over her naked body. Police, social workers, and the NSPCC failed to treat warning signs sufficiently seriously—prematurely ending a child protection investigation based on a paediatrician's mistaken diagnosis that scars on her skin were caused by scabies.

After Victoria's treatment was finally exposed, both Kouao and Manning were jailed for murder at the Old Bailey, several social workers at Haringey Council were sacked, and three major investigations were launched: by the council, the Independent Police Complaints Commission (IPCC), and a public inquiry chaired by former Chief Inspector of Social Services Lord Laming. Reporting in January 2003, he made seventeen recommendations for reforming child protection procedures. The most significant are listed in table 17B to be found on the **Online Resource Centre**.

The government's response was a famous Green Paper, *Every Child Matters*. It outlined four key aims for improving child protection:

- increasing the focus on supporting families or carers—described as 'the most critical influence on children's lives';
- ensuring that necessary intervention takes place before children reach crisis point and that they are protected from falling through the net;
- addressing underlying problems identified by the report into Victoria Climbié's death—weak accountability and poor integration; and
- ensuring that people working with children are valued, rewarded, and trained.

Following a widespread public consultation and a further paper, *Every Child Matters: The Next Steps*, many of Lord Laming's recommendations came into force under the 2004 Act. They revolved around five 'Every Child Matters' outcomes, which set out to enable all children to:

- be healthy;
- stay safe;
- enjoy and achieve;
- make a positive contribution; and
- achieve economic well-being.

To pursue these ends, the government created *children's trusts*: multidisciplinary teams comprising various professionals involved in child protection. To improve coordination of children's services on the ground, trusts would bring together various professionals at single locations in the local community, such as children's centres or schools. Between them, these agencies would:

- conduct joint needs assessments of children in need;
- reach shared decisions on priorities relating to children's well-being;
- identify all available resources suited to improving children's well-being; and
- collaboratively deploy resources, to avoid duplication or overlap.

Even before trusts were in place everywhere, plans were unveiled in June 2008 for their remit to be widened to encompass aspects of youth justice previously overseen by the Police Service and Prisons Service Agency. Then Children's

Secretary Ed Balls increased collaboration between the Youth Justice Board and trusts over the care of the 2,900 under-18s in young offender institutions, private secure training centres, and council-run secure units. His stated aim was to replace the then punitive approach to youth justice with early-intervention strategies designed to 'catch' potential career criminals early and prevent repeat offending. The policy—branded 'Integrated Resettlement Support' (IRS)—evoked the 'tough on crime, tough on the causes of crime' view vocally espoused by Tony Blair in his days as Shadow Home Secretary.

To steer Labour's changes to child protection policy, an independent **Children's Commissioner for England** was appointed in March 2005. The Commissioner, currently Anne Longfield, former chief executive of families charity 4Children, is responsible for:

- promoting awareness of children's views and interests among all sectors;
- collaborating with organizations that take decisions affecting all aspects of children's lives, including police, schools, hospitals, and voluntary groups;
- enforcing the framework of the five 'Every Child Matters' outcomes and children's rights under the 1989 UN Convention on the Rights of the Child; and
- protecting children in accordance with the United Nations Convention on the Rights of the Child (UNCRC).

In the run-up to the first Commissioner's appointment, consultation among children found that their main concerns were bullying, personal safety, and pressure in education (especially exams). Difficulties associated with deprived and minority social backgrounds were also raised. More recently, the Children and Families Act 2014 extended the Commissioner's remit to allow her to provide advice and assistance directly to children living in care or otherwise away from home. Crucially, it also gave her (or an appointed agent) powers to enter premises other than private dwellings to interview a child or inspect the quality of care being provided to him or her. Inclusion of this clause was prompted, in large part, by the slew of revelations about historical abuse of juveniles in institutional care which emerged in the wake of the scandal over alleged serial sex attacks by late television presenter Jimmy Savile. There is a separate Children's Commissioner for Wales; a Northern Ireland Commissioner for Children and Young People; and a Children and Young People's Commissioner for Scotland.

A further significant reform flowing from 'Every Child Matters' was the requirement placed on children's services departments to develop integrated systems to coordinate needs assessments, planning, early intervention, and periodic reviews of local services. As of April 2006, social care for under-16s was removed from the general social services arena and combined with education provision under this new all-embracing umbrella. The Act also stipulated that every authority—with the initial exception of those with 'excellent' ratings under the then government performance monitoring regime (Comprehensive Area Assessment/CAA)—must publish periodic 'children and young people's plans' (CYPPs), to which every local agency should contribute. These should detail all local services for children and young people, and the shared objectives of partner organizations for improving them.

The council-run boards demanded by Lord Laming were introduced in the guise of **local safeguarding children's boards (LSCBs)**. These are charged with coordinating the various agencies involved in delivering services and monitoring their collective effectiveness. The Act defined three levels of action to be taken by boards, as outlined in table 17C, entitled 'Three levels of responsibility of local safeguarding children's boards', to be found on the **Online Resource Centre**. In Scotland, the role of LSCB is taken by local multi-agency *child protection committees (CPCs)*.

To further facilitate a more joined-up approach to caring for and supporting vulnerable children, a short-lived database, ContactPoint, was launched in 2009 enabling communication and expertise to be exchanged between different agencies involved in a child's care. Controversially, its aim was to keep on record basic identifying details for each child in England up to their eighteenth birthdays—from their names, addresses, genders, dates of birth, and unique identifying numbers, to the contact details of every service or professional to whom they were known. Amid widespread concerns about the potential for security breaches, the Coalition switched off ContactPoint in August 2010, although, in a sign of their determination to introduce their own changes to better safeguard children, ministers ordered a swift review of child protection by Eileen Munro, a professor of social policy at the London School of Economics. Published in April 2011, this argued for abandoning a top-down, target-driven approach to protecting children in favour of locally driven strategies based on past experiences and professionals' 'expert' judgments. It made the following recommendations, most of which were swiftly accepted by ministers:

- specific legal requirements for assessments of children's needs to be completed within rigid, centrally determined timescales should be scrapped;
- adapting child protection services to specific local needs and liberating them from 'nationally prescribed ways of working', with professionals trusted to redesign services based on informed research and feedback from families;
- dropping the punitive approach to serious case reviews (SCRs), instead placing more emphasis on learning from how mistakes were made and why professionals behaved as they did, rather than simply naming and shaming culprits, with Ofsted's ability to evaluate SCRs removed;

- introducing a new 'duty' for all local services to make an 'early offer of help' to families who may not (yet) meet criteria for intervention under child protection legislation, to prevent situations escalating to the point at which they do meet those criteria;
- improving Ofsted inspections of children's services, to put more weight on feedback from children and families themselves and observing social workers in action;
- encouraging experienced social workers to continue to work part-time on the front line, to ensure that their expertise is passed down directly to junior levels; and
- that each children's services authority should appoint a principal child and family social worker to report regularly the views and experiences of front-line staff to management.

To begin the process of enabling councils to adopt many of Ms Munro's recommendations, ministers confirmed that future council funding settlements would include provision for a (non-ring-fenced) **early intervention grant** (see 11.2.1.1).

Besides abandoning ContactPoint, the Coalition went on to modify certain other elements of Labour's joined-up approach to children's services. On 31 October 2010, it withdrew statutory guidance on children's trusts, allowing individual authorities more flexibility about precisely how they met the need to coordinate child protection in their areas. Although councils and their partner bodies still had to retain collaborative children's trust *boards* to manage their collective caseloads, many areas went on to adopt arrangements known as **children's partnerships**: essentially, forms of collaboration structured in less prescriptive, one-size-fits-all ways. The aim of these is to allow councils and their partners to adapt to the specific needs of their areas—harmonizing the configurations of their child protection arrangements with those of their local health and well-being boards (see 6.2.1). Additionally, the stipulation that all areas must produce CYPPs was removed, although trusts or partnerships were permitted to maintain them if doing so 'makes sense locally'.

In addition to having their own children's commissioners, each of the devolved nations has recently gone some way towards matching—if not exceeding—the levels of protection offered to juveniles by the 2004 Act. Scotland's latest safeguarding agenda—dubbed 'Getting it Right for Every Child'—has seen each child allotted their own 'named person' from 31 August 2016. This is usually a health visitor for pre-school children and a teacher or head-teacher for those of school age up to 18 (or older if they remain in school beyond that). Named persons act as points of contact for children themselves, their families, and anyone else concerned about their well-being. While the Scottish changes were introduced in the Children and Young Persons (Scotland) Act 2014, increased protection for both children and adults was the subject of the Social Services and Well-being (Wales) Act, which paved the way for the introduction of a new joint *National Independent Safeguarding Board* and All Wales Child Protection Procedures (AWCPPs). As in Scotland, this blizzard of reforms was, in part, the outcome of a series of national child protection reviews and 'action plans' for tackling child sexual exploitation—as with the recent changes in England, precipitated by the belated disclosure of historical allegations of abuse and neglect of minors in institutional care. A single *Safeguarding Board for Northern Ireland* has been responsible for coordinating child protection across the province since 2012.

17.1.3 **Care orders**

The reforms described so far illustrate the extent to which children's services and other child protection agencies have become increasingly interventionist—in part because of pressure from media, public, and families themselves. But sometimes they are required to be more proactive still, in the interests of children they fear are at serious risk of abuse or neglect if they remain with their parents or guardians. The Climbié case highlighted what can happen if early warning signs are not noted or acted upon. Similar allegations were later levelled at the same council over the death of 17 month-old Peter Connelly (known initially as 'Baby P') after eight months of abuse by his step-father and a family lodger in Haringey—just streets away from where Climbié had perished. The scandal led to the sacking of Haringey's director of children's services, Sharon Shoesmith, and the resignations of its leader and cabinet lead member for children and young people. More recently, children's services departments (and other agencies, including the police) have been vilified for failing to prevent groups of men and boys systematically grooming and abusing vulnerable girls in a number of English towns, including Rotherham, Doncaster, Keighley, and Oxford.

While lambasting the system for any failure to identify abuse, the media is equally quick to criticize conscientious social workers who, fearing that children are living in abusive environments, intervene overzealously to remove them.

Perhaps the most infamous example of heavy-handed intervention occurred in Cleveland in 1987, when 121 cases of suspected child abuse were diagnosed by two Middlesbrough-based paediatricians, Marietta Higgs and Geoffrey Wyatt. Social workers removed several children from their families during the ensuing investigation, using a power introduced under the Children and Young Persons Act 1969: a 'place of safety order'. In the end, twenty-six children from twelve families were found by judges to have been wrongly diagnosed, and cases involving another ninety-six were dismissed by the courts.

More recently, several newspapers—notably the *Daily Mail*—castigated Portsmouth City Council for being too ready to take children into care following the drowning of a 17-month-old girl, Anna Hider, in her foster parents' swimming pool, allegedly during a family party. But the pendulum swung back the other way yet again when news broke in April 2009 of a vicious attack by two brothers, aged 10 and 11, on two other boys in Edlington, south Yorkshire. An SCR concluded that the violent sexual assault might have been prevented had thirty-one chances to intervene with the families not been missed by nine agencies over a fourteen-year period. The case review launched by Doncaster Council under pressure from its local paper, the *Doncaster Free Press*, marked the tipping point in a five-year period during which seven children had died in and around the town—despite being registered as 'at risk'.

Recent Acts have seen successive governments attempt to walk the tightrope between guaranteeing high standards of child protection and preventing cavalier intervention by social workers and other agencies. Since the 1989 Act, the principal means by which councils have been able to take children into care for indefinite periods—often against their parents' or guardians' wishes—is by applying to family courts for **care orders**. Under these circumstances, parents or guardians must still be allowed 'reasonable access' (unless explicitly prohibited by the court), but authorities assume parental responsibility in law and have powers to determine the *degree* of contact. Occasionally, the need to safeguard a child's welfare is perceived as so urgent that a council can apply to a court for a fast-tracked order to remove him or her from a domestic threat. This is known as an **interim care order** or **emergency protection order**. Initially granted for up to eight days, and renewable for a further week, these may be granted only if a court judges there to be 'reasonable cause to believe that the child is likely to suffer considerable harm' if left alone. Since the Family Law Act 1996, emphasis has switched to removing 'the source of danger', rather than the child (for example applying for a 'non-molestation order' against another named individual will lead to his or her removal from the situation).

Councils also have the power to apply for a lesser 'supervision order'—a device enabling them to 'supervise' parents or guardians more closely than normal to ensure that children potentially at risk are properly cared for. Under the 1989 Act, a court may make an order only if satisfied that:

- a child is suffering or likely to suffer significant harm; and
- the harm or likelihood of harm is attributable to care given (or likely to be given) being below what it is 'reasonable to expect a parent to give' or the child's being 'beyond parental control' (persistently truanting from school and/or acting antisocially or criminally).

Under supervision orders, it is councils' duty to 'advise, assist, and befriend' children and approach courts for variations—converting them into care orders if they prove insufficient in practice. Likewise, councils may apply for court orders to be lifted when no longer necessary. Where requests for orders specifically relate to children's non-attendance at school or their parents' refusal to send them, a local education authority (LEA) may apply for a specific *education supervision order*.

17.1.4 Taking children into care

There are various ways, then, in which children can be removed from their homes, should professionals and courts be sufficiently concerned for their well-being. But where do these 'looked-after children' actually *live* while under protection?

Whether children are subject to emergency protection or full care orders, they will normally be accommodated either by:

- registered community children's homes; or
- foster parents.

17.1.4.1 Children's homes

As with other forms of residential accommodation for vulnerable groups, today's children's homes may either be run directly by councils or other 'registered providers', from private companies to specialist charities like Barnardo's. Although far removed from the grim Victorian orphanages and homes of yesteryear, many of those operating today still contain shared dormitories, as well as individual rooms. They tend to take both boys and girls, rather than being single-sex, and can house 100 or more children at once (although most limit their intakes to double figures).

Children's homes are designed to:

- keep young people safe;
- give them consistent boundaries and routines;
- give them assistance in accessing education;
- promote their health and well-being; and
- provide quality of life—for example games, leisure activities, and external trips.

Like adult care homes, children's homes used to be inspected by councils, but this role has shifted to a succession of quangos in recent years and is currently the responsibility of the Office of Standards in Education, Children's Services, and Skills (Ofsted—14.3.1). In Scotland, all social care inspections, including those of organizations involved in child protection, have been carried out by the Social Care and Social Work Improvement Scotland (SCSWIS, commonly known as the 'Care Inspectorate') since 2011, when it supplanted several separate bodies. The Scottish Social Services Council (SSSC) is charged with raising standards in both adult and child social care. In Wales, these functions are discharged by the Care and Social Services Inspectorate Wales (CSSIW) and the Care Council for Wales respectively; in Northern Ireland, all health and social care is regulated by a single body: the Regulation and Quality Improvement Authority (RQIA).

In July 2012, serious questions were raised about both the quality of care in children's homes and the manner in which responsible councils allocated vulnerable juveniles to them, following a highly critical report by then deputy children's commissioner Sue Berelowitz, commissioned after nine men were jailed in Rochdale for grooming and sexually abusing young girls, including one in care. This concluded that the high turnover of young people in children's homes provided a 'constant flow of vulnerable children for perpetrators to exploit'. It also highlighted the difficulty of tracking down those who went missing from care because of the absence of clear statistics on the subject.

Ms Berelowitz's report came a month after an all-party parliamentary group investigating the plight of children who vanish from care homes revealed that 46 per cent of juveniles were placed by councils miles (if not hundreds of miles) away from their native communities and support networks, with large concentrations of homes clustered in north-west and south-east coastal resorts. Condemning the 'very serious weaknesses' exposed in both reports, then Children's Minister Tim Loughton ordered councils to revise placement policies to ensure juveniles were placed locally whenever possible. Ministers also established an expert group to improve data-gathering and data-sharing to address significant disparities between official council figures for the number of children who go missing from care for twenty-four hours or more and incidents relating to vulnerable juveniles recorded by police.

In its first ever stand-alone annual report into the social care side of its remit, published in October 2013, Ofsted condemned the standard of child protection offered by twenty English councils as 'unacceptably poor' and said that only one in four councils was doing enough to safeguard children. Its chief inspector, Sir Michael Wilshaw, singled out Birmingham City Council—which failed inspections on seven separate judgments—as 'a national disgrace'. Ofsted has since overhauled its own inspections to ensure that it is picking up on child protection issues, following several recent reports of bullying and abuse by staff in schools and care homes.

17.1.4.2 Fostering

Fostering can be arranged on a long-term or short-term basis by children's services, often working with independent foster agencies. Councils tend to view it as preferable to keeping children in community homes because the involvement of designated foster parents places them in familiar, domestic-style settings, rather than impersonal institutions. Children placed in long-term foster care are normally located with 'parents' who have at least one child themselves. They may continue living in this environment for some years, although if they leave home at the age of 16, their foster carers will no longer have legal rights over them. If their stay becomes long-term, however, the foster parents may apply at some stage to adopt them. Assuming that such applications are successful, the foster carers then become the legal parents.

There are various forms of foster arrangement. The main ones are explained in table 17D to be found on the **Online Resource Centre**. The strict vetting procedure for prospective foster parents is outlined in table 17E to be found on the **Online Resource Centre**.

As with adoptive parents, there is a national shortage of foster carers. A survey published by the Fostering Network in January 2016 estimated that 9,070 more were needed to provide for all of the youngsters waiting to be placed at that time—with particular shortages of carers willing to take on teenagers, disabled children, sibling groups, and unaccompanied asylum-seeking minors.

Despite this, all foster carers qualify for allowances to cover the basic costs of clothing, feeding, and otherwise providing for children. If an arrangement is negotiated through an agency, it will set the level of allowance, usually dependent on the child's age, with carers of older juveniles qualifying for more. Since April 2007, guaranteed minimum allowance levels for children in different age groups now exist, as outlined in table 17F to be found on the **Online Resource Centre**.

Foster parents have also qualified, since 2003, for income tax allowances, enabling them to 'earn' up to £10,000 a year, tax-free, from foster payments. In addition, they receive tax reliefs of up to £200 a week for under-11 year-olds and £250 a week per child over 11 for every week or part-week for which the minor remains in their care. In addition, there is a National Insurance (NI) backed scheme called 'Home Responsibility Protection', which ensures that long-term foster parents will not retire on less than State Pension—a contributory benefit—even if they have made too few NI contributions to qualify under normal rules.

17.1.5 Adoption

The distinction between fostering and **adoption** is that while the former is (in theory) a temporary arrangement, the latter is permanent. At any point, up to 4,000 children across Britain are looking for adoptive parents. By law, children can be adopted only through adoption agencies—either councils or government-approved registered adoption societies (voluntary agencies). Most cover radiuses of around fifty miles from their offices. Not all arrange placements themselves, but they may carry out adoption assessments to ensure that prospective adoptive parents are suitable.

Who, then, is entitled to adopt? Until recently, the right was largely restricted to married heterosexual couples, with those under the age of 40 more likely to be successful than older applicants. But much of this changed with the Adoption and Children Act 2002, which opened adoption up to single people, as well as individual partners in unmarried couples (whether straight or gay). The law was further tweaked in 2005, enabling unmarried couples to apply jointly—effectively giving them the same rights as married ones. For gay

Table 17.1 Criteria for prospective adopters

Criterion	Meaning
Age	Must be over 21 and able to prove they will make space in their lives for child, and are patient, flexible, energetic, and determined to make difference to child's life. No official upper age limit, although agencies can favour younger people.
Criminal background checks	Must not have been convicted of serious child-related offence. More minor offences must be looked into, but may not preclude adoption.
Relationship status	Couples married or in civil partnerships, single people, or individual partners in unmarried couples (heterosexual, lesbian, or gay) may adopt. Unmarried couples may apply to adopt jointly. Ban on gay and unmarried couples adopting in Northern Ireland overturned by Supreme Court in December 2013.
Good health	Prospective adopters must have medical examinations and health issues (including hereditary conditions) should be explored.
Ethnic/cultural background	People of all ethnic backgrounds may adopt. Since Children and Families 2014, preferential treatment no longer given to prospective parents of same racial/religious identity as child (influenced by research into well-being of minority-adopted adults who grew up with families who did not match their ethnicities).
Disability access	People with disabilities may adopt, subject to case-by-case conditions.

couples, the procedure is normally quicker if they are married or in civil partnerships, but provided that they live together they stand as much chance of success as straight couples. Qualifying conditions for adopters are listed in Table 17.1.

Today, anyone wishing to adopt a child faces a two-stage process: 'Stage One' involves a number of preliminary checks on their suitability; 'Stage Two', which follows once they have been provisionally approved, is the serious business of matching them up with a child. The different steps involved in this process are outlined in Table 17.2. In theory, the two stages should take no more than six months to complete, but there is some variation in practice, and the procedure has been known to take longer in England than in Wales, Scotland, and Northern Ireland.

Once prospective adopters have negotiated earlier hurdles in the process, they can find themselves facing delays that are beyond their control. If a child's natural parents are willing for them to be adopted—for example if they were conceived during rapes or by mothers below the age of consent (16) who feel unable to take on the responsibility of raising them—adoption orders can be issued fairly simply by the courts. However, if the natural parents *object* to the child being adopted, agencies must apply to the courts for *freeing orders*—removing them from their parents' custody against their wishes.

Table 17.2 Adoption process

Procedure	What happens
Initial meeting(s)	Following application through agency, prospective adopter(s) meets social worker, together and individually (if in a couple), on several occasions.
Background investigation	Prospective adoptive parents' personal backgrounds investigated and they are asked reasons for adopting. Confidential enquiries made through local children's services department and police.
Personal references	Supplied by at least two friends of adopter(s), and prospective adopter(s) undergoes GP medical examination.
Independent adoption panel	Hearing by panel (linked to agency through which prospective adopter(s) has applied) considers case and decides if it should progress to final stage: opportunity to meet panel in person.
Provisional care agreed	Once adopters approved in principle, child put into their provisional care (children's services authorities or adoption panels must be notified if done through approved adoption society).
Adoption order confirmed	Decision made by family proceedings court, sitting in private, three months after notification to authority.
Contact order established (if relevant)	Court orders that contact be allowed (or not) with former parents or guardians, under clearly specified circumstances

Growing adoption waiting lists—the number of children placed with adoptive families fell by 15 per cent between March 2009 and 2010—prompted a wide-ranging review by the Coalition. Then Education Secretary Michael Gove, who was adopted himself, issued liberalized guidance for councils to speed up the process—particularly for black children, who take up to twice as long to be placed as those from other groups—while improving scrutiny of the 76 per cent of agencies then recently rated 'good' or 'outstanding'. It was nearly a year before Mr Cameron formally detailed government plans to introduce a 'foster to adopt' system and a 'faster, fairer' vetting process, focusing on measures to make it easier for white parents to adopt black children (and vice versa) and forcing social workers to consult the national adoption register to fast track placements if they failed to find adoptive families locally within three months. The new fast-track system was formally introduced with the issuing of new statutory guidance to authorities and agencies in July 2013, followed by the Children and Families Act 2014. This formally removed the requirement for adoption authorities to give 'due consideration' to the 'ethnic match' between adopted child and adoptive parents; the introduction of personal budgets (see 17.2.3) for adoptive families; and a new right of access to the adoption register for prospective adopters. In addition, the Act brought in a new system of 'post-adoption contact' to minimize the disruption to a child that can be caused by contact with their former parents or guardians, with courts given powers to order that contact is (or is not) permitted—and under precisely what circumstances.

17.1.6 Childminding

Daycare provision for children outside nursery, preschool, or school is known as childminding. Registered childminders look after children in their own homes, normally while their parents or guardians are working. Under the Care Standards Act 2000, regulation of childminding is overseen by Ofsted (and its Scottish, Welsh, and Northern Irish equivalents), rather than councils. Ofsted's role is to:

- provide a register of professionals paid for looking after those under the age of 5 on an area-by-area basis; and
- inspect the homes of anyone applying to be registered as a childminder to ensure that there are adequate facilities, including toilets and play equipment.

Registration is subject to various conditions covering facilities to be provided, number of staff and their qualifications or experience, and the maximum number of children who may be minded at once (particularly those aged under 12 months). If conditions are breached, it can be revoked or modified to reduce the maximum number of children minded.

17.1.7 The Protection of Children Act 1999

Introduced following a series of high-profile scandals about child abuse in residential care homes, the Protection of Children Act 1999 saw the launch of a statutory list of all people considered unsuitable to work with children. The Consultancy Service Index, a list along these lines, had been kept by Secretaries of State since 1993, but the 1999 Act—in Scotland, the Protection of Children (Scotland) Act 2003—formalized the process by enforcing it as a statutory list, to which all existing names were added.

It requires childcare organizations to inform the government if:

- they transferred or dismissed someone who had harmed a child or put one at risk; or
- an individual evaded disciplinary action along these lines by resigning or retiring.

17.2 Adult social services and the rise of community-based care

Although children's services account for the bulk of councils' social care budgets—and attract the most media coverage—councils retain significant responsibilities towards the elderly and working-age adults with enduring physical and mental illnesses or disabilities.

Until relatively recently, much of the care provided for people falling into these categories was delivered in institutional environments: long-stay care homes (like adult versions of children's homes) or nursing homes for those who could no longer look after their own basic needs alone.

People with mental disorders severe enough to prevent them continuing to live at home were often transferred for prolonged periods into NHS-run mental hospitals or specialist secure asylums managed by councils. The oldest of these facilities had been established in the early 1800s, and many continued in more or less uninterrupted use for the best part of 200 years. But under Margaret Thatcher and John Major, a revolution occurred that transformed the culture of social care for both the mentally ill and all other categories of adult 'service-user'.

This transformation came in the form of the National Health Service and Community Care Act 1990, which restyled patients as 'clients' and ushered in the now-notorious policy of 'Care in the Community'. In simple terms, it aimed to:

- place greater emphasis on **community care**—providing support for elderly people and those with illnesses or disabilities in their homes, enabling them to remain in 'community' settings for longer, reducing pressure on acute wards and residential facilities; and
- improve cost-effectiveness of social care, and increase choice for 'service users', by means of greater involvement of private and voluntary-sector providers.

Although few opposed the idea of empowering the vulnerable to continue living in community settings in *theory*, many were alarmed by the way in which the NHS and councils began implementing the Act in practice. Long starved of funding for the 'Cinderella service' of mental health, and with many homes and asylums severely under-occupied (and therefore uneconomical), many councils and NHS trusts used freedoms granted by the Act to shut down half-empty units—discharging inpatients to return to 'the community' irrespective of their personal support networks or ability to fend for themselves.

Tabloid newspapers reported a slew of scare stories about assaults, and even killings, by prematurely discharged mental patients. Most infamous was the 1992 murder of musician Jonathan Zito by someone suffering paranoid schizophrenia, who had been released from mental hospital just weeks earlier under 'Care in the Community'. Mr Zito's death prompted his wife, Jayne, to set up the Zito Trust, which continues to campaign for changes to mental health policy in the best interests of patients and public. Other high-profile cases included the 1996 murders of Lin Russell and her 6 year-old daughter, Megan, by Michael Stone on a country lane in Kent. Stone, who had a severe personality disorder, had been out of prison, under 'community care' arrangements, since 1992.

At the time of the murders, it was not only the 1990 Act that attracted media condemnation, but also the Mental Health Act 1983, which, opponents claimed, contained a loophole preventing mental health professionals providing care for people suffering from untreatable conditions, such as Stone's, even when they asked for help (he had repeatedly pleaded to be admitted to Broadmoor). More recently, in July 2010, it emerged that fugitive gunman Raoul Moat—who led police on a week-long manhunt after murdering his ex-partner's boyfriend, and shooting both her and a police constable—had asked Newcastle City Council social workers to refer him to a psychiatrist months before his rampage.

But not every aspect of the renewed emphasis on community care has proved negative. For many elderly and disabled people, the channelling of social services funding into care packages tailored to their individual needs, and home adaptations to make their domestic environments more comfortable and user-friendly, has proved liberating—enabling them to spend crucial extra years living near friends and family, which would have been 'lost' had they been prematurely admitted to residential care.

The responsibilities with which councils are charged under the 1990 Act in relation to community care are listed in table 17G to be found on the **Online Resource Centre**.

Nonetheless, the 'Care in the Community' controversy proved so enduring that, when Labour returned to power, it scrapped it (although in practice the 1990 Act remains the main legal basis underpinning adult social care). Community care is still ministers' preferred option for caring for the elderly and disabled, until such time as they require full-time nursing, although the balance has been redressed somewhat between domiciliary and residential care.

Ensuing reforms included:

- the Health Act 1999, which introduced a new NHS structure and partnerships with the private sector, formally abolishing the joint consultative committees (JCCs) established in 1977; and
- the National Carers' Strategy, which built on the Carers (Recognition and Services) Act 1996, giving statutory recognition to the work of unpaid relatives or friends looking after people receiving community care in their homes and enabling these informal carers to access their own support.

17.2.1 Community care: the limits of state provision

Councils are duty-bound to assess the needs of people requiring care as a result of age, infirmity, or disability. If assessments indicate these people require services, their needs must be determined, along with the extent to which they can be expected to contribute to their own care. Some authorities have been accused of raising the bar with 'eligibility criteria' owing to budgetary concerns, but courts have ruled it appropriate for councils to take their financial resources into account when setting those criteria.

The principal community care services that can be accessed through councils—many means-tested, and most now delivered by charities, voluntary organizations or private agencies, rather than councils themselves—include:

- home help (assistance with washing, dressing, and/or cleaning the home);
- hot meals ('meals on wheels');
- help with shopping and financial management;
- advocacy (advice and support with accessing other services, paying bills, etc.);
- telephone access;
- cheap travel (bus passes and free transport to appointments);
- free and accessible parking by means of the 'disabled badge holder' scheme;
- day-care (access to day centres for structured activities, day trips, etc.);
- respite care; and
- home modifications and aids to daily living (stair lifts and hoists are usually provided by housing departments, while wheelchairs and other mobility aids are often accessed through the NHS or charities).

In addition, training and employment can be provided for disabled people in sheltered workshops, while day nurseries and centres are available for their children.

These days, community care 'packages' are arranged by individuals' key workers. Because most social care professionals now work in multidisciplinary teams designed to improve coordination between social services, NHS, and the other agencies, these may be social workers, community psychiatric nurses (CPNs), or occupational therapists (OTs). The OTs' expertise lies in assessing individuals' capacity to perform basic tasks for themselves and providing support in carrying them out where needed. In Scotland, Wales, and Northern Ireland, the extent of this collaborative working is far more extensive—as is that in relation to children's social services—because of the progressively more integrated approach to health and social care provision adopted in each nation (see 6.2.3). So far, full integration of NHS and social care services in England has been limited to the newly liberated Greater Manchester Combined Authority (and, prospectively, the other major metropolitan authorities due to adopt similar powers from 2017), but an important agent of this change across the rest of the country is a new single, pooled £5.3bn-a-year 'Better Care Fund' launched by ministers in the 2013 spending round with a specific emphasis on providing more community-based care for older and disabled people. This budget—a collaboration between NHS England, the Department of Health, the Department for Communities and Local Government, and LGA, and backed by an online information-sharing resource, the 'Better Care Exchange'—is intended to fund working projects that involve the NHS and local authorities delivering services together. As of the 2015 spending review, an additional £1.5bn per year was pledged for the fund by 2019–20, as a mark of the then Cameron government's commitment to furthering health and social care integration in coming years.

Key workers have a statutory duty to produce—and regularly update—'care plans' individually tailored to their clients' needs. These should be made available to them or their carers in writing, on request, and should include the following details:

- services to be provided (and by whom), when and where this will happen, and what the services are intended to achieve;
- contact details for dealing with problems about service delivery; and
- information on how to ask for a review of services if circumstances change.

Specific concerns about the plight of people with serious mental health issues led to the introduction, in 1991, of a more rigorous care plan procedure, known as the 'care programme approach' (or 'care plan approach'). This is broken down into four stages, as follows.

1. Initial assessment of the client's needs.
2. Consultation with all professionals involved, any informal carer, and (depending on their degree of mental capacity) the client themselves.
3. Appointment of a key worker.
4. Coordination of services agreed on the basis of the initial assessment by that professional.

As with residential care, the quality of domiciliary care (home care) for the elderly has encountered repeated criticism. In March 2012, consumer group *Which?* branded much of that offered to older people in their homes 'disgraceful', referring to a litany of missed visits by professionals, soiled beds, and food being left out of reach as illustrations of typical complaints detailed in diaries kept by thirty service-users and carers that January. Although the organization declined to 'name and shame' errant providers, it highlighted the growing issue of disinterested private care agencies. In a separate survey, half the respondents said that prearranged home visits had been missed in the previous six months—with six out of ten receiving no prior warning. Four months later, a survey of 739 companies providing domiciliary care by the UK Homecare Association concluded that three-quarters of councils were 'rationing' home visits for budgetary reasons by demanding that they be completed within half an hour. One in ten imposed time limits of just fifteen minutes. A knock-on effect of shabby homecare provision can be rises in emergency hospital admissions for vulnerable people that might otherwise have been avoided—trends that pile pressure on the NHS (see Chapter 6). In its fifth '*State of Care*' report, published in November 2015, the Care Quality Commission (CQC—see 17.2.5) found that, while 'many' providers had improved their performance in the previous year, some vulnerable people were still receiving care that was 'unacceptable', with 13 per cent of hospitals, one in ten adult social care services, and 6 per cent of GP practices inspected in 2014–15 rated 'inadequate for safety'.

17.2.2 Home carers

Britain's rapidly ageing population, coupled with the growing emphasis on community-based care, has led to a huge rise in the number of carers—people who spend part of their lives looking after elderly or disabled relations in their or the other person's home. According to Carers UK, as of June 2014 there were 6.5 million unpaid carers in Britain. Of these, 175,000 or more were aged 18 or under and 1.5 million were over 60.

Long-running campaigns by carer support groups led to belated recognition of their work, initially through the 1996 Act (entitling them to limited respite care), and the ten-year National Carers' Strategy established by the Blair–Brown governments.

In practice, although they improved the situation for some, these strategies were just that. Recent studies suggest that carers still feel isolated, undervalued, and bewildered by the often labyrinthine network of services and providers theoretically available to them, and the bureaucratic processes involved in accessing them. A 2013 report by Carers UK, entitled *Prepared to Care*, found that the burden of caring had led 42 per cent of carers to suffer relationship breakdowns with family members, while six out of ten struggled to maintain friendships. A similar proportion suffered from depression, while 92 per cent of respondents said that their caring roles had left them feeling more 'stressed'.

17.2.3 Choice in community care: the rise of direct payments

As if service-users and carers did not already face a tough enough task in navigating the maze of community care options available to them, recent governments have put them more directly in the driving seat as part of their 'choice' agenda (see Chapter 6). The Tories introduced this concept, in the Community Care (Direct Payments) Act 1996, which enabled councils to make cash payments to dependent individuals, so they could 'buy' their own services from providers of their choice. The approach was not mandatory, and councils were required to ensure that individuals to whom they paid money had the capacity to take informed decisions about their needs and access suitable services. In some cases—when evidence suggested they had spent the money on things other than services related to their 'needs', such as alcohol or gambling—councils could halt direct payments and even require payments to be refunded.

Since 2006, when Labour embraced the idea of these individual budgets in its own White Paper, they have gone through various transformations (and changes of name)—from 'personal budgets' to 'direct payments'—and many English social care authorities now require those eligible for means-tested financial help to hold their own purse strings, or have the money transferred to a trust that can be managed on their behalf by a carer. Ironically, a device predicated on the concept of choice has become mandatory—infuriating some campaigners for the elderly and mentally, not to mention service-users themselves who do not always feel up to the task of shopping around for care. Though individual budgets have slowly been introduced elsewhere in the UK, notably in Scotland, the degree of compulsion used to introduce them has tended to be less: in other words, in the spirit of choice, people have been allowed to 'opt out' of the system if they so wish.

17.2.4 Care homes, nursing homes, and the rise of the private sector

When people are no longer well enough to continue living in their own homes, or with carers, they are normally moved into either long-term residential care homes or those with nursing provision ('nursing homes'). The former are usually 'low dependency' environments, in which residents can enjoy relatively independent lifestyles in the company of other people of similar age or with comparable physical or mental needs. Nursing homes, in contrast, are targeted at individuals with more severe physical or mental impairments—often the very old or those at advanced stages in the progression of their conditions—who require care provided or supervised by registered nurses.

Broadly speaking, the process followed when elderly people reach the point of requiring residential accommodation is as follows:

- Assessment by key workers in multidisciplinary teams, followed by placement in homes suited to their needs (council, voluntary, or private) Where private homes are chosen, their ability to pay 'the full economic cost' of their care is assessed—taking into account the value of any property in their name, which might be sold to contribute to home fees.

Since the late 1980s, there has been a marked increase in the amount of residential care provided by private companies, rather than councils. In many areas, homes are no longer maintained by councils directly: all are owned and managed by the private or charitable sectors.

In tandem with the expansion of private provision and rising fees, Mr Major's government risked infuriating the 'grey vote' with new moves to divide the cost of residential care between state and individual. Under the 1990 Act, anyone with assets of £16,000 or more—including the home in which he or she lived until going into care—was expected to pay for themselves up to the point at which that money was exhausted (at which stage, the state took over). In practice, this meant many people—particularly widows and widowers whose homes were entirely their own—were 'forced' to sell houses and flats for which they had spent much of their working lives paying. The 'capital/assets limit' remains in place, but has been raised incrementally over time to £23,250, although anyone with assets of £14,250 or more must contribute £1 for every £250 that they own above that amount. Mr Cameron's government legislated to introduce a new 'care cap' from April 2016—in essence, a ceiling on the maximum amount any over 65 year-old or younger adult with disabilities should be expected to pay for their own care of £72,000—but in July 2015 ministers delayed this until 2020, after worried councils warned them that implementing the policy at that time would have left them with a £4.3bn 'black hole' in their budgets by the end of the decade. Also postponed were other plans in the Care Act 2014, including a commitment to lifting the threshold above which people have to start contributing to their own care costs to £17,000, while raising the upper assets limit fivefold, to £118,500.

In the meantime, devolution has already seen the emergence of variations in this system, with the Welsh Assembly introducing a slightly higher upper means test threshold (currently £24,000) and the Scottish Parliament, an even more generous one (£25,750). Since 2002, families of care home residents in Scotland have also benefited from government guidance directing councils to introduce 'deferred payment' schemes, under which the balance of any contribution owed is paid from the beneficiary's estate after his or her death.

For all the procrastination over reforms in England, an unexpected boost to the funding of adult social care came in the November 2015 Comprehensive Spending Review, when Chancellor George Osborne introduced a 'social care precept' allowing local authorities to raise Council Tax by 2 per cent without a referendum provided the money was spent on adult social services (see 11.2.4.3).

Another source of tension that emerged in the 1990s was that between social services departments and the NHS over how to provide for people not yet in need of residential care, but who experienced frequent, sometimes prolonged, bouts of ill health necessitating in-patient treatment. Hard-pressed acute hospitals, already struggling with long waiting lists, increasingly became the subject of news reports about 'bed-blockage' ('bed-blocking')—the need to cater for vulnerable patients too sick to be sent home, but for whom residential care was either unavailable or not yet deemed necessary.

Given that more than half of those over the age of 65 now have a disabling condition requiring long-term care, and that Britain's population is ageing fast, it is no wonder that bed-blocking remains a serious issue as councils struggle to find enough care home places to meet demand—particularly for those with unusual or debilitating ailments. Yet critics argue that governments have merely intensified pressure, by getting tough with councils found 'guilty' of contributing to bed-blocking, rather than concentrating on boosting residential care places. Under the Community Care (Delayed Discharges etc.) Act 2003, NHS hospitals may fine councils up to £120 a day for every 'blocked' bed. The Act was motivated, in part, by a 2001 Audit Commission report that found that two out of three patients in English hospitals at any one time were over 65, with around 5,000 people on any given day unnecessarily stuck on acute wards. But hospitals have lately found themselves in a Catch-22: to discourage them from discharging patients prematurely, then Health Secretary Mr Lansley announced in 2010 that those having to readmit the same individuals within a month of sending them 'home' would receive no extra funding for additional treatment.

Whether the incipient integration of health and social care in England will address some of these issues remains to be seen, but the example of Wales—where this is already largely the case—suggests that integration is unlikely to be a magic bullet. In January 2016, Welsh health boards were awarded an extra £2.5m by the Cardiff government to alleviate bed-blocking, after a record 435 people were left stranded on the wards the previous month due to a lack of space in care homes and delays in carrying out community assessments.

17.2.5 Regulating social care

The regulator charged with ensuring high-quality care standards throughout England is the **Care Quality Commission (CQC)** (see also 6.2.2). In the social care field, it inspects day centres, care homes, domiciliary care agencies, nurses' agencies, children's homes, and residential special schools.

All residential care and nursing homes must be formally registered under the Registered Homes (Amendment) Act 1991 (previously the Registered Homes Act 1984), but since 2004 the 18,500 listed homes have also had to register separately with the CQC. On inspection, all care organizations (including agencies) are rated under a star system. The meanings of these classifications are as follows:

- no stars—poor;
- *—adequate;
- **—good; and
- ***—excellent.

Following an inspection (or subsequent investigation), the CQC may either demand that an organization meets specified 'conditions to improve', bringing it up to agreed minimum standards, or—in extreme cases—order its closure. Since July 2014, homes requiring urgent action short of closure have also been subject to 'special measures', in the same way as ailing hospitals, GP practices, and failing schools (see 14.3.1). In addition, instances of abuse or neglect may be referred to the police and Crown Prosecution Service (CPS). The Commission is especially vigilant in relation to adults with serious disabilities or impairments that put them at greater risk of abuse—in line with the 'Protection of Vulnerable Adults' (POVA) scheme introduced in July 2004. As with cared-for children, anyone directly caring for vulnerable adults must undergo periodic CRB checks and there are bans preventing those who have harmed such people previously from working with them again.

Although the CQC has tightened regulation of the increasingly disparate social care 'market', serious concerns have been repeatedly raised about the rigour with which inspections are carried out. In June 2008, an investigation by Radio 4's *Today* programme found that many of the Commission's own inspectors were unhappy with the frequency and quality of its inspections. More than 200 employees of the then Commission for Social Care Inspection (CSCI)—now absorbed into the CQC—participated in an anonymous questionnaire, with one commenting: 'I wouldn't leave my dog in 90 per cent of our care homes.'

Criticism of social care regulation has been sharpened following a slew of deeply critical reports published since 2011 exposing the poor quality of residential and inpatient provision for elderly people. The first to attract media attention collated ten investigations into inadequate care by English NHS trusts and two GP practices carried out by then Parliamentary and Health Service Ombudsman Ann Abraham. In October 2011, the CQC concluded that more than half of the 100 hospitals it had inspected were 'failing' older people, with one in five inadequately catering for their 'dignity' or nutritional needs: two benchmarks emphasized in revised standards introduced a year earlier. Its findings prompted Mr Lansley to fast track inspections for 500 nursing homes, inviting Age UK to recruit past and present service users to participate. Two months later, the first ever 'National Audit of Dementia'—covering 210 hospitals in England and Wales—identified 'problems across practically every aspect of care for patients admitted to hospitals'. It pinpointed the impersonal manner of staff, poor training and supervision, and patients' feelings of being ignored as key issues—despite the fact that separate figures suggested one in four hospital beds was occupied by people with dementia.

Long-term care homes have come in for even harsher criticism. In February 2012, a commission set up by Age UK, the NHS Confederation, and the Local Government Association (LGA) published a report, *Delivering Dignity*, in which they issued 'a call to arms to the whole health and social care system'—recommending that residents be directly involved in day-to-day management decisions, that ageist language be stamped out, and that a new rating system be introduced to inform future CQC inspections. The report's overarching emphasis was on improving the quality of the care home experience, by moving beyond a utilitarian approach to running homes—whereby efficiency was measured purely in terms of the speed with which tasks such as washing, dressing, and feeding were performed—toward one in which residents were enabled to lead more active, fulfilling lives. Other recommendations included the establishment of a Nursing and Care Quality Forum (subsequently established) to raise standards of professionalism in older people's care and improve training for everyone from front-line care workers to managers.

In addition to formal regulation, since the Health and Social Care Act 2012 the social care sector has been subject to the advice and oversight of the recently renamed National Institute of Health and Care Excellence (NICE—see 6.2.2). Its primary role is to develop and publish statutory guidance and quality standards for all aspects of social care, based on an 'evidence-based' model drawing on examples of good (and bad) practice in the field. The first five aspects of social care that it was charged with reviewing (based on concerns arising from then recent scandals) were home care, the care of older adults with long-term conditions, improving the transition from NHS to social care settings for older people, improving the transition from children's to adult services, and handling cases of child abuse and neglect.

17.2.6 'Sectioning' the mentally ill

Since the Mental Health Act 1983, councils have had limited powers to detain mentally infirm adults not in residential care in specialist hospitals or units: a process known as 'sectioning' after the appropriate sections in this and subsequent Acts. The procedures by which they may do so are outlined in table 17H to be found on the **Online Resource Centre**.

17.2.7 The Mental Health Act 2007

Before it finally received royal assent in July 2007, Labour's Mental Health Bill endured one of the rockiest rides of any piece of legislation in recent memory. At the heart of the Bill were two key proposals that provoked fury among mental health and human rights campaigners and an award-winning campaign by *The Independent on Sunday*:

- new powers enabling doctors to detain people with serious mental health conditions who might pose potential risks to themselves or others, primarily for public protection; and
- authority for clinicians (GPs and psychiatrists) to 'impose' treatment on the severely mentally ill, regardless of their wishes and even if they were judged to have mental capacity to make their own decisions.

At various stages, the Bill was opposed by campaign groups—most notably, the Mental Health Alliance, a coalition of seventy-eight organizations, including

Mind, the King's Fund, and various bodies representing practitioners. It was eventually watered down, although the ability of doctors to prescribe enforced medication remained in the final version.

The Act's other main features are listed in table 17I to be found on the **Online Resource Centre**.

Prior to the Act, Labour introduced a marginally less controversial reform in the guise of the Mental Capacity Act 2005, which enshrined the rights of people with severe mental health issues to exercise power over their own care that had previously existed only in common law. The Act covered only England and Wales, but similar provisions had earlier been made under the Adults with Incapacity (Scotland) Act 2000.

The 2005 Act also introduced:

- an Independent Mental Capacity Advocate Service (IMCAS) for England and another for Wales from 2007;
- criminal offences of 'wilful neglect' and 'ill-treatment';
- the ability of service users to nominate 'substitute decision-makers' to their nearest relatives under a new lasting power of attorney (LPA); and
- a Court of Protection with extended powers.

As well as addressing concerns about the financial means tests for those needing long-term residential care, the Care Act 2014 also introduced several new measures designed to protect adults with mental health issues and/or learning difficulties. Specifically, it required all social services authorities to establish **safeguarding adults boards (SABs)**, to match their existing LSCBs, which will be responsible for 'helping and protecting' adults in need of 'care and support' and/or 'experiencing', or 'at risk' of, 'abuse or neglect'. Those moving from one council area to another also have a right to an immediate needs assessment to ensure that they do not miss out on services to which they are entitled—an innovation known by the buzzword 'portability'.

Topical feature idea

The following is a hard news story published in the *Birmingham Mail* on 11 February 2016, focusing on a 'bed-blocking crisis' at one of the city's acute hospitals. Your news editor asks you to explain the background to this story in a feature, 'humanizing' it by finding and/or contacting some of the families affected—suggesting that you crowd-source this information. What social media and other tools might you use to do this, and what are the ethical issues you might come up against in deciding whether, and how, to use information sourced in this way? Who else would you need to contact to build up your story, and ensure it is balanced?

Article published in *Birmingham Evening Mail*, 11 February 2016

Bed blocking crisis as number of patients 'trapped' in hospitals DOUBLES in year

By Anuji Varma

Birmingham Mail

11 February 2016

Web link: **http://www.birminghammail.co.uk/news/midlands-news/bed-blocking-crisis-number-patients-10876109**

A bed-blocking crisis is looming after figures revealed numbers of patients 'trapped' at one Birmingham hospital trust because of social care cuts has soared by 125 per cent.

Research shows the Heart of England NHS Foundation Trust (HEFT) is already struggling to move older people out of its hospitals and back into their homes.

New figures show delayed discharges—people stuck in hospitals often due to lack of social care—at the Trust are four times worse than the national average.

In the twelve months to November 2015 there were 10,151 delayed days, compared to 4,516 the previous year, a rise of 125 per cent. Nationally there was a 28 per cent rise.

Reduced social care services—including a lack of beds at residential homes—means more patients are unable to be discharged promptly.

HEFT runs Heartlands, Good Hope and Solihull hospitals.

MP Liam Byrne warned the 'battering of Birmingham' could spark a local hospitals crisis, following news the council will not benefit from a £300 million windfall to help struggling authorities.

He added:

> ‘The battering of Birmingham has got to stop. While rich Tory shires are getting a £300 million bung, we're being asked to make the biggest cuts in local government history. What's now clear is that this will spark a social care crisis that may throw our hospitals into crisis, because they simply can't get older people off the wards and back into their homes.’

New research has also showed more older people are attending A&E, with nearly 5,000 extra patients at HEFT compared to last year.

There were 59,393 emergency attendances by patients aged over 60 in 2014/15 compared to 54,772 the previous year.

This week the Government confirmed dramatic cuts to Birmingham funding, which will force the city council to make savings of £258 million.

Local Government Secretary Greg Clark told the House of Commons he was pressing ahead with the cuts, despite a campaign by city MPs and the Birmingham Mail urging him to think again.

And David Cameron was accused of a 'shameless attempt to buy votes' after it emerged most of the extra cash set aside to help councils cope with funding changes is going to Conservative areas—while Birmingham gets nothing.

✷ Current issues

- **Enhanced powers for the Children's Commissioner in England** The Children and Families Act 2014 gave the Children's Commissioner new powers to enter premises other than dwellings to interview juveniles and/or verify the quality of care they are receiving, and allowed her to directly contact children to offer them support and assistance.

- **Gradual integration of adult social care in England** The 2013 spending round introduced the 'Better Care Fund' to finance collaborative projects between the NHS and social services departments focused on providing community-based services for older and disabled adults. The £3.5bn annual fund has since been increased, with additional money coming from the new 2 per cent 'social care precept' on Council Tax.
- **Delays in introducing the 'care cap' and higher asset thresholds before adults have to pay for their own residential care** The Care Act 2014 was to have raised exempted adults from contributing to their own care costs unless they have assets of £17,000-plus, and raised the threshold above which they no longer qualified for any state assistance to £118,500—while capping the costs they could be asked to pay at £72,000. But pressure from councils persuaded ministers to delay the changes until 2020.

Key points

1. Councils responsible for social care now have two departments overseeing this: children's services and adult social services.
2. Child protection is overseen by children's services departments, collaborating with children's trusts or partnerships, based at centralized locations where families may access professionals from various agencies, and local safeguarding children boards, which meet regularly to ensure that all 'children in need' are adequately protected.
3. When children are taken into care, family environments are favoured over institutional ones. Short-term care arrangements are known as 'fostering', and long-term ones (in which carers become children's legal parents) as 'adoption'.
4. Care of disabled or elderly adults can either be provided at home or in institutional settings. Typical home care involves home help (assistance with washing, dressing, and cooking) and 'meals on wheels', while most residential care is provided in privately owned homes.
5. Regulation of adult social care in England is overseen by the Care Quality Commission (CQC), while Ofsted inspects child protection services. Scotland, Wales, and Northern Ireland have their own CQC counterparts, each overseeing both adults and children.

→ Further reading

Ayre, P. and Preston-Shoot, M. (2010) *Children's Services at a Crossroads: A Critical Evaluation of Contemporary Policy for Practice*, Lyme Regis: Russell House Publishing. **Incisive overview of the tensions between intervention and family-centred policies in contemporary child protection.**

Blackman, T., Brody, S., and Convery, J. (eds) (2001) *Social Care and Social Exclusion: A Comparative Study of Older People's Care in Europe*, Basingstoke: Palgrave Macmillan. **Thoughtful and informative comparisons between different approaches taken by six states—including Britain—to providing social care for the elderly.**

Gray, A. M. and Birrell, D. (2013) *Transforming Adult Social Care: Contemporary Policy and Practice*, Bristol: Policy Press. **Critical evaluation of the current issues and debates in social care for vulnerable adults.**

Philpot, T. (2007) *Adoption: Changing Families, Changing Times*, London: Routledge. **Examination of the British adoption laws, focusing on real-life stories and recent changes to open up the process to same-sex and unmarried couples.**

Online Resource Centre

www.oxfordtextbooks.co.uk/orc/Morrison5e/

Visit the Online Resource Centre that accompanies this book for web links and regular updates.

18

Transport, environment, leisure, and culture

As previous chapters have shown, local authorities' primary focus is raising and allocating funds, administering the planning process, and managing (if not always directly delivering) core services like schools, housing, and social care. But beyond these complex and costly areas, councils have various other responsibilities: maintaining roads; licensing pubs and nightclubs; inspecting hotels and restaurants; and providing museums, theatres, and libraries. This broad sweep of service areas—covering everything from public transport to environmental health and trading standards—is where the basic utilitarian needs represented by the core spending areas give way to services designed to improve people's quality of life.

18.1 Highways and public transport

A prime motivator for the introduction of the earliest local authorities was the promotion of production and trade, and the need to service the rapidly evolving agricultural and manufacturing economy ushered in by the Industrial Revolution. To this end, embryonic nineteenth-century councils became preoccupied with two broad areas of policy designed to facilitate economic expansion:

- *highways and transport*: specifically, the movement of workers and goods from country to town, and between markets, and the maintenance of proper roads; and
- *public health*: the provision of housing and sanitation of sufficient quality to cater for the workers on whose labour the new economy rested—responsibilities split today between councils' housing (see Chapter 16),

environmental health, and waste management functions, and their recently re-acquired public health role (see 18.2.4).

For hundreds of years, the only highways of navigable standard were the remains of Roman roads and others built from the Tudor era onwards by local parish councils. But the growth of commerce and long-distance trade in the eighteenth century meant that industrialists and merchants soon recognized the need for their goods to be transported speedily and safely. This prompted a dramatic boost in private investment in highways, motivated by pure self-interest.

The main developments early in the history of highways and public transport are outlined in table 18A to be found on the **Online Resource Centre** that accompanies this book.

18.1.1 Types of road and the highways authorities responsible for them

Construction and maintenance of Britain's labyrinthine road network is today divided between several authorities. Minor roads and those linking two or more towns are usually maintained by county councils, unitary authorities, or metropolitan boroughs, but the longest and widest (A-roads and M-roads/motorways) are normally overseen by the Secretary of State for Transport. Upkeep of these primary roads falls to a government-owned company, **Highways England**—formerly an executive agency of the Department for Transport (DfT) called the Highways Agency (HA). While highway maintenance may sound like a dull subject for news stories, inadequate street lighting, potholes, and general road disrepair are among the most common causes of complaints to councils (which actually makes them very newsworthy). The main road designations and authorities responsible for them are outlined in Table 18.1.

New highways are usually either the result of deliberate local and/or central government road-building schemes—in which case, they are automatically 'adopted' by the relevant authority once built—or incidental outcomes of house-building programmes. In the latter case, a scheme's developer will normally sign a formal agreement with the planning authority to ensure that it can hand over responsibility for the roads when building is complete. Such agreements are backed with 'bonds' issued by banks or building societies to ensure that, if the developer enters receivership or defaults, the roads will be finished without costing local taxpayers.

In some circumstances, however, highways—normally footpaths or bridleways—may be closed or diverted to enable development. There are two main ways in which this is done:

- If a highway is being closed because it is no longer used, the authority must apply to magistrates for an 'extinguishment order' under the Highways Acts.

Table 18.1 Types of road and authorities responsible for them

Road type	Definition	Authority
Trunk roads (M- and major A-roads)	Major roads linking towns/cities and/or connecting them to ports/airports. Normally divided into dual carriageways, biggest are multilane motorways. M25 in process of becoming 8-lane motorway, with junctions 12–14 boasting 10 and another stretch (junctions 14–15) 12 lanes.	Transport Secretary and Highways England
County roads (A-roads)	Major arterial roads (almost all A-roads) linking smaller towns, normally within single county.	County councils, unitary authorities, metropolitan borough councils, and London boroughs
Secondary roads (B-roads), and public bridleways and footpaths	B-roads and smaller rural and urban roads, particularly those linking villages, hamlets, and minor settlements. Bridleways and footpaths—often just dirt tracks—following medieval/ Roman/ancient routes and paths through fields and woodland.	Councils (as county roads)
Private roads	Highways contained within boundaries of private estates such as Canary Wharf, east London, or City of London.	Private estates and related businesses (e.g. Canary Wharf)—unless road formally adopted by relevant council under Private Street Works Act 1892

- A highway can be *realigned* to run around, rather than through, a development, by granting a 'public path diversion order' under various Town and Country Planning Acts.

Developers must conduct detailed research before embarking on their plans, to ensure they have applied for any necessary extinguishment or diversion orders. This is done by consulting a 'definitive rights of way map' maintained by the council.

18.1.2 The Secretary of State and Highways England

Because of their major infrastructural significance, motorways are designated 'special roads' by government. In relation to both motorways and trunk roads, the Transport Secretary is responsible for:

- *overall policy*—approving new M-/A-roads, the use of tolls and other road-pricing, and the balance between road-building and investment in passenger transport via the railways and airports;

- *planning, improvement, and maintenance*—the logistics of building, repairing, and maintaining major roads, and implementing policies on the ground; and
- *financing and controlling* the trunk road and motorway programme through taxation.

In practice, many important decisions were traditionally taken in (recently abolished) regional government offices, with most maintenance and improvement overseen by the Highways Agency, which, in turn, subcontracted hands-on engineering work to private companies. In addition, although county councils and unitaries have long undertaken road maintenance on the government's behalf, this too is franchised out to contractors.

There is also an increasingly complex system by which primary, secondary, and unclassified roads can be 'designated' to lower-tier authorities to take control of their day-to-day maintenance, ensure smooth traffic flows, and tackle congestion and pollution from noise and petrol fumes. The Transport Secretary can 'designate' responsibility for maintaining motorways and major A-roads to London boroughs, while county councils do likewise to boroughs/districts. When roads are designated downwards, this is known as 'de-trunking'.

From 1994 to 2015, responsibility for building and maintaining England's major road network was down to the Highways Agency, which had its own board and a chief executive latterly earning upwards of £330,000. However, as part of a £15 billion 'road investment strategy', the Lib Dem–Conservative Coalition renamed the HA Highways England and turned it into a government-owned company, in an effort to give it the fleet-footedness to operate more quickly and efficiently, in the manner of a commercial firm—a move some critics viewed as a form of backdoor roads privatization akin to the creation of Railtrack twenty-five years earlier (see 7.5.1.4). Highways England has the following responsibilities in relation to England's A- and M-roads:

- promoting economic growth by improving the road infrastructure;
- managing traffic;
- tackling congestion;
- providing information to road users;
- improving journey times, road safety, and reliability; and
- minimizing the impact of the road network on the environment.

As with other aspects of planning (see Chapter 15), the aim of introducing Highways England was to remove much of the bureaucracy previously associated with gaining approval for major infrastructural projects. However, significant schemes still need to go through certain key planning stages, as outlined in table 18B to be found on the **Online Resource Centre**. In addition, Highways England's conduct is overseen by both a new statutory regulator, the *Office of Rail and Road*, and a consumer watchdog, **Transport Focus**, which, as well as representing road users and bus passengers, encompasses the oversight role previously held by *Passenger Focus* in relation to rail (see 7.5.1.4).

In the past, road projects have seldom gone smoothly. Numerous high-profile protests have been raised against major projects, among the most famous being the campaign against the 'Newbury Bypass'—a 9-mile stretch of dual carriageway built around the market town of Newbury, Berkshire. From January to April 1996, 7,000 protestors—ranging from hardcore environmentalists to middle-aged professionals and pensioners—picketed a 360-acre site in an effort to thwart the building programme, which involved felling 120 acres of ancient woodland. In the end, the work went ahead—but not before the cost of policing the protest (dubbed 'Operation Prospect') topped £5 million, and that of hiring private security firms to erect fences and patrol the perimeter reached £24 million. Other notable protests include those over the construction of the A30 between Exeter and Honiton in Devon, which saw a network of tunnels and tree houses built at a camp near Fairmile. Highways England's role does not encompass the capital, where Transport for London is in charge of keeping the city running (**see** 10.5.1). A similarly overarching transport agency exists north of the border, in the form of Transport Scotland, while major roads in Wales are overseen directly by the Welsh Assembly and those in Northern Ireland by the Department of Regional Development, Northern Ireland.

Road-building continues to be a sensitive issue across Britain, not least because there is little evidence that continuing expansion of the network has eased congestion. Studies suggest that funnelling government spending away from public transport and into road-building programmes *increases* traffic jams—by encouraging more people to drive. A 2002 review by transport consultant Halliburton predicted an increase in congestion in the M25 corridor of a third by 2016 unless radical steps were taken to persuade people to use public transport, such as charging tolls or introducing a luxury bus service around the motorway. In the event, the M25's western arm had become so congested by 2016 that Highways England floated some 250 radical ideas for relieving pressure on the road—including a 'double-decker' section of motorway between junctions 10 and 16 and a new high-speed rail link between Heathrow and Gatwick airports.

Concern about road policy is arguably one of the rare issues to unite supporters and opponents, albeit from different perspectives: to environmental campaigners, congestion causes serious pollution and long-term ecological damage, while to motorists and long-distance hauliers traffic jams are a source of discomfort and frustration. Ministers have launched numerous initiatives in recent years to address congestion and pollution, as listed in table 18C to be found on the **Online Resource Centre**.

18.1.3 Local traffic management, road-pricing, and congestion charging

The term 'traffic management' was, for years, synonymous with little more than road crossings, signs, lights, and 'lollipop ladies': in short, bread-and-butter mechanisms used to direct traffic from A to B, help pedestrians to cross it safely, and 'warn' motorists about everything from changes in speed limits to steep slopes, sharp bends, and bumpy surfaces. To a large extent, councils remain preoccupied with these and other humdrum concerns—many of which continue to excite the attention of local journalists. The more workaday responsibilities of highways departments include planning, installing, and monitoring everything from traffic lights, roundabouts, and 'sleeping policemen' (speed bumps) to positioning road signs, cycle and bus lanes, and one-way systems, and introducing free 'park and ride' bus services to and from town centres.

In recent years, traffic management has entered a new phase, as pedestrians' and motorists' frustration with mounting congestion has sparked growing calls from both environmentalists and businesses for radical action to address the unsustainable growth in private car ownership. Environmentalists' prime concerns remain pollution caused by carbon monoxide exhaust fumes and noise generated by heavy traffic. Business leaders, meanwhile, are increasingly alarmed by the impact of lengthy traffic delays on the smooth running of the economy. A 2016 survey for TomTom, a manufacturer of satellite navigation (satnav) systems for vehicles, found that the average UK commuter wasted five days a year in traffic jams.

Faced with the prospect of roads becoming even more clogged and associated quality-of-life issues, successive governments have looked to other countries for inspiration on encouraging greater use of public transport. Given the high cost of travelling by rail and severe congestion on many train routes—particularly in south-east England—the 'carrot' of public transport has historically made little impact on car usage, so policymaking has shifted towards adopting a 'stick' approach, focusing on mechanisms such as congestion charging and road-pricing (tolls).

18.1.3.1 Congestion charging

Introduced in Singapore in 1975, congestion charging is the system by which flat-rate fees are charged to drivers entering specified 'congestion charge zones' (usually in or around urban centres) between specified hours on given days. In Britain, the most famous example—although not the first, which was introduced in Durham—was initiated by former London Mayor Ken Livingstone in February 2003, within a limited central zone defined by the capital's inner ring road. This zone was extended to cover much of west London in February 2007, although in December 2010 Mr Livingstone's successor, Boris Johnson, scrapped the extension as a 'Christmas present' to local people. The charge operates between 7 a.m. and 6 p.m., Monday to Friday, and is currently set at £11.50 a day for all vehicles, although a £1.50 reduction is available to those paying in advance. Drivers may now pay over the phone by credit or debit card, by text message, via a dedicated website, or in shops equipped with PayPoint facilities. Non-payers are fined.

The congestion charge has won praise from both business leaders and green lobbyists, with various reports suggesting it has cut jams in central London by up to 20 per cent. It has won fans in the medical community, too: according to a 2008 study in *Occupational and Environmental Medicine* magazine, its impact on pollution may have 'saved' up to 1,888 extra 'years of life' among London's 7 million residents. Perhaps unsurprisingly, however, it has infuriated many motorists—including shift workers required to arrive at (or leave) work in central London at unsocial hours, when little public transport is available.

Nonetheless, its perceived success has seen cities from New York to Stockholm imitating it, and before leaving office Labour (initially sceptical of Mr Livingstone's plans) had committed itself to replicating it elsewhere. In June 2008, the then Transport Secretary Ruth Kelly approved what would have been the biggest congestion charge scheme anywhere in the world, in the form of a dual-ring zone around Greater Manchester, covering an area twelve times bigger than the original London zone. However, in December 2008, the plan was thrown into disarray when local residents rejected it by 79 to 21 per cent in a referendum. The policy has since been revived by the recently established Greater Manchester Combined Authority, but progress towards gaining public approval, let alone implementing it, has been slow. Advanced plans for other cities, including Bristol, later stalled, following the then Coalition Transport Secretary Philip Hammond's decision in June 2010 to suspend the Transport Innovation Fund used to co-finance the schemes.

In addition to congestion charging, in 2008 Mr Livingstone introduced a 'low-emission zone' (LEZ) encompassing all 610 square miles (1,580 km^2) of Greater London. The worst polluting lorries, buses, and coaches were fined £200 per day for entering the capital between 7 a.m. and 6 p.m. on weekdays, excluding public holidays, with drivers starting journeys late in an evening and ending them early the following morning forced to pay for two days, not one. On entering office, Mr Johnson, who had condemned the charge as 'the most punitive, draconian fining regime in the whole of Europe', moved to suspend it, but in practice it has continued. Indeed, in January 2012 LEZ emissions standards were made even stricter, with new classes of vehicle affected, including larger vans, minibuses, motor caravans, motorized horseboxes, and 4×4 utility vehicles registered as new before 1 January 2002. Meanwhile, individual councils—including some in London—have experimented with even more novel ways of penalizing 'gas-guzzling' vehicles. In January 2007, Richmond became the first of nine London boroughs to introduce higher-rate residents' parking permits for owners of 'Chelsea tractors' and other cars with larger engines. Although the scheme was replicated elsewhere, after years of protest from residents and motoring organizations such as the Automobile Association (AA), Westminster scrapped it in July 2010.

18.1.3.2 Road-pricing

Congestion charging may be popular among councils seeking to battle traffic problems (and raise the odd million for investment), but the idea of forcing motorists to pay up front to use roads is hardly new. In Britain, 'road-pricing' was first mooted by John Major's Conservative government, which proposed introducing a network of privately financed toll roads on major routes, modelled on systems used in France and other mainland European countries. To date, Britain has only one private toll motorway: a 27-mile stretch of the M6 between Coleshill, Warwickshire, and Cannock, Staffordshire, which opened in December 2003. In July 2004, the then Transport Secretary Alistair Darling announced plans for two 50-mile 'pay as you go' expressways between Wolverhampton and Manchester, but these have remained unrealized, in light of figures published by the Campaign for Better Transport in August 2010 revealing that the M6 toll's then private operator, Midland Expressway Ltd, had been running it at an annual £25 million loss. So acute had the road's financial problems become by 2013, that it was acquired by a consortium of overseas banks, including French-based Credit Agricole, in a complex debt restructuring transaction. But when even this failed to turn around its fortunes, the road was formally put up for sale in February 2016. At the time, the extent of motorists' ongoing resistance to road-pricing was starkly exposed by figures showing that just 48,000 vehicles a day were using it, compared to an original target of 72,000.

18.1.3.3 'Speed' cameras

The days of roadside safety cameras—used to photograph the number plates of vehicles exceeding official speed limits on roads and to award their drivers fixed penalties for speeding—have been fast fading since the early days of the Coalition, when slashed police and local authority budgets saw many forces and councils vote with their feet and cease to operate them. In July 2010, Oxfordshire County Council became the first major authority to stop funding them. Its decision to end its contributions to the collaborative Thames Valley Safer Roads Partnership, encompassing several counties, saw speed camera enforcement in Oxfordshire stop immediately. Other areas followed suit, including Warwickshire and London, where three-quarters of all 754 speed cameras had been switched off by June 2012. Across Britain, 1,522 of the 3,189 cameras were no longer actively used.

While councils and police forces decided to dispense with speed cameras for largely pragmatic reasons—regarding their retention as a costly luxury, given the relatively small sums that fines generated—there have been conflicting reports about the 'policy's' impact on road safety. According to figures published in *The Sun* in June 2012, the number of accidents in which speed was a factor in Avon and Somerset actually fell after sixty-nine of the area's cameras were switched off in April the previous year. In contrast, statistics released to *Highways* magazine and the *Salisbury Journal* in February 2012 showed that accidents in which people were injured rose by nearly a quarter in Wiltshire between June and August 2011. This followed the closure a year earlier of the Wiltshire and Swindon Road Safety Partnership and the camera switch-off that accompanied it.

More recently, though, speed cameras have slowly begun to reappear: barely a year after all 305 film-based fixed speed cameras were switched off in the West Midlands, in February 2014 a digital camera pilot scheme was launched at selected sites in Birmingham and Solihull.

18.1.3.4 Lighting, minor road maintenance, and pathways

Street lighting tends primarily to be the preserve of county and unitary councils, except where, as with parking policy (see Table 10.1), districts or boroughs have delegated responsibility for maintaining and repairing roads and pathways within towns (along with the budgets required to contract out the necessary work). Under Tony Blair's government, some parish councils judged to be operating efficiently were, for a time, designated 'quality' parish councils and given responsibility for overseeing the maintenance of individual roads in smaller towns, villages, and rural settlements. Even today, it is not unusual for parish, town, and community councils to be delegated budgets by higher-tier authorities to manage the lighting of pathways, public bridleways, and other minor rights of way within the villages and small towns in which they are based.

18.1.3.5 Public transport

Since the publicly owned National Bus Company was privatized in the 1980s, followed by the subsequent deregulation of local routes and introduction of dedicated passenger transport authorities (PTAs) in metropolitan areas, councils have generally played a diminishing role in providing public transport. As in many policy areas, they have largely been reduced to 'commissioner' or mere 'enabler' status—monitoring provision of bus, tram, Underground, and river boat services by the free market, and stepping in as 'providers of last resort' where unacceptable service gaps or inconsistencies emerge.

Since 1985, when Margaret Thatcher's government replaced existing metropolitan county councils with metropolitan boroughs and scrapped the Greater London Council (GLC), independent passenger transport authorities (later renamed integrated transport authorities) were created in major urban areas, the most famous being Transport for London (TfL—see Table 10.3). At the same time, these councils' responsibility for providing transport links to and from airports or docks was transferred to new joint boards. The 1972 Act's one abiding legacy was the transfer of highways and transport responsibilities from boroughs or districts to counties. Once again, the strategic transport framework in metropolitan areas is currently undergoing a transformation, however, with Greater Manchester Combined Authority assuming this responsibility in that conurbation (through the aegis of its own version of TfL: Transport for Greater Manchester) and other emerging combined authorities set to do likewise in the North East, South Yorkshire, and elsewhere.

The privatization of bus transport was formalized in the Transport Act 1985, with councils expected to provide only 'socially necessary' services directly—for example those linking villages and smaller towns—and only then when the market failed to do so. A year later, the system was formally deregulated, allowing any number of bus companies to compete on 'registered bus routes'—provided that they first obtained 'public service operator's licences' from one of the *Traffic Commissioners for Great Britain*. Trams, such as those operating in urban centres from Manchester to Croydon, had to be similarly licensed.

Under the present licensing regime, there are seven regional Commissioners. Their responsibilities are to:

- license operators of delivery lorries or heavy goods vehicles (HGVs), buses and coaches (or 'public service vehicles' (PSVs));
- register local bus services; and
- grant vocational licences, and take action against drivers of HGVs and PSVs if necessary.

The Traffic Commissioner for Scotland has additional powers that, in England and Wales, are exercised individually by officers in council highways departments. These include determining appeals against taxi fares, and removing improperly parked vehicles in Edinburgh and Glasgow.

One side-effect of deregulating local bus services was to undermine councils' ability to subsidize public transport. While, in some areas, introducing competition did improve services by pushing down fares, in others the loss of council-run buses deprived residents of heavily subsidized tickets that found no replacement in the privatized marketplace. Among the most celebrated local services were the cut-price buses ushered in by Mr Livingstone in the days of the GLC and the record-breaking 2 pence fares introduced by future Home Secretary David Blunkett while leader of Sheffield City Council in the 1970s.

Contracting out bus services has also been blamed for the increasing isolation of some communities, particularly those in remote villages and hamlets, because—shorn of state subsidies—private companies have been reluctant to maintain, let alone to initiate, unprofitable routes. While bus licensing long ago passed to the Commissioners, counties, unitaries, and metropolitan boroughs retain responsibility for issuing licences to taxi operators and minicab firms, including Hackney carriages outside London (where they are licensed by the Commissioner of the Metropolitan Police). In major conurbations, all such responsibilities will soon have transferred to the newly established combined authorities (**see** 10.2.4).

Although bus deregulation may have produced a patchy to non-existent service in many areas, recent years have seen the introduction of generous **concessionary fare schemes** for those meeting certain criteria, such as students, the disabled, and pensioners. Councils fund these schemes by subsidizing local bus operators with the equivalent of the full fares they are 'losing' by implementing the schemes. Since April 2006, all councils have had to provide a bare minimum of free off-peak bus fares for pass-holders, while from April 2008 pensioners and the disabled were entitled to free off-peak (9.30 a.m.–11.00 p.m.) travel anywhere in England and Wales, rather than simply in their local authority areas. Both Scotland and Northern Ireland have equivalent schemes. Despite speculation that ministers might remove subsidies for better-off pensioners, as part of a wider drive to save money by means-testing certain benefits that currently apply universally, including the Winter Fuel Payment (see 8.5.1), for now the bus pass remains.

While major transport infrastructural projects have traditionally been overseen by central government, recent years have seen a trend towards devolving them to local and regional authorities, particularly in metropolitan areas (as explained earlier). At the decisive turning point, in June 2010, the then Coalition government shelved or abandoned a raft of long-awaited projects (together worth £5.2 billion), including a network of electric 'trolleybuses' powered by overhead cables in Leeds and phase one of a Tees Valley Metro system linking Teesside to Darlington (though this was later revived on a smaller scale in the absence of Whitehall funds).

18.1.3.6 Car parking

Responsibility for administering and policing car parking is broadly divided between councils, as outlined in Table 18.2.

Parking responsibilities used to be split fairly clearly in two-tier areas between boroughs or districts and counties, with the former managing off-road

Table 18.2 Types of council responsible for car parking services

Type of parking	Local authority
On-street and residents' parking	Nominally county councils and unitary authorities, but now administered by all types of council (subject to local arrangements)
Open-air car parks on public or council-owned land	Traditionally, district/borough councils and unitary authorities, but now depends on local arrangements
Multistorey car parks	Private firms such as National Car Parks Ltd (NCP)
Car parks at hospitals, colleges, universities, and business premises	Run by organizations themselves, increasingly using private contractors

car parks and the latter on-street parking. In many areas, these distinctions are blurred today, with some districts entering into 'agency agreements' with neighbouring counties, and vice versa, effectively contracting out these functions to the other. To confuse the public further, while fixed-penalty fines tend to be administered by counties or unitaries, placing penalty notices on parked vehicles has traditionally been performed by traffic wardens employed by the police. This recently changed, with council-employed parking attendants (later redesignated 'civil enforcement officers') taking over the role in most areas.

As with traffic management, parking issues have a habit of raising motorists' blood pressure—and consequently provide raw material for endless news stories. A common misconception is that wardens and attendants are paid commissions or 'bonuses' related to the number or value of fixed-penalty notices that they issue. In fact, the government legislated to prevent this happening in the Traffic Wardens and Parking Attendants Act 2005. So combustible has the car parking issue become in recent years, nonetheless, that parking ticket recipients may now appeal to a National Parking Adjudication Service (NPAS).

A particular parking management 'scandal' to receive media attention recently was Westminster's highly controversial decision to introduce a blanket charge of up to £4.80 an hour in the evenings and on Sundays—a move condemned by an unlikely alliance of local residents and businesses, West End theatres, religious leaders, and London's *Evening Standard* newspaper. A High Court ruling in December 2011 forced the council to put what the then Mayor Mr Johnson described as a 'nightlife tax' on hold until at least after the August 2012 London Olympics. It has yet to be revived.

18.1.4 **Transport for London (TfL)**

The quango TfL is charged with managing (if not directly running):

- London buses, Croydon Tramlink, and Docklands Light Railway (DLR);
- London Underground network (the 'Tube');
- Transport for London Road Network (TLRN); and
- London River Services—licensed passenger ferries along and across the Thames.

It also:

- regulates taxis and minicabs;
- coordinates Dial-a-Ride and Taxicard schemes, providing door-to-door services for people with mobility problems;
- installs and maintains traffic lights across London; and
- promotes safe use of the Thames for passenger and freight movement.

In 1998, a Transport Committee for London was set up by the GLA to replace the four pre-existing bodies responsible for overseeing the Tube, buses, taxis, main roads through the capital, and the DLR (a privately owned company).

While all of this may sound harmonious, at times the process of taking decisions about the future of London's transport network has been anything but. Between 1997 and 2001, Tony Blair's government was locked in a tortuous stalemate with Mr Livingstone and the then London Transport Commissioner Bob Kiley over its insistence on 'part-privatization' of the Underground. Despite widespread criticism about the shambolic sell-off of the national rail network, ministers went to huge lengths to persuade the Mayor to accept a public–private partnership (PPP—see 7.6), which saw a near-identical model adopted for the Tube, with franchises to run services on individual lines contracted out to competing companies, while tracks, signals, stations, and even rolling stock remained in the hands of a separate authority (in this case TfL). In the Underground's case, the proposed management/ownership split was three-way, rather than two-way as with rail—with companies contracted to carry out the £13 billion, fifteen-year programme of improvements on its infrastructure given a stake in it too. More recently, TfL was involved in protracted negotiations over Crossrail—the upcoming £16 billion overland train link that, once completed, should connect thirty-seven stations, from Heathrow Airport and Maidenhead in the west to Canary Wharf and Shenfield, Essex, in the east, bringing twenty-four overland peak-time rail services an hour through the heart of London. Crossrail was finally approved in September 2007, after a decade of deliberation, and work commenced on the biggest engineering project in Europe, with the construction of 21 km twin-bore tunnels stretching under central London in spring 2012. Its central section is due to open in 2018.

18.2 Waste management and environmental health

Public health has been on the local agenda for longer than almost anything else. A rundown of major Public Health Acts and other relevant legislation is given in table 18D to be found on the **Online Resource Centre**.

The task of ensuring that housing, businesses, and local amenities conform to basic hygiene and safety standards falls to district or borough and unitary environmental health departments. Of their myriad responsibilities, by far the most costly and complex are those related to the effective organization of waste management—an area so broad that it requires the active involvement of every type of council.

18.2.1 Waste collection, recycling, and waste disposal

There are two overriding aspects to waste management:

- *waste collection*—the responsibility of districts or boroughs, unitaries, and metropolitan or London boroughs; and
- *waste disposal*—the responsibility of counties, unitaries, and metropolitan or London boroughs.

18.2.1.1 Waste collection

Households and businesses have traditionally benefited from weekly door-to-door waste collections. In recent years, however, a number of councils have introduced fortnightly collections to save money, while the nature of 'rubbish collecting' has changed, with more emphasis on recycling, rather than the simple disposal of refuse at 'tips' (landfill sites).

As with most areas of local service delivery, waste collection is periodically put out to tender (see 12.1.4), with the result that many 'binmen' (and women) are now employed not directly by councils, but by private contractors. Having started out with kerbside recycling points at supermarkets, parks, and other public amenities, many English and Welsh collection authorities now operate at least fortnightly door-to-door recycling services. Operators contracted to collect standard 'black bin' household and/or business waste (food waste, plastics, etc.) may not be the same ones picking up the ('green bag') recycling.

Despite having dramatically increased its recycling levels in recent years, Britain was slow to embrace 'green waste' compared to most European countries. As a result, Labour ministers considered increasingly fiendish ways of cajoling householders and businesses to recycle more. Most controversial was the mooted introduction of 'pay as you throw' fines for people who chucked away too much, with 'rebates' for those who made most use of their recycling bins. The then Environment Secretary David Miliband announced plans to give councils powers to charge for excessive black bin waste in May 2007, as part of the then Labour government's drive to force councils to recycle at least 40 per cent by 2010 and 50 per cent by 2020. Under the Climate Change Act 2008, trials of bin taxes began in 2009 in five pilot areas, policed by new quangos known as 'joint waste authorities', which would potentially be able to set new taxes. Not content to wait for the outcome of the pilots, some councils proactively launched pay-as-you-throw schemes: in September 2006, Woking Borough Council was accused of snooping on households after installing electronic chips capable of weighing 'residual' (non-recyclable) waste in wheelie bins. But, on entering office, the Coalition abandoned this approach.

Whether carrot or stick wins out in the end, British councils face an uphill struggle to meet EU recycling targets over the coming decade: a 1999 directive stipulated that the amount of biodegradable waste dumped in UK landfill (equivalent to 18.1 million tonnes in 2003–4) should be cut to 13.7 million tonnes by 2010, 9.2 million tonnes by 2013, and 6.3 million tonnes by 2020. Failure to meet these targets would see the government fined £180 million a year by the European Commission. Figures released in March 2013 gave cause for hope, though—showing that Britain's recycling rates had risen faster than those of any other European country in the 1990s, with 39 per cent of its waste being recycled by 2010 (putting it ahead of target). It also met its 2013 target and is expected to be recycling half of all its recyclable waste by 2017—two years ahead of the 2020 deadline. Some areas are significantly better than others at recycling, though: in February 2013, Wales recycled 54 per cent of its waste, putting it well ahead of England.

18.2.1.2 Waste disposal

The Environmental Protection Act 1990 required all waste disposal authorities to form arm's-length local authority waste disposal companies (LAWDCs) to dispose of refuse on their behalf. In turn, these were required to 'hire' waste disposal contractors (in practice, either the company itself or another franchisee) to:

- provide waste transfer and landfill sites to which householders can take large items (for example electrical goods) for landfill or destruction;
- dispose of items collected from local people's homes by collection operators; and
- recycle or sell waste for scrap.

Contractors running waste disposal sites on behalf of councils must obtain waste management licences (WMLs) from the Environment Agency (EA) in England and Wales. In Scotland, applications are made to the Scottish Environmental Protection Agency (SEPA); in Northern Ireland, to the Department of the Environment (Environment and Heritage Service).

Because the European Union has toughened its recycling targets, the issue of straightforward rubbish dumping has become acutely politically sensitive. Faced with rapidly dwindling capacity at Britain's existing landfill sites, successive governments have sought to deter councils from continuing to dump waste in the age-old tradition. The most contentious mechanism they have used is the Landfill Tax. Introduced in the Finance Act 1996, this was initially levied on councils, waste disposal companies, and other organizations involved in dumping rubbish, at a standard rate of £7 a tonne and a reduced rate of £2 a tonne. In its 1999 Budget, Labour raised the standard rate to £10 a tonne and introduced a 'Landfill Tax accelerator' designed to increase it by a further £1 a tonne each year until 2004, and the then Chancellor Gordon Brown announced further planned increases in 2002. For 2016–17, the two rates were:

- *standard rate*: £84.40 a tonne for household waste that may decay and/or contaminate land; and

- *reduced rate*: £2.65 a tonne for rocks and soils, ceramics and concrete, unused minerals, furnace slag, ash, low-activity inorganic compounds, and water.

To dilute the impact of the tax on site operators, successive governments have introduced discounts for those who demonstrate other forms of 'green' behaviour: Mr Major's government brought in a Landfill Tax credit scheme to reward them with a 90 per cent tax credit against any donations made to environmental bodies registered with the scheme's regulator; and Labour launched a Landfill Allowance Trading Scheme (LATS), allowing individual waste disposal authorities with surplus landfill space to 'sell' it to those in 'deficit', in the manner of carbon trading.

18.2.2 Air quality, noise pollution, fly-tipping, and dog fouling

The council officials charged with inspecting domestic and business premises to ensure they meet statutory environmental health standards are **environmental health officers**. One of their main duties is to investigate complaints relating to waste collection and disposal—or rather *lack* of collection and disposal when it is meant to have taken place. They also investigate reports of 'fly-tipping': the practice of dumping rubbish on someone else's doorstep or in fields or alleyways after missing collection days or to avoid the cost of disposing of larger items at landfill sites. In extreme cases, rotting waste that has been inadequately stored or left out for days may attract vermin, necessitating direct intervention by environmental health 'pest controllers' to remove them. The cost of ridding an area of vermin will normally be passed straight to the offending party—and they can be prosecuted and fined for non-compliance.

Another menace accorded greater priority in recent years is dog fouling. After years of campaigning by environmental groups and others concerned about the potential danger that contact with dog mess poses to young children, so-called 'poop scoops' and dog litter bins had become a common feature of most parks and public rights of way by the late 1990s. Yet many areas remained so blighted by it that some councils went so far as to use CCTV cameras to spy on errant dog owners who failed to clean up after their pets, until this practice was banned by the Coalition. Councils' ability to do this (using anti-terror measures introduced in the Regulation of Investigatory Powers Act 2000) sparked a media outcry when it emerged in June 2008. In January 2011, the then Home Secretary Theresa May confirmed that they would no longer be permitted to snoop on residents for 'bin crimes' or other such minor infringements—except in cases in which alleged offences carried custodial sentences. Even then, this would be possible only if councils first obtained formal approval from a magistrate. Reports of such 'spying', however, persisted.

Other menaces continue to be the subject of strict statutory powers. In response to growing pressure on Britain to conform to EU directives, the

Pollution Prevention and Control Act 1999 made councils responsible for exercising 'local authority pollution prevention and control' (LAPPC) in relation to so-called 'Part B' industrial installations in their areas. These include smaller power plants, glassworks, waste disposal sites, sewerage works, and municipal and hospital incinerators. More major polluting installations—for example oil refineries, nuclear power stations, steelworks, and large chemical plants—were designated as 'Part A1' and placed under 'integrated pollution prevention and control' (IPPC) orders overseen by the EA, SEPA, or Northern Irish Department of the Environment. There is also a third category of process ('Part A2'), which relates to medium-range installations. This, like Part B, is policed by councils as follows:

- Applications for a process to be carried out must be made to the relevant authority (if refused, appeals can be lodged with the Environment Secretary).
- If an enforcing authority believes that an operator has breached an authorization, it can serve an enforcement notice specifying the nature of the breach, steps that need to be taken to rectify it, and a deadline for their completion.
- If external factors are creating an imminent risk of serious pollution (even if unconnected with the process itself), it can serve a prohibition notice.

Another newsworthy issue recently has been the growing intolerance of noise pollution. In certain circumstances, councils may even seize offending equipment, such as stereos or drills. The Noise Act 1996 empowered them to send officers to investigate sources of excessive noise at night and to 'measure' noise levels. Wherever these exceed statutory limits, warning notices may immediately be served on those responsible. Failure to comply is a criminal offence and officers may subsequently enter properties without warrants to seize offending equipment. Prosecution often also follows.

Noise pollution has also been a notable target of government crackdowns on 'antisocial behaviour' (see 10.7.1.2). In March 2005, Andrew Gordon and his 18 year-old son, Phillip, were banned from their own home in Dunfermline for three months under the Antisocial Behaviour (Scotland) Act 2004 because of noise and disruption caused by drinking, cursing, fighting, and drug-taking at the house when Mr Gordon was away.

Action taken against unpleasant smells has also made numerous headlines. One contentious case involved an award-winning vegetarian cafe in Greenwich, which was ordered to stop serving cooked food in June 2008 after neighbours complained about the smell.

Environmental health officers also oversee various other areas, as listed in table 18E to be found on the **Online Resource Centre**.

18.2.3 Environmental health and food safety

A key duty of environmental health officers (or 'inspectors') is their role in promoting food safety by ensuring that restaurants, cafes, pubs, and shops serving food are preparing, cooking, and storing meat and other items of suitable quality and under appropriate conditions. This role—memorably satirized in the classic 'Basil the Rat' episode of BBC1 sitcom *Fawlty Towers*—covers all aspects of food hygiene, including its sale, importation, preparation, transportation, storing, packing, wrapping, displaying, serving, and delivery.

The Food Standards Act 1999 set up a Food Standards Agency (FSA) to oversee hygiene and animal husbandry issues nationally, while building on existing legislation to introduce two criminal offences for businesses failing to meet minimum standards: rendering food 'injurious to health' or selling produce 'unfit for human consumption'. There are now separate bodies performing the same functions in all three devolved nations: namely the FSA in Wales, the FSA in Northern Ireland, and Food Standards Scotland. The Act also introduced new, all-encompassing council environmental services departments, specifying that environmental health officers were responsible for:

- inspecting and seizing suspicious food;
- issuing improvement notices to owners of food businesses;
- serving emergency prohibition notices to close down businesses in the case of perceived serious health risks;
- liaising with the NHS to address potentially communicable disease risks; and
- issuing additional enforcement notices dictated by central government in instances of sudden crisis—for example the ban on the sale of beef on the bone caused by the late 1980s/early 1990s bovine spongiform encephalopathy (BSE), or 'mad cow disease', crisis.

The BSE 'outbreak' presented one of the biggest instances in recent memory of environmental health issues affecting the wider public health arena. The alarm generated by early diagnoses of BSE in cattle in November 1986 and subsequent identification of symptoms of Creutzfeldt-Jakob disease (CJD) in several Britons became an international concern—leading to a ten-year ban on the export of UK beef on the bone to the rest of the EU, lasting from 1996 to 2006.

Other examples of recent environmental health scares have included a succession of outbreaks of foot-and-mouth disease in British livestock. The major one occurred in 2001, leading to a mass cull of sheep and cattle—including tens of thousands of healthy animals—in what was widely portrayed in the media as a panicky, unnecessarily costly government reaction. There were two further localized outbreaks in 2007, attracting more measured responses. Under the law, where landowners suspect outbreaks of communicable (infectious or contagious) diseases among their animals, they must inform police, council, and the Department for Environment, Food & Rural Affairs (Defra). Once outbreaks are confirmed, any movement of animals 'from the land' or 'within and beyond the local area' is prohibited, other than under licence granted by inspectors.

More usually, environmental health officers are called in to individual business premises to remove samples of food for laboratory analysis on receiving public complaints about food poisoning, unpleasant tastes or odours, or outdated food labels. Among the more commonplace—if potentially dangerous—food safety issues arising is the identification of bacteria such as *E. coli* or salmonella. In a notorious example of government overreaction to the latter, in 1988 the then Junior Health Minister Edwina Currie provoked widespread alarm (and her own resignation) by erroneously telling reporters:

> 'Most of the egg production in this country, sadly, is now affected with salmonella.'

Food safety authorities also oversee the regulation of slaughterhouses in accordance with EU rules and inspect the quality of meat bought from them. They are also authorized to provide their own public slaughterhouses, cold stores, and refrigerators.

Environmental health officers are not the only officials involved in policing outbreaks of diseases such as foot-and-mouth, *E. coli*, and salmonella. Trading standards officers (employed by unitary and county councils) and other Defra-approved contractors also have duties in such instances, albeit primarily in relation to animal welfare. Trading standards departments (see 18.3) inspect livestock for signs of illness or poor treatment, and help to enforce UK and EU legislation relating to safe and humane animal transportation. Meanwhile, a 2007 EU directive introduced a requirement for formal 'competence assessments' to be carried out, on Defra's instructions, on anyone intending to transport livestock, horses, or poultry for more than 65 km.

18.2.4 The future of public health at local level

Amid the wholesale franchising out of most local services promoted by the Coalition, it came as a surprise when ministers announced plans to give councils *additional* powers in relation to one area of policy: public health. The initiative—which revives the tradition that existed prior to the NHS of councils being held responsible for promoting healthy lifestyles and environments—was formalized in a national Public Health Outcomes Framework published in January 2012. Councils are now responsible for everything from encouraging local people to lose weight and give up smoking to promoting breastfeeding, cutting tooth decay in children, and reducing rates of heart disease, strokes, cancer, and serious falls among those aged over 65. From April 2013, funding for local initiatives to achieve these ends has been drawn from a new public health grant (see 11.2.1.1)—one of only two ring-fenced payments by central government into their revenue budgets to survive the Coalition's reforms of council finance (initially worth £5.2 billion a year).

18.3 Trading standards and the licensing laws

While environmental health officers are responsible for verifying the *safety* of food sold to the public, wider consumer protection duties relating to its sale and presentation fall to **trading standards officers**. Under the Food Safety Act 1990, there are two main criminal offences relating to trading standards:

- selling food 'not of the nature or substance or quality demanded by the purchaser'; and
- 'falsely describing or presenting food'—usually without advertisement or labelling.

Trading standards officers are also responsible for ensuring that businesses comply with government policy in the following areas.

18.3.1 General consumer protection

Consumer protection involves monitoring the accurate description of goods, the use of credit, and product safety for items ranging from household tools to kitchen appliances to children's toys. Trading standards departments are also responsible for ensuring that local trade is carried out 'fairly', under terms set out by the Competition and Markets Authority (CMA—see 7.3.2.1). So time-consuming and costly can this work be that some authorities have even established dedicated consumer advice departments to pool resources with their local Citizens Advice Bureaux and Consumers' Association.

The Fair Trading Act 1973 introduced a Director General of Fair Trading, authorized to ask any business 'acting in a way detrimental to the interests of consumers' to give assurances about its future conduct. If it fails to do so, the Director General can take individuals to county courts or the Restrictive Practices Court, which has authority to accept an assurance that an offence will not be repeated—or to make an order. Civil claims under the Sale of Goods Act 1979 must be brought by individuals through county courts.

18.3.2 Weights and measures

Each authority must appoint a 'chief inspector of weights and measures' to ensure that all local traders comply with authorized weights and measures (the 'metric system' of metres and litres used throughout the EU, rather than the previous 'imperial system' of yards and ounces).

The history of Britain's reluctant conversion to metric standards is almost as long and tangled as its relationship with the EU itself. It began in earnest with the passage of the Weights and Measures Act 1963, which formally redefined yards and pounds in terms of metres and kilograms, and abolished such archaic imperial measurements as 'scruples', 'rods', and 'minims'. In 1965, under pressure from industry, the then President of the Board of Trade committed Britain to adopting the metric system fully within a decade, and by 1968 a Metrication Board had been established to promote it. The pledge was reaffirmed on Britain's entry into the European Economic Community (EEC) in 1973.

Despite several concrete moves, such as the decimalization of the UK's currency in 1971, subsequent governments further delayed full implementation of metrication, and it was only after two EU directives—in 1995 and 2000, respectively—that Britain was finally ordered to introduce the metric system, first for packaged and then bulk-sold goods (for example fresh fruit and vegetables sold on market stalls).

This diktat did not stop some traditionalists resisting. The first few years after the introduction of metrication in fruit and vegetable markets were marked by high-profile court cases that captured the imagination of the popular press—with so-called 'metric martyrs' continuing to label their goods in pounds and ounces in defiance of EU law. In September 2007, enduring public defiance finally scored a pyrrhic victory when the EU Commissioner responsible for the single market, Günther Verheugen, announced that they would be permitted to continue labelling their items in imperial measures after all—provided they also did so in metric measurements. The EU subsequently relaxed its stance even more, allowing most traders to continue using only imperial measures, but some councils still prosecute those who do so. A victory of sorts for the metric martyrs finally came when, in October 2008, the then Department for Innovation, Universities, and Skills (DIUS) issued new guidelines urging councils to take only 'proportionate' action against refuseniks.

In addition to checking that goods are itemized in metric measures, inspectors regularly vet market stalls and shops to ensure food is not sold in 'short weight': that is, that scales are used correctly and consumers are sold the correct quantities of goods. Short weight is a criminal offence. Weights of manufactured goods are checked at factories, while those of loose food, fuel, and beer are checked at point of sale.

18.3.3 Sunday trading

The Deregulation and Contracting Out Act 1994 marked a major liberalization of Britain's retail laws, which up to that point had been among the strictest in Europe—with most shops commonly opening only between 9.30 a.m. and 5.30 p.m. six days a week, and few allowed to trade on Sundays out of respect for Christian worshippers. The 1994 Act gave individual traders freedom to decide their own opening hours and other employment practices on weekdays and Saturdays. Most remaining restrictions were finally removed in the Sunday Trading Act 1994, which stipulated that:

- 'large shops'—those with internal sales areas of 280 m^2 (3,000 sq ft) or more—could open for up to six hours between 10 a.m. and 6 p.m. on Sundays, but must remain closed on Easter Sunday and Christmas Day (if the latter falls on a Sunday);
- smaller shops could open as and when they chose to; and
- shop workers who did not wish to work on a Sunday for religious reasons should have some protection from discipline or dismissal.

In 2012, Sunday trading laws were relaxed even further (albeit only for eight weeks, from 22 July) to enable larger shops across England and Wales to open longer than the traditional six hours during the Olympics and Paralympics. However, a bid by Mr Cameron's Conservative government to radically extend Sunday opening, by allowing local authorities to permit any shop to stay open longer if there was sufficient local demand, was defeated by 317 to 286 votes in the Commons in March 2016, thanks to something of an unholy alliance between normally uncooperative Labour and Scottish Nationalist MPs and twenty-six backbench Tory rebels. The vote's outcome proved controversial, in that the SNP's decisive contribution to a government defeat on a legal change that would only have applied to England and Wales once more raised the spectre of the West Lothian Question—a constitutional anomaly supposedly addressed by reforms to the passage of English/Welsh-only bills following the 2014 Scottish independence referendum (see 1.3.6). The party justified its intervention by arguing that, had the proposed changes been introduced, shop workers around the UK would have lost any entitlement to premiums for agreeing to work on Sundays, as the new law would have had the effect of making the rules around Sunday trading indistinguishable from those applying on any other day. Critics pointed out, however, that there was a whiff of hypocrisy about the party's stance, given that, under devolution, Scottish shops are allowed to open for as long as they like on Sundays. Rules around Sunday shopping are strictest in Northern Ireland, where the Sunday Trading (Northern Ireland) Order 1997 tends to limit opening hours to 1–6 p.m., so as not to interfere with the timing of most church services.

18.3.4 Trade descriptions

It is a criminal offence under the Trade Descriptions Acts 1968 and 1972 for 'false descriptions' to be ascribed to goods or 'false indications' given of their sale prices: for example, for labelling not to include value added tax (VAT) as part of the cover price.

18.3.5 The licensing of pubs and clubs, and drinking by-laws

The Licensing Act 2003, which finally came into force in February 2005, ushered in so-called '24-hour drinking' in England and Wales, by allowing pubs and bars to apply to vary their existing liquor licences so that they could open until later than the customary 11.00 p.m. closing time on weekdays and Saturdays, and 10.30 p.m. on Sundays. Nightclubs and restaurants were allowed to apply for 'late licences' allowing them to stay open beyond their usual 2 a.m. shutdown. In liberalizing the drinking laws, the then Labour government's stated aim was to tackle Britain's rising epidemic of 'binge drinking' by ending the frantic 'last orders' culture, which often saw drinkers racing to buy multiple drinks just before closing time. The hope was that this more relaxed approach to buying and drinking alcohol would instead foster a Continental-style 'cafe culture', with a steadier stream of drinkers drifting in and out of bars at different times, and fewer explosions of violence and rowdy behaviour at 'chucking out' times.

The 2003 Act also introduced significant changes in the way licences were issued and policed. Until 2005, local magistrates' courts were responsible for awarding and varying liquor licences, but the Act transferred this duty to unitary authorities, London/metropolitan boroughs, and district/borough councils in two-tier areas. They now work together with police to ensure the terms of licences are adhered to, and apply to magistrates for formal orders to revoke them if they are breached.

The new licensing laws had a mixed reception from licensees, public, and police alike. A common complaint from landlords and nightclub owners in the early days related to the complexity of the revised system. Rather than simply having to apply for a personal licence to serve alcohol between stated hours on stated days and a single public entertainment licence giving them freedom to stage occasional events, such as concerts or stand-up comedy, they were now required to apply for both the former and a separate premises licence or temporary event notice for each occasion on which they planned to stage any entertainment—whether a live acoustic band or karaoke competition.

Following a high-profile run-in between the Musicians' Union, various other groups representing performers, and the Department of Culture, Media, and Sport (DCMS)—the ministry implementing the reforms—the Act was tweaked to avoid any unintended consequences, such as deterring pubs from putting on shows or plays. In rationalizing this aspect of the law, however, ministers unwittingly made it easier for licensed premises to put on all manner of other performances: lap dancing, for example, was recategorized alongside more innocuous forms of public entertainment, meaning that premises no longer needed to apply for separate 'sexual encounter' licences to stage it. Perhaps unsurprisingly, this led to a significant increase in the number of clubs and bars offering shows involving at least partial nudity—with the pressure group

Object identifying some 300 by the mid-Noughties, compared to just a handful ten years earlier. The Licensing Act has also been criticized by police forces and residents for allegedly turning some town centres into 'no-go areas' for older residents, particularly on Friday and Saturday nights. In its 2008 submission to a government review of the impact of the 2003 Act, the Local Government Association (LGA) described it as 'a mistake', and its then chairman, Sir Simon Milton, told the *Daily Telegraph* that it had 'failed miserably'. A Freedom of Information Act 2000 request by the *Daily Telegraph* to all forty-three police forces in England and Wales, just ahead of the publication of the Home Office's official review in February 2008, appeared to support their reservations, by uncovering official statistics confirming that twelve forces had seen a 46 per cent rise in antisocial incidents since the Act was enforced—with sixteen reporting an increase of 5 per cent in alcohol-related assaults, harassment, and criminal damage. Nationwide, serious violent offences in the early hours had risen by a quarter.

When it was finally published, in March 2008, the government's review recommended retaining the 'new' licensing regime—but with a new 'two-strikes rule' designed to deter off-licences from selling alcohol to underage drinkers. As for the '24-hour' aspect of the legislation, despite the initial expectation that all-night drinking would become a feature of most town centres, statistics obtained from 86 per cent of licensing authorities in November 2007 found that fewer than 500 English and Welsh pubs and clubs had ever been granted 24-hour licences. Most 'late licences' tended to cover only an additional hour or two of business, and then only at weekends generally. Of the 5,100 venues operating 24-hour licences between April 2006 and March 2007, 3,300 were hotels, 910 were supermarkets, and 460 were pubs and clubs. Nonetheless, concerns about the links between late-night drinking and unruly behaviour remain—prompting the Coalition to signal a 'complete review' in May 2010. At the time of writing, however, licensing laws in England and Wales remained unchanged.

Licensing laws in Scotland, administered by local *licensing boards*, have become somewhat stricter than elsewhere in Britain in recent years. The Licensing Act (Scotland) 2005 and later laws, notably the Alcohol etc. (Scotland) Act 2010 and Criminal Justice and Licensing (Scotland) Act 2010, have introduced additional conditions surrounding the presence of children in pubs, including requirements that those admitting families provide baby-changing facilities and only serve parents who order meals as well as drinks. This is part of a wider picture of toughening attitudes towards alcohol north of the border, reflected in a 2014 Scottish statutory instrument, which sharply reduced the 'drink-drive' limit, and the Alcohol (Minimum Pricing) (Scotland) Act 2012, which introduced a minimum unit price (initially of 50p)—an oft-mooted measure repeatedly kicked into the long grass in England and Wales. At the time of writing, however, the latter Act had yet to be implemented, due to an ongoing legal challenge by the Scotch Whisky Association, which, following a hearing in the Court of Justice of the European Union (see 9.3.4), was due to return shortly to Scotland's highest appeal court: the Court of Session. The Licensing (Northern Ireland) Order 1996 covers all aspects of licensing in the province. In addition to national licensing laws, councils across the UK have long had powers under various statutes to curb public drinking. In the early 1990s, Plymouth and Bristol city councils were among the first to invoke by-laws forbidding public consumption of alcohol in specified locations, and similar measures have since been widely implemented. Additional powers were introduced under the Criminal Justice and Police Act 2001, enabling councils to pass alcohol-free zone orders—or, to use their official title, 'alcohol consumption in designated public places orders'—again related to specified locations. The recent Scottish Acts confer similar powers on councils to curb alcohol-related antisocial behaviour in Scotland. Once a zone is in place, police officers may require individuals spotted drinking there to stop immediately and, where necessary, may confiscate their alcohol. In the last resort, those failing to comply may be prosecuted and, if convicted, fined up to £500. Some authorities have gone still further: within weeks of his election as London Mayor, Mr Johnson banned all drinking from London Underground and other public transport throughout the capital.

Various other initiatives have been used to clamp down on antisocial drinking—from Labour's 'alcohol disorder zones', for which extra policing was funded by licensees, to increased fines introduced by the Coalition for pubs, clubs, and off-licences that sell alcohol to children. Licensing authorities may also now set 'late-night levies' for pubs and clubs whose decisions to stay open into the night result in more costly policing arrangements. Meanwhile, 'early morning restriction orders' (EMROs) introduced by Labour to limit sales of alcohol between 3 a.m. and 6 a.m. have been toughened up to allow councils to impose them from midnight.

18.4 Leisure and cultural services

Providing for citizens' quality of life arguably means more than managing public transport, clearing up refuse, and maintaining a social environment relatively free of crime and disorder. 'Softer services' traditionally offered by councils include those falling under the broad umbrellas of leisure and culture. These terms—increasingly fused by some councils—cover everything from maintaining local swimming pools and sports centres to providing theatres, museums, and galleries, and financing festivals, like the Edinburgh International Festival or England's largest equivalent: the Brighton Festival.

18.4.1 Swimming pools, leisure centres, parks, and playgrounds

Under the Local Government (Miscellaneous Provisions) Act 1972, councils were given discretion to raise funds for and to provide 'such recreational facilities as they think fit'. These included:

- sports centres;
- pitches for team games and athletic events;
- swimming pools;
- tennis courts;
- stadiums, and premises for athletic and other sporting clubs;
- golf courses and bowling greens;
- riding schools;
- campsites;
- facilities for gliding, boating, and waterskiing; and
- staff (including instructors) for any of these.

As in most other areas of local service provision, compulsory competitive tendering (see 12.1.4) was introduced under Mrs Thatcher to force councils to compete with private contractors for franchises to run leisure centres. Wearing another 'hat', however, they still have responsibility for ensuring that *standards* of service meet statutory requirements, not least in health and safety, and disabled access.

18.4.2 Libraries, museums, galleries, and the performing arts

Under the Public Libraries Act 1850, emerging councils were empowered to *provide* libraries, but not actually to stock them with books. This changed under the Public Libraries 1919 Act, which allowed them to 'spend more than a rating limit of one penny in the pound on books'. Today, there is no statutory limit, and councils are obliged to offer 'a comprehensive and efficient library service' covering everything from books, newspapers, and periodicals, to records, CDs, and DVDs. Public libraries have also been required to offer free Internet access to the public since 2002.

There were fears that libraries might become the latest in a long line of 'added value' services to fall prey to the Coalition's public spending squeeze when the DCMS announced plans to shake up local library services in August 2010. With statistics showing that only 29 per cent of British people any longer regularly visited their libraries and many local branches were housing dwindling, outdated stocks of books, the then Culture Minister Ed Vaizey launched a Future Libraries Programme both to generate cost savings and attract more users by reorganizing services in ways better suited to the pressures and routines of modern living. Among the ideas he floated was relocating libraries to premises other than conventional ones, such as shops and pubs—suggestions that swiftly attracted more than fifty submissions for support involving 100-plus councils. Ten of these were followed up in the initial phase, in counties ranging from Northumberland and Durham in the north-east to Cornwall and Devon in the south-west.

But libraries remain a sensitive topic. According to a BBC survey published in March 2016, 343 UK libraries had been closed for good in the six years since the Conservatives had returned to power, initially in Coalition with the Lib Dems—with another 111 due to shut within the year. Although 174 libraries had been 'saved', at least temporarily, by being transferred to community groups, with a further fifty taken over by private providers, more than 8,000 salaried staff had lost their jobs, largely to be replaced by an unpaid army of 15,500 volunteers. The news brought instant condemnation from award-winning authors including Philip Pullman and Alan Gibbons, who described the situation as 'the greatest crisis in [the library service's] history'.

Although their statutory requirements to do so are less stringent, councils are 'allowed' to provide museums and galleries, and to require neighbouring authorities to contribute to their upkeep. Museum 'activities' beyond collecting, maintaining, and displaying objects—for example public events like readings or classes—are currently overseen by Arts Council England (ACE). The Local Government Act 1972 also gave councils powers to establish theatres, concert halls, and other entertainment venues, to maintain bands or orchestras, and to foster arts and crafts.

Use of the broad-brush term 'cultural services' to encapsulate these varied 'quality of life' provisions has been increasingly criticized—not least by those directly employed by the organizations concerned. At times (like the present) when ministers offer councils a less-than-generous financial settlement, such 'non-essential' services are invariably the first to suffer, as authorities scrabble to protect 'core' areas such as education and social services. The museums sector has increasingly dwindled, as long-serving curators have retired without being replaced, while councils have sought to make economies by introducing job-shares and substituting specialist staff with generalists.

Hard-pressed councils are often also 'forced' to withdraw funding from theatres and other venues. In 2007, Derby City Council withdrew a £40,000 grant for Derby Playhouse, criticizing the theatre's poor management and 'unsustainable' losses.

In addition to their overarching role in promoting cultural venues and local events, councils are charged with encouraging tourism and monitoring its effects on their local economies, in partnership with the national tourist promotion quango Visit Britain.

Topical feature idea

The following is the full text of a consultation document published online by Wirral Metropolitan Borough Council in 2016, asking local residents for their views on proposals to make savings in local library provision by replacing paid staff with volunteers. With an hour to your deadline, your news editor on the *Liverpool Echo* has told you to develop this into a bigger story about a threat to the survival of cultural services in the area. Who would you contact first and how would you develop the angle(s) contained in this document?

'Savings proposal for consultation—libraries re-provision', Wirral Metropolitan Borough Council, 2016

Saving in 2016–2017

£203,000

Summary of option

Wirral must and will ensure we always enable and provide a comprehensive and efficient library service, and one which meets the needs of our communities. This proposal would see the council make a relatively small saving through working with community organizations and volunteers to increase their involvement in running council-funded library buildings.

We do not believe we will have to close any library buildings as part of this proposal. We are already seeing many community organizations, groups and volunteers take an active role in running their local library; we believe we can encourage more of this work and allow the council to make the savings we need while keeping the facilities open for the communities who want them.

Context

The Public Libraries and Museums Act (1964) places a general duty on every local authority to provide a comprehensive library service. Councils need to meet the Act through paying particular regard to securing a sufficient number, range and quality of avenues to access content, by any appropriate means. We are also required to encourage people to use library services, and access advice and support.

The broad definition of a library is 'a collection of sources of information and similar resources, made accessible to a defined community for reference or borrowing. It provides physical or digital access to material, and may be a physical building, a room, a virtual space, or a combination of them all.'

Our vision is of a library service in Wirral which meets community needs through: Enabling Wirral residents to have access to a lively and engaging reading offer, to make sure that they can access relevant resources, information and support and that they can be supported to get online.

Some key pieces of insight and information related to our current library offer include:

- residents have told us that libraries, and related areas such as arts, culture and museums, should not be among our highest priorities—only 9% of residents have indicated libraries as being most important to them
- library usage is falling throughout the country as people find new ways to access books and content
- Wirral has more libraries than the national comparator and all but one of our regional neighbouring authorities

- Wirral has more libraries per head of population than the national comparator and all but one of our regional neighbouring authorities

The library is important for all communities in Wirral, and it is an offer we believe we can invest resources into in a different way, to expand and make it more widely available. We can build upon our current approach to open up new channels to access the core library offer of accessing books and content.

Why this option has been put forward

We must be clear on the future of the service and—particularly—how we deliver the offer to residents. We want residents to be able to access a library service which is comprehensive and efficient, but also for it to be delivered in a way which is designed according to their needs. We believe we can do these across four main themes:

Our view of the future scope of the service is covered in four themes:

Visit the library

We know people enjoy, they value and they sometimes rely on the traditional library building. They go there to read books, meet friends, access the internet and a wide range of other support. We must and will retain a major element of this in our future service model.

Have the library come to you

We also know that a library building isn't right for everyone, and that bringing the library offer closer to the community will help us support literacy, access to books and access to content to those neighbourhoods who most need that support. A modern, agile outreach service should play a key role in delivering on our vision in the future.

A library in your home, or on your phone

The use of traditional libraries is falling year-on-year and people want different ways to access content and read books; we need to move with the times and think differently too. 86% of Wirral residents have access to the internet; with 6 in 10 having access to a home laptop or PC. This access will continue to rise and we must make sure our offer keeps up with this demand through continuing to improve and refine our digital library service.

A library you can run

Only one in ten Wirral residents say they would not consider volunteering, and half say they would if they knew what was available. Over 1 in 4 residents are already volunteering in some form. We must capitalise on this community spirit and harness it to find new ways of providing the library offer.

How we will deliver

Implementing this proposal will over time see an improved library offer, with a redefined and strengthened purpose, which has a greater reach into the community. It will see less council-funded library buildings, but instead an equivalent library service that is supported by an enhanced outreach and digital offer and a much greater volunteer and community owned provision.

To get there, we will begin discussions with stakeholders: including individuals, community groups and other organisations who have indicated they are willing to work with us as we transform the service.

This approach is not, and cannot, be about simply deciding which libraries we keep and which libraries we close. We are not approaching it in that way. We know we can deliver this service in a different way and that we can make sure our library service more than meets our statutory obligations, that it delivers the right outcomes for residents and that it is financially stable and sustainable in the longer-term.

Moving more libraries into community ownership will mean we have more volunteers, and therefore we require less staff and over the course of the next year we believe we can be in a position to transfer up to 12 of our current physical library buildings into community ownership. That means we can start to open up new access points for library services—in other council buildings, other partner buildings such as health centres and begin to grow our digital offer.

Next steps

Over 10,000 residents have taken part in a survey to tell us their views about the various budget proposals and the general principles we have used to put them together. The survey closed on Friday 29th January and the findings will be included in a report that will be considered by Councillors when they set the budget in February.

© Wirral Metropolitan Borough Council 2016

✷ Current issues

- **The 'privatization' of major road networks and the new transport regulation regime** The longstanding Highways Agency has been replaced in England by Highways England, a government-owned company limited by shares, charged with fast tracking major road infrastructure projects. Rail and road regulation in the country has now been combined, under a new Office of Rail and Road (ORR).
- **Devolution of strategic transport policy in metropolitan areas to new combined authorities** The Greater Manchester Combined Authority has become the first to take over responsibility for planning, building, and maintaining its own public transport infrastructure, including bus services. As of 2017, its newly elected mayor will assume similar responsibilities to those of current London Mayor Sadiq Khan, with other combined authorities soon following suit.
- **Continued mass library closures** According to a March 2016 BBC survey, between May 2010 and 2017 some 454 local libraries will have been closed down across the UK, with hundreds of those remaining now run by volunteers, rather than paid staff. Blue Peter Award-winning children's author Alan Gibbons has described the position of the library service as 'the greatest crisis in its history'.

Key issues

1. Responsibility for building and maintaining many roads through and between towns and villages rests with county councils or unitary authorities and metropolitan/combined authorities or London boroughs. A-roads and M-roads (motorways) in England are built and maintained by a new government-owned company, Highways England, with Transport Scotland, the Welsh Assembly, and Department of Regional Development, Northern Ireland, doing so elsewhere.

2. Responsibility for waste collection rests with districts/boroughs in two-tier areas, with counties disposing of waste. Waste is either recycled or deposited in landfill sites.
3. Environmental health officers, employed by districts/boroughs in two-tier areas, are responsible for ensuring that shops and restaurants are clean and hygienic in handling food, but trading standards officers (unitary authorities) are charged with making sure that food is labelled (and weighed) accurately.
4. Leisure and cultural services are overseen by counties in two-tier areas. These include everything from swimming pools and sports centres to theatres and museums.
5. County councils, unitaries, and London or metropolitan boroughs have a statutory duty to provide 'comprehensive' library services, though many libraries are now staffed by volunteers.

→ Further reading

Black, G. (2011) *Transforming Museums in the Twenty-First Century*, London: Routledge. **Apposite examination of the challenges and opportunities facing museums and galleries as they adapt to lower state funding and a harsher commercial environment.**

Cahill, D. (2010) *Transport, Environment, and Society*, Buckingham: Open University Press. **Acclaimed critique of Britain's overreliance on the car, and the impact of cuts in public transport on social inequality and exclusion.**

Docherty, I. and Shaw, J. (2008) *Traffic Jam: Ten Years of Sustainable Transport in the UK*, Bristol: Policy Press. **Lively critique of the successes and failures of attempts to introduce a more integrated and sustainable transport policy under New Labour.**

Lane, K. (2006) *National Bus Company: The Road to Privatisation*, Shepperton: Ian Allan. **Affectionate account of the last years of the National Bus Company monopoly, and the revolution in public passenger transport ushered in by the Thatcher government's privatization and deregulation reforms.**

Morgan, S. (2009) *Waste, Recycling, and Reuse*, London: Evans Brothers. **Practical evaluation of the West's mounting waste management problem, with suggested solutions, focusing on 'three Rs'—reducing, reusing, and recycling.**

Waters, I. and Duffield, B. (1994) *Entertainment, Arts, and Cultural Services*, London: Financial Times/Prentice Hall. **Informative look at changes in the provision and funding of arts, entertainment, and other aspects of cultural services during the 1990s, emphasizing the tensions between different parts of the sector.**

@ Online Resource Centre

www.oxfordtextbooks.co.uk/orc/Morrison5e/

Visit the Online Resource Centre that accompanies this book for web links and regular updates.

19

Freedom of information

Most of this book has been concerned with explaining how Britain is governed—both politically, and through the nuts and bolts of public administration. This final chapter is the exception, as it focuses not on who wields power, what that power amounts to, or how it is exercised, but on the means by which journalists (and taxpayers) can find out more about decisions taken on their behalf.

19.1 The origins of the Freedom of Information Acts: what is FoI?

The concept of 'freedom of information' (FoI) rests on the notion that, in a democracy, citizens should be entitled to know as much as possible about the actions and decisions of the politicians elected to represent them, and the officials they appoint to implement policy. More important still is the principle that participating citizens should be able to find out how public money—largely derived from the taxes they pay—is spent on their behalf.

Freedom of information took a long time to emerge in Britain. At least seventy other states had enshrined their citizens' rights to find out about the inner workings of power long before the Freedom of Information Act 2000 and Freedom of Information (Scotland) Act 2002 received royal assent. It was not until Tony Blair's election in 1997 that a British government committed to implementing such reforms. Even then, it was several years into his first term before this manifesto pledge was put into action—and in a watered-down form at that. Not until 1 January 2005, towards the end of Mr Blair's second term, did the full force of the new law come into effect, under the then Department of Constitutional Affairs (now the Ministry of Justice).

Freedom of information is a long-cherished concept in the United States, which has a nationwide Freedom of Information Act based on the principle of democratic accountability and numerous state-specific laws governing access to public documentation and records of tax-levying entities—Acts collectively known as 'sunshine laws'. Elsewhere in Europe, where FoI legislation is commonplace, Acts are generally known as 'open records'. The European Union (EU) as a whole is governed by Regulation 1049/2001, passed by the European Parliament and Council of Ministers on 30 May 2001. This sets out a detailed system of rules regarding public access to EU institutions.

Lest blinkered constitutional historians try to convince us that Britain is the seat of democracy, it is worth noting that the earliest known 'open record' was passed in Sweden in the late eighteenth century. And while some might scoff at the idea of openness and accountability operating under dictatorships, it is intriguing to note that, since 1 January 2008, even China has had an FoI law (at least nominally): the Regulations of the People's Republic of China on Open Government Information.

Given the huge number of FoI laws in force globally, perhaps unsurprisingly there is little conformity in their exact provisions. Most share general traits, however—notably, the principle that the 'burden of proof' falls on institutions from which information is being sought, rather than individuals seeking it. In other words, people making requests are not normally required to explain *why* they want information, but organizations questioned must give valid reasons for failing to supply details requested. What, then, constitutes a 'valid' excuse?

19.1.1 Information that the act covers—and exempts

The UK's FoI legislation applies to more than 100,000 'public authorities', ranging from individual schools and hospitals, to councils, quangos, and entire government departments. If legitimate requests are made under either Act, authorities asked must first tell the questioners whether they hold the relevant information and then, assuming that they do, supply it within twenty working days.

Authorities may, however, *refuse* to confirm or deny the existence of information—and/or to provide it—if any of the following conditions apply:

- information requested is 'exempt';
- requests are 'vexatious' or similar to previous ones; and/or
- the costs of compliance exceed 'appropriate limits'.

The term 'exemption' might invite the idea that any authority possessing information can freely refuse to disclose it, but according to the Acts even exempt material should sometimes be made available. There are two broad classes of legitimate exemption: 'absolute' and 'qualified'. While the former may not be disclosed under any circumstances, the latter may be if the 'public interest' in revealing it outweighs that in keeping it secret. For example, authorities involved in security policy might legitimately refuse to disclose exempt information that could compromise public safety by jeopardizing counter-terrorism operations, but would be hard-pressed to do so if the information that they were withholding could *improve* safety—by, for example, revealing the expected time or location of an impending terrorist attack.

In addition to absolute and qualified exemptions, several entire categories of information are exempt. Authorities may also refuse requests that they consider 'likely to prejudice' law enforcement or Britain's interests abroad. The three categories of exemption are listed in Table 19.1.

Even when none of the above exemptions applies, journalists should proceed with caution before reproducing certain information wholesale in the media. Under the Re-use of Public Information Regulations, introduced in July 2005, some details disclosed by authorities under FoI remain subject to their legal copyright. This means that, while requesters are entitled to answers, they do not necessarily have 'automatic rights' to reuse the information, other than for the purposes for which it was originally produced by the authorities concerned. Although theoretically these Regulations could be used by disingenuous authorities to delay or prevent journalists disclosing perfectly 'free' information, in practice they tend to be invoked to protect intellectual property rights

Table 19.1 Exemptions under the Freedom of Information Act 2000

Absolute	Qualified
Information supplied by/relating to bodies dealing with security matters.	Intended for future publication.
Court records and information related to impending prosecution.	Related to national security (other than information supplied by/relating to named security organizations).
Information that would infringe parliamentary privilege.	Which might limit defence of British Isles, or 'capability, effectiveness, or security' of Armed Forces.
Personal information either: 1. relating to person making request, which could be obtained under Data Protection Act 1998; or 2. about another individual, if it would breach data protection principles.	Potentially prejudicial to international relations between UK and another state/international organization/court or its interests abroad.
Information held by Commons or Lords that may be prejudicial to effective conduct of public affairs.	Information that might prejudice relations between administrations within UK.

Table 19.1 (*continued*)

Absolute	Qualified
Information provided in confidence.	Information likely to prejudice UK's financial and/or economic interests.
Prohibitions on disclosure where prohibited by enactment or would constitute contempt of court.	Information relating to investigations and proceedings conducted by public authorities.
	Information likely to prejudice law enforcement—defined as prevention or detection of crime, prosecution of offenders, assessment of taxes, etc.
	Information relating to public authority with audit functions in relation to another public body (e.g. Audit Commission).
	Information relating to formulation of government policy, communications between ministers, or operations of ministerial office.
	Information held by public authorities other than Commons or Lords that may be prejudicial to effective conduct of public affairs.
	Information relating to communications between Queen, ministers, and/or other public bodies, including those relating to honours system.
	Information likely to endanger health and/or safety of individuals.
	Environmental information authority is obliged to make public under s. 74 of the Act.
	Personal information believed by institution not to breach data protection principles, but in relation to which individual who is subject of request serves notice that disclosure would cause 'unwarranted substantial damage or distress'.
	Subject to legal professional privilege.
	'Trade secrets' or information liable to prejudice individual's/authority's commercial interests.

of third parties whose work is included in disclosed material: for example freelance photographers, architects, or designers.

These, then, are the exempt categories of information—but what of the Acts' definitions of 'public authority'? Are any organizations or individuals that one might expect to fall under this umbrella exempted from FoI requests? In short, yes.

19.1.1.1 The Queen and Royal Household

The Royal Family's website defines the status of the Queen and Royal Household thus:

> ‘The Royal Household is not a public authority within the meaning of the FOI Acts and is therefore exempt from their provisions.’

It goes on to cite the 'fundamental constitutional principle' that communications between reigning sovereigns and ministers or other public bodies remain confidential—to ensure that royals do not compromise their 'political neutrality'. As the site stresses, however, the fact that the Royal Household is not bound by FoI does *not* mean that it is unwilling to make certain information available voluntarily. To this end, it is happy to 'account openly for all its use of public money'. It does this by posting online every July a consolidated report, including a full annual account and breakdown of the sovereign grant. Additionally, the Prince of Wales voluntarily publishes details of his income from the Duchy of Cornwall—both before and after tax—on his website (see 1.2.3.1).

What the sites fail to emphasize is the fact that no information about the Royal Household's funding was made public until 2001, when it was persuaded to agree to greater openness while negotiating with HM Treasury a new ten-year funding settlement. Perhaps even more remarkable is the amount of detail about its dealings that the Royal Family still will *not* disclose. For example, nowhere will British taxpayers access details about other aspects of the royals' personal finances, such as incomes derived by several members of the family from the Armed Forces, the Duchess of York's royalties for her series of *Budgie the Little Helicopter* children's books and numerous television talk show appearances, or the dividends and profits derived from family members' investments. Soon after the 2010 election, the Coalition gave the National Audit Office greater access to the Queen's accounts, but this has yet to yield any major revelations.

The list of specific FoI exemptions for the Queen and the Royal Household are detailed in Table 19.2. The special treatment the Queen and her immediate family enjoy in relation to FoI became the subject of a public dispute in January 2012 between the Scottish Government and Scotland's then newly installed Information Commissioner, Rosemary Agnew. Interviewed in *Scotland on Sunday*, she criticized former First Minister Alex Salmond's proposal to turn the 'qualified' exemption covering royal communications north of the border into an 'absolute' one.

Table 19.2 Specific FoI exemptions relating to the Royal Household

Exemption	Details
Financial and other personal matters	Information relating to personal affairs of sovereign/ family members—including private finances and personal activities—exempt under s. 40 of FoI Act and s. 38 of Scottish FoI Act (Data Protection Act provisions).
Royal communications	'Absolute' exemption for correspondences sent by/on behalf of/to Queen, heir to throne, or second in line introduced under Constitutional Reform and Governance Act 2010, with same exemption expected to be introduced in Scotland under Freedom of Information (Amendment) Bill. 'Qualified' exemptions apply to communications with other Royal Household/family members under s. 37 of FoI Act 2000. Latter may be disclosed only if 'balance of public interest' deems this necessary. All exemptions apply for whichever longer of twenty years or five years after death of family member concerned.
Correspondences with family members now deceased	Personal information on recently deceased family members relating to communications with Queen, other members of Royal Household/family. If contained in records less than thirty years old, may be exempt under s. 37 of UK FoI Act (s. 41 of Scottish FoI Act).
Other information relating to deceased royals	Information relating to recently deceased family members, disclosure of which would damage 'right to family life' of deceased's relatives, may be exempt under s. 44 of UK FoI Act and s. 26 of Scottish FoI Act, and s. 8 ('Private Life and Family') of Human Rights Act 1998.

The introduction, in 2010, of a similar absolute exemption across the rest of Britain, however, failed to silence *The Guardian* over its then five-year quest to use FoI to force publication of twenty-seven correspondences from Prince Charles to ministers—dubbed the 'black spider memos' because of his illegible handwriting—purportedly showing that the heir to the throne had lobbied them to change government priorities. This long-running saga led to a showdown between the paper and the then Coalition Attorney General Dominic Grieve in 2013, when he refused to disclose the letters' contents on the grounds that they could cast doubt on the Prince's political neutrality—creating constitutional difficulties for him when he acceded to the throne. Mr Grieve had defied a ruling by the Information Tribunal that the public were entitled to see the letters under the FoI Act 2000 and under the Environmental Information Regulations 2004. However, in March 2014, the Master of the Rolls, Lord Dyson, and two other senior judges overruled him—once again, paving the way for the letters' release and forcing ministers to launch a further appeal to suppress them, this time to the Supreme Court. As the government continued to drag its collective heels, choice nuggets of information began seeping out via other sources: in interviews for a June 2014 BBC Radio 4 documentary, *The Royal Activist*, ex-Labour Education Secretary David Blunkett claimed that Prince Charles had lobbied him to extend the grammar school system in the 1990s, while a former Environment Minister, the late Michael Meacher, disclosed that he and Prince Charles 'would consort together quietly' to try to persuade then Prime Minister Tony Blair to introduce more radical policies to combat climate change and abandon investment in genetically modified (GM) crops. When the letters were finally published, in May 2015, they proved something of an anticlimax: generally written in a gracious and diplomatic, rather than insistent, tone, they largely focused on a mixture of well-known and more obscure pet concerns of the Prince. These ranged from worries that about the heavy-handed nature of EU regulation of complimentary medicines (of which he is famously in favour) to criticisms of the negative impact of supermarket food pricing on struggling farmers, to the much more curious suggestion to the then Culture Secretary Tessa Jowell that Antarctica ought to be considered a British territory.

Despite this array of exemptions, placing Britain's Royal Household in a significantly more privileged position than any other, recent annual disclosures of its public accounts have shed light on the huge lengths to which members appear to go to defend FoI applications. According to its 2006–7 accounts, it spent £180,000 of taxpayers' money in that one year shielding itself from FoI requests. Buckingham Palace claimed that the sum was spent 'reminding' government departments of the exemption to prevent them from releasing details of private communications.

Nonetheless, resourceful journalists have found ways of circumventing royals' exemptions. In June 2008, an ingenious FoI request to the Ministry of Defence unearthed the cost of Prince William's controversial flight in an RAF Chinook helicopter to an exclusive stag party on the Isle of Wight. The trip—one of five 'familiarization exercises' undertaken by the prince, which saw him stop off en route to pick up his brother, Prince Harry, in London—set taxpayers back £8,716. Embarrassing disclosures teased out of communications with the Royal Household covered only by qualified exemption have included the revelation that, in 2004, the Queen asked ministers for grants worth £60 million to improve the energy efficiency of Buckingham Palace—from a pot of money specifically targeted at low-income households (see 16.2.2). Among hundreds of other letters obtained by *The Independent* in September 2010 was one exposing a row between the Queen and ministers over who should profit from the sale of land around Kensington Palace.

19.1.1.2 Utilities, train companies, and other passenger transport operators

Controversially, the privatized utilities—water, electricity, gas, telecommunications, and rail-operating companies—were excluded from automatic coverage by the FoI Acts when they entered their final draft stages. After being included in the remit of the government's 1997 White Paper *Your Right to Know*, hopes were high that they would be subject to scrutiny when the Acts were passed. But after intensive lobbying by the companies concerned—on the basis that exposure to FoI could jeopardize commercially sensitive operations—they were omitted.

The decision to exclude companies involved in supplying British taxpayers with such vital 'natural monopolies' as energy and water was enough to infuriate many, but more baffling was the fact that even Network Rail—the not-for-dividend company formed to take over maintenance of the railway infrastructure after the collapse of private firm Railtrack in 2001—was exempted. In a test ruling in January 2007, the **Information Commissioner**—the individual who hears FoI appeals (see 19.1.5)—clarified that it was a 'private company', not a 'public authority' under the Act's terms. His ruling came in response to an appeal against the company's refusal to answer a May 2005 request, under the Data Protection Act 1998, regarding information about a flood by a railway line. As of 24 March 2015, though, this situation changed, when Network Rail was formally made subject to the FoI Act. In addition, the latest government-owned company to be formed in relation to transport, Highways England, is also bound by the Act. However, following a major government-initiated review of the Act, published by an Independent Commission on Freedom of Information in March 2016, ministers declined to extend the remit of FoI to cover the growing number of commercial companies and charities involved in delivering public services—to the frustration of hopeful transparency campaigners.

Although utility companies and private contractors with public service franchises remain immune to FoI, the regulators set up to monitor them—such as the Office of Gas and Electricity Markets (Ofgem) and Office of Communications (Ofcom)—are *not*. The fact that it is possible for press and public to access significant amounts of information from utilities *indirectly* has been used as an argument by the Confederation of British Industry (CBI) and other business lobbyists for retaining the 'light touch' approach to the utilities that currently remains.

19.1.1.3 Academies

Until recently one of the most contentious categories of organization exempt from FoI was academies—'independent' secondary schools operating within the state sector (see 14.2.2). Their exemption—granted because of the involvement of private sponsors in setting them up and running their ancillary services—was widely viewed as a double standard, as it enabled them to avoid revealing performance data that all other state schools were expected to publish. Some even suggested that the exemption was a convenient way of masking academies' initially sluggish academic progress (when introduced in 2002, they were trumpeted as a way of turning round 'failing' comprehensives by pumping in private capital). Up to January 2011, when the law was amended to bring them within the ambit of FoI by the then Education Secretary Michael Gove, Labour's academies were allowed to publicize their exam results in a different way from other schools—omitting details of the subjects in which GCSE A*–C grades had been obtained, thereby making it hard for parents to take informed decisions about their relative performance.

Critics also pointed to a clear contradiction between the government's public insistence that, despite being largely privately financed, academies remained in the public sector—as opposed to representing the start of creeping privatization of the state schooling system. In addition to bringing the first wave of academies under FoI, in September 2010 Mr Gove extended the Act's remit to cover all those formed under the Coalition.

19.1.1.4 The British Broadcasting Corporation (BBC)

As a publicly funded organization, the BBC is subject to FoI in relation to much of its activities. However, given that a large part of its remit is to produce, commission, and broadcast programmes and other creative content (on television, radio, and the Internet) for public consumption, there are areas of its operation that are exempt. The scope of the Act as it applies to the Corporation is therefore defined as relating to information 'held for purposes other than those of journalism, art or literature'—in other words, requests for disclosure are not allowed to interfere with the BBC's own editorial decisions and output, which themselves might often involve FoI-related enquiries. Such exempt information will also be excluded from the versions of the BBC's annual report and accounts, which are made publicly available on its website through its own publication scheme.

19.1.1.5 The Security Service, MI6, and other intelligence agencies

Just as most security-related material is exempt from FoI, there is a blanket exemption for any information relating to the work of the Security Service (MI5), MI6, and other British intelligence agencies. Similar exemptions apply to Special Forces, such as the Special Air Service (SAS) and Royal Marines Special Boat Squadron (SBS).

19.1.2 How to make an FoI request—and how not to

Around 120,000 FoI requests are made each year—six out of ten by the public, a fifth by businesses, and around one in ten by journalists. That said, the exhaustive nature of some enquiries has taken its toll on authorities' time and resources. In 2005, the year the 2000 Act came into force for the general public, the overall cost of complying with media-related FoI requests was estimated at £35.5 million.

But how does one make a request? Although the exact procedure varies from authority to authority, it entails writing either by email or post, detailing specific question(s) to which an answer(s) is requested. Any ambiguity in wording should see authorities enter into dialogues with requesters to clarify the question(s) and supply information as quickly as possible—provided it is not exempt. Authorities are also expected, where relevant, to supply additional explanatory material if this will clarify complex or confusing information and avoid the need for prolonged correspondence with requesters. As in other states, requesters must give their names and contact details when filing requests, but are not expected to divulge their motivations. In principle, FoI requests are free, and it is highly unusual for organizations to charge for answering them.

In addition to the aforementioned exemptions, authorities may refuse to respond to requests for other reasons. If a single request to a government department or body is likely to cost more than £600 in terms of time and/or staffing needed to locate the information (£450, in the case of other authorities), it may be refused. Alternatively, authorities may send requesters notice that they will be charged fees up to the cost of gathering and supplying requested information. If requesters pay, material must then be provided. Authorities may also decline to answer 'vexatious' requests—defined as ones:

- imposing a 'significant burden' on authorities in terms of expense or distraction *and* not having any serious purpose or value;
- being designed to cause disruption or annoyance;
- having the effect of harassing the authority; or
- being otherwise obsessive or manifestly unreasonable.

Examples of 'vexatious' cases have included that of an individual refused information by Birmingham City Council after making more than seventy previous requests. In another case, West Midlands Transport Executive spent 175 hours responding to one person's enquiries. Transport for London (TfL), meanwhile, received so many letters from a single enquirer that it had had to devise a new internal management strategy to cope. But perhaps the most burdensome FoI addict to date was the individual who sent no fewer than 347 requests to police forces, 412 to the Ministry of Defence, and 22 to the Cabinet Office.

Just as authorities are allowed to reject vexatious requests, they may also refuse to answer 'repeated' ones—those identical to others that they have previously answered in full, particularly if they originate from the same individual or organization.

19.1.3 The Environmental Information Regulations 2004

The FoI Act was not the only new legislation designed to promote greater government openness to take effect in 2005. Under EU law, the Environmental Information Regulations (EIR) 2004—in Scotland, Environmental Information (Scotland) Regulations 2004—came in simultaneously, giving the public access to information about the state of their natural environment, particularly in relation to potential hazards such as pollution.

Unlike FoI, EIR requests—also generally made by post or email and subject to twenty-day response times—may be lodged verbally, rather than in writing. They also cover various private-sector organizations currently beyond the FoI Acts' remit. For example, EIR requests may be made to privatized utilities, such as water and electricity companies, responsible for activities with direct impact on the environment. Environmental information covered by the Regulations may relate to:

- the state of 'elements of the environment'—air, water, soil, land, fauna (including human beings);
- emissions and discharges, noise, energy, radiation, waste, and other such substances;
- measures and activities such as policies, plans, and agreements affecting, or likely to affect, the state of the environment;
- reports, cost–benefit, and economic analyses;
- the state of human health and safety, and contamination of the food chain; and
- cultural sites and built structures—to the extent that they may be affected by the state of the elements of the environment.

As with the FoI Acts, there are certain 'absolute' and 'qualified' exemptions to the EIR's provisions, as outlined in Table 19.3.

Enquiries made under EIR tend to incur fees for requesters, provided these are set at a 'reasonable' level and authorities publish a schedule of their charges. Requests may not, however, be refused on cost grounds alone.

Table 19.3 Exemptions under the Environmental Information Regulations 2004

Absolute	Qualified
Information not held by authority (if so, it has 'duty' to refer request to relevant body).	Release would breach confidentiality of legal proceedings.
Request 'manifestly unreasonable'.	Might prejudice international relations between Britain and other states/international bodies, public security, or national defence.
Request 'too general' (although authority should still fulfil duty to advise and assist).	Might jeopardize course of justice and right of citizens to fair trial.
Requests for unfinished documents or data (in which case, estimated time for completion must be given).	Commercially confidential information.
Requests for internal communications.	Certain information related to intellectual property rights.
Related to personal/voluntary data.	Related to environmental protection work.

19.1.4 FoI versus data protection

The Data Protection Act 1984, as amended by the Data Protection Act 1998, relates to the notion of protecting individuals' privacy, as its name suggests. Superficially, this may appear to conflict with more 'free for all' aspects of information disclosure ushered in by FoI. In practice, however, the two Acts largely consolidate one another—a fact assured by the ministers' decision to give the task of policing both of them to the Information Commissioner in 2005.

The 1998 Act relates to 'personal data'. This is 'any data which can be used to identify a living person'—including names, addresses, telephone, fax, and mobile phone numbers, email addresses, and birthdays. It applies, however, only to data that is or is intended to be held on computer or in another 'relevant filing system'. The Act's scope is fairly broad in this latter context: individuals' paper diaries may be considered 'relevant filing systems' if used commercially. The Act is underpinned by seven 'key principles', as outlined in Table 19.4.

The Act gives anyone whose personal data is processed the right to:

- view any data held by an organization, for a small ('subject access') fee;
- request incorrect information be corrected—and if the organization ignores his or her plea, a court may order data to be corrected or destroyed and compensation to be paid;
- require data not be used in a way that causes 'damage or distress'; and
- require that his or her data is not used for direct marketing.

Table 19.4 Conditions relating to use of personal data under the Data Protection Act 1998

Condition	Details
Focus	Data may be used only for specific purposes for which collected.
Privacy	Data must not be disclosed to other parties without consent of individual concerned, unless legislation/other overriding legitimate reason requires information to be shared (e.g. crime prevention/ detection). It is an offence for other parties to obtain data without authorization.
Accessibility	Individuals have right to access information about them, subject to certain exceptions (e.g. crime prevention/detection information).
Time-sensitivity	Data may be kept no longer than necessary.
Protection	Data may not be transmitted outside European Economic Area (EEA) unless individual to whom it relates consents or adequate protection exists (e.g. use of prescribed form of contract). Entities holding personal information required to have adequate security—e.g. technical measures (such as computer firewalls) and organizational ones (such as staff training).
Regulation	Almost all entities that process personal information must register with Information Commissioner.

So how do the two Acts—governing 'data protection', on the one hand, and 'freedom of information', on the other—coalesce in practice?

First, many enquiries that individuals might think of making under the FoI Act in relation to information about themselves will be exempt. However, this is only because the correct procedure for accessing such information actually falls under the 1998 Act. That said, if individuals seek to make requests relating to themselves that will disclose information about third parties, the correct law to use *is* likely to be the FoI Act. Confusingly, though, authorities asked to supply such information must consider 'data protection principles' applicable under FoI before deciding whether to release it.

Because many FoI requests concern what might be termed 'corporate' information—procedural, statistical, and/or constitutional matters—rather than personal data, in practice the number of serious conflicts between the FoI and Data Protection Acts is limited. There have, however, been notable altercations between journalists and councils—particularly in relation to the salaries and perks of senior officers. Councils have often tried to hide behind data protection legislation when asked for such details under FoI, arguing that, because officers are not elected representatives, they constitute information of a personal nature and should be treated as confidential. The Commissioner has clarified the legal position surrounding this, by distinguishing between information relating to public officials' private lives (exempt) and public duties (covered). Sections 34 and 35 of the 1998 Act exempt individuals from data protection if the data requested consists of information that authorities handling requests are obliged to publicize by law, or if court orders or other 'rules of law' require its disclosure. Either of these can override personal data protections otherwise guaranteed by Section 40 of the FoI Act.

A landmark ruling by the Commissioner in June 2011 raised the prospect of a more free-for-all approach to disclosing information about public servants' salaries. Defying a Cabinet Office attempt to protect the identities of twenty-four senior civil servants earning more than £150,000 each, he ordered that their names be publicized—raising the prospect that a strongly resisted request by the then Communities Secretary Eric Pickles for councils to publish the names and salaries of all officers earning £58,200-plus (see 11.4) might return to haunt them. While the Cabinet Office had tried to avoid releasing certain figures, ministers had already taken significant steps towards throwing open the books in relation to mandarins earning more than the prime minister a year before the Commissioner's ruling. The most recent figures issued in what has since become something of an annual 'naming and shaming' ritual were published in December 2015. They revealed that, if anything, the superannuation of senior public servants had inflated over the five years since the first details were published—despite almost all other public-sector employees enduring years of pay freezes amounting to real-terms cuts in income. It disclosed that 319 officials earned more than the prime minister, thirty-five of these working in senior roles on the London-to-Midlands High-Speed 2 (HS2) rail-building project. Among them was its chief executive, Simon Kirby, who earned £750,000.

19.1.5 FoI appeals and the Information Commissioner

Anyone refused FoI information has a right to appeal, initially through the authorities' own internal review procedures, but ultimately to the Information Commissioner's Office (ICO). In addition to its central London headquarters, the ICO has three offices in the capitals of the devolved nations: Edinburgh, Cardiff, and Belfast.

It is the Information Commissioner's job to ensure that the twenty-three current exemptions are not abused by authorities seeking to keep secret information that they regard as embarrassing, but which is not exempt. In Scotland, where *both* Acts apply (the Scottish one binds only devolved public authorities), complaints are made to the Scottish Information Commissioner. And citizens there have a further right to appeal beyond even the Commissioners: to an *Information Tribunal*.

To aid authorities in complying with the FoI Acts, the ICO has published 'Ten Top Tips'. These are listed in table 19A to be found on the **Online Resource Centre**.

Complaints may be made to the ICO if authorities fail to:

- provide information requested;
- respond to requests within twenty working days (or explain why longer is needed);
- give proper advice and help;
- give information in forms requested;
- properly explain reasons for refusing requests; or
- correctly apply exemptions.

Complainants must provide the following material:

- a covering letter, detailing the complaint;
- details of the initial request;
- a copy of the authority's initial response '(the 'refusal notice');
- a copy of the complaint made to the authority's internal review or complaints procedure;
- a copy of the authority's response;

- any other information that they think relevant; and
- their contact details.

Stories in which the Commissioner has played a prominent role have had more to do with data protection than FoI. In June 2008, he served formal enforcement notices—the toughest sanctions available—against both HM Revenue and Customs (HMRC) and the Ministry of Defence (MoD) over 'deplorable failures' leading to 'serious data breaches'. He was referring to two (then recent) data protection fiascos. In November 2007, HMRC confessed to losing two unencrypted discs containing personal details of 25 million Child Benefit recipients—every British family with a child under the age of 16. The information—including names, addresses, birthdates, National Insurance (NI) numbers, and bank details—had been en route from HMRC's offices at Waterview Park, Sunderland, to the National Audit Office in London.

The second breach, revealed in January 2008, concerned the theft of an MoD laptop containing confidential details of 600,000 service personnel. In reporting the crime in a Commons statement, the then Defence Secretary Des Browne revealed that two further thefts of departmental laptops had also occurred since 2005.

There is a welter of guidance on the ICO's website about the rights of public and media to access information under the Acts it administers. One of the most useful for journalists is the 'Guidance Notice explaining how authorities should weigh the 'public interest' of a request against potential qualified exemptions' (see Table 19.5).

Table 19.5 Priority types of information covered by the FoI 'public interest test'

Category	Definition
Matters of public debate	Issues about which public debate has been generated and debate cannot properly take place without information disclosure; issues affecting many individuals/companies; government has put views on record; issues that may affect legislative process.
Public participation in political debate	Situations in which local interest groups need sufficient information to represent those interests and requests relate to facts behind major policy decisions.
Accountability for public funds	Matters relating to government accountability for sale of public assets or legal aid spending; need for openness relating to tender processes/prices for public spending and services; misappropriation of public funds; accountability of elected officials whose propriety called into question; need for public bodies to obtain value for money in spending taxpayers' cash.
Public safety	Information relating to air safety, nuclear plant security, and public health, contingency plans in emergencies, and potential environmental damage.

19.2 Freedom of information and the headlines: some case studies

Perhaps unsurprisingly, reporters working on everything from local weekly free sheets to national dailies have embraced FoI as a source of potential stories—not least because they enable a modicum of what might loosely be termed 'investigative journalism' to be carried out within the increasingly restrictive confines of modern newsrooms. Widespread cutbacks—from the offices of regional publishers to those of major nationals—have seen the size of many papers' reporting staffs dwindle in recent years. Papers face growing competition from the Internet and other forms of new media, and as a result new recruits are expected to 'multitask' as everything from video journalists and photographers, to designers, subeditors, and bloggers. At the same time, ever-tighter economies imposed on newsrooms mean that what conventional reporting is still being done is increasingly carried out over the telephone and/or email, rather than in the face-to-face, hands-on fashion of times past.

Freedom of information therefore offers a means by which journalists with suitably forensic minds can hold authorities accountable 'on the cheap'. Whereas once they might have had to invest significant resources into rooting out information that organizations were keen to keep secret, much of this can now be obtained (at least theoretically) by sending a simple email. FoI legislation has also spawned several 'amateur' journalism websites almost entirely dedicated to using it as an investigative tool (notably **http://helpmeinvestigate.com**, **www.whatdotheyknow.com**, and **www.opendemocracy.net**).

The FoI bonanza did not begin in earnest until January 2005. Within days of the 2000 Act coming into force, *The Observer* ran a story listing a 'who's who' of celebrities and business people who had been wined and dined by the then Prime Minister Mr Blair at his country retreat, Chequers, since 2001. The luminaries—whose names it obtained under FoI—included entertainer Des O'Connor, former Spice Girl Geri Halliwell, television presenter Esther Rantzen, Lord Lloyd Webber, Olympic champion rower Sir Steve Redgrave, and then Tesco chief executive Sir Terry Leahy.

That August, BBC2's *Newsnight* used an FoI request to expose the fact that Harold Macmillan's government sold Israel sufficient quantities of uranium 235 and heavy water to enable it to develop its nuclear weapons programme. In a statement to the International Atomic Energy Agency (IAEA), then Foreign Office Minister Kim Howells denied that Britain had been a party to any such sale, but in March 2006 *Newsnight* used a further request to expose sales of plutonium to Israel under Harold Wilson.

Perhaps even more shocking was the disclosure, in December 2005, of a hushed-up report by Scotland Yard detective Tom Hayward into a brutal torture camp operated by British forces in post-war Germany. *The Guardian* used

FoI to obtain a copy of the document, detailing the outcome of interrogations of 372 men and forty-four women at the Bad Nenndorf camp, near Hanover. Among the grisly details was an account of how two men suspected of being Communists were starved to death, another beaten to a pulp, and numerous others seriously injured. Four months later, the paper published images of emaciated prisoners after winning an appeal against the MoD's refusal to release photographs of the victims contained in the report.

But FoI requests do not always produce such sensational outcomes. In most cases, they 'unearth' humdrum information—much of it unexciting and lacking in any obvious news value. Indeed, there is a feeling in some quarters—not least the offices of less well-staffed authorities—that journalists have come to rely on FoI too heavily. Before the concept of 'freedom of information' passed into British law, reporters were forced to rely on those tried-and-tested qualities—guile, ingenuity, and perseverance—to tease out material that organizations wanted to keep hidden from public view. If they received tip-offs that councillors were fiddling their expenses or public officials taking overseas flights using taxpayers' money, they would often have to confront press officers (or officials themselves) head on, using arguments about the 'public interest' and 'public domain' to remind them of their obligations to confirm or deny such activities, and where necessary supply details. Reluctant though authorities invariably were to expose themselves to criticism by admitting such abuses, more often than not they grudgingly disclosed them. Today, able to hide behind the cloak of having to 'dig out the information' or 'go through the files', the same authorities can cheerfully take far longer to make disclosures—using the cover of the statutory twenty-day time limit to craft polished excuses and put off answering questions until any newsworthiness derived from them has dwindled or passed.

Seasoned FoI users—particularly those experienced enough to know the difference between stories requiring the Act and those that can be stood up using more conventional tactics—cite the counterargument that, given the relative ease and effectiveness of the legislation, too few journalists are taking advantage of it. Used in a targeted way, it is certainly true that FoI provides an excellent source of off-diary stories (which, in this pressure-cooker, 24/7 age, are more prized by news editors than ever).

19.3 The future of FoI—and moves to extend (or restrict) it

New Labour initially made a big noise about its commitment to FoI, but later on it appeared to regret laying itself open to quite so much scrutiny. Ministers' discomfort with outcomes of some FoI requests began emerging in May 2007, when

Conservative backbencher David Maclean introduced a private member's Bill (PMB) into the House of Commons—the Freedom of Information (Amendment) Bill—which proposed exempting members of Parliament (MPs) from the 2000 Act (ostensibly to protect details contained in their personal correspondences, including the addresses of private individuals). It would also have incorporated the cost of time that officials spent 'thinking' about whether to disclose information within the £600 limit above which requests become chargeable.

The issue came to a head that June after the Commons provisionally approved the Bill and ministers began seeking a sympathetic peer to 'sponsor' it through the Lords. When none volunteered, and the Bill was condemned by both the Commons Constitutional Affairs Select Committee and Lords Constitution Committee, it finally fell—but not before the then Leader of the House, Jack Straw, issued new guidelines urging authorities to ensure that MPs' personal details were not compromised by releasing correspondences with their constituents.

It is not only public authorities that occasionally gripe about FoI. In May 2007, the Commissioner used his address to the annual Freedom of Information Conference to urge people to act with 'restraint' when making requests. He cited an enquiry about how much the Foreign Office spent on Ferrero Rocher chocolates and another asking about the number of eligible bachelors in the Hampshire Police Force as examples of frivolous queries. Significantly, years after these events, Mr Blair confessed in an interview that introducing FoI was one of his biggest regrets.

Despite such reservations, in addition to the minor extensions to FoI outlined above, in relation to Network Rail and Highways England, it has recently been rolled out to cover some functions of bodies that are not strictly public authorities, but nonetheless involved in delivering public policy. The Freedom of Information (Designation of Public Authorities) Order 2011 requires the Universities and Colleges Admissions Service (UCAS), a registered charity, to answer FoI requests in relation to its role as a central coordinator of university applications, although not its other areas of responsibility. The same order brought the Association of Chief Police Officers (ACPO) and the Financial Ombudsman Service (FOS) fully within the scope of the Act.

FoI campaigners continue to lament the lack of any meaningful extension of FoI's scope, however, while warning of the ongoing danger that *existing* levels of openness might be curtailed by ministers and/or senior civil servants determined to close ranks to protect 'state secrets'. It was in this spirit of wariness that they greeted the publication in March 2016 of a report by an Independent Commission on Freedom of Information set up some months earlier by Mr Cameron's then newly elected Conservative government. In the event, the report stopped short of recommending some measures that had been feared—including introducing routine charges for making requests, which critics argued would disenfranchise those without the money to pay.

However, it did make twenty-one recommendations, which at the time of writing were still under consideration by ministers. These included:

- giving authorities an additional twenty-day maximum period to reply to FoI requests that it would be 'impracticable to respond to' in the usual time period 'because of the complexity or volume of the requested information';
- new legislation to require all authorities liable to the Act and employing 100-plus people to publish statistics on their FoI compliance;
- the introduction of an exemption for information that would disclose internal communications relating to government policy;
- legislation to 'put beyond doubt' the fact that it has the power to 'veto' the release of information under the Act—with the proviso that information should only be vetoed where the 'accountable person' takes a different view to the Information Commissioner in relation to the 'public interest';
- the removal of a right to appeal to the First Tier Tribunal in respect of decisions made by the Commissioner in relation to the Act;
- a review of the adequacy of resources available to the Commissioner.

By far the most contentious of the suggestions (many of which arguably strengthened the protections available to citizens) was that potentially permitting the government to veto the release of certain information—a suggestion many campaigners saw as an attempt to prevent future disclosures along the lines of that surrounding the Prince of Wales's letters. It remains to be seen, though, whether any or all of these recommendations will be implemented, given then Cabinet Office Minister Matthew Hancock's statement that no wholesale change to the existing FoI Act was necessary and, more recently, Mr Cameron's replacement as prime minister by Theresa May.

19.4 FoI and the European Union

Under the bureaucratically named 'Regulation 1049/2001', any EU citizen may request a copy of a document produced by the European Commission, whether it has previously been published or not. On the online Register of Commission Documents—available on the https://ec.europa.eu website—draft legislation and other published documents can usually be searched and downloaded from a database by clicking on an accompanying link. However, it is also possible to request a copy of any unpublished document listed on the register by clicking on the box beneath the online reference and completing a form. But while this may sound open and transparent, the EC has come in for some criticism for the various caveats it attaches to citizens' FoI rights. It has been known to request copies of identity documents from requesters before granting them access, and the online register lists a wide range of classes of information to which it will not usually grant access, including papers relating to EU 'pilots', state aid, court cases, competition, mergers, and 'infringements'.

19.5 Other sources of information: accessing historical records

For decades, there has been a rule (still present under the FoI Acts) absolving British governments from making public Cabinet papers and other official documents until thirty years after they were written. However, in 2010, this was changed to twenty years. The reform—which fell short of a fifteen-year limit for secrecy proposed by an inquiry headed by *Daily Mail* editor Paul Dacre—has since been gradually phased in, in a ten-year process that will take until 2023—allowing 2 million additional documents to be transferred to the National Archives (formerly the Public Records Office) at Kew, west London, at a rate of two years' worth of records per year. There will be some exceptions, though: as under FoI, communications with reigning monarchs and their heirs are absolutely exempt from disclosure, while documents concerning British government policy and activities in Northern Ireland during 'The Troubles' will remain secret for thirty years, as before.

Although, by definition, they will relate to events that took place up to two decades earlier, records released under the new 'twenty-year rule' are likely to provide magnets for journalists—if documents published under the old ones are anything to go by. Previous disclosures have revealed everything from detailed preparations made by Margaret Thatcher's administration in 1981 for the possibility of nuclear war with the Soviet Union, to a private admission by her predecessor, James Callaghan, that his fatal decision to delay an election that he might have won in autumn 1978 was inspired by his 'malicious' delight at confounding the Tories' expectations.

Topical feature idea

Your local newspaper editor has given you three weeks to find an off-diary exclusive using the Freedom of Information (FoI) Act. With plenty of financial and other information already available on your council's website, to which other public authorities could you direct your enquiry? How would you frame your FoI request to dig out the most newsworthy lead?

✷ Current issues

- **Incremental extension of the scope of FoI** Network Rail was finally made subject to FoI in March 2015, with the Act also applying to the body that replaced the Highways Agency: Highways England. Piecemeal extensions continue in relation to other quangos, executive agencies, and government-owned companies.
- **The belated release of the 'black spider memos'** Following a ten-year battle between *The Guardian* and successive governments, twenty-seven letters from Prince Charles to ministers—dubbed the 'black spider memos'—were finally published in May 2015. They proved less than electrifying, with most focusing on uncontroversial issues known to be close to the Prince's heart, such as complimentary medicine and the plight of struggling farmers.
- **Publication of an independent FoI review** A much-anticipated review of existing FoI legislation, published in March 2016, made twenty-one recommendations for improvements in the existing regime—but stopped short of suggesting that charges were introduced for making requests, as FoI campaigners had feared. It did, however, recommend that ministers should legislate to formalize their power to veto the release of certain information.

Key points

1. The Freedom of Information (FoI) Act 2000 and Freedom of Information (Scotland) Act 2002 allow individuals to make free, written applications for financial and other data to more than 100,000 UK 'public authorities'.
2. FoI requests must be made in writing (usually via post or email) and should be responded to within twenty working days of being received.
3. Certain categories of information held by public authorities are 'exempt', either on an 'absolute' or 'qualified' basis. The former includes information that might be prejudicial to court cases or national security, and letters written to or by the Queen or heir and second in line to the throne.
4. Rules about how FoI should be applied are laid out by the Information Commissioner. People believing that they have been refused information unlawfully may appeal to him or her or, if still dissatisfied, the Information Tribunal.
5. The Commissioner also oversees the Data Protection Act 1998, under which individuals are entitled to access personal information that organizations hold about them—for a small fee—and the Environmental Information Regulations (EIR) 2004, which entitle people to access information on the state of their natural environment.

→ Further reading

Birkinshaw, P. (2010) *Freedom of Information: The Law, the Practice, and the Ideal*, Cambridge: Cambridge University Press. **Excellent overview of the theory and prac-**

tice of FoI law in Britain, and the conflicts between the need for secrecy in intelligence and crime prevention and open government.

Brooke, H. (2006) *Your Right to Know: A Citizen's Guide to the Freedom of Information Act*, 2nd edn, London: Pluto Press. **Step-by-step guide to making effective FoI requests by the journalist who exposed the MPs' expenses scandal. Includes an introduction by Ian Hislop, editor of *Private Eye*, on his magazine's prolific use of the FoI Acts.**

Burgess, M. (2015) *Freedom of Information: A Practical Guide for UK Journalists*, Abingdon: Routledge. **As its title suggests, an indispensable and up-to-date guide to how to get the most out of the FoI Acts in their current forms.**

Wadham, J., Harris, K., and Metcalfe, E. (2013) *Blackstone's Guide to the Freedom of Information Act 2000*, 5th edn, Oxford: Oxford University Press. **Revised fifth edition of popular, user-friendly FoI guide, which contains clear pointers to making worthwhile requests, what not to bother requesting under the Acts, and full explanation of various exemptions.**

Online Resource Centre

www.oxfordtextbooks.co.uk/orc/Morrison5e/

Visit the Online Resource Centre that accompanies this book for web links and regular updates.

Glossary

A

academy Labour's successor to Conservatives' **city technology colleges (CTCs)**, these semi-independent state schools (many funded by private capital) are allowed to specialize and deviate from the **National Curriculum**. Initially targeted at 'failing' comprehensives, academy status is now available to all state schools, including primaries. Up to 10 per cent of pupils may be selected on the basis of aptitude in an academy's specialism(s).

additional member system (AMS) Hybrid electoral system used for Scottish Parliament and Welsh Assembly elections. Each elector has two votes: one for his or her constituency and another for a regional party 'top-up list' designed to ensure fair representation for parties with few winning constituency candidates but relatively high numbers of votes.

adoption Process by which registered 'children in need' are taken into the permanent care of a family other than their biological one. Adopters become their legal parents, and recent reforms have extended adoption rights to gay and unmarried heterosexual couples, as well as married people. *Cf.* **fostering**

Advisory, Conciliation, and Arbitration Service (ACAS) **Quango** charged with mediating between employers and employees in industrial disputes. It is often asked to intervene by one of two parties to prevent industrial action, such as strikes, being taken in the first place.

agenda Outline of items to be considered in a meeting of a subcommittee, committee, full council, **cabinet** (executive), or other body.

alternative vote (AV) Electoral system used in Australia and proposed by the Coalition as a potential replacement for 'first past the post' (FPTP) elections for British members of Parliament (MPs). Like FPTP, AV returns only one member per **constituency**, but rather than casting a single vote, electors place candidates in order of preference. If no candidate wins half or more of the votes cast on first count, the lowest-placed contender is struck off the ballot paper and his or her second-preference votes are distributed among the other candidates. The process is repeated until someone achieves a simple majority. A form of AV is used in Labour leadership elections.

area of outstanding natural beauty (AONB) Geographical area designated for special legal protection from development and commercial exploitation because of its natural beauty and/or rare flora and fauna.

Assembly member (AM) Elected representative in the **National Assembly for Wales**. There are sixty AMs—forty representing **constituencies** and four for each of five larger regions.

B

backbencher Term referring to majority of MPs in the House of Commons, who represent **constituencies**, but have no additional job title or responsibilities in government or Opposition, and therefore sit on 'back benches' (seats behind the front row on either side of the House).

background paper Document or file produced by a local government officer for consideration as support for a policy proposal to be considered at a subcommittee, committee, cabinet, or full council meeting.

balance of payments Difference in value between imports to and exports from UK in given financial year, including *all* types of payment. This encompasses both 'visible' items (e.g. cars and refrigerators) and 'invisible' ones (such as legal and financial services), as well as financial transfers and debt payments to foreigners. If the value of imports exceeds that of exports, Britain is in 'balance of payments deficit'; if the reverse is true, it is in 'balance of payments surplus'. *Cf.* **balance of trade**

balance of trade Difference in value between imports to and exports from UK in given year, excluding financial transfers and debt repayments to foreigners. If Britain is importing goods and services worth more than those it is exporting, it is in 'trade deficit'; if the reverse is true, it is in 'trade surplus'.

Bank of England Britain's central bank, based in the City of London. It has its own governor and was given independence from government by the then Chancellor Gordon Brown in 1997.

basic allowance Standard fee (usually modest) paid to **councillors** out of local authorities' revenue budgets. It can vary from area to area.

Big Society Capital State-sponsored, but independent, bank set up by Coalition to invest in projects launched by charities, community groups, and voluntary organizations to address 'major social issues' in their areas.

billing authority Local authority that sends out **Council Tax** bills to households, collects money, and keeps a register of who has paid. This is the responsibility of **district councils** or **borough councils** and unitary authorities. *Cf.* **precepting authority**

borough council Type of local authority with same powers as a **district council**, but which has right to call itself a 'borough' because of its historical connection to the Crown.

Boundary Commissions **Quangos** responsible for periodically reviewing the sizes and boundaries of English, Welsh, Scottish, and Northern Irish parliamentary **constituencies** to ensure they cover approximately the same number of voters. In devolved nations, Commissions also review boundaries for assembly constituencies. The next boundary reviews are due by 2018.

brownfield site Area of land (usually in a built-up area) previously used for development, which may still have extant buildings on it. *Cf.* **greenfield site**

Budget Annual statement of accounts of 'UK plc', beginning with the Budget Statement made by the Chancellor of Exchequer, in which tax and spending plans for the coming year are set out. This is followed by a Finance Act enshrining these changes in law.

budget deficit Overspends by governments, local authorities, and other bodies within a given financial year: when expenditure exceeds income. See also **cyclical** and **structural deficits**.

building permission/regulations Additional consent required by private individuals or developers on top of **planning permission** in relation to work on extant buildings, normally addressing internal structural alterations. To attain *building permission*, developers must meet *building regulations* relating to health and safety, energy efficiency, etc.

by-election Poll called in a single parliamentary or devolved assembly constituency, or local authority ward, following the death, resignation, or deselection of a sitting member.

by-law Form of delegated legislation that may be invoked by a local authority to combat a specific problem. Many councils have invoked by-laws allowing them to ban alcohol consumption in streets to improve public order. *Cf.* **statutory instrument**

C

Cabinet Committee of senior government ministers, which meets at least weekly in Downing Street. *Cf.* **cabinet**

cabinet Form of executive arrangement introduced under the Local Government Act 2000, mimicking Westminster **Cabinet** system. Most local cabinet members are drawn from parties with the most seats on their councils, with each member handed a specific 'portfolio'/brief (e.g. housing).

Cabinet committees Subsets of **Cabinet**, usually comprising groups of three or more senior ministers with related departmental responsibilities. Three types exist: standing (permanent); ad hoc (temporary); and ministerial (permanent, but composed not of ministers but senior civil servants from related spending departments).

capital expenditure Share of local authority's annual budget spent on building and repairing infrastructure, such as roads, schools, care homes, and libraries. *Cf.* **revenue expenditure**

capping Process by which central government has sometimes stopped councils raising **Council Tax** above a certain level. It has also occasionally been used to cap specific types of spending.

care order Umbrella term for a type of court order used by local authorities to remove children from their parents and place them in protective care. This can be a temporary arrangement (**fostering**) or permanent (**adoption**).

Care Quality Commission (CQC) Regulator established in April 2009 to handle complaints about NHS treatment and conduct regular inspections of health and social care services in England and Wales, including residential homes, hospitals, and GP surgeries.

Chairman of the Conservative Party Title held by an official (often an MP) responsible for masterminding the public image of the party and coordinating its national fundraising and membership recruitment.

chief constable Most senior officer in the local police force, responsible for hiring and firing junior officers and ensuring resources are spread effectively across the force area. He or she is held accountable by his or her local **police and crime commissioner**.

chief executive Most senior **officer** working for a local authority. The chief executive often takes the role of 'acting **returning officer**' for his or her area at local, general, and European elections.

child protection plan Formerly the 'child protection register', this is a list of all recognized 'children in need' in each local authority area, which is shared between various public, private, and voluntary organizations involved in protecting them.

Children's Commissioner for England Government regulator appointed under the 'Every Child Matters' agenda to ensure all professionals and organizations involved in protecting children in need discharge their duties effectively.

children's partnerships Collaborative, multi-agency partnerships involved in overseeing child protection locally.

children's trust All-in-one local body comprising a multidisciplinary team of professionals involved in child protection, including social workers, paediatricians, and child psychologists. Since 31 October 2010, some areas have adopted looser arrangements adapted to their localities, known as **children's partnerships**.

city council Honorary title bestowed on certain **district councils, borough councils**, unitary authorities, and metropolitan borough councils granted Royal Charter status.

city technology college (CTC) Type of semi-independent state secondary school, introduced by John Major's Tory government to specialize in maths, sciences, and information technology (IT), often with hands-on private-sector involvement.
Cf. **academy**

clinical commissioning groups (CCGs) New consortia of general practitioners (GPs) and other health professionals that commission NHS services from trusts and other providers, in place of Labour's primary care trusts (PCTs).

coalition government Form of Westminster government comprising ministers drawn from two or more parties, formed when no single party wins a working majority at a **general election**. Britain's FPTP electoral system tends to return majority governments because it produces 'winner takes all' outcomes in each **constituency**, but the 2010 poll resulted in a Liberal Democrat–Conservative coalition: Britain's first since the wartime 'National Government' ended in 1945.

code of conduct Rule system governing the behaviour of **councillors** and **officers** that, since the LGA 2000, each council has adopted. It must set out details of unacceptable conduct and any penalties incurred.

collective responsibility Principle that all members of a parliamentary party's front bench (especially the government's) should either 'sing from the same hymn sheet' publicly, whatever their personal views on some party policies, or be prepared to resign. Late Labour **Leader of the House** Robin Cook resigned in 2003 in protest at the UK's impending invasion of Iraq. *Cf.* **individual ministerial responsibility**

combined authorities New metropolitan councils covering large conurbations and other areas encompassing a number of smaller neighbouring authorities. They will be run by elected mayors, with sweeping devolved powers over strategic planning, policing, and, potentially, their local NHS.

Commission for Local Administration or Local Government Ombudsmen Three independent officials, each covering a different region, who investigate complaints from public, businesses, and other organizations about alleged incompetence by local government officials.

Commission of the European Union, or European Commission European Union's Civil Service, spread over thirty-three departments known as 'Directorates-General' (DGs). Unlike the British Civil Service, it *initiates* policy as well as implementing it on behalf of elected politicians. Each DG is headed by a Commissioner.

committee stage Third stage of a Bill's passage through Parliament, this gives a committee of **backbenchers** the chance to scrutinize the Bill line by line and suggest amendments. The type of committee that examines Bills is a **public Bill committee** (formerly 'standing committee') and normally sits in a room outside main Commons chamber. Emergency legislation, however, and committee stages of international treaties due to be incorporated into British law are usually heard in Commons itself—a so-called 'Committee of the Whole House'. *Cf.* **report stage**

community care Umbrella term for social care provided to the elderly and adults with mental health issues in their homes or those of friends or relatives. Help available under community care includes 'meals on wheels'.

community protection notice (CPN) Order requiring a person to do, or stop doing, a specified act considered antisocial: e.g. writing graffiti or leaving excess refuse outside his or her home.

community school Term used for LEA-controlled secondary schools under 'New Labour'. Some community schools are known as 'community colleges' because they provide adult education and evening classes on top of their main role as day schools.

Competition and Markets Authority (CMA) New super-regulator formed in April 2014 from merger of the Competition Commission, which vetted prospective company mergers and acquisitions, and Office of Fair Trading (OFT), which policed the fair day-to-day operation of competitive markets.

comprehensive school Colloquial term referring to all types of LEA-run maintained secondary school other than **grammar schools**.

compulsory purchase order (CPO) Enforceable statutory order used by planning authorities to force homeowners or businesses to sell up property, so that it can be demolished to make way for new development.

concessionary fare schemes Types of discount bus fare scheme, often operated by individual councils and passenger transport authorities, allowing qualifying individuals—such as children, pensioners, or students—to travel at reduced rates. Labour launched a nationwide concessionary fare scheme in April 2008, allowing all pensioners to travel free on local buses anywhere in the UK.

conservation area District of city, town, or village characterized by buildings of particular historical and/or architectural vintage, and offered statutory protection from unsympathetic alteration (particularly to exterior appearance).

Conservative Campaign Headquarters (Conservative Central Office) National headquarters of the Conservative Party and the building it occupies at Victoria Street, Westminster.

constituency Geographical area represented by an MP. There are 650 (soon to be 600) constituencies in the present Commons and all members (including ministers) must stand for re-election when a **general election** is called.

Consumer Council for Water Consumer watchdog overseeing water industry.

consumer price index (CPI) Government's preferred measure of **inflation**, this charts movement in the value of a notional 'basket' of goods regularly bought by typical British households. Unlike the **retail price index (RPI)**, it does not include mortgage payments, so its readings tend to be lower than the RPI.

contributory benefits Umbrella term for more generous social security benefits to which British people are entitled (subject to meeting other criteria) if they have made sufficient **National Insurance (NI)** contributions during previous periods in work. For example, **Employment and Support Allowance (ESA)** is a contributory benefit related to illness and disability. *Cf.* **non-contributory benefits**

council constitution Each local authority has been obliged to adopt its own constitution since the LGA 2000, outlining its chosen form of executive decision-making arrangements and other procedural matters.

Council of Europe Alliance of forty-seven European member states formed in 1949, prior to the European Union. It aims to promote common legal and ethical standards in all member states, and its most celebrated achievement is the European Convention on Human Rights (ECHR).

Council of Ministers of the European Union, or Council of the European Union European Union's supreme decision-making body. Composed of senior ministers from each member state, its precise composition varies according to the issue debated. If health policy is on the **agenda**, each state sends its most senior health minister. The Council is chaired by a leading politician from the country holding the EU presidency, which rotates on six-monthly basis.

Council Tax Form of local taxation currently paid by UK residents. It is charged to households and is predominantly property-based (under a system of banding A–H, related to the capital values of homes), but with elements of a 'head tax'. It was introduced in 1993 to replace the unpopular Community Charge (or 'Poll Tax').

councillors Politicians elected at four-year intervals to represent local authority **wards** or electoral/county divisions. Councillors determine policies to be implemented by **officers**.

county council 'Upper-tier' local authority in parts of England and Wales that retain a two-tier, rather than unitary, structure. Counties are responsible for service areas including children's and adult social services, schools, and highways.

county road Major arterial road—normally an A-road linking one town or city to another—the whole length of which falls within boundaries of single county. *Cf.* **trunk road**

Court of Justice of the European Union (CJEU) Main EU legal body which ensures EU law is correctly implemented in member states. Each state contributes one judge—twenty-eight in all—although only fifteen ever sit in session together. Only major cases go to full Court, with others heard by a General Court. Warring parties have their cases presented to judges by one of eleven advocates-general.

crime prevention injunction (CPI) 'Fast-track' antisocial behaviour order (ASBO) introduced by Coalition for lower-level antisocial behaviour. These can be imposed more quickly (within days or hours of an 'offence') and require lower standards of proof than the ASBO.

criminal behaviour order (CBO) One of two orders introduced by the Coalition to replace antisocial behaviour orders (ASBOs), these empower police and local authorities to impose 'bans' on antisocial conduct, if necessary forcing miscreants to attend programmes designed to improve their behaviour.

cross-benchers Peers who sit as independents (i.e. with no party affiliation) in the House of Lords.

cyclical deficit Occasional budget deficits incurred in years when there is economic turbulence (e.g. recessions).

D

debt charge Money councils must set aside each year in revenue budgets to repay interest on outstanding loans taken out for capital projects.

declaration of interest Admission made by a **councillor** on being elected or at beginning of business in full council, committee, subcommittee, or **cabinet**, that he or she has an outside vested interest in an issue to be debated. He or she must leave the meeting for the duration of that item.

dedicated schools grant (DSG) **Ring-fenced grant** payment made from central government to local authorities on condition it is spent only on school staffing and maintenance.

devolution Constitutional concept of delegating a degree of power from central parliament to regional and/or local assemblies. In the UK, Scotland, Wales, and Northern Ireland were all granted devolution in 1998. The Scottish gained most powers, including the right to vary income tax by up to 3 pence (later 10 pence) in the pound and near-complete control of its domestic policy following its 2014 **independence** referendum. Devolution is distinct from independence, which is the handover of full sovereignty.

direct taxes Umbrella term for taxes, such as income tax and corporation tax, taken directly from an individual or company, normally at a progressive rate determined by their income levels in given financial year. *Cf.* **indirect taxes**

directly elected mayor (DEM) Most senior and powerful local politician in towns and cities that have voted in a local **referendum** to adopt one of two forms of executive arrangement introduced by LGA 2000. They run their administrations with the aid of a **cabinet**. Ken Livingstone, inaugural Mayor of London, was Britain's first DEM.

dissolution Procedure by which Parliament is formally 'dissolved' following a government's resignation before a **general election**.

district council Lower-tier local authority in two-tier areas, responsible for services including housing, development control, environmental health, and **Council Tax** collection.

E

early intervention grant New specific local authority revenue grant introduced by Coalition ministers at the behest of the Liberal Democrats, to fund initiatives designed to improve life chances of disadvantaged children. Although not ring-fenced, it is meant to fund a variety of schemes, including the continuation of **Sure Start**.

election deposit Deposit of £500 by each candidate who stands in a **general election**. The payment is lost if he or she fails to poll votes from more than 5 per cent of the registered electorate in a **constituency**. It was introduced in 1929 as a deterrent to 'frivolous candidates', but has been criticized recently for being too affordable.

Electoral Commission **Quango** responsible for ensuring that the correct procedures are followed in parliamentary, local, and European elections, and for enforcing rules on party finance. Its responsibilities include keeping campaign spending by election candidates within agreed statutory limits, and it may refer cases to the Crown Prosecution Service (CPS) if it feels electoral law has been broken.

electoral division Term used for **constituencies** represented by county and some unitary authority **councillors**. Each has between one and three councillors, depending on the size of its population.

electoral register Official list of all electors registered to vote in local, general, and European elections in a local authority area. It is compiled by the electoral registration **officer** employed by a **district council/ borough council** or unitary authority.

emergency planning officer **Officer** employed by a **county council** or unitary authority to oversee strategic planning for civil emergencies, such as floods.

emergency protection order, or interim care order Type of **care order** allowing a local authority to take a child into care immediately because of a perceived threat to his or her well-being. Initially applies for eight days, but may be renewed for a further week.

Employment and Support Allowance (ESA) Introduced by Labour to replace Incapacity Benefit for individuals judged too sick or disabled to work. Since October 2013, ESA has been gradually absorbed into **Universal Credit**.

enlargement Term referring to expansion of the European Union. It has been enlarged three times in the past decade, with several ex-Soviet countries joining for the first time: ten new states joined in 2004, a further two—Bulgaria and Romania—in 2007, and Croatia in 2013.

Environment Agency **Executive agency** of Department of Environment, Food, and Rural Affairs (Defra) responsible for regulating the quality and safety of water in rivers and streams, and strategic planning for flood protection.

environmental health officer **Officer** employed by a **district council, borough council**, or unitary authority to investigate complaints about environmental health hazards, such as vermin infestation, rotting waste, and noise pollution, and inspect the hygiene standards of businesses serving food.

Equality and Human Rights Commission (EHRC) **Quango** formed from amalgamation of the Commission for Racial Equality (CRE) and Equal Opportunities Commission (EOC) to ensure the equal treatment of employees in the workplace, regardless of their gender, race, or age.

euro (€) Single European currency, introduced in all EU member states bar the UK, Denmark, and Sweden on 1 January 2002. Since 2008, the 'eurozone' (the nineteen countries using the euro) has been in crisis over the sovereign debts of Greece and other member states.

European Central Bank (ECB) Based in Frankfurt, the central bank of the EU, which issues the **euro**.

European Commission *See* **Commission of the European Union**

European Council Newly recognized as one of five EU governing institutions following ratification of the Treaty of Lisbon, this is a periodic gathering of the heads of state or most senior politicians in member states, headed by a permanent president. Charged with charting the future strategic direction of the European Union, it is not to be confused with either the **Council of Ministers** or **Council of Europe**.

European Court of Human Rights (ECtHR) Based in Strasbourg, the ultimate court of appeal for citizens of states that have signed up to the European Convention on Human Rights (ECHR) and passed it into their own domestic law. Britain belatedly ratified the Convention by passing the Human Rights Act 1998. The Court was established by the Council of Europe and has no link to the European Union.

European Economic Area (EEA) A loose extension of the European Union's single-market zone, membership of which is negotiated on a state-by-state basis. The EEA presently encompasses three non-EU states – Liechtenstein, Iceland, and Norway – and is a possible home for the UK after Brexit.

European Parliament (EP) Based primarily in Brussels, but moving to Strasbourg for one week every month, the European Parliament is elected every five years. **Members of the European Parliament (MEPs)** sit in political groupings, rather than along national lines—for example the British Labour Party sits with the Socialist Group.

excepted hereditary peerage Peerages that pass from one generation to next. Until 1999, every hereditary peer was entitled by birthright to sit in the House of Lords, but all except ninety-two (ninety of whom have since been elected to remain by colleagues) had this privilege removed under the House of Lords Act 1999.

executive agency Subset of large government spending department, staffed by civil servants, charged with delivering particular area or areas of its policy. Examples include the **Health and Safety Executive** within the Department of Health (DoH) and **Highways England** within the Department for Transport (DfT).

F

faith schools Umbrella term for schools run by particular religious communities, including non-Christian groups. There are at least 7,000 faith schools in England, Wales, and Northern Ireland, many of which receive state funding.

federalism Flip side of **subsidiarity**, an idea promoted by Eurosceptics that further extension of EU powers will lead to individual member states surrendering autonomy for their internal affairs to centralized institutions, turning the Union into a 'United States of Europe'. The 2014 Scottish **independence referendum** sparked debate about whether Britain should be transformed into a federal democracy, with citizens governed by a hierarchy of national and regional parliaments.

Financial Conduct Authority (FCA) Part of the new, tougher, tripartite regulatory system set up by the Coalition to avert future banking collapses. Established under the Financial Services Act 2012, this polices the overall conduct of every financial company authorized to provide services to the public.

Financial Policy Committee (FPC) Modelled on the existing **Monetary Policy Committee (MPC)**, in March 2012 this new committee of the **Bank of England** took over responsibility from the Financial Services Authority (FSA) for identifying risks to the stability of Britain's economy and taking pre-emptive action to combat them.

first reading Formal introduction of a proposed Bill to Commons. The reading usually consists solely of full title of Bill being read out by a minister. *Cf.* **second reading**; **third reading**

Fiscal Compact Commonly used name for the Treaty on Stability, Coordination, and Governance in the Economic and Monetary Union—agreed by all EU countries apart from Britain and the Czech Republic in December 2011. It requires signatory states to maintain balanced budgets or budget surpluses, or face fines from the **European Central Bank (ECB)**.

forward plan List of upcoming **key decisions** due to be taken by a local authority. It must be made public at least a month in advance.

fostering Practice of placing vulnerable children into care with another family, often for a short period of time, while a more permanent situation is sought. *Cf.* **adoption**

foundation school Like the Conservative Party's grant-maintained (GM) schools, this is a self-governing state secondary school, permitted to spend its budgets as it pleases, within certain conditions set by central government. Money is allocated to it via its local education authority (LEA), but it may hire and fire its own staff, and set its own admissions and disciplinary policies distinct from those of local LEA-run schools.

foundation trust Form of NHS hospital, ambulance service, or mental health trust permitted full autonomy over its own financial and contractual affairs, regulated by **NHS Improvement**. The majority of trusts now have 'foundation status'.

free schools Key plank of Conservative education policy and its 'Big Society' vision of government, and based on a model devised in Sweden, these are a new generation of publicly funded secondary schools that parents, teachers, and other members of their community are setting up and running for themselves.

FT100 Share Index (Footsie) The Financial Times Stock Exchange 100 Share Index (to use its full title) is the most famous of a number of 'indices', or lists, of major companies listed on the London Stock Exchange (LSE). It lists the 100 highest-valued companies at any time in order of share value.

further education (FE) Umbrella term for post-compulsory education and training provided by tertiary colleges and school sixth forms. It can encompass resits of A levels and other qualifications aimed at those of school age, but primarily focuses on vocational courses and diplomas.

G

general block grant Generic term for revenue grants paid by central government to local authorities that may be used for any service area, according to local needs and priorities, which enjoyed resurgence under Coalition. Often used as a synonym for the **revenue support grant (RSG)**.

general committee Umbrella term for the three types of temporary parliamentary committee formed to scrutinize prospective legislation: a **public Bill committee**, a **private Bill committee**, and a **grand committee**.

general election Name denoting elections for the House of Commons. Since May 2015, general elections are held at fixed five-year intervals following reform introduced by the Coalition. The electoral system used to elect UK MPs is first past the post (FPTP).

globalization Term describing the gradual convergence of national economies into a bigger international whole. Used increasingly in relation to the ideas of free trade, free movement of labour between countries, and the expansion resulting from the Internet.

grammar school Type of maintained secondary school, phased out in much of the UK, which admits only pupils who have passed an academic test known as the '11-plus'. Those who fail are admitted to standard **comprehensive schools**.

grand committee One of three types of **general committee** in Parliament, this is convened to debate the impact of prospective legislation on specific UK regions or to scrutinize Bills in the Lords on occasions on which they are not debated in the House—or to consider Bills designated by the Speaker as concerning England (or England and Wales) only.

Greater London Authority (GLA) London's overarching 'council', established in 2000 at the same time as the capital gained its first **directly elected mayor (DEM)**. Individual London boroughs retain their own councils to run local services at ground level, but the GLA is responsible for taking strategic decisions for London as a whole.

Green Investment Bank New Edinburgh-based financial institution, set up in autumn 2012, and backed by a £3 billion capitalization fund. It addresses private-sector market failings by financing environmentally sustainable infrastructure projects.

Green Paper Consultation document on tentative government policy proposal that may, in time, evolve into a **White Paper**, and from there into a Bill. All government Bills (other than emergency legislation) go through at least one Green Paper stage, although if public and/or interest groups oppose strongly, are unlikely to go further.

greenbelt Designated zones around towns and cities that have deliberately been kept free of development to prevent urban sprawl and to protect wildlife.

greenfield site Area of land on which there has been little or no prior development. *Cf.* **brownfield site**

gross domestic product (GDP) Total profit from all goods and services generated in Britain in a financial year, irrespective of which state benefits from them. *Cf.* **gross national product (GNP)**

gross national product (GNP) Total profit from all goods and services generated by British-based companies in a financial year, irrespective of where they are physically produced—for example Far Eastern call centres owned by UK companies like BT or Virgin would still contribute to Britain's GNP. *Cf.* **gross domestic product (GDP)**

growth Increase in the gross domestic product (GDP) measure from one month, quarter, or year to another, usually characterized by rises in bank lending/consumer spending and falling unemployment.

G8 (Group of 8) Loose organization or forum devoted to promoting economic free trade and **globalization**, made up of the world's eight leading industrial nations—currently the United States, Britain, Japan, France, Germany, Italy, Canada, and Russia.

G20 (Group of 20) Loose organization or forum comprising world's twenty leading industrial powers.

H

Hansard Official record of all parliamentary business in Parliament. Protected by legal privilege and now available to read online, it is nonetheless not an entirely verbatim record of proceedings (except for words used by the **prime minister**).

head of the paid service *See* **chief executive**

Health and Safety Executive (HSE) **Executive agency** of the Department of Health (DoH), charged with setting and enforcing health and safety legislation in the workplace across the UK. It recently merged with the Health and Safety Commission (HSC), which previously drew up health and safety rules.

health and wellbeing boards Local bodies formed by all 152 English local authorities with social care and public health responsibilities to promote integrated approaches to improving health, bringing together all commissioners of health and social care in each area, along with local representatives of **Healthwatch**, including local **councillors**.

health service scrutiny committee Statutory body set up by a **county council** or unitary authority, comprising fifteen members, including a chairperson, local **councillors**, and representatives from relevant voluntary sector organizations.

Healthwatch National 'consumer-led' regulator of health services in England, with local branches based on the local involvement networks (LINks) setup inherited from Labour.

High Representative for Foreign Affairs and Security Policy Influential new permanent **European Commission** post created under the 2007 Treaty of Lisbon. The first postholder, backed by a diplomatic corps known as the 'European External Action Service' (EEAS), was Britain's former EU Trade Commissioner Baroness Ashton of Upholland.

higher education (HE) Level of education provided by universities for those who have acquired the right qualifications at post-compulsory/tertiary level (such as A levels). Begins with undergraduate 'Bachelor' degrees (of Arts (BA) or of Science (BSc) etc.) and progresses to postgraduate degrees (Masters (MA) and doctorates (PhD)) and beyond.

Higher Education Funding Council for England (HEFCE) **Quango** that channels public money for teaching and research into universities.

Highways England **Executive agency** of the Department for Transport (DfT) responsible for building and maintaining Britain's major roads. Formerly *Highways Agency*.

Historic England National **quango** (formerly English Heritage) responsible for managing heritage monuments and properties, such as Stonehenge, on the government's behalf. It also administers the **listed buildings** programme.

honours list Generic term used for two annual lists of individuals chosen to be honoured with ceremonial titles by the Queen in recognition of their worldly achievements. Lists are compiled by ministers and shadow ministers and honours awarded in the Queen's Birthday Honours List and New Year Honours List.

House of Lords Appointments Commission **Quango** that vets potential candidates for **life peerages** after they have been nominated by party leaders. It may have an enhanced role as and when the last hereditary peers are finally removed from the Lords.

housing association (HA) Not-for-profit organization formerly overseen by the Housing Corporation **quango**. Housing associations are principal providers of social housing in Britain today, often working with, or on behalf of, councils.

hung parliament Outcome of a **general election** that leaves no single party with an overall majority and the largest one facing the prospect of either ruling as a minority administration or forging a coalition with one or more others. The May 2010 election produced Britain's first hung parliament since 1974.

hybrid structure Type of local government structure in some English and Welsh counties, in which the **two-tier structure** remains in certain areas while others have adopted the newer **unitary structure**. East Sussex is an example of a hybrid county: Lewes is covered by both a **district council** and a **county council**, while neighbouring Brighton and Hove has a unitary **city council**.

I

Income Support Basic level of benefit paid to a range of people who satisfy certain needs-based criteria, but have paid insufficient prior **National Insurance (NI)** contributions to qualify for **contributory benefits**. It is available to certain people aged between 16 and 60 who are not in full-time work, such as carers or single parents. As with all other benefits paid to low earners and the unemployed, it is slowly being subsumed into **Universal Credit (UC)**.

independence Constitutional arrangement whereby a constituent part of a state, such as a region or country, is granted full powers of self-government as a sovereign entity. A national **referendum** was held in Scotland on extending the country's devolved powers to full independence on 18 September 2014. Residents voted to remain in the UK.

Independent Parliamentary Standards Authority (IPSA) New regulator created in 2009 to police MPs' and peers' allowance claims and to pay their salaries. This **quango**, which began work in earnest only after the 2010 election, replaced the in-house Fees Office following the long-running scandal over parliamentary expenses, which led to several resignations and successful prosecutions.

Independent Police Complaints Commission (IPCC) National **quango** responsible for investigating complaints against **chief constables** and/or their forces. The Commission automatically launches investigations whenever civilians are killed by police officers.

Independent Press Standards Organization (IPSO) Independent, self-regulatory body responsible for handling complaints from public about newspapers and magazines. It replaced the Press Complaints Commission (PCC) following the Leveson Inquiry into Press Standards, sparked by the *News of the World* phone-hacking scandal.

independent remuneration panel Body comprising at least three non-**councillors**, set up in each local authority area under the Local Government Act 2000 to adjudicate independently on any application by a council to increase its member allowances.

indirect taxes Often referred to as 'hidden' or 'stealth' taxes, these are embedded in costs of items bought by individuals or companies. VAT and excise duties on tobacco and alcohol are indirect taxes. Because they are charged at flat rates on relevant items, they are regressive: that is, they do not take account of individuals' or companies' ability to pay. *Cf.* **direct taxes**

individual ministerial responsibility Principle that the **secretary of state** should 'fall on his or her sword' and resign if a major failing is exposed in his or her department. In practice, ministers often have to be pushed by the **prime minister** (as happened with the then Chancellor Norman Lamont after 'Black Wednesday' in 1992). *Cf.* **collective responsibility**

inflation Rises in the prices of goods and services from one month to next. This is calculated using either the **consumer price index (CPI)** or **retail price index (RPI)**, which monitor fluctuations in values of notional 'baskets' of goods containing items regularly bought by typical British households.

Information Commissioner Statutory official appointed to police implementation of the Freedom of Information (FoI) Act 2000 and adjudicate on complaints from individuals and organizations of public authorities' lack of transparency in response to legitimate FoI requests.

interest rates Instrument of monetary policy used to promote saving and investment, and reduce consumer spending. Since 1980s, raising interest rates has been the preferred method of controlling **inflation**. The **Bank of England**'s **Monetary Policy Committee (MPC)** meets monthly to decide whether to raise or lower interest rates.

interim care order *See* **emergency protection order**

internal market Term describing internal commissioning structure of the National Health Service in England since the 1990s: today **clinical commissioning groups** commission from **NHS trusts** and other service providers, including private companies and charities.

J

Jobcentre Plus Government body responsible for administering benefits of all kinds, from **Jobseeker's Allowance (JSA)** and **Income Support** to sickness- and disability-related benefits.

Jobseeker's Allowance (JSA) Benefit paid to people over 16 who are registered unemployed and 'actively seeking work'. There are two types of allowance: contributions-based—related to prior **National Insurance (NI)** payments—and income-based. It is in the process of being replaced by **Universal Credit**.

K

key decision Policy decision affecting two or more **wards** or **electoral divisions** in a local authority area and likely to involve 'significant expenditure' if approved. These are judged so significant that they must be presented for the final say to a full council and cannot be taken solely in **cabinet** unless delegated to the individual portfolio-holder.

L

leader of the council Most senior and powerful local politician in authorities that have either adopted the second new executive arrangement under the LGA 2000 or retained their existing one. Like the **prime minister**, they are normally the leader of the party with the most seats on the council.

Leader of the House Minister responsible for organizing the weekly Commons timetable and proposing changes to its working hours and order of business.

life peerage Honorary peerages conferred on individuals for life in one of two annual **honours lists**. As their name suggests, these titles die with the recipients and cannot be passed on to their children. *Cf.* **excepted hereditary peerage**

listed building Individual building or small group of buildings (such as a Georgian crescent) offered statutory protection against alteration or demolition because of a link to specific historical personalities, events, or architectural movements. There are three levels of listing: grades I, II*, and II.

local development documents (LDDs) Main types of forward plan produced by planning authorities in England and Wales, stipulating where development is permitted in their areas for periods of up to twenty years.

local enterprise partnerships (LEPs) Alliances of local councils, businesses, and voluntary organizations introduced by the Coalition to boost commercial investment in local areas, these were local-level replacements for Labour's regional development agencies (RDAs).

local government associations (LGAs) Regional coalitions of local authorities that lobby Parliament and central government. There is also a national Local Government Association (LGA).

Local Government Boundary Commission for England (LGBCE) National **quango** tasked with periodically reviewing the boundaries between **wards** and **electoral divisions** to ensure that each is represented by the correct number of **councillors** relative to its population size.

Local Government Ombudsman *See* **Commission for Local Administration**

Local Housing Allowance (LHA) Formula used to determine how much Housing Benefit the unemployed and low earners may claim to help with rental costs. Ultimately paid by **Jobcentre Plus**, it is administered by **district councils** or **borough councils** and unitary authority housing offices. Since April 2008, Housing Benefit payments have been calculated relative to average rental prices in each postcode area (the LHA formula), rather than based on assessments of the value of specific homes rented by claimants.

local safeguarding children's board (LSCB) Committee set up by every **county council** and unitary authority under the Children Act 2004 to coordinate all organizations involved in looking after children in need.

local services support grant (LSSG) Replacing Labour's area-based grant, local authorities have received this non-formula, unfenced payment to spend as they wish (within certain parameters) since 31 March 2011.

Lord Speaker Recently introduced post designed to mimic that of the Commons **Speaker**. This title is given to a peer elected by his or her colleagues in the Lords to chair debates in chamber.

Lords Spiritual Collective term for the twenty-six most senior Church of England bishops, led by the Archbishop of Canterbury, who remain entitled to sit in the Lords.

M

marine plans Form of offshore forward plan, introduced by the Coalition, which outlines where permitted development may take place in each of eleven marine plan areas around English coast.

mayor Ceremonial title traditionally rotated annually between **councillors** on local authorities. The recipient spends twelve months chairing full council meetings on a non-partisan basis and attending civic events.

means-tested benefits Umbrella term for social security benefits targeted at individuals and families on the basis of financial need.

member of the European Parliament (MEP) Elected representative who sits in the **European Parliament**, of which there are 754, elected every five years. Each state contributes a number of members reflecting its population size.

member of the Legislative Assembly (MLA) Elected representatives to the **Northern Ireland Assembly**. There are currently 108, chosen in four-yearly elections using the **single transferable vote (STV)** system of **proportional representation (PR)**.

member of Parliament (MP) Elected representative to the House of Commons. As of the May 2010 election, there were 650 MPs, each representing on average 65,000 constituents.

member of the Scottish Parliament (MSP) Elected representatives in the **Scottish Parliament**. There are 129 MSPs at any one time, elected every four years using the additional member system (AMS) form of **proportional representation (PR)**.

minister of state Umbrella term for all ministers in government departments, including junior ministers.

Ministerial Code Document outlining ten key 'principles' of conduct for ministers, including avoiding real or apparent conflicts of interest, and stipulating that the **prime minister** should refer any alleged breach by a minister to the Independent Adviser on Ministerial Interests.

minutes Written record of the proceedings of a meeting of a subcommittee, committee, full council, **cabinet/** executive, or other body.

Monetary Policy Committee (MPC) Committee of the **Bank of England** that meets once a month to decide whether to raise or lower **interest rates**, on the basis of the previous month's **inflation** figures.

monitoring officer Senior local authority **officer** responsible for monitoring **councillors**' and officers' compliance with their council's **code of conduct**, and recording and reporting to members any cases of suspected maladministration.

N

1922 Committee Often referred to as 'the influential 1922 Committee', this is made up of all backbench Conservative MPs at any one time. The 'mood' of the Committee is a crucial test of the likely lifespan of its leadership and it was widely credited with delivering the knockout blow to Margaret Thatcher's premiership after she was challenged by Michael Heseltine in 1990.

National Assembly for Wales Full title of Wales' devolved assembly, based in a purpose-built chamber in Cardiff Bay.

National Curriculum Compulsory content that must be taught in maintained (state) schools in Britain in certain core subjects, such as English language and maths.

National Executive Committee of the Labour Party (NEC) Often referred to as 'Labour's ruling NEC', a senior policy committee composed of representatives of all main branches of Labour Party, including MPs, **constituency** party members, and trade unionists. Major changes to the party's constitution must be approved by this committee.

National Institute for Health and Care Excellence (NICE) **Quango** that vets medication before it is made available on the NHS, carries out its own research into potential cures and treatments, and publishes good practice guidance for social care providers. It is headed by a chief medical officer.

National Insurance (NI) System of contributory payments deducted from employees' wages and topped up by employers to finance future benefit and pension entitlement. The system was originally set up in 1911 to protect workers from poverty should they become unable to work because of sickness or injury.

national minimum wage (NMW) Minimum hourly rate to be paid to all employees in the UK, introduced by Labour in 1998. There are lower NMW rates for 16–18 year-olds and 18–20 year-olds. The escalating new higher rate of NMW introduced in 2016 is known as the *national living wage*.

national non-domestic rates (NNDR) *See* **uniform business rates (UBR)**

National Offender Management Service (NOMS) **Executive agency** of the Ministry of Justice (MoJ) responsible for recruiting and employing the UK's 48,000 prison staff and overall policy on day-to-day running of its 135 jails. The Prison Service is now part of NOMS and is responsible only for publicly funded jails.

national parks Fourteen geographical areas of Britain designated for the highest degree of protection from development or commercial exploitation possible under UK law.

national service framework (NSF) NHS designation for nine clinical conditions considered to be national priorities in terms of prevention and treatment. These include coronary heart disease and cancer.

Natural England **Quango** responsible for conserving, protecting, and managing the natural environment in England for current and future generations.

neighbourhood plan New form of local development plan devised by a community itself. The local authority must adopt this plan in place of its own proposals if approved in local **referendum**—provided 51 per cent or more of residents who turn out to vote approve of it.

Network Rail Not-for-dividend company set up by government in 2001 to take over the repairs and maintenance of UK overland rail network (tracks, signals, and stations) from

Railtrack—the private monopoly initially given those responsibilities following privatization of British Rail in early 1990s.

NHS England National **quango** that commissions primary care and specialist health services at regional and nationwide levels.

NHS Improvement Independent regulator of NHS **foundation trusts**, formerly known as *Monitor*.

NHS trust Umbrella term for hospitals, ambulance services, and mental health services provided by NHS. The term 'trust' was coined in early 1990s and relates to new levels of autonomy given to these bodies to run their own affairs. Each has its own board, like a company, and is designated a service 'provider'—rather than 'commissioner', like primary care trusts (PCTs).

non-contributory benefits Umbrella term for lower-level social security benefits to which British people are entitled (subject to meeting other criteria) irrespective of their previous **National Insurance (NI)** contributions. **Income Support** is an example of a purely 'needs-based', non-contributory benefit paid to people in lieu of higher-level entitlement. *Cf.* **contributory benefits**

North Atlantic Treaty Organization (NATO) Military alliance made up of twenty-six predominantly Western powers, NATO was formed with signing of North Atlantic Treaty in Washington DC in 1949. It was initially designed to act as a bulwark against the expansion of the Soviet Union and Warsaw Pact during the Cold War.

Northern Ireland Assembly Based at Stormont, this is the devolved chamber for Northern Ireland. Since March 2007, when power was restored by the British government to devolved institutions, it has been elected every four years.

O

Office for Budget Responsibility (OBR) **Quango** set up by the Coalition to produce independent economic forecasts and comment on likely impact on jobs and **inflation** of government budgetary decisions. For its first three months, it was overseen by Sir Alan Budd, former economic adviser to Margaret Thatcher and founder member of the **Bank of England**'s **Monetary Policy Committee (MPC)**.

Office of Communications (Ofcom) **Quango** dubbed a 'super-regulator' because of its all-embracing responsibilities for overseeing telecommunications, broadcast media industries (radio, television, and the Internet), and now postal services. Ofcom may fine broadcasters, including the BBC, for breaking rules governing taste and decency, and it monitors their public service content (such as current affairs and news output).

Office for Fair Access (OFFA) Regulator charged with ensuring that **higher education (HE)** institutions that charge tuition fees above the 'standard level' produce 'access agreements' detailing practical steps for attracting students from disadvantaged backgrounds.

Office of Gas and Electricity Markets (Ofgem) Regulatory **quango** that oversees Britain's privatized energy market to ensure there is free and fair competition between suppliers, and that bills are kept within acceptable bounds. It is headed by a Director General of Gas and Electricity Markets.

Office of the Qualifications and Examinations Regulator (Ofqual) Independent national regulator established in 2008 to monitor standard of qualifications, exams, and tests in England. It is headed by a ruling committee.

Office of Rail and Road Recently established joint regulator for Britain's rail and road networks. It awards rail franchises to train operating companies and monitors the performance of Network Rail.

Office of the Schools Adjudicator (OSA) **Quango** charged with ruling on disputes about local authority plans to change school admissions arrangements and to resolve disputes over school reorganization by councils.

Office for Standards in Education, Children's Services, and Skills (Ofsted) Central government inspectorate, headed by a Chief Inspector of Schools, which visits most maintained schools, preschools, education providers, and **further education (FE)** colleges on a rolling basis to monitor standards of teaching and administration, and awards grades from 'unsatisfactory' to 'outstanding'. Schools rated outstanding are now visited only if inspections are triggered by requests to Ofsted from parents or teachers.

Office of Water Regulation (Ofwat) *See* **Water Services Regulatory Authority**

officers Civil servants employed by local authorities to implement policies agreed by elected **councillors**.

Order in Council One of three types of **secondary legislation**, this is a legal instrument enacted by the monarch on the advice of the **Privy Council**.

overnight residency requirements Coalition's replacement for night-time curfews of up to sixteen hours that Labour used to restrict the movements of terrorist suspects in a community. The new system will limit the duration of overnight curfews to ten hours.

overview and scrutiny committee Overarching 'super-committee' adopted by some local authorities under the Local Government Act 2000, which scrutinizes the workings of council departments and **cabinet** and senior **officers**' decisions. There are normally several scrutiny subcommittees—or panels—focusing on specific policy areas.

P

parish meeting Lowest form of local authority, this de facto parish council convenes once a year in small villages to discuss the provision of local services and to make representations to statutory authorities on behalf of local people.

Parliamentary Commissioner for Administration or Parliamentary and Health Service Ombudsman (PHSO) Also responsible for overseeing administration in the NHS, the Commissioner hears complaints from the public and organizations about alleged maladministration by Parliament, rather than corruption.

Parliamentary Commissioner for Standards Post created on the recommendation of the Nolan Inquiry, which was prompted by a series of 'sleaze' scandals involving Conservative MPs in the early 1990s—including the 'cash for questions' affair, when Neil Hamilton was accused of taking payments from Harrods owner Mohamed Al Fayed to ask parliamentary questions on his behalf. The Commissioner polices the rigorous system of disclosure of outside interests introduced after these scandals.

Parliamentary and Health Service Ombudsman (PHSO) *See* **Parliamentary Commissioner for Administration**

Parliamentary Labour Party (PLP) Labour's equivalent of the Conservative Party's **1922 Committee** and a collective term for all Labour **backbenchers**.

parliamentary private secretary (PPS) Very junior government post often offered to an upcoming MP judged to have ministerial potential. The post is a 'link' between senior ministers and ordinary **backbenchers** in a party, and is frequently used to float potential policy ideas to 'test the water' among parliamentary colleagues.

parliamentary privilege Constitutional convention allowing MPs and peers to speak freely within their respective chambers, even criticizing named individuals without fear of being prosecuted for defamation. Even under parliamentary privilege, however, certain terms are banned in reference to fellow MPs or peers, including the word 'liar'.

parliamentary sovereignty Constitutional principle derived from the 1689 Bill of Rights that elevated Parliament to a position of supremacy over the sovereign in governing England and Wales (and, in due course, the whole UK).

parliamentary under-secretary Lowest rank of government minister, a junior minister below the level of **minister of state** and **secretary of state**.

parole Procedure by which prisoners are released early from sentences for 'good behaviour'. Those convicted of more minor offences are usually granted automatic early release after serving half of the total length of their sentences, but serious offenders, including rapists and serial murderers, usually serve twenty-plus years.

permanent secretary Most senior civil servant in government department, he or she offers day-to-day advice to the **secretary of state** and other ministers, and therefore occupies a **politically restricted post**.

Personal Independence Payment (PIP) New, non-means-tested benefit introduced to replace Disability Living Allowance (DLA) for disabled people needing care and/or help with mobility. Recipients are subject to new eligibility tests similar to **work capability assessments (WCAs)**.

planning inquiry Public inquiry held into contentious development proposal to which there is strong opposition. It will be chaired by an independent inspector appointed by the **Secretary of State** for Communities and Local Government, and those immediately affected by a proposal will be allowed to speak at it.

planning obligations, or planning contribution, or planning gain Offer by a developer of added value for a local authority in exchange for being granted **planning permission** for a major project—for example a developer may offer to finance a new playground for children in a deprived **ward** as a form of 'sweetener' to help its bid to build a new supermarket.

planning permission Consent given to an individual, company, or other organization to build new premises, or to extend or adapt existing ones. Can be 'outline' or 'detailed'.

police and crime commissioners (PCCs) Elected officials who replaced police authorities on 15 November 2012. As with their precursors, they are responsible for overseeing and holding to account their local police forces, with powers to hire and fire chief constables.

police community support officers (PCSOs) Semi-trained officers employed as auxiliary police, with powers to arrest and issue some minor punishments, such as fixed-penalty fines for antisocial behaviour.

policy and resources committee Traditionally, the most powerful local authority committee, because it controls a council's overall budget and must be consulted on major decisions (such as to build new roads) because it has to approve funding.

political sovereignty Constitutional concept of an institution or individual holding political supremacy (or 'sovereignty') over a nation's citizens. In Britain, political sovereignty originally rested with the reigning monarch ('sovereign'), but passed to Parliament after the 1689 Bill of Rights.

politically restricted post Contractual position held by senior public officials (civil servants and local government **officers**) barred from canvassing openly for a political party at elections, or from standing for office, because of their close day-to-day working relationships with politicians.

postal vote Means of casting votes in elections by post, rather than in person. The British government is committed to extending rights to vote by post across the UK, following several recent pilots, but this has provoked criticism from some quarters because of the perceived risk of fraud in multi-occupancy households.

postcode lottery Term denoting the unequal availability around the country of public services theoretically on offer throughout Britain—most commonly used to refer to NHS treatments.

precepting authority All councils that receive revenue funding through **Council Tax**. The term 'precept' refers to the 'invoice' that such authorities present to the **billing authority**, outlining the sum that they wish to raise through Council Tax in the coming financial year.

prerogative powers The mixture of ceremonial and actual powers (e.g. the authority to declare war and appoint ministers) deriving from the **royal prerogative** that are exercised by the monarch directly or on his or her behalf by ministers.

prescribed function Role and responsibility formally delegated by a council to its committees, subcommittees, **cabinet**/executive, and individual cabinet members. These will normally be spelt out in the council's constitution.

President of the European Council Recently created permanent post at the helm of the **European Council**, a powerful body comprising most senior politicians from each EU member state. Introduced under the 2007 Treaty of Lisbon, its inaugural holder, former Belgian Prime Minister Herman van Rompuy, was re-elected for a further two-and-a-half-year term in March 2012.

primary legislation Bills and Acts of Parliament (and their equivalents in the devolved assemblies).

prime minister (PM) Commonly used title of the senior minister who chairs the **Cabinet**, officially the 'First Lord of the Treasury'. The 'PM', or 'premier', is constitutionally seen as 'first among equals', in that he or she is an elected **constituency** MP like any other, but with more power than all others.

private Bill Type of primary legislation introduced by government minister(s) for the purpose of conferring specific powers or duties on a particular organization or regional entity. The Act permitting Formula One racing in Birmingham stemmed from a private Bill.

private Bill committee Temporary Commons committee convened to scrutinize a prospective **private Bill**—one of the three types of **general committee**.

private finance initiative (PFI) Main way in which major capital projects are now funded, this is an arrangement between a public authority (such as a council or government department) and a private company, under which the latter foots most of the initial bill and the former pays it back (with interest) over a period of years. *Cf.* **public–private partnership (PPP)**

private member's Bill (PMB) Bill proposed by an individual **backbencher**, normally on an issue close to his or her heart, and/or one that concerns his or her constituents. While they may cast the media spotlight onto an issue, most PMBs are never allotted sufficient parliamentary time to pass into law—but there have been exceptions, including the 1967 Abortion Bill, introduced by future Liberal leader David Steel.

Privy Council Ancient committee of state, originally formed as a group of close confidantes for the reigning monarch to counteract the power of the Great Council, or *Magnum Concilium*, composed of the peers of the realm. Today, all serving and past **Cabinet** ministers and leaders of the Opposition are appointed members for life and advise the monarch on matters such as use of the Privy Purse (the monarch's personal pot of money, derived from the Duchy of Lancaster estate) and the issuing of **Orders in Council**.

proportional representation (PR) Umbrella term for electoral systems alternative to the 'first past the post' (FPTP) process used in British **general elections**. Most Western countries use PR, including Ireland, which uses the **single transferable vote (STV)**. Liberal Democrats have been campaigning for STV to be adopted in Britain, arguing that it is fairer than the UK system, because the number of seats won by the party tends to bear stronger relationship to votes cast for them than does FPTP.

prorogation Term denoting the procedure by which Parliament is temporarily suspended (or 'prorogued') at the end of a parliamentary session.

Prudential Regulatory Authority (PRA) Created as subsidiary of the **Bank of England** in 2013 to prevent banks, building societies, or other financial companies taking imprudent risks with their investors' money, the PRA is part of the new tripartite regulatory regime for the finance sector.

public Bill Primary legislation introduced by government minister(s) to change the law of the land. Public Bills usually begin with a **Green Paper**, then a **White Paper**, before going through a series of readings, the **committee stage**, the House of Lords stage, and finally **royal assent**.

public Bill committee Temporary parliamentary committee convened to scrutinize and debate a Bill or another prospective Act of Parliament. Formerly known as a 'standing committee' because, being only temporary, its members were notionally not in a post for long enough to warrant permanent seats at the committee table, this is one of three types of **general committee**.

Public Health England National **quango** charged with promoting public health initiatives across England, backed by a £4 billion fighting fund to finance locally run projects.

public health grant (PHG) New ring-fenced revenue grant introduced by the Coalition from April 2013 to help councils to take over the funding of initiatives aimed at improving the well-being of their communities—for example by encouraging people to quit smoking.

public limited company (plc) Type of larger registered company in the UK which issues shares that the general public can buy by 'floating' itself on the London Stock Exchange (LSE). It has legal obligation to maximize profits for its shareholders and to pay them dividends. Most household-name companies in Britain are plcs (for example BP).

public–private partnership (PPP) Financial arrangement used to fund major capital projects, such as roads and prisons, whereby a government department or other public authority will share the cost of initial outlay with a private company or companies. The bulk of the upfront investment is usually made by the private sector and the public sector will pay it off (with interest) over a period of years. The PPP is 'New Labour's' successor to the Conservatives' **private finance initiative (PFI)**.

public sector net cash requirement (PSNCR) Formerly the 'public sector borrowing requirement' (PSBR), this is the sum of money that the British government will need to borrow by means of commercial loans or from the public in a given financial year to meet its public spending commitments—that is, the difference between the total taxation that the Exchequer expects to raise in the year and actual outgoings.

Public Works Loan Board (PWLB) Body that can lend money to local authorities for major capital projects at a lower rate than those offered by the banking sector. The PWLB is part of the UK Debt Management Office, an HM Treasury **executive agency**.

pupil premium Additional funding, introduced by the Coalition, allocated annually to schools with high numbers of pupils from disadvantaged backgrounds and/or on free school meals. The aim is to use one-to-one tuition and other strategies to intercept potential education inequalities.

Q

qualified majority voting (QMV) System of voting in the **Council of Ministers of the European Union** that enables certain issues to be decided by majority vote in favour or against, rather than unanimously. Under QMV, each member state is allocated a certain number of votes in proportion to its population, meaning that some have substantially more say in matters than others and that decisions are taken on a 'qualified' majority basis. The UK, for example, has twenty-nine votes, while Malta has just three.

quango or quasi-autonomous non-government organization Non-departmental body set up by a government department and partly funded by taxpayers, to regulate, monitor, or otherwise oversee a particular area of policy delivery. UK quangos have their own executive boards, like companies, and include Arts Council England and the **Equality and Human Rights Commission (EHRC)**.

quantitative easing (QE) Practice by which central banks—in Britain, the **Bank of England**—purchase bonds or equities from retail banks to increase the prices of those assets and to reduce the **interest rates** payable on them. The aim is to 'free up' finance for businesses and individuals in the wider economy by encouraging banks to lend more and at lower rates.

Queen's Speech Annual address given by the Queen at the State Opening of Parliament. The speech is actually a list of legislation to be proposed by the government during the coming parliamentary session (year), and is written not by the monarch herself, but by the sitting **prime minister** and **Cabinet**.

Question Time Sessions of parliamentary business during which **backbenchers** and/or peers on all sides have the opportunity to question individual departmental ministers on the conduct of their ministerial business. Major spending departments each have a question time session at least once a fortnight, while the most famous is 'Prime Minister's Questions' (PMQs), held every Wednesday lunchtime.

R

rateable value Sum of money that a business premises would be able to earn on the rental market. Both **uniform business rates (UBR)** and rates—the property-based domestic tax that preceded the Community Charge—are (or were) based on rateable values.

recession Economic term used to describe rapid economic slowdown or negative **growth**. Technically, it refers to a period of two successive quarters during which the economy has 'shrunk'—that is, consumers have stopped spending, sales of goods and services have dwindled, and manufacturers have reduced production.

refer back Term used for when a local authority **cabinet**/executive and/or full council meeting asks a committee or subcommittee to rethink its recommendations. It is also used in the context of recommendations made by **general committees** of the House of Commons.

referendum Public vote on a single issue. In Britain referendums are rare, but a national referendum was held in 1975 on the question of whether the country should remain in the European Community, and the people of Scotland, Wales, and Northern Ireland were consulted in referendums about whether they wanted devolved government. The most recent referendum was held on 23 June 2016 to determine whether the UK should leave the European Union.

register of members' financial interests (formerly register of members' interests) Register of the outside 'interests' (directorships, share holdings, etc.) of MPs and peers, introduced to improve transparency in 1974. Local authorities have been required to keep similar registers for their **councillors** since the passage of the Local Government Act 2000.

relative needs formula (RNF) Calculation used by central government to decide how much to allocate each local authority in formula grants each financial year. It is based on an assessment of the precise demographic factors in each area, including not only size of local population but its *nature* (for example the number of pensioners).

relative resource amount (RRA) Calculation used by central government to estimate how much money each local authority is able to raise itself for revenue spending in given financial year. The RRA is subtracted from the **relative needs formula (RNF)** to calculate the level of formula grants.

report stage Stage immediately after the **committee stage**, when a **public Bill committee's** chairperson 'reports back' to Commons with its recommendations.

resolved items Matters concluded at the end of a committee, full council, or **cabinet**/executive meeting. A vote will normally be taken on the final decision.

retail price index (RPI) Measure of **inflation** (changes in prices of goods and services) preferred by most economists to the **consumer price index (CPI)**, this charts movement in the value of a notional 'basket' of goods regularly bought by typical British households. Because it includes mortgage payments, it is usually higher than the CPI.

returning officer Official responsible for overseeing local and **general election** procedures on the day of a poll, ordering recounts where necessary and announcing the result. Officially, this post is held by the chairperson or **mayor** of a neighbouring or coterminous local authority, but a senior council **officer** will usually perform the duties in practice—often the **chief executive** or electoral registration officer.

revenue expenditure Share of local authority's annual budget spent on day-to-day running costs of schools, libraries, offices, and other services. *Cf.* **capital expenditure**

revenue support grant (RSG) One of three types of formula grant allocated to local authorities by central government for their revenue spending, this was traditionally the biggest single chunk of money that they received. It is calculated on the basis of a formula relating to the demographic make-up of a local area and may be used by councils in any area of revenue spending. Also known as the **general block grant**, the proportion of funding channelled through the RSG increased under the Coalition.

ring-fenced grant One of two types of **specific grant** for local authority revenue spending that must be used for the purpose stipulated by central government. All but two ring-fenced grants—the **dedicated schools grant (DSG)** and the new **public health grant**—were scrapped by the Coalition. *Cf.* **unfenced grants**

royal assent 'Rubber stamp' given to a Bill by the reigning sovereign to make it an Act. In practice, royal assent is a formality today and no monarch has refused to give it since Queen Anne attempted to do so in 1707.

royal prerogative Constitutional term used to refer to the (now largely notional) idea that power in the UK derives from the authority of the reigning sovereign. In practice, today most **prerogative powers** rest with the elected **prime minister** of the day.

rule of law Constitutional principle, derived from 1215's Magna Carta, stipulating that no one is 'above the law of the land', including (in theory) the sovereign.

S

safeguarding adults board (SAB) Adult equivalent of **local safeguarding children's board (LSCB)** introduced under the Care Act 2014. English social services authorities must establish these to safeguard vulnerable adults at risk of, or experiencing, neglect or abuse.

Schengen Agreement Collective term for two EU treaties—signed in 1985 and 1990 respectively—formally abolishing passport controls between member states.

Scottish Government, or Scottish Executive Title used by the devolved administration in Scotland.

Scottish Parliament Scotland's devolved assembly, based in a purpose-built parliamentary building at Holyrood in Edinburgh.

second reading First stage at which the main principles of a Bill are formally read out in Parliament and debated. It normally takes place within a few weeks of the **first reading** and may lead to an early vote on some aspects of Bill. *Cf.* **third reading**

secondary legislation 'Lower-tier law', derived from a parent Act, which may be implemented by ministers without the need to pass further Bills. There are three main types: **statutory instruments, by-laws**, and **Orders in Council**. Also known as delegated or subordinate legislation.

secretary of state Umbrella term for the most senior government minister in a spending department—for example the Secretary of State for Health.

select committee Permanent parliamentary committee charged with scrutinizing the day-to-day workings of a government department and other public authorities related to the responsibilities of that department—for example the Culture, Media, and Sport Select Committee examines the work of the Department for Culture, Media, and Sport (DCMS), as well as that of the BBC.

selection The means by which **grammar schools** admit pupils, based on their performance in a test known as the '11-plus'. **Academies** and specialist schools are also permitted to select up to 10 per cent of their intake based on aptitude in their subject specialisms.

separation of powers Principle stipulating that the three main seats of constitutional authority in a state—executive, legislature, and judiciary—should be kept separate to avoid concentrating power in too few hands. In practice, in the UK there are overlaps, with the **prime minister** and **Cabinet** (executive) also sitting in Parliament (legislature).

single transferable vote (STV) Form of **proportional representation (PR)** used in **general elections** in the Republic of Ireland and long favoured by Lib Dems for Westminster polls. Candidates are ranked in order of preference and all those who achieve 'quotas' of votes up to a predetermined number are elected to multimember **constituencies**. If too few candidates achieve the quota, the lowest-ranked candidate is struck off the ballot papers and second choices are redistributed among remaining contenders until enough reach the required level.

site of special scientific interest (SSSI) Area judged to have special or unique natural features. There are two types: *biological SSSIs* (those with rare or unusual flora and/or fauna), and *geological SSSIs* (those of particular physiographic interest).

sovereign grant All-in-one method of financing the Royal Household from taxpayers' money, covering both day-to-day living costs previously funded through the Civil List, and the upkeep of occupied palaces and royal transport traditionally paid as grants-in-aid.

Speaker **Member of Parliament** elected by his or her peers, traditionally on a motion moved by the Father of the House (the member with the longest unbroken service to the chamber) following **general election**, to serve as chairperson of debates and to maintain discipline in the Commons.

special responsibility allowance Top-up fee added to the **basic allowance** for **councillors** in recognition of additional responsibilities, such as sitting on, or chairing, a local authority committee. The allowance can vary according to the level of responsibility.

special school State school dedicated to teaching children with learning difficulties and/or mental or physical disabilities.

specialist school Generic term for all state schools permitted to specialize in one or more subjects over and above teaching the **National Curriculum**. **Academies** are, by nature, specialist schools—but in practice many **community schools** also have subject specialisms.

specific grant One of two different categories of non-formula grant given to local authorities each year to help with revenue spending. Specific grants can either be **ring-fenced grants** or **unfenced grants**.

Spending Review Method used by HM Treasury to encourage individual spending departments to plan strategically for the future by announcing how much money it intends to allocate to them on a three-yearly basis, rather than annually through the **Budget**. Three spending reviews—in 1998, 2007, and 2010—have been dubbed 'comprehensive' because of their more detailed nature.

spin doctor Layperson's term for the type of special adviser usually employed by a senior figure in a political party to put positive 'spin' on its policies to public and media. Alastair Campbell, former Downing Street director of communications, became one of Britain's most infamous spin doctors during Tony Blair's ten years in power.

Standard Attainment Tests (Sats) Academic tests taken by state school pupils at three Key Stages in their **National Curriculum** learning. Key Stages 1, 2, and 3 take place at the ages of 7, 11, and 14, respectively.

standards committee Committee set up by each local authority under the Local Government Act 2000 to monitor **councillors**' and **officers**' compliance with the council's **register of members' financial interests** and **code of conduct**. Committees must have at least one lay member.

standing order System of rules adopted by individual local authorities to govern the day-to-day conduct of business in full council, and its committees, subcommittees, and/or **cabinet**.

statutory instrument Most common form of **secondary legislation**, this refers to the rules and guidelines issued by departmental ministers to implement the changes introduced in a new Bill on the ground.

structural deficit An ongoing form of budget deficit incurred by governments, local authorities, and other bodies when their spending outstrips their incomes over prolonged periods of time.

subsidiarity Loose constitutional principle underpinning the European Union, which holds that member states retain primary sovereignty over their internal affairs, with the Union acting as a 'subsidiary' institution and the last port of call if individual self-determination falters.

supplementary estimate Additional sum that a local authority department might ask for when it has underestimated the level of revenue funding it will need in the next financial year to fund its projected spending.

Supreme Court of the United Kingdom Britain's final court of appeal for civil cases, and the highest for criminal matters in England, Wales, and Northern Ireland, this was established in October 2009 in an effort to emulate the constitutional **separation of powers** in the United States. It replaced the Appellate Committee of the House of Lords—previously the UK's ultimate court—which had been the seat of the 'Law Lords' for centuries. There are twelve Justices of the Supreme Court, all currently former Law Lords.

Sure Start Government programme launched in 1999 to improve access for low-income families to early years teaching and other support services.

T

tactical voting Type of strategic voting by electors voting in 'first past the post' (FPTP) elections, which sees them vote for candidates other than their 'sincere preferences', knowing that their preferred options would be 'wasted votes'. Tactical voters instead opt for their 'least worst option'—choosing a 'bearable' third party to stop the candidate whom they most oppose from winning.

tax-increment financing (TIF) Form of capital finance for councils, allowing them to borrow money for infrastructural or other capital investment against likely future income generated through business rates from companies likely to be attracted by that investment.

Ten-minute rule One of three ways in which **private members' Bills (PMBs)** may be introduced, and the one that most often grabs headlines. The MP must have his or her idea for a Bill proposed and seconded by colleagues, and obtain another eight members' signatures, and will then be given ten minutes in which to introduce the proposals to the Commons. An MP who opposes the Bill will then have the same amount of time in which to make a speech outlining his or her objections.

terrorism prevention and investigation measure (TPim) Coalition's replacement for control orders used by Labour to restrict the movements of those suspected (but not yet convicted) of terrorism plots. Unlike control orders, they lapse after two years.

third reading Final stage of a Bill's passage through the Commons. It is at third reading that MPs are confronted with the final version of the Bill's wording, so it is an occasion for any major disagreements to be fought out in a formal vote. *Cf.* **first reading**; **second reading**

trading standards officer **Officer** employed by a **county council** or unitary authority to ensure that local businesses adhere to regulations regarding issues such as product labelling, and weights and measures.

Traffic Commissioner One of seven regional commissioners employed to license public transport routes and operators, and long-distance haulage companies.

Transport Focus Consumer watchdog (previously *Passenger Focus*) representing the interests of overland rail and bus commuters/passengers.

Transport for London (TfL) **Quango** responsible for the strategic planning and day-to-day running of London's transport network, including London Underground, Docklands Light Railway, city bus services, and river ferries.

trunk road Major arterial road—A-road or motorway—linking towns and cities, and sometimes crossing the boundaries between counties. *Cf.* **county road**

trust school Form of **foundation school** introduced under the Education and Inspections Act 2006, these primary and secondary schools are supported by charitable trusts, which employ staff, manage assets, and set admissions policies.

trust special administrator Senior Department of Health (DoH) officials appointed to intervene on the Health Secretary's behalf to close or downgrade hospital accident and emergency (A&E) departments, maternity units, and other hospital services if they are having a detrimental effect on neighbouring trusts' finances.

two-tier structure Type of local government structure established under the 1974 local reorganization, in which there are two levels of council operating in the same area: **district councils** and/or **borough councils** responsible for services such as waste collection, housing, and environmental health; and an overarching **county council** providing countywide services such as education and highways (roads).

U

unfenced grant One of two types of **specific grant** for local authority revenue spending, it may be spent however the council sees fit, subject to certain conditions. Unfenced grants have come back into fashion under recent Tory-led governments, after years of ring-fencing. *Cf.* **ring-fenced grant**

uniform business rates (UBR) Local taxation paid by companies, the bills of which are calculated according to the **rateable values** of business premises and a national multiplier set each year by government (such as 50 pence in the pound). Money is collected locally, and has traditionally then been funnelled through HM Treasury and redistributed around the country according to need. A growing proportion is now kept by local authorities to be spent in the areas in which it was collected.

UNISON Main local government trade union, it counts among its members many departmental officers, social workers, and health professionals.

unitary structure Type of local government structure that has replaced the **two-tier structure** in many areas. A single—unitary—local authority is responsible for all local services, from waste collection to education and social care.

United Nations (UN) Global peace-making body formed in 1945, as successor to the defunct League of Nations established after the First World War. Headquartered in New York, its main constitutional bodies include the UN General Assembly and UN Security Council (which debates international conflict).

universal benefits Umbrella term for social security benefits paid to anyone meeting age or other needs-based criteria, irrespective of how wealthy they are (e.g. child benefit traditionally).

Universal Credit (UC) New 'all-in-one' welfare payment for the low-paid and unemployed, due to supplant all other benefits between October 2013 and 2017, brought in as part of the Coalition's efforts to reduce the social security bill and complexity in the system.

university technical colleges (UTCs) Vocational colleges introduced by the Coalition to train 14–19 year-olds in the skills needed to 'rebalance' the British economy towards technology.

V

virement Process allowing councils limited discretion to transfer money from one spending area to another during a given financial year, if the former is in surplus and the latter in deficit. Councils' ability to use virement has been severely curtailed as a result of the rollout of **ring-fenced grants**.

voluntary school Type of school in the state sector whose land and buildings are owned by a charity or local church. Voluntary-aided schools receive some local authority funding, but retain significant autonomy (for example employing their own staff and setting their own admissions policies), while voluntary-controlled schools are run directly by local education authorities (LEAs).

W

ward **Constituency** represented by **district council** or **borough council**, and some unitary authority **councillors**. Each has between one and three councillors, depending on population size.

Water Services Regulatory Authority, or Office of Water Regulation (Ofwat) One of three statutory regulators of the privatized water industry, Ofwat monitors the transparency of individual water companies' accounts and share policies.

Welsh Assembly Government (formerly Welsh Executive) Title adopted by the elected devolved administration in Wales.

whips MPs and peers with the job of 'whipping into line' their parliamentary colleagues, making sure that the latter attend important debates and votes, and 'toe the party line'.

White Paper Crystallized version of a **Green Paper**, containing more concrete proposals. If a proposed government Bill has got this far, it will normally proceed further to become a formal draft Bill and may well subsequently become an Act.

work capability assessment (WCA) Periodic medical test, introduced by Labour and continued under the Coalition and Conservatives, to determine whether individuals claiming **Employment and Support Allowance (ESA)** are fit for work.

Bibliography

A

Adonis, A. (2012) *Education, Education, Education: Reforming England's Schools*, Kindle edn, London: Biteback Publishing.

Atkinson,H. (2012) *Local Democracy, Civic Engagement and Community: From New Labour to the Big Society*, Manchester: Manchester University Press.

Ayre, P. and Preston-Shoot, M. (2010) *Children's Services at a Crossroads: A Critical Evaluation of Contemporary Policy for Practice*, Lyme Regis: Russell House Publishing.

B

Bale, T. (2016) *The Conservative Party: From Thatcher to Cameron*, 2nd edn, Cambridge: Polity Press.

Bartholomew, J. (2014) *The Welfare State We're In*, London: Biteback Publishing.

Bayliss, J., Smith, S., and Owens, P. (2010) *The Globalization of World Politics: An Introduction to International Relations*, 5th edn, Oxford: Oxford University Press.

Betty, S. (2011) *The PFI; 'Teething Problems or Fundamentally Flawed?' A Critical Analysis of the UK's Private Finance Initiative*, Bury St Edmunds: Lambert Academic Publishing.

Bennett, O. (2016) *The Brexit Club: The Inside Story of the Leave Campaign's Shock Victory*, London: Biteback Publishing.

Birbalsingh, K., Gove, M., Hill, S., Hunter, M., Johnson, D., Martin, J., Lewis, O., Womersley, D., Woodhead, C., and Young, T. (2013) *The Gove Revolution: Transforming England's Schools*, London: Standpoint.

Birkinshaw, P. (2010) *Freedom of Information: The Law, the Practice, and the Ideal*, Cambridge: Cambridge University Press.

Black, G. (2011) *Transforming Museums in the Twenty-First Century*, London: Routledge.

Blackman, T., Brody, S., and Convery, J. (eds) (2001) *Social Care and Social Exclusion: A Comparative Study of Older People's Care in Europe*, Basingstoke: Palgrave Macmillan.

Blais, A. (ed.) (2008) *To Keep or to Change First Past the Post? The Politics of Electoral Reform*, New York: Oxford University Press.Bochell, H., Powell, M., and Bochell, H.M. (eds) *The Coalition Government and Social Policy: Restructuring the Welfare State*, Bristol: Policy Press.

Bogdanor, V. (2009) *The New British Constitution*, Oxford: Hart Publishing.

Bower, T. (2016) *Broken Vows: Tony Blair - The Tragedy of Power, London: Faber* & Faber.

Bowles, N., Hamilton, J., and Levy, D. A. L. (2013) *Transparency in Politics and the Media: Accountability and Open Government*, London: I .B. Tauris.

Brooke, H. (2006) *Your Right to Know: A Citizen's Guide to the Freedom of Information Act*, 2nd edn, London: Pluto Press.

Brown, C. and Ainley, K. (2005) *Understanding International Relations*, 4th edn, Basingstoke: Palgrave Macmillan.

Budge, I., Crewe, I., McKay, D., and Newton, K. (2007) *The New British Politics*, 4th edn, London: Longman.

Burnham, J. and Pyper, R. (2008) *Britain's Modernised Civil Service*, Basingstoke: Palgrave Macmillan.

Burgess, M. (2015) *Freedom of Information: A Practical Guide for UK Journalists*, Abingdon: Routledge.

C

Cahill, D. (2010) *Transport, Environment, and Society*, Buckingham: Open University Press.

Caless, B. and Owens, J. (2016) *Police and Crime Commissioners: The Transformation of Police Accountability*, Bristol: Policy Press.

Clegg, N. (2016) *Politics: Between the Extremes*, London: Bodley Head. Colling, T. and Terry, M. (2010) *Industrial Relations: Theory and Practice (Industrial Revolutions)*, Oxford: Wiley Blackwell.

Cooper, K. and Macfarland, C. (2012) *Clubbing Together: The Hidden Wealth of Communities*, London: ResPublica.

Cowley, P. and Ford, R. (2014) *Sex, Lies, and the Ballot Box: 50 Things You Need to Know about British Elections*, London: Biteback.

Crewe, I. (ed.) (1998) *Why Labour Won the General Election of 1997*, London: Frank Cass.

Cribb, J., Jesson, D., Sibieta, L., Skipp, A., and Vignoles, A. (2013) *Poor Grammar: Entry into Grammar Schools for Disadvantaged Pupils in England.* Available online at: www.suttontrust.com/researcharchive/poor-grammar-entry-grammar-schools-disadvantaged-pupils-england/

Crossman, R. (1979) *The Crossman Diaries: Selections from the Diaries of a Cabinet Minister, 1964–1970*, London: Book Club Associates.

Cullingworth, B., Nadin, V., Hart, T., Navoudi, S., Pendlebury, J., Vigar, G., Webb, D., and Townshend, T. (2014) *Town and Country Planning in the UK*, 15th edn, Abingdon: Routledge.

D

Denver, D., Carman, C., and Johns, R. (2012) *Elections and Voters in Britain*, 3rd edn, Basingstoke: Palgrave Macmillan.

Dillon, D. and Fanning, B. (2012) *Lessons for the Big Society: Planning, Regeneration, and the Politics of Community Participation*, Kindle edn, Farnham: Ashgate.

Docherty, I. and Shaw, J. (2008) *Traffic Jam: Ten Years of Sustainable Transport in the UK*, Bristol: Policy Press.

Driver, S. (2011) *Understanding British Party Politics*, Cambridge: Polity Press.

E

Exworthy, M., Mannion, R., and Powell, M. (2016) *Dismantling the NHS? Evaluating the Impact of Health Reforms*, Bristol: Policy Press.

F

Farrell, D. (2011) *Electoral Systems: A Comparative Introduction*, 2nd edn, Basingstoke: Palgrave Macmillan.

Fischel, W. A. (2005) *The Homevoter Hypothesis: How Home Values Influence Local Government Taxation, School Finance, and Land-Use Policies*, Cambridge, MA: Harvard University Press.

G

Gallent, N. and Robinson, S. (2013), *Neighbourhood Planning: Communities, Networks, and Governance*, Bristol: Policy Press.

Geddes, A. (2013) *Britain and the European Union*, Basingstoke: Palgrave Macmillan.

Golding, P. and Middleton. S. (1982) *Images of Welfare*, Oxford: Mark Robertson.

Gray, A. M. and Birrell, D. (2013) *Transforming Adult Social Care: Contemporary Policy and Practice*, Bristol: Policy Press.

Gumbrell-McCormick, R. and Hyman, R. (2013) *Trade Unions in Western Europe: Hard Times, Hard Choices*, Oxford: Oxford University Press.

H

Ham, C. (2009) *Health Policy in Britain: The Politics and Organisation of The National Health Service*, 6th edn, Basingstoke: Palgrave Macmillan.

Hanley, L. (2013) *Estates: An Intimate History*, London: Granta Books.

Hansen, R. S. (2001) *Citizenship and Immigration in Post-war Britain: The Institutional Origins of a Multicultural Nation*, Oxford: Oxford University Press.

Hennessey, P. (2001) *The Prime Minister: The Job and its Holders since 1945*, London: Penguin.

Hollis, G., Davies, H., Plokker, K., and Sutherland, M. (1994) *Local Government Finance: An International Comparative Study*, London: LGC Communications.

J

Jackson, R. and Sorensen, G. (2012) *An Introduction to International Relations: Theories and Approaches*, Oxford: Oxford University Press.

Johnston, R. and Pattie, C. (2006) *Putting Voters in Their Place: Geography and Elections in Great Britain*, Oxford: Oxford University Press.

Jones, B. (2010) *Dictionary of British Politics*, 2nd edn, Manchester: Manchester University Press.

Jones, B. and Norton, P. (2013) *Politics UK*, 8th edn, London: Longman.

Jones, N. (2002) *The Control Freaks: How New Labour Gets Its Own Way*, London: Politico's Publishing.

Jowell, J., Oliver, D., and Ocinneide, C. (2015) *The Changing Constitution*, 8th edn, Oxford: Oxford University Press.

K

Kenealey, D., Peterson, J., and Corbett, R. (eds) (2015) *The European Union: How Does it Work?*, 4th edn, Oxford: Oxford University Press.

Klein, R. (2013) *The New Politics of the NHS: From Creation to Reinvention*, 7th edn, Abingdon: Radcliffe Publishing.

L

Lane, K. (2006) *National Bus Company: The Road to Privatisation*, Shepperton: Ian Allen.

Leach, S. (2010) *Managing in a Political World: The Life Cycle of Local Authority Chief Executives*, Basingstoke: Palgrave Macmillan.

Leyland, P. (2016) *Constitution of the United Kingdom: A Contextual Analysis*, 3rd edn, Oxford: Hart Publishing.

Leys, C. and Player, S. (2011) *The Plot Against the NHS*, Perth: Merlin Press.

Loughlin, M. (2013) *The British Constitution: A Very Short Introduction*, Oxford: Oxford University Press.

Lund, B. (2011) *Understanding Housing Policy*, 2nd edn, Bristol: Policy Press.

M

Malpass, P. (2005) *Housing and the Welfare State: The Development of Housing Policy in Britain*, Basingstoke: Palgrave Macmillan.

Meisler, S. (2011) *United Nations: A History*, New York: Grove Press/Atlantic Monthly Press.

McCormick, J. (2014) *Understanding the European Union: A Concise Introduction*, 6th edn, Basingstoke: Palgrave Macmillan.

Michie, R. C. (2001) *The London Stock Exchange: A History*, Oxford: Oxford University Press.

Midwinter, A. F. and Monaghan, C. (1993) *From Rates to the Poll Tax: Local Government Finance in the Thatcher Era*, Edinburgh: Edinburgh University Press.

Monbiot, G. (2001) *Captive State: The Corporate Takeover of Britain*, London: Pan Books.

Morgan, S. (2009) *Waste, Recycling, and Reuse*, London: Evans Brothers.

Mullin, C. (2010) *View from the Foothills*, London: Profiles Books.

Murie, A. (2016) *The Right to Buy? Selling off Public and Social Housing*, Bristol: Policy Press.

N

Newman, I. (2014) *Reclaiming Local Democracy: A Progressive Future for Local Government*, Bristol: Policy Press.

Norman, J. (2010) *The Big Society: The Anatomy of the New Politics*, Buckingham: University of Buckingham Press.

Norton, P. (2013) *Parliament in British Politics*, 2nd edn, Basingstoke: Palgrave Macmillan.

O

Olechnowicz, A. (2007) *The Monarchy and the British Nation, 1780 to the Present*, Cambridge: Cambridge University Press.

P

Phillips, R. and Furlong, J. (2001) *Education, Reform and the State: Twenty-Five Years of Politics, Policy, and Practice*, London: Routledge Falmer.

Philpot, T. (2007) *Adoption: Changing Families, Changing Times*, London: Routledge.

Pratchett, L. (2000) *Renewing Local Democracy? The Modernisation Agenda in British Local Government*, London: Frank Cass.

Pugh, M. (2011) *Speak for Britain! A New History of the Labour Party*, London: Vintage.

R

Reiner, R. (2010) *The Politics of the Police*, 4th edn, Oxford: Oxford University Press.

Ricketts, S. (2012) *Localism and Planning*, Haywards Heath: Bloomsbury Professional.

Rogers, R. and Walters, R. (2015) *How Parliament Works*, 7th edn, London: Longman.

S

Sanders, A. (2010) *Criminal Justice*, 4th edn, London: LexisNexis UK.

Seymour, R. (2016) *Corbyn: The Strange Rebirth of Radical Politics*, London: Verso Books.

Smith, D. (2016) *Something Will Turn Up: Britain's Economy, Past, Present, and Future*, London: Profile Books.

Stevens, A. (2006) *Politico's Guide to Local Government*, 2nd edn, London: Politico's Publishing.

Stewart, J. (2003) *Modernising British Local Government: An Assessment of Labour's Reform Programme*, Basingstoke: Palgrave Macmillan.

Stiglitz, J. (2010) *Freefall: Free Markets and the Sinking of the Global Economy*, London: Penguin.

T

Turpin, C. and Tomkins, A. (2011) *British Government and the Constitution: Text and Materials*, 7th edn, Cambridge: Cambridge University Press.

W

Wadham, J., Griffiths J., and Harris, K. (2007) *Blackstone's Guide to the Freedom of Information Act 2000*, 3rd edn, Oxford: Oxford University Press.

Waters, I. and Duffield, B. (1994) *Entertainment, Arts, and Cultural Services*, London: Financial Times/Prentice Hall.

Wilson, D. and Game, C. (2011) *Local Government in the United Kingdom*, 5th edn, Basingstoke: Palgrave Macmillan.

Wilson, D., Ashton, J., and Sharpe, D. (2001) *What Everyone in Britain Should Know about the Police*, 2nd edn, London: Blackstone Press.

Index